Ubiquitous Computing:
Design, Implementation, and Usability

Yin-Leng Theng
Nanyang Technological University, Singapore

Henry B. L. Duh
National University of Singapore, Singapore

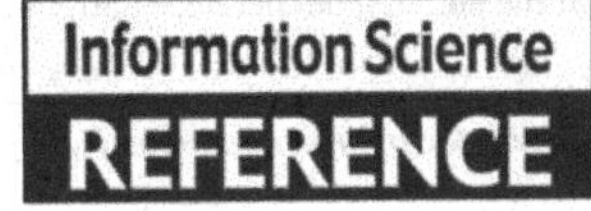

INFORMATION SCIENCE REFERENCE
Hershey · New York

Acquisitions Editor: Kristin Klinger
Development Editor: Kristin Roth
Senior Managing Editor: Jennifer Neidig
Managing Editor: Jamie Snavely
Assistant Managing Editor: Carole Coulson
Copy Editor: Jeannie Porter
Typesetter: Carole Coulson
Cover Design: Lisa Tosheff
Printed at: Yurchak Printing Inc.

Published in the United States of America by
Information Science Reference (an imprint of IGI Global)
701 E. Chocolate Avenue, Suite 200
Hershey PA 17033
Tel: 717-533-8845
Fax: 717-533-8661
E-mail: cust@igi-global.com
Web site: http://www.igi-global.com

and in the United Kingdom by
Information Science Reference (an imprint of IGI Global)
3 Henrietta Street
Covent Garden
London WC2E 8LU
Tel: 44 20 7240 0856
Fax: 44 20 7379 0609
Web site: http://www.eurospanbookstore.com

Library of Congress Cataloging-in-Publication Data

Ubiquitous computing : design, implementation, and usability / Yin-Leng Theng and Henry Duh, editors.

p. cm.

Summary: "This book highlights usability theories, techniques, tools and best practices in these environments. It shows usable and useful systems are able to be achieved in ways that will improve usability to enhance user experiences. Research on the usability issues for young children, teenagers, adults, and the elderly is presented, with techniques for the mobile, ubiquitous, and virtual environments"--Provided by publisher.

ISBN-13: 978-1-59904-693-8 (hardcover)

ISBN-13: 978-1-59904-695-2 (e-book)

1. Ubiquitous computing. I. Theng, Yin-Leng, 1961- II. Duh, Henry.

QA76.5915.U259 2008

004--dc22

2007051616

British Cataloguing in Publication Data
A Cataloguing in Publication record for this book is available from the British Library.

Table of Contents

Preface xv

Section I
Introduction to Ubiquitous Computing and Related Works

Chapter I
Ubiquitous Computing, History, Development, and Future Scenarios 1
Jimmy Chong, Nanyang Technological University, Singapore
Stanley See, Nanyang Technological University, Singapore
Lily Leng-Hiang Seah, Nanyang Technological University, Singapore
Sze Ling Koh, Nanyang Technological University, Singapore
Yin-Leng Theng, Nanyang Technological University, Singapore
Henry B. L. Duh, National University of Singapore, Singapore

Chapter II
Pervasive Computing: What is it Anyway? 9
Emerson Loureiro, Federal University of Campina Grande, Brazil
Glauber Ferreira, Federal University of Campina Grande, Brazil
Hyggo Almeida, Federal University of Campina Grande, Brazil
Angel Perkusich, Federal University of Campina Grande, Brazil

Section II
New User Issues

Chapter III
Convergence Broadcast and Telecommunication Services: What are Real Users' Needs? 37
Raquel Navarro-Prieto, Fundació Barcelona Media, Spain
Nídia Berbegal, Universitat Pompeu Fabra, Spain

Chapter IV
Warranting High Perceived Quality of Experience (PQoE) in Pervasive Interactive Multimedia Systems 53
Anxo Cereijo Roibás, SCMIS, University of Brighton, UK

Chapter V
Interacting with Interaction Histories in a History-Enriched Environment 72
Yoshinari Shirai, University of Tokyo, Japan and NTT Corporation, Japan
Kumiyo Nakakoji, University of Tokyo, Japan and SRA Key Technology Laboratory, Inc., Japan
Yasuhiro Yamamoto, University of Tokyo, Japan

Chapter VI
A User Acceptance Study on a Plant Mixed Reality System for Primary School Children 87
Charissa Lim Mei-Ling, Nanyang Technological University, Singapore
Yin-Leng Theng, Nanyang Technological University, Singapore
Wei Lui, National University of Singapore, Singapore
Adrian David Cheok, National University of Singapore, Singapore

Chapter VII
Human-Based Models for Ambient Intelligence Environments 98
Giovanni Acampora, Università degli Studi di Salerno, Italy
Vincenzo Loia, Università degli Studi di Salerno, Italy
Michele Nappi, Università degli Studi di Salerno, Italy
Stefano Ricciardi, Università degli Studi di Salerno, Italy

Section III
New Supporting Technological Issues

Chapter VIII
Wireless Technologies for Mobile Computing 114
Biju Issac, Information Security Research (iSECURES) Lab and Swinburne University of Technology–Sarawak Campus, Malaysia
C.E. Tan, University Malaysia Sarawak, Malaysia

Chapter IX
Context Sensitive Mobile Services 130
Indranil Bose, The University of Hong Kong, Hong Kong
Xi Chen, The University of Hong Kong, Hong Kong

Chapter X
Wireless Ad Hoc Networks: Design Principles and Low Power Operation....144
Veselin Rakocevic, City University, UK
Ehsan Hamadani, City University, UK

Chapter XI
TeleTables and Window Seat: Bilocative Furniture Interfaces....160
Yeonjoo Oh, Carnegie Mellon University, USA
Ken Camarata, KDF Architecture, USA
Michael Philetus Weller, Carnegie Mellon University, USA
Mark D. Gross, Carnegie Mellon University, USA
Ellen Yi-Luen Do, Georgia Institute of Technology, USA

Chapter XII
Using Multimedia and Virtual Reality for Web-Based Collaborative
Learning on Multiple Platforms....172
Gavin McArdle, University College Dublin, Ireland
Teresa Monahan, University College Dublin, Ireland
Michela Bertolotto, University College Dublin, Ireland

Chapter XIII
Leveraging Pervasive and Ubiquitous Service Computing....204
Zhijun Zhang, University of Phoenix, USA

Section IV
New Usability Engineering Approaches

Chapter XIV
A Software Engineering Perspective on Ubiquitous Computing Systems....222
Emerson Loureiro, Federal University of Campina Grande, Brazil
Loreno Oliveira, Federal University of Campina Grande, Brazil
Frederico Bublitz, Federal University of Campina Grande, Brazil
Angelo Perkusich, Federal University of Campina Grande, Brazil
Hyggo Almeida, Federal University of Campina Grande, Brazil

Chapter XV
When Ubiquitous Computing Meets Experience Design:
Identifying Challenges for Design and Evaluation....238
Ingrid Mulder, Telematica Instituut and Rotterdam University, The Netherlands
Lucia Terrenghi, Vodafone Group R&D, Germany

Chapter XVI
Building Applications to Establish Location Awareness: New Approaches to Design, Implementation, and Evaluation of Mobile and Ubiquitous Interfaces....................................253
D. Scott McCrickard, Virginia Polytechnic Institute and State University (Virginia Tech), USA
Miten Sampat, Feeva Technoology, Inc., USA
Jason Chong Lee, Virginia Polytechnic Institute and State University (Virginia Tech), USA

Chapter XVII
Interactive Tables: Requirements Design, Recommendations, and Implementation........................266
Michael Haller, Upper Austria University of Applied Sciences–Digital Media, Austria
Mark Billinghurst, Human Interface Technology Laboratory New Zealand–University of Canterbury, New Zealand

Chapter XVIII
A Case Study of Icon-Scenario Based Animated Menu's Concept Development............................288
Lim Chee Koon, Motorola Electronics Pte. Ltd., Singapore
Henry B. L. Duh, National University of Singapore, Singapore

Chapter XIX
Formalizing Patterns with the User Requirements Notation 301
Gunter Mussbacher, University of Ottawa, Canada
Daniel Amyot, University of Ottawa, Canada
Michael Weiss, Carleton University, Canada

Appendix..320

Compilation of References 336

About the Contributors...361

Index..369

Detailed Table of Contents

Preface xv

Section I
Introduction to Ubiquitous Computing and Related Works

Chapter I
Ubiquitous Computing, History, Development, and Future Scenarios 1
Jimmy Chong, Nanyang Technological University, Singapore
Stanley See, Nanyang Technological University, Singapore
Lily Leng-Hiang Seah, Nanyang Technological University, Singapore
Sze Ling Koh, Nanyang Technological University, Singapore
Yin-Leng Theng, Nanyang Technological University, Singapore
Henry B. L. Duh, National University of Singapore, Singapore

Chapter I gives a brief history of ubiquitous computing, highlights key issues, and assesses ubiquitous computing research and development under the broad categories of design architecture and systems, implementation challenges, and user issues. Using Singapore as a case example, the chapter then concludes with selected scenarios, presenting exciting possibilities in the future ubiquitous landscape.

Chapter II
Pervasive Computing: What is it Anyway? 9
Emerson Loureiro, Federal University of Campina Grande, Brazil
Glauber Ferreira, Federal University of Campina Grande, Brazil
Hyggo Almeida, Federal University of Campina Grande, Brazil
Angel Perkusich, Federal University of Campina Grande, Brazil

This chapter introduces the key ideas related to the paradigm of pervasive computing. The authors discuss its concepts, challenges, and current solutions by dividing it into four research areas. Such division enables further understanding of what is really involved in pervasive computing at different levels. Within this context, this chapter can be helpful for researchers of pervasive computing, mainly for the beginners, and for students and professors in their academic activities.

Section II
New User Issues

Chapter III
Convergence Broadcast and Telecommunication Services: What are Real Users' Needs?................37
Raquel Navarro-Prieto, Fundació Barcelona Media, Spain
Nídia Berbegal, Universitat Pompeu Fabra, Spain

The aim of this chapter is to present an example of the user-centered design cycle for the development of innovative convergence services and technology of broadcast and mobile networks. The authors' research will explain how combining different methodological approaches (that is, contextual research, experimental studies, and usability tests) has proven to be very useful in gathering and validating user needs, scenarios, and interfaces for these complex services. Overall, the authors highlight that technology developers have to be careful about the amount of information presented, since users are very sensitive to information overload both for mobile TV and for alerting systems. Once again, for mobile services, less is more.

Chapter IV
Warranting High Perceived Quality of Experience (PQoE) in Pervasive
Interactive Multimedia Systems 53
Anxo Cereijo Roibás, SCMIS, University of Brighton, UK

This chapter presents an overview of diverse ethnographic praxis intended to know users and understand how the usage scenarios can influence the quality of their experiences when interacting with pervasive communication systems. Data gathering and evaluation techniques from users' perspective, future interfaces, and applications for pervasive interactive multimedia systems (an evolved state of mobile and pervasive iTV) are discussed. This chapter also focuses on well-established ethno-methodologies that study users and their context in field living labs, cultural probes, focus groups, and on-the-field enactments, integrated within the participatory design process to create future scenarios and applications for pervasive interactive multimedia systems.

Chapter V
Interacting with Interaction Histories in a History-Enriched Environment.......................................72
Yoshinari Shirai, University of Tokyo, Japan and NTT Corporation, Japan
Kumiyo Nakakoji, University of Tokyo, Japan and SRA Key Technology Laboratory, Inc., Japan
Yasuhiro Yamamoto, University of Tokyo, Japan

A ubiquitous computing environment would capture a large amount of interaction histories of objects in the environment over a long period of time. Such interaction histories serve as valuable sources of information for people to solve problems and make decisions in the present time. The authors' approach is to enrich the space by providing interaction history information through noticeable wear expressed within a physical environment. A history-enriched environment (HEE) allows people to use interaction histories of people, things, and places on demand, and to obtain relevant information by tracing links among objects. This chapter describes how to design an HEE through the Optical Stain environment, which we designed as an HEE.

Chapter VI
A User Acceptance Study on a Plant Mixed Reality System for Primary School Children 87
Charissa Lim Mei-Ling, Nanyang Technological University, Singapore
Yin-Leng Theng, Nanyang Technological University, Singapore
Wei Lui, National University of Singapore, Singapore
Adrian David Cheok, National University of Singapore, Singapore

Based on initial findings of Study I (Theng et Al., 2007) on the authors' Plant Mixed Reality System (PMRS), designed for primary school children (11-12 years old), this chapter describes Study II employing the well-established Technology Acceptance Model (TAM) to investigate participants' perceptions of usefulness and usability, identified as key determinants of participants' intention to use the system. Preliminary results seemed to indicate participants' intention to use the PMRS for learning, and this intention was influenced directly by perceived usefulness, and indirectly through perceived usability and social influence. System quality, personal innovativeness and compatibility were found to be important external factors. The chapter concludes with a discussion of implications on the design of mixed reality systems for education.

Chapter VII
Human-Based Models for Ambient Intelligence Environments 98
Giovanni Acampora, Università degli Studi di Salerno, Italy
Vincenzo Loia, Università degli Studi di Salerno, Italy
Michele Nappi, Università degli Studi di Salerno, Italy
Stefano Ricciardi, Università degli Studi di Salerno, Italy

Ambient Intelligence gathers best results from three key technologies: Ubiquitous Computing, Ubiquitous Communication, and Intelligent User Friendly Interfaces. Two critical issues, common in most of applications, are (1) how to detect in a general and efficient way context from sensors and (2) how to process contextual information in order to improve the functionality of services. Here, the authors describe agent-based ambient intelligence architecture able to deliver services on the basis of physical and emotional user status captured from a set of biometric features. Abstract representation and management is achieved thanks to two markup languages, H2ML and FML, able to model behavioral as well as fuzzy control activities and to exploit distribution and concurrent computation in order to gain real-time performances.

Section III
New Supporting Technological Issues

Chapter VIII
Wireless Technologies for Mobile Computing 114
Biju Issac, Information Security Research (iSECURES) Lab and Swinburne University of Technology–Sarawak Campus, Malaysia
C.E. Tan, University Malaysia Sarawak, Malaysia

Mobility and computing were two concepts that never met a decade or two ago. But with the advent of new wireless technologies using radio propagation, the impossible is now becoming possible. Though there are many challenges to be overcome in terms of improving the bandwidth and security as with a wired network, the developments are quite encouraging. This chapter briefly explores some popular wireless technologies that aid in mobile computing, like 802.11 networks, Bluetooth networks, and HomeRF networks. Under 802.11 networks, the authors investigate the details of both infrastructure and ad hoc networks and its operations. The reader is thus made aware of these technologies briefly along with their performance, throughput, and security issues, and the chapter concludes with the user preferences of these technologies.

Chapter IX
Context Sensitive Mobile Services 130
Indranil Bose, The University of Hong Kong, Hong Kong
Xi Chen, The University of Hong Kong, Hong Kong

Advancements in mobile technologies make the collection of customers' context information feasible. Service providers can now incorporate context information of customers when providing personalized services to them. This type of service is called context sensitive mobile services (CSMS). Context refers to the environment around customers when there are business transactions between customers and service providers. Location, time, mobile device, services, and other application specific information are all possible components of context. Compared to other types of mobile services, CSMS can fit to customers' demands better. CSMS can follow push model or pull model. Different context sensitive services are sensitive to different context information with different degrees of sensitivity. In the future, CSMS can find good support from data mining approaches to understand customers better. Security is currently an important issue for CSMS.

Chapter X
Wireless Ad Hoc Networks: Design Principles and Low Power Operation 144
Veselin Rakocevic, City University, UK
Ehsan Hamadani, City University, UK

Seamless communication between computing devices is an essential part of the new world of ubiquitous computing. To achieve the concept of a "disappearing computer," it is necessary to establish reliable and simple communication principles to enhance the usability and the efficiency of the ubiquitous computing devices. It is also important to use wireless links and to enable devices to quickly create and manage networks ad hoc, without any need for network infrastructure. This chapter presents the design principles for such networks. The main features of these networks are analysed, including the principles of medium access control and routing, along with the current standardisation and development activities. Special attention is paid to the low power design of wireless ad hoc networks. Low power design is important because of the predicted self-organisation, small size, and extended scalability of ubiquitous computing networks. In such an environment, it is important to extend the network lifetime by deploying power sensitive network algorithms and protocols.

Chapter XI
TeleTables and Window Seat: Bilocative Furniture Interfaces 160
Yeonjoo Oh, Carnegie Mellon University, USA
Ken Camarata, KDF Architecture, USA
Michael Philetus Weller, Carnegie Mellon University, USA
Mark D. Gross, Carnegie Mellon University, USA
Ellen Yi-Luen Do, Georgia Institute of Technology, USA

People can use computationally-enhanced furniture to interact with distant friends and places without cumbersome menus or widgets. This chapter describes computing embedded in a pair of tables and a chair that enables people to experience remote events in two ways: the TeleTables are ambient tabletop displays that connect two places by projecting shadows cast on one surface to the other. The Window Seat rocking chair through its motion controls a remote camera tied to a live video feed. Both explore using the physical space of a room and its furniture to create "bilocative" interfaces.

Chapter XII
Using Multimedia and Virtual Reality for Web-Based Collaborative
Learning on Multiple Platforms 172
Gavin McArdle, University College Dublin, Ireland
Teresa Monahan, University College Dublin, Ireland
Michela Bertolotto, University College Dublin, Ireland

Since the advent of the Internet, educators have realised its potential as a medium for teaching. With the introduction of wireless networks, mobile devices are also being investigated as a medium to present learning content. Currently the use of 3-Dimensional (3D) graphics is being explored for creating virtual learning environments online. Virtual Reality (VR) is already being used in multiple disciplines for teaching various tasks. This chapter focuses on describing some VR systems and also discusses the current state of e-learning on mobile devices. The authors also present the VR learning environment that we have developed, incorporating many of the techniques mentioned above for both desktop and mobile devices.

Chapter XIII
Leveraging Pervasive and Ubiquitous Service Computing 204
Zhijun Zhang, University of Phoenix, USA

The advancement of technologies to connect people and objects anywhere has provided many opportunities for enterprises. This chapter will review the different wireless networking technologies and mobile devices that have been developed, and discuss how they can help organizations better bridge the gap between their employees or customers and the information they need. The chapter will also discuss the promising application areas and human-computer interaction modes in the pervasive computing world, and propose a service-oriented architecture to better support such applications and interactions.

Section IV
New Usability Engineering Approaches

Chapter XIV
A Software Engineering Perspective on Ubiquitous Computing Systems 222
Emerson Loureiro, Federal University of Campina Grande, Brazil
Loreno Oliveira, Federal University of Campina Grande, Brazil
Frederico Bublitz, Federal University of Campina Grande, Brazil
Angelo Perkusich, Federal University of Campina Grande, Brazil
Hyggo Almeida, Federal University of Campina Grande, Brazil

We are now facing a migration from the traditional computing, based on personal computers, to an era of pervasiveness, on which computing devices will be spread all around us, seamless integrated to our lives. It is this new stage of computing that researchers have named of ubiquitous computing, also known as pervasive computing. There is no doubt that this vision is certainly a promising computing paradigm for the 21st Century. However, its completely new characteristics have an impact on the way that software is developed. The purpose of this chapter is then to review the challenges involved in ubiquitous systems development as well as present a software engineering perspective for tackling such challenges. In addition, it will also be presented the way these techniques have been used, by outlining some of the current ubiquitous computing solutions.

Chapter XV
When Ubiquitous Computing Meets Experience Design:
Identifying Challenges for Design and Evaluation..238
Ingrid Mulder, Telematica Instituut and Rotterdam University, The Netherlands
Lucia Terrenghi, Vodafone Group R&D, Germany

This chapter provides an overview of the main implications of emerging ubiquitous computing scenarios with respect to the design and evaluation of the user experience. In doing that, the authors point out how these implications motivate the evolution of the Human-Computer Interaction discipline towards a more interdisciplinary field of research requiring a holistic approach as well as new adequate research methods. Challenges for design and evaluation are identified and different classes of methods to cope with these challenges are considered. Within their discussion, the authors support the idea that ubiquitous technology provides new means for the study of human experiences as well as human deliberate engagement with technology; the latter as an alternative to automation and invisible technology.

Chapter XVI
Building Applications to Establish Location Awareness: New Approaches to Design, Implementation, and Evaluation of Mobile and Ubiquitous Interfaces 253
D. Scott McCrickard, Virginia Polytechnic Institute and State University (Virginia Tech), USA
Miten Sampat, Feeva Technoology, Inc., USA
Jason Chong Lee, Virginia Polytechnic Institute and State University (Virginia Tech), USA

An emerging challenge in the design of interfaces for mobile devices is the appropriate use of information about the location of the user. This chapter considers tradeoffs in privacy, computing power, memory capacity, and wireless signal availability that accompany the obtaining and use of location information and other contextual information in the design of interfaces. The increasing ability to integrate location knowledge in our mobile, ubiquitous applications, and their accompanying tradeoffs requires that we consider their impact on the development of user interfaces, leading to an Agile Usability approach to design borne from agile software development and usability engineering. The chapter concludes with three development efforts that make use of location knowledge in mobile interfaces.

Chapter XVII
Interactive Tables: Requirements Design, Recommendations, and Implementation........................266
Michael Haller, Upper Austria University of Applied Sciences–Digital Media, Austria
Mark Billinghurst, Human Interface Technology Laboratory New Zealand–University of Canterbury, New Zealand

Interactive tables are becoming increasingly popular. In this chapter, the authors describe a collaborative tabletop environment that is designed for brainstorming meetings. After describing the user requirements, they demonstrate different possible solutions for both the display and the tracking implementation, and summarize related work. Finally, they conclude with a more detailed description of the Shared Design Space. Using a digital pen, participants can annotate not only virtual paper, but also real printouts. By integrating both forms of physical and digital paper, the authors combine virtual and real drawings, three-dimensional models, and digital data in a single information space. They discuss the unique way that we have integrated these devices and how they can be used efficiently during a design process.

Chapter XVIII
A Case Study of Icon-Scenario Based Animated Menu's Concept Development...........................288
Lim Chee Koon, Motorola Electronics Pte. Ltd., Singapore
Henry B. L. Duh, National University of Singapore, Singapore

This chapter will first describe the development workflow of graphical user interface (GUI) design and the implementation that is adopted across a 2G platform. It describes the development workflow of graphical user interface (GUI) design and the implementation that is adopted across a 2G platform. The authors then describe the implementation process of developing Icon-Scenario Based Animated Menu GUI. The same design process developed is implemented in the other models when the authors develop another set of GUIs for different customers using the same workflow. The chapter concludes by describing the concept development process of the phone's menu enhanced by the use of a captivating Icon-Scenario Based Animated Menu, followed by demonstrating how it takes usability into consideration, bringing delight to users.

Chapter XIX
Formalizing Patterns with the User Requirements Notation 301
Gunter Mussbacher, University of Ottawa, Canada
Daniel Amyot, University of Ottawa, Canada
Michael Weiss, Carleton University, Canada

Patterns need to be described and formalized in ways that enable the reader to determine whether the particular solution presented is useful and applicable to his or her problem in a given context. This chapter describes the User Requirements Notation (URN), and demonstrates how it can be used to formalize patterns in a way that enables rigorous trade-off analysis while maintaining the genericity of the solution description. URN combines a graphical goal language, which can be used to capture forces and reason about trade-offs, and a graphical scenario language, which can be used to describe behavioral solutions in an abstract manner. Although each language can be used in isolation in pattern descriptions (and have been in the literature), the focus of this chapter is on their combined use.

Appendix 320

Compilation of References 336

About the Contributors 361

Index 369

Preface

Institutions are investing millions of dollars implementing ubiquitous services and technologies to ride on the next wave of computing power to enhance computing use by making computers available but effectively invisible to the users throughout the physical environment. Ubiquitous computing is challenging and interdisciplinary, and it is important that various research communities coordinate and communicate to explore the frontiers of computing as it moves beyond the desktop and becomes increasingly interwoven into the fabrics of our lives. Ubiquitous computing has significant advantages in that computational devices are distributed in the physical world, giving us boundless access to communication and information channels, with users' knowledge built based on collaboration, communication, and experimentation.

History has taught us that inadequate understanding of users, scenarios of use, and technologies have led to failures of many research and development computing projects. As we have problems producing good conventional interactive systems, it is reasonable to anticipate that we may have problems creating good ubiquitous computing systems. Mark Weiser, father of ubiquitous computing, points out that getting the computer out of the way is not easy. The challenge in ubiquitous computing is to "create a new kind of relationship of people to computers, one in which the computer would have to take the lead in becoming vastly better at getting out of the way so people could just go about their lives" (retrieved 26 Oct 2005, http://ubiq.com/htpertext/weiser/UbiCACM.html).

The editors would like to thank the authors and reviewers for their excellent contributions and insights, without which this book would not have been possible. We are also grateful to Idea Group Publishing for the opportunity to publish this book focusing on design, implementation, and usability issues in ubiquitous computing.

ORGANISATION

The book is written for academics, practitioners, and undergraduate/postgraduate students and organized around six sections into chapters with the following major themes:

1. Introduction to Ubiquitous Computing and Related Works
2. New User Issues
3. New Supporting Technological Issues
4. New Usability Engineering Approaches
5. Selected Readings—New Applications and Future Trends

References in each chapter as well as an appendix of further resources on human-computer interaction research and related disciplines at the end of the book provide additional information to readers to pursue a more detailed study of any particular aspect.

OVERVIEW

Section I gives a brief overview of ubiquitous computing, related works, and underlying concepts, and discusses design and implementation issues, highlighting scenarios in the future ubiquitous landscape. Section I consists of two chapters.

Chapter I "Ubiquitous Computing History, Development and Future Landscape" by Jimmy Chong, Stanley See, Lily Seah Leng-Hiang, Koh Sze-Ling, Yin-Leng Theng, and Henry Duh Been-Lim, gives a brief history of ubiquitous computing, highlights key issues, and assesses ubiquitous computing research and development under the broad categories of design architecture and systems; implementation challenges; and user issues. Using Singapore as a case example, the chapter then concludes with selected scenarios, presenting exciting possibilities in the future ubiquitous landscape.

In **Chapter II**, "**Pervasive Computing: What is it Anyway?**" Emerson Loureiro Glauber Ferreira, Hyggo Almeida, and Angelo Perkusich introduce key ideas related to the paradigm of pervasive computing. Concepts, challenges, and current solutions are also discussed. The introductory chapter is helpful to those who are beginning to explore pervasive computing and the underlying concepts.

Section II focuses on "**New User Issues,**" that is, user issues relating to new applications in domain-specific areas. Section II consists of five chapters, and they highlight challenges faced by designers and developers in designing user-centred applications.

Chapter III, "Convergence Broadcast and Telecommunication Services: What Are Real Users' Needs?" by Raquel Navarro-Prieto and Nídia Berbegal**,** presents an example of the user-centred design cycle for the development of innovative convergence services and technology of broadcast and mobile networks. The authors describe three main phases: (1) validation of the scenarios developed as well as requirements gathering for the services portrayed in the scenarios, taking into consideration cultural differences among countries; (2) in-depth requirements for specific services (mobile TV and personalized alerting); and (3) usability test in three countries to test navigational aspects, users' understanding of icons and menus, and user acceptance of the mock-up. Using a combination of different methodological approaches (that is, contextual research, experimental studies, and usability tests), this chapter demonstrates the importance of gathering and validating user needs, scenarios and interfaces for these complex services.

In **Chapter IV**, Anxo Cereijo Roibás discusses the "**Warranting High Perceived Quality of Experience (PQoE) in Pervasive Interactive Multimedia Systems.**" The chapter presents an overview of diverse ethnographic praxis intended to know the users and understand how the usage scenarios can influence the quality of their experiences when interacting with pervasive communication systems. This chapter focuses on ethno-methodologies that study users and their context on the field living labs, cultural probes, focus groups, and on-the-field enactments, integrated within the participatory design process to create future scenarios and applications for pervasive interactive multimedia systems.

Chapter V by Yoshinari Shirai, Kumiyo Nakakoji and Yasuhiro Yamamoto on "**Interacting with Interaction History in a History-Enriched Environment**" describes an approach to enrich the space by providing interaction history information through noticeable wear expressed within a physical environment. The authors postulate that a history-enriched environment (HEE) allows people to use interaction histories of people, things, and places on demand, hence obtaining relevant information by tracing links among objects. They also argue that taking into account two aspects of people's cognitive activities—situated encountering and information-triggered information needs—is key to building an HEE. As an illustration, this chapter describes the design of an HEE through the Optical Stain environment.

Chapter VI, **"A User Acceptance Study on a Plant Mixed Reality System for Primary School Children"** by Charissa Lim Mei-Ling, Yin-Leng Theng, Liu Wei, and Adrian David Cheok, describes Study II, a follow-up study, employing the well-established Technology Acceptance Model (TAM) to investigate participants' perceptions of usefulness and usability, identified as key determinants of participants' intention to use the system, of a Plant Mixed Reality System (PMRS) designed for primary school children (11 to 12 years old). Preliminary results seemed to indicate participants' intention to use the PMRS for learning, and this intention was influenced directly by perceived usefulness, and indirectly through perceived usability and social influence. System quality, personal innovativeness, and compatibility were found to be important external factors. The chapter concludes with a discussion of implications on the design of mixed reality systems for education.

In **Chapter VII, "Human-Based Models for Ambient Intelligence Environments,"** Giovanni Acampora, Vincenzo Loia, Michele Nappi, and Stefano Ricciardi describe an agent-based ambient intelligence architecture based on technologies in ubiquitous computing, ubiquitous communication, and intelligent user friendly interfaces to deliver services on the basis of physical and emotional user status captured from a set of biometric features.

Section III examines **"New Supporting Technological Issues"** focusing on the "how" aspects of ubiquitous systems with regard to algorithms, techniques, and/or methods. Discussions on pertinent technological issues and results for comparisons serve as useful lessons learnt and provide a gauge of the efficiency and effectiveness of the implementation. Section III consists of five chapters.

Chapter VIII, **"Wireless Technologies for Mobile Computing,"** by Biju Issac and Chong Eng Tan, briefly explores some popular wireless technologies that aid in mobile computing, like 802.11 networks, Bluetooth networks, and HomeRF networks. Under 802.11 networks, the authors investigate into the details of both infrastructure and ad hoc networks and its operations. Though there are many challenges to be overcome in terms of improving the bandwidth and security as with a wired network, the developments are quite encouraging, and the authors conclude by highlighting user preferences of these technologies.

The advancements in mobile technologies make the collection of customers' context information feasible. Service providers can now incorporate context information of customers when providing personalized services to them. This type of services is called context sensitive mobile services (CSMS). Equipped with advanced mobile technologies, sophisticated context sensitive mobile services could be provided to customers now and in future.

In **Chapter IX**, **"Context Sensitive Mobile Services,"** by Indranil Bose and Chen Xi, the authors introduce the definition of context and its explanation in context sensitive mobile services (CSMS). The chapter then discusses the business models of CSMS and strategies which services providers of CSMS can follow, the classifications of CSMS and relationships between context and each type of CSMS. Although CSMS is powerful, the authors argue that it cannot replace other types of services and should be integrated into the whole business strategy of a firm so that it can work seamlessly with other types of services.

Seamless communication between computing devices is an essential part of the new world of ubiquitous computing. To achieve the concept of a "disappearing computer," it is necessary to establish reliable and simple communication principles to enhance the usability and the efficiency of the ubiquitous computing devices. It is also important to use wireless links and to enable devices to quickly create and manage networks ad hoc, without any need for network infrastructure.

Chapter X, **"Wireless Ad Hoc Networks: Design Principles and Low Power Operation,"** by Veselin Rakocevic presents the design principles for such networks. The main features of these networks are analysed, including the principles of medium access control and routing, along with the current standardisation and development activities. Special attention is paid to the low power design of wireless ad hoc networks. Low power design is important because of the predicted self-organisation, small size and extended scalability of ubiquitous computing networks. In such an environment, it is important to extend the network lifetime by deploying power sensitive network algorithms and protocols.

Chapter XI, **"TeleTables and Window Seat: Bilocative Furniture Interfaces,"** by Yeonjoo Oh, Mark D Gross, Ellen Yi-Luen Do, Michael Philetus Weller, and Ken Camarata, describe two computationally enhanced furniture pieces, a pair of tables and a chair, built to support experiencing remote events with everyday objects. With embedded computation in the furniture, people can interact with distant friends and places without cumbersome menus or widgets. The TeleTables are ambient bidirectional tabletop displays that connect two particular distant places by projecting shadows cast on one table across the Internet to the other. Window Seat is a rocking chair that can be tied to a particular remote place by controlling a remote camera tied to a live video feed through the motion of the rocking chair. Both these projects explore the use of the physical space of a room and its furniture to create bilocative interfaces that allow information navigation without screen-based GUIs and menus.

Chapter XII, **"Using Multimedia and Virtual Reality for Web-Based Collaborative Learning on Multiple Platforms,"** by Gavin McArdle, Teresa Monahan, and Michela Bertolotto, describes virtual reality systems, and also discusses the current state of e-learning on mobile devices. The authors also present the virtual reality learning environment developed, incorporating established techniques both desktop and mobile devices.

Zhijun Zhang, in **Chapter XIII**, **"Leveraging Pervasive and Ubiquitous Service Computing,"** reviews the different wireless networking technologies and mobile devices that have been developed and discusses how they can help organizations better bridge the gap between their employees or customers and the information they need. The chapter also discusses the promising application areas and human-computer interaction modes in the pervasive computing world, and proposes a service-oriented architecture to better support such applications and interactions.

In a workshop on "Evaluation Methodologies for Ubiquitous Computing" in the Ubicomp 2001 conference, it was agreed that interactive systems, and in particular, ubiquitous computing posed complex evaluation methodologies. To date, not much known research is being carried out to determine what constitutes good ubiquitous services and technologies, and positive user interactions and experiences. Designers often design for themselves unless they are trained to realise that people are diverse, and that users are unlikely to be like them. The more errors that can be avoided "up front" by the right method, the less work both test-users and designers will have to put in for refinement to improve design, use, and usability. Hence, **Section IV** examines **"New Usability Engineering Approaches,"** focusing on usability evaluation techniques employed in the design and development of ubiquitous systems, addressing users, requirements, and context of use. Section IV consists of five chapters.

We are now facing a migration from the traditional computing, based on personal computers, to an era of pervasiveness, on which computing devices will be spread all around us, seamlessly integrated into our lives. It is this new stage of computing that researchers have named of *ubiquitous computing*, also known as *pervasive computing*. There is no doubt that this vision is certainly a promising computing paradigm for the 21st Century. However, its completely new characteristics have an impact on the way that software is developed. We should emphasize that, for example, to achieve the seamless integration characteristic of ubiquitous computing environments, applications must implement mechanisms for discovering the needs of users, in order to present them with relevant information at the right place and on the right time. This, and other intrinsic features of ubiquitous computing systems, makes necessary the use of different software engineering techniques. Within this scope, Emerson Loureiro, Frederico Bublitz, Loreno Oliveira, Angelo Perkusich, and Hyggo Almeida in Chapter XVI, "A Roadmap of Software Engineering for Ubiquitous Computing Systems," claim that service-oriented computing, component-based development, plug-in-based architectures, event-based systems, and dynamic software evolution are the main techniques that can be used in the development of ubiquitous systems. The purpose of this chapter is then to review the challenges involved in ubiquitous systems development as well as present a software engineering perspective for tackling such challenges. In addition, the author's also present the way these techniques have been used by outlining some of the current ubiquitous computing solutions.

In **Chapter XV**, "**When Ubiquitous Computing Meets Experience Design: Identifying Challenges for Design and Evaluation,**" Ingrid Mulder and Lucia Terrenghi provide an overview of the main implications of emerging ubiquitous computing scenarios with respect to the design and evaluation of user experience. The authors identify challenges for design and evaluation and consider different classes of methods to cope with these challenges. These challenges are illustrated with examples in which ubiquitous technology is used both for the design and for the study of the users' everyday life. In this chapter, the authors argue that ubiquitous technology provides new means for the study of human experiences as well as human deliberate engagement with technology; the latter as an alternative to automation and invisible technology.

An emerging challenge in the design of interfaces for mobile devices is the appropriate use of information about the location of the user. **Chapter XVI**, "**Building Applications to Establish Location Awareness: New Approaches to the Design, Implementation and Evaluation of Mobile and Ubiquitous Interfaces,**" by Scott McCrickard, Miten Sampat, and Jason Chong Lee, considers tradeoffs in privacy, computing power, memory capacity, and wireless signal availability that accompany the obtaining and use of location information and other contextual information in the design of interfaces. The increasing ability to integrate location knowledge in our mobile, ubiquitous applications and their accompanying tradeoffs requires that we consider their impact on the development of user interfaces, leading to an Agile Usability approach to design borne from agile software development and usability engineering. The chapter concludes with three development efforts that make use of location knowledge in mobile interfaces.

Interactive tables are becoming increasingly popular. **Chapter XVII**, "**Interactive Tables: Requirements, Design, Recommendations and Implementation,**" by Michael Haller, describe a collaborative tabletop environment that is designed for brainstorming meetings. After describing the user requirements, the author demonstrates different possible solutions for both the display and the tracking implementation, and summarizes related work. Finally, the author concludes with a more detailed description of the Shared Design Space. Using a digital pen, participants can annotate not only virtual paper, but also real printouts. By integrating both forms of physical and digital paper, the authors combine virtual and real drawings, three-dimensional models, and digital data in a single information space. The authors then discuss the unique way in which these devices are integrated together and how they can be used efficiently during a design process.

Chapter XVIII, "A Case Study of Icon-Scenario Based Animated Menu's Concept Development," by Chee Koon Lim and Henry Duh Been-Lim, describes the development workflow of graphical user interface (GUI) design and the implementation that is adopted across a 2G platform. The authors describe the implementation process of developing Icon-Scenario Based Animated Menu GUI. The same design process developed is implemented in the other models when the authors develop another set of GUI for different customers using the same workflow. The chapter concludes by describing the concept development process of the phone's menu enhanced by the use of a captivating Icon-Scenario

Based Animated Menu, followed by demonstrating how it takes usability into consideration, bringing delight to users.

Patterns need to be described and formalized in ways that enable the reader to determine whether a particular solution presented is useful and applicable to his or her problem in a given context. However, many pattern descriptions tend to focus on the solution to a problem, and not so much on how the various (and often conflicting) forces involved are balanced. **Chapter XIX, "Formalising Patterns for the User Requirements Notation,"** by Gunter Mussbacher, Daniel Amyot, and Michael Weiss, describes the user requirements notation (URN), and demonstrates how it can be used to formalize patterns in a way that enables rigorous trade-off analysis while maintaining the genericity of the solution description. URN combines a graphical goal language, which can be used to capture forces and reason about trade-offs, and a graphical scenario language, which can be used to describe behavioral solutions in an abstract manner. Although each language can be used in isolation in pattern descriptions (and have been in the literature), the focus of this chapter is on their combined use. It includes examples of formalizing design patterns with URN together with a process for trade-off analysis.

Yin-Leng Theng and Henry B. L. Duh
21 September 2007

Section I
Introduction to Ubiquitous Computing and Related Works

Chapter I
Ubiquitous Computing History, Development, and Scenarios

Jimmy Chong
Nanyang Technological University, Singapore

Stanley See
Nanyang Technological University, Singapore

Lily Leng-Hiang Seah
Nanyang Technological University, Singapore

Sze Ling Koh
Nanyang Technological University, Singapore

Yin-Leng Theng
Nanyang Technological University, Singapore

Henry B. L. Duh
National University of Singapore, Singapore

ABSTRACT

This chapter gives a brief history of ubiquitous computing, highlights key issues, and assesses ubiquitous computing research and development under the broad categories of design architecture and systems, implementation challenges, and user issues. Using Singapore as a case example, the chapter then concludes with selected scenarios, presenting exciting possibilities in the future ubiquitous landscape.

INTRODUCTION

History and Vision of Ubiquitous Computing

Technology in computing has undergone extensive changes over the years. In the early 1970s, mainframe computers dominated the computing scene based on the principle of one computer serving many people. In the 1980s, mainframe computers gave way to personal computers and notebooks, and, in contrast, the emphasis was one computer to one person. In the 1990s, with increased computing powers available at affordable prices, we are witnessing a new era of personal computing, that is, a phenomenon in which multiple computers are serving one person.

Through the ages, technology has dramatically transformed our lives, changing the way we learn, live, work, and play. Technology shrank transistors to such microscopic sizes that they enable computer chips to be found in the things we use daily, even down to a pair of shoes made by Adidas (McCarthy, 2005). Technology also connects computers around the world breaking down geographical boundaries as people are able to "travel" virtually everywhere, collaborate with others online, and be connected with loved ones virtually even though they may be miles away physically.

Mark Weiser (1991; 1993a; 1993b), father of "ubiquitous computing" (or "ubicomp" in short), coined the term "ubiquitous" to refer to the trend that humans interact no longer with one computer at a time, but rather with a dynamic set of small networked computers, often invisible and embodied in everyday objects in the environment. Keefe and Zucker (2003) see ubicomp as a technology that enables information to be accessible any time and anywhere and uses sensors to interact with and control the environment without users' intervention. An example often cited is that of a domestic ubicomp environment in which interconnected lighting and environmental controls incorporate personal biometric monitors interwoven into clothing so that illumination and heating conditions in a room might be modulated according to "needs" of the wearer of such clothing.

Other examples of ubiquitous environment include applications in homes, shopping centres, offices, schools, sports hall, vehicles, bikes, and so forth. The principle guiding ubicomp is the creation of technology that brings computing to the background and not the foreground, making technology invisible. Philosophers like Heidegger (1955) called it "ready-to-hand" while Gadamer (1982) coined it "horizon." This means that people do not need to continually rationalize one's use of an ubicomp system, because once having learned about its use sufficiently, one ceases to be aware of it. It is literally visible, effectively invisible in the same way, for example, a skilled carpenter engaged in his work might use a hammer without consciously planning each swing. Hence, ubicomp defines a paradigm shift in which technology becomes invisible, embedded and integrated into our everyday lives, allowing people to interact with devices in the environment more naturally.

CURRENT RESEARCH CHALLENGES

Research challenges in ubicomp remain interdisciplinary, and this is evident as we trace the development of the Ubicomp Conference Series into its ninth year in 2007. The conference series began as Handheld and Ubiquitous Computing in 1999, focusing on areas relating to the design, implementation, application, and evaluation of ubicomp technologies, a cross-fertilization of a variety of disciplines exploring the frontiers of computing as it moves beyond the desktop and becomes increasingly interwoven into the fabrics of our lives. Over the years, the Ubicomp Conference Series from 1999 – 2006 has grown in participation by region, with papers addressing more

Table 1. Breakdown of participation by region, application areas and technologies ubicomp conference series from 1999-2006

Ubicomp Conf	Region			Application Areas					Technologies				
	Asia Pacific	Europe	U.S. & Canada	Education	Health Care	Tourism	Gen	Others	Mobile Devices	Internet	Wireless	Several Devices	Others
1999 (53 paper)	4	39	10	1	1	3	40	8	13	3	-	5	32
2000 (18 paper)	2	8	8	-	1	-	14	3	3	1	-	2	12
2001 (30 paper)	1	12	17	2	-	3	23	2	2	3	2	10	13
2002 (29 paper)	2	14*	15*	1	2	2	19	5	1	1	-	5	22
2003 (26 paper)	-	8	18	1	2	1	19	3	2	-	1	7	16
2004 (26 paper)	3	7*	17*	2*	2*	1	17	5	-	-	1	4	21
2005 (22 paper)	2	10*	12*	-	3	-	16	3	4	-	1	1	16
2006 (30 paper)	4*	7	20*	-	4	2	19	5	7	1	1	2	19

Note: * *in 2002: 2 papers written by Europe-U.S. authors*

* *in 2004: 1 paper written by Europe-U.S. authors; 1 paper can be applied both in education and health care*

* *in 2005: 2 papers written by Europe-U.S. authors*

* *in 2006: 1 paper written by Asia-U.S. authors*

diverse application areas, as well as innovative supporting technologies/media (see Table 1).

In the following sections, we highlight key issues and assess the current situation of ubicomp research and development under the broad categories of design architecture and systems and implementation issues.

Design Architecture and Systems

For the ubicomp vision to work, we need an infrastructure supporting small, inexpensive, robust networked processing devices. Current contemporary devices giving some support to this vision include mobile phones, digital audio players, radio-frequency identification tags and interactive whiteboards. For a fully robust ubicomp implementation, we also require a better understanding of the yet-to-emerge "natural" or intuitive interaction paradigms.

Challenges facing design architecture and systems also include issues relating to the wireless network, power component, and standards for service discovery. In the ubicomp world, anyone can interact with thousands of wirelessly connected devices, implying implicit mobility. Hence, mobility and density of data transferred require a robust network infrastructure in place. Such networks should have the capacity to transmit and receive wireless data at ultrahigh speed virtually anywhere and everywhere.

Different standards are currently adopted by different countries, for example, the U.S. standards include analog and digital services; GSM, the European standard, is meant for wide area cellular service; Japan uses CDMA, and so forth, and hence pose problems in interoperability. In order to build a better wireless network environment, some countries are working towards adopting the WiMAX wireless broadband technology in cooperation with telecommunications operators to create wireless broadband cities. Examples include Mobile-Taiwan project (Mobile Taiwan Initiative, 2004) and Singapore SG@Wireless project (Wireless@SG, 2006). Increased use of wireless networks and mobile devices has also resulted in increasing need to manage and administer the interconnection of networked devices with less complexity. Wireless and mobile infrastructure will play a major role in achieving the ubicomp vision; hence, more research should be done to resolve current issues.

Design and Implementation Challenges

The ubicomp paradigm presents a novel interpretation of the post-desktop era, and these interfaces thoroughly integrated into everyday objects and activities have to take on different forms. This means that users "using" ubicomp devices engage themselves in many computational devices and systems simultaneously, and may not necessarily even be aware that they are doing so when performing these ordinary activities. Hence, models of contemporary human-computer interaction describing command-line, menu-driven, or GUI-based interfaces may seem inadequate. The challenges facing designers are in making access easy for users to retrieve information on the Internet through either desktops or handheld devices.

We discuss some of these challenges in design and implementation:

- **Smaller screen display.** Designers need to work within constraints of smaller screen sizes when displaying information (Want & Pering, 2005). Scalable interfaces are also explored as applications extend to desktops, PDAs, and even phone interfaces (Abowd, 1999).
- **Location-based and context-sensitive data.** Many ubicomp applications "push" information based on the location of users and display information implicitly to users on a mobile device (Rogers, Price, Randell, Fraser, & Weal, 2005). Hence, designing ubicomp systems also requires designers to consider context awareness. Information needs to be personalized according to user's location, time, mood, and history (Abowd, 1999).
- **Cultural differences.** Users are diverse and they can come from all over the world. We need to have in place some degree of standardization to prevent diverse cultural conflicts (Rosson & Carroll, 2002).
- **Privacy.** With widespread use of wireless broadband, we have to be vigilant in protecting our personal information and our personal network access. Users should be educated that tapping into other people's wireless network is unethical and that detailed tracking of individuals accessing illegally is possible (IDA, 2005b). Yamada (2003) highlighted privacy management considerations asking three fundamental questions: (i) "where" to store personal data (network centric or end-user centric); (ii) "who" to manage the privacy (user, network operator or service provider); and (iii) "how" to protect privacy (principle of minimum asymmetry, pawS system or P3P). Designers of ubicomp applications need to address carefully these important privacy questions.
- **Security.** Bardram (2005) discussed tradeoffs between usability and security. In the ubicomp environment, we have many public computers serving individual computers. For context awareness systems, users' details and profiles need to be captured. New design challenges involve understanding security tradeoffs of having users logging into the public computers as opposed to not having authentication where users enjoy access into these various systems.

To address these design and implementation challenges, Jones and Marsden (2006) see designers/developers as playwrights developing "scripts" with scenarios and use cases on how technologies are used. Carroll (2000) stresses the importance of maintaining a continuous focus on situations of and consequences for human work and activity to promote learning about the structure and dynamics of problem domains, thus seeing usage situations from different perspectives, and managing tradeoffs to reach usable and effective design outcomes.

Design is difficult and is never completely "done," resulting in the task-artifact cycle dilemma (Carroll, 2000). This is so because at the start of any software development, tasks help articulate requirements to build artifacts, but designed artifacts create possibilities (and limitations) that redefine tasks. Hence, managing the task-artifact cycle is not a linear endeavour with different starting and ending points. There will always be a further development, a subsequent version, a redesign, a new technology development context. That is, the design scenarios at one point in time are the requirements scenarios at the next point in time. Claims analysis was later developed by Carroll (2000) to enlarge the scope and ambition of scenario-based design approach to provide for more detailed and focused reasoning. Norman's influential Model of Interaction (Norman, 1988) is used as a framework in claims analysis for questioning the user's stages of action when interacting with a system in terms of goals, planning, execution, interpretation, and evaluation.

SINGAPORE AS A CASE EXAMPLE: DISCUSSION OF SCENARIOS IN EDUCATION

In Singapore, the IT initiatives underwent three phases of implementation in the early 1990s through the Civil Service Computerization Plan, the National IT Plan, and IT 2000. The IT2000 Master Plan was launched in 1992 (National Computer Board, 1992), just 6 months after Weiser's seminal article on ubicomp in Scientific America (Weiser, 1991). The IT2000 vision in Singapore aimed to provide a nationwide information infrastructure to link every home, school, and workplace in Singapore, creating an intelligent island (Choo, 1997). In 2005, the IT 2000 vision was revised and the Singapore Government Intelligent Nation 2015(iN2015) is a 10-year blueprint to enable every individual to have seamless access to intelligent technology (IDA, 2005). The goal was to create smart, sentient entertainment spaces with networked, embedded spaces padded with sensory and distributed intelligence characterized by human-friendly computing as well as business-efficient automation.

In the 2006 survey (IDA Survey, 2006), the high mobile penetration rate of 104.6% of infocomm usage in households and individuals showed that the Internet and mobile phones had perpetually been weaved into the daily activities of Singaporeans. Some examples of innovation usage included (IDA Infocomm Survey, 2006): (i) distributing critical information to the entire population during crisis situations; (ii) voting in contests, donating money during charity events; (iii) booking services for movie or taxi; and (iv) electronic road pricing system utilizing unique vehicle identification units, smart cards, distributed data collection points, and a centralized data centre to provide variable pricing information to drivers going into the central district areas and highways.

In education, we are witnessing applications/services being implemented in some schools in Singapore towards the 2015 vision of making learning truly global and out of the classroom, to align with Singapore's 10-year Infocomm Plan iN2015 (IDA, 2005a, 2005b, 2006). We illustrate in the following scenarios how different personas could interact with the ubiquitous ecosystem and the contactless smart badge/card as a wearable computer concept that communicates with sensors in the surrounding.

Scenario 1

Presently, all school-going students in Singapore possess built-in smart cards, serving as identity cards as well as as cash cards. Kiosks are set up in some schools where students could pay for food using their student cards. These kiosks also record purchasing habits of students. Parents could go online to check expenditures incurred and eating habits of their children, attendance records, and homework details.

Scenario 2

In the near future, perhaps smart badges with built-in Radio Frequency Identification (RFID) could replace the traditional student card. The smart card storing students' personal particulars with RFID could automatically send out a unique identifier to sensors located on walls and ceilings in schools. Hundreds of interconnected closed circuit televisions (CCTVs) and images could be installed at every corner in the school to survey and record daily activities, and keep track of incoming or out-going students.

Scenario 3

Classrooms could be fully equipped with computing resources involving multimedia features such as screen, pen stylus, and table could be neatly arranged like a Swiss army knife at the side of a chair, and students could scan their smart badges to activate resources. Upon activation, the online learning portal could be launched. The computer could be interconnected to all fellow students and the teacher-in-charge during the class. The portal could allow students to learn, work on their assignments, and take tests or exams in an interactive way. Instead of carrying bags containing books, students could carry tablet PCs, capable of communicating wirelessly with other devices.

Scenario 4

Perhaps teachers could also have smart badges with built-in RFIDs and tablet PCs. At the start of school each morning, the tablet PC could automatically take attendance of students in class, and start "tracking down" the absentees. After 15 minutes, it could send a text message via mobile phones to parents concerned. Similarly, parents could remotely find out about their children's well-being and whereabout. For example, if a parent wishes to check whether her youngest child at school is having a fever, she could do so by logging onto a portal to activate the smart card for the body temperature to be taken.

CONCLUSION

With all the hype about ubicomp, one could easily get carried away with the lure of benefits it promises to bring. With these challenges, ubicomp also brings along many unknowns and changes radically the way people interact with one another and with the environment. As technology becomes embedded in everyday artefacts, the modes of interaction change constantly.

Although Weiser (1991) started the ubicomp vision more than a decade ago, current ubicomp literature keeps revolving around Weiser's vision for the future of implementing ubicomp applications or services that could provide a seamless interconnected environment. In fact, Bell and Dourish (2006) suggest that we stop talking about the "ubicomp of tomorrow" but rather at the "ubicomp of the present." Doing so, they advocate getting out of the lab and looking at ubicomp as it is being developed rather than what it might be like in the future.

Hence, this chapter highlighted key issues and assessed the current situation of ubicomp development in design architecture and systems, implementation issues, and challenges. Selected scenarios in the Singapore's education landscape were also described, presenting possibilities and challenges in the future ubiquitous landscape.

To conclude, there is perhaps no need for heroic engineering; the heterogeneous technologies could be utilised as well. We are already living in the world of ubicomp. Gibson (1999), father of cyberpunk fiction, rightfully pointed out "the future is here, it is just not evenly distributed" (retrieved on March 11, 2007 from http://en.wikiquote.org/wiki/William_Gibson).

ACKNOWLEDGMENT

The authors would like to thank the 2006-2007 Usability Engineering Class in the M.Sc. (Information Systems) programme at the Division of Information Studies (Nanyang Technological University) for their discussion on ubiquitous computing.

REFERENCES

Abowd, G. (1999). *Software engineering issues for ubiquitous computing.* ACM Press.

Bardram, J. (2005, July 23). *The trouble with login: On usability and computer securityin ubiquitous computing.* Springer-Verlag London Limited.

Bell, G., & Dourish, P. (2007, January). Yesterday's tomorrows: Notes on ubiquitous computing's dominant vision. *Personal Ubiquitous Computing, 11*(2), 133-143.

Carroll, J. (2000). *Making use: Scenario-based design of human-computer interactions.* The MIT Press.

Choo, C.W. (1997). IT2000: Singapore's vision of an intelligent island. In P. Droege (Ed.), *Intelligent environments.* North-Holland, Amsterdam.

Gadamer, H.G. (1982). *Reason in the age of science* (Trans.). Cambridge: MIT Press.

Heidegger, M. (1955, 1977). The question concerning technology (Trans.). In *The question concerning technology and other essays* (pp. 3-35). New York: Harper & Row Publishers.

IDA. (2005a). *Enhancing service, enriching experience, differentiating Singapore.* iN2015 (p. 14). Retrieved January 16, 2008, from http://www.in2015.sg/download_file.jsp?file=pdf/11_Tourism_Hospitality_and_Retail.pdf

IDA. (2005b). *Innovation. Integration. Internationalisation.* iN2015 (p. 92). Retrieved January 16, 2008, from http://www.in2015.sg/download_file.jsp?file=pdf/01_iN2015_Main_Report.pdf

IDA. (2006). iN2015. Retrieved January 16, 2008, from http://www.in2015.sg/about.html

IDA Infocomm Survey. (2006). Annual survey of Infocomm usage in households and individuals 2006. Retrieved January 16, 2008, from http://www.ida.gov.sg/doc/Publications/Publications_Level2/2006_hh_exec%20summary.pdf

Jones, M., & Marsden, G. (2006). *Mobile interaction design.* John Wiley & Sons Ltd.

Keefe, D., & Zucker, A. (2003). Ubiquitous computing projects: A brief history. In *Ubiquitous Computing Evaluation Consortium.* Arlington, VA: SRI.

McCarthy, M. (2005). *Adidas puts computer on new footing.* Retrieved January 16, 2008, from_http://www.usatoday.com/money/industries/2005-03-02-smart-usat_x.htm

Mobile Taiwan Initative. (2004). Retrieved January 16, 2008, from http://www.roc-taiwan.org/uk/TaiwanUpdate/nsl022005h.htm

National Computer Board. (1992). *A vision of an intelligent island: IT2000 report.* Singapore: National Computer Board.

Norman, D. (1998). *The psychology of everyday things.* Basic Books.

Rogers, Y., Price, S., Randell, C., Fraser, D. S., & Weal, M. (2005). Ubi-learning integrates indoor and outdoor experiences. *Communications of the ACM, 48*(1), 55-59.

Rosson, M. B., & Carroll, J. M. (2002). Usability engineering in practice. In *Usability Engineering-Scenario-Based Development of Human-Computer Interaction* (pp. 349-360). San Francisco: Morgan Kaufmann Publishers.

Want, R., & Pering, T. (2005). System challenges for ubiquitous & pervasive comput-ing. In *ICSE'05, ACM* 1-58113-963-2/05/00.

Weiser, M. (1991). The computer for the twenty-first century. *Scientific American, 265*(3), 94-104.

Weiser, M. (1993a). Some computer science issues in ubiquitous computing. *Communications of the ACM, 36*(7), 75-84.

Weiser, M. (1993b). Ubiquitous computing. *IEEE Computer, 26*(10), 7 1-72.

Wireless@SG project. (2006). Retrieved January 16, 2008, from http://www.ida.gov.sg/Infrastructure/20070202144018.aspx

Yamada, S. (2003). *Overview of privacy management.* Ubiquitous Computing Environments, National Institute of Informatic.

Chapter II
Pervasive Computing:
What is it Anyway?

Emerson Loureiro
Federal University of Campina Grande, Brazil

Glauber Ferreira
Federal University of Campina Grande, Brazil

Hyggo Almeida
Federal University of Campina Grande, Brazil

Angel Perkusich
Federal University of Campina Grande, Brazil

ABSTRACT

In this chapter, we introduce the key ideas related to the paradigm of pervasive computing. We discuss its concepts, challenges, and current solutions by dividing it into four research areas. Such division is how we were able to understand what really is involved in pervasive computing at different levels. Our intent is to provide readers with introductory theoretical support in the selected research areas to aid them in their studies of pervasive computing. Within this context, we hope the chapter can be helpful for researchers of pervasive computing, mainly for the beginners, and for students and professors in their academic activities.

INSIDE CHAPTER

The recent advances in hardware and wireless technologies have leveraged the creation of the first experimental pervasive computing scenarios. Due to the belief that these scenarios will be an integral part of future living, research in this field is increasing at a fast pace. Therefore, theoretical and mainly practical studies are of great use as a way of supporting this belief.

Performing such studies, however, implies identifying the intricacies behind pervasive computing. Although its concept is quite simple, understanding these intricacies is a task which scatters across different research fields. Computer networks, distributed and cognitive systems, software engineering, and user interface design are some of these fields.

Therefore, in this chapter our main objective is to identify and discuss, at an introductory level, some of these intricacies. More specifically, we define four major research areas in pervasive computing, namely pervasive networking, context awareness, pervasive systems development, and pervasive computing middleware. Based on this view, we then take the reader on a journey through the universe of pervasive computing, discussing concepts, challenges, and current solutions.

INTRODUCTION

Today, computing is facing a significant revolution. There is a clear migration from the traditional desktop-based computing to the ubiquitous era, where computing will be spread all around us and seamlessly integrated into our lives. It is this new stage of computing that researchers have named pervasive computing. We can say that it is the accomplishment of the so-called concept of *calm technology* (Weiser & Brown, 1995), or as Weiser (1993) has said, it "envisions computation primarily in the background where it may not even be noticed" (p. 1). Not surprisingly, these ideas require us to view computers in a totally different way, not only as something we log onto, work on, and log out of when we are finished (Saha & Mukherjee, 2003). Instead, we should see a computer as a portal to a repository of computational resources, making use of them to work on the background and fulfill tasks according to our needs and preferences.

Pervasive computing, also known as ubiquitous computing (Weiser, 1991), has been recognized as the third wave in computer science, following the mainframe and the personal computer ages. Therefore, even if not fully conceived, pervasive computing will be the prevailing paradigm of the 21st century. Observing the graph shown in Figure 1[1], one can see the sales associated with ubiquitous computing devices follow a fast exponential growth. As more and more facilities, or services,

Figure 1. Sales of mainframes, personal computers, and ubiquitous computing devices

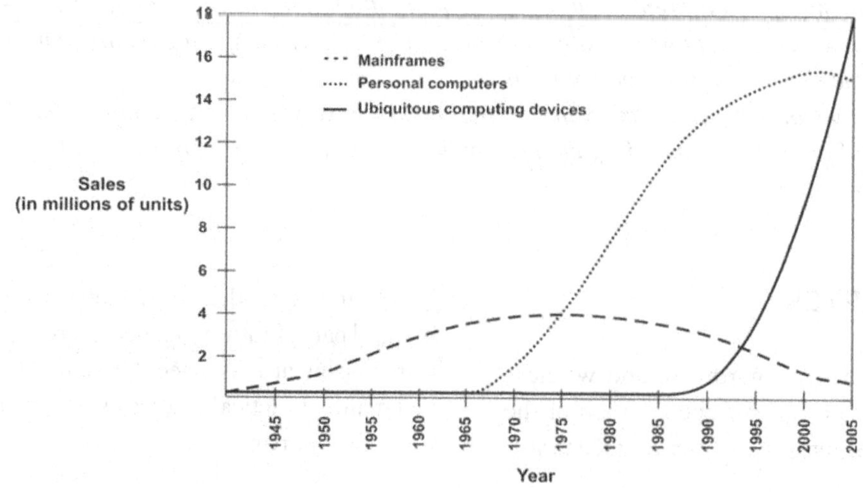

Figure 2. Overview of the chapter

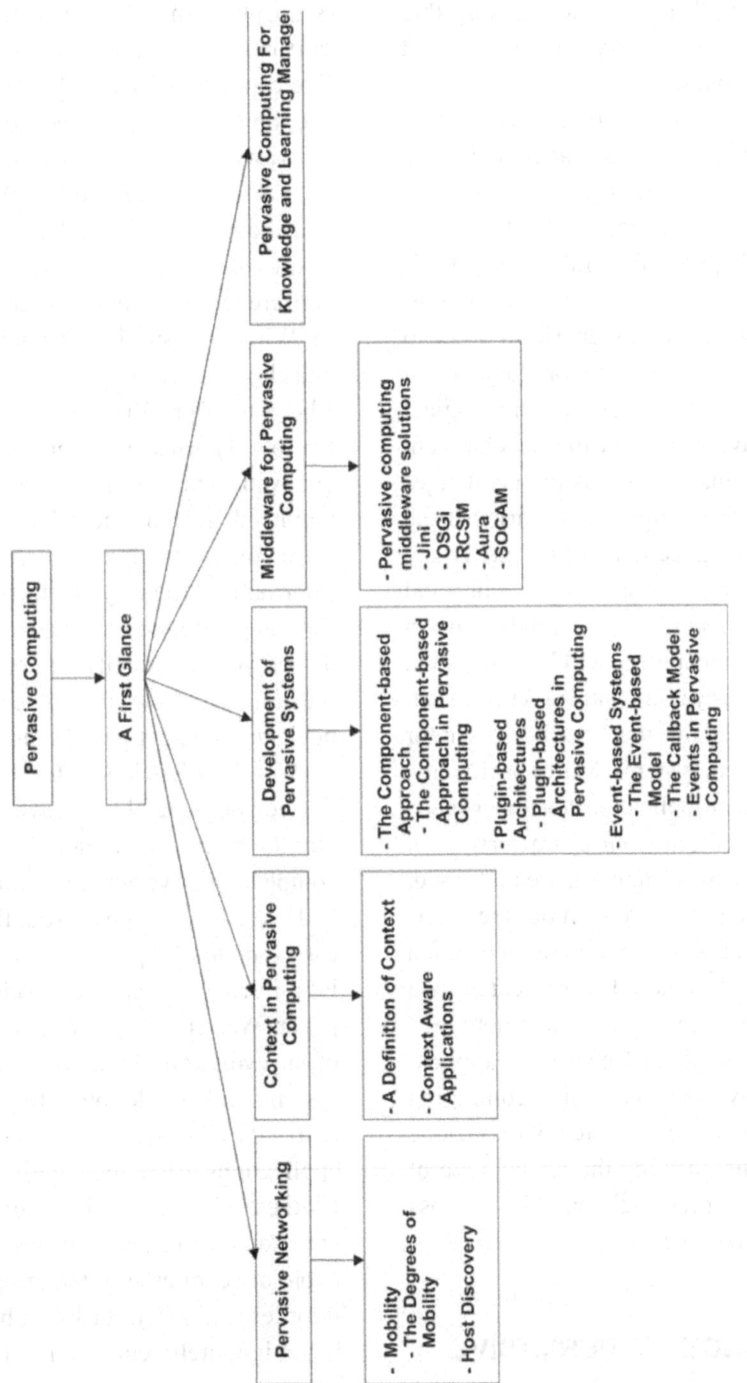

will be available for users of such devices, this growth, even that in a lower rate, will be expected to continue. After all, it is not for nothing that academy and mainly industry are so confident on the pervasive computing paradigm.

Getting a ride on this new trend, the purpose of this chapter is to conduct the reader behind the scenes of pervasive computing, introducing the main concepts and challenges involved in it. The structure of the chapter is illustrated in Figure 2. We start with a first glance at pervasive computing by describing a sample scenario in order to provide the reader with the general concepts. It is presented as an overview of the technological advances that have leveraged the development of pervasive systems, as well as the challenges imposed by pervasive computing scenarios. In the Pervasive Networking section, we present two key concepts for pervasive environments, mobility and host discovery. The notion of context and its importance to pervasive computing will be outlined in the Context in Pervasive Computing section. Next, we present some methods that have been used for developing pervasive systems. More specifically, some techniques that application developers need in order to deal with the inherent characteristics of software for pervasive computing are discussed. Based on this discussion, we then outline in the Middleware for Pervasive Computing section the main features that should be presented by a pervasive computing middleware and how they can aid the development of pervasive applications. Additionally, some pervasive computing middleware solutions are presented. We conclude the chapter by summarizing the actual state of pervasive computing research, and also discuss possible future directions.

A FIRST GLANCE AT PERVASIVE COMPUTING

Imagine yourself porting a mobile device, like a handheld, while walking through a shopping mall. Now imagine you are very interested in having a cappuccino. You think it is a pity there is no place in this mall offering cappuccinos. Fortunately, your handheld "knows" that you like cappuccino, and it becomes aware that the shopping mall has just opened a coffee shop. And guess what? Cappuccinos are sold there. Based on this information, your mobile device notifies you about this news, and now you can have your desired cappuccino. While you are savoring it, you are reminded of that book you are interested in. Without hesitation, you take your device out and check to see if any store in the mall has such a book to offer. When the search is finished, you find out that two bookstores are selling the book you want. The search returns all the information you need, such as the price of the book in both stores, discounts, and payment options. With such information at hand, you select the offer best suited for you and request the book. From your mobile device, you provide all the information to complete the purchase. Now, all you need to do is go to the bookstore and get your brand new book.

Wonderful, is it not? Just by porting a mobile device you were able to savor a cappuccino and buy the book you wanted. And both tasks were completed in a very natural way, as if computing had been fully woven into our lives. This is a typical example of a pervasive computing scenario. First introduced by Mark Weiser in his seminal paper (Weiser, 1991), pervasive computing is part of an evolution chain consisting of distributed systems and mobile computing (Satyanarayanan, 2001). It envisions a world where computing and applications are embedded in everyday objects. Clothes, televisions, air conditionings, and cars are examples of such objects. They will be capable of seamlessly interacting with each other in order to perform tasks on behalf of the users by taking intelligent actions or making available relevant information at the right place and at the right time.

Weiser affirmed that pervasive computing can be achieved through three major technologies:

Table 1. The introductory literature that has been used and their main contributions

Reference	Main Contribution
(Weiser, 1991) (Weiser, 1993) (Saha & Mukherjee, 2003)	Overview of pervasive computing
(Satyanarayanan, 2001)	Challenges brought on by pervasive computing
(Weiser & Brown, 1995)	The concept of calm technology
(Garlan, Siewiorek, Smailagic, & Steenkiste, 2002) (Stanford, Garofolo, Galibert, Michel, & Laprun, 2003) (Esler, Hightower, Anderson, & Borriello, 1999) (Loureiro, Bublitz, Barbosa, Perkusich, Almeida, & Ferreira, 2006)	Some current solutions for pervasive computing

cheap and low-power devices, a network infrastructure for communicating these devices, and pervasive applications. At the time this was said, hardware technology was not fully available to support pervasive computing. Wireless networking, as we have today, was neither available nor deployed in mobile devices. Consequently, pervasive applications could not be developed.

This started to change with the introduction of more powerful mobile devices, such as the current smart cellular phones and handhelds, that allowed for the development of more complex applications for such devices. Also, the embedding of wireless networking technologies, like Bluetooth (Bray & Sturman, 2000) and Wi-Fi (Reid & Seide, 2002), on mobile devices has promoted the availability of mobile applications. These technologies have permitted us to give the first steps toward the vision of pervasive computing. This has caused a rush for the first solutions in the field, and many works with this purpose have been developed. Oxygen (*http://www.oxygen.lcs.mit.edu*), Aura (Garlan, Siewiorek, Smailagic, & Steenkiste, 2002), Smart Space (Stanford, Garofolo, Galibert, Michel, & Laprun, 2003), Portolano (Esler, Hightower, Anderson, & Borriello, 1999), and Wings (Loureiro, Bublitz, Barbosa, Perkusich, Almeida, & Ferreira, 2006) are some examples of works related to the branch of pervasive computing.

However, a long road is still ahead. Despite the hardware advances in the last years, there are still a new set of problems associated with software systems for pervasive environments. For pervasive computing to become a true reality, applications need to have full access to the information about the users and the environments in which they are situated. This is in a broad sense what has been named *context*, although many variations for the concept exist nowadays. The current lighting condition, temperature level, and the number of users around a mobile device are some examples of the information associated with the word *context*. The great challenge that remains within this scope is how to model context information, and mainly how to effectively exploit it. The effective use of context information is one of the key issues to achieve Weiser's vision of invisible computing (Satyanarayanan, 2001). Still, acting on behalf of users requires pervasive systems to be ready for changes in their interests. Changes in the local and remote resources available should also be considered, as they are important for achieving such pervasiveness.

Going down to the networking level, we find that mobility and host discovery are two important features for pervasive environments. Whereas the former allows embedded applications to perform their tasks uninterruptedly; that is, even when the user is moving through different networks, host discovery permits a device to discover network hosts, and also to be discovered by them. Due to the discovery of such hosts, a device is then able to query for the information and resources they share, informing the user about the most relevant ones.

It is clear the preceding challenges need to be first well understood and solved. Only then can dependable pervasive systems emerge. Therefore, from this point on, we start delineating such challenges, as well as mentioning some of the current solutions for them. However, if any of the introductory ideas are not clear enough, the reader can refer to the literature presented in Table 1, where we indicate the contribution of references used throughout the first two sections.

PERVASIVE NETWORKING

Pervasive networking is about the plumbing involved in the communication of devices in pervasive computing environments. Therefore, studies within this area range from the design and energy consumption techniques of wireless interfaces to the development of high level protocols, such as routing and transport ones. At this high level, mobility and host discovery play fundamental roles as enablers of pervasive environments. Research in these areas has considerably advanced, and as a result, some practical solutions are already available today. Therefore, in this section we present a review of the concepts associated with mobility and host discovery.

Mobility

You probably receive your mail at your residence, right? Now, consider that you are moving to a new house. Among other concerns, you would probably want to change the mailing address associated with correspondences like your credit card bill. In this case, you must notify your credit card company that you have just moved, and that consequently your mailing address has changed. Either you do this or your credit card bill will be delivered to the old address, which is not a desirable situation.

A scenario similar to the above one is basically what happens in computing environments enhanced with mobility. In other words, mobility must allow a device to change its physical location and still be capable of receiving network packages from the other hosts. Note that, by physical location, we are referring to the network a device is connected to. Therefore, moving through different networks is what requires a node to have its address changed.

Mobility is certainly a fundamental element for pervasive environments. The possibility for providing users with *on the move* networking enables applications to work in the background by invisibly searching for some relevant content. However, the use of mobility in computing systems inherently leads them to face a set of new and challenging problems, which can be grouped in the following way (Satyanarayanan, 1996):

- **Resource poverty of mobile computing devices:** It is a fact that mobile devices are resource-poor when compared to personal computers. Processor speed and memory/disk capacities are considerably higher in static computers than in mobile ones. Therefore, software for mobile computing need to be well designed in order to save processor usage and storage space.
- **Energy restrictions:** Static computers are plugged to some energy network, which is theoretically an unlimited source of energy. Mobile devices, on the other hand, depend on limited capacity batteries. Therefore, techniques for saving energy should be applied in mobile applications.

- **Variability of wireless links:** Wireless connectivity is still highly variable in terms of performance and reliability. Whereas some buildings provide high-bandwidth and reliable wireless connections, others may provide considerably less bandwidth and reliability. This can be even worse in an open environment, where connection may be shared by lots of users. Undoubtedly, these changes in wireless connectivity need to be addressed in pervasive computing systems by, for example, implementing some network congestion control algorithm.
- **Security of wireless connections:** Due to the broadcast nature of wireless links, they are easier to eavesdrop with than wired ones. Therefore, if security is already an important feature of fixed networks, for wireless ones it is an even more important feature.

The Degrees of Mobility

The different degrees of mobility have a direct impact over the topology of a network. The more mobile are the network nodes, the more flexible the network needs to be. In the case of Ethernet networks, for example, nodes are too static. Therefore, only in sporadic situations is it necessary to change the network address of a node. Consequently, the network topology does not necessarily need to be flexible. In this case, protocols like DHCP (dynamic host configuration protocol) seamlessly solve the problem of delivering new network addresses to nodes. At the other extreme, a network may be populated by highly mobile nodes. Such a level of mobility allows users to move around areas that, for various reasons, have no fixed network coverage. In these situations infrastructureless networks are more appropriate. That is, nodes should be capable of establishing connections with each other whenever needed. In this case, the network would be formed opportunistically as more and more mobile devices get together.

Within this context, as Sun and Savoula (2002) have already pointed out, three modes of communication can be distinguished when it comes to the degree of mobility: *nomadic, cellular*, and *pervasive communication*. In the first case, no connection is necessary when the device is migrating from one network to another. A typical example of the nomadic communication is a user who uses a notebook for connecting to a network both at work and at home. Note that there is no need to keep network connections while the users are moving from work to their house. Only when getting home should the notebook receive a new address for accessing the network. In the cellular communication mode, the network is organized in cells, where each cell is located adjacent to a set of others. All cells have a central element, which provides connectivity for the nodes within them. Therefore, a mobile device can move through different cells and maintain a connection with their central element, becoming thus accessible even when moving. Current mobile telephony networks are an example of this kind of communication, where the base stations act as the central elements. Finally, pervasive communication can be mainly characterized by the lack of a fixed network infrastructure different from the two previous ones. Therefore, nodes should establish connections directly with each other whenever they come close enough. These features are what characterize the so-called ad hoc networks (Chlamtac, Conti, & Liu, 2003), and will be of great importance in the deployment of pervasive computing environments.

Among the current solutions for mobility, we could cite Mobile IP (Perkins, 1997), GPRS (General Packet Radio System), and Bluetooth. Basically, Mobile IP and GPRS are mobility solutions respectively for IP and mobile telephony networks. Bluetooth, on the other hand, is a standard for short-range and low-cost wireless communication in an ad hoc way. Further description concerning these technologies can be found on the Web sites listed in the Useful URLs section.

Figure 3. Host discovery approaches

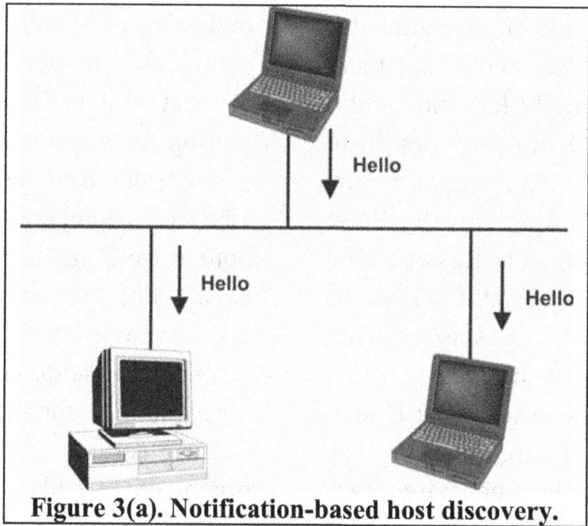

Figure 3(a). Notification-based host discovery.

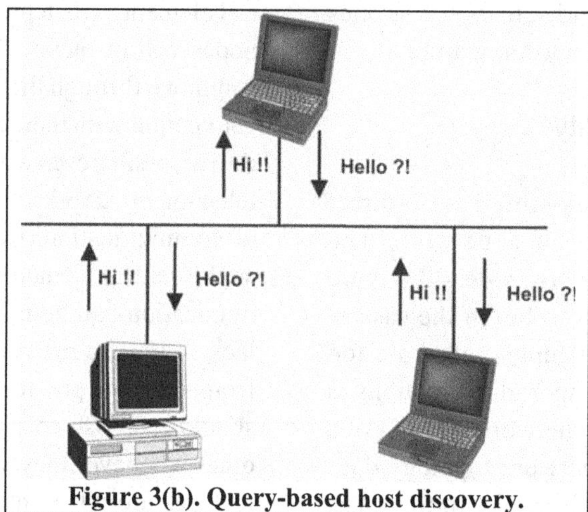

Figure 3(b). Query-based host discovery.

Host Discovery

Putting it simply, host discovery is about finding other hosts in the network, and also being found by them. This apparently simple concept is of great importance for pervasive computing environments, and can be found in technologies such as Bluetooth and UPnP (Universal Plug and Play). As an example of its usage, consider the acquisition of context information in decentralized environments, such as the available services. By using host discovery, a device can, for example, find the available hosts in the environment and query them for the services they provide. This is the service discovery mechanism used by the Bluetooth technology.

Host discovery can be performed either by using a *notification*-based approach or a *query*-based one. In the former, a host is discovered when it notifies itself to the others. This requires the host to send its advertisement through the network, so that the others can be aware of it. Such advertisements contain information such as the address, name, and description of the hosts. The advertising task can be executed a singe time (e.g., when the host joins the network) or periodically (e.g., each second). The notification-based host discovery is illustrated in Figure 3(a). On the other hand, the query-based approach, illustrated in Figure 3(b), is based on sending *discovery messages* and waiting for their responses, which contain information about the discovered hosts. Therefore, by retrieving the information contained in these responses, a host is able to contact the discovered hosts.

CONTEXT IN PERVASIVE COMPUTING

A fundamental functionality of pervasive computing applications is to present users with relevant information or services at the right place and in the right time, in a seamless way. Such information can be, for instance, a landmark for tourists to visit based on their preferences. In this process, two key inputs are involved: the needs and interests of the user and the information available both in the environment and in their devices. The former allows the applications to define what sort of information would be relevant to the user. The latter is the source from where such information will be retrieved. Let us get back to our first example, the one presented in the First Glance on Pervasive Computing section. In that case, your desire for a cappuccino and the book you wanted to buy were your needs and interests. Whereas the former could be acquired, for instance, by keeping historic information of your preferences, the information about the book has been explicitly provided by you. Based on both information, the application running in the handheld was able to determine what would be considered relevant information for you. By gathering information from the environment, the application decided that the opening of a new coffee shop and the bookstores in the surrounding area were relevant enough information to present you.

A Definition of Context

The preceding discussion should provide at least a first impression of what *context* really means. In pervasive computing literature, context has been defined in a number of ways. Some researchers have defined context by categorizing the different information associated with it. Gwizdka (2000), for example, identifies two types of context: *internal* and *external*. Internal context provides information about the state of the users, such as their current emotional state. External context, on the other hand, describes the environment on which a user is immersed, for example, informing about the current noise or temperature level. In the work of Petrelli, Not, Strapparava, Stock, and Zancanaro (2000), two types of context are identified: *material* and *social*. Material context is associated with location (e.g., at home), devices (e.g., a handheld, a cellular phone) or the available infrastructure (e.g., available networks). Social context, on the other hand, encapsulates the information about the current social state of the user, for example, in a meeting or a movie theater. Another work, by Schilit and Theimer (1994), defines three categories for grouping context information: *computing context*, *user context*, and *physical context*. A refinement of these categories is presented by Chen and Kotz (2000), through the addition of a fourth category, *time context*. The information associated with each category is presented as follows.

- **Computing context:** Network bandwidth, the cost involved in communication, and available resources, such as printers, displays, and workstations.

- **User context:** People in the vicinity and the location, profile, and current social situation of the user.
- **Physical context:** Lighting and noise levels, current temperature, and traffic conditions.
- **Time context:** Time of the day, day of the week, month and season of the year.

Note that the above ideas do not really define what is context, but instead try to give it a meaning by enumerating the sort of information that could be related. The problem in defining context in this way is that it may be hard to affirm whether some information can be considered context information or not. Additionally, a more general definition of context would certainly enable a better understanding of its role in pervasive computing. Therefore, for the purposes of this chapter, we consider a context as defined by Dey (2001, p. 45).

Context is any information that can be used to characterize the situation of an entity. An entity is a person, place, or object that is considered relevant to the interaction between a user and an application, including the user and applications themselves.

Context Aware Applications

Considering the current context for determining the actions that can be taken is very natural for us. We commonly use information such as the place we are at and the people around us to guide our actions. When we are in a movie theater, for example, we know how bothersome it is to speak loudly, and so most of us generally do not do so. In this scope, applications that make use of this kind of information are called *context aware applications*. Such applications, however, require functionalities for acquiring and interpreting the context information, and to choose and execute an action based on it. More precisely, three elements are involved throughout this process: *context acquisition, context representation*, and *context reasoning*.

Context acquisition concerns the way context information is obtained, namely *sensed, derived*, or *explicitly provided* (Mostéfaoui, Rocha, & Brézillon, 2004). Sensed context information is gathered from physical sensors, such as lighting or temperature ones. Derived context information is computed on demand, like the time of the day and the number of people around. Finally, when context information is explicitly provided, the user is responsible for providing it. An example of this acquisition can be viewed on applications which provide a form for users to fill in with their preferences (i.e., favorite kinds of books, movies, food, and entertainment).

Once acquired, context information needs to be made available to the interested applications. This implies that it must be represented in an agreed format, so that the interested applications can "understand" the information they received from the providers. As already pointed out by Held, Buchholz, and Schill (2002), the representation of the context should be *structured, interchangeable, composable/decomposable, uniform, extensible*, and *standardized.* Structuring is important for enabling applications to filter pieces of information from the context. Interchangeability is related to the possibility of applications to exchange context information with each other. Therefore, in order to provide this characteristic, a context representation must be serializable. Composition and decomposition enables to compose and decompose context information from different sources. This allows transferring only sub-parts of the information, for example, when it has been updated, to avoid sending the whole context representation. Uniformity claims that different kinds of context information (e.g., user's profile, device profiles, resource profiles) should be represented in a similar manner in order to ease interpretation by the applications which use them. As the number of terms and variables of a context is difficult to predict, even in quite restricted domains, extensibility is also a fundamental characteristic for context information representation. Finally, as devices and applications can come from different vendors, context information must be based on standards. This would certainly improve the exchanging of context information among pervasive computing applications. Current solutions for pervasive computing represent context in different ways; for example, using key-value pairs, XML documents (Boyera & Lewis, 2005; Ryan, 1999), object-oriented models (Henricksen, Indulska, & Rakotonirainy, 2002), and ontology-based models (Chen, Finin, & Joshi, 2003; Henricksen, Livingstone, & Indulska, 2004; Masuoka, Labrou, Parsie, & Sirin, 2003).

Considering that the context information is represented in a way that applications understand, it is possible to make use of this information and perform context reasoning. Basically, context reasoning is the use of contextual information for guiding the actions an application will take. As Satyanarayanan (2001) has already pointed out, the effective use of context information is a fundamental element in pervasive computing, as a means for achieving the invisibility feature envisioned by Weiser. The context reasoning mechanism of a pervasive computing system can be as simple as *if-then-else* statements, or as complex as rule-based (Nishigaki, Yasumoto, Shibata, Ito, & Higashino, 2005) and case-based methods (Ma, Kim, Ma, Tang, & Zhou, 2005). An important characteristic of context reasoning systems is the ability to deal with uncertain context information. As the information acquired by sensors (i.e., sensed context information) is prone to errors, applications should consider the quality of the acquired context information when performing their reasoning tasks. To this end, different approaches have been proposed using, for example, Bayesian networks (Gu, Pung, & Zhang, 2004a) and Fuzzy logic (Ranganathan, Muhtadi, & Campbell, 2004).

DEVELOPMENT OF PERVASIVE COMPUTING SYSTEMS

Based on our discussion until now, it is easy to realize that the intrinsic features of pervasive computing have an impact on the way software is designed and developed. For example, adaptability, customization, and context sensitivity are some of the characteristics that are constantly associated with pervasive computing systems (Raatikainen, Christensen, & Nakajima, 2002). Different software engineering techniques have been used when dealing with them. In this way, we will now review some of these techniques, as well as how they can be applied in pervasive computing systems. More precisely, we will discuss how the component and plugin-based approaches can be used to provide such systems with adaptability and customization. In addition, we show how they can be aware of changes in the context, through the generation and notification of events.

The Component-Based Approach

Component-based software engineering addresses the development of systems as an assembly of components. More precisely, its focus is on the development of components as reusable entities, as well as on the maintenance and upgrade of systems through the customization and replacement of such components. The main advantages of this reuse and assembly-based paradigm is a more effective management of complexity, reduced time to market, increased productivity, and improved quality (Crnkovic, 2001).

In a general way, a component is a software implementation which can be executed in a logic or physical device and can be reused in several applications of the same domain (Bachman, Bass, Buhman, Dorda, Long, Robert, Seacord, & Wallnau, 2000). The well-defined interface of the component describes the services or events that implement its functionalities. Such inter-

Figure 4. Component-based architecture

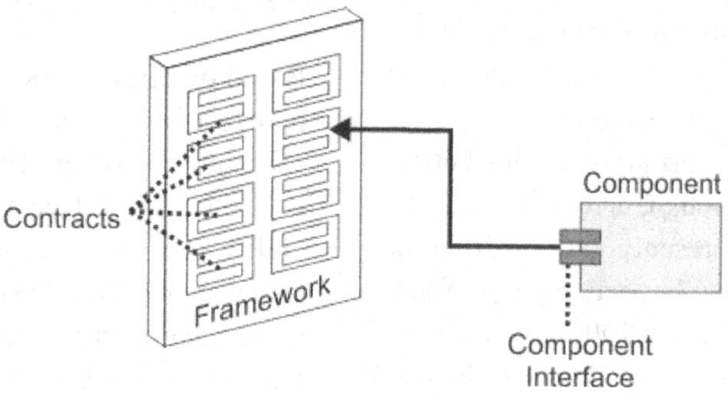

face enables encapsulation of the component's functionalities, reducing the coupling among them, and also improving the flexibility of the software design.

Because the components must be connected to assemble the application, it is necessary software to ensure the interaction among components, managing their service and event dependencies. Generally, such entity is implemented as a software framework. To guarantee the components will behave as expected by the framework, some interfaces, called *contracts*, are defined (see Figure 4). These contracts, which components are forced to implement, guarantee that the development of independent components satisfies certain standards, allowing the framework to use such components without being aware of their internal implementation details (Bachman et al., 2000).

The Component-Based Approach in Pervasive Computing

Within the scope of pervasive computing, the application of the component-based approach is straightforward in the development and maintenance of software. Due to the dynamics and heterogeneity they present (e.g., different services available, several kinds of protocols, devices with different processing power, and storage capabilities), the reuse and flexibility characteristics of components are mandatory in pervasive computing software design. The combination of these features provides an efficient way for enabling an application to seamlessly adapt. This can be performed either by dynamically changing a component by an equivalent, or by assembling a new functionality to the application.

In this context, reuse is important, for example, due to the increasing number of technologies related to pervasive networking, such as Bluetooth, UPnP, Zeroconf (Guttman, 2001), and JXTA (Gong, 2001). Since such technologies are based on standard protocols, they can be implemented as software components in order to be reused in several applications. Reuse is not only interesting for communication technologies. Components can also be implemented for many other purposes, such as audio and video streaming and context information retrieval, and yet provide the same reuse feature.

Examples of pervasive computing systems which make use of the component approach include Aura (Garlan, et al., 2002), Runes (Costa, Coulson, Mascolo, Picco, & Zachariadis, 2005), and PCom (Becker, Handte, Schiele, & Rothermel, 2004).

Plug-in-Based Architectures

Applications based on the plug-in approach are characterized by having a functional core with well-defined hooks where extensions (i.e., plug-ins) can be dynamically plugged (see Figure 5) (Mayer, Melzer, & Schweiggert, 2002). The functional core contains only the minimum set of functionalities the application needs to run. Plug-ins, on the other hand, are intended to enhance the application by adding features to it. Therefore, plug-in-based applications can be executed even when no extensions have been installed. Besides, features that are not in use can be safely removed, by plugging out the associated plug-in.

A more revolutionary view of plug-in-based architectures is to consider everything as a plug-in. In this new form of plug-in architectures, the application becomes a runtime engine for managing each plug-in's life cycle. As a consequence, end user functionalities are entirely provided by means of plug-ins. For such kinds of application, the extension of plug-ins through other plug-ins is thus a fundamental feature (Birsan, 2005).

Plug-in-Based Architectures in Pervasive Computing

The application of the plug-in approach in pervasive computing systems provides them with the needed characteristic of customization. From minimum, but functional software, users can gradually download specific plug-ins to their daily activities, choosing the ones which best supply their needs. Take as an example an environment filled with services of video streaming, delivered in *avi* format. Consider now a mobile device, with a video player installed, capable of receiving video streaming through the network and displaying it to the user. Such a player, however, can only decode *mpeg* formats, and the environment delivers video in *avi*. Once the user wants to play some movie available in the environment, the player has to transparently find out a way of playing *avi* video formats. Therefore, considering that Internet access is available in the environment, the video player can download an *avi* plug-in from a repository, install it, and play the required video in a transparent way. Note that, although the player did not know the user would ever need to receive a video stream in *avi* format, it was prepared for such situation, permitting it to fulfill the process smoothly.

It is interesting to note how the pure plug-in approach fits well when applied in pervasive computing. The plug-in runtime environment, obviously equipped with other features, like context sensitivity, can be mapped to a pervasive computing infrastructure. Applications would then be viewed as plug-ins, which could be extended by other plug-ins, and so on. Therefore, plug-ins, in

Figure 5. General view of a plug-in-based architecture

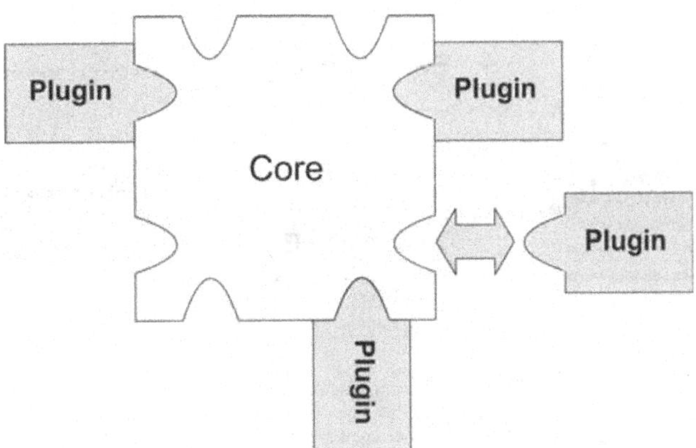

this case, applications, could be installed in the user's device on demand, and be removed from it when no longer needed.

Within this scope, the fact that plug-ins can be removed without affecting its host application is also important for pervasive computing. Mobile devices are restricted concerning disk and memory capacity, and thus it would be helpful to remove non-used plug-ins in order to save some space.

Practical examples concerning the usage of the plug-in concepts in pervasive computing can be found in middlewares like Wings (Loureiro, et al., 2006), BASE (Becker, Schiele, Gubbels, & Rothermel, 2003), ReMMoC (Coulson, Grace, Blair, Duce, Cooper, & Sagar, 2005), and Plugin-ORB (dAcierno, Pietro, Coronato, & Gugliara, 2005).

Event-Based Systems

An event-based system is the one in which the communication among some of its components is performed by generating and receiving events. In this process, initially a component fires an event, and after that, such an event will be delivered to all the components interested in it. In an event-based system, a component can assume the role of *producer*, *consumer*, or both. The producer is responsible for generating and firing events. The consumer, on the other hand, is a component which registers itself for the occurrence of a particular event, and is notified when such event occurs.

The process of event notification can be performed in two ways: through the event-based or the callback cooperation models (Fiege, Mühl, & Gärtner, 2002). In the former, a key element is the *event service*. Such an element is responsible for receiving an event from a producer and forwarding it to consumers. To exemplify this process, we have presented an example, which is illustrated in Figure 6. In such a figure, we have six components (A, B, C, D, E, and F), the event service, and two kinds of events (X and Z). Some components act only as producers (components A and C) whereas others only as consumers (components B, D, and F). Finally, component E acts as both a producer and a consumer. The arrows in the figure indicate the flow of event announcements and notifications

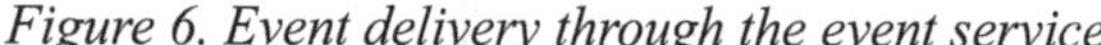

Figure 6. Event delivery through the event service

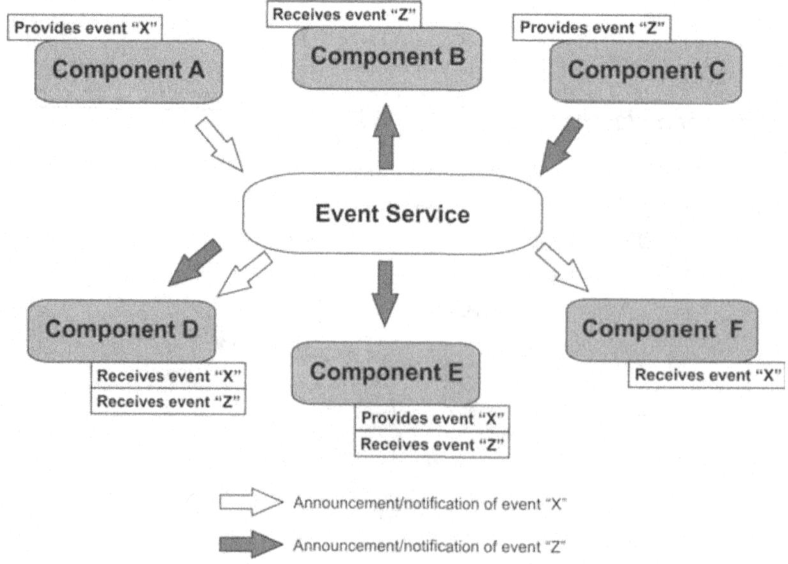

within the system. In the callback model, on the other hand, the consumer subscribes directly to the provider of the event. Therefore, the provider must keep track of the consumers for each event it provides. When some component is interested in various events, it must thus subscribe to each component providing the event. The so-called *Observer* design pattern (Gamma, Helm, Johnson, & Vlissides, 1995) is an abstraction of the callback event cooperation model.

The Event-Based Approach in Pervasive Computing

In the context of pervasive computing, the event-oriented approach can be very helpful in the notification of changes in the context. An example would be a user, located in a shopping mall, who is interested in book discounts. Applications dispersed in the environment could frequently deliver events associated with the discounts available in the mall. Through a handheld, the users could then register their interests on events associated, for example, with books discounts. As soon as one of such events is generated by some application, a centralized event service would be able to deliver the event to the user's handheld, which in turn would notify the user. The event could then provide the user with information such as the store offering the discounts and the associated books.

Another use of events in pervasive computing is for notifying applications about the battery level of a device. In this scenario, through the callback cooperation model, an application could specify a value associated with the remaining battery (e.g., 5%) and register itself to an event which is fired every time the battery level reaches such a value. In this way, an application could be notified when the device is about to be run out of energy, in order to save some critical data before the battery be completely consumed.

The event approach has been successfully used in the development of pervasive software systems. Maybe the best example we can cite is the UPnP specification. Its event mechanism, which uses the General Event Notification Architecture (GENA) (Cohen, Aggarwal, & Goland, 2000), permits the notification of changes in a device, such as the services that have been inserted or removed from it. Other examples include the Scooby (Robinson & Wakeman, 2003) and Solar (Chen & Kotz, 2002) pervasive computing middlewares.

MIDDLEWARE FOR PERVASIVE COMPUTING

The task of building pervasive computing applications can be too tedious if performed from scratch. In other words, the developer will need to deal with low level networking protocols, the way the context is acquired and monitored, notification of changes in the context, and methods for enabling flexibility in their applications. This, of course, deviates the attention of the developers to tasks that are not the purpose of the application. Instead, they should only concentrate on the application logic, that is, the tasks the application must perform. This is where middleware for pervasive computing comes in.

By providing a high level abstraction for application developers, middlewares can considerably speed up development time and also decrease the number of errors in software implementation (Mascolo, Capra, & Emmerich, 2002). Besides abstracting low level details, an ideal middleware should also provide the developer with robustness, efficiency, and security (Aldestein, Gupta, Richard, & Schwiebert, 2005).

These are, however, characteristics that should be presented by any kind of middleware, targeted at pervasive computing or not. From the discussion we have presented until now, it is clear that pervasive computing middleware should not stop at this point. Adaptability, for example, is part of any application in pervasive environments, and consequently, pervasive computing middlewares should present it. Take as an example the RPC (remote procedure call) protocols they use for invoking remote services available in the environment. Considering the diversity of such protocols (e.g., XML-RPC, RMI, SOAP), the middleware could be faced with situations in which it does not implement the RPC protocol used by a certain service. Middlewares for pervasive computing should be capable of transparently overcoming this problem, by downloading the specific RPC protocol implementation, installing it, and finally invoking the service. Moreover, middlewares for pervasive computing should naturally support the development of flexible applications on top of it. In other words, they should provide all the necessary tools for developers to build inherently adaptable applications. Based on our previous discussions, the component and plug-in-based approaches can be very effective, both for the middleware and the applications running over it.

Another characteristic is that pervasive computing middlewares need to provide a way for applications to retrieve information from the context, and also to be notified about changes related to it. In middlewares for traditional distributed systems this was not required, as the context on which they were executed was too static. Therefore, the sporadic changes in the context could be easily managed by the middleware, with no need to be exposed to the applications. As a result of the dynamics involved in pervasive environments, middlewares can not efficiently take decisions on behalf of applications (Mascolo et al., 2002). It is more reasonable, thus, to expose the context to applications and let them take their own actions. At this point, context representation and event notification are very useful for pervasive computing middlewares.

Pervasive Computing Middleware Solutions

Current solutions for pervasive computing middlewares have been focused on different aspects, such as service discovery, service composition, context sensitivity, and networking heterogeneity. These solutions range from general purposes middlewares, like Jini (Waldo, 1999) and Aura (Garlan, et al., 2002), to application domain specific ones, such as healthcare (Bardram & Christensen, 2001) and e-learning (Apostolopoulos & Kefala, 2003). Due to their importance in the development of pervasive computing applications, in this section we outline some of these solutions.

Jini

Jini is a middleware focused on service discovery and advertisement. Jini services are advertised in service catalogs through a Java interface. When the service catalog address is known a priori, Jini clients make requests directly to the service catalog in order to discover services. The service catalog returns a proxy for each discovered service, which is used by clients for remotely invoking it. If the service catalog address is not known, requests are performed in order to find it. As the service provider—and consequently its services—may not be available in the network, Jini implements a lease mechanism to help clients avoid finding unavailable services. Therefore, when providing a service, its provider receives a lease, which must be renewed at a specified time interval. If the lease is not renewed, the service is removed from the service catalog, and thus can no longer be found by Jini clients.

OSGi

The open services gateway interface (OSGi) is a specification supporting the development of Java service-based applications through the deployment of components known as *bundles* (Lee, Nordstedt, & Helal, 2003). A major advantage of the OSGi specification is that such bundles can be installed, uninstalled, and updated without the need to stop and restart the Java applications. In the scope of pervasive computing, this is a fundamental feature, as it enables pervasive computing systems to adapt themselves in a completely transparent way to their users.

The main idea behind OSGi is the sharing and discovery of *services*. In other words, bundles are able to advertise and discover services. When advertising a service, a bundle can define a set of key-value pairs, representing the service's properties. Such properties can thus be useful for other bundles, in order to discover the services they need. These advertisement and discovery processes are both performed through a registry, managed by the OSGi implementation. In this way, it is able to keep track of all services currently advertised and being used, thus enabling a bundle to be updated even when other bundles are executing and using its services.

RCSM

Reconfigurable context-sensitive middleware (RCSM) (Yau, Karim, Yu, Bin, & Gupta, 2002) addresses context-awareness issues through an object-based framework. The context-independent information of an application is implemented in programming languages such as C++ and Java. The context-sensitive information is implemented as an interface, using the context-aware interface definition language (CA-IDL). This interface has a mapping of what actions should be executed according to each activated context. In this way, the application logic is isolated from the context specification.

SOCAM

Service-oriented context-aware middleware (SOCAM) (Gu, Pung, & Zhang, 2004b) supports the development of context-aware services where ontologies are used for representing context information. There are two types of ontologies: *high-level ontologies* describe generic concepts which are domain-independent, such as person, activity, location, and device, and *domain-specific ontologies* define concepts which concern specific domains, such as vehicle and home domains.

Aura

The main focus of Aura is to minimize the distraction of users by providing an environment in which adaptation is guided by the user's context and needs. This project, developed at the Carnegie Mellon University, has been applied in the implementation of various applications, such as a wireless bandwidth advisor, a WaveLan-based people locator, an application which captures the user's intent in order to provide task mobility among different environments. All these applications use components provided specifically by the Aura project, as well as other components, such as the service registry functionalities provided by Jini and Coda (Satyanarayanan, 2002).

CURRENT AND FUTURE TRENDS IN PERVASIVE COMPUTING RESEARCH

Undoubtedly, research in the pervasive computing field has considerably advanced. At the networking level, for example, wireless communication is already possible through technologies like Bluetooth, Wi-Fi, and Zigbee. Wi-Fi, although providing a data rate of up to 54 Mbps, has high energy consumption. Bluetooth and Zigbee consume considerably less energy than Wi-Fi, but provide less transmission rates, respectively of 1 Mbps and 250 Kbps at most. The tradeoff of these characteristics must then be analyzed when deploying a pervasive computing environment. Despite these advances, enhancements must still be achieved in this area. Among them, we could point out the power consumption of wireless interfaces. Are current solutions well suited for today's appliances? Can power consumption be improved? Or better, can the relation between power consumption and transfer rate of a wireless interface be improved? Considering this variability of power consumption and transfer rate in wireless interfaces, what would be an ideal configuration for the network and the appliances (i.e., the set of wireless interfaces in the environment and the devices) to minimize power consumption and maximize the transfer of data?

Mobility and ad hoc networking protocols have also been developed, like Mobile IP, GPRS, UPnP, and Zeroconf. The mix of wireless interfaces and these protocols have already leveraged the deployment of some experimental pervasive environments. One point to be considered in this scope is the degree of pervasiveness of such solutions. In other words, how seamless are they concerning configuration, initialization, and finalization? Do we need to start and stop them all the time? One could still think about the performance of these solutions in current mobile devices. Do they consume too much energy? If yes, how can they be improved?

When considering the context-awareness, undoubtedly some efforts have been made in specific application domains. As examples, we could cite tourist information, healthcare, sports, learning, multimedia, and intelligent houses. However, context is far from being used as it is intended. For example, some of the current solutions focus on discovering needed services, but do not well address the assembly of new functionalities based on the requirements of the users and the resources available. In this case, what sort of methods should be applied in order to improve this assembly? Is the context information represented in a reasonable way, so that it simplifies such assembly? Work in this area should involve more precise representation of the context, including the resources and the interests of the user, as well as more intelligent methods for better determining what is relevant to the users, and what is not. Determining what is relevant to the user also requires the application to be capable of capturing the user's preferences, needs, and different states (i.e., social, emotional, physical). User preferences are mostly acquired by providing forms which users fill in. However, how boring can it be for a user to update such forms? Considering that this is a boring task, are they willing to pay this price for some degree of pervasiveness? Concerning the needs of the user, they are commonly obtained explicitly; that is, the users provide to the system what functionality they are interested in. Can this acquisition be enhanced? Is it possible to draw a profile of the user from its reoccurring needs in order to enable pro-activity? What about the information concerning the states of the user? Is it reasonable to require the users to explicitly set them in their personal devices? Can this information be acquired in a different way, through sensors placed in the user's body for example?

Another point to be analyzed concerns the social impact pervasive computing may cause. Consider, for example, the way people will react to sensors that detect their presence and suggest actions for them. Will they be pleased for these suggestions or angry because there is always some boring gadget telling them what to do? One should consider also whether people will accept having sensors in their bodies for obtaining information like their health and emotional state. Will you? What about privacy and security? Many people are still mistrustful of checking their banking accounts through the Internet, what would they say about sharing personal information in an open environment inhabited by all kinds of people? Certainly, all these social factors are as important as technological ones, and thus, must be deeply investigated.

PERVASIVE COMPUTING FOR KNOWLEDGE AND LEARNING MANAGEMENT

As we have seen throughout this chapter, the evolution that has taken place in hardware and networking technologies, along with the dissemination of mobile devices like cellular phones, make pervasive computing the prevailing paradigm for the next computing systems. Within the scope of this trend, one of the aspects that pervasive computing can greatly contribute is knowledge management, mainly when we consider the increased demand for learning independently of time and place (Lytras, Pouloudi, & Poulymenakou, 2002). The use of information technology (IT) in the context of knowledge management is already commonplace. As already stated by Marwick (2001), many different IT solutions can be used for this purpose, with the goal of enabling knowledge to be acquired, created, and disseminated by transforming it from tacit to explicit forms and vice-versa. One of the great advantages of IT, in this case, is the possibility to transpose the barriers of time and space. Based on this, it is not hard to realize how pervasive computing can aid in further transposing such barriers. With pervasive computing technology, members of an organization are able to establish meetings, anytime and anywhere, with the goal of sharing their knowledge. In this scenario, video and audio over the Internet could be used to give the impression that the members are in a real meeting. Therefore, people from organizations geographically distributed would not need to travel to meet each other. Another use of pervasive computing technology is for the generation of reports with the intent of disseminating someone's knowledge. With the possibility of having Internet connection whenever needed, members of an organization could prepare reports about a specific topic and then distribute them to the others, no matter where they are. Within this process, any needed document, either internal or external to the organization, could also be accessed, enabling knowledge to be acquired, created, and disseminated in a ubiquitous way.

Due to this possibility of extending the limits of knowledge acquisition, creation, and dissemination, it is not surprising to see the first solutions trying to combine pervasive computing and knowledge management. An example is the work of Will, Lech, and Klein (2004), which proposes a tamagotchi-based solution for supporting mobile workers in finding relevant information for the work they perform. Basically, this solution works by enabling a mobile device to interact with information suppliers in a seamless way, through a continuous and proactive matching between the information they provide and the one needed by the mobile workers. Another work in this category is the p-learning Grid, also known as the pervasive learning Grid (Liao, Yang, & Hsu, 2005). As its name indicates, the p-Learning Grid is targeted to support mobile learners in pervasive environments. The overall idea of this work is to represent learning objects (LOs) using Grid services (Foster, Kesselman, Nick, & Tuecke, 2002), distributing them among several connected computers (i.e., Grid infrastructure). In this way, through such an infrastructure, LOs can be dynamically discovered by client devices, using, for example, the current learning needs of users. Other solutions in this field include the work of Amman, Bright, Quirchmayr, and Thomas (2003) and the GetSmart system (Marshall, Zhang, Chen, Lally, Shen, Fox, & Cassel, 2003).

CONCLUSION

In this chapter, we have discussed some concepts surrounding pervasive computing. We have provided the reader with a high level understanding of the pervasive computing paradigm at different levels, and thus we have ranged from networking to software engineering issues. By using this approach, we presented a broad vision related to pervasive computing to aid researchers, students, and professors in research and teaching activities.

Based on the concepts we have discussed, it is possible to conclude that the application of pervasive computing in the real world is still in its beginning. Many efforts have still to be made in order to bring the primary vision of pervasiveness to real life. One could ask whether such vision will really be conceived. This is, for now, a question which is still unanswered. Answering it will require deep theoretical and, mainly, practical studies. This is what researchers should focus on, and thus, this work has been an introductory theoretical contribution to this end. We believe the concepts presented here will be summed up in other works, and also be useful when developing real world applications, with the intent of reaching a reasonable vision of pervasive computing.

REFERENCES

Aldestein, F., Gupta, S.K.S., Richard, G.G., & Schwiebert, L. (2005). *Fundamentals of mobile and pervasive computing.* McGraw-Hill.

Amann, P., Bright, D., Quirchmayr, G., & Thomas, B. (2003). Supporting knowledge management in context aware and pervasive environments using event-based co-ordination. *In Proceedings of the 14th International Workshop on Database and Expert Systems Applications*, Prague, Czech Republic.

Apostolopoulos, T.K., & Kefala, A. (2003). A configurable middleware architecture for deploying e-learning services over diverse communication networks. In V. Uskov (Ed.), *Proceedings of the 2003 IASTED International Conference on Computers and Advanced Technology in Education* (pp. 235-240). Rhodes, Greece. Acta Press.

Bachman, F., Bass, L., Buhman, C., Dorda, S.C., Long, F., Robert, J., Seacord, R., & Wallnau, K. (2000). *Technical concepts of component-based software engineering* (vol. 2). Pittsburgh, PA. EUA: Carnegie Mellon Software Engineering Institute. Retrieved October 10, 2006, from http://www.sei.cmu.edu/pub/documents/00.reports/pdf/00tr008.pdf

Bardram, J.E., & Christensen, H.B. (2001). Middleware for pervasive healthcare: A white paper. In G. Banavar (Ed.), *Advanced topic workshop: Middleware for mobile computing*, Heidelberg, Germany.

Becker, C., Handte, M., Schiele, G., & Rothermel, K. (2004). PCOM: A component system for pervasive computing. In *Proceedings of the 2nd IEEE International Conference on Pervasive Computing and Communications* (pp. 67-76). Orlando, FL: IEEE Computer Society.

Becker, C., Schiele, G., Gubbels, H., & Rothermel, K. (2003). BASE-A micro-broker-based middleware for pervasive computing. In *Proceedings of the First IEEE International Conference on Pervasive Computing and Communications* (pp. 443-451). Fort Worth, USA: IEEE Computer Society.

Birsan, D. (2005). On plug-ins and extensible architectures. *ACM Queue, 3*(2), 40-46, 197-207.

Boyera, S., & Lewis, R. (2005, May 2). *Device independence activity.* Retrieved October 10, 2006, from http://www.w3.org/2001/di

Bray, J., & Sturman, C.F. (2000). *Bluetooth: Connect without cables.* Prentice Hall.

Chen, H., Finin, T., & Joshi, A. (2003). An ontology for context-aware pervasive computing environments. *Knowledge Engineering Review, 18*(3), 197-207.

Chen, G., & Kotz, D. (2000). *A survey of context-aware mobile computing research* (Tech. Rep. No. TR2000-381). Hanover: Dartmouth College.

Chen, G., & Kotz, D. (2002). *Solar: A pervasive computing infrastructure for context-aware mobile applications* (Tech. Rep. No. TR2002-421). Hanover: Dartmouth College.

Chlamtac, I., Conti, M., & Liu, J.J.N. (2003). Mobile ad hoc networking: Imperatives and challenges. *Ad hoc Networks, 1*(1), 13-64.

Cohen, J., Aggarwal, S., & Goland, Y.Y. (2000, September 6). *General event notification architec-*

ture base: Client to arbiter. Retrieved October 10, 2006, from http://www.upnp.org/download/draft-cohen-gena-client-01.txt

Costa, P., Coulson, G., Mascolo, C., Picco, G. P., & Zachariadis, S. (2005). The RUNES middleware: A reconfigurable component-based approach to network embedded systems. In *Proceedings of the 16th Annual IEEE International Symposium on Personal Indoor and Mobile Radio Communications* (pp. 11-14). Berlin, Germany.

Coulson, G., Grace, P., Blair, G., Duce, D., Cooper, C., & Sagar, M. (2005). *A middleware approach for pervasive grid environments.* Paper presented at the Workshop on Ubiquitous Computing and E-research, Edinburgh, Scotland.

Crnkovic, I. (2001). Component-based software engineering: New challenges in software development software. *Software Focus, 4*, 127-133.

dAcierno, A., Pietro, G.D., Coronato, A., & Gugliara, G. (2005). Plugin-orb for applications in a pervasive computing environment. In *Proceedings of the 2005 International Conference on Pervasive Systems and Computing.* Las Vegas, Nevada: CSREA Press.

Dey, A.K. (2001). Understanding and using context. *Personal and Ubiquitous Computing, 5*(1), 4-7.

Esler, M., Hightower, J., Anderson, T., & Borriello, G. (1999). Next century challenges: Data-centric networking for invisible computing (The Portolano Project at the University of Washington). In *Proceedings of the 5th International Conference on Mobile Computing and Networking* (pp. 24-35). Seattle, Washington: ACM Press.

Fiege, L., Mühl, G., & Gärtner, F.C. (2002). Modular event-based systems. *The Knowledge Engineering Review, 17*(4), 359-388.

Foster, I., Kesselman, C., Nick, J., & Tuecke, S. (2002). Grid services for distributed system integration. *Computer, 35*(6), 37-46.

Gamma, E., Helm, R., Johnson, R., & Vlissides, J. (1995). *Design patterns: Elements of reusable object-oriented software.* Addison-Wesley Professional.

Garlan, D., Siewiorek, D., Smailagic, A., & Steenkiste, P. (2002). Project Aura: Toward distraction-free pervasive computing. *IEEE Pervasive Computing, 1*(2), 22-31.

Gong, L. (2001). JXTA: A networking programming environment. *IEEE Internet Computing, 5*(3), 88-95.

Gu, T., Pung, H.K., & Zhang, D.Q. (2004a). A Bayesian approach for dealing with uncertain contexts. In G. Kotsis (Ed.), *Proceedings of the 2nd International Conference on Pervasive Computing,* Vienna, Austria. Austrian Computer Society.

Gu, T., Pung, H.K., & Zhang, D.Q. (2004b). Toward an OSGi-based infrastructure for context-aware applications. *IEEE Pervasive Computing, 3*(4), 66-74.

Guttman, E. (2001). Autoconfiguration for IP networking: Enabling local communication. *IEEE Internet Computing, 5*(3), 81-86.

Gwizdka. J. (2000). *What's in the context?* (Position Paper for Workshop on the What, Who, Where, When, Why, and How of Context-Awareness). The Hague: The Netherlands.

Held, A., Buchholz, S., & Schill, A. (2002). Modeling of context information for pervasive computing applications. In *Proceedings of the 6th World Multiconference on Systemics Cybernetics and Informatics,* Orlando, Florida.

Henricksen, K., Indulska, J., & Rakotonirainy, A. (2002). Modeling context information in pervasive computing systems. In F. Mattern & M. Naghshineh (Eds.), In *Proceedings of the First International Conference on Pervasive Computing* (pp. 167-180). Zurich, Switzerland: Springer-Verlag.

Henricksen, K., Livingstone, S., & Indulska, J. (2004). Towards a hybrid approach to context modeling, reasoning, and interoperation. In *Proceedings of the First International Workshop on Advanced Context Modeling, Reasoning, and Management,* Nottingham, UK (pp. 54-61). ACM Press.

Lee, C., Nordstedt, D., & Helal, S. (2003). Enabling smart spaces with OSGi. *IEEE Pervasive Computing, 2*(3), 89-94.

Liao, C. J., Yang, F. C., Hsu, K. (2005). A service-oriented approach for the pervasive learning grid. *Journal of Info. Science and Engineering, 21*(5), 959-971.

Loureiro, E., Bublitz, F., Barbosa, N., Perkusich, A., Almeida, H., & Ferreira, G. (2006). A flexible middleware for service provision over heterogeneous networks. In *Proceedings of the 4th International Workshop on Mobile Distributed Computing,* Niagara Falls, New York. IEEE Computer Society. (Accepted for publication)

Lytras, M., Pouloudi, A., & Poulymenakou, A. (2002). Knowledge management convergence: Expanding learning frontiers. *Journal of Knowledge Management, 6*(1), 40-51.

Ma, T., Kim, Y.D., Ma, Q., Tang, M., & Zhou, W. (2005). Context-aware implementation based on CBR for smart home. In *Proceedings of IEEE International Conference on Wireless and Mobile Computing, Networking and Communications,* Montreal, Canada (pp. 112-115). IEEE Computer Society.

Marshall, B., Zhang, Y., Chen, H., Lally, A., Shen, R., Fox, E., & Cassel, L. (2003). Convergence of knowledge management and e-learning: The GetSmart experience. In *Proceedings of the Joint Conference on Digital Libraries,* Houston, Texas (pp. 135-146). IEEE Computer Society.

Marwick, A.D. (2001). Knowledge management technology. *IBM Systems Journal, 40*(4), 814-831.

Mascolo, C., Capra, L., & Emmerich, W. (2002). Mobile computing middleware. *Advanced Lectures on Networking* (pp. 20-58). Springer-Verlag.

Masuoka, R., Labrou, Y., Parsia, B., Sirin, E. (2003). Ontology-enabled pervasive computing applications. *IEEE Intelligent Systems, 18*(5), 68-72.

Mayer, J., Melzer, I., & Schweiggert, F. (2002). Lightweight plug-in-based application development. In M. Aksit, M. Mezini, & R. Unland (Eds.), *Revised Papers from the International Conference on Objects, Components, Architectures, Services, and Applications for a Networked World,* Erfurt, Germany (pp. 87-102). Springer-Verlag.

Mostéfaoui, G.K., Rocha, J.P., & Brézillon, P. (2004). Context-aware computing: A guide for the pervasive computing community. In F. Mattern & M. Naghshineh (Eds.), *Proceedings of the 2004 IEEE/ACS International Conference on Pervasive Services,* Beirut, Lebanon (pp. 39-48). IEEE Computer Society.

Nishigaki, K., Yasumoto, K., Shibata, N., Ito, M., & Higashino, T. (2005). Framework and rule-based language for facilitating context-aware computing using information appliances. In *Proceedings of the First International Workshop on Services and Infrastructure for the Ubiquitous and Mobile Internet* (pp. 345-351). Columbus, Ohio: IEEE Computer Society.

Perkins, C.E. (1997). Mobile IP. *IEEE Communications, 35*(5), 84-99.

Petrelli, D., Not, E., Strapparava, C., Stock, O., & Zancaro, M. (2000). Modeling context is like taking pictures. In *Proceedings of the Workshop on Context Awareness.* The Hague: The Netherlands

Raatikainen, A.K., Christensen, H.B., & Nakajima, T. (2002). Application requirements for middleware for mobile and pervasive systems.

Mobile Computing Communication Review, 6(4), 16-24.

Ranganathan, A., Muhtadi, J.A., & Campbell, R.H. (2004). Reasoning about uncertain contexts in pervasive computing environments. *IEEE Pervasive Computing, 3*(2), 62-70.

Reid, N.P., & Seide, R. (2002). *Wi-Fi (802.11) network handbook.* McGraw-Hill.

Robinson, J., & Wakeman, I. (2003). The scooby event based pervasive computinginfrastructure. In *Proceedings of the Postgraduate Networking Conference*, Liverpool, UK.

Ryan, N. (1999, August 6). *ConteXtML:* Exchanging contextual information between a mobile client and the FieldNote server. Retrieved October 10, 2006, from http://www.cs.kent.ac.uk/projects/mobicomp/fnc/ConteXtML.html

Saha, D., & Mukherjee, A. (2003). Pervasive computing: A paradigm for the 21st century. *Computer, 36*(3), 25-31.

Satyanarayanan, M. (1996). Fundamental challenges in mobile computing. In *Proceedings of the 15th Annual ACM Symposium on Principles of Distributed Computing* (pp. 1-7). Philadelphia: ACM Press.

Satyanarayanan, M. (2001). Pervasive computing: Vision and challenges. *IEEE Personal Communication, 8*(4), 10-17.

Satyanarayanan, M. (2002). The evolution of coda. *ACM Transactions on Computer Systems, 20*(2), 2-25.

Schilit, B., & Theimer, M. (1994). Disseminating active map information to mobile hosts. *IEEE Network, 8*(5), 22-32.

Stanford, V., Garofolo, J., Galibert, O., Michel, M., & Laprun, C. (2003). The NIST smart space and meeting room projects: Signals, acquisition, annotation and metrics. In *Proceedings of the 2003 IEEE Conference on Acoustics, Speech, and Signal Processing*, Hong Kong, China. IEEE Computer Society.

Sun, J.Z., & Savoula, J. (2002). Mobility and mobility management: A conceptual framework. In *Proceedings of the 10th IEEE International Conference on Networks* (pp. 205-210). Singapore: IEEE Computer Society.

Waldo, J. (1999). The Jini architecture for network-centric computing. *Communications of the ACM, 42*(7), 76-82.

Weiser, M. (1991). The computer for the 21st century. *Scientific American, 265*(3), 94-104.

Weiser, M. (1993). Ubiquitous computing. *Computer, 26*(10), 71-72.

Weiser, M., & Brown, J.S. (1995). Designing calm technology. *PowerGrid Journal, 1*(1). Retrieved October 10, 2006, from http://www.ubiq.com/weiser/calmtech/calmtech.htm

Will, O.M., Lech, C.T., & Klein, B. (2004). Pervasive knowledge discovery: Continuous lifelong learning by matching needs, requirements, and resources. In *Proc. of the 4th International Conf. on Knowledge Management*, Graz, Austria.

Yau, S.S., Karim, F., Yu, W., Bin, W., & Gupta, S.K.S. (2002). Reconfigurable context-sensitive middleware for pervasive computing. *IEEE Pervasive Computing, 1*(3), 33-40.

ENDNOTE

1 Courtesy of the Xerox Palo Alto Research Center - http://www.ubiq.com/hypertext/weiser/UbiHome.html

APPENDIX I: INTERNET SECTION: UBIQUITOUS COMPUTING GRAND CHALLENGE

The Ubiquitous Computing Grand Challenge is a community of researchers from different parts of the world targeting ubiquitous computing (*http://www-dse.doc.ic.ac.uk/Projects/UbiNet/GC*). Their research is focused at different levels of ubiquitous computing, from social to technological. With this purpose, this community has been proposing a set of, as they call it, *foothill projects,* within the scope of ubiquitous computing. This community still provides a mailing list used by their members to discuss the projects and directions of the community, among other adjacent topics. The registration to the list is open.

Interaction

Select one of the foothill projects presented on the Ubiquitous Computing Grand Challenge Web site and prepare one of the following items:

1. A research paper with at least 3000 words, without counting images, or
2. A presentation at least 40 minutes long.

Both the paper and the presentation should present in what way the selected project contributes to the ubiquitous computing research, the state of the art, and practical applications. Remember that it could be helpful to access the mailing list, for example, to generate some interesting discussion concerning the selected foothill project.

APPENDIX II: CASE STUDY

A Usual Day with Pervasive Computing

At half past six in the morning, Jessica's alarm clock wakes her up, as programmed. As soon as she gets off the bed, the curtains of the bedroom are automatically opened and the alarm clock stops yelling. Within one hour, she dresses for work, takes her breakfast, gets her stuff, and leaves.

When arriving at work, a camera positioned at the entrance of the parking lot recognizes Jessica and her car, and thus, the gates are automatically opened. She greets the gateman and enters. At this point, her car automatically selects the best parking options. She chooses one of them, and leaves the parking lot.

Jessica is about to enter the company when a sensor in the entry of the building detects her presence, and by knowing the elevator she usually takes to go up, warns her that it is on maintenance. Based on the number of people waiting at each elevator, it suggests the best option for Jessica.

Finally, Jessica gets to her office, and at this moment environmental conditions, like lighting or air conditioning levels or curtains opening, are automatically adjusted according to her preferences. Furthermore, a coffee machine, which knows that Jessica usually drinks a cup of coffee in the morning, greets her and asks if she would like some. She has a meeting within a few minutes, but she thinks she has enough time to taste her daily coffee. Then, through a voice command, Jessica orders the machine to prepare it. After finishing the coffee, she then leaves the room for another day of work.

Late in the night, Jessica gets ready to return home. When leaving the parking lot, her car informs her that the usual way she takes home is too congested and it automatically provides an alternative route.

On her way home, she receives a phone call on her cellular phone. As she is currently driving, the phone redirects the caller's talk to an audio output located in the car. Jessica can use an available microphone to talk to the caller by forwarding the audio streaming to the cellular phone. Therefore, the focus on the driving is not compromised.

When she gets home, the mail box identifies her and notifies her about the three letters left in it. She takes the correspondences and enters her home, when again the environment is adjusted according to her preferences. Furthermore, the answering machine detects her presence and automatically informs her of missed calls. Through a voice command, Jessica starts listening to each message left. She then finds a message by her mother, asking her to return the call as soon the she gets home. Jessica stops listening to the missed calls and orders the answering machine to dial her mother's number through her cellular phone. After talking to her, Jessica has dinner and finally gets ready to sleep. She lies down on her bed, and automatically the air conditioning is turned on, the curtains are closed, and the alarm clock is set to wake her up in the morning to have one more usual day with pervasive computing.

Questions

1. What other pervasive computing features would be helpful for Jessica's daily activities? For each feature provide a detailed description of how it would be fit into the above scenario.
2. Do you think the current society is ready for this kind of technology? Explain your answer.
3. Considering the hardware and software technologies we have today, identify/describe issues of creating the pervasive computing scenario described.

APPENDIX III: USEFUL URLS

UPnP Forum Web site
http://www.upnp.org

Wi-Fi Alliance
http://www.wi-fi.org

Bluetooth Special Interest Group
https://www.bluetooth.org

What is General Packet Radio Service?
http://www.gsmworld.com/technology/gprs/intro.shtml

Zigbee Alliance
http://www.zigbee.org

Home Networking with Zigbee
http://www.embedded.com/showArticle.jhtml?articleID=18902431

Mobile IP for IPv4
http://www.ietf.org/html.charters/mip4-charter.html

Zero Configuration Networking (Zeroconf)
http://www.zeroconf.org

OSGi Alliance
http://www.osgi.org

APPENDIX IV: FURTHER READING

Banavar, G., & Bernstein, A. (2002). Software infrastructure and design challenges for ubiquitous computing applications. *Communications of the ACM, 45*(12), 92-96.

Gupta, R., Talwa, S., & Agrawal, D.P. (2002). Jini home networking: A step toward pervasive computing. *Computer, 35*(8), 34-40.

Kallio, P., Niemelä, E., Latvakoski, J. (2004). *UbiSoft – pervasive software.* Retrieved October 10, 2006, from http://www.it.lut.fi/kurssit/04-05/010651000/Luennot/T2238.pdf

Kindberg, T., & Fox, A. (2002). System software for ubiquitous computing. *IEEE Pervasive Computing, 1*(1), 70-81.

Landay, J.A., & Borriello, G. (2003). Design patterns for ubiquitous computing. *Computer, 36*(8) 93-95.

Milanovic, N., & Milutinovic, V. (2003). Ad hoc networks and the wireless Internet. In V. Milutinovic & F. Patricelli (Eds.), *Mastering e-business infrastructure* (pp. 255-335). Kluwer Academic Press. Retrieved October 10, 2006, from http://informatik.hu-berlin.de/~milanovi/chapter6.zip

Plymale, W.O. (2005). Pervasive computing goes to school. *EDUCAUSE Review, 40(1), 60-61.*

Tarkoma, S., Balu, R., Kangasharju, J., Komu, M., Kousa, M., Lindholm, T., Mäkelä, M., Saaresto, M., Slavov, K., & Raatikainen, K. (2004). *State of the art in enablers of future mobile wireless Internet. HIIT Publications.* Retrieved October 10, 2006, from http://www.hiit.fi/publications/pub_files/fc-state-of-the-art-2004.pdf

Weiser, M. (1994). The world is not a desktop. *Interactions*, *1*(1), 7-8.

Weiser, M., Gold, R., & Brown, J.S (1999). The origins of ubiquitous computing research at PARC in the late 1980s. *IBM Systems Journal*, *38*(4), 693-696.

APPENDIX V: POSSIBLE PAPER TITLES/ESSAYS

- Pervasive computing: a utopia of human mind or a promising paradigm for everyday life?
- Social impacts of pervasive computing
- Bringing pervasiveness to the real world: practical applications of pervasive computing
- Dealing with privacy of context information in pervasive computing systems
- The impact of pervasive computing on software development

This work was previously published in Ubiquitous and Pervasive Knowledge and Learning Management: Semantics, Social Networking and New Media to Their Full Potential, edited by M. Lytras and A. Naeve, pp. 1-34, copyright 2007 by IGI Publishing, formerly known as Idea Group Publishing (an imprint of IGI Global).

Section II
New User Issues

Chapter III
Convergence Broadcast and Telecommunication Services: What are Real Users' Needs?

Raquel Navarro-Prieto
Fundació Barcelona Media, Spain

Nídia Berbegal
Universitat Pompeu Fabra, Spain

ABSTRACT

The aim of this chapter is to present an example of the user-centered design cycle for the development of innovative convergence services and technology of broadcast and mobile networks. We will describe three main phases that encompass our work. During the first phase, we focused on the validation of the scenarios developed as well as requirements for the services portrayed in the scenarios, taking into consideration cultural differences among countries. Then we studied in-depth requirements for specific services (mobile TV and personalized alerting). Last, we performed a usability test in three countries to test navigational aspects, users' understanding of icons and menus, and user acceptance of the mock-up. We will explain how combining different methodological approaches (that is, contextual research, experimental studies, and usability tests) have proven to be very useful in gathering and validating user needs, scenarios, and interfaces for these complex services. In general, we would like to highlight that technology developers have to be careful about the amount of information presented, since users are very sensitive to information overload both for mobile TV and for alerting systems. Once again, for mobile services, less is more.

INTRODUCTION

This chapter will describe the work that has been carried out in the INSTINCT project (2004-2006) in order to define users' needs for mobile broadcasting services (e.g., mobile TV). Our goal was to illustrate how a combination of diverse methodologies during different phases of convergence service development could be very fruitful, even when the technology is in the early stages of definition.

INSTINCT is a European project with the goal of assisting DVB in realizing the commercial provision of convergent services in mobility with a special focus on the DVB-T, DVB-H and DVB-MHP standards in conjunction with the concept of wireless communications networks (notably GPRS and UMTS) combined with terrestrial DVB broadcast networks. Converged technologies are seen as the new leap forward in integrating the latest advances on various digital mobile radio networks. Nevertheless, the new levels of flexibility that these technologies could introduce raise the complexity for the users and potentially lower the usability, especially for services like mobile TV. Therefore, our studies are critical for understanding and properly meeting user needs for these services.

USER-CENTERED DESIGN (UCD) IN DESIGNING MOBILE SERVICES

The UCD process is a well-known approach to bringing user expectations and needs into technology development, shifting the emphasis in a project from the development of technology "for technology's sake" to the development of systems that support particular user needs in an accessible and usable way. It is widely recognized that there is a big shift from a device-driven world to a service and experience-centered world. Therefore, how the users perceive the service and the emotional impact and pleasure that the service creates and maintains is becoming more and more important.

In recent years there has been an increasing amount of research in applying UCD in mobile services in general, and some on convergence services. Nevertheless, after a review of 102 publications of major journals and proceedings in the area, Kjeldskov and Graham (2003) concluded that there is bias towards building systems and a lack of research for understanding user requirements for these technologies. Even when user studies are performed, they seem to be a "trial and error" strategy for mobile technology development. For instance, field studies are mostly being used for the purpose of evaluation, instead of for the exploration of use context and users needs to guide technology development. Their data revealed that most (71%) mobile device evaluations were done in laboratory settings. Among possible reasons for this, the authors claim that the data reflects the strong bias towards engineering and evaluating systems in the two fields where mobile human computer interaction (HCI) has strong roots, namely, computer science and human computer interaction. The bias could be due to the difficulties of finding appropriate methodology for

For instance, Kjeldskov and Graham's (2003) data could be interpreted as data collection techniques such as think aloud, video recording or observations being difficult in the field. Because of that, we consider very important to focus mobile HCI research into the development of efficient and well recognized methodologies for gathering information that can inform the development of mobile contexts.

In recent years, we have started to see publications focused on methodologies for users' studies for mobile technology. For instance, Kaikkonen, Kallio, Kekäläinen, and Kankainen (2005) conducted several studies comparing the trade off between effort and quality of the information gathered between laboratory studies and field testing. One usability of a consumer application was tested in two environments: in a laboratory and in a field with a total of 40 test users. Interestingly, they tested an application designed for consumers. Kaikkonen et al. (2005) claimed that

the users may not have any specific and clear goals during their free time, or the goal can be vague, for example, time killing or entertainment. Users of consumer applications can also be more explorative and creative with their actions than professional users. Being explorative and non-task oriented may require more from the user in real mobile contexts than in the laboratory settings.

Although their focus is still on testing, their conclusions are very informative. They found that although a contextual study would not be very worthwhile to test interface flaws to improve user interaction, the combination of these studies and usability testing is very informative for the design of these services. Other example of methodological work is the study reported by Jambon (2006), where the author reported the methodological approach, data collection and analysis when evaluating the usability of a mobile device in a quasirealistic context. He used two different methodological approaches that he named analogical and digital.

The analogical data collection refers to classic usability laboratory data collection: video of the context (DV camcorder), voice of the user (wireless microphone) and PDA screen (VNC-like tool). The digital data collection refers to the recording of user actions on the device, system feedbacks and device localization in the building.

The main conclusion of this study is that although it is possible to test the usability without recording video, usability problems may remain uncovered and will need other methods that complement the digital data collection. Nevertheless, all these works are still focus on testing rather than gathering user requirements.

As for methods to study the sociological aspects of mobile phone usage, McGuigan (2005) compares the strength and weakness of social demography, political economy, conversation, discourse and text analysis, and ethnography. Other authors are trying to create new ways to gather contextual information to update the design of mobile applications. Page (2005) presents a new method called Discount User Observations. This method is based on Contextual Inquiry sequence model evolved into a timeline associated with data points, location, and social context with photos.

A lot of the research about mobile multimedia convergence services has been focused on services around mobile TV. Although most of the work on mobile TV has been from the technology development perspective, a thorough study has been reported from Södergård (2003). After performing contextual research and lab usability studies with a prototype, they gathered evidence that mobile TV was considered "suitable for public spaces—where it has to compete with other media—as a time killer, a filler of empty moments and a buffer for privacy." Contrary to their expectations, the trial users considered the service to be a television as opposed to a multimedia service, underlying the importance that the new service to be rooted in the old one.

With the exception of this work, most of the work in mobile TV (as in mobile HCI in general) has been focused on testing technology developments. When user field trials on mobile TV have been reported, the results are presented in terms of the percentage of answers to surveys. For instance, very recently, a press release from Nokia (2006) summarizes the main findings in mobile TV pilots that have been carried out during 2005 and 2006 across Europe (i.e., in Finland, UK, Spain, and France). For instance, in Finland, with 500 users involved, 58% of the participants are reported to believe that mobile TV services would be very popular. In the UK, 83% of the participants seemed to be satisfied with this service; this number is 72% in France.

While these data could be quite useful to understand customer demand, there is a gap of knowledge for detailed information about users' contextual needs and the quality of service required by the users.

Recent studies have also tried to understand the convergence between TV in home environments and mobile technologies. For instance, Barros, Zuffo, and Benini (2006) looked at the UI of mobile phones and TV sets and they claim the two devices each have their own navigational style and incompatible input devices. The authors argue for the need of a level of consistency amongst these to facilitate the convergence of devices for the end-user that they call User Interface Continuum. Turner, Cairns, and Jones (2006) used the results of a television planning diary study to develop and evaluate design concepts that should "allow users to learn about potentially interesting programmes via their mobile as well as using recommendations from family and friends."

PHASES IN HF WORK IN INSTINCT

Requirements gathering for innovative mobile convergence technology and services is complex, as we are trying to learn about technology before it is even built. Therefore, our approach has been to use an iterative process involving users, technologists, and designers. In order to carry out this process, we needed to select some methods to learn about the users and work with them. As we have seen previously, many methods have been developed and HCI researchers are constantly working on new methods to help gain a better understanding of user activities, including activities that do not exist but will be enabled by future technologies. We propose that these methods could be used in combination depending on the phase of the technology development that we are trying to understand. Our Human Factors work for this project was divided in three phases illustrated in Figure 1.

During the first phase, we focused on the validation of the scenarios developed as well as requirements gathering for the services portrayed in the scenarios. The goal of the second phase was to provide in-depth requirements for specific services, namely the mobile TV and personalized alerting services. In the third and last phase, we performed a usability test in three countries to test the navigational aspects, the users understand of the icons and menus, the interaction device, and user acceptance of the mock-up.

First Step: Scenarios Validation

Scenario-based requirement gathering techniques have been used in Human Computer Interaction research as an effective way to capture, analyze, and communicate users' needs for technology (Carroll & Rosson, 1992; Carroll, 2000). The basic principle of this approach is that presenting scenarios of use of technology, or the foreseen technology, to users and developers can bridge the gap between the user's tasks and the design of new technology to accomplish these tasks. Several specific systematizations of the process of showing the scenarios to users have been proposed.

Figure 1. Phases in human factor's work in INSTINCT

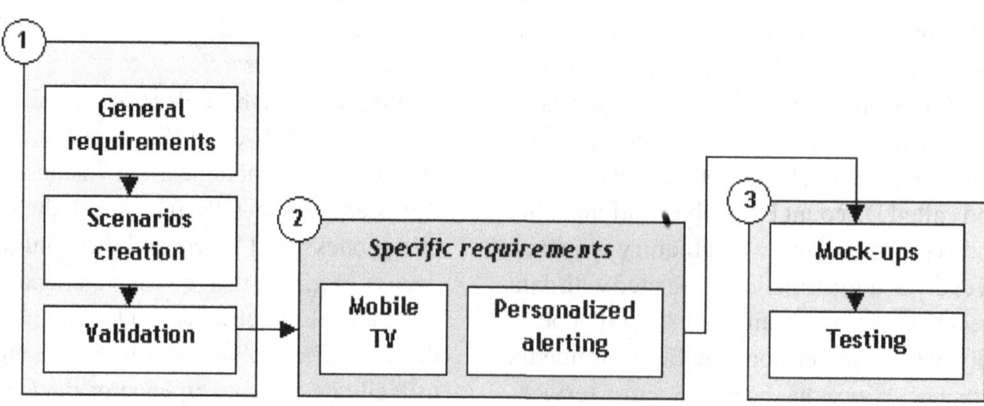

For instance, Carroll (2000) used the scenarios in workshops with users and developers proposing system features and creating "claims" (a set of possible positive and negative consequences of the implementation of this particular feature of technology component).

Three user scenarios, each one based on a merger of broadcast and telco mobile applications, have been developed within the project, and are currently being used by the INSTINCT partners to derive requirements and deliver specifications to the overall project (e.g., service announcement and delivery mode, protocols, architectures, terminals, hybrid network dimensioning, business models). Two scenarios were based on economical, social, and technological aspects of developed countries. The third scenario, developed by Brazilian INSTINCT partners, focusing on low-income users, has an approach to social and digital inclusion.

A complete description of each scenario can be found at Sicre, Duffy, Navarro-Prieto et al. (2004). In order to introduce to the reader to the type of services studied in ICING, we will present here an extract of one of the two scenarios based on a European commuter target user group:

John Doe lives in Saint-Malo and works in Rennes (France). He spends quite a lot of time commuting by train. This Saturday he decided to take the plunge and buy a bi-mode INSTINCT handset and changed to a new operator. Back at home, he connected to the INSTINCT portal to discover the whole range of provided services among them is real-time notification. After authenticating, he updated his user profile page subscribing to the sport notification service and managing the alerts levels in order not to be disturbed by overly intrusive pop-ups. Today, John woke up as his handset rings smoothly. His preferred TV "INSTINCT" programme starts giving the morning news, the handset screen shows him the list of SMS and alert messages he received during the night. He switches on the sport alert service, as well as the weather windsurf driven alert. While preparing his breakfast, John accepts a text alert informing him that the Ireland rugby team won the international tournament in Australia by defeating New Zealand and that *TV.Instinct.com* proposes a 1.30-minute video stream of the most remarkable actions of the game. John immediately grabs his INSTINCT terminal. Thanks to the link provided, he has access, in one click, to the rugby TV channel. John Doe is very enthusiastic. This new terminal enables him to enjoy his daily 40-minute journey to work. John browses the broadcast portal to see which services are available; he accesses the TV programme guide. As tonight's programme does not seem very attractive, John connects to the "Movies On Demand" mobile portal and, after authenticating, orders a movie for the evening. He indicates that the movie must be downloaded before 8:00 p.m. to his home. While browsing the INSTINCT portal, John receives a weather alert telling him that strong wind is forecasted. Immediately, John clicks on the link provided within the alert to get more specific information. Then he clicks on the weather Web cam service available through the INSTINCT portal; this service allows him to check weather conditions at "La Hoguette" beach, which is his favourite windsurfing spot.

After the draft of the scenarios was developed, the first step in the design of the scenario-based requirement gathering study was the definition of the questions about the scenarios (i.e., the services and the situations depicted) that are most relevant for the project. The production of these questions was based on several sources. First, each step of the scenarios, the services, and the technology requirements involved was studied in-depth. Furthermore, several questions were gathered from discussions and e-mails (internal to the work package and from exchanges between work packages). In our case, we were interested in the validation of the scenarios, that is, gathering direct feedback from the users about the situations and services portrayed in our scenarios. For this reason, the questions that we presented to the users, illustrated in Table 1, were oriented to

Table 1. Example of mapping between the step in the scenario, the scenario components and the questions for the participants

Slide Number	Reception situation	Service component	Access/ Delivery Mode	Scenario Components	Questions for participants
Slide 8	On the move	TV service	DVB-T	John switches to TV programme	- Can you give us an example of a situation when you would like to watch TV and/or watch a video clip, or an audio file? -Are the situations for one or another different? - Frequency? - Can you give us an example of the content that you would like to see in this kind of service
	On the move	Enhanced TV	DVB push + Telco IP	John enjoys the news with multimedia enrichment: an URL linking to additional Web pages related to the ongoing news	

get them to imagine themselves in the proposed situation, in order to understand the usefulness of the services envisioned in INSTINCT. After the set of questions had been developed, they were merged by mapping each one of them according to the user experience of the services. Therefore, the grouping of questions about services was NOT based on the technology behind a service, but on the service that the user would experience. The networks aspect was not neglected, as the network used for one service makes an impact on the services. Because of that, questions regarding the differences between receiving services on a broadcast network and receiving services on a Telco network were asked. The next task was to write the questions avoiding any kind of technical terms and to be able to engage the users in providing information about their own lives. This step was finalised by prioritising the questions and taking the final decision about which questions would be definitely asked to the participants of the study.

The second step was to map the research questions to the steps in the scenarios in order to get detailed user feedback about particular research questions in the context of these scenarios. The method chosen to present the scenarios to the users and to gather their feedback was paired interviews. Open questions in semistructured interviews (e.g., what are your expectations about a particular service) allow the Human Factors specialist to gather rich information without constraining the user to predetermined answers. In this way, no unexpected answers and particularities provided by each participant were lost. Paired interviews, where two users are questioned at the same time, have been shown to minimize the problems associated with asking the users to think-aloud about their usage of technology and to enhance the amount of information gathered (Wildman, 1995).

Each scenario was implemented as a presentation in Power Point to make it possible to share it with prospective end users. The goal of this mock up was NOT to present to the users how the user interface for the system or the services should be.

These illustrations (an example is presented in Figure 2) had two main goals:

- To present the scenarios to the users as a useful technique to trigger user needs and validate the scenarios. This method has shown to be especially useful for technologies that are under development (Navarro-Prieto & Conaty, 2003).
- To engage technology developers and human factors engineers in a dialog to specify and describe the interactions of the users with the technology.

Figure 2. Example of the slide used to illustrate the scenarios

elmundo.es
BODA
REAL
Los Principes visitan Cuenca y Albarracin antes de ir a Zaragoza en su luna de miel
John switches to TV programme and enjoys the news with multimedia enrichment: an URL linking to additional Web pages related to the ongoing news.

Towards this goal, the teleco-driven and the broadcast-driven scenarios were presented to prospective end users. Our target users were young urban customers, corporate users, and the general public on the move, walking, in public transport, or transiting through any public areas. These two scenarios have been tested with the same methodology with three different samples, namely a Spanish, English, and Brazilian sample, with a total of 66 potential citizens participating in these studies.

The analysis performed of the data gathered was divided into two stages. The first one was focused on the steps of the "discourse analysis approach" and began with the transcription of the handwritten notes for each session. During this transcription, both the answer and the topic that was asked during the question were annotated. That helped enormously in grouping all the answers that the users gave for each of the topics. The scenario elements in the service components column (third column presented in Table 2) were used as the topics.

Second, the analysis was followed up by consolidating the answers that were agreed amongst more than one user. Therefore, the entire answer grouped by question and by the different types of answers provide to each question is available. In some occasions, a consensus in the answers was found, with small differences. Other times, it was realized that there were several groups of answers to one scenario component.

The information gathered was very encouraging, as the data confirmed that Telco-broadcast convergence, in the mobile world, offers real opportunities and that the markets induced have an interesting future. From the analysis of these data we were able to create the list of services that were most wanted from each country, and also detected a few of them for which there is not, at present, a real need in people's day-to-day life. More importantly, we gather concrete information about when, how, and why they would like to use these services.

The data collected confirmed that the participants would like to have a portal that integrates the available services and allows them to access the services in any context but with different devices for each context (mobile phone, PDA, tablet PC, laptop, TV, etc.). Not surprisingly, the participants expressed their concern about the way the information is presented to them. This is true for every system that a user interacts with, but particularly relevant in the mobile context. One particular concern of users is the information overload—*not too much stuff.* An interesting solution proposed by the users was placing the alerts in a folder where the users could recover them when they want. Likewise our participants provided us with examples of how they would use these services to fill some needs that are not currently catered to by the services available to them now. Other services that have been found useful and attractive have been the use of profiles, authentication before using some services, voting services, subscription to newspapers, forums, online shopping, and context based information.

We found interesting cultural differences among the three countries involved in the study. We would like to highlight two differences. First, that mobile TV seems to be more wanted by the European participants, while in the Brazilian sample only a small part of the participants expressed that they would like it. There is an interesting difference between the Spanish and Brazilian sample, in comparison with the English sample, concerning the importance that they give to receive sport news. This service seems to be only required by the English sample.

Second Step: Specific Requirements

The goal of the second phase was to provide in-depth requirements for specific services, the mobile TV, and intelligent alerting services. We conducted one study to understand which variables are important for the user's acceptance for each of these services.

Mobile TV

For this service, we investigated what video quality was acceptable. After reviewing the existing standards and the problems with their application, we decided to create our own experimental design and session planning. We proposed an innovative methodology adapted from classical psychophysics, to discover the functions relating physical quality to perceived quality.

After reviewing the methods for absolute rating in a 5-point scale, McCarthy, Sasse, and Miras (2004) also concluded that these methods were not suitable for multimedia content. They presented an innovative approach for testing users' acceptance on multimedia technologies. According to McCarthy et al. (2004), "this metric tackles many of the drawbacks of alternative approaches." This method was based on gradually increasing and decreasing video quality within a single video to identify the threshold level at which quality becomes acceptable or unacceptable to the users. The users' task was to say when the quality starts to be acceptable or unacceptable. The clips users watched were 210 seconds in length and the quality was increased or decreased in discrete steps every 30 seconds. Users were not aware of this quality structure, the authors simply told them they would be watching films that "varied in quality." In our case, we used an experimental design where we manipulated four variables to understand their impact on the subjective ratings. These variables are presented in Table 2.

In order to make sure that all the conditions are presented the same number of times in all the possible positions of the conditions, we used a counterbalance across all the subjects in a Graeco Latin Square Design. These variables are manipulated within subjects, which means that each of the subjects passes through the three levels of the variable video both in an increasing quality order and in a decreasing quality order.

Our users' sample was similar to the sample in the first part of our project, namely, young users but not teens, white collar workers, commuters. There were a total of 24 participants in the study.

We performed statistical analysis (ANOVA) for each of the compression bit rate conditions with

Table 2. Description of the variables manipulated to understand their influence on Mobile TV acceptance

Variable Name	Number of values	Values
Compression scheme and screen size	2	▪ high-compression bit rate (MPEG4) & mobile phone screen, 160x128 pixels ▪ low-compression bit rate (MPEG2) & PDA screen size (352x288 pixels)
Gradient of quality[1]	2	▪ increasing quality ▪ decreasing quality
Video Content[2]	3	▪ Source clip A: Music clip ▪ Source clip B: Football sequence ▪ Source clip C: News from a TV news program
Quality	4	▪ For high compression bit rates (MPEG4) values: 100, 175, 250,and 325 Kbps ▪ For low compression bit rates (MPEG2) values: 0.45, 0.8, 1.15, and 1.45 Mbps

2X3X4 experimental design, with all the variables manipulated within subjects design (Gradient of the quality X Content X Video Quality).

We would like to highlight two major conclusions, the first one regarding the methodology and the second regarding the results found in the study. First, we can conclude that the methodology based on psychophysics introduced by McCarthy et al. (2004) for multimedia assessments of sport sequences has proven to be very useful for mobile TV quality assessment with a variety of content.

Regarding the main results found with this methodology, we will remark that:

- Specific thresholds for the required quality from the user perspective for each of the compression rate and videos presented were gathered. It is out of the scope of this chapter to present each of these thresholds.
- We found that it is not possible to have a "one size fits all" for the quality of video in which content should be presented to users for mobile TV services because of dependencies on the content.
- Special attention should be paid to the transmission of news content and specifically to the transmission of the text part of the video, which seems to be the main problem with video in small screens.
- Finally, we also found that users did not like the content when it was just "miniturase" for a small screen, but adapted to this new format.

Personalized Alerting

We consider important an evaluation of personalized alerting services because they are at risk of being rejected by the market if they are judged to be intrusive. We know from our requirements gathering work that unwanted passive alerting, that is, SMS message with information, is considered intrusive. On the other hand, personalized alerting that provides links to information and offers a "one click" access to a service may be seen as useful and not intrusive, especially if it contains personalized information. In addition, it can be changed and disabled very easily. Our goal was to understand when personalized alerting is considered acceptable, and to study under which circumstances users trust the system to select only the relevant alerts.

After reviewing what it is known about these services, we agreed to test the impact of three variables on the users' acceptance of the alerting system explained below:

- **The task that the user is performing:** We asked the users to perform three different tasks (watching a film, taking a phone call, and participating in a videoconference) which lasted for 7 minutes. The last two tasks were simulated in an experimental environment and were not live conversations although we instructed the users to imaging that they were real conversations.
- **The number of alerts the user receives during each task:** We had three levels of alerts, a low level with one message, a medium level with two messages, and the highest level with five messages (see Figure 3 for an example of the alerts users received).
- **The relevance of the alerts according to interests and profile:** We gave the users a list of preferences for some types of information (for instance music and news) and asked them to fill this profile in a prototyped UI. We instructed them to imagine that this profile was their own profile. Based on this profile, we classified the alerts between relevant or irrelevant for the participant.

We have chosen different topics to provide the users a wide range of alerts. The topics used have been: news (three messages), weather, public transport, music (two messages), and travel information (one message). All the alerts had three layers: a first one with a very brief summary of the alert, a second one with a more extended explanation, and finally a link to a Web resource. Figure 3 provides some examples of the alerts used:

The relevance of the message was manipulated between groups. The rest of the variables were manipulated within groups.

We created an experimental design that controlled the order in which each task was presented to each user. While they were doing these tasks, the users received different numbers of alerts according to the three levels described. Half of the users received relevant alerts according to their profile; for the other half, the alerts were irrelevant for their interests. All the conditions were presented the same number of times in all the possible positions of the conditions.

We measured users' acceptability and trust of the alerting system through questionnaires:

- **Acceptability test:** After each of the three tasks were completed the participants were asked to fill out a brief questionnaire (questionnaire B2, attached as an Annex) in order to gather a subjective numeric evaluation about the acceptability of the intelligent alerting and the grade of confidence the users have in the system.

Figure 3. Example of an alert used in our study

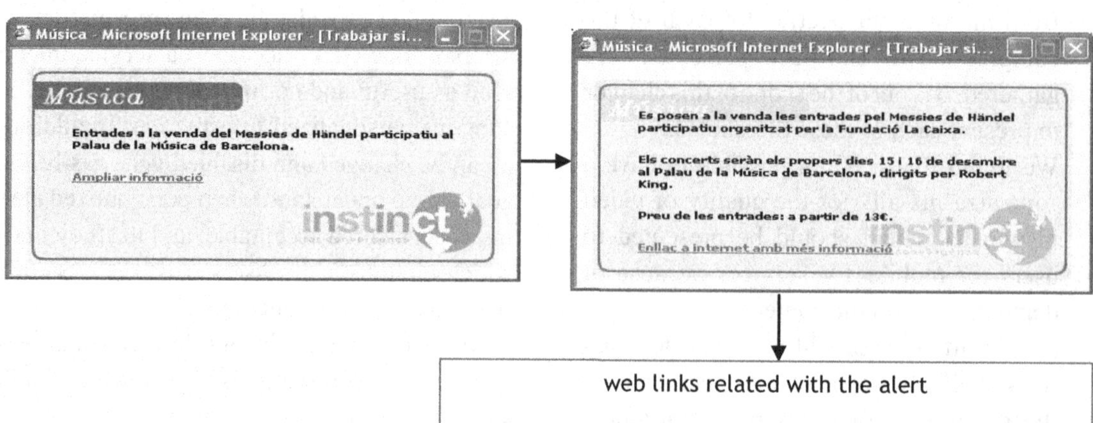

- **Trust in the system question:** After they completed the three tasks, the users were asked a question to measure their trust in the system in terms of providing alerts relevant to their profiles (in questionnaire B2, attached as an Annex).
- **Post test questionnaire:** After the participants performed the three tasks, and the post test, another questionnaire was given to allow us to get more information about in which circumstances would they be willing to use INSTINCT services and especially mobile TV.

We would like to highlight a summary of the results of the acceptability and the trust test. Regarding the acceptability test, we found significant some of the variables that we thought were important for the acceptance of the alerts, but we did not find evidence about the effect of other variables.

First, the type of task that the users are performing has shown to affect the acceptance ratings on the system, although our initial assumptions have not been validated. The task with the least acceptable rating was watching a short film, then the voice conference, and then the reading (simulated call). We considered that we need more research with other tasks in order to fully understand why the short video was the task during which the users considerd more irritable to be interrupted by an alert. His effect is stronger for the group with relevance alerts, probably explained by the fact that because the participants were interested in these alerts, they paid more attention to them.

In relation with the number of alerts, we found that receiving only one alert was the most accepted of all the levels, averaging across all the tasks, while there were no differences at all between receiving two or five alerts. This data indicates that we need to restrict the number of alerts that a service of these characteristics would show.

The type of task have also shown an effect (although not significant) on the acceptability of the different number of alerts. We found that the task for which there was the most difference in the acceptability ratings, and with the lower ratings, was the simulated phone call (reading task). In the case of the phone call task, with more alerts the system was less acceptable, and with five alerts, the system was rated unacceptable (1.75 over a 5 point scale).

We would like add to the conclusions the significant effect that we found of the relevance or not of the alerts presented in the level of trust that the users have that the system is selecting the alerts correctly for them, and in the acceptance of these alerts. Even with a small sample of alerts and with the users focus on different tasks, that is to say, their attention was mainly in performing the task that we asked then to perform, they clearly noticed whether the system was not showing what they demanded. This result has implications in the design of these systems because it validates the idea that unless we can make sure that the alerts we present are relevant, users will not use this service.

Finally, we would like to highlight that we found that participants did not like (2.3 on a 5 point scale) that the alerts were presented following the windows style getting in front of the task that they were doing. These data agree with the data found during the validation of the scenarios and suggest that we need to find less intrusive ways of presenting the alerts, for instance, an icon flashing (as was suggested by the participants).

MOCK-UP AND USABILITY EVALUATIONS

The main goal of this third phase of our work was to understand users' navigation though the mock-ups in order to test how well they could access and understand different services and parts of the interface for the different services specified in the scenarios. Three UI prototypes were developed, one for each of the scenarios developed in the project, according to the user requirements gathered in the previous two phases. The scenario developed specifically for the Brazilian population was tested in Brazil, in which the users navigated within a TV set using a specifically built remote control and mobile phone. The other two scenarios, developed for the European population, were prototyped for a mobile phone screen (test performed in U.K.) and tablet PC (test performed in Germany). A total of 10 searching tasks were defined in order to gather precise information about time and accuracy of the users using the different menus and navigation structures. Five of these tasks were common to all three scenarios (including one free navigation task) and another five were created to test the services that were specific to each scenario.

Table 3 lists the entire tasks that were created for these tests. A brief description of the tasks and which scenario was used is also presented in Table 3.

The same methodology was used in three usability tests in three different countries: Germany (15 users), the United Kingdom (15 users), and Brazil (19 users). Our users' sample was similar to the sample used in the previous studies of our project.

The metrics used and the data that we intended to gather for each of them are described below:

- Icon Recognition test tested how easily the icons and labels used in the UIs were understood. The material used for this test was a printout of the UI screens with blank spaces where the participants filled in what they thought the function of each icon was. This test was performed twice; after a free navigation task of 5 minutes, and after they had finished all the tasks. We wanted to measure if after performing several tasks with our UIs; the users had learned what the icons meant, even if they did not know at the beginning (an example is shown in Figure 5).
- The time needed to perform each task: The idea behind this measure was to gather data about which tasks were easy to perform and which ones needed more time.
- Successful task completion: it was important for us to be able to compare the average task completed across scenarios. If several users were unable to complete that task at all (within what was consider a "reasonable

Table 3. User tasks for each scenario

TASK	Broadcast Scenario	Telco Scenario	Brazilian Escenario
TASK 1: Free navigation task (Fix duration of 5 minutes)	YES	YES	YES
TASK 2: Understanding the portal/Services start page	YES	YES	YES
TASK 3: Finding content pages and reading/watching them	YES	YES	YES
TASK 4: Accessing the EPG and interacting with TV programs	NO	YES	YES
TASK 5: Reconfiguring INSTINCT account	NO[3]	YES	YES
TASK 6: Write and e-mail to one friend	NO	NO	YES
TASK 7a and 7b: Find a bus schedule (7a) table and a video (7b) and transfer it to your mobile phone	NO	NO	YES
TASK 8: Read the latest news about football club Hertha BSC	YES	NO	NO
TASK 9. Planning a day trip	YES	NO	NO
TASK 10: Find an article saved under archive and delete it	YES	NO	NO

Table 4. Questions of the user satisfaction questionnaire for the mock-ups

Questions of the user satisfaction questionnaire
Screen layouts make tasks easier
Amount of information that can be displayed on a screen
Arrangement of information on the screen
Sequence of screens
Next screen in a sequence
Going back to the previous screen
Colours of the screen
Beginning, middle, and end of tasks
Are you able to find sufficient information to help you understand the services?
How easy do you find it to use?
Do you find it easy the services in the portal?
Did you follow what was happening on the TV screen?
Overall reactions to the system: Not useful to Useful
Overall reactions to the system: Frustrating to Satisfying
Overall reactions to the system: Difficult to Easy

Figure 5. Printout of the UI screen with blank spaces to fill in by the users

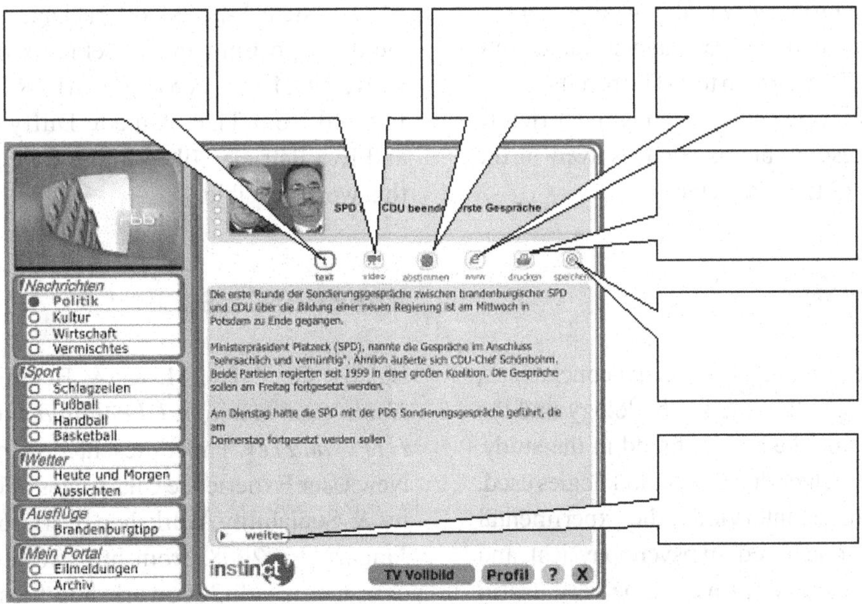

interval" of 5 minutes), the design interface elements involved in that task were considered problematic. The errors committed during each task by the users were also recorded and analyzed.
- User satisfaction questionnaire that was filled out after all the test's tasks were done. Table 2 presents the questions asked in this questionnaire.

Quantitative analyses were done comparing the average completion time, the successful task completion, and the errors across scenarios, among tasks and among countries, informing us of the specific strong and weak points of our UI prototypes.

The user satisfaction test and the users' performance of the tasks showed that there are a lot of positive aspects of the mock-up that were tested. Despite this, the results also pointed out that, in general, the navigation was not clear enough. The users had problems understanding where they were and how to go back or forward in the task. Another problem was the arrangement of the information in the screen that was rated quite low in the user satisfaction test. The results for the common tasks were similar among the different countries. These problems where solved in the new iteration of these interfaces.

CONCLUSION

We would like to highlight two major conclusions, the first one regarding the methodology and the second regarding the results found in the study. First, we can conclude that the methodologies used, the scenario-based interviews, the experimental work (like the one based on psychophysics), and usability studies, have proven to be very useful for mobile TV quality assessment and a variety of services. Moreover, altogether the data gathered during these studies are very complementary and have allowed us to have a complete picture from general scenarios to detailed perception thresholds.

Regarding our results, we have presented an overall view of the data found in each study. In general, we would like to highlight that users have demanded, across different services, that they require the service's options to be simple, with easy to use interfaces. In addition, technology developers will have to be careful about the amount of information presented to the users, since users are very sensitive to information overload both for mobile TV and for alerting systems. Once again, for mobile services, less is more.

ACKNOWLEDGMENT

The authors acknowledge the support for this work that is funded by the EU under the IST program as the project INSTINCT (IP-Based Networks, Services and TermINals for Converged SysTems), IST-507014. The authors also want to acknowledge all partners in INSTINCT, especially in the ECO-System Aspects work package. In particular, we thank to Emmanuel Tsekleves from Brunel University, Jean-Luc Sicre from FTRD, Veronique Leturcq from TDF, Annette Duffy from RBB, and Eva Patricia Gil from the UOC, who made this work possible.

REFERENCES

Barros, G., Zuffo, M. K., & Benini, J. (2006). *Home entertainment UI continuum:Cell phone, HTPC and iTV.* Paper presented at Investigating New User Experience Challenges in iTV: Mobility & Sociability Workshop, CHI'06. Retrieved January 16, 2008, from http://soc.kuleuven.be/com/mediac/chi2006workshop/files/home_entertainment_ui_continuum.pdf

Bouch A., & Sasse, M. A. (2001, August 20-24). A user-centered approach to Internet quality of service: Why value is everything. In *Proceedings of IT-COM'2001,* Denver, Colorado.

Carroll, J. M. (2000). *Making use: Scenario-based design of human-computer interactions.* Cambridge, MA: Massachusetts Institute of Technology Press.

Caroll, J. M., & Rosson, M. B. (1992). Getting around the task-artifact cycle: How to make claims and design by scenario. *ACM Transactions on Information Systems, 10*(2), 181-212.

INSTINCT Project home page. Retrieved January 16, 2008, from http://www.ist-instinct.org/

Jambon, F. (2006, Aoruk 22-27). Reality testing of mobile devices: How to ensure analysis validity? In *Proceedings of CHI 2006,* Montreal, Canada.

Kaikkonen, A., Kallio, T., Kekäläinen, A., Kankainen, A., & Cankar, M. (2005, November). Usability testing of mobile applications: A comparison between laboratory and field testing. *Journal of Usability Studies, 1*(1), 4-16.

Kjeldskov, J., & Graham, C. (2003). A review of mobile HCI research methods. In *Proceedings of 5th International Mobile HCI Conference*, Udine, Italy. Springer-Verlag.

McCarthy, J., Sasse, M. A., & Miras, D. (2004, April 20-24). Sharp or smooth? Comparing the effects of quantization vs. frame rate for streamed video. In *Proceedings of CHI 2004*, Vienna, Austria.

McGuigan, J. (2005, April). Towards a sociology of the mobile phone. *Human Technology.* Retrieved January 16, 2008, from http://www.humantechnology.jyu.fi/archives/april05.html

Navarro-Prieto, R., & Conaty, G. (2003). User requirements for SDR terminals. In M. Dillinger, K. Madani & N. Alonistioti (Eds.), *Software defined radio: Architectures, systems and functions* (pp. 27- 45). John Wiley & Sons.

Nokia press release. (2006, March 8). *Mobile TV set to be very popular*. Retrieved January 16, 2008, from http://press.nokia.com/PR/200603/1038209_5.html

Page, C. (2005). Mobile research strategies for a global market. *Communications of ACM, 48*(7), 42-48.

Sicre, J. L., Duffy, A., Navarro-Prieto, R. et al. (2004, November 3-4). Three user scenarios on the joint usage of mobile telco and TV services for customers on the move. In *WWRF12 meeting – WG1.* Toronto, Canada.

Södergård, C. (2003). *Mobile television - technology and user experiences. Report on the Mobile-TV project.* Espoo: VTT Information Technology.

Turner, N., Cairns, P., & Jones, M. (2006). *Dispersing the interactivity: Mobiles and electronic programme guides.* Paper presented at the Investigating New User Experience Challenges in iTV: Mobility & Sociability Workshop CHI'06. Retrieved January 16, 2008, from http://soc.kuleuven.be/com/mediac/chi2006workshop/files/dispersing_the_interactivity.pdf

Wildman, D. (1995, July). Getting the most from paired user testing. *Interactions.*

KEY TERMS

Convergence Services: Services that are possible through new technologies that provide convergence between digital broadcasting and mobile networks (i.e., mobile TV thought DVB-H protocol).

Experimental Methodologies for Evaluation of Mobile TV Quality Acceptance: An innovative approach for testing users' acceptance of multimedia technologies based on gradually increasing and decreasing video quality within a single video to identify the threshold level at which quality becomes acceptable or unacceptable to the users. The users' task was to say when the quality starts to be acceptable or unacceptable.

INSTINCT Project: A European project with the goal of assisting DVB in realizing the commercial provision of convergent services in mobility with a special focus on the DVB-T, DVB-H, and DVB-MHP standards in conjunction with the concept of wireless communications networks (notably GPRS and UMTS) combined with terrestrial DVB broadcast networks.

Personalized Alerting: An alert sent to the user through their mobile phone that provides links to information, and offers a "one click" access to a service may be seen as useful and not intrusive, especially if it contains personalized information. Pesonalized alerting can be changed and disabled very easily.

Quality Acceptance Threshold: The threshold from which the user considers a particular audiovisual content as acceptable for a particular content.

Scenarios: Portrayals of alternative futures, usually in the form of written descriptions, but which could include graphs and illustrations. Scenarios may be broad or may focus on a particular aspect of life but always represent a person or several persons and a sequence of steps using a particular technology or application. Scenarios may often include a story of how that future came to develop, outlining anticipated key events, choices, and consequences.

Scenario-Based Requirement Gathering: Scenario-based requirement gathering techniques have been used in Human Computer Interaction research as an effective way to capture, analyze, and a communicate user's needs for technology (Carroll, 2000; Carroll & Rosson, 1992). The basic principle of this approach is that presenting scenarios of use of technology, or the foreseen technology, to users and developers can bridge the gap between the user's tasks and the design of new technology to accomplish these tasks.

User Centred Design: A well-known approach to bringing user expectations and needs into technology development, shifting the emphasis in a project from the development of technology "for technology's sake" to the development of systems that support particular user needs in an accessible and usable way.

User Interface Evaluation: A test where the user needs to perform a number of tasks with the interfaces with the goal of understanding user acceptance and the user experience with this user interface.

User Requirements: The description of the technical and nontechnical characteristics that will need to have a system in other to fulfil real user needs.

ENDNOTES

1 The proposed four discrete steps would be of 30 seconds, since that is the proven length for users to note differences in quality.

2 According to previous literature, one of the most important variables regarding the video content for quality assessments is the amount of movement in the sequence We used sport, news, and video clips, as they were important contents for the project.

3 Because of problems with the interface implementation

Chapter IV
Warranting High Perceived Quality of Experience (PQoE) in Pervasive Interactive Multimedia Systems

Anxo Cereijo Roibás
SCMIS, University of Brighton, UK

ABSTRACT

This chapter presents an overview of diverse ethnographic praxis intended to know users and understand how the usage scenarios can influence the quality of their experiences when interacting with pervasive communication systems. Data gathering and evaluation techniques from users' perspective, future interfaces, and applications for pervasive interactive multimedia systems (an evolved state of mobile and pervasive iTV) are discussed. This chapter also focuses on well-established ethnomethodologies that study users and their context in field living labs, cultural probes, focus groups, and on-the-field enactments, integrated within the participatory design process to create future scenarios and applications for pervasive interactive multimedia systems.

INTRODUCTION

Data gathering and evaluation activities that aim to understand the users' point of view and their experiences when using a technology are a central element of user-centered design approaches such as Participatory Design and play a key role in the assurance of optimal user experiences (Douglas et al., 1993).

Identifying appropriate requirements to make interactive systems accessible is not enough to ensure the relevance and personal satisfaction of the designed system for users. "Designers need more soft data about users such as they problems, preferences, lifestyles and aspirations" (Newel, 2006, p. 112). Traditional data gathering and evaluation methodologies such as focus groups, interviews, observation, usability labs, and expert based evaluation (e.g., heuristic evaluation) together with new experimental techniques such as in-situ evaluation (e.g., living labs, observation, and mobile probes) can help to understand the user experience in the people's real contexts (for example, in their homes, at work, and on the move). At the same time, these techniques can be useful to identify design requirements and to assess the usage quality of the proposed applications and interfaces in terms of usability, accessibility, and last but not least, acceptance. Data gathering and evaluation activities need to assess specific experience of the users in their specific physical, system, and social context (e.g., community aspects in daily life, social cohesion, and social identity), in diverse situations and circumstances (e.g., leisure, government, and health care). At the same time it is crucial to verify the overall user acceptance of the applications proposed (e.g., using models such as the uses and gratifications).

However, the main concerns in obtaining design requirements and evaluating these systems are: first how to observe people's usage of these systems without making them feel controlled, as this might influence their natural usage of the system; and second, to avoid the subjective position of the ethnographers due to their cultural background, views, position, and understanding as well as their direct interaction with the environment and with the observed subjects and therefore their distortion of the data (Anderson, 1994).

This chapter discusses the application of different data gathering and evaluation approaches such as expert based evaluations, lab-based user experience tests, in-situ evaluations such as living labs (e.g., in home Wizard of Oz deployments), and video observation on the move to identify requirements and to deliver first feedback on the interface designs of prototypes and user-centeredness of the applications. It also explores how these methods can gain in reliability when combined with other experimental data gathering methods such as mediated data collection, mobile probes (do it), data logs (use it), video observation (wear it), and simulations such as prototype tests, scenarios, heuristics, and enactments such as role-playing and storyboarding. The aim of this analysis is to understand which research tools can be more appropriate to ensure a high quality of experience (QoE) for users interacting with pervasive interactive multimedia systems (Alben, 1996). Finally, the chapter illustrates the methodology that has been used in this research project aiming to unfold future scenarios of pervasive interactive multimedia systems, focusing on commuters.

THE QUALITY OF EXPERIENCE IN PERVASIVE INTERACTIVE MULTIMEDIA SYSTEM

The assumption of pervasive interactive multimedia systems is that users can, in any situation, select the most suitable interface to produce (or have access to) multimedia content and to share it with others. For example, taking a video with a mobile phone, editing it in a PC, and from there broadcasting or narrowcasting it on iTV or allowing users to download it in an ambient display at home or in a MP3-player gives the idea of pervasive computing. In fact, the quick diffusion of powerful handhelds with multimedia features together with the increasing interoperability between devices that enables interconnection dialogue between different interfaces are stimulating the genesis of domestic pervasive multimedia systems. This concept considers not only handhelds as possible interfaces to create and share but also receive and interact with multimedia content but it also includes the potential use of a whole system of interfaces (TV, PC, mobile phones, public digital displays, etc.) that can be indiscriminately used in different contexts (Cereijo et al., 2005) to achieve a tasks.

In an ideal scenario of pervasive computing, the computer would even disappear from our awareness (Weiser, 1993). However, rather than being a simple means for communication, interfaces (PC's, mobile phones, PDAs, etc.) often become the focus of attention. This attention could be even accentuated with some unhappy approaches to enhancing accessibility, such as interfaces like human assistants (Tesler, 1991) or the intimate computer (Kay, 1991).

According to this, lessening the protagonist role of the computer in favour of the users' task and context can increase the quality of the user experience. We can define the quality of experience (QoE) as the ensemble of emotions, feelings, perceptions, and opinions of people when they interact with a system. Different elements can contribute to make this experience enjoyable or displeasing and frustrating: the technology (e.g., quality of transmission or QoT), the service (quality of the service or QoS), the look and feel of the interface, the context, and physical and social environment (Watson et al, 1996). In fact, the QoE can be different in diverse contexts, albeit dealing with the same interface. Moreover, it is a subjective feature that is affected by a number of attributes of the user such as cultural background, education, believes, gender, education, aesthetic preferences, and so forth, and for this reason it would probably be more appropriate to focus on the perceived quality of experience (PQoE). The PQoE cannot be measured in terms of technical appropriateness or adherence to physical standards. It is an abstract evaluation or judgment of a product that is formed from intrinsic attributes of the product and extrinsic attributes that are not part of the actual physical product. Especially in the case of commercial artifacts, the reputation of designers of the system—or brand—can also enhance the PQoE, becoming close to the marketing concept of perceived value. Perceived value can be defined as the consumer's overall assessment of the utility of a product based on what is received and what is given. However, this definition embraces many highly personal and distinctive notions of value. In fact, it includes high-level abstractions such as convenience in addition to quality (Zeithaml, 1988). Therefore designing systems with a high QoE is not an easy task and requires an accurate analysis of the users (feelings, expectations, requirements, etc.) and their context.

In areas that are normally characterized by strong innovation-driven approaches, industry has often failed to understand and forecast users' needs and expectations. Many companies have developed products or applications using inappropriately ICT resources that imply massive modifications in users' habits, thus resulting in perceptive and cognitive overload. Consequently, the market's response to investments in developing new products (e.g., mobile TV broadcasting) has not been very positive to date. Rapid changes in users' habits and technological advances have generated enormous uncertainties and call for innovative R&D methodologies. For example, some network operators in Europe, the USA, Japan, Korea, and Canada begin to broadcast TV on handhelds, commonly defined as mobile TV. However, there are several facts related to the user experience that might undermine the success of these deployments. The first one is related to the intrinsic physical diversity between both interfaces (TV and handhelds) making them unsuitable for the same mode of delivering of content. The second concerns the context of use: TV is traditionally used in a domestic private environment (Spigel, 1992) and often involves social sharing (Morley, 1986) while mobile phones are mainly used in public environments and entail an individual experience (Perry, O'Hara, Sellen, Harper, & Brown, 2001). Moreover, users are becoming increasingly nomadic, spending less time at home and in the office. This implies a mounting need for performing our daily tasks whilst on the move (Leed, 1991). Therefore, unlike TV, handhelds are regularly used in different situations and with different purposes; they are likely to be used as an auxiliary tool to assist users' in a main activity (Harper, 2003). In addition, mobile services can be related to the specific context of the user (context awareness). Finally, there are operability differences: TV (including interactive TV) is considered a passive or low interactive medium while handhelds entail high interactivity and connectivity. These dissimilarities influence the way each medium is used and therefore imply distinct interaction patterns and content as well as different service formats and features.

Mobile and pervasive communications occur in physical and social spaces. When considering the user experience, the concept of place prevails over the concept of space. In fact, spaces are characterized by physical properties, while places are also characterized by social properties (Dourish, 2001). A place implies a sense of personal and cultural meaning and this meaning needs to be caught by designers as having a strong influence on the use of a system (for example, during this research it has been acknowledged how some users felt embarrassed to use a camera-phone when travelling by train). Therefore, considering the PQoE when designing user interfaces for pervasive systems implies to take into account not only users' characteristics but also other people and objects in the domain. Somehow designing such interactive systems can be compared to producing a play in theatre. It needs to know and take into account holistically the whole environment in the stage (light, acoustic, furniture, etc.) (Laurel, 1991). In fact, three elements need to be taken into consideration in order to design appropriate ubiquitous systems: the characteristics of the users, the attributes of the interfaces, and the properties of the context. Cognitive psychology and human factors research seems to fail to provide adequate solutions to pervasive communication systems. In fact, focusing on users and their human information-processing abilities disregards an important aspect of the user experience, which is the physical and social context.

BACKGROUND

The level of usability and accessibility are important factors when evaluating the quality of mobile and pervasive interactive systems. However, ensuring an acceptable QoE implies to assess also users' overall experience with the system. This includes getting information about their emotions and feelings. McCarthy and Wright argue that the user experience must take into consideration the emotional, intellectual, and sensual aspects of our interactions with technology.

Today we don't just use technology, we live with it. Much more deeply then ever before we are aware that interacting with technology involves us emotionally, intellectually and sensually. So people who design, use, and evaluate interactive systems need to be able to understand and analyze people's felt experience with technology. (McCarthy & Wright)

According to them, the felt experience of technology can be understood according to a framework of four threads of experience: sensual, emotional, compositional, and spatio-temporal. With the notion of threads, the authors try to capture the multifacetted, interweaved nature of the different aspects of human experience, which are continually "active" in parallel and more or less perceived as a "unity." As a tool for analyzing experience, the authors address the following six processes: anticipating, connecting, interpreting, reflecting, appropriating, and recounting. (McCarthy et al., 2004).

Ethnographic studies and the activity theory aiming to analyze the use of systems in the users' real environments have been applied in industrial design (Wasson, 2002). In fact, a number of different data gathering techniques—most of them within the ethnographic praxis—have been more or less successfully employed to take into account the context of use in mobile and pervasive systems. In fact, ethnography came to existence in order to understand how cultures experienced opposed to the traditional anthropology practice that was focused on what communities or civilizations did. To do this, surveys and interviews started to be combined to immersive fieldwork such as observation and participation. The development of complex interactive systems such as pervasive computing and CSCW demanded the use of Participatory Design methodologies in HCI and at the same time, encouraged the use of new research techniques that could go beyond the analysis of the user interacting with the computer, and considered the whole system (Button, 2000).

A traditional methodology for data collection in user centred design projects consists of direct observation in the "workplace" (Kjeldskov et al., 2004). The strength of this approach is that it does not focus exclusively on tasks but analyzes in a holistic way users' interaction in their real contexts. Considering aspects such as the physical and social environment as well as the users' threads of experience such as emotions and feelings during their interaction with the system potentially enhances the consistency and relevance of the results.

The recording and self-recording of everyday experiences with special emphasis to the users emotional aspects is nothing new for the social science. In this sense, "experience sampling" consists of empirical methods aimed to enable users to collect in the field their thoughts, feelings, and actions. In computerized experience sampling studied users are asked to carry a communication device (e.g., a PDA) that at different intervals solicits some feedback about the experience. This methodology is also called diary methods, real-time reporting techniques, daily process methods, and ecological momentary assessment (Larson et al., 1978). These self-reporting techniques can be arduous and disrupting for users when it aims to collect their feelings and reactions when interacting with a system.

In-the-field analysis can be a complex activity when the interaction happens in a more private environments such as the users' home or when the space is not fixed to a specific place, but can be anywhere as it happens with pervasive communication systems. In these situations, users are usually moving and carrying out different activities at the same time, making the observation intrusive interfering with the normal course of these tasks or, if distant, not reliable. In fact, such a research approach needs to balance the privacy and autonomy of participants with the need of gathering accurate data (Hagen, Robertson, Kan, & Sadler, 2005). A better solution could be to complement in-situ evaluation techniques with traditional laboratory evaluations (Beck et al., 2003).

Creation of usage scenarios is a diffused ethnographic technique used to identify requirements and concept assessment, often combined with laboratory evaluation (Carroll, 2000). The Creative Research environment for Air Traffic Management Project shows a Participatory Design approach through different kind of scenarios during the different stages of the project lyfe-cycle: activity scenarios (e.g., based on experiential narratives) are useful during preparatory fieldwork early in the design process; mock-up scenarios aim to understand how the designed system suits users' activities; prototype evaluation scenarios that aim to evaluate the interface models of the system; integration scenarios that simulate the effect of the finished design (e.g., Wizard of Oz testing).

The uses and gratifications (U&G) theory aims to understand users' motivations and concerns when using a specific technology (McGuire, 1974). Some researches have used the U&G theory to understand the users' experience with mobile technologies (Massoud & Gupta, 2003). "Consumer perception and attitude toward mobile communication," International Journal of Mobile

Communications 1(4), pp. 390-408. U&G is used in user-centered approaches and can be defined as the satisfaction reported by users, concerning their active use of a system. However, its application assumes a reiterative use of the media in question and it is usually used by industry to evaluate consumer demands and/or consumer attitudes. As it analyzed what people do with media, it can only be used in the case of rather mature technologies. For example, it has been used to explore the user experience related to mobile services (Stafford, 2003).

Hagen (Hagen et al., 2005) groups the data gathering techniques into three categories. The first one is called "Mediated Data Collection" and includes those techniques where users either do the data collection; for example, self-reporting, diaries, cultural probes (Gaver et al., 2004), experience clips (Isomursu et al., 2004), and mobile probes (Hulkko, Mattelmäki, Virtanen, & Keinonen, 2004), or use some technology that collects the data automatically as a consequence of using the device (for example, use/data logs), or, finally, wear mobile recording devices such as cameras or sensors (for example, video observation, use/data logs). In all three cases, the data collection happens in the users' natural settings. The second category is labelled "Simulations and Enactments," and involves a form of pretending to allow the data collection. Simulations usually are held in labs and aim to imitate aspects of the use in the real contexts (e.g., lab tests, prototypes, emulators, simulators, scenarios, and heuristics). Enactments instead involve a sort of role-playing including visual imagery or storytelling (e.g., scenarios, role-playing, prototyping and storyboarding). Finally, in "Combinations," existing methods such as questionnaires, focus groups and interviews, and/or mediated data collection and/or simulations and enactments are combined to allow access to complementary data.

All these data-gathering techniques can be used to both identify plausible usage scenarios and for evaluating the user experience with applications that have been developed for these scenarios.

DESIGN IMPLICATIONS, CONTROVERSIES, AND PROBLEMS

The Experience Clip is an example of mediated data collection (self-reporting) using mobile camera phones used to capture video and audio during the use of a mobile application providing in-situ evaluation information is. The methodology involved pairs of users who were visiting the city center of Oulu together so one of them used the application to be assessed—a mobile context aware city information service—and the other one documented the experience with camera phone. Users could decide what to capture and this fact implied that the information collected could be biased towards specific experiences, disregarding other crucial facts (for example, many users did not want to record their failures) (Isumursu et al., 2004). Although this experiment is a good engaging technique in a participatory design approach as it enables users to document and share their own ideas with a community of users "creating a communal construction of meaning" (Goldman-Segall, 1992), (Buur et al., 2000) and provided some valuable in-the-field user experience information (such as emotions, data, and feelings evoked by the application), it disrupts users from normal routines affecting the usage situation, it is not easy to aim at the user and at the application at the same time, and it would be arduous to involve certain categories of users such as older users, as the documenting process with a camera phone can be very demanding.

Automated data collection techniques such as use/data logs are the less intrusive and demanding technique for the user. However, it might pose serious ethical issues if privacy aspects are not properly managed and at the same time, the technical sophistication of the system required can make this research tool rather expensive.

An example of click-stream data logs consist in embed an small camera and a microphone in the handheld to collect audio-visual data during its use (Engestrom, 1999).

In-situ evaluation techniques have been used in several projects regarding the design of interactive systems in public or semipublic environments such as the evaluation of ambient displays at work and in the university (Mankoff et al., 2003), to evaluate ambient displays for the deaf that visualize peripheral sound in the office (Ho-Ching et al., 2003), to evaluate a sound system to provide awareness to office staff about events taking place at their desks (Mynatt, Back, Want, Baer, & Ellis, 1998), and to evaluate a system of interactive office door displays that had the function of electronic post-it notes to leave messages to the office occupant then they are not there (Cheverst, Dix, Fitton, & Rouncefield, 2003).

An example of data gathering considering older users in private environments such as their homes[1] regards the evaluation of a computer supported collaborative care (CSCC) ambient display aimed to help day-by-day the local members of an elder's care network by using augmented digital picture frame to give information about elders. This evaluation combined heuristic evaluation with an in-home Wizard of Oz evaluation and aimed to analyze eldercare from the entire support network's view point, taking into account the social context further the family and close friends. It also considered other people peripherically involved in the elder's care in order to observe possible problems in the eldercare process such as miscommunication, misunderstanding, unequilibrated distribution of responsibilities, distrust, unmet care needs, and so forth. The concept was to focus on the older users instead of the caring process as a whole. In this way crucial issues related to the use of the supporting technology such as emotion, trust, and privacy might easily arise (Consolvo et al., 2004). Research team members collected the data used in the displays by calling the elders and their parents or caregivers several times each day; the evaluators then updated the displays remotely using a Web-based tool. However, this practice created on many older users a perception of being over-surveyed and thus not always providing sincere or accurate information.

Simulations and enactments are very useful when the usage contexts make particularly difficult the mediated data collection due to highly privacy, technical, or legal issues (e.g., military environments) or when the system is at a very experimental level. Simulations using proof of concept mock-ups or explorative prototypes in labs have been largely used to evaluate the usability and accessibility of interactive systems. Although they might provide valuable information about the user experience with a certain interface, they tend to disregard the contextual and emotional aspect of the interaction. Moreover, they can only be used when the conceptual model of the system reaches an adequate level of maturity as they presume the use of a sort of prototype. Enactments, not necessarily involving the use a prototype, can be used at the early stages of concept development. Unlike simulations, they aim to take into account the physical and social environment and cultural context of the users and their affective reaction to the system, that is, how technology is experienced in its context of use.

Experiential narratives are an interesting form of enactments if investigated from a conversation analytic perspective. Conversation analysts study "the way in which stories are embedded within conversation and interaction" rather than "the isolated story or the events with in it" (Goodwin, 1990, p. 234) focusing on their sequential location in conversation instead of on the structure of stories. Narratives usually take the form of storytelling as "stories are not produced in a vacuum, but their telling is always situated within an interactional and sequential context" Hutchby and Wooffitt (1998, p. 131). In fact, "people tell stories to do something—to complain, to boast, to inform, to alert, to tease, to explain, or excuse, or justify," Schegloff (1997, p. 97), and when people tell stories they enact their daily practices, habits, and social intercourses. Therefore, experiential narratives can be used to construct experience scenarios. In fact, the "analysis of narrative in human and social sciences has mostly ignored the interactional business that people might be doing in telling them" (Edwards, 1997, p. 265). Scenarios are can become a useful tool for designers as they "show a critical potential to enable forms of creative design that do not aim at solving specific problems but rather at shaping new activities that could not exist without the system being designed" (Rizzo et al., 2004). Storytelling and information design can successfully amalgamate in analyzing the user experience with modern technologies (Meadows, 2003). When designing useful systems that consider individual or societal awareness, scenarios based on experiential narratives can provide a valuable openness that help designers to balance artistic and esthetic quality and functionality in their prototypes (Gaver et al., 2000).

Theatre is gradually being used as a successful enactment technique in design development. Theatre is an effective way to promote the self-knowledge of a culture, to encourage its openness to be , and to elicit its curiosity to observe another cultures[2]. Theatre techniques can involve the potential users in the performance or make use of professional actors (Howard et al., 2002; Stato, 1999). Theatrical performances are a valuable technique to collect data and identify requirements and other crucial information from users such as feelings and emotions because the user's self-esteem is not directly into play so inhibiting factors like embarrassment or shyness are not elicited. Moreover, users do not get the sensation of being under examination.

The use of drama can be an effective tool in participatory design as it facilitates the dialogue between designers and users. According to Newell, it can cross boundaries of technical language and knowledge, allowing potential users to be involved effectively in the process of design at the pre-prototyping stage (Newell, 2006).

Live play gives the audience the possibility of interacting directly with the actors, providing feedback about the feasibility and realism of the situation played, but in the case of budget restrictions the use of video can be an effective alternative.

This methodology is somehow similar to the creation of scenarios as both of them are based on storyboards of experiential narratives that take into account the physical and social context of the user. However, the drama not only includes the crucial issues to be discussed and shared by the audience of users but it is performed real time or in video—usually in a tragicomic style in order to increase the engagement of the public—with frequent use of exaggeration and a special focus in the emotional aspects of the user experience. The design issues treated in Newell's films were based on events, conversations and observations. The emotional aspects include the impact on the users of possible mistakes when using the system (Newell, 2006), the feelings when interacting the system in the presence of other users, and so forth. Short plays containing just a few issues each have proved to be more effective to encourage debate among the audience and keeping the discussion focused on specific aspects. However, too simplistic scenarios might underestimate the effect of synergies between components.

METHODOLOGY FOR THE DESIGN OF SCENARIOS IN MOBILE AND PERVASIVE INTERACTIVE MULTIMEDIA SYSTEMS

Due to the high uncertainness about technological trends and users' future needs and expectations, analysing the user experience in future scenarios of mobile and ubiquitous interactive multimedia systems is not an easy task. In fact, as outlined above, rapid changes in users' habits and technological advances have generated enormous uncertainties and call for innovative research and development methodologies (Cereijo et al., 2006). In order to understand how these pervasive systems could be universal, that is, naturally adaptable according to the specific user requirements, this project considered two disparate categories of users: the young and the seniors. Moreover, as shown in the previous analysis, ethnographic techniques that might work with young users might not be appropriate when examining older users and vice verse.

This research is structured in two main directions that ran in parallel: the first one aimed to unfold what users would expect from interactive multimedia systems for leisure while on the move through their mobile phones. We have denominated these interactive multimedia systems "Mobile iTV" in order to use an easily comprehensible concept for the users; however, we made clear that this notion should be abstracted from the traditional model of TV broadcasting. The second part intended to understand how crucial issues for this media—especially in nomadic and parapetic situations—such as sociability and context sensibility could be solved with mobile phones.

Methodologically, the work presented uses systematically an user-centered approach-based study of documentation and ethnographic data collection and analysis from studies of user panels, observation, focus groups, interviews, and mapping of users' movements and experimental techniques such as cultural probes and enactments. In order to take fully into consideration all aspects of the users' social and physical context in pervasive communication environments (e.g., goals, processes, inputs and outputs, experience, constraints, physical and social elements, tools in use, relationships, etc.), different frameworks for data collection have been considered in the first phase. For example the person, objects, situations, time, and activity (POSTA) framework, Richard Saul Wurman's location, alphabetical, time, category hierarchy (LATCH), the activities, environments, interactions, objects, users (ABOU), and the Robinson (1993) framework (space, actors, activities, objects, acts, events, goals, feelings). From all these frameworks, Robinson's was chosen as the most appropriate to the scope of this work in terms of simplicity and completeness. Although each element of the framework needs to be accurately described and understood, it is especially crucial to observe the possible relations between these elements.

The work has followed the following main stages:

1. Analysis of the usage scenario and existing technologies. This phase used ethnographic research such as interviews, focus groups, cultural probes, observation, mapping of users' movements, and questionnaires with some representatives of the target group of users as the main research methodology. Observation (video recording in-the-field and video-data analysis) provided useful information about new uses of mobile phones as multimedia communication tools.
2. Study of documentation regarding theories about models of interaction and successful interactive experiences with users. In this new design, patterns suitable for interacting with a distributed system of interfaces have been studied and refined.
3. Validation of scenarios. As part of the participatory design process, users' representatives have been systematically involved also in the assessment of the experiential scenarios hypothesized. To do this, dramatizations (theatre) have been organized in India (Carmichael et al., 2005).
4. Finally, thanks to explorative prototypes—or better, proof of concept mock-ups—relevant and plausible applications are been tried,

making use of the practice of pretending in the field.

The first phase has been carried out in collaboration with the BT Mobility Research Centre in the UK. The methodology consisted of two initial focus group sessions with some representatives of the users (mainly aged over 58 with a broad mix of cultural and educational backgrounds and a quite dynamic lifestyle). Each workshop involved around 12 participants living in England and aimed to get the users view about trends on multimedia mobile applications, TV at home and on the move, new forms of content for mobile TV, advanced interaction possibilities, and finally, possible interconnections between handhelds and other devices. Participants were asked to bring real and fictional stories (experiential narratives) regarding the subject.

This activity has been combined with a theoretical investigation of existing technologies and successful interactive user experiences in other areas (e.g., games). This phase also included experimental ethnographic research using Cultural Probes (and questionnaires) and naturalistic observation (photo/video recording in-the-field and data analysis) and mapping of users movements.

The cultural probes aimed to get inspirational responses to understand beliefs, desires, aesthetic preferences, and cultural concerns of users without observing them directly. This technique that was initially used by Gaver to find new features in community design (Gaver, Dunne, & Pacenti, 1999) has been recently exported to HCI (Hulkko et al., 2004). Six selected users have been given a pack with the probes material under condition of returning it back completed after two weeks. Each pack (Figure 1) included four main items with the following indications:

- **Maps:** World (Where would you imagine having a daydream?); City (Where would you like to go but you can't?); House (Where would you like to be alone?, Where would you like to meet people?); Family, friends, and colleagues relationships (Show frequency and nature of contacts).
- **Questionnaires:** A set of 11 postcards aimed to provide a very informal and open approach, encouraging instinctive and casual replies about the users' vision on the topic and were distributed to 12 target users.
- **Camera:** Take a picture of an image/video you would like to take with your mobile.
- **Media Diary:** Record TV, cinema, and radio use (what, when, where, with whom).
- **Photo album and color pencils:** Collect things, images, and stories of your week; make sketches.

Observation has been done for a period thereof 3 months in the city of London and in trains

Figure 1. Cultural probes packs

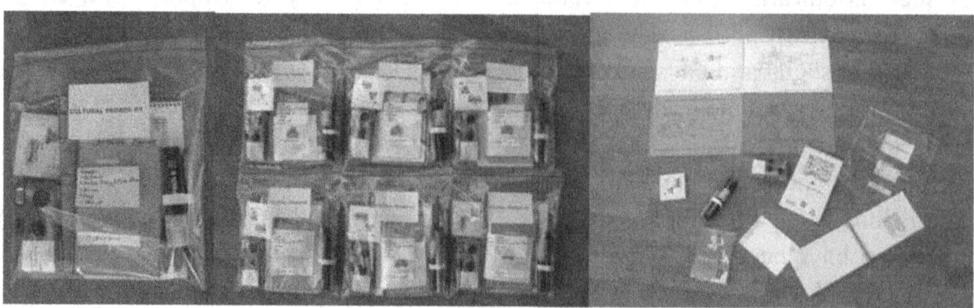

between London and Brighton (a frequently used route by this typology of users during the whole year). The data has been by the observer collected in pictures, videos, and hand-written notes. During this activity, it was also possible to map the movements of users in spaces of aggregation such as stations and parks. These maps considered an average period of 2 hours and were a valuable source of information regarding the sociability processes in public spaces as well as the effect of technology (mobile phones mainly) in this phenomenon.

While the discussion and the storytelling activities during the focus groups has been very useful in the creation of the scripts for the scenarios. The analysis of documentation and study-cases have been good sources of functional and data requirements, Cultural Probes (and questionnaires) provided good information about users' requirements, and finally, in-the-field observation and mapping of movements has been a very valuable technique to identify environmental and usability requirements.

Once the scenarios have been constructed, three validation sessions have been organized consisting in in-situ theatre performances following the scripts of the scenarios. The plays were performed in public environments (mainly squares in the city) by some of the users while the others could comment on what they were watching. The advantage of these in-situ enactments is that they provided precious information about some contextual factors that had not been identified in the research process (for example, some users found unnatural recording video with their mobile phones in a crowded square as they were very concerned about thefts).

The last part of the project uses horizontal proof of concept mock-ups to assess relevant and plausible applications that have been identified during the research. This phase consist in an evaluation—through the practice of pretending—in the field.

These very early prototypes incite experimentation, are easy to use and adopt, encourage discussion between users and designers, and have a very low cost. However, due to their low-Fi appearance, they might result unconvincing raising criticism by the users. Moreover, they focus excessively on functionality if not tested in the real usage contexts.

REVIEW OF RESULTS

In order to address complex issues such as understanding, emotion, security, trust, and privacy, the data gathering techniques presented in this chapter focused on users rather than on their tasks or objectives with the analyzed interfaces. This research showed how the physical and social contexts have a strong impact in the users' attitudes towards mobile interactive multimedia applications: the context influences in a positive or negative way the users' emotions and feelings towards the interaction process, persuading, or discouraging its use (Kjeldskov et al., 2004). For example, during the in-the-field assessment of the proof of concept mock-ups, some users found unsafe recording video with their mobile phones in a crowded street, as they were very concerned about thefts.

The cultural proves and focus groups proves a clear users' desire of using their handhelds to create self-authored content to TV with two main purposes: as an enhanced democratic tool (e.g., voting on public issues or having "five minutes of glory in TV") and to leave their "signature" along the way (e.g., by putting down personal-digital content on public digital board in monuments and places). This is not a new HCI issue. In fact, applications regarding exchange of multimedia content with objects and places have been explored in different contexts: visiting a city (Cheverst et al., 2004), playing pervasive games (Benford et al., 2004), leaving signs, and building communities

(Burrell et al., 2002). They also exposed users' preferences when receiving multimedia content on their handset from people, places or things: "If on the move, better if related to my context." In this sense, context awareness technologies enable customized information that can be defined as the right information in the right place and in the right time.

Observations and mapping of movements provided qualitative information about how the social context influences the use of mobile phones in public spaces. For example, it evinced how mobile phones encouraged their owners to temporarily disconnect from a social group (such a group of friends) during the time of its use (for example, while reading a message).

The experiential narratives that participants presented during the focus groups raised the following issues for mobile interactive multimedia systems: socialibility (e.g., to allow users traveling together share the experience of viewing of a video with their mobile phones), collaboration (enable users who are in different places to exchange moods, share information and even work together), context awareness (both services and content should be customized and related to the specific users' context), creativity (enable nomadic and peripatetic users to produce self-authored multimedia content), high interactivity (interfaces need to grant a high level of interactivity, by using new modalities such as gestures), convergence (enable users to use the most plausible and appropriate interface in each context: iTV, mobile phones, in-car-navigators, and Internet), and connectivity (enable different ways of communication among users: one to one and one to many).

This field research uncovered a scarce users' appeal in having broadcasting of traditional TV formats on their mobile phones (except some exceptions such as brief life updates of a decisive football match or extraordinary news). Therefore, the definition of mobile or pervasive iTV will likely have more to do with the emerging of mobile communities that are a sort of "DIY producers" of multimedia content: they will create content in multimedia formats and share it with others. Therefore the concept of mobile and pervasive multimedia systems will likely have more to do with the emerging of mobile communities that are a sort of "DIY producers" of multimedia content: they will create multimedia content in specific contexts and with precise purposes and share it with others.

First Conceptual Prototypes

The scenarios elaborated in the previous phase provided the basis for identification of possible implementation settings and verify the system requirements. Once potential interfaces and applications were determined, assessing their quality in the field required the development of proof of concept mock-ups. Since this work focused on the nomadic and peripatetic aspects of users, ambient and home interfaces have not been considered. Following there is a description of the different applications that have been assessed in form of Low-Fi experimental prototypes. Several of the devices and applications described below are not original; however, the presentation of the whole as a pervasive interactive multimedia system is innovative. In fact, if any of the identified interfaces or applications had been already developed (e.g., a multimedia mobile phone), we have considered appropriate to incorporate it in the system instead of creating a new one. The proof of concept mock ups have been made combining paper, cardboard, and real mobile-phones. The envisaged pervasive interactive multimedia system consists of five interfaces; a mobile phone, an interactive map, public interactive displays, an in-car multimedia system and a memory pin.

Handheld

This mobile device has a traditional clamshell design with a pivotable color display, photo and

Figure 2. Proof-of-concept mock-up for the digital memory-box

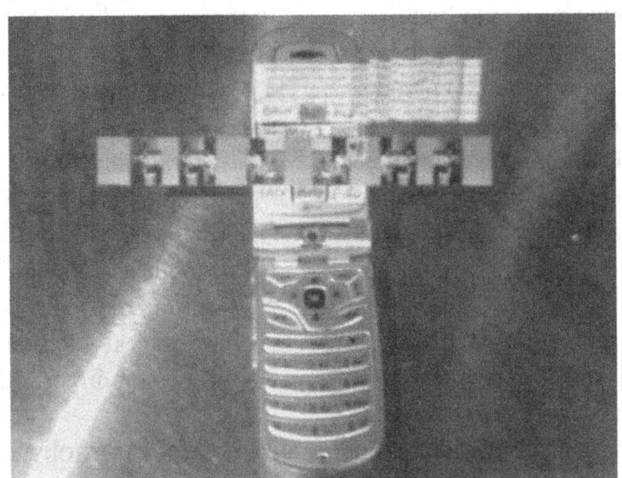

video camera, and keypad-based standard interaction as well as voice-based interaction.

In addition, a small transmitter inside the device enables it to serve as a pointer and allows interaction with TV screens, public digital displays (much like how a mouse is used to point to a computer display), and with intelligent objects such as bust stops (to get information from them).

Also envisaged is the possibility of combining two devices to double the size screen and permit enhanced navigation, which would increase the sociability potential of this application.

Applications for this device include:

- Context aware infotainment such as local video news, visualization of user's position on a map, reception of in-situ multimedia alert messages from things, places (landmarks, building, etc.), and events. Distance vision such as enabling a remote life-cam activation and control (zoom, positioning) or request of other user's phone remote cam activation and control (zoom, positioning).
- Customized multimedia content such as a embedded mobile live-encyclopedia with patterns recognition search engine (linked to TV-video content).
- Self-authoring system enabling recording, editing and sharing, broadcasting or narrowcasting of personal videos, life TV video debate in videoconferencing, mobblogging and coproduction of reality-TV channels, notification of a live event or TV series, video clip summary of a TV show, and the possibility of storing, editing, or sharing it to other users.
- "Memory box" that enables users to register self-authored multimedia content (memories) that would be delivered in specified future occasions such as birthdays or graduation-day to their younger relatives or friends, to keep their presence alive even when they have passed away. Figure 2 shows the experimental prototype of a mobile "memory box." This is one of applications that this work has identified and consists in a mobile multimedia tool that can help the users to register self-authored multimedia content (memories) that would be delivered in specified future occasions such as birthdays or graduation-day to their younger relatives or friends, to keep their presence alive even when they have passed away.

- Socialization and social awareness system such as matchmaking system to find users with desirable profiles, shared whiteboard, locator of buddies. New interaction models for this application include the possibility of pointing the mobile towards a person to get info about them, and exchange of personal information by shaking hands between users.
- Electronic Diary Guide where users can manage their daily appointments as well as checking whether their friends or relatives are currently engaged in any sort of interaction with the system (e.g., discussion group, etc.).

Public Interactive Display

Interactive digital billboard that displays customized info based on profiles of passersby with a pointing-based interaction system and voice-based interaction capabilities. Although similar interfaces have been already developed in other projects, the scenarios showed that it was crucial in terms of completeness to integrate if in the proposed system (Gaver, 1990; Mynatt et al., 1998).

Applications for this device include:

- Storage and display of digital messages from people that have been there before, public interactive discussion board (using one's mobile as both pointing device and content editing tool), display of incoming personal messages (video, text, or voice through sonic cones for direct sound to the user).

Personal Interactive Map

This device is best described as electronic foldable paper with full touch-screen display, voice based interaction, and GPS location based system (see Figure 3).

Applications for this device include:

- Mapping and routing services such as local maps and interactive ads

Figure 3. Interactive map

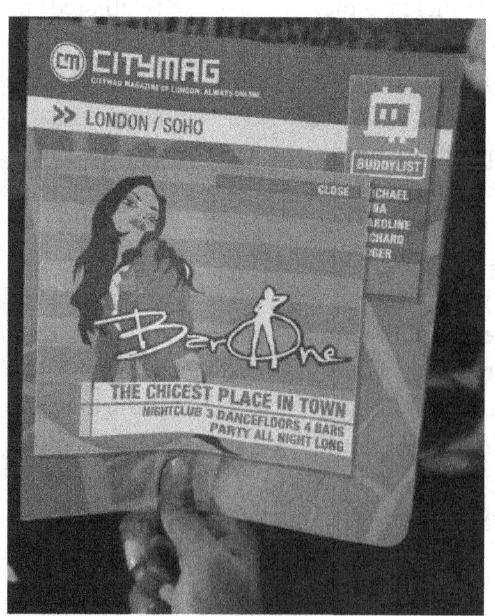

- Social and context awareness such as location of the user, other people, things, and places, routing system with multimedia information about nearby people, things and places including an instant messaging system (IM).
- Micropayment e-commerce applications such as the possibility of making bookings or purchases related to the above (e.g., concert) and forwarding the information to someone else.
- Display of self-authored content such as users edited travel guides and maps.

In-Car Multimedia Communication System

When the users sits in the driver's seat of a car with this built-in system, all of their mobile communications automatically route through it. The system consists of an adjustable monitor and semitransparent projection (for the driver's use) in the front glass (Figure 4), touch-screen capabilities, and voice-based interaction

Applications for this device include:

- Context aware infotainment such as local video news, local satellite maps (and possibility of forwarding the location to someone with a voice/text message).
- Social awareness such as localization of other people.
- Busitainment applications such as video message and videoconference system, retrieval of personal/work files, automatic addressing of messages, different "screening" modes: family, personal, work, very-urgent-only.

Memory Pin

This device is simply a small, low-cost storage container capable of interacting with a user's mobile on request in order to store a wireless download of self-authored multimedia content. The "pin" is then attached to a desired object (as shown in Figure 5) and ready to upload its multimedia content to nearby devices (PID, e-paper).

Applications for this device include:

- Downloading of text, sounds, and movies from a mobile.
- Uploading of the registered video-quote on a user's device (digital book, PC, PID, electronic paper) by simple touch.

The Low-Fi prototypes representing these interfaces and applications have been tested in the field. However, safety concerns in the case of the in-car system, obliged us to do the assessment

Figure 4. Semitransparent projection in the car windshield

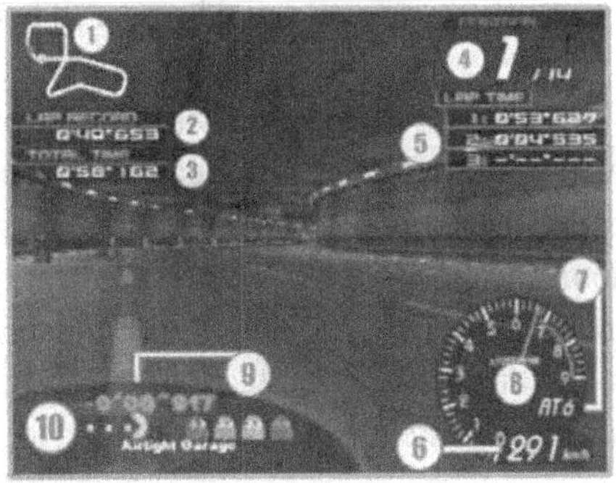

Figure 5. Memory pin: interfaces as containers of information

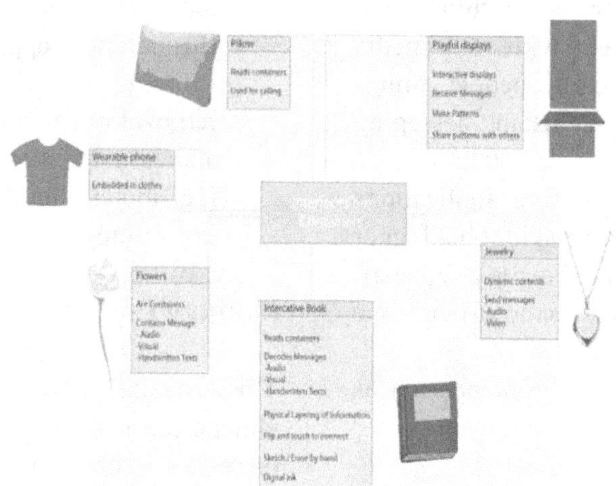

in a motionless vehicle. This unrealistic testing context has strongly put in discussion the validity of the results. However, a semitransparent GUI projection in the front glass elicited users' worries about safety and security.

In the other cases, when the evaluation considered the real context of use, it provided crucial information about how the physical and social environment can influence the use of the system. For example, the interactive map raised concerns about the management of the privacy, and the mobile multimedia phone about embarrassment in crowded areas. During the in-the-field assessment of the proof of concept mock-ups, the experience with some applications (like the "memory box") has been highly praised.

FUTURE WORK

The user-centered approaches illustrated by this chapter are based on ethnomethods and user studies of new and emerging behaviour and needs, focusing on several multidisciplinary and cross-disciplinary domains of pervasive interactive multimedia systems such as socialibility, context awareness, creativity, interactivity, interoperability, and connectivity (one to one and one to many).

Beyond these areas, it is imperative to explore how the new technological paradigms will affect the PQoE in pervasive interactive multimedia systems. These paradigms include hybrid artefacts, advanced interaction modalities, new forms of content, and novel environments intelligent environments, immersive environments such as collaborative virtual environments and multi-user environments. In this sense, an examination of the contributions that disciplines such as the interactive arts, space technology, medicine, and games could give to this area might offer significant insights. However, to achieve satisfactory PQoE standards in these new territories, new immersive field research instruments need to be explored.

Other areas also deserve attention in future pervasive multimedia systems are: the psychological and sociological impacts of multiple viewer scenarios; the implications of issues such as personalisation; gender issues; social inclusion and concerns about privacy and security; technological innovation; and socio-economic issues related to the management and production of interactive services; and convergent media. In addition, special attention must be given to aspects related to copyright, industrial property, and other legal, editorial, and production issues. To conclude, other critical areas of study are related to technological innovation implications for users and require an understanding of: users (early to late) adoption of new technologies, economic technological changes and relationship with the market, sustainability of business models related to the new systems, and how to economically sustain the proposed systems.

CONCLUSION

Technological advancements in mobile phones transformed them into tools for creation, editing, and diffusion of personalized and personal multimedia content on pervasive communication systems. A convergence of powerful and usable multimedia mobile devices with other nearby devices such as ambient deployments, printers, public Displays, i-TV, and so forth, will generate pervasive communication scenarios for self-authored interactive multimedia content and this calls for a new research approaches capable to understand the interconnections between the users' physical, technological, and social contexts.

Traditional data gathering and evaluation techniques based on cognitive psychology focus on the human machine interaction system disregarding a crucial aspect in the process: the context of the users. The physical and social context might have a strong impact in the PQoE of the analyzed interfaces: it influences in a positive or negative way the users' emotions and feelings towards the interaction process, persuading or discouraging its use.

This research tries to understand the mutual influence between technology and society. Just as technology shapes society, we also need to investigate how society shapes technology. In making predictions about new technology, it is crucial to explore the critical disconnections between the ways in which such technologies are produced and the ways in which they are consumed, naturalized, and rejected (Fischer, 1992; Lee et al., 2004).

Handsets are becoming tools for creation, editing, and diffusion of personalized and personal multimedia content and this attribute allows users to become a sort of "DIY producers" of digital content (Cereijo et al., 1994). Users will be able to create their own multimedia contents and share them with other users. Therefore, new communities will find themselves in new communication contexts and in new expressive situations: they will be able to create their own "movies" and share them with other users, places (real and virtual environments), and objects (intelligent objects and other digital-physical hybrids). This expression of users' creativity needs to be corroborated by interfaces that support some form of social interaction (Preece et al., 2003). Open, diffuse, and pervasive interactive multimedia systems can provide an exceptional virtual platform that might foster and enhance the development of new communities of creative users that can share moods, content, and collaborate with different purposes such as work, entertainment, or government.

REFERENCES

Alben, L. (1996). Quality of experience: Defining the criteria for effective interaction design. *Interactions, 3*(3), 11.

Anderson, R. (1994). Representation and requirements: The value of ethnography in system design. *Human-Computer Interaction, 9*(2), 151-182.

Benford, S., Flintham, M., Drozd, A., Anastasi, R., Rowland, D., Tandavanitj, N., et al. (2004, July). Uncle Roy all around you: Implicating the city in a location-based performance. In *Proceedings of ACM Advanced Computer Entertainment, Singapore*. ACM Press.

Burrell, J., & Gay, G.K. (2002). E-graffiti. Evaluating realworld use of a context-aware system. *Interacting with Computers, 14.*

Button, G. (2000). The ethnographic tradition and design. *Design Studies, 21*, 319-332.

Cereijo, R.A., & Johnson, S. (2006). Unfolding the user experience in new scenarios of pervasive interactive TV. In *Proceedings of CHI 2006, Interact.* Inform. Inspire.

Cereijo, R.A., & Sala, R. (2004, March-April). Main HCI issues for the design of interfaces for ubiquitous interactive multimedia broadcast. *Interactions Magazine*, 51-53. ACM.

Cheverst, K., Dix, A., Fitton, D., & Rouncefield, M. (2003). Out to lunch: Exploring the sharing of personal context through office door displays. In S. Viller & P. Wyeth (Eds.), *Proceedings of the 2003 Australasian Computer-Human Conference, OzCHI 2003, CHISIG, Canberra, Australia* (pp. 74-83).

Cope, B., Kalantzis, M., & New London Group. (2000). Multiliteracies: *Literacy learning and the design of social futures.* South Yarra, Vic: Macmillan.

Dey, A.K., & Abowd, G.D. (1999). *Towards a better understanding of context and context-awareness* (GVU Tech. Rep. GIT-GVU-99-22). College of Computing, Georgia Institute of Technology. Retrieved January 18, 2008, from ftp://ftp.cc.gatech.edu/pub/gvu/tr/1999/99-22.pdf

Fischer, C.S. (1992). *America calling: A social history of the telephone.* Berkeley, CA: University of California Press.

Gaver, W.W., Dunne, A., & Pacenti, E. (1999). Cultural probes. *Interactions Magazine, vi*(1), 21-29.

Hagen, P., Robertson, T., Kan, M., & Sadler, K. (2005). Emerging research methods for understanding mobile technology use. In Proceedings of the 19th Conference of the Computer-Human Interaction Special Interest Group (CHISIG) of Australia on Computer-human Interaction, *ACM International Conference Proceeding Series* (Vol. 122). Camberra, Australia.

Harper, R. (2003). People versus information: The evolution of mobile technology. In L. Chittaro (Ed.), *Human computer interaction with mobile devices* (pp. 1-15). Berlin, Germany: Springer, Berlin.

Hulkko, S., Mattelmäki, T., Virtanen, K., & Keinonen, T. (2004). Mobile probes. In *Proceedings of the Third Nordic Conference on Human-Computer Interaction* (pp. 43-51). ACM Press.

Kress, G.R., & Van Leeuwen, T. (2001). *Multimodal discourse: The modes and media of contemporary communication.* London: Hodder Headline.

Lee, B., & Lee, R.S. (1995). How and why people watch TV: Implications for the future of interactive television. *Journal of Advertising Research, 35*(6).

Leed, E.J. (1991). *The mind of the traveller.* New York: Basic Books.

Lull, J. (1980). The social uses of television. *Human Communication Research, 6*(3).

Morley, D. (1986). *Family television. Cultural power and domestic leisure.* London, UK: Comedia.

Mynatt, E.D., Back, M., Want, R., Baer, M., & Ellis, J.B. (1998). Designing audio aura. In *Proceedings of CHI '98, Los Angeles,* California (pp. 566-573). ACM.

Palen, L., Salzman, M., & Youngs, E. (2000). Going wireless: Behavior of practices of new mobile phone users. In *Proceedings of CSCW 2000* (pp. 201-210).

Pascoe, J., Ryan, N.S., & Morse, D.R. (1999). Issues in developing context-aware computing. In

Proceedings of the International Symposium on Handheld and Ubiquitous Computing (pp. 208-221). Karlsruhe, Germany: Springer-Verlag.

Perry, M., O'Hara, K., Sellen, A., Harper, R., & Brown, B.A.T. (2001). Dealing with mobility: Understanding access anytime, anywhere. *ACM Transactions on Computer-Human Interaction, 4*(8), 1-25. ToCHI.

Pooley, C.G., Turnbull, J., & Adams, M. (2005). *A mobile century? Changes in everyday mobility in Britain in the Twentieth Century.* Aldershot, Hampshire: Ashgate.

Preece, J., & Maloney-Krichmar, D. (2003). Online communities: Focusing on sociability and usability. In J.A. Jacko & A. Sears (Eds.), *Handbook of human-computer interaction.* London: Lawrence Erlbaum Associates Inc.

Spigel, L. (1992). *Make room for TV: Television and the family ideal in postwar America.* Chicago: University of Chicago Press.

Watson, A., & Sasse, M.A. (1996). Evaluating audio and video quality in low-cost multimedia conferencing systems. *Interacting with Computers, 8*(3), 255-275.

Weiss, S. (2002). *Handheld usability.* New York: Wiley.

Zeithaml, V.A. (1988, July). Consumer perceptions of price, quality, and value: A conceptual model and synthesis of research. *Journal of Marketing, 52*, 2-22.

ENDNOTES

1 Older people are a particularly delicate typology of users due to their intrinsic physical and physical limitations together with a pessimistic approach towards innovation and a cultural endorsement of the practice of direct intercourse and personal trust. Moreover, "they can have a negative attitude to new technologies, but also be very positive about the prototypes which are presented to them. If they cannot cope with technology, they tend to blame themselves, and their own incompetence, rather than poor design. Their confidence in their ability to use technology can also be very fragile, and it is important not to put older people in a position which threatens any confidence they may be" (Newel, 2006, p. 112). Low self-esteem, predisposition to frustration and fear of failure in public creates a genuine reluctance to change.

2 For example, the European Social Fund in collaboration with the Spanish Ministry of Work and Social Affairs have recently organized several theatre workshops in Madrid aimed to encourage the integration among teenagers of different ethnic origins and to better understand the phenomena of emigration. http://www.entredosorillas.org/

Chapter V
Interacting with Interaction Histories in a History-Enriched Environment

Yoshinari Shirai
University of Tokyo and NTT Corporation, Japan

Kumiyo Nakakoji
University of Tokyo and SRA Key Technology Laboratory, Inc., Japan

Yasuhiro Yamamoto
University of Tokyo, Japan

ABSTRACT

A ubiquitous computing environment would capture a large amount of interaction histories of objects in the environment over a long period of time. Such interaction histories serve as valuable sources of information for people to solve problems and make decisions in the present time. Our approach is to enrich the space by providing interaction history information through noticeable wear expressed within a physical environment. A history-enriched environment (HEE) allows people to use interaction histories of people, things, and places on demand, and to obtain relevant information by tracing links among objects. We argue that taking into account two aspects of people's cognitive activities—situated encountering and information-triggered information needs—is key to building an HEE. This chapter describes how to design an HEE through the Optical Stain environment, which we designed as an HEE.

INTRODUCTION

Omnipresent sensors and cameras placed in a real world make it possible to keep track of objects, such as people, things, and places, in a large space over a long period of time. We envision that a ubiquitous computing environment would be one that is *enriched* with such information, where the descriptor *ubiquitous* refers not only to the spatial aspect but also to the temporal aspect. Just like footprints left on a mountainside help trekkers decide which path to take, and signs of wear on a university telephone directory help to locate pages listing faculty members, the ubiquitous computing environment would help us find ways to solve problems, to make decisions, or, to put it simply, to relax, feel better, and enjoy life.

People do not always engage in consciously purposeful activities. They become interested in what they encounter in certain situations (Suchman, 1987). For example, when a person walks by a restaurant that smells good, that person may become interested in knowing more about the restaurant. This does not preclude a purposeful activity such as looking for an appropriate restaurant for a birthday party. However, people often experience situations such as these in their everyday lives; for example, just by walking by a place, a person may become interested in knowing more about it.

A person's information needs do not always arise from well-planned problem-solving steps. Often, a person does not become aware of information needs until the person becomes aware of the existence of relevant information (Fischer & Nakakoji, 1991; Nakakoji & Fischer, 1995). New information often triggers a person to become aware of more information needs, and such information needs cannot be predicted a priori because they are situated, depending on an unspecifiable context (Winograd & Flores, 1986). For instance, if a person becomes aware of a restaurant that he/she is passing by, that person may examine a menu placed in front of the entrance. If the menu looks appealing, that person may then look inside the restaurant through a window to see whether it is crowded. In everyday life, finding information should not be regarded as a one-time affair. Presenting information in response to an initial information request should be treated as a trigger to subsequent information exploration steps.

A ubiquitous computing environment would capture a large amount of data from a physical environment over a long period of time. Such data would serve as a valuable source of information for people to solve problems and make decisions. We argue that taking into account the above two aspects of people's cognitive activities, *situated encountering* and *information-triggered information needs*, is key to building an information-enriched ubiquitous computing environment.

THE TEMPORAL ASPECT OF UBIQUITY

Time, History, and Social Settings

Capturing a large amount of data from a physical environment over a long period of time necessarily deals with three factors: time, history, and social settings.

Time, or, more precisely, the timestamp of information, has been regarded as an important element to locate, understand, and coordinate the information. A prototypical example is TimeMachine Computing by Rekimoto (1999), which describes the time-centric approach for organizing electronic information stored on a personal computer. Rekimoto's (1999) TimeScape uses several visualization techniques to explore the timestamped information space, and his TimeCasting links heterogeneous objects by using the temporal information. Time is also used to coordinate people's activities. Timewarp (Edwards & Mynatt, 1997), for instance, uses explicit and editable timelines to coordinate collaboration among team members. These approaches primarily use temporal information as indices to the information, and they view time as metadata for managing information.

In addition, tools have been developed to use activity data recorded over a long period of time to support an individual by serving as a memory aid. The Forget-me-not project (Lamming & Flynn, 1994) uses ParcTab, a personal digital assistant (PDA) that records a user's activities, such as where the user was previously, which telephone number called, whom the user saw, and which documents the user sent to whom. The user can then use the collected data to remember past events by browsing the history of those activities and searching for certain events.

More recent projects include MyLifeBits (Gemmell, Lueder, & Bell, 2003), which records a variety of activities in which a user has engaged, such as browsed Web pages and telephone calls. The user then uses the record to remember past events and produce an autobiography. Memory Prosthesis (Vemuri, Schmandt, Bender, Tellex, & Lassey, 2004) uses an iPAQ to help a user record audio together with physical location data, which is determined via proximity to 802.11b base stations. The user browses the recorded data along the timeline by using keyword search and by zooming in and out through a visualization mechanism. Another example is Rememberer (Fleck, Frid, Kindberg, O'Brian-Strain, Rajani, & Spasojevic, 2002), which helps a user to record exhibition visits at a museum. The user can create a record of an exhibition visit, consisting of pictures and notes that later become browsable as a Web page. Fleck et al. (2002) detail how technologies support the recording of exhibition visits by using radio-frequency identification (RFID) tags and activated cameras to take photos of a user at the exhibit.

These approaches primarily use a history of an individual's activities over a long period of time to support the user in remembering past events.

The use of footprints left on a mountainside to decide which path to take can be viewed as using the history of activities in a social setting. Social navigation systems use data accumulated within a social setting to help users find information and make decisions (Dieberger, Dourish, Höök, Resnick, & Wexelblat, 2000).

A classical example of such a system is Edit Wear and Read Wear by Hill, Hollan, Wroblewski, and McCandless (1992). The document editor for this application uses an attribute-mapped scrollbar, which is an augmented scrollbar with a histogram-like representation that shows areas within a document that had been viewed and modified more frequently than others. Using the same notion of history-rich digital objects, Wexelblat and Maes (1999) developed a framework for representing interaction history and built a series of tools, called Footprints tools. Footprints tools, including maps, paths, annotations, and signposts, aid Web page browsers by using other users' history information to contextualize Web pages that the user is presently viewing. Maps, for instance, show the Web site traffic of other users, and Paths show which path each user took from one page to another. CoWeb visualizes the similar information of access history within a Web page that is being browsed (Dieberger & Lönnqvist, 2000).

History of activity data collected in social settings is used to make recommendations. Social information filtering in general makes personalized recommendations to a user based on similar users' activities (Shardanand & Maes, 1995). PHOAKS (People Helping One Another Know Stuff) by Terveen, Hill, Amento, McDonald, and Creter (1997) has extended the notion by making Web resource recommendations that *reuse* existing online Usenet news messages.

Hill et al. (1992) state, "By graphically depicting the history of author and reader interactions with documents, these applications offer otherwise unavailable information to guide work" (p. 3). Our approach is to apply the same notion to a physical environment by graphically depicting history collected from a physical space over a long period of time.

History-Enriched Environments

Hill and Hollan (1993) describe the notion of history-enriched digital objects as similar to the physical "wear" left by usage. Physical wear is quite limited in terms of being informative and useful. Physical wear obeys physical laws. We cannot leave footprints on a paved walkway. Physical wear is "an emergent property and though it generally remains unremarked upon until it causes a problem, it is also tattooed directly on the worn object, appearing exactly where it can make an informative difference" (Hill & Hollan, 1993).

Our approach is to make a physical environment *history-rich* by using ubiquitous computing technologies. We use the notion of "history-rich" in a manner similar to that of Wexelblat and Maes (1999), who explain the notion by saying that "physical objects may be described as history-rich if they have associated with them historical traces that can be used by people in the current time" (p. 270).

By using various kinds of presentation technologies, such as ambient displays and personal information devices, we could depict history collected from a physical space over a long period of time to enrich the environment by offering otherwise unavailable information to guide people's living. We could artificially express wear on a physical space to be used by people in the current time.

We envision that a ubiquitous computing environment collects and stores an interaction history of each individual object such as a person, a thing, and a place, in a real-world setting over a long period of time. Such a ubiquitous computing environment is enriched by enabling people (1) to use interaction histories of people, things, and places on demand; and (2) to obtain relevant information by tracing the links among objects connected based on their interaction histories.

Each interaction record of an object is time-stamped, denoting one or more objects with which that object has interacted. For instance, an interaction history of a *person* stores interaction records including when and where that person saw whom; when and what that person used; or when and where that person visited. An interaction history of a *thing* stores interaction records, including when, how, and by whom that thing was used; when and to where that thing was moved; or when, by whom, and with what other objects that thing was used. An interaction history of a specific *place* stores interaction records, including when and who visited or left that place; when and what came to that place; or when and who did what at that place.

We call such a ubiquitous computing environment a *history-enriched environment* (HEE). In an HEE, we could use the interaction history of an object to know the object better. We could use the interaction history of a person when we see that person to know what the person has been doing in the past. We could use the interaction history of a thing to know how the thing has been used. Or, we could use the interaction history of a place when we visit there to know what other people have done at that place. For instance, a person walking by a restaurant building over a period of time could determine how popular the restaurant was everyday, whether the restaurant ever has a waiting line, and what day of the week and what time of the day the waiting line is the longest.

TOWARD BUILDING HISTORY-ENRICHED ENVIRONMENTS

The design of how people interact with the interaction history in the HEE affects the utility of the HEE because it may encourage and benefit, or discourage and prohibit, taking advantage of being in a history-enriched environment. Our study takes the interaction design approach. Interaction design refers to "determining the representations and operations of an application system by considering what representations the user needs to interact with, through what operations" (Yamamoto & Nakakoji, 2005, p. 514).

Our interaction design of an HEE aims at supporting people's cognitive activities in everyday situations, specifically *situated encountering* and *information-triggered information needs.* In the design of an HEE, we have identified the following issues to address, related to how people can take advantage of being in an HEE:

1. How to help people become aware of the existence of the interaction history of the place. It is important that a person who is interested in knowing about the interaction history of a place should be able to become aware of its existence, access it, and examine it at the place.
2. How to let people further investigate information relevant to the interaction history. A person who becomes interested in the interaction history of a place should be able to further investigate information relevant to the interaction history.
3. How not to distract those who are not interested in knowing more about the interaction history. Constantly presenting the interaction history of the place and making it available for use at the place might be beneficial for some people but simultaneously disturbing and annoying for others. Different types of people can concurrently *occupy* a physical place, including both those who are interested in the interaction history of the place and those who are not.
4. How to adapt to different needs of individuals. People's desires to examine and explore aspects of the interaction history will differ, depending on their personal needs and situations. In addition, people would want to explore related information in a variety of ways.
5. How to guide people to explore related information as a personal engagement once they become aware of the existence of the interaction history in a public space. Even though a person may start accessing the interaction history of a place at the place (which may likely be a publicly accessible space), the person might want to further examine and explore the interaction history privately, without being watched by other people.
6. How to preserve private activities without bothering others also present at the place. A disinterested person would likely not want to be bothered by someone else's process of examining specific aspects of the interaction history.

Our goal is to design an HEE that supports *situated encountering* and *information-triggered information needs*, where the space is enriched by providing interaction history information as noticeable wear that might be helpful for people to find ways to solve problems, make decisions, and enjoy life.

Although some systems exist that display some historical information of physical objects on top of the physical objects, none of them explicitly supports people to further explore related information once they find the information interesting. For instance, TouchCounters (Yarin & Ishii, 1999) displays the usage history of plastic storage containers stacked on a shelf by using a two-dimensional (2D) light-emitting diode (LED) display attached to each container. Skog (2004) has developed 2D visualizations for a large display showing activity levels at a local cafe over a week by analyzing sound captured by microphones at the cafe. Memory-rich garments, such as a dress, shirt, or skirt (Berzowska & Yarin, 2005) show where and when they have last been touched by illuminating LEDs sewn on their surface. They display information as a one-time affair with little support for *information-triggered information needs.*

An HEE is a physical, real-world place that is accessible by multiple people who are often strangers to each other. At the same time, recognition of the interests and information needs of each person has a personal, private nature. If someone is interested, he or she should be able to know more about the place by exploring the relevant information. Even though it is important that people become aware of the existence of the interaction history, it is also important that its presentation would not annoy or disturb those who are present at the site but not interested in using it. Personal interests and information needs often emerge successively; a person may not be interested in looking at an interaction history until he/she actually sees part of it.

To address these issues, we rely on the existing studies in the area of Ambient Display research, specifically in two themes: *public displays* and *calm technologies*.

Public Displays

Research in ambient displays, which explores ways to move information off the more conventional screens into the physical environment (Streiz et al., 2003), studies the different types of information to be displayed for different types of users by making a balance between displays for public and those for personal use. These displays use different phases and modes to distinguish different levels of a user's interest and attention.

For instance, Vogel and Balakrishnan (2004) propose the four-phased model for publicly located ambient displays, consisting of Ambient Display Phase, Implicit Interaction Phase, Subtle Interaction Phase, and Personal Interaction Phase. They argue that it is important that users be able to seamlessly move from implicit interaction with public information to explicit interaction with their personal information. Their approach focuses on the transition from public to personal in terms of a user's interaction and the information to be displayed by using interaction techniques such as hand gesture recognition, body orientation, and position cues.

Streiz et al. (2003) use Hello.Wall (a large public display) and ViewPorts (personal mobile devices) to allow users to move among three zones: Ambient Zone, Notification Zone, and Cell Interaction Zone. The zones are determined based on the distance of a user from the display detected by position sensors attached to Hello.Wall. Hello.Wall changes what it displays depending on the zone in which a user is standing. When standing in the Cell Interaction Zone, a user can use a ViewPort to engage in a more personal interaction with a cell, which is a small area on the display with which the user can specifically interact.

Neither of these approaches, however, is concerned with how the result of the personal interaction might affect others in the public, even though they occur in the public space. In an HEE, wear should not look different even when another person is engaging in exploring the wear. A personal exploration of relevant information should remain personal, and not disturbing to other people.

Calm Technologies

We want to design a *calm* HEE (Weiser & Brown, 1996). Weiser and Brown (1996) argue that an encalming technology, in contrast with enraging one, "engages both the center and the periphery of our attention, and in fact moves back and forth between the two" (Weiser & Brown, 1996). They use the notion of *periphery* to denote what people are "attuned to without attending to explicitly." They argue that the notion is not related to being unimportant:

"What is in the periphery at one moment may in the next moment come to be at the center of our attention and so be crucial. The same physical form may even have elements in both the center and periphery" (Weiser & Brown, 1996).

Situated encountering and *information-triggered information needs* imply that there may be those who are not situated to encounter and there are situations when people do not become aware of information needs even if they are presented with the information. For those who are present at the place but not interested in the history information, the presentation of the history information should remain in the *periphery*.

Thus, in supporting *situated encountering* and *information-triggered information needs*, the HEE needs to be encalming by allowing people to move back and forth between the periphery and the center of their attention. This poses two challenges: (1) how to design a periphery display, and (2) how to support the transition from periphery to center.

Existing studies have argued that physical and tangible displays are suitable for presenting information as peripheries. In their design of Ambient Displays, Wisneski, Ishii, and Dahley (1998) use subtle changes in light, sound, and movement for displaying information so that it can be processed in the background of awareness. Other examples include BusMobile, which uses a physical token to display the location of the next bus (Mankoff, Dey, Hsieh, Lederer, & Ames, 2003), and InfoCanvas, which is a paint-like display, parts of which correspond to some types of personal information that are adaptable by users (Stasko, Miller, Pousman, Plaue, & Ullah, 2004).

Matthews, Dey, Mankoff, Carter, and Rattenbury (2004) argue that a peripheral display must support three key characteristics: abstraction (so that it is easier to grasp), notification levels (so that a person would know how important it is), and transitions (so that a person would become aware of the changes). We agree that these three key characteristics are important to keep people aware of and to keep them from missing potentially important information; however, an HEE is not meant to keep people informed, but to make the information available when they want to find it. Therefore, the latter two characteristics are of little relevance in the design of an HEE.

Wisneski et al. (1998) argue that the transition from the background (i.e., periphery) to the foreground (i.e., center) should be controlled by a person when the information presented comes to that person's attention. We argue that, in addition, when moving the attention to the foreground, a person should be able to incrementally explore more personal, detailed, specific information (Mankoff et al., 2003).

The aforementioned projects by Vogel and Balakrishnan (2004) and Streitz et al. (2003) use context awareness techniques, such as identifying phases and zones, to control the transition. In contrast, we want to give complete control to a person to engage in an HEE. *Situated encountering* cannot be interpreted by anybody else: It is a personal cognitive activity.

Based on these considerations, our approach is first to present the existence of the interaction history of a place as peripherally as possible within the place. We then allow a person to explore related information in a more personal, but more attention-consuming, *foreground* setting if the person is interested in knowing more about it. Such personal exploration of information should not be visible to others because the person may want it to be private; even if the person dose not care about privacy, others might be disturbed by such presence.

The following section describes how we realized this through using mechanisms that overlay an invisible light projection on top of a visible light projection on the physical space.

THE OPTICAL STAIN ENVIRONMENT

Optical Stain keeps an interaction history of a physical bulletin board in an office space by using a camera (Figure 1). When a poster is removed from the bulletin board, Optical Stain projects a simple impression of the removed poster as a

Figure 1. The optical stain environment

trace of the poster on the bulletin board by using visible light (Figure 2). Optical Stain simultaneously projects detailed information of the removed poster on top of the poster impression on the bulletin board by using infrared light, which is invisible to the naked eye but becomes visible by looking through an infrared camera (Figure 2). The invisibly projected information includes the timestamp of when the poster was removed, and the QR code, which is a type of 2D barcode (see http://www.denso-wave.com/qrcode/index-e.html). By using a laptop computer equipped with an infrared camera, one can capture the QR code, and retrieve the associated picture (i.e., the snapshot taken at the time and stored in the history database) on the laptop computer.

System Overview

Figure 3 illustrates the mechanisms of Optical Stain. Optical Stain (Shirai, Nakakoji, Yamamoto, & Giaccardi, 2005; Shirai, Owada, Kamei, & Kuwabara, 2003) allows people to interact with the interaction history of a bulletin board located in an office. The bulletin board is mainly used for posting conference posters and announcements of presentations.

Optical Stain uses a camera to record an interaction history of the bulletin board by taking a picture of the bulletin board every 30 seconds. The series of pictures taken are then analyzed to identify which posters have been placed when and where (i.e., the position on the bulletin board) and which posters have been removed when from

Figure 2. Two overlaid projections: (a) with visible light; (b) with infrared light

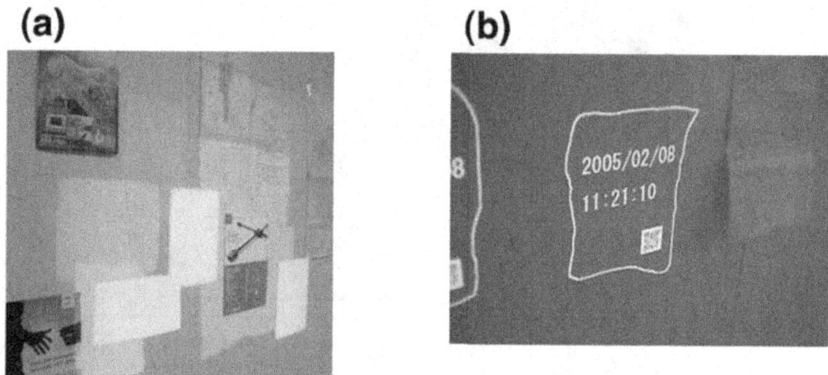

Figure 3. Mechanisms of optical stain

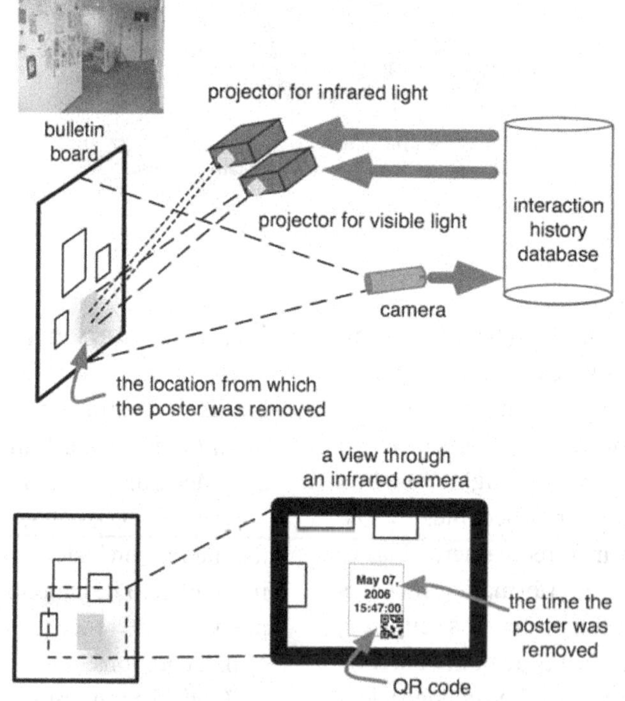

where. This information is stored in the interaction history database. The content for each poster is currently manually coded in the database.

The system then uses two types of projectors to present information on the bulletin board, one for projecting visible light and the other for projecting invisible, infrared light. The two projected results can be overlaid on each other.

The system projects the information about the poster on the bulletin board for the duration of one day with strong visible light right after the poster is removed, and gradually diminishes the light over the duration of a week. Thus, a newly removed poster impression would be more visible than one that had been removed earlier (Figure 2). The invisible (infrared) projection lasts as long as the corresponding visible projection remains.

The Optical Stain Design

Optical Stain is designed as an HEE that both supports *situated encountering* and nurtures *information-triggered information needs* (Figure 4). By using Optical Stain, anyone who visits the bulletin board may first become aware that a poster has been removed by viewing a poster impression. If that person is interested in knowing more about the missing poster, he/she can look at the poster impression through the infrared camera to obtain more information. The person may also download more relevant files by using the QR code. Conversely, if the person is not interested in knowing more about the poster impression in the first place, he/she may simply ignore it without taking any further action. Thus, the environment supports (1) *on-location awareness* of the interaction history of the bulletin board (i.e., previously posted posters), and (2) *personal exploration of relevant information* without disturbing those who are not interested in knowing more about the interaction history of the place.

Supporting On-Location Awareness

Existential information about the interaction history of a place must be presented at the place so that people who visit the place can become aware of its existence. This supports people to engage in *situated encountering*.

Optical Stain presents information about the poster at the place the poster was located, which supports on-location awareness. More detailed information is also projected at the same place but with invisible light, allowing access only to those who are interested in knowing more about it, by looking through the infrared camera.

Presenting information as peripheral or *background* to one's attention requires visual cues to be as subtle and seamless with the surrounding environment as possible. We have conducted preliminary user studies and examined different design options for presenting the existence of the history information as a peripheral presentation projected with visible light so that it does not disturb those who are not interested in it. Figure 5 shows four different options we have produced:

Figure 4. How optical stain supports on-location awareness and personal exploration of relevant information

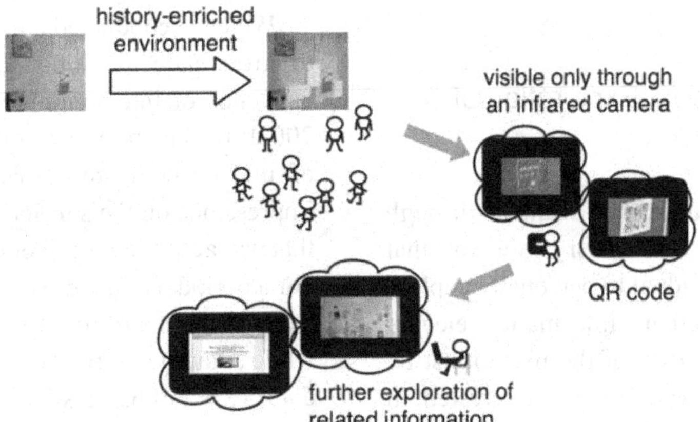

Figure 5. Design options for presenting the existence of the interaction history as periphery

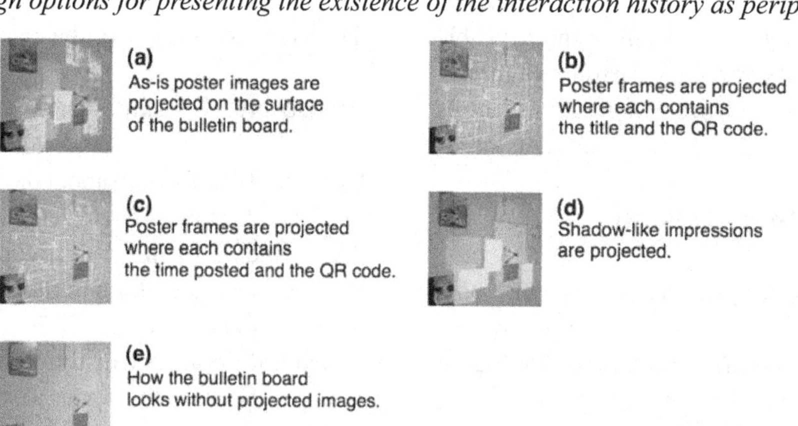

(a)
As-is poster images are projected on the surface of the bulletin board.
(b)
Poster frames are projected where each contains the title and the QR code.
(c)
Poster frames are projected where each contains the time posted and the QR code.
(d)
Shadow-like impressions are projected.
(e)
How the bulletin board looks without projected images.

(a) the as-is-poster image, (b) the poster title, (c) the time when the poster was removed, and (d) the shadow-like poster frame impression. Figure 5 (e) shows how the bulletin board looks without projected images for comparison.

As is obvious from Figure 5, presenting exact poster images interferes with the currently displayed posters, and thus does not serve as periphery information. Presenting only the title or the timestamps is not as disturbing as the first option, but the information was found to be too specific and visually disturbing. Such specific information was not demanded most of the time because people were not interested in the poster in the first place. The shadow-like poster impression was most preferred as a peripheral presentation, but people were not able to distinguish one poster from the others.

Supporting Personal Exploration of Relevant Information

Relevant information must be available through the presented interaction history in a way that would allow an individual to personally explore it without bothering others. Information relevant to the interaction history of the place must be available for those who become interested in knowing more about the interaction history. An interested person should be able to explore the relevant information as his/her interests arise, which nurtures *information-triggered information needs.*

Optical Stain allows a person to know more about the presented history information by overlaying the infrared projection. Projecting different levels of detailed information in the same place by using the infrared camera lets a viewer go from the initial presentation to the more detailed information smoothly and quickly. At the same time, what one sees through the infrared camera is not visible to others who are not looking through infrared cameras. This makes the information presentation maintain the balance between being informative and yet less disturbing to others.

We have conducted a preliminary user study to investigate the influence of presenting the existence of interaction histories (Shirai et al., 2003). In the study, we projected the existence of interaction histories by using shadow-like impressions on the surface of the bulletin board that was actually used in our laboratory building. For a period of 6 days, we videotaped the area in front of the board to observe people's behavior while standing there. According to the recorded data, 13.5% of passers-by in front of the bulletin board looked at the board when the system projected interaction histories through shadow-like impressions, whereas only 4.6% of passers-by took looked at the board when the system did not project them. We also found that 1.76% of passers-by paused in front of the bulletin board when the system projected interaction histories, whereas 1.07% of passers-by paused when the system did not project them.

In another user study, we observed three users' behaviors when they looked at the interaction histories displayed in the four different options mentioned in Figure 5, which were projected not only by visible light but also by infrared light. The participants looked at the interaction histories, and we asked them make comments. They were instructed to use an infrared-sensitive camera if they wanted to look at the interaction histories projected by infrared light. We observed that all of the participants put the camera close to the surface of the bulletin board, and zoomed in. Comments we collected include:

- "Interaction histories projected by visible light are more conspicuous than interaction histories projected by infrared light";
- "The bulletin board becomes messy and it is difficult to recognize posters, when the number of as-is poster images increased"; and
- "I cannot understand what kinds of posters were presented through the shadow-like impressions."

CONCLUDING REMARKS

This chapter has presented our attempt to build an HEE by focusing on its interaction design—how people should interact with the interaction histories in an HEE. A number of core technical issues need to be addressed to realize an HEE, such as how one can extract different types of meaningful information from the plain history data of each object, how one should identify associations among interaction histories of different objects, and how one handles the privacy issue (such as when and who visited where in a physical world). Although we are aware that each of these issues requires a vast amount of research, we have argued that without considering the design of such a ubiquitous computing environment, its true virtue can never be achieved.

Although this chapter focuses specifically on the interaction history of a place, our goal is to let users "hop around" in an HEE by following links among various types of interaction histories, including people and things. If we could link them with the interaction histories of informational/digital objects, such as Web pages, file systems, and software systems, we could achieve an integrated ubiquitous computing environment.

For instance, with the Optical Stain environment, if the interaction history of the poster is associated with who had stood by and looked at the poster, when, and for how long, we could collect a list of people who might have been interested in the poster. By using this history information, we could establish an anonymous mailing list that would allow the person who became interested in the poster to communicate with those who had been interested in the same poster.

An HEE collects and stores interaction histories of people, things, and places. Rather than designing a priori how to use potentially collectable data in ubiquitous computing environments, our approach is to first collect interaction history data that are as simple, plain, and generic as possible. The approach then focuses on the design of how people ought to interact with such data within an HEE with their emerging, gradually identified needs.

As illustrated with the Optical Stain environment, we have designed an HEE so that it allows people to engage in *situated encountering* of potentially useful information, and to deal with *information-triggered information needs.* Interaction history data collected in a ubiquitous computing environment over a long period of time would serve as a rich source of information for people to solve problems and make decisions. Our goal is to enrich the environment by artificially expressing wear in physical worlds through interaction history data. If people become interested in knowing more about the wear, the environment provides ways to explore relevant information in a more personal setting. Thus, such an HEE displays the interaction history information in an objective, neutral manner so that an individual can interact with the information subjectively without disturbing others.

As modern developments in the world progress, there are fewer and fewer natural things, and we have fewer and fewer occasions to experience physical wear. In some sense, the world is getting less tolerant of physical wear by regarding it as something we want to avoid. Physical wear, or a partial trace of interaction histories, however, has been helping humans in many ways in their everyday lives. History-enriched ubiquitous computing environments should be able to complement this valuable loss of physical wear by embedding interaction histories in the environment.

ACKNOWLEDGMENT

We thank Mitsunori Matsushita and Takeshi Ohguro for their contributions on the design of the Optical Stain environment. We would also like to thank Yunwen Ye and Elisa Giaccardi for the valuable discussions we had on the topic. This research is partially supported by the Ministry of Education, Science, Sports and Culture, Grant-in-Aid for Scientific Research (A), 16200008, 2004-2007.

REFERENCES

Berzowska, J., & Yarin, P. (2005). Memory rich garments: Body-based displays. In *Proceedings of the ACM SIGGRAPH 05 Electronic Art and Animation Catalog*, Los Angeles, CA (pp. 168-171).

Dieberger, A., Dourish, P., Höök, K., Resnick, P., & Wexelblat, A. (2000). Social navigation: Techniques for building more usable systems. *Interactions*, *7*(6), 36-45.

Dieberger, A., & Lönnqvist, P. (2000). Visualizing interaction history on a collaborative Web server. In *Proceedings of Hypertext'2000* (pp. 220-221).

Edwards, W. K., & Mynatt, E. D. (1997). Timewarp: Techniques for autonomous collaboration. In *Proceedings of Conference on Human Factors in Computing Systems (CHI'97)* (pp. 218-225), New York: ACM Press.

Fischer, G., & Nakakoji, K. (1991). Making design objects relevant to the task at hand. In *Proceedings of the Ninth National Conference on Artificial Intelligence (AAAI-91)* (pp. 67-73). Cambridge, MA: AAAI Press/The MIT Press.

Fleck, M., Frid, M., Kindberg, T., O'Brien-Strain, E., Rajani, R., & Spasojevic, M. (2002). Rememberer: A tool for capturing museum visits. In *Proceedings of Ubicomp 2002* (pp. 48-55).

Gemmell, J., Lueder, R., & Bell, G. (2003). The MyLifeBits lifetime store. In *Proceedings of ACM SIGMM 2003 Workshop on Experiential Telepresence*.

Hill, W., & Hollan, J. (1993). History-enriched digital objects. In *Proceedings of Computers, Freedom: And Privacy (CFP'93)*. Retrieved January 18, 2008, from http://archive.cpsr.net/conferences/cfp93/hill-hollan.html

Hill, W. C., Hollan, J. D., Wroblewski, D., & McCandless, T. (1992). Edit wear and read wear. In *Proceedings of ACM Conference on Human Factors in Computing Systems (CHI'92)* (pp. 3-9). New York: ACM Press.

Lamming, M., & Flynn, M. (1994). Forget-me-not: Intimate computing in support of human memory. In *Proceedings of the FRIEND21 Symposium on Next Generation Human Interfaces* (pp. 125-128).

Mankoff, J., Dey, A. K., Hsieh, G., Kientz, J., Lederer, S., & Ames, M. (2003). Heuristic evaluation of ambient displays. In *Proceedings of ACM Conference on Human Factors in Computing Systems 2003, CHI Letters, 5* (pp. 169-176). New York: ACM Press.

Matthews, T., Dey, A. K., Mankoff, J., Carter, S., & Rattenbury, T. (2004). A toolkit for managing user attention in peripheral display. In *Proceedings of the Symposium on User Interface Software and Technology (UIST2004)* (pp. 247-256).

Nakakoji, K., & Fischer, G. (1995). Intertwining knowledge delivery, construction, and elicitation: A process model for human-computer collaboration in design. *Knowledge-Based Systems Journal: Special Issue on Human-Computer Collaboration, 8*(2-3), 94-104. Oxford, UK: Butterworth-Heinemann Ltd.

Rekimoto, J. (1999). Time-machine computing: A time-centric approach for the information environment. In *Proceedings of the ACM Symposium on User Interface Software and Technology (UIST'99)* (pp. 45-54).

Shardanand, U., & Maes, P. (1995). Social information filtering: Algorithms for automating word of mouth. In *Proceedings of the ACM Conference on Human Factors in Computing Systems (CHI'95)* (pp. 210-217). New York: ACM Press.

Shirai, Y., Nakakoji, K., Yamamoto, Y., & Giaccardi, E. (2005). A framework for presentation and use of everyday interaction histories. In *Proceedings of 1st Korea-Japan Joint Workshop on Ubiquitous Computing and Networking Systems (ubiCNS2005)* (pp. 257-261).

Shirai, Y., Owada, T., Kamei, K., & Kuwabara, K. (2003). Optical stain: Amplifying vestiges of a real environment by light projection. In *Proceedings of the 10th International Conference on Human-Computer Interaction (HCI International 2003), 2* (pp. 283-287).

Skog, T. (2004). Activity wallpaper: Ambient visualization of activity information. In *Proceedings of the 2004 Conference on Designing Interactive Systems (DIS2004)* (pp. 325-328).

Stasko, J. T., Miller, T., Pousman, Z., Plaue, C., & Ullah, O. (2004). Personalized peripheral information awareness through information art. In *Proceedings of Ubicomp 2004* (pp. 18-25).

Streitz, N., Prante, T., Rocker, C., Alphen, D.V., Magerkurth, C., Stenzel, R., et al. (2003). Ambient displays and mobile devices for the creation of social architectural spaces. In K. O'Hara et al. (Eds.), *Public and situated displays: Social and interactional aspects of shared display technologies* (pp. 387-409). Dordrecht, The Netherland: Kluwer Academic Publisher.

Suchman, L. A. (1987). *Plans and situated actions: The problem of human-machine communications.* Cambridge, UK: Cambridge University Press.

Terveen, L., Hill, W., Amento, B., McDonald, D., & Creter, J. (1997). PHOAKS: A system for sharing recommendations. *Communications of the ACM, 40*(3), 59-62.

Vemuri, S., Schmandt, C., Bender, W., Tellex, S., & Lassey, B. (2004). An audio-based personal memory aid. In *Proceedings of Ubicomp2004* (pp. 400-417).

Vogel, D., & Balakrishnan, R. (2004). Interactive public ambient displays: Transitioning from implicit to explicit, public to personal, interaction with multiple users. In *Proceedings of ACM Symposium on User Interface Software and Technology (UIST2004)* (pp. 137-146).

Weiser, M., & Brown, J. S. (1996). Designing calm technology. *PowerGrid Journal, 1*(1).

Wexelblat, A., & Maes, P. (1999). Footprint: History-rich tools for information foraging. In *Proceedings of Conference on Human Factors in Computing Systems (CHI'99)* (pp. 270-277). New York: ACM Press.

Winograd, T., & Flores, F. (1986). *Understanding computers and cognition: A new foundation for design.* Norwood, NJ: Ablex Publishing Corp.

Wisneski, C., Ishii, H., & Dahley, A. (1998). Ambient displays: Turning architectural space into an interface between people and digital information. In *Proceedings of International Workshop on Co-operative Buildings (CoBuild'98)* (pp. 22-32).

Yamamoto, Y., & Nakakoji, K. (2005). Interaction design of tools for fostering creativity in the early stages of information design. *International Journal of Human-Computer Studies (IJHCS), 63*(4-5), 513-535.

Yarin, P., & Ishii, H. (1999). TouchCounters: Designing interactive electronic labels for physical containers. In *Proceedings of Conference on Human Factors in Computing Systems (CHI'99)* (pp. 362-369). New York: ACM Press.

Chapter VI
A User Acceptance Study on a Plant Mixed Reality System for Primary School Children

Charissa Lim Mei-Ling
Nanyang Technological University, Singapore

Yin-Leng Theng
Nanyang Technological University, Singapore

Wei Liu
National University of Singapore, Singapore

Adrian David Cheok
National University of Singapore, Singapore

ABSTRACT

Based on the initial findings of Study I (Theng, Lim, Liu, & Cheok, 2007) on our plant mixed reality system (PMRS), designed for primary school children (11-12 years old), this chapter describes Study II, employing the well-established technology acceptance model (TAM) to investigate participants' perceptions of usefulness and usability, identified as key determinants of participants' intention to use the system. Preliminary results seemed to indicate participants' intention to use the PMRS for learning, and this intention was influenced directly by perceived usefulness and indirectly through perceived usability and social influence. System quality, personal innovativeness, and compatibility were found to be important external factors. The chapter concludes with a discussion of implications on the design of mixed reality systems for education.

MIXED REALITY APPLICATIONS IN EDUCATION

Mixed reality (MXR), the incorporation of virtual computer graphics objects into a real three-dimensional scene, or alternatively the inclusion of real world elements into a virtual environment (Pan, Cheok, Yang, Zhu, & Shi, 2006) is one of the newest technologies explored in edutainment that promises the potential to revolutionise learning and teaching, making learners' experience more "engaging." But, history has shown that as new technologies evolve before maturing and succeeding in penetration and acceptance in our daily lives, there is a need to carry out empirical studies to understand users' perceptions of usability and usefulness of such technologies as early as possible to avoid expensive remedial work later (Mikropoulos, Chalkidis, Katsikis, & Emvalotis, 1998; Theng et al., 2007).

However, little known work has been done to understand students' acceptance of the mixed reality technologies for learning, and it is believed that formal investigation into the area of *acceptance* of mixed reality in the context of education could yield a better understanding of the criteria that are important to users, in this case, students, in using such technology for their learning.

Hence, in this chapter, we describe Study II, a follow-up investigation to Study I (Theng et al., 2007), being conducted to investigate initial students' perceptions of usefulness and usability of the system. In Study II, we applied a modified technology acceptance model (TAM) to understand the factors that may motivate/hinder the acceptance of the system. The chapter will also discuss the implications of the findings in relation to the design and implementation issues for PMRS, as well as mixed reality applications in general.

PLANT MIXED REALITY SYSTEM (PMRS)

In this section, we briefly revisit the development of PMRS so that their methods and findings can provide a background for the body of this chapter, and the issues explored within.

PMRS, developed by the Mixed Reality Lab of the National University of Singapore (NUS), was selected as a case study to understand users' perceptions of mixed reality systems since this is one of the first known educational mixed reality programs designed according to the local school syllabus and deployed in a local primary school (School X) in Singapore. It was designed for Primary Five students (11-12 years old), who were taught seed germination, plant reproduction, seed dispersion, and photosynthesis in their science lessons. The PMRS was developed together with a group of teachers from a primary school in Singapore. Physical objects were used in this project to give pupils the "tangible" experience. PMRS was designed to be suitable for the classroom environment and at same time for self-learning. By projecting the display on a big screen, a teacher can use this system as a general teaching tool. For self-learning, texts and sounds were added in this system to help students to better comprehend the contents. In addition, the MXR technology also aims to bring the entertainment elements to the learning process, allowing pupils to learn in a more interesting way.

Unlike immersive VR, the PMRS interfaces allow users to see the real world at the same time as virtual imagery attached to real locations and objects. In a PMRS interface, the user views the world through a hand-held or head-mounted display (HMD) through overlays of graphics on video of the surrounding environment. The most unique character of PMRS is that the interface allows people using physical objects to interact with virtual world in a tangible way. PMRS aims to provide totally different learners' experiences in education by:

- Supporting seamless interaction between real and virtual environments;
- Using a tangible interface metaphor for object manipulation; and
- Switching smoothly between reality and virtuality.

As shown in Figure 1, using a physical spade, pupils can add virtual soil in the real flower pots. They can also add virtual seeds using spade and add virtual water using watering can. By pressing

Figure 1. Adding virtual soil in the flower pot

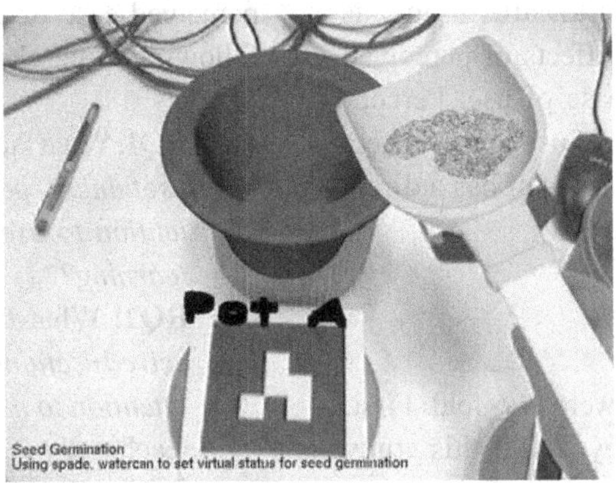

Figure 2. A healthy bud germinated

a button, pupils can observe the seed germination process under different conditions.

Figure 2 shows germination and growth of a healthy bud with enough water, suitable temperature, and light. Through observing and using PMRS, students can learn about seed germination from their own experience under a teacher's instruction.

The whole development process included two prototypes and an earlier user study in which PMRS was verified according to the feedback from students and teachers. In this study, PMRS was ready to be tested in a real classroom.

THE STUDY

Motivation and Theoretical Model

In the context of education, technology acceptance model (TAM) has been applied to educational technologies such as Web-based learning systems and digital libraries, in a higher education setting. Over the years, a significant body of research has focused on identifying various factors that influence user acceptance behaviour. In the context of user acceptance of IT, TAM has received considerable attention. TAM, as originally conceived, proposes that IT usage is determined by behavioural intention. Behavioural intention is, in turn, affected by attitude towards usage, as well as direct and indirect effects of perceived usefulness and perceived ease of use. Perceptions of usefulness and ease of use jointly affect attitude. Perceived ease of use itself has a direct impact on perceived usefulness.

Objectives

The objectives of the study were two-fold. First, using constructs modeled by TAM, this study investigated factors that might influence the acceptance of PMRS as a tool for teaching and learning in education, as perceived by primary school students. Second, the determinants of students' perceptions were also investigated. Using the TAM constructs of perceived usefulness, perceived ease of use and intention to use, the following research questions were formulated:

- **RQ1:** What factors affect *students' perceived usefulness, perceived ease of use,* and *intention to use* mixed reality programs for *learning*?
- **RQ2:** What factors affect *educators' perceived usefulness, perceived ease of use,* and *intention to use* mixed reality programs for teaching?
- **RQ3:** *How receptive* are students and educators towards the use of mixed reality programs, based on these factors and constructs?

Table 1. List of external factors used

Factor	Description	Referenced Studies
Interactivity	The degree to which the student perceives the virtual environment to be interactive.	Roussou (2004); Stuart (2001); Winn (1997)
Perceived Enjoyment	The extent to which the activity of using a specific system is perceived to be enjoyable in its own right, aside from any performance consequences resulting from system usage.	Agarwal and Karahanna (2000); Chin and Gopal (1995); Teo et al. (1999)
Interest and Engagement	The degree to which the student feels interested and absorbed by the activity.	Agarwal and Karahanna (2000); Stuart (2001)
System Quality	The perceived quality of the system and its output, taken here to refer to the graphics and the ability of the system to detect and respond to the student's actions.	Lederer et al. (2000); Lucas and Spitler (2000); Venkatesh and Davis (2000)
Personal innovativeness	The willingness of an individual to try out any new information technology.	Agarwal and Prasad (1998); Robinson et al. (2005)
Compatibility	The degree to which an innovation is perceived as being consistent with the existing values, needs, and past experiences of potential adopters.	Chin and Gopal (1995); Dishaw and Strong (1999); Premkumar and Potter (1995)
Gender	Male or female. Has been found to influence TAM as both an external factor and a moderating factor.	Ong and Lai (2006); Venkatesh and Morris (2000)
Self-Efficacy	The belief that one has the capability to perform a particular behaviour (Lee, Kozar, & Larsen, 2003), taken here to refer to being comfortable with using technologies such as computers.	Compeau et al. (1999); Fenech (1998); Ong and Lai (2006)
Attitude Towards Topic	The degree to which the student likes the topic.	Hidi and Renninger (2006); Schiefele (1991)
Social Influence	Person's perception that most people who are important to him think he should or should not perform the behaviour in question. Also known as subjective norms. Here, taken to refer to peer influence.	Chung (2005); Venkatesh and Davis (2000)

Figure 3. Research model: Modified TAM for students' acceptance of mixed reality for learning

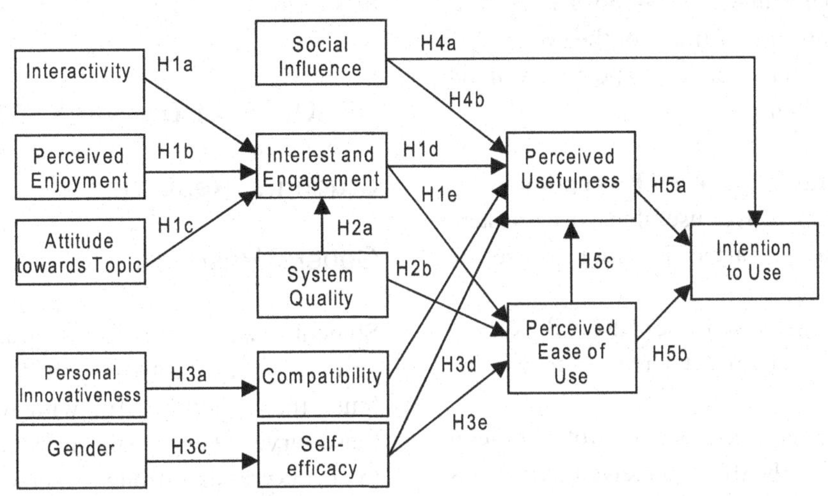

Modified Technology Acceptance Model and Hypotheses

The questionnaire, using a 5-point Likert scale, was designed according to the factors in Table 1. A research model, with five corresponding sets of hypotheses, was developed using these factors (Figure 3). The factors and relationships were derived from literature on TAM, mixed reality, and virtual environments, and also learning.

Five sets of hypotheses were formulated:

Set H1 Hypotheses: Experience-related

- **H1a:** Interactivity of the system will positively affect the level of interest and engagement provided by the system.
- **H1b:** Perceived enjoyment from using the system will positively affect the level of interest and engagement provided by the system.
- **H1c:** Attitude (liking) towards the topic will positively affect the level of interest and engagement provided by the system.
- **H1d:** The level of interest and engagement provided by the system will positively affect the perceived usefulness of the system.
- **H1e:** The level of interest and engagement provided by the system will positively affect the perceived ease of use of the system.

Set H2 Hypotheses: System-related

- **H2a:** System quality will positively affect the level of interest and engagement provided by the system.
- **H2b:** System quality will positively affect the perceived ease of use of the system.

Set H3 Hypotheses: Individual-related

- **H3a:** Personal innovativeness will positively affect compatibility with the system.
- **H3b:** Compatibility with the system will positively affect the perceived usefulness of the system.
- **H3c:** Males will report greater self-efficacy than females.
- **H3d:** Self-efficacy will positively affect the perceived usefulness of the system.
- **H3e:** Self-efficacy will positively affect the perceived ease of use of the system.

Set H4 Hypotheses: Social influence-related

- **H4a:** Social influence will positively affect the perceived usefulness of the system.
- **H4b:** Social influence will positively affect intention to use the system.

Set H5 Hypotheses: Overall Perception

- **H5a:** The perceived usefulness of the system will positively affect intention to use the system.
- **H5b:** The perceived ease of use of the system will positively affect intention to use the system.
- **H5c:** The perceived ease of use of the system will positively affect perceived usefulness of the system.

Protocol

The study took place from July 7-8, 2006, at the Excel Fest, an annual exhibition organized by the Ministry of Education. Forty-four students at the exhibition took part in the study. The students came from various schools in Singapore. Students from School X were stationed at the exhibition booth to give demonstrations of the program. They were organized into groups and each group took shifts in manning the booth. Visitors to the booth were asked to watch a demonstration and then interact with the program, after which they could fill in a survey form and participate in a lucky dip.

RESULTS AND ANALYSES

Students' Response

General Response

Students' general response towards the Plant program was very positive. Almost all the students found the program useful, with 40.9% (n=19) of those surveyed expressing agreement and 56.8% (n=25) expressing strong agreement that the program was useful for learning about plants. The students were slightly less positive towards ease of use. 50% (n=22) reported agreement and 31.8% (n=14) strong agreement that the program was easy to use. The remaining students were either neutral (n=6; 13.6%) or disagreed (n=2; 4.5%) that it was easy to use. Thus, the mean score for ease of use was slightly lower at 4.09 compared with 4.52 for usefulness.

Regarding the intention to use the program, 86.3% (n=38) wanted to have the program in their school with 72.7% (n=32) expressing strong agreement while the remaining 13.6% (n=6) were neutral. 90.9% (n=40) said that they would use the program if it were available in their school.

Table 2. Hypotheses with significant results

Hypothesis	Result of Correlation	Result of Regression
H1b	r = .492, p = .001	p = .003, B = .297
H1c	r = .499, p = .001	p = .002, B = .303
H2b	r = .635, p = .000	p = .000, B = .735
H3a	r = .423, p = .004	p = .004, B = .480
H3b	r = .335, p = .026	p = .017, B = .287
H4a	r = .435, p = .003	p = .007, B = .337
H5a	r = .660, p = .000	p = .000, B = .718
H5c	r = .596, p = .000	p = .000, B = .401

Experience-Related Response

The students reported a positive experience. Ninety-seven percent (n=43) felt that the program was interesting, with 84.1% (n=37) expressing strong agreement with this. Ninety point nine percent (n=40) found it engaging. Ninety-five point four percent (n=42) felt that the program was interactive. Ninety point nine percent (n=40) enjoyed using the program, and liked this science topic.

System-Related Response

The quality of the program, in terms of graphics quality and sensitivity of the program, was generally perceived to be good but the latter to a lesser extent: (a) 90.9% (n=40) of the students found the graphics attractive, while only 72.7% (n=32) felt that the program was able to detect actions easily (sensitivity); (b) 6.8% (n=3) disagreed, and (c) 20.5% (n=9) were neutral regarding the sensitivity of the program. Thus, the mean score for sensitivity was lower at 3.98 while that for attractiveness of the graphics was 4.43.

Individual-Related Response and Profiles

Mixed reality was largely compatible with their existing needs, values and experiences: (a) 90.9% (n=40) felt that multimedia CD-ROMs, Web sites, or other learning technologies were useful for studies although a slightly lower 81.9% (n=36) reported that they used such technologies; (b) 77.3% (n=34) liked computer games, arcade games, or console games; (c) 97.8% (n=43) reported that they liked experimenting with new technology, showing that students' personal innovativeness towards technology is high; (d) nearly all of them (97.7%; n=43) were comfortable with using technology such as computers, showing high computer self-efficacy. Both genders were roughly equally represented, with 52.3% (n=23) of the students surveyed being male and 47.7% (n=21) female. Only 15.9% (n=7) of the students found the subject

Figure 4. Research model with significant results (see full lines)

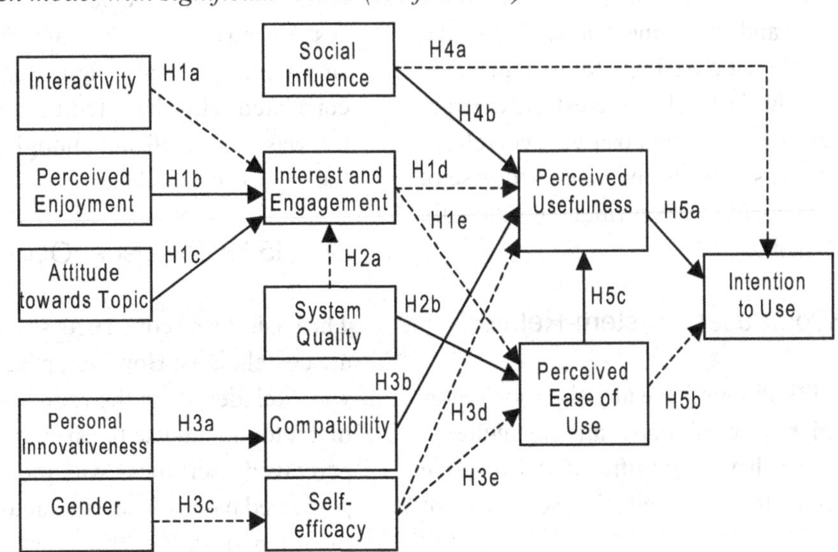

difficult. The respondents ranged from Primary 1 to Secondary 3 students where 18.2% (n=8) were in lower primary, 59.1% (n=26) in upper primary, and 22.8% (n=10) in secondary school.

Social Influence-Related Response

The majority of the students perceived that their friends would be receptive towards the program. While 95.4% (n=42) felt that their friends would find this system useful for learning, only 88.6% (n=40) felt that their friends would want to use this system.

Hypotheses Testing

Some hypotheses showed significant correlation, but were not significant when regression was applied. Hypotheses with significant results for both correlation and regression are shown in Table 2 and Figure 4.

Set H1 Hypotheses: Experience-Related

Interactivity, perceived enjoyment, and attitude towards the subject were all significantly and positively correlated with interest and engagement. However, when using these factors to predict the level of interest and engagement, it was found that interactivity did not contribute to the regression model. Similarly, the level of interest and engagement was significantly and positively correlated with perceived usefulness and perceived ease of use, but this factor did not contribute significantly to either of them.

Set H2 Hypotheses: System-Related

System quality did not have any significant correlation with the level of interest and engagement. It did, however, have a significant and positive relationship with the perceived ease of use of the system.

Set H3 Hypotheses: Individual-Related

Personal innovativeness and compatibility were significantly and positively correlated, which could indicate that students with greater propensity towards trying out IT innovations will tend to have more positive attitudes and behaviours towards multimedia CD-ROMs, Web sites, and technology-related games. Compatibility was found to be significantly and positively correlated with the perceived usefulness of the system and contributed to the regression model.

There was no significant difference between self-efficacy reported by males and females. Both reported that they were comfortable with using technology such as computers (with a mean of 4.78 for the boys and 4.76 for the girls).

Self-efficacy had a significant and positive relationship with perceived usefulness, but was not significant enough to be included in the regression model. It did not have any significant correlation with perceived ease of use and was not included in the regression model.

Set H4 Hypotheses: Social influence-related

Social influence had a significant and positive relationship with the perceived usefulness of the system and this was also supported by the regression model. It was also significantly and positively correlated with the intention to use the system, but was not significant enough to be included in the regression model.

Set H5 Hypotheses: Overall Perception

The basic TAM constructs showed the appropriate correlations. However, perceived ease of use was excluded from the regression model to predict intention to use the system. This means that perceived usefulness was more important than perceived ease of use as a factor in determining intention to use. In other words, the benefits perceived to be gained from using the system figured more prominently in students' acceptance of the system than the perceived effort or cost of using it. At the same time, however, perceived ease of use indirectly influenced intention to use through perceived usefulness.

DISCUSSION AND DESIGN IMPLICATIONS

Experience-Related Findings

The PMRS was considered interactive, enjoyable, interesting, and engaging, as was the case for many other reports such as Mikropoulos et al. (1998), where interest, engagement, and enjoyment were noted. *Attitude towards the topic* was found to predict *interest and engagement*, which reflected the notion of students taking interest in activities related to a topic they like.

System-Related Findings

The program rated well on attractiveness of graphics, but less so on system sensitivity. Though other aspects of system quality (such as ease of navigation and ease of learning) were mentioned in Mikropoulos et al. (1998) as needing improvement, our findings are reflective of a general situation where technology is still developing. *System quality* was found to affect *perceived ease of use*, consistent with Leow (2005), although the factor was defined differently. The system sensitivity aspect of system quality would affect how hard it was for the student to invoke the appropriate response from the system. It did not affect *interest and engagement* as hypothesized, possibly due to the brevity of the interaction and the novelty of the technology.

Individual-Related Findings

Mixed reality was generally *compatible* with existing needs, values, and experiences, which in turn affected *perceived usefulness. Personal innovativeness* was high. Being more open to new technologies seemed to lead to mixed reality being more compatible with the students' values and attitude, which led to perceived usefulness. Leow's (2005) study reported that students liked using computers, however, the students gave only a lukewarm response towards their AR lesson.

Computer self-efficacy was high and was not affected by *gender*, unlike in Venkatesh and Morris (2000). This could be due to the fact that in the Information Age, children in Singapore are generally exposed to IT, regardless of gender and that the gender-biased thinking that boys are better than girls when it comes to IT has not been perpetuated to them. *Computer self-efficacy* did not affect *perceived usefulness* or *ease of use.*

Social Influence-Related Findings

The majority felt that their friends would find this system useful for learning and, hence, want to use this system. Unlike Venkatesh and Davis (2000) and Chung (2005), this *social influence* did not affect *intention to use* directly. It affected *intention to use* indirectly through *perceived usefulness*, a relationship that was also found in Venkatesh and Davis (2000). This could indicate that the opinions of peers affect their own perceptions, but that students would not adopt certain behaviour simply because "their friends do it."

TAM-Related Findings

Overall, students found the program useful, easy to use, and indicated that they would want to use it. This is in keeping with the general observations from other studies, which reported factors such as enthusiasm, usefulness, and effectiveness, ease of interaction, and so forth (Hughes, Stapleton, Hughes, & Smith, 2005; Mikropoulos et al., 1998; Shin et al, 2003). The relationships among the TAM constructs were consistent with past studies. *Perceived usefulness* was found to have had a significant relationship with *behavioural inten-*

tion in 74 studies, while only 58 studies showed a significant relationship between *perceived ease of use* and *behavioural intention* (or behaviour). Sixty-nine studies found a significant relationship between *perceived ease of use* and *perceived usefulness* (Lee et al., 2003).

CONCLUSIONS AND FUTURE WORK

Study II shows that students' intention to use mixed reality for learning was influenced directly by perceived usefulness and indirectly by perceived ease of use and social influence. System quality, personal innovativeness, and compatibility were also found to be important external factors. This is on-going work for us. As this study focuses on perceptions of prospective student users as they related to the acceptance of mixed reality in education, there could be further investigation into the actual learning effects of mixed reality, as used in the classroom.

ACKNOWLEDGMENT

We would like to thank the participants for taking part in the study, the Ministry of Education for funding the development of the Plant Mixed Reality System, and NTU's AcRF grant (RG8/03) for funding the user studies.

REFERENCES

Agarwal, R., & Karahanna, E. (2000). Time flies when you're having fun: Cognitive absorption and beliefs about information technology. *MIS Quarterly, 24*(4), 665-694.

Chung, D. (2005). Something for nothing: Understanding purchasing behaviors in social virtual environments. *CyberPsychology & Behavior, 8*(6), 538-554.

Hughes, C.E., Stapleton, C.B., Hughes, D.E., & Smith, E.M. (2005). Mixed reality in education, entertainment, and training. *IEEE Computer Graphics and Applications, 25*(6), 24-30.

Lee, Y., Kozar, K.A., & Larsen, K.R.T. (2003). The technology acceptance model: Past, present, and future. *Communications of the Association for Information Systems, 12*, 752-780.

Leow, M.C.L. (2005). *Exploring effectiveness of augmented reality for learning geometry in primary schools: A case study.* Unpublished masters thesis, Nanyang Technological University, Singapore.

Mikropoulos, T.A., Chalkidis, A., Katsikis, A., & Emvalotis, A. (1998). Students' attitudes towards educational virtual environments. *Education and Information Technologies, 3*, 137-148.

Pan, Z., Cheok, A.D., Yang, H., Zhu, J., & Shi, J. (2006). Virtual reality and mixed reality for virtual learning environments. *Computers & Graphics, 30*, 20-28.

Shin, Y.S. (2003). Virtual experiment environments design for science education. In *Proc. Int'l Conference on Cyberworlds 2003, IEEE Computer Society* (pp. 388-395).

Theng, Y.L., Lim, M.L., Liu, W., & Cheok, A. (2007, July 22-27). Mixed reality systems for learning: A pilot study understanding user perceptions and acceptance. Full Paper. Accepted to HCI International 2007 (HCII2007), Beijing, China.

Venkatesh, V., & Davis, F.D. (2000). A theoretical extension of the technology acceptance model: Four longitudinal field studies. *Management Science, 46*(2), 186-204.

Venkatesh, V., & Morris, M.G. (2000). Why don't men ever stop to ask for directions? Gender, social influence, and their role in technology acceptance and usage behavior. *MIS Quarterly, 24*(1), 115-139.

KEY TERMS

Education: Encompasses learning and teaching specific skills.

Immersive Digital Environment: An artificial, interactive, computer-created scene of the "world" within which a user can immerse themselves.

Mixed Reality: The merging of real and virtual world to produce new environments and visualisations where physical and digital objects co-exist and interact in real time.

Tangible Interaction: A user interface in which a person interacts with digital information through the physical environment/object.

Technology Acceptance Model (TAM): An information system theory that models how users come to accept and use a technology

Usability: How well a user can use a system, product, and so forth.

Virtual Reality: Technology which allows a user to interact with a computer-simulation (generate by computer graphics) environment, be it a real or imagined one.

Chapter VII
Human-Based Models for Ambient Intelligence Environments

Giovanni Acampora
Università degli Studi di Salerno, Italy

Vicenzo Loia
Università degli Studi di Salerno, Italy

Michele Nappi
Università degli Studi di Salerno, Italy

Stefano Ricciardi
Università degli Studi di Salerno, Italy

ABSTRACT

Ambient intelligence gathers best results from three key technologies, ubiquitous computing, ubiquitous communication, and intelligent user friendly interfaces. The functional and spatial distribution of tasks is a natural thrust to employ multi-agent paradigm to design and implement AmI environments. Two critical issues, common in most of applications, are (1) how to detect in a general and efficient way context from sensors and (2) how to process contextual information in order to improve the functionality of services. Here we describe an agent-based ambient intelligence architecture able to deliver services on the basis of physical and emotional user status captured from a set of biometric features. Abstract representation and management is achieved thanks to two markup languages, H2ML and FML, able to model behavioral as well as fuzzy control activities and to exploit distribution and concurrent computation in order to gain real-time performances.

INTRODUCTION

When designing ambient intelligence (AmI) environments (Aarts, 2004), different methodologies and techniques have to be used, ranging from materials science, business models, network architectures, up to human interaction design. However, as key technologies, AmI is characterized by:

- **Embedded.** Devices are (wired or unwired) plugged into the network (Ditze, 2004). The resulting system consists of several and multiple devices, compute equipments and software systems that must interact among them. Some of the devices are simple sensors; others are actuators owning a bunch of control activities in the environment (central heating, security systems, lighting system, washing machines, refrigerator, etc.). The strong heterogeneity makes it difficult a uniformed policy-based management.
- **Context awareness.** This term appeared for the first time in Schilit (1994), where the authors defined the context as locations, identities of nearby people and objects, and changes to those objects. Many research groups have been investigating on context-aware applications, but there is no common understanding on what context and context awareness exactly means.
- **Personalized.** AmI environments are designed for people, not generic users. This means that the system should be so flexible as to tailor itself to meet human needs.
- **Adaptive.** The system, being sensible to the user's feedback, is capable of modifying the corresponding actions that have been or will be performed (Astrom, 1987).

We have designed and implemented an intelligent home environment populated by intelligent appliance agents skilled to perform distributed and adaptive transparent fuzzy control. The agents interact and coordinate their activities using the Fuzzy Markup Language (FML) (Loia, 2005) as an abstract protocol over shared resources independently from hardware constraints. The agents compose an abstract layer that binds the instrumental scenario with the services, ensuring efficiency and adaptivity. This approach allows AmI designers to achieve useful goals:

- To customize the control strategy on a specific hardware through an automatic procedure;
- To distribute the fuzzy control flow in order to minimize the global deduction time and better exploit the natural distributed knowledge repositories; and
- To acquire at run time the user's behavior and the environment status in order to apply context-aware adaptivity.

This chapter proposes an ambient intelligence architecture being able to distribute personalized services on the basis of physical and emotional user status captured from a set of biometric features and modeled by means of a markup language based on XML. This language, namely *H2ML*, is a new tool to model human information usable at different abstraction levels inside the AmI architecture so as to reach transparency, uniformity, and abstractness in bridging multiple sensors properties to flexible and personalized actuators.

In this chapter we show that several layers composing the overall AmI architecture are used to achieve the aforesaid goal. Different layers serve to link the low-level details (the hardware layer) with the high-level view (software layer) by employing two classes of markup languages: FML and H2ML.

FUZZY MARKUP LANGUAGE

Initially, FML has been designed to act like a middleware between the legacy fuzzy environment and the real implementation platform. Legacy fuzzy environment module allows creating a fuzzy controller using a legacy representation (Acampora, 2005). An example of legacy fuzzy environment module is Matlab™ that produce a *.fis* file to represent the fuzzy control system. The obtained legacy fuzzy controller is passed to the FML converter module that translates it into a markup-based description (FML).

The next step concerns the real implementation of the fuzzy controller on a specific hardware. The Initial version of FML used XSLT languages translator to convert FML fuzzy controller in a general purpose computer language using an XSL file containing the translation description. At this level, the control is compilable and executable for the proposed hardware. Actually, FML can be considered as a standalone language used to model the fuzzy controllers from scratch. Now, the FML compiler is based on the integration of different techonologies to instantiate a run-time fuzzy controller without additional work. These technologies are: the *TCP/IP client/server application* and the *JAXB XML binding technology*. In particular, the JAXB XML binding technology allows generating a Java class hierarchy starting from the FML control description. The TCP/IP client/server application allows separating the real control from the controlled devices so as to obtain the total independence of the devices from the language used to code the fuzzy controller. In particular, a TCP server instantiates a Java objects collection representing the FML controller starting from the class hierarchy generated by a JAXB module. Using this object collection, the server will be able to apply the inference operators on the objects representing the fuzzy rule base, generating, in this way, a set of defuzzificated values representing the control results. The TCP Client, hosted on the controlled devices, is a simple standard TCP client able to send the sensor's values to server and to receive the control results; from this point of view, the Client does not know the details about the fuzzy control, it sees only a bidirectional data flow. The client/server communication is performed obviously by TCP sockets. Figure 1 shows the architecture of the proposed system. This choice allows obtaining a high level of abstraction showing one only gap: The client and the server have to agree on the exchange data format. In particular, the server has to know exactly the data format coming from the client and vice versa. The proposed system uses the classic string data type to solve the problem. In order to exchange the sensors' values and the inferred results, the client and server have to choose a special character to create a communication data string. While the client uses this character to compose a string containing the sensors data, the server uses the same character to infer and to create a string containing the fuzzy control results. Client and server simply have to split the received string in order to use the data in a normal fashion. Figure 2 shows the communication step performed during a control iteration. In order to perform the JAXB/TCP/FML controller, it is necessary to create a TCP endpoint to identify in a direct and unambiguous way the FML server on the Internet. TCP defines an endpoint to be a pair of integers (host, port), where the host is the IP address for the FML server host and port is a TCP port where the server is executed on that host. The IP address depends on the network which hosts the FML server; the TCP port has to be defined in a univocal way to allow the FML clients to contact the server without problems. The FML server port is defined considering the concatenation of ASCII codes related to F, M and L characters modulo 65536 (available TCP ports) obtaining, in this way, the integer port number 12330. Some examples of FML/TCP endpoints are: (192.168.0.4, 12330), (193.205.186.85, 12330).

Fuzzy Markup Language and Fuzzy Logic Control

Since Zadeh's coining of the term fuzzy logic (Zadeh, 1965) and Mamdani's early demonstra-

Figure 1. FML TCP/JAXB architecture

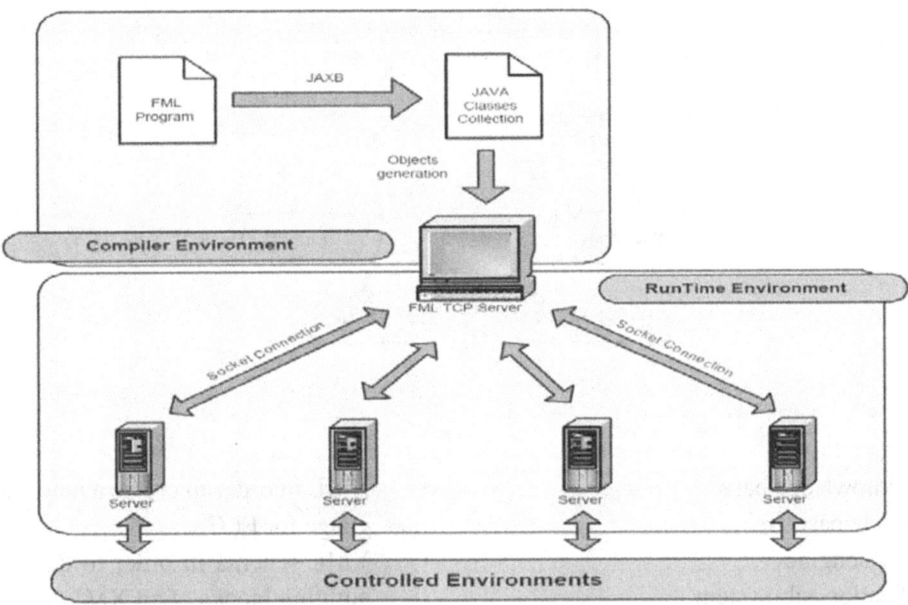

Figure 2. FML TCP/JAXB inference step

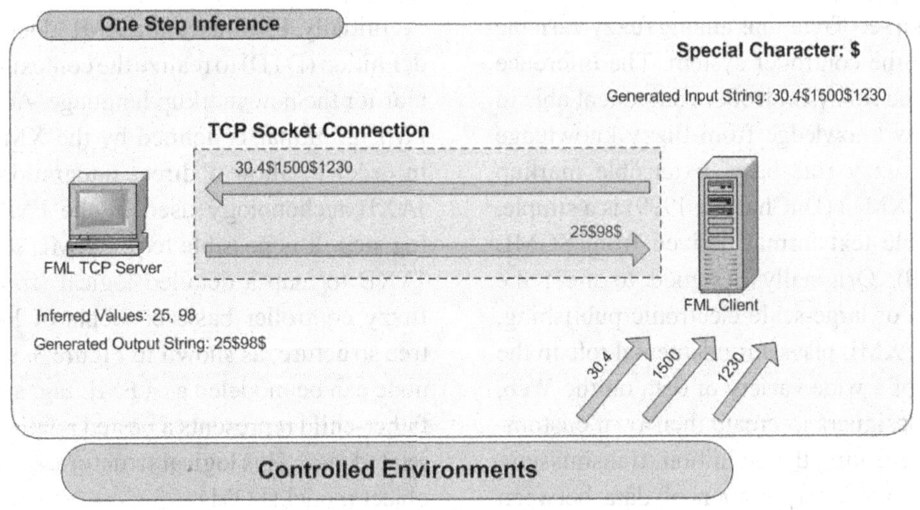

tion of fuzzy logic control (FLC) (Mamdani, 1974), enormous progresses have been made by the scientific community in the theoretical as well as application fields of FLC. Trivially, a fuzzy control allows the designer to specify the control in terms of sentences rather than equations by replacing a conventional controller, say, a PID (proportional-integral- derivative) controller with linguistic IF-THEN rules. The main components of a fuzzy controller are:

Figure 3. Fuzzy control tree

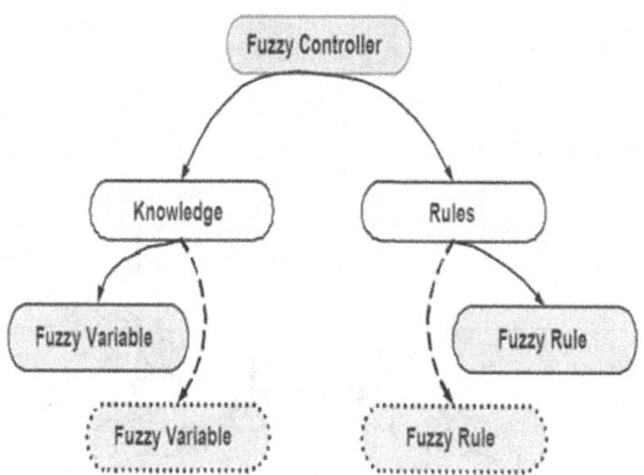

- Fuzzy knowledge base
- Fuzzy rule base
- Inference engine
- Fuzzification sub-system
- Defuzzification sub-system

The fuzzy knowledge base contains the knowledge used by human experts. The fuzzy rule base represents a set of relations among fuzzy variable defined in the controller system. The inference engine is the fuzzy controller component able to extract new knowledge from fuzzy knowledge base and fuzzy rule base. Extensible markup language (XML) (DuCharme, 1999) is a simple, very flexible text format derived from SGML (ISO 8879). Originally designed to meet the challenges of large-scale electronic publishing, nowadays, XML plays a fundamental role in the exchange of a wide variety of data on the Web, allowing designers to create their own customized tags, enabling the definition, transmission, validation, and interpretation of data between applications, devices, and organizations. If we use XML, we take control and responsibility for our information, instead of abdicating such control to product vendors. This is the motivation under FML proposal: to free control strategy from the device. FML uses:

- XML in order to create a new markup language for FLC
- XML schema in order to define the legal building blocks of an XML document
- XSLT in order to convert fuzzy controller description into a programming language code

Initially, FML used the XML document type definition (DTD) to realize the context free grammar for the new markup language. Actually, the FML grammar is defined by the XML schema in order to allow a direct integration with the JAXB techonology used in the FML compiling step. It is possible to use XML schema and JAXB to map a detailed logical structure of a fuzzy controller basic concepts of FLC into a tree structure, as shown in Figure 3, where each node can be modeled as a FML tag, and the link father-child represents a nested relation between related tags. This logical structure is called fuzzy object model (FOM).

Currently, we are using FML for modeling two well-known fuzzy controllers: Mamdani and Takagi-Sugeno-Kang (TSK) (Takagi, 1985).

In order to model the controller node of fuzzy tree, the FML tag <FUZZYCONTROL> is created (this tag opens any FML program). <FUZZYCON-

TROL> uses three tags: type, defuzzify method, and ip. The type attribute permits to specify the kind of fuzzy controller, in our case Mamdani or TSK; defuzzify method attribute defines the defuzzification method; ip can be used to define the location of controller in the computer network and, in the case of <FUZZYCONTROL> tag it defines the first member of TCP endpoint pair. Considering the left sub-tree, the knowledge base component is encountered. The fuzzy knowledge base is defined by means of the tag <KNOWLEDGEBASE> which maintains the set of fuzzy concepts used to model the fuzzy control system. <FUZZYVARIABLE> defines the fuzzy concept, for example, luminosity; <FUZZYTERM> defines a linguistic term describing the fuzzy concept, for example, low; a set of tags defining the shapes of fuzzy sets is related to fuzzy terms. The attributes of <FUZZYVARIABLE> tags are: name, scale, domainLeft, domainRight, type, ip. The name attribute defines the name of fuzzy concept (e.g., time of the day); scale defines how to measure the fuzzy concept (e.g., hour); domainLeft and domainRight model the universe of discourse of fuzzy concept in terms of real values (e.g., [0000, 2400]); the role of variable (i.e., independent or dependent variable) is defined by type attribute; ip locates the position of fuzzy knowledge base in the computer network. <RULEBASE> permits to build the rule base associated with the fuzzy controller. The other tags related to this definiton are: <RULE>, <ANTECEDENT>, <CONSEQUENT>, <CLAUSEA>, <CLAUSEC>, <VARIABLE>, <TERM>, and <TSKPARAM>. The meaning of these tags appears evident and we do not further detail them here.

Distributed Fuzzy Control

Just to give a concrete example, considering automatic lighting system, we can model the knowledge base and rule base FML code portion, and in particular the lamp light level as shown in Listing 1 (Mamdani method).

This bunch of FML code is useful to understand how it is possible to associate a fuzzy control activity (knowledge base and eventually the rule base) on a single host (in our example, localhost). In this naive example, a centralized Mamdani fuzzy controller is produced, but in real cases, a distributed approach is performed, as illustrated in Figure 4. This feature is useful to obtain several advantages:

- To parallelize the fuzzy inference engine reducing inference time and minimizing knowledge base and rule base occupancy;
- To manage distributed knowledge environment, that is, environments in which the global knowledge is shared on many points of interested environment, as often happens in AmI;
- To exploit mobile agents as a natural and efficient technology to share data distribution and dispatch running code on a network.

In order to distribute fuzzy controller components on different hosts, we need to characterize the independent members of controller. In particular, working with Mamdani we identify the following components:

- Fuzzy controller
- Knowledge base
- Fuzzy variable
- Rule base
- Fuzzy rule

The default value of ip attribute of <FUZZYCONTROL> tag is localhost. The Internet address value of the fuzzy controller is distributed toward the bottom in the parse tree related to fuzzy program. From this point of view, the Internet address of other independent components (knowledge base and rule base), if not defined, is overlapped by network address from <FUZZYCONTROL> tag. This distributive concept also is extended to the nodes of the parse tree related to the rule base and knowledge base: Each member of the controller is spread in a scalable and distributed way, as shown in Figure 4. Comparing Figures 3 and 4, we better note the strong differences between a centralized controller and a distributed one. In Figure 3, all components of the centralized controller are connected by straight lines indicating that all components (knowledge base, rule base, and related sub components) are maintained on the same host at the same time. Figure 4 shows a distributed fuzzy controller, whose members, connected by dotted lines, can be treated concurrently by different processes. In particular, Figure 4 shows a distributed fuzzy controller with luminosity and time of the day concepts hosted on 192.168.0.4, dimmer concept hosted on 192.168.0.8, and the rule base shared on 192.168.0.5, 192.168.0.6, and 192.168.0.7. In this way, we can distribute fuzzy rule base in the network and exploit distributed processing by minimizing inference. In order to address in a high-level way the issues of delocalization and concurrency, we map the distributed fuzzy model coded in FML on a multi-agents system. In particular, the agents that compose the system are: stationary fuzzy agent set, registry agent, and inference agent. The set of stationary fuzzy agent is used to manipulate in a distributed way the concept coded in FML program and modeled in the distributed fuzzy controller. These agents

Listing 1. FML sample program

```
<DOCTYPE FUZZYCONTROL SYSTEM "fml.dtd">
<FUZZYCONTROL defuzzifymethod= "CENTROID"
ip = "localhost" type = "MAMDANI">
<KNOWLEDGEBASE IP = "localhost">
<FUZZYVARIABLE
      domainleft = "0" domainright = "1"
      ip = "localhost" name = "Luminosity"
      scale = "Lux"type = "INPUT">
      <FUZZYTERM name="low">
            <PISHAPE
                  param1 = "0.0"
                  param2 = "0 .45">
            </PISHAPE>
      </FUZZYTERM>
      <FUZZYTERM name="MEDIUM">
            <PISHAPE
                  param1 = "0.49999999999999994"
                  param2 = "0.44999999999999996">
            </PISHAPE>
      </FUZZYTERM>
      <FUZZYTERM name= "HIGH">
            <PISHAPE
                  param1 = "0.5501" param2 = "1">
```

continued on following page

Listing 1. continued

```
            </PISHAPE>
        </FUZZYTERM>
    </FUZZYVARIABLE>
    </KNOWLEDGEBASE>
    <RULEBASE
        inferenceengine = "MINMAXMINMAMDANI"
        ip = "localhost">
        <RULE connector = "AND" ip = "localhost"
            weight = "1">
            <ANTECEDENT>
                <CLAUSE not = "FALSE">
                        <VARIABLE> Luminosity </VARI-
ABLE>
                        <TERM> low </TERM>
                </CLAUSE>
                <CLAUSE not = "FALSE">
                    <VARIABLE> hour </VARIABLE>
                        <TERM> morning </TERM>
                </CLAUSE>
            </ANTECEDENT>
            <CONSEQUENT>
                <CLAUSE not = "FALSE">
                    <VARIABLE>dimmer</VARIABLE>
                        <TERM>medium</TERM>
                </CLAUSE>
            </CONSEQUENT>
        </RULE>
    ▷▷▷
    </RULEBASE>
    </FUZZYCONTROL>
```

Figure 4. Distributed fuzzy control tree

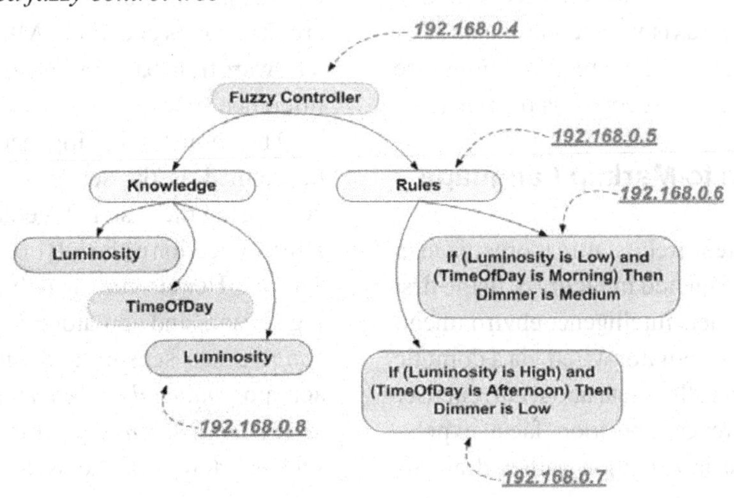

Figure 5. Mobile agent fuzzy improvements using three agents

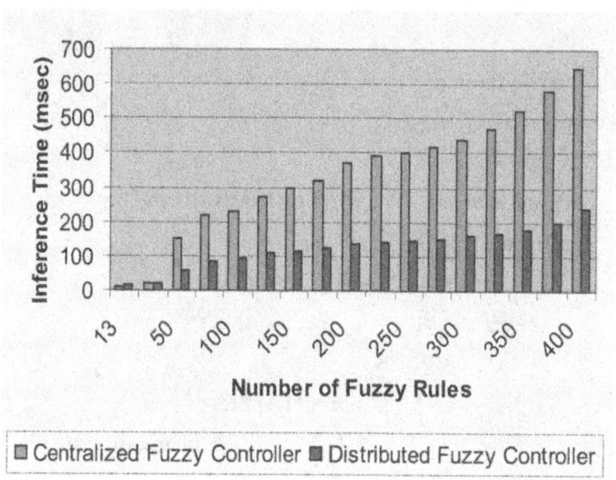

represent the run time containers able to execute the fuzzy logic operator on a modeled entity. Stationary fuzzy agents are hosted on the different hosts of the network; these hosts represent the fuzzy control network (FCN). The inference agent is a migrating agent able to apply the classic inference operator, like *Mamdani MinMaxMin* or *Larson Product* on hosts running the stationary agents. Due to the delocalization of rules, it is necessary to collect the partial inference results. This is done by the migration of inference agent that gathers the partial results available on each stationary. Just to give an idea of the gain from shifting a centralized to a decentralized evaluation, we give in Figure 5 the results from a testbed done by spreading the control over three computational nodes. On the axis x we report the number of fuzzy rules evaluated, the required inference time, expressed in milliseconds, is on axis y.

H2ML: Human to Markup Language

The proposed system architecture is organized in several layers, as depicted in Figure 6. In the first layer from top, ambient intelligence environment, a set of sensors and actuator wired via a domotic protocol is used to gather data about current user status (temperature, gait, position, facial expression, etc.). Part of information gathered at this stage is handled by morphological recognition subsystems (i.e., facial recognition eubsystem [8]) resulting in a semantic description. These kinds of information, together with the remaining information retrieved in the environment, are organized in a hierarchical structure based on XML technology in order to create a new markup language, called human to markup language (H2ML). H2ML is a new tool to model human information allowing a transparent use in different intelligent frameworks.

The other layer, multilayer controller, based on the hierarchical fuzzy control, represents the core designed to distribute appropriate services related to the information contained in H2ML representation. Each fuzzy controller used in our architecture is coded in FML in order to achieve hardware transparency and to minimize the fuzzy inference time.

The ambient intelligence environment can be defined as the set of actuators and sensors composing the system together with the domotic interconnection protocol (Lontalk+IP in our case). The AmI environment is based on the following sensors and actuators: *internal* and *external temperature* sensors and *internal temperature* actuator, *internal* and *external luminosity* sensor and *internal luminosity* actuator, *indoor presence sensor*. Moreover, the system relies on a set of

Figure 6. Ambient intelligent architecture

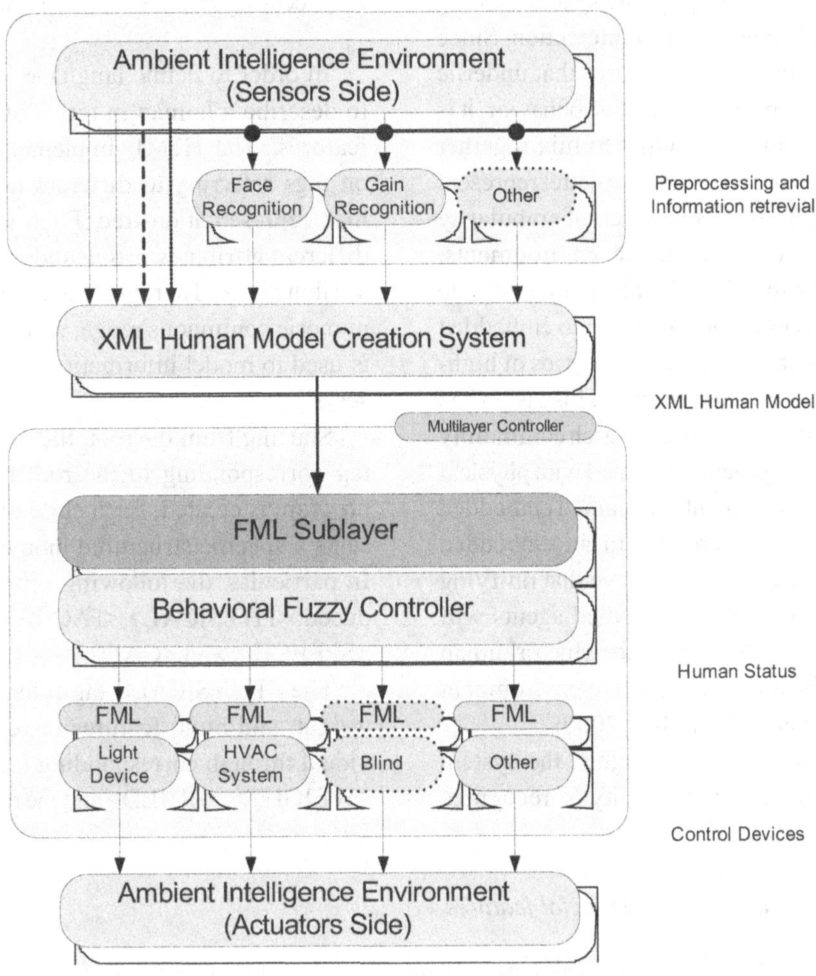

color cameras to capture information about gait and facial expression, and an infrared camera to capture thermal images of the users.

Recently, some approaches have been proposed to model the human aspect by using specific languages. Virtual human markup language (VHML) (Marriot, 2002), and multi-modal presentation markup language (Prendinger, 2004) are examples of languages proposed to simplify the human-computer interaction through a virtual Web assistant. While the mentioned languages are based on a high-level description of human status (i.e., happy and fear face concepts), H2ML is focused on detailed, low-level description of physical human features (i.e., closed and opened eyes or mouth). These features are important for AmI scenarios, in two wide applications:

- **Embodied conversational agents.** Conversational agents will be an integral part of ambient intelligent environments since they add a social dimension to man-machine communication and thus may help to make such environments more attractive to the human user. Earlier agent-based applications were characterized by a clear separation between the user's and the agent's world. Recently, there has been a trend, however, to merge the virtual and the physical space enabling completely new forms of interaction. Since agents embody inner features that underlie adaptive, robust and effective behavior, it is more natural for designer to mix together heterogeneous techniques to better represent and handle, at different levels of granularity and complexity, dynamic environments. Furthermore, the possibility to integrate useful pieces of intelligence into embedded artifact makes realizable scenarios of high-level ubiquitous computing. This vision has strongly stimulated the research community in envisaging agents stemmed with physical devices. These agents are named embedded agents, which were run in an embedded system or device. We believe that unifying conversational with embodied agents will represent a new paradigm for which a human is immersed in the proactive environment and vice versa (Churchill, 2000).

- **Context awareness.** Roughly, the system should own a certain ability to recognize people and the situational context, by processing human-oriented features.

In order to define language lexicon we have to describe a human in terms of morphological features. The H2ML implementation is based on tags referring to different nodes of the human representation tree. Each tag can use two different attributes: *value* and *status*. The value attribute is used to represent human features by a numeric continuous range, while status attribute is used to model information through a discrete set of labels.

Starting from the root, the <INDIVIDUAL> tag corresponding to the root tag of a H2ML program is created. Each child of this tag represents a specific structured biometric descriptor. In particular, the following set of tags is introduced: <PHYSICAL>, <FACE>, <THERMAL>, <SPEECH>, and <GAIT>.

The <PHYSICAL> tag refers to the height, weight, and build features of represented individual through corresponding tags <HEIGHT>, <WEIGHT>, <BUILD> and the related attributes

Figure 7a. H2ML used to handle facial features

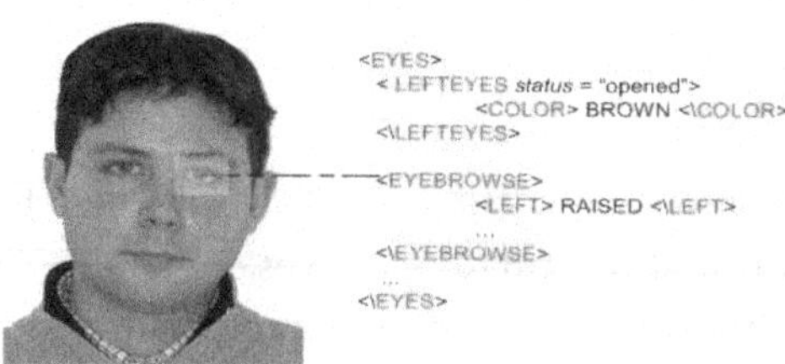

Figure 7b. H2ML used to handle body features

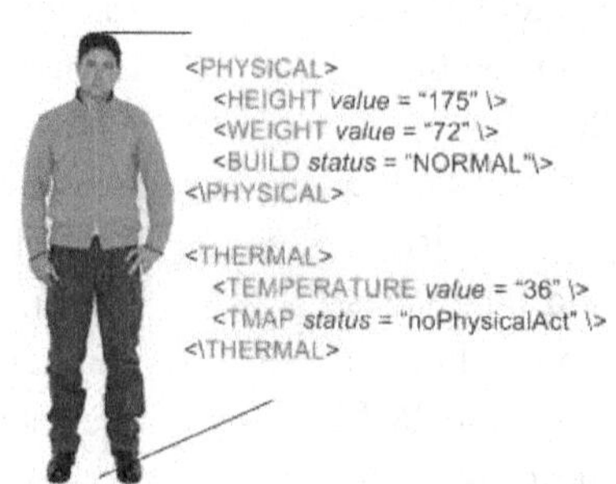

value and *status*. The <FACE> tag is used to handle facial features. Such features are modeled by <EYES>, <EYEBROWS>, and <MOUTH> tags. The <EYES> tag has two child tags: <RIGHT-EYE>, <LEFTEYE>. Eye features are modeled by <COLOR> tag. <EYEBROWS> tag is the root of a morphological subtree containing <LEFT> and <RIGHT> tags modeling the corresponding eyebrow. Finally, the <MOUTH> tag and its *status* attribute models the mouth-lips shape.

Body thermal features are represented through <TEMPERATURE> and <TMAP> tags nested in the <THERMAL> branch of the morphological tree. These tags use the *value* and *status* attribute to respectively model temperature and thermal distribution. The <SPEECH> tag represents voice features by <ACOUSTIC> and <SPECTRAL> nested tags. The last morphological subtree models motion features through the <GAIT> tag. Its child tags <POSITION>, <VELOTICY>, <ACCELERATION>, and <MOTION> are used to represent related physical properties. While the first three tags use the *value* attribute, the fourth one uses the *status* attribute to model the motion pattern property. Figures 7a and 7b show some examples of H2ML codes.

Vertical and Horizontal Fuzzy Distribution

The hierarchical structure of the proposed fuzzy controller is suited to apply a "divide et impera" strategy to the controlled system. Main goals are decomposed into sub-goals by partitioning the input space into a finite number of regions, each one featuring a specific sub-controller.

The divide et impera strategy leads to two different kinds of fuzzy rulebase distribution: *vertical* and *horizontal* distribution.

By "vertical fuzzy distribution" we mean a collection of dependent *control blocks* each ones represented by a single fuzzy controller or a set of horizontally distributed fuzzy controllers. The *dependency* relationship between control blocks is defined as follows: given a finite set of control block $\{CB_1, CB_2, \ldots, CB_i, \ldots, CB_n\}$ the output returned from the CB_i control block depends from the output computed from CB_{i-1} control block and so on. In particular, the defuzzified output of control block CB_{i-1} represents a fuzzy cutter for the aggregated, but not defuzzified, output of control block CB_i. The aim of the proposed vertical fuzzy distribution scheme is to separate fuzzy concepts not semantically related, emphasizing the fuzzy reasoning properties.

Through the "horizontal fuzzy distribution," we can parallelize inferences on different hosts, splitting a large semantically related rulebase by mobile agent technology, thus minimizing the fuzzy inference time (see the Fuzzy Markup Language section).

Experimental Results

Our scheme of fuzzy distribution allows separating the fuzzy variables related to human behavior from those related to domotic devices (vertical distribution). This distinction is thus used to parallelize the fuzzy inference applied to domotic controllers (horizontal distribution). More precisely, the first control block (vertical wise), named *behavioral fuzzy controller*, basically: (1) operates on H2ML program; (2) parses it; and (3) infers information about human status. The system adopts *singleton* fuzzy variables to model the behavioral concepts in fuzzy terms. *Sleeping*, *working*, and *relaxing* are only some examples of singleton behavioral fuzzy variables; the following rules are examples of behavioral rules:

IF velocity is LOW AND leftEye is CLOSED AND RightEye is CLOSED AND Speech is LOW AND Position is BED
THEN SLEEPING is ON

IF velocity is LOW AND leftEye is OPENED AND RightEye is OPENED AND Speech is LOW AND Position is Desk AND Acceleration

Figure 8. FML / H2ML application view

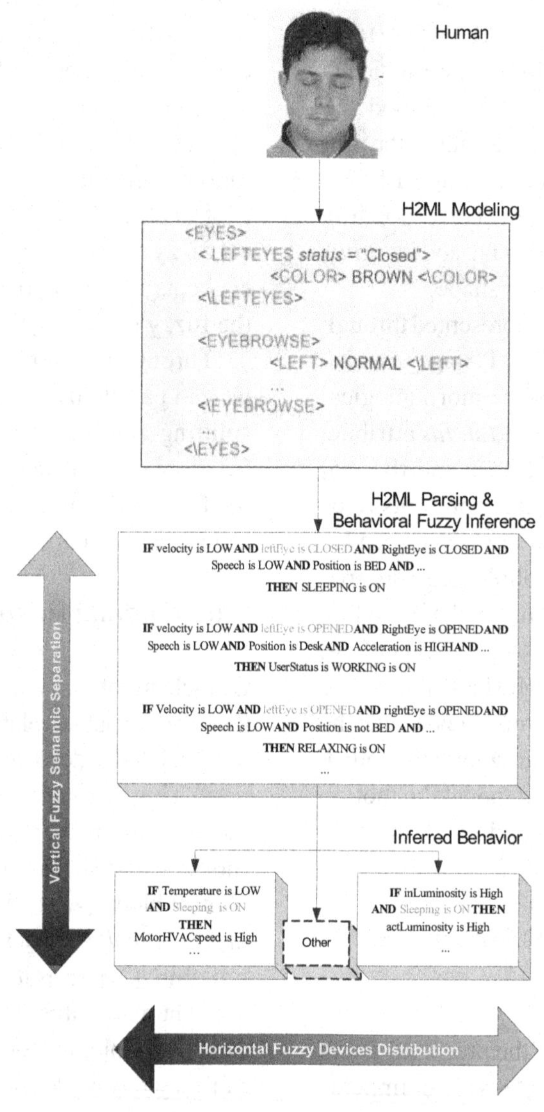

is HIGH

THEN UserStatus is WORKING is ON

IF Velocity is LOW AND leftEye is OPENED AND rightEye is OPENED AND Speech is LOW AND Position is not BED

THEN RELAXING is ON

...

The information inferred at this stage will be used in the next level to control the actuator devices.

The second control block (vertical wise) is a set of semantically related controllers distributed using horizontal scheme. At this hierarchical level the system uses classic fuzzy controllers coded in FML. In particular, we code a whole fuzzy ambient intelligence controller distributing the related rules (e.g., HVAC rules or lighting system rules) on different hosts. Some examples of devices control distributed fuzzy rules are shown:

IF Temperature is LOW AND Sleeping is ON
THEN MotorHVACspeed is High

IF inLuminosity is LOW AND
Working is ON THEN actLuminosity is High
...

It is simple to note that information related to behavior inferred from root layer of hierarchic intelligence scheme is used merely to cut the fuzzy set composing the consequent part of rules so as to influence the device's operation. An application view of our framework is shown in Figure 8.

CONCLUSION

The importance of human body monitoring is fundamental for many sectors such as health, rehabilitation and gerontology, as well as domestic environments. In most cases, it is crucial to evaluate many indexes of activities, such as movement or acceleration of body segments, frequency of posture change, walking speed, and so forth. For this purpose, we find a growing set of instruments capable of capturing and tracking the human features. Even though many efforts are made for solving the several practical drawbacks arising from the use of these devices, minor experiences are reported to provide the abstract and problem-independent description model useful for the interoperability and adaptive control strategies. This issue is crucial for intelligent environment applications, but it is not fully supported by the currently available technologies. Sun JINI and Microsoft UPnP are two popular examples of network specifications for easy connection to home information appliances and computers, but they are rather primitive and demand a lot of complex works (in terms of several software layers) so as to bridge the framework with the sensor software level. Only recently, the scientific community is paying much attention to the problem of flexible and uniform utilization of sensors in advanced programmable controllers. The markup languages or in more general the formal conceptual description have played a key role in this direction. For the sake of simplicity we cite just two works (Noguchi, 2003; Fodor, 1998). In Noguchi (2003), the authors made a choice using XML to implement the sensor network middleware. This choice: allows achieving remarkable benefits for network transparency and flexible sensor management. A wider perspective has been deepened in Fodor (1998), where the concept and implication of an ontological controller are discussed. The ontological controller supervises a programmable controller in order to: (1) detect dynamically when the programmable controller is in a critical situation due to a violation of ontological assumptions and (2) move (when possible) the programmable controller into such a state from which it can regain its control (recovery operation). The combination of FML and H2ML in a multi-layered architecture represents a strong improvement for abstraction representation and efficient control management for real hardware AmI implementation (Echelon Lonworks, X10, Konnex, etc.). Moreover, the FML layer allows distributing fuzzy controller components on different hosts, thus providing a simple platform for real ubiquitous computing system.

REFERENCES

Aarts, E. (2004, January-March). Ambient intelligence: A multimedia perspective. *IEEE Multimedia, 11*(1), 12-19.

Acampora, G., & Loia, V. (2005a, May 22-25). Using fuzzy technology in ambient intelligence environment. In *Proceedings of the IEEE International Conference on Fuzzy Systems*, Reno, NV.

Acampora, G., & Loia, V. (2005b). Fuzzy control interoperability and scalability for adaptive domotic framework. *IEEE Transactions on Industrial Informatics, 1*(2), 97-111.

Astrom, K. J. (1987). Adaptive feedback control. *Proceedings of the IEEE, 75*(2), 185-217.

Churchill E. (Ed.). (2000). *Embodied conversational agents*. Cambridge, MA: The MIT Press.

Ditze, M., Kamper, G., Jahnich, I., & Bernhardi-Grisson, R. (2004, June 24-26). Service-based access to distributed embedded devices through the open service gateway. In *Proceedings of the 2nd IEEE International Conference on Industrial Informatics*, Berlin, Germany (pp. 493-498).

DuCharme, B. (1999). *XML: The annotated specification*. Upper Saddle River, NJ: Prentice Hall.

Fodor, G. A. (1998). *Ontologically controlled autonomous systems: Principles, operations, and architecture*. Kluwer Academic.

Mamdani, E. H. (1974). Applications of fuzzy algorithms for simple dynamic plants. *Proceedings of IEEE, 121*, 1585-1588.

Marriott A., & Stallo, J. (2002, July 16).VHML: Uncertainties and problems, a discussion. In *Proceedings of the AAMAS-02 Workshop on Embodied Conversational Agents*, Bologna, Italy.

Noguchi, H., Mori, T., & Sato, T. (2003, October). Network middleware for utilization of sensors in room. In *Proceedings of IEEE/RSJ International Conference on Intelligent Robots and Systems*, Las Vegas, NV (Vol. 2, pp. 1832-1838).

Prendinger, H., Descamps, S., & Ishizuka, M. (2004). MPML: A markup language for controlling the behavior of life-like characters. *Journal of Visual Languages and Computing, 15*, 183-203.

Schilit, B., & Theimer, M. (1994). Disseminating active map information to mobile hosts. *IEEE Network, 8*(5), 22-32.

Takagi, T., & Sugeno, M. (1985) Fuzzy identification of systems and its applications to modeling and control. *IEEE Transactions on Systems, Man and Cybernetics, 15*(1), 116-132.

Zadeh, L. A. (1965). Fuzzy sets. *Information and Control, 8*, 338-353.

This work was previously published in Artificial Intelligence and Integrated Intelligent Information Systems: Emerging Technologies and Applications, edited by X. Zha, pp. 1-17, copyright 2007 by IGI Publishing, formerly known as Idea Group Publishing (an imprint of IGI Global).

Section III
New Supporting Technological Issues

Chapter VIII
Wireless Technologies for Mobile Computing

Biju Issac
Information Security Research (iSECURES) Lab and Swinburne University of Technology–Sarawak Campus, Malaysia

C.E. Tan
University Malaysia Sarawak, Malaysia

ABSTRACT

Mobility and computing were two concepts that never met a decade or two ago. But with the advent of new wireless technologies using radio propagation, the impossible is now becoming possible. Though there are many challenges to be overcome in terms of improving the bandwidth and security as with a wired network, the developments are quite encouraging. It would definitely dictate the way we do transactions in future. This chapter briefly explores some popular wireless technologies that aid in mobile computing, like 802.11 networks, Bluetooth networks, and HomeRF networks. Under 802.11 networks, we investigate the details of both infrastructure and ad hoc networks and its operations. The reader is thus made aware of these technologies briefly along with their performance, throughput, and security issues, which finally concludes with user preferences of these technologies.

INTRODUCTION

Wireless networks are generally implemented with a transmission system that uses radio waves for the carrier and this implementation usually is done at the physical layer of the network. These networks allow you to eliminate messy and intertwined cables. Wireless connections offer great mobility options, but on the negative side there can sometimes be other radio interference that might block or distort the original signal. Wireless networks can be commonly found on college campuses, offices, and in public places like airports, coffee cafes, and so forth. Among the myriad of applications and services that are executed by mobile devices, network and data services are on the rise. According to a recent study by Cahners In-Stat Group, the number of subscribers to wireless data services will grow rapidly from 170 million worldwide in 2000 to more than 1.3 billion or more in 2004 and later years and the number of wireless messages sent per month will rise from 3 billion in early 2000 to 244 billion or more by 2005 and later years. That clearly trumpets the fact that mobile computing cannot be ignored! We plan to briefly investigate some selective wireless technologies that help mobile computing, like 802.11 networks (with infrastructure mode and ad hoc mode), Bluetooth, and HomeRF.

IEEE 802.11 INFRASTRUCTURE WIRELESS NETWORK

The IEEE 802.11 family consists of different standards. The initial standard was approved in 1997 and it backed wireless local area network medium access control (MAC) and physical layer (PHY) specifications that supported 1 Mbps and 2 Mbps data rate over the 2.4 GHz ISM band using frequency hopping spread spectrum (FHSS) or direct sequence spread spectrum (DSSS) as radio technologies, along with infrared technologies as well. WLAN (wireless local area network) configurations vary from simple, independent, peer-to-peer connections between a set of PCs, to more complex, intrabuilding infrastructure networks. There are also point-to-point and point-to-multipoint wireless solutions. A point-to-point solution is used to bridge between two local area networks and to provide an alternative to cable between two geographically distant locations. Point-to-multipoint solutions connect several, separate locations to one single location or building. Both point-to-point and point-to-multipoint can be based on the 802.11 standard. In a typical WLAN infrastructure configuration, there are two basic components: access points and wireless stations. An access point/base station connects to a local area network (LAN) by means of Ethernet cable. Usually installed in the ceiling or other specific locations, access points receive, buffer, and transmit data between the WLAN and the wired network infrastructure. A single access point supports on the average, 20 users and has a coverage varying from 20 meters in areas with obstacles (walls, stairways, elevators) and up to 100 meters in areas with clear line of sight. A building may require several access points to provide complete coverage and allow users to roam seamlessly between access points. A wireless network adapter connects users via an access point to the rest of the LAN. A wireless station can be a PC card in a laptop, an ISA, or PCI adapter in a desktop computer, or can be fully integrated within a handheld device. Security of a WLAN is of great concern with wired equivalent privacy (WEP) encryption design weakness. EAP-RADIUS server with temporal key integrity protocol (TKIP) is proposed as an interim solution to mitigate security attacks. As a long term solution, 802.11i is working on making advanced encryption standard (AES) as the future encryption standard (Gast, 2002). 802.11n provides higher throughput improvements and is intended to provide speeds up to 500 Mbps. We would like to investigate the co-existence scenarios of different 802.11 standards.

802.11 WLAN STANDARDS AND CO-EXISTENCE ANALYSIS

There are different wireless LAN technologies that the IEEE 802.11 standard supports in the unlicensed bands of 2.4 and 5 GHz. They share the same medium access control (MAC) over two PHY layer specifications: direct-sequence spread spectrum (DSSS) and frequency-hopping

Table 1. Popular IEEE 802.11 comparisons

Features	802.11 (Legacy)	802.11a	802.11b	802.11g	802.11n
Speed	1 Mbps to 2 Mbps	54 Mbps	11 Mbps	54 Mps	~200Mbps (with multiple antennas)
Frequency	2.4 GHz	5 GHz	2.4 GHz	2.4 GHz	2.4 GHz and/or 5 GHz
Year of inception	1997	1999	1999	2003	2006
Modulation and Antenna	FHSS and DSSS	OFDM	DSSS	OFDM	Alamouti coding with MIMO
Interference risk	High	Low	High	High	Low/High
Range (Indoor)	~25m	~30m	~35m	~35m	~70m
Range (Outdoor)	~75m	~100m	~110m	~110m	~160m

spread spectrum (FHSS) technologies. Infrared technology though supported, is not accepted by any manufacturer. Data rates of up to 2 Mbps were achieved initially by IEEE 802.11 systems operating at the 2.4 GHz band. Their wide acceptance initiated new versions and enhancements of the specification. The different extensions to the 802.11 standard use the radio frequency band differently.

Some of the popular 802.11 extensions are as follows. IEEE 802.11b specifies the use of DSSS at 1, 2, 5.5 and 11 Mbps. The 802.11b products were quite popular with its voluminous production at the onset of wireless network market. 802.11a specifies the use of a frequency multiplexing scheme called as orthogonal frequency division multiplexing (OFDM) and it uses a physical layer standard that operates at data rates up to 54 Mbps. As high frequencies attenuate more, one needs more 802.11a access points compared to using 802.11b access points. 802.11g specifies a high speed extension to 802.11b that operates in 2.4 GHz frequency band using OFDM to obtain data rates up to 54 Mbps and as well as backward compatible with 802.11b devices. 802.11i recognizes the limitations of WEP and enhances wireless security. It defines two new encryption methods as well as an authentication method. The two encryption methods designed to replace WEP include TKIP and advanced encryption standard (AES). The authentication is based on the port-based 802.1x approach defined by a prior IEEE standard. Other 802.11 extensions include 802.11c that focuses on MAC bridges, 802.11d that focuses on worldwide use of WLAN with operation at different power levels, 802.11e that focuses on Quality of Service, 802.11f that focuses on access point interoperability, and 802.11h that focuses on addressing interference problems when used with other communication equipments (Held, 2003). 802.11n, which is one of the newest standards produces higher throughput using multiple input multiple output (MIMO) antennas and uses a coding scheme to transmit multiple copies of a data stream across a number of antennas. Table 1 shows the comparison of the popular 802.11 standards.

Network simulation is performed for the performance and co-existence analysis of different 802.11 standards (Issac, Hamid, & Tan,

Figure 1. The topology used in the scenario where 802.11g nodes with AP (on right) co-exist with 802.11b nodes with AP (on left)

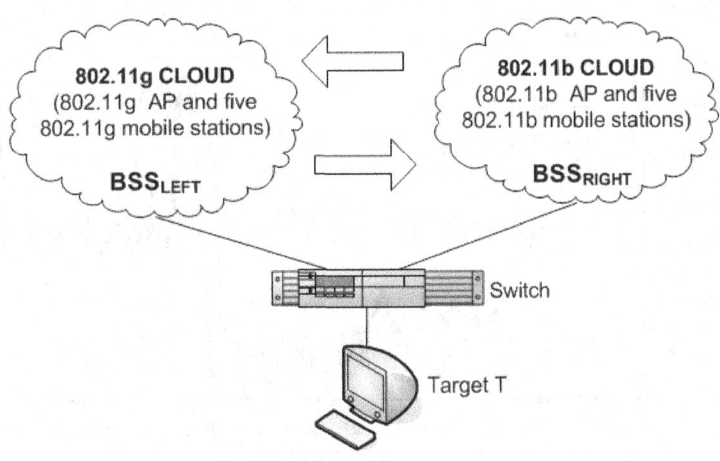

Figure 2. The throughput measured on the target station T in different WLAN configurations like 802.11b, 802.11g, 802.11 b with g and 802.11a

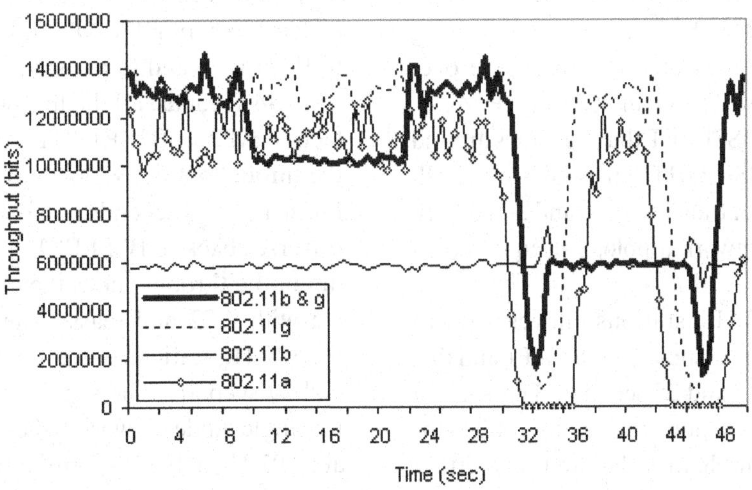

2006). We considered 802.11a, 802.11b, 802.11g, 802.11b with g, and 802.11a with g, along with other configurations. Comparisons are done in terms of throughput when they work in single and mixed mode. The trajectory timing is generally set between 0 and 49 seconds. Different scenarios of wireless networks were created for simulation like 802.11 b and g co-existing, WLAN with only 802.11b nodes, WLAN with only 802.11g nodes, WLAN with only 802.11a nodes, and other mixed modes. The data traffic dropped and throughput were measured. An 802.11b with g WLAN was created that consisted of two Basic Service Set (BSS) networks: BSSLEFT and BSSRIGHT. The data rate of 802.11g mobile node is set to 54Mbps and that of 802.11b node is set to 2Mbps. The nodes communicate to a Target Station T that is connected to an Ethernet LAN where the access points

Figure 3. The data traffic dropped in throughput measurement in 802.11b, 802.11g, 802.11 b with g and 802.11a networks

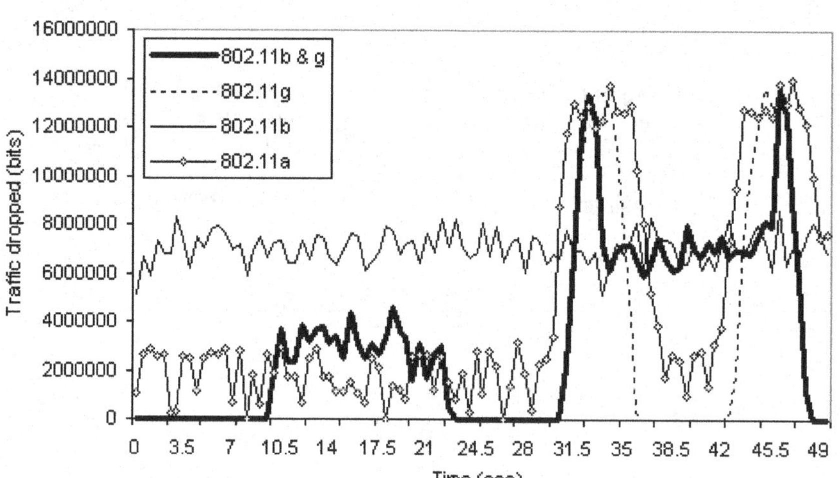

of BSSLEFT and BSSRIGHT are connected. In the initial setup, BSSLEFT consist of five 802.11g stations that transmit data (set to transmit over 2Mbps per node) to T and an 802.11g AP (AP1). The total load of BSSLEFT thus becomes around 13 to 14 Mbps. BSSRIGHT consist of five 802.11b stations that do not transmit data and an 802.11b AP (AP2). The network topology used is shown in Figure 1.

The five 802.11b stations moves toward BSSLEFT and gets associated with AP1 and this happens between 5 and 25 seconds. The 802.11g station in BSSLEFT now have to use "CTS-to-self" protection mechanism before transmitting their data frames at 54Mbps because the newly arrived 802.11b stations cannot decode 802.11g data. This and association of 802.11b stations to BSSLEFT causes the throughput rate to drop from 14Mbps to 10Mbps during 10 to 21 seconds. Later the five 802.11b stations traverses back to BSSRIGHT and re-associates with AP2 during 21 to 30 seconds. Now the throughput rises to 14Mbps as BSSLEFT becomes an all-11g WLAN. The five 802.11g stations do the reverse. They move toward BSSRIGHT and associate with AP2 during 30 to 33 seconds. Now the throughput drops down as they are disassociated with AP1 and are scanning for AP2. It later gets back and to BSSLEFT and re-associates with AP1. From 33 to 44 seconds, all the five 802.11g stations attach to AP2 in BSSRIGHT. As AP2 is 802.11b, the throughput drops down to less than 6Mbps. From 44 to 49 seconds, the five 802.11g stations traverses back to BSSLEFT. This causes a short dip in the throughput as they have to disassociate with AP2 and reassociate with AP1. Thus the 802.11g stations move to and fro between 30 and 49 seconds. The same scenario is repeated for single mode networks where 802.11a, 802.11b and 802.11g networks were simulated and performance measured.

Figure 2 shows the processes of 802.11b with 802.11g co-existence in detail and shows the ups and downs in the throughput graph. The throughput is comparable for all 802.11g and all 802.11a networks that support 54Mbps. For all 802.11b networks, the throughput is lower. In the other simulation models, the 802.11 standard is changed on the devices to accommodate comparison of standards. The graph for data traffic dropped is shown in Figure 3.

The drop is quite severe and uniform for all 802.11b networks. For other configurations, the drops are comparable (Issac et al., 2006).

Security Issues

Highly sensitive antennas (with high level of directional sensitivity) can be used by anyone to pick up the RF signals of wireless LAN, to a great distance. If sufficient numbers of frames are captured, static WEP key can be reconstructed using software application programs like Airsnort, WEPCrack, AirCrack, and so forth. The attacker can also pretend to be a legitimate user of the network, say through medium access control (MAC) spoofing. Certain bits could be flipped in the wireless frame by the attacker, changing the Integrity Check Value without the knowledge of the user. In denial of service (DoS) attack, the intruder floods the network with either valid or invalid messages affecting the availability of the network resources. Because the cost of access points has fallen, many organizations face the threat of rouge access points that joins the company's network. In ARP (Address Resolution Protocol) poisoning, an attacker creates illegitimate packets with a spoofed IP address which claims that IP belongs to his own computer's MAC address. Session hijacking within a wireless network is said to occur when an attacker causes the user to lose his connection, and the attacker assumes his identity and privileges for a period. An attacker disables temporarily the user's system, say by DoS attack or a buffer overflow exploit. General precautions for WLAN security includes use strong encryption scheme like TKIP or AES, use of mutual authentication through authentication server (like RADIUS server), use of nondictionary passwords, use of virtual private network (VPN) over WLAN, use of intrusion detection software (IDS) and use of network monitoring with accounting facilities.

IEEE 802.11 AD HOC WIRELESS NETWORK

The connections in an ad-hoc network are essentially wireless links. The network is termed ad hoc because any node is free to forward data to any other adjacent node, through dynamic decisions based on network topology and connectivity. Three different types of wireless ad hoc networks include mobile ad hoc networks (MANETs), wireless sensor networks (WSNs), and wireless mesh networks (WMNs). A mobile ad hoc network (MANET) is a self configuring network of mobile routers along with associated hosts connected by wireless links. This union of network nodes or devices forms an arbitrary topology. The routers are free to move randomly and organize themselves arbitrarily, making unpredictable changes in network's wireless topology. A wireless sensor network (WSN) is a network that is made up of autonomous devices that uses one or more sensors and a transceiver to gauge the atmospheric or environmental factors such as sound, temperature, pressure, and so forth, at various locations. Mesh is a communication infrastructure that is cooperative in nature between a good number of individual wireless transceivers. Mesh networks are also highly reliable, as each node is connected to several other nodes and if one node shuts down for some reason, its neighbouring nodes would find another route. Wireless mesh networking (WMN) is mesh networking that is implemented over a wireless LAN.

When there is a scope for dynamic environments in which people or vehicles need to be temporarily connected in areas without a pre-existing communication infrastructure, or where infrastructure cost is not justified, the solution is to have the 802.11 ad-hoc networks. Hence, operating in this mode, the stations are said to form an independent basic service set (IBSS) or an ad-hoc network. After a synchronization phase, any station that is within the transmission range of any other can start interacting with each other. There is no need for access point and if one station working in ad-hoc mode is connected to a wired network, stations forming ad hoc network have a wireless access to Internet. IEEE 802.11 technology can be used to implement single-hop ad hoc networks where the stations need to be in the same transmission radius to be able to communicate. But in multihop ad hoc networking, routing mechanisms can be enabled to extend the range of the ad hoc network beyond the transmission radius of the single source station. Routing solutions for wired network do not apply to ad hoc networks because of its dynamic topology. Each node is free to move around while interacting with other nodes and the topology of such a network is quite dynamic in nature due to the constant movement of the participating nodes, causing intercommunication patterns among nodes to change all the time.

Some common problems that affect ad-hoc network performance (though relevant to other forms of wireless networks) are as follows:

1. The wireless medium has fuzzy boundaries and outside these boundaries the stations cannot receive network frames.
2. As the channel is open to all the signals to come in, there can be interference.
3. The channel has time varying and asymmetric propagation properties.

Ad-hoc routing protocols are getting popular with the increase in mobile computing. Ad-hoc networks include resource-starving devices, low bandwidth, high error rates, and a topology that is continuously changing. Some of the design goals with ad hoc routing protocols are minimal control overhead, minimal processing overhead, multihop routing capability, dynamic topology maintenance, and loop prevention. The protocols should operate in a distributed manner. The nodes should operate either in proactive or reactive mode. Proactive protocols are table-based and maintain routes for the entire network within each node. The nodes must be fully aware of the changing topology. For topologies that are overtly dynamic, this approach can introduce a considerable overhead. Reactive or on-demand protocols trade off this overhead with increased delay. A route to destination is established when it is needed based on an initial discovery between the source and destination. Security of ad hoc networks are a great concern with flawed WEP (128 bits) encryption, but 802.1x authentication along with other improved encryption schemes offer some temporary solution (Basangi, Conti, Giordano, & Stojmenovic, 2004).

Demand Driven Routing Protocols in Ad hoc Networks

A brief description of some selective demand driven routing protocols is given below: Destination-sequenced distance vector (DSDV) is a different version of the Bellman-Ford algorithm to take care of time dependent topologies. DSDV is table driven and each node maintains a routing table with the next hop entry for each destination and metric for each link. The overhead with this protocol is high and this limits the number of nodes in the network. *Ad hoc on-demand routing (AODV)* is a variation of DSDV algorithm. When a node wants to establish a communication link, it does a path-discovery process to locate the other node. The source node broadcasts a route request (RREQ) packet with its IP address, Broadcast ID, and the sequence numbers of source and destination nodes. The receiving nodes set a backward pointer to the source and generate a route replay (RREP) unicast packet if it is the destination. As RREP is routed back to source, intermediate nodes set up forward pointers in their routing tables. AODV favors the least congested route and uses hello messages to maintain node connectivity. *Dynamic source routing (DSR)* uses source based routing rather than table based and it is source initiated rather than hop-by-hop. A node wishing

Table 2. Demand-driven protocol comparison

Parameters	AODV	DSR	TORA
Routing philosophy	Flat	Flat	Flat
Routes stored in	Route Table	Route Cache	Route Table
Multicast option	Yes	No	No
Multiple routes	No	Yes	Yes
Routing metric (path)	Most Fresh and Shortest	Shortest	Shortest
Loop-free network	Yes	Yes	Yes
Route re-configuration approach	Delete route – and notify source	Delete route – and notify source	Link reversal – and route repair

to communicate issues a Route Request to all its neighbors and each neighbor in turn rebroadcasts this Request adding its own address in the header of the packet. When a Request is received by the destination node or by an intermediate node in the path to destination, a Route Reply is sent back to the sender along with addresses accumulated in the Request header. Thus the entire route is maintained in the packet header. DSR is not that scalable to large networks. *Temporally-ordered routing algorithm (TORA)* is a distributed and adaptive protocol that can operate in a dynamic network. For a particular destination, it uses the "height" parameter to determine the direction of a link between any two nodes. Thus multiple routes are often present for a given destination. For a node to start communication, it broadcasts a Query to all its neighbors, which is rebroadcast through the network until it reaches the destination. This node would reply with an Update that includes its height with respect to the destination, which is propagated back to the sender. Each node that receives the Update sets its own height to one greater than that of the neighbor that sent it, which results in a series of directed links from sender to destination in the order of height values (Aaron & Weng, 2001).

A comparison summary on the three simulated protocols can be given as follows. Table 2 (Royer & Toh, 1999) shows the details in a nutshell. As DSR packets need to contain full routing information, the memory overhead is more compared to AODV. But it does not make use of periodic router advertisement which saves some bandwidth and power consumption. As DSR allows multiple routes to the destination, in the event of a link failure, the other valid routes can be checked and this can prevent route reconstruction, hastening the route recovery. As DSR assumes small network diameter, it is not scalable to large networks. The requirement to place the route in both route replies and data packets increases the control overhead much more than in AODV.

AODV overhead is much less in comparison to DSR as the route replies need to carry only the destination IP address and sequence number. This also reduces the memory overhead in comparison to DSR. AODV also uses a route discovery mechanism that is similar to DSR. A big advantage of AODV is its support for multicast communication. TORA is a link-reversal algorithm that is suitable for densely populated network with a large number of nodes. It creates directed acyclic graphs (DAG) to help route creation and supports multiple routes for single source-destination pair. TORA needs synchronized clocks for its operation and, if the external time source fails, the protocol would fail. Even route rebuilding can incur lengthy delays because of synchronization related oscillations (Royer et Al., 1999)

Performance Analysis of Demand Driven Protocols

Network simulation was performed to do a performance comparison of demand driven protocols within an ad hoc network and the setup is shown in Figure 4. As shown, first a wireless server is configured with DSR and 40 mobile nodes are configured as work stations (that can generate application traffic) running DSR. They are placed as 20 nodes on one side and remaining 20 nodes on the other side. The simulation is done for 30 minutes (1800 sec). The setup is similar for other scenarios as well. The wireless nodes can communicate to each other within a cloud or to the server. They can also communicate with the wireless nodes in the other cloud. The mobile nodes are configured to eliminate all receivers that are over 1500 meters away. In all cases, the throughput of the network that runs some applications like Telnet, e-mail, or FTP sessions is checked. Second, the wireless server is configured with TORA and mobile nodes are configured as work stations running TORA. Third, the wireless server is configured with AODV and mobile nodes are configured as work stations running AODV. This is done in the default mode. Later the same exercise is done with reduced or light traffic. Parameters set for AODV (to reduce routing traffic) are as follows: Route Discovery Parameter: Gratuitous Reply-Enabled, Active Route Timeout: 30 sec and WLAN data rate: 1Mbps.

Figure 4. The general wireless ad hoc network topology used for simulation

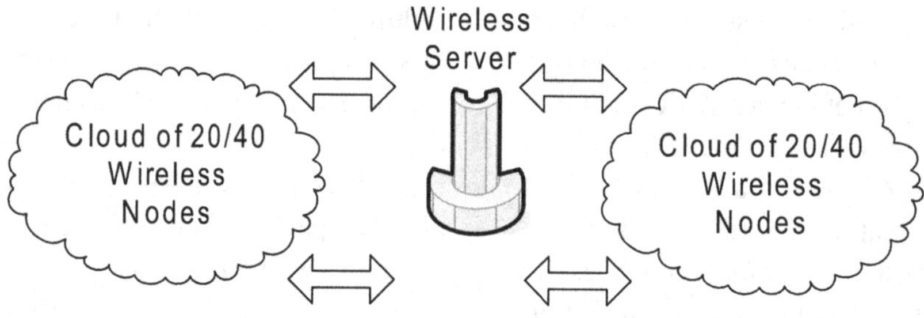

Figure 5. Throughput for ad hoc network when using DSR, TORA, and AODV (default and low traffic (LT)

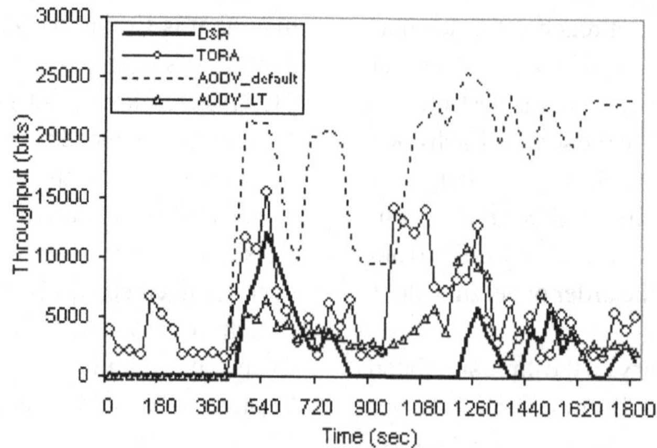

Figure 5 shows the throughput comparison of all 3 protocols: DSR, TORA, and AODV. AODV with gratuitous reply enabled (light traffic/LT option) and DSR shows comparable throughput. Default AODV shows a greater throughput and TORA is in between (Issac et al., 2006). Many of the security issues mentioned under Infrastructure WLAN in the previous section, are applicable here also.

BLUETOOTH NETWORK

The popularity of Bluetooth capable devices has been driven by the increase of portable personal devices which require short range communications. Bluetooth provides a convenient way to connect and exchange information between devices such as personal digital assistants (PDAs), mobile phones, laptops, printers, digital cameras, and so forth, via a secure, low cost, globally available short range radio frequency. It aims to be a cable replacement technology. The basic unit of networking in Bluetooth is a piconet. A device can be either slave or master in a piconet and can thus be part of more than one piconet. This network overlapping is called scatternet. The frequency hopping (FH) used in Bluetooth provides resistance to interference and multiple path effects and provides multiple accesses from colocated devices in different piconets. The security mechanism in Bluetooth uses a 48-bit address defined by IEEE, a 128-bit authentication key, a 128-bit symmetric encryption key and a generated random number. In order to add more values to this fantastic radio technology, two potential aspects should be looked into to strengthen the Bluetooth platform for future applications; they are Bluetooth-enabled secure access to wide area networks and the interference issues with other devices operating within the same frequency band. In recent years, the research communities have been looking into the possibility of expanding the coverage of Bluetooth networks for greater coverage and applications. More efficient architectures for the formation of scatternet and routing protocols for interconnecting Bluetooth devices across multiple scatternets have been the main attention among researchers. The driving force is to push Bluetooth radio technology into the next level where users with existing Bluetooth capable devices can reach further such as smooth access to the Internet just likes WiFi. Several initiatives have been proposed such as the BLUEPAC (Albrecht, Frank, Martini, Schetelig, Vilavaara, & Wenzel, 1999), the BWIG (Rouhana & Horlait, 2002), and the BlueStar (Cordeiro, Abhyankar, Toshiwal, & Agrawal, 2003) to enable Bluetooth devices to connect to the Internet. All of these proposals have their own advantages toward delivering IP packets aim to work in their predescribed scenarios. To make all this possible, new architectures are essential to allow the transport of IP packets seamlessly from the Bluetooth piconet to the Internet. Bluetooth by itself is not designed for wide area access; hence, it requires an intermediate network with wide area access ability to complement it for wide area access. The intermediate networks can be either a wireless LAN, an Ethernet backbone, or even a 3G cellular network. The issue now will be on how to route the IP data packets in a heterogeneous network environment efficiently with minimum interference especially when interconnected with wireless LANs. Some of the major contributions in enabling wide area access for Bluetooth devices are discussed below.

The BWIG Architecture

The Bluetooth Web Internet Gateway (BWIG) architecture is based on a client/proxy/server model where Bluetooth clients send the requested HTTP URLs over the Bluetooth L2CAP stack to the Bluetooth gateway, which in turn will use the TCP/IP stack to contact the requested Web server. Upon receiving a reply from the Web server via TCP/IP, the Bluetooth gateway will redirect the reply to the Bluetooth client using the conventional

Bluetooth stack. The application-level proxy is used at both Bluetooth client and server to intercept the original requests send by Bluetooth user to the local TCP/IP stack and redirect them over the local Bluetooth stack to the Bluetooth gateway. At the gateway, the proxy server takes care of the requests just like any other HTTP requests. The implementation is less complicated since there is no TCP/IP stack involved in the Bluetooth part of communication but this will also restrict Bluetooth clients from higher user mobility.

The Bluetooth Public Access Reference Network Architecture

The Bluetooth public access reference network architecture has been proposed and called the Bluetooth Public Access (BLUEPAC) network (Albrecht et al., 1999). The reference network architecture defines a BLUEPAC area that consists of Bluetooth devices, BLUEPAC base stations, a BLUEPAC agent, an application server, a network gateway/proxy, and a BLUEPAC LAN, which interact based on the BLUEPAC IP protocol concept. The BLUEPAC reference network architecture, shown in Figure 6, is aiming to provide seamless wide area connectivity for Bluetooth-enabled devices and address the mobility issues using a concept derived from Mobile IP called the BLUEPAC IP protocol model. The BLUEPAC IP addresses the issues of local IP assignment, mobile IP, and handoff supports. If a Bluetooth device carries its own IP address and has a Mobile IP home agent, upon entering the BLUEPAC network, the device can request the BLUEPAC foreign agent to provide communication in a Mobile IP fashion.

The BlueStar Architecture

The BlueStar architecture aims at a larger scale of network sharing among wireless and wired devices for both local and wide area networks particularly for Bluetooth-.enabled devices by taking advantages of IEEE 802.11 wireless LANs.

Figure.6 The BLUEPAC reference network architecture

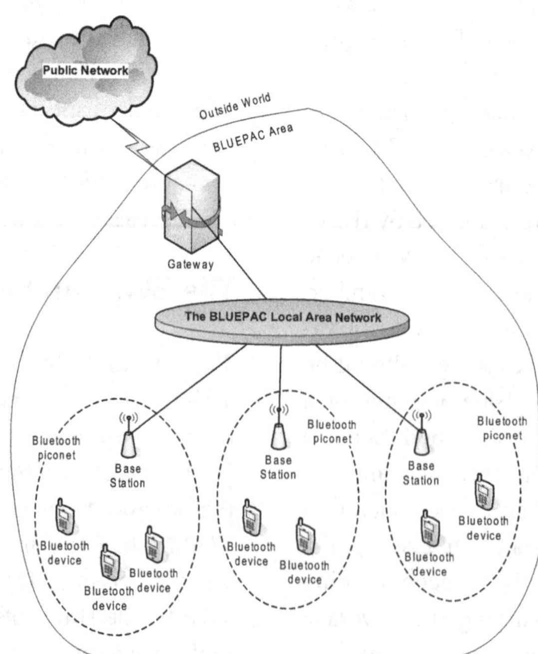

Selected devices which possess both Bluetooth and WLAN interfaces are used as the Bluetooth Wireless Gateways (BWGs) to allow access to local WLANs from a Bluetooth device in a piconet.

Figure 7 shows the BlueStar architecture proposed in (Cordeiro et al., 2003). Once access to local WLANs is established, further access to MANs or WANs will be a straightforward step and hence Bluetooth devices would be able to communicate with almost any entity in the Internet. BlueStar makes use of the existing point-to-point protocol (PPP) in mobile devices to deliver IP packets which eliminated the need for additional protocol stacks for this interconnection purpose. Since the BWGs need to coordinate the multiplexed receiving and sending of packets carefully in order to provide efficient and concurrent operation as they both employ the same 2.4GHz frequency band, BlueStar employs a unique hybrid approach of an adaptive frequency hopping (AFH) to mitigate persistent interference and the Bluetooth carrier sense (BCS) scheme to take care of the intermittent interference. The BlueStar architecture claimed to have doubled the performance of the regular Bluetooth in which the Bluetooth and WLAN systems operate independently with no information exchange between the two systems.

The Interference and Security Issues

The major challenge for Bluetooth- wide area access via WLANs will be the persistence interference between them since both technologies operate in the same 2.4GHz frequency band. At the same time, Bluetooth devices will also experience intermittent interference between multiple piconets in the same physical location. Interference among radio devices operating in the same frequency band has been a serious issue since decades ago. Bluetooth, WiFi, and microwave ovens are technologies that operate in the 2.4GHz range and they are prone to interference with each other when operating within the same physical location. Even with several independent piconets

Figure 7. The BlueStar architecture

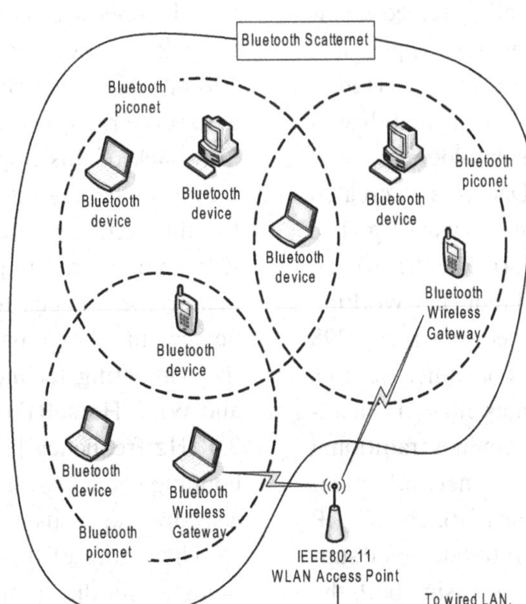

operate in the same area; interference raised will degrade the overall network performance. For a smooth and successful adoption of Bluetooth technology for more serious applications, interference survey and studies must be conducted and precautions must also be taken.

Bluetooth was initially designed for small number of devices operating in a piconet, with large number of participation scatternet will be formed and increased popularity in Bluetooth embedded devices, the security issues for this type of ad hoc nature network will be a major concern. Bluetooth is based on SAFER+ algorithm for key generation. Hence authorization and key management are critical in securing the Bluetooth networks since the trusted third party and identity-based schemes for key agreement are the most potential point of attack. Other potential attacks on Bluetooth are authentication attacks, encryption attacks, and communication attacks.

HOMERF NETWORK

HomeRF was proposed to fill the gap in home communications where it can be implemented to carry voice and data. HomeRF created a new class of mobile consumer devices using personal computers and the Internet. It is also referred to as the last 50 meters access. The availability of high speed last mile access technologies such as xDSL, cable modem, and ISDN has also created a high speed demand on home networking. The shared wireless access protocol (SWAP) has been developed by the Home Radio Frequency Working Group (HomeRF WG) launched in March 1998 as a single specification for consumer devices interoperability. SWAP operates either as an ad-hoc peer to peer network that provides traditional data networking or as a managed network under the control of a connection point (CP). The SWAP medium access control (MAC) provides good support for voice and data service by using both the TDMA and the CSMA/CA access mechanisms. It supports four high quality voice connections and up to 1.6Mbps data rate. The data security feature, node power management, and a 24-bit Network ID are also part of the specification.

The increasing bandwidth demand of home applications such as high quality audio and video transmission has pushed for a new specification, the HomeRF 2.0. HomeRF 2.0 can deliver Ethernet equivalent bandwidth to support wider wireless voice and data networking applications at home. It allows 800 kbps for isochronous voice and a maximum of 10 Mbps for asynchronous data transfer. The standard categorizes the HomeRF devices into 3 types: Asynchronous data device (also called A-node), Streaming data device (S-node), and Isochronous data device (I-node). The CP provides service management for the A-node, S-node, and I-node. The HomeRF standard defines two kinds of network topologies: Ad hoc network and Managed Network. An ad hoc network is a distributed network in which the devices can make a peer-to-peer communication that includes only A-nodes without any CP. The Managed Network is a network managed by the CP and the devices can either communicate peer-to-peer (data services) or can establish communication through the CP (voice services) depending on the type of HomeRF devices used. HomeRF 2.0 supports 128 bit encryption so that all the data traveling across the radio waves is encrypted. The major drawback of this implementation is the lack of a centralized key management for the network. But this is not a concern for home users because it is common assumption that the manual key management needs to be done only for a few devices in a home network. Similar to some of the competing technologies such as Bluetooth and WiFi, HomeRF operates in the license free 2.4GHz frequency band and utilizes frequency hopping spread spectrum technology to achieve a secure and robust communication.

The future of this technology is difficult to predict with the competition from similar technologies such as Bluetooth, WiFi, and HiperLAN2.

The success of this technology is also dependent on the adoption of the manufacturers to promote its advantages. To date, the wide acceptance of WiFi and Bluetooth has overwhelmed HomeRF as the major home networking technology. Major industrial players such as Intel and Proxim have started to discontinue their HomeRF products, which accelerate the obsoleteness of HomeRF technology.

USER ACCEPTANCE OF WIRELESS TECHNOLOGIES

It would be good to look at how users perceive and accept these technologies. A comparison of the technologies that we discussed is given in Table 3.

As of now, IEEE802.11g is the popular wireless fidelity (WiFi) technology with users because of its larger distance range (as it operates on the lower 2.4 GHz frequency band) and greater data rate of 54 Mbps, compared to the related IEEE wireless technologies. It is backward compatible with 802.11b devices. Despite its major acceptance, 802.11g suffers from interference problems as with 802.11b, in the already crowded 2.4 GHz range. Microwave ovens, Bluetooth devices, and cordless telephones operate in this frequency range. 802.11b though had the initial acceptance with users now falls back because of it lower speed of 11Mbps. 802.11a is also a good bargain, but its higher frequency band of operation (around 5 GHz) lessens its coverage area. But 802.11a can be popular with corporate organizations which needs more channels to operate with, who may be tolerant with pricing. 802.11n builds upon previous 802.11 standards by adding multiple-input multiple-output (MIMO) that uses multiple transmitter and receiver antennas to allow for increased data throughput through spatial multiplexing and increased range by exploiting the spatial diversity. Bluetooth is quite useful for short range wireless solution like wireless keyboard, wireless mouse, wireless printer, and so forth. HomeRF may not be a popular choice with wireless users as 802.11 technologies can perform better with higher speeds.

CONCLUSION

In this chapter we provide the details on some selected wireless technologies that aid in mobile computing. Mobile computing incorporating the technologies outlined would make computing on the move a reality along with other cellular technologies like GPRS, EDGE, 3G, and so forth. We also present some analysis on the performance and security aspects wherever it is relevant. The

Table 3. Wireless technology comparison

	802.11a/b/g	802.11n	Bluetooth	HomeRF
Modulation	DSSS	DSSS	Adaptive FHSS (Gaussian FSK)	FHSS (2 or 4 Level FSK)
Frequency Range	2.4 GHz (b/g) and 5.8 GHz (a)	2.4 GHz or 5 GHz	2.4 GHz	2.4 GHz
Distance Range	~30 to ~100 m	~50 to ~100 m	~10 m	~150 feet
Network Type	IP and Peer-to-Peer	IP and Peer-to-Peer	Peer-to-Peer	Peer-to-Peer
Data Rate	2 Mbps to 54 Mbps	~200 Mbps	~1 Mbps to ~3 Mbps	~800 kbps to ~10 Mbps

field of mobile networking is rapidly growing and changing so dynamically that there are many challenges to be met, in terms of the interoperability and security of different technologies. The convergence of all these wireless technologies to form one single network is the greatest challenge ahead, as they all use different technologies or network architectures. Though an imminent solution on convergence of networks is not in the horizon, research is aggressively moving ahead, and that could take us to a world where seamless and ubiquitous computing will become a definite reality—in every sense.

REFERENCES

Aaron, A., & Weng, J. (2001). *Performance comparison of ad-hoc routing protocols for networks with node energy constraints.* Retrieved January 19, 2008, from http://ivms.stanford.edu/~amaaron/ee360/EE360_FINAL_PAPER.pdf

Albrecht, M., Frank, M., Martini, P., Schetelig, M., Vilavaara, A., & Wenzel, A. (1999). IP services over Bluetooth: leading the way to a new mobility. In *Proceedings of 24th Annual Conference on Local Computer Networks (LCN'99)* (pp. 2-11).

Basangi, S., Conti, M., Giordano, S., & Stojmenovic, I. (2004). *Mobile ad-hoc networking.* Wiley InterScience.

Cordeiro, C., Abhyankar, S., Toshiwal, R., & Agrawal, D. (2003). A novel architecture and coexistence method to provide global access to/from Bluetooth WPANs by IEEE 802.11 WLANs. In *Proceedings of IEEE Performance, Computing and Communications Conference (IPCCC 2003)* (pp. 23-30).

Gast, M.S. (2002). *802.11 wireless networks–the definitive guide.* CA: O'Reilly.

Held, G. (2003). *Securing wireless LANs.* Sussex: John Wiley & Sons.

Issac, B., Hamid, K., & Tan, C.E. (2006a). Analysis of demand driven ad-hoc routing protocols on performance and mobility. In *Proceedings of the International Wireless and Telecommunication Symposium 2006 (IWTS 2006)*, Malaysia (136-141).

Issac, B., Hamid, K., & Tan, C.E. (2006b). Analysis of single and mixed 802.11 networks and mobility architecture. In *Proceedings of the International Conference on Computing and Informatics (ICOCI 2006)*, Malaysia.

Kelsey, J., Schneier, B., & Wagner, D. (1999). Key schedule weaknesses in SAFER+. In *Proceedings of the 2nd Advanced Encryption Standard Candidate Conference* (pp. 155-167).

Lim, Y., Kim, J., Min, S., & Ma, J. (2001). Performance evaluation of the Bluetooth based public Internet access point. In *Proceedings of the 15th International Conference on Information Networking (ICOIN 2001)* (pp. 643-648).

Myers, E. (2003). *HomeRF overview and market positioning.* Retrieved January 19, 2008, from http://www.palowireless.com/homerf/

Rouhana, N., & Horlait, E. (2002). BWIG: Bluetooth Web Internet Gateway. In *Proceedings of IEEE Symposium on Computer and Communications (ISCC 2002)* (pp. 679-684).

Royer, E.M., & Toh, C-K. (1999). A review of current routing protocols for ad hoc mobile wireless networks. *IEEE Personal Communications*, 46-55.

KEY TERMS

802.11 Networks: Wireless networks developed by the IEEE LAN/MAN Standards Committee (IEEE 802) in the 5 GHz and 2.4 GHz radio bands. 802.11 specify an over-the-air interface between wireless devices like a wireless client and a base station or between two wireless clients.

Access Point: The central or master device through which an infrastructure wireless node makes a connection to the local area network. It acts more like a bridge between wireless node and LAN.

Ad hoc network: A decentralized 802.11 wireless network where the wireless stations form a self-organized wireless network among themselves with routing capabilities, without a central server or station.

Bluetooth: An industry standard for wireless personal area networks. It provides a way by which devices such as mobile phones, laptops, PCs, printers, scanners, digital cameras, and so forth, communicate over a globally unlicensed short-range radio frequency.

Connection Point: The homeRF system can operate either as an ad hoc network or as a managed network under the control of a Connection Point, which is required to coordinate the system. The Connection Point also provides the gateway to the PSTN network which can be connected to computers.

Direct Sequence Spread Spectrum: A form of spread spectrum in which each bit in the original signal is represented by multiple bits in the transmitted signal, using a spreading code.

Encryption: To convert plain text or data into unreadable form by means of a reversible mathematical computation.

Frequency Hopping Spread Spectrum: A spread-spectrum method of transmitting radio signals by rapidly switching a carrier among many frequency channels, using a pseudorandom sequence known to both transmitter and receiver.

HomeRF: Short form for "home radio frequency." It is designed specifically for wireless networks in homes, in contrast to 802.11, which was created for use in businesses.

Orthogonal Frequency Division Multiplexing: A digital modulation process in which a signal is divided into several narrowband channels at different frequencies. It is thus a digital multicarrier modulation scheme which uses a large number of closely spaced orthogonal subcarriers, which are eventually modulated.

Piconet: A small network of communication devices connected in an ad hoc fashion using Bluetooth technology.

Scatternet: A scatternet is collection of piconets connected through sharing devices.

Wireless Local Area Network: The same as 802.11 networks, developed by IEEE that operates in 5 GHz and 2.4 GHz radio bands, where wireless devices can operate in centralized (infrastructure) mode or decentralized (ad hoc) mode.

Wireless Station: The client computer (i.e., a workstation or laptop) that gets connected to an access point in an infrastructure network and to other wireless stations in an ad hoc network.

Chapter IX
Context Sensitive Mobile Services

Indranil Bose
The University of Hong Kong, Hong Kong

Xi Chen
The University of Hong Kong, Hong Kong

ABSTRACT

The advancements in mobile technologies make the collection of customers' context information feasible. Service providers can now incorporate context information of customers when providing personalized services to them. This type of services is called context sensitive mobile services (CSMS). Context refers to the environment around customers when there are business transactions between customers and service providers. Location, time, mobile device, services, and other application specific information are all possible components of context. Compared to other types of mobile services, CSMS can fit to customers' demands better. CSMS can follow push model or pull model. Different context sensitive services are sensitive to different context information with different degrees of sensitivity. In the future, CSMS can find good support from data mining approaches to understand customers better. Security is currently an important issue for CSMS.

INTRODUCTION

Due to the fast penetration of mobile phones, mobile telecommunication services are becoming more and more popular. From the research done by Gartner Dataquest (Businessweek, 2005), it is known that there will be more than one billion mobile service subscribers in the Asia/Pacific region. It is expected that the number will reach 1.4 billion in 2009. Research analysts of Gartner Dataquest also estimated that over 39% of the people in China will use mobile phones at that time. In another country in Asia, India, the penetration rate of mobile phones is also expected to increase from 7% in 2005 to 28% in 2008. The Yankee Group has also reported a growing trend of mobile service revenues from 2003 to 2009 not only in the Asia-Pacific region but also in the U.S. It is further expected that the market for m-commerce will reach $25 billion in 2006. With the mature wireless and mobile technologies, more and more information about the environment that the customers are in can be collected easily and rapidly with higher accuracy. The existence of this type of information can help service providers picture the context of services and context of customers so that they can understand customers' demands better. These types of services, which take into consideration the contextual information of customers, are called context sensitive mobile service (CSMS). According to the studies done by Analysys (2001), the number of people who subscribe to CSMS such as location services will reach 680 million by 2006. It is also estimated that in Europe the revenue from location services will be over 32 billion Euro by 2005 (Strategies Group, 2000).

In this chapter, we discuss the following issues. What is context in general? What are the key elements of context for CSMS? Why do we need CSMS? What is the business model of CSMS? What types of CSMS are there in reality? And finally, what business strategies can be adopted with regard to CSMS. This chapter is organized as follows. First, we give some background information about CSMS by providing the definition of context and the benefits of CSMS. Then we discuss CSMS as a type of information manufacturing system as well as the pull and push models of CSMS. The third part of the chapter discusses the classification of CSMS. We also provide analysis on the relationship between context and each type of CSMS in the fourth part of the chapter in order to find suitable strategies for carrying out CSMS. The fifth part of the chapter is the discussion on the future development of context sensitive mobile services. The last part provides a summary of this chapter.

BACKGROUND

Mobile services are services delivered to customers via mobile technology artifacts such as mobile networks and mobile devices. One characteristic of mobile services is that they can be delivered to customers anytime and anywhere due to the ability of mobile technology. Thus, it is believed that mobile services are highly related to the environment that the customers are in at the time the services are needed. Location may be one of the most important factors used to describe environment. People may have different needs when they are in different places. For example, when a person is driving, what he wants is the direction to get to his destination, whereas when he is in the office what he wants is important information related to his business. Location-based services can be defined as "services that integrate a mobile device's location or position with other information so as to provide added value to a user" (Spiekermann, 2004). However, there are other elements in environment besides location, such as time which is related to "context." In fact, in Spiekermann's (2004) definition we notice the mention of "other information." "Context" may be defined as "any information that can be used to characterize the situation of entities that are considered relevant to the interaction between a user and an application, including the user and the application themselves." Context is typically the location, identification, and the state of people, groups, and computational and physical objects" (Dey, Abowd, & Salber, 2001). This definition actually gives a very complete list of components of context. Since this definition is not provided for mobile services the question still remains: what should be included as part of context for mobile services? Zhang (2003) mentioned that there are preferences of mobile services users, mobile devices, and the wireless network. Rao and Minakakis (2003) suggested that time, reason customers are in the location, means by which customers come to this location, and preferences of customers, and so forth, are also important information besides location. Abowd and Mynatt (2000) pointed out specifically that context should include the "five W": who, what, where, when, and why. By "who," Abowd and Mynatt (2000) meant not only the type of roles people played in context but also the identification of them. For example, it is not enough to identify that a person is a customer. To be more complete, this person's past actions and service related background should also be identified. "What" refers to the activities done by people involved in the context and interactions between them. "Where" is about location information. "When" concerns the time. "Where" and "When" are closely related to each other. "Why" is about the reason that "who" does "what." "Why" is a very complicated idea and it is actually the operating principle of the whole context sensitive information systems.

Based on the aforementioned literature, we consider the following elements as important components of context for context sensitive mobile services. Location is the first element. Providing location based services is the first task of context sensitive mobile services. Time is the second element of CSMS because people are moving and therefore location is changing with time. The third element of CSMS is mobile technology. By mobile technologies we refer to the hardware and the software that allows transmission of data between mobile devices or between mobile and fixed devices wirelessly. These elements are inter-related. Mobile technologies work as an enabler of CSMS. Mobile technology enables CSMS not only by providing mobile devices but also by connecting these devices so that services can be sent to people anywhere and anytime. On the other hand, the characteristic of mobile technology is also a part of the context. Services delivered via mobile networks should be displayable or executable on customers' mobile devices. By mobile technologies, it is also possible to get information about customers' locations. Again, timing is indispensable from location. Customers' needs vary at different time. Also, the status of location and mobile network condition also changes from time to time. For example, a main road becomes crowded at office hour while it remains almost empty at midnight. There are other elements which can be used to describe the context, such as information about service itself, which is what CSMS delivers to customers. It is relatively difficult to name them because different applications have different characteristics. After all, customers' interests should also be taken into consideration because customers are the center of all these business applications.

The elements we proposed here are instances of the five "Ws" as mentioned in Abowd and Mynatt (2000). Location and time correspond to "where" and "when." These two elements have almost the same meaning as the original definition in Abowd and Mynatt (2000). Mobile technologies and context sensitive services correspond to "what" people use and "what" people do in CSMS. Service providers and CSMS customers are the "who" in CSMS. The providers should know the preferences of customers and use it as their support to provide suitable services. In other words, context sensitive mobile services should be sensitive to customers' needs and interests, which is the principle of CSMS' business model and is therefore the "why" of CSMS.

Benefits of Context Sensitive Services

Various mobile services are available in the market at the present time. But all these mobile services are not CSMS. Only those services which are provided to customers based on the context of customers using mobile communication technologies can be regarded as CSMS. The appearance of CSMS is driven by the development of mobile technologies. First, the bandwidth of mobile telecommunication network is ever increasing. Currently, the most popular mobile telecommunication networks are those based on global system for mobile (GSM).

However, the speed of global system for mobile (GSM) is only 9.6 kilobits per second (kbps). Based on GSM, general packet radio service (GPRS) can help the users have mobile connection with speed about 56 to114 kbps. The implementation of 3G networks brings with it new visions about the capability of mobile telecommunication networks. It is believed that the speed of 3G will be as fast as 2 megabits per second (mbps). The increasing of bandwidth provides support for multimedia and more sophisticated services such as mobile video conference call and mobile TV. Second, technologies such as global positioning system (GPS) and radio frequency identification (RFID) can support location sensitive functions which make the extracting of customers' context information possible. GPS is the only fully-functional navigation system based on satellite technologies. Europe and China are developing their navigation system based on satellites but their system is not completed as yet. Compared to GPS, RFID is a tracking technology with much lower cost of implementation. RFID technology makes use of specially made tags which can emit signals and scanners that can detect the signals from tags. By combining RFID and wireless telecommunication technologies, it is possible to track the location of people and products. Mobile telecommunication technologies such as code division multiple access (CDMA) and GSM can also be upgraded to support GPS (Kurkovsky & Harihar, 2006). Another critical driver of the development of CSMS is the customers' need for more sophisticated and personalized services. Compared with services delivered through traditional channels such as telephone and Internet, CSMS takes advantage of mobile technology for connecting people anytime and anywhere. Service providers can reach customers directly and immediately. Similarly, customers can also respond to service providers rapidly. This benefit makes the interaction between service providers and customers easy and frequent. Compared to other mobile services, CSMS makes use of context information. Having information about the environment or situation customers are currently in, service providers can understand customers' demands in addition to just knowing what they want. Thus, services or solutions to customers' requests that fit closely with the desire of customers can be provided.

Compared to services provided via other channels such as mail, CSMS is comparatively cost effective and quick. Compared to services provided by telephone, CSMS can be less interruptive. Compared to services delivered via Internet, CSMS can reach people anytime and anywhere and do not require customers to sit before a computer. Also, without the support of mobile technologies, it is difficult to get information about customers' context. Therefore, to some extent, CSMS can be a replacement for other types of marketing channels such as mail, telephone, or Internet based services. Services information sent via Internet can now be sent via a mobile device. When we talk about benefits, we should also look at the other side of CSMS, the limitations. One of the limitations of CSMS is that due to the limited size of screens of mobile devices, only brief information can be provided in mobile marketing solicitations while e-mail or mail marketing can provide very detailed information. On the other hand, although telephone based services require good communication skills of telesales, once they have the skills, the interaction between service providers and customers is more quick and effective. Finally, CSMS is not capable of every thing. It is obvious that we cannot have our hair cut via mobile networks. But, it is possible for us to get expert opinions on our hair styles or dressings via mobile services with video aids.

BUSINESS MODELS FOR CMCS

The business process for CSMS involves interactions between CSMS providers and customers. Usually, the interaction takes the form of transferring different types of information: customer

Figure 1. Operational model of CSMS

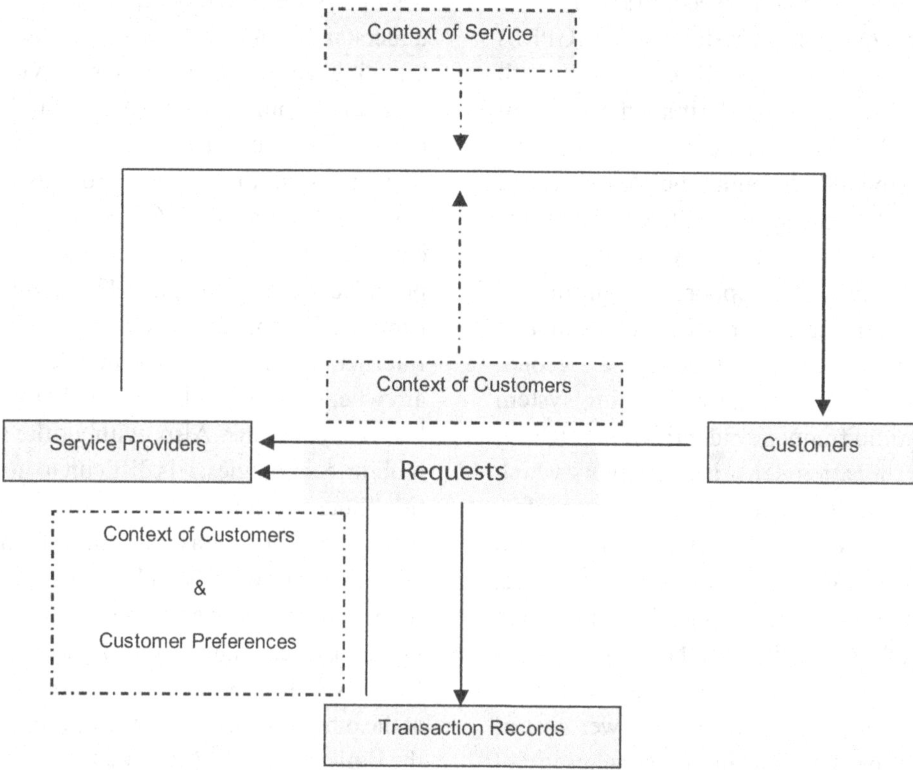

information, service information, and information on other elements of context. In Ballou, Wang, Pazer, and Tayi (1998), the authors referred to information systems as an information product manufacturing systems that produce predefined information products. The information manufacturing system model proposed by them has five components: data vendor block, processing block, data storage block, quality block, and customer block, with the processing object called data unit, whose component is context-dependent. CSMS can also be seen as an information product manufacturing system with context information. The service providers collect service related data, process the data to obtain useful information, store the information, and deliver the information to customers with acceptable quality. What is special for CSMS is the key role of context information in the CSMS business model. The operations of CSMS usually involve three main jobs as shown in Figure 1.

1. Collection of service related information. This is the "manufacture" process of service providers. Service related information are collected and organized in a "ready-for-use" format. The "production" of service information should be ready before requests are made by customers and should be sent out before the information has lost its usability. For example, driving direction service will have to collect traffic information and maps of different regions; shopping guides will have to prepare information about goods and shopping malls. These service related information forms the context of services.
2. Collection of information about customers. The customer is the revenue generator in

the business model of CSMS. Providing personalized CSMS is a key to help CSMS providers to achieve success. Thus, collecting information about customer is very important. The quality of information collected would influence customers' satisfaction of the services directly. There are mainly two types of information about customers for CSMS: customers' context information and information about customers themselves. Customers' context information contains information about customers' location, their mobile devices, and the time. The context information of customers can be collected from customers' request of services or previous transaction records. Information about customers themselves include their gender, occupation, age, and past purchasing records, and so forth, which are useful for estimating customers' preferences of services.

3. Providing services to customers. Customers' context information is compared with the whole context information of services in order to find possible solutions. For example, in driving direction services, a customer' location is compared with map of the region to see which area he or she is in. Then the traffic information and road information of this area are extracted in order to find possible routes for the customer. Usually this will be the end of this transaction. However, service providers can do something additional if they have collected enough information to know the customers interests. For example, service providers may find this customer is not in his hometown and he usually goes to the current area for business and will stay overnight from past transaction records. Then, besides providing the direction information this customer wants, service providers can provide additional information, such as hotel promotions.

CSMS and Information Quality

From the above discussion, it is worth noting that the information quality (IQ) is very critical to the success of CSMS. We all know that garbage in is garbage out. Strong, Lee, and Wang (1997) identified four categories of characteristics of information quality patterns: intrinsic IQ, accessibility IQ, contextual IQ, and representational DQ. Ballou et al. (1998) considered four attributes of information products: timeliness, data quality, cost, and value. Cappiello, Francalanci, and Pernici (2003) defined a mathematical model to evaluate time-related measures of data quality. The authors proposed that the data can be measured along four dimensions: data relevance, data accuracy, data format or ease of interpretation, and data privacy, security, and ownership. They focus their research on three quality dimensions: currency, accuracy, and completeness. Interested readers can refer to related works by Strong et al. (1997), Ballou et al. (1998), and Cappiello et al. (2003).

Generally, timeliness, completeness, accessibility, and accuracy, and so forth, are important issues related to information quality. For CSMS, time is also a key element of context. The completeness and accuracy of service information are related to the quality of service and the quality of information about customer is related to good understanding of customers' preferences.

The above analysis provides an overview of the operation model of CSMS. If we study it with more detail, we observe that the process of delivering CSMS to customers can follow two models: push and pull. Push and pull models originate from the area of marketing and advertising. It is also widely used in the field of electronic commerce. The two models represent two different logics of interaction with customers.

Push Model

Push model sends service to customers without the request of customer. In order to apply push model for CSMS, the service providers should have good knowledge on customers' context and their interests. Since the customers will not give their context information at the time services are provided, service providers will have to guess or estimate the status of customers' context and preferences. One way to find strong support for their guess is to look for useful information from past records on customers' location and transaction. Using mobile technologies, it is possible to record the customers' location at different time. From these records, service providers can find some moving patterns of customers from which they can infer the current location of customers. However, the tracking of customers' location requires permission from them otherwise there will be legal problems. Customers' preference can also be inferred from their past transaction records. It is even more helpful if the transaction record can be linked with the moving patterns. In this case, service providers can make judgments on where customers are at that time and therefore, what they may want. In push model, marketers would also like to consider the capability of customers' mobile device to make sure that the format of information delivered to them is displayable.

Pull Model

In pull model, service providers of CSMS wait for the customer to send a request for services or information about services. In the case of CSMS following pull model, the customers usually know what they want and what type of functions their mobile device supports. Also, customers will provide information about their context or allow service providers to collect related information from their mobile device. Thus, in contrast to CSMS following push model, service providers do not have to guess the customers' preferences and status of context. However, customers who request services are usually in movement therefore they want instant response from service providers. So service providers need to prepare related information before hand. For example, if a customer is driving and requests a route guide, then the service provider should have collected traffic information in that area at that time and a map of that area. The significance of pull model is that the information from customers is very useful for understanding customers' preferences, such as the preferred service time and interests.

Classification of CSMS

CSMS can be applied in various forms. Spiekermann (2004) divided location based services (LBS) into two big categories: person-oriented and device-oriented. Under the category of person-oriented LBS, there are five types of applications: communication, information, entertainment, mcommerce, and advertising. Under the category of device-oriented LBS, there is one type of application: tracking. However, Spiekermann's (2004) classification may still bring confusion. For example, her definition of communication services can also perform tracking of friends. On the other hand, tracking is always "person-oriented" since the tracking request is always placed by person. Rao and Minakakis (2003) also provided a classification of context sensitive mobile services. They divided the CSMS according to the demand level: consumer demand, niche consumer and business, and industrial demand. However, the niche consumer and business demand is a vague concept because whether it is niche or not is a relative term. With the evolution of business models in modern society, niche demand in the past can become mainstream demand in the future. In this chapter, we only consider consumer based CSMS. Based on the previous study, we classify CSMS according to the type of intrinsic value these services can bring to service providers. The four types of CSMS we identify are "help desk" services, location services, marketing and advertising services, and entertainment services.

- **Help desk services.** In reality, help desks exist in varies occasions such as conferences, exhibitions, library, shopping malls, and even in a residence community, and so forth. The function ofhelp desks is to provide customers information about facilities and events in current occasions. Context sensitive "help desk" services act like mobile help desks which can answer customers' questions anytime and anywhere. Shopping guide is one type of possible "help desk" services. Shopping guide services can tell customers where the products they want are, what types of promotional events are going on, and where the functional facilities such as toilet and food court are located. Academic conferences are also very good occasions for applying CSMS. CSMS of conferences can provide typical services such as finding lecture rooms and schedule checks. More advanced CSMS can also be provided such as dynamic program organizing (Okoli, Ives, Jessup, & Valacich, 2002). Dynamic program organizing is very meaningful for academic conferences. During the conference period, it is quite common that attendants may be inspired by other speakers so that they may want to organize spontaneous or instant meetings in order to discuss with other attendants. These meetings cannot be planned beforehand. Dynamic program organizing supported by CSMS can be a good solution.
- **Location services.** Location services focus on finding physical positions. It can be the position of a customer himself, the position of target building, the position of personal assets such as a car, or the position of children. One basic task of location services is searching, such as driving direction guide. Customers ask for feasible routes to their destination. Service providers search their database containing map information and traffic information to find answers. Another more advanced task is tracking. Tracking services require support from tracking techniques such as global position system (GPS). Devices that support GPS are installed with items or people who are going to be tracked. Of course, tracking of people should be carried out with great care in order to avoid legal issues. There are some ad hoc applications of tracking services such as golf assistant and fish finder services (Rao & Minakakis, 2003). Golf assistant can tell golf players the landform of the golf course and other information that can influence the game such as speed of wind. Fish finders can tell fishing fans the location of nearest shoal as well as the latest weather condition.
- **Marketing and advertising.** Context sensitive marketing and advertising services send product information, promotion, and coupons with discounts, and so forth, to customers. Compared to traditional marketing and advertising activities, CSMS based marketing and advertising requires more sophisticated understanding of customers and their context (Hristova & O'Hare, 2004). The time of sending mobile information needs to be appropriate as well. It would be very helpful if service providers can collect enough information from customers' past transaction records to estimate where a customer may go and what he or she may want at a certain time. For example, Mr. X usually goes shopping on Sunday afternoon at Shopping Mall ABC. After analyzing the previous transaction records, managers of ABC can find such a rule. They can then send promotional information to Mr. X sometime during his visit to ABC. A real case of context sensitive marketing and advertising service has been conducted in Hong Kong by "Three." "Three" in Hong Kong is trying to send promotion information about mobile phones to customers and inform them the closest shop of "Three"

when customers are detected to be close to shopping centers. This type of marketing or advertising services has a high possibility to stimulate the buying urge of customers. There are some other factors that should be paid attention to. The content delivered to customers should be displayable on their mobile device. The most important concern for context sensitive mobile marketing and advertising services is the issue of privacy. For those services following the push model, customers' information on their location will be collected and used for commercial purpose without their tacit knowledge. Permission from customers is necessary before any solicitations can be sent to them. Otherwise, customers may feel uncomfortable with the services provided to them.

- **Entertainment.** Context sensitive entertainment services can connect people within similar context for games or other entertainment services. The comparison of similarity is based on one or more of the several elements of context. For example, context sensitive game services can group players within the same region and can also group players according to their online time. Also it is possible to group players with similar preferences. Maitland, Van der Kar, When de Montalvo, and Bouwman (2005) reported a location-based mobile game called Botfighter which is claimed to be the first context sensitive mobile game in the world. The game is played using standard GSM phone with SMS functions. Players design their own "robot" on the Internet and send instructions via their mobile phones. When two players are close in physical location, the game system will notify them by their mobile phone and then they can fight each other. This type of services requires certain functions on mobile phones to support the services, such as SMS. Also, the quality of network should also be taken into consideration to reduce the time lag. Timeliness is also very important. The commands sent by players should be processed and responded immediately.

These four types of services contribute different values to the service providers. "Help desk" services act as a supplementary means to enhance the value of core services. In contrast, marketing and advertising services usually act as the causal factors that can influence customers' purchasing behaviors. Location services and entertainment services usually act as the core revenue generator for the service providers.

Strategies for CSMS

Different services can follow different models, push or pull. They are sensitive to different elements of the context and to customers' demands. Spiekermann (2004) provided an analysis on the relationship between location based services (LBS) and the accuracy of location information. The analysis showed that different applications have different requirements for the accuracy of location information. However, their analysis used specific examples of location based services and cannot be generalized to other applications. Second, they only analyzed the relationship between location information and applications. For CSMS, location information is only one component of context information. Further, accuracy can only reflect one aspect of information quality. To overcome these limitations, we divide the CSMS applications into four types according to their functions. We include not only the location information but also other elements of context. We used "sensitivity" to reflect the influence of information quality on CSMS applications. The more sensitive the CSMS applications are to a certain element the more influence they get from that element. In the following section, we discuss the different models the aforementioned services can follow and also indicate what elements of context are likely to play an important role for the execution of the services. "Help desk" services usually follow the pull model. They are mildly sensitive to the location of customers because the scale of area is within a building. Timing is an important element for "help desk" services because there are various events occurring over time. For example, CSMS in conferences can help organizing spontaneous and instant meetings. Whenever there are such meetings, related information should be updated. "Help desk" services can also follow push models. For example, when a customer asks for the location of a certain product, besides the required information, additional information on similar products can also be provided. But additional information should be designed very carefully so that it will not hinder customers from getting what they requested for. When push model is used for "help desk" services, customers' personal preferences should be taken into consideration.

Location services usually follow the pull model. They are strongly sensitive to the location of customers and also to the time when the customers send their requests. For example, in a driving direction guide the current location and customer's target is critical for finding feasible routes. The traffic status at that time also influences the selection of routes, such as whether there are traffic jams, or whether a road is one-way or two-way at that time. Sometimes, other information about service related environment also influences the implementation of services. Fish finder services have to consider the weather condition when selecting target shoals.

Context sensitive marketing and advertising services can follow either push or pull model. CSMS for marketing and advertising are strongly sensitive to the needs of customers. If the information provided to customers is about products they want, chances are large that they will buy the products. However, if the information is about unwanted products, customers may have negative experience of the service. If too many negative experiences are accumulated, service providers will lose that customer. When push model is used, service providers should be aware of the most appropriate time and frequency for sending marketing information to customers. If the information is given too frequently, customers consider the promotion messages to be a nuisance. If the information is given too seldom, the customers may forget about it. Pull model is relatively rare for CSMS but this type of service is indispensable because it provides information on customers' demands and their preferences about time and location. CSMS for marketing and advertising are not very sensitive to location information but combining location information will be very helpful for these services because customers' demands are usually linked to a particular location. When a customer wants to find a restaurant, he or she may want one closer to where he or she lives. Knowing the location of the customer's residence, service providers such as restaurant marketers can advertise restaurants that are close to the customer and can satisfy the customer's demands.

Context sensitive entertainment services usually follow the pull model. Service providers have to wait for the subscription from customers. For game related applications, location and timeliness are very critical for the players' satisfactory gaming experience. Also service providers should design appropriate gaming interface so that as many as possible customers can join the game without upgrading their mobile device. Network condition will also be an important factor. But there will be a tradeoff between the requirements for mobile device and network bandwidth and the requirements for a good gaming interface. Friendly graphic game interface usually means sophisticated handset functions and availability of large bandwidth. However, with the rapid development in handset and telecommunication network, designers may achieve better balance between them in the future.

We summarize our discussion on the relationship between context elements and different types of CSMS in Table 1. The first row contains the types of CSMS. The left most column is the list of context elements. "Strong," "mild," "slight" represent the degree of sensitiveness to the context elements. These labels are assigned on a relative basis based on the comparison among the four types of application. For timeliness, marketing and advertising has the least strict requirement than other three types of CSMS because marketing and advertising activities usually will last for a period to strengthen their influences on customers. On the other hand, customers also need time to make decisions. However, "help desk," location, and entertainment services always require instant communication with service providers. For location information, location services and entertainment services require accurate locating of customers positions. In contrast, marketing and advertising activities are usually not that concerned about customers' location. For customer preferences, since "help desk" and marketing services can follow the push model, they have to estimate the preferences of customers carefully and make changes to their services accordingly. Location and entertainment services usually follow the pull model. These types of services vary relatively little after they are designed. Thus, we conclude that location services and entertainment services are less sensitive to customer preferences than "help desk" services and marketing and advertising services. For the service itself, location services rely heavily on customers' requests while "help desk," marketing and advertising, and entertainment services rely on the interactions between customer and the content of services provided to them, for example, how attractive the services are to the customers. Therefore, we believe that location services are relatively less sensitive to service related information than the other three types of CSMS.

Whatever model one may use when carrying out CSMS for marketing, one issue must always be kept in mind and that is explicit permission from customers (Bayne, 2002). Mobile technology makes connections so direct that it can interfere with customers' privacy very easily. Therefore, sending advertising or promotion information to people will cause trouble if permissions are not sought before solicitations or customers wishes about not receiving a solicitation are not respected.

FUTURE TRENDS

In this chapter, we discussed several issues on context sensitive mobile services. We identified the main components of context and the key actors in CSMS. We also discussed the influence of information quality on context and key actors. Then we classified CSMS into four categories: "help desk" services, location services, mobile

Table 1. Relationship between context and CSMS

	Help desk	**Location**	**Marketing and advertising**	**Entertainment**
Time	Strong	Strong	Mild	Strong
Location	Mild	Strong	Slight	Strong
Customer preferences	Strong	Mild	Strong	Mild
Device	Slight	Strong	Slight	Mild
Service related information	Strong	Slight	Strong	Strong
Other context information	Other people's needs	Weather, wind, traffic	N/A	N/A

marketing and advertising services, and entertainment services. We analyzed the relationship between CSMS applications and contextual elements and the strategies for different types of CSMS applications.

The mobile technologies will advance further in the future. New technologies will enable new kinds of services. For example, the implementation of the third generation (3G) wireless systems will make the bandwidth much larger than that in current networks. In fact, the fourth generation of mobile telecommunication network (4G) will be implemented in the future and this will provide higher speed and better support to various new applications (Bose, 2006). On the other hand, the device will have a larger screen with higher resolution. These two together will make new services possible such as interactive audio, or even interactive video services, and mobile office services (Fjermestad, Pattern, & Bartolacci, 2006). New services may be provided in new formats and can come with new contexts. However, the principle is still not only to know what customers want, but also to know when, where, and what type of services they may want. Sophisticated customer analysis techniques such as data mining techniques could be used in the future to find customer behavior patterns with time and location factors. Data mining techniques has been used widely in direct marketing for analyzing customers' interests and preferences to target customers (Ling & Li, 1998). There are also data mining techniques for clustering customers such as Self-Organizing-Map (SOM) (Kohonen, 1995; Min & Han, 2005) and techniques for discovering customer behavior such as association rules mining (Agrawal & Srikant, 1994). In the future, the availability of huge amounts of data on customers will compel marketers to adopt strong data mining tools to delve deep into customers' nature. On the other hand, data mining techniques can also be used to dig out useful information from customers' context such as their moving paths (Lee & Wang, 2003) which will be very helpful for application of the push model. CSMS technologies can help companies with their management of stuff and also in handling the logistics of materials and products. "Three" Hong Kong is planning to provide a context sensitive mobile workforce management solution called "WorkPlace" (Three.com.hk, 2006). By installing more than 2000 mobile information transmitters throughout Hong Kong, "WorkPlace" will enable managers and dispatchers to easily locate their employees equipped with mobile handsets in real time. With supporting software, "WorkPlace" will allow companies to manage the mobile workforce effectively.

The future of CSMS is bright. However, challenges still exist. Security is one important issue (Lyytinen et al., 2004) because context sensitive services are highly personalized services. During the transaction, confidential information may be transferred between service providers and individual customers. However, the wireless medium is not fully secure and is subject to different types of vulnerabilities. Designing sophisticated security mechanisms such as authentication mechanism, innovative encryption, and safer communication protocols may be necessary to reduce the risk of information leakage. Privacy is another important issue. This issue has bothered the marketers in electronic commerce and it also exists for context sensitive mobile services. Robust and complete legislation is needed to make the business deals among customers, sellers, and services providers more reliable and secure and to protect the privacy of customers.

CONCLUSION

Equipped with advanced mobile technologies, sophisticated context sensitive mobile services could be provided to customers now and in the future. In this chapter, we introduced the definition of context and its explanation in CSMS. We discussed the business models of CSMS and strategies which services providers of CSMS can follow. We also discussed the classifications of CSMS and relationships between context and each type of CSMS. In future, new types of CSMS will appear and expand to various industries. Although CSMS is powerful, it cannot replace other types of services and should be integrated into the whole business strategy of a firm so that it can work seamlessly with other types of services.

REFERENCES

Abowd, G..D., & Mynatt, E.D. (2000). Charting past, present, and future research in ubiquitous computing. *ACM Transactions on Computer-Human Interaction, 7*(1), 29-58.

Agrawal, R., & Srikant, R. (1994). Fast algorithms for mining association rules. In *Proceedings of the 20th International Conference on Very Large Databases* Santiago, Chile (pp. 487-499).

Analysys. (2001). Mobile location services and technologies. Retrieved January 21, 2008, from http://www.gii.co.jp/english/an6596_mobile_location.html

Ballou, D., Wang, R., Pazer, H., & Tayi, G. (1998). Modeling information manufacturing systems to determine information product quality. *Management Science, 44*(4), 462-484.

Bayne, K.M. (2002). *Marketing without wires: Targeting promotions and advertising to mobile device users.* New York: John Wiley & Sons Ltd.

Bose, I. (2006). Fourth generation wireless systems: A review of technical and business challenges for the next frontier. *Communications of AIS, 17*(31), 693-713.

Businessweek. (2005, November 21). Special advertising section: 3G the mobile opportunity [Asian ed.]. *BusinessWeek,* 92-96.

Cappiello, C., Francalanci, C., & Pernici, B. (2003). Time-related factors of data quality in multichannel information systems. *Journal of Management Information Systems, 20*(3), 71-91.

Dey, A.K., Abowd, G.D., & Salber, D. (2001). Toolkit for supporting the rapid prototyping of context-aware applications. *Human-Computer Interaction, 16*, 97-166.

Fjermestad, J., Pattern, K., & Bartolacci, M.R. (2006). Moving towards mobile third generation telecommunications standards: The good and bad of the anytime/anywhere solutions. *Communications of AIS, 17*, 71-89.

Hristova, N., & O'Hare, G.M.P. (2004). Ad-me: Wireless advertising adapted to the user location, device and emotions. In *Proceedings of the 37th Annual Hawaii International Conference on System Science.*

Kohonen, T. (1995) *Self-organizing maps.* Berlin, Germany: Springer.

Kurkovsky, S., & Harihar, K. (2006). Using ubiquitous computing in interactive mobile marketing. *Personal and Ubiquitous Computing, 10*(4), 227-240.

Lee, A.J., & Wang, Y-T. (2003). Efficient data mining for calling path patterns in GSM network. *Information Systems, 28*, 929-948.

Lyytinen, K., Varshney, U., Ackerman, M.S., Davis, G., Avital, M., Robey, D. et al. (2004). Surfing the next wave: Design and implemenmtation challenges of ubiquitous computing environments. *Communications of AIS, 13*, 697-716.

Maitland, C.F., Van der Kar, E.A.M., Wehn de Montalvo, U., & Bouwman, H. (2005). Mobile information and entertainment services: Business models and service networks. *International Journal of Management and Decision Making, 6*(1), 47-63.

Min, S.-H., & Han, I. (2005). Detection of the customer time-variant pattern for improving recommender systems. *Expert Systems with Applications, 28*(2), 189-199.

Okoli, C., Ives, B., Jessup, L.M., & Valacich, J.S. (2002). The mobile conference information system: Unwiring academic conferences with wireless mobile computing. *Communications of AIS, 9*, 180-206.

Rao, B., & Minakakis, L. (2003). Evolution of mobile location-based services. *Communications of the ACM, 46*(12), 61-65.

Spiekermann, S. (2004). General aspects of location-based services. In J. Schiller & A. Voisard (Eds.), *Location-based service* (pp. 9-26). California: Morgan Kaufmann.

Strategies Group. (2000). *European wireless location services.* Retrieved January 21, 2008, from http://www.findarticles.com/p/articles/mi_m0BFP/is_2000_April_10/ ai_61430512

Strong, D.M., Lee, Y.W., & Wang, R.Y. (1997). Data quality in context. *Communications of the ACM, 40*(5), 103-110.

Three.com.hk. (2006). *Location-based mobile workforce management (WorkPlace).* Retrieved January 21, 2008, from http://dualband.three.com.hk/website/template? pageid=d81240&lang=chi

Zhang, D. (2003). Delivery of personalized and adaptive content to mobile devices: a framework and enabling technology. *Communications of AIS, 12*, 83-202.

Chapter X
Wireless Ad Hoc Networks: Design Principles and Low Power Operation

Veselin Rakocevic
City University, UK

Ehsan Hamadani
City University, UK

ABSTRACT

Seamless communication between computing devices is an essential part of the new world of ubiquitous computing. To achieve the concept of a "disappearing computer," it is necessary to establish reliable and simple communication principles to enhance the usability and the efficiency of the ubiquitous computing devices. It is also important to use wireless links and to enable devices to quickly create and manage networks ad hoc, without any need for network infrastructure. This chapter presents the design principles for such networks. The main features of these networks are analysed, including the principles of medium access control and routing, along with the current standardisation and development activities. Special attention is paid to the low power design of wireless ad hoc networks. Low power design is important because of the predicted self-organisation, small size, and extended scalability of ubiquitous computing networks. In such an environment, it is important to extend the network lifetime by deploying power sensitive network algorithms and protocols.

INTRODUCTION

Ubiquitous computing paradigm assumes the existence of networks of computing devices capable of processing and exchanging data. Since the essence of ubiquitous computing is the invisibility of the computing system, it is paramount that these networks use wireless links, that they are easy to implement and easy to scale, and that they provide reliable and robust communication capabilities. Recent advances in both hardware and software have initiated a small revolution in wireless devices able to communicate without any help from network infrastructure, that is, in a so-called ad hoc mode. They are characterized by high flexibility and scalability, ease of deployment, and simplified network management.

Ad hoc networks have initially been used in military applications. The need for rapid deployment of a communication network in environments that have no infrastructure support was the main motivation behind the projects such as PRNet and SURAN (Freebersyser & Leiner, 2001) and LPR (Fifer & Bruno, 1987). During the last decade, with the emergence of cheap hardware solutions, the research in mobile ad hoc networking has in addition concentrated on non-military applications. Typical applications for wireless ad hoc networks include their use in sensor networks, especially in medical applications, for emergency services, in commercial use for "smart home" networking, for location-aware applications, for environment monitoring, agriculture, production, and so forth.

Ad hoc networks are especially interesting because their independent nature enables us to think about tailored design of network protocols and interfaces. For example, if the key requirement for a sensor network is for a network to be active for as long as possible, the network protocols must be designed to minimise the power consumption regardless of other, more traditional requirements for maximising the throughput, or minimising the delay. On the other hand, if the key requirement is the reliability of communication, the network has to be designed in a way that ensures that the data must arrive at the destination point regardless of the increased delay or the decreased throughput (this can be done for example by increasing the number of link-layer retransmissions). This approach is fundamentally different from the typical approach to networking inherited from TCP/IP networks, where the long process of standardization forced researchers to think globally and work toward unique solutions with ubiquitous application.

Recent experience in ubiquitous systems prototyping has taught us that the key issue in successful connection of computing devices does not lie in their battery life, processing power, or low-level network connectivity, but in the fact that devices could not work together unless they have been specifically programmed to talk to each other (Edwards, Newman, Sedivy, & Smith, 2005). This important fact is crucial for understanding the complexity of network design for ubiquitous computing. However, throughout this chapter, we will focus on the principles of networked communication specific for the wireless ad hoc environment. We assume that interoperability, middleware design, and interfacing will be covered in more detail in other chapters and will focus on general networking principles such as routing, medium access control, and, especially, power management.

To start with, we can say that the main characteristics of ad hoc networks include:

- The lack of network infrastructure
- Mobility of connected nodes
- Multihop routing of data packets
- Need for low power consumption

Ad hoc networks do not depend on any established network infrastructure. This has great impact on network design—there is no centralised intelligence responsible for network management, traffic engineering, and network security. Node discovery and connectivity mechanisms have to be distributed which puts greater strain on limited processing power in connected nodes. Mobility of the nodes stems either from the independent movement of the nodes or from the external activities and/or phenomena that influence the mobility (e.g., sensor nodes thrown from an airplane are highly mobile because they are thrown around by winds). The mobility of nodes creates numerous problems for successful network protocol design.

Network topology becomes highly dynamic—this is exactly opposite to the underlying principle of legacy computer networks. The impact of dynamic network topologies is in the problems with network robustness and reliability—it is a great challenge to design transport protocol that can establish reliable data delivery when intermediate routers can disappear from the network at any time. This is closely connected to the third characteristic of ad hoc network mentioned above. Every node in a multihop network has to operate as a router as well as a processing node. Data packets are forwarded from one node to another until they reach the destination. Routing protocols for ad hoc networks have to be highly dynamic and have to have quick and reliable mechanisms for rerouting packets. Finally, majority of ad hoc networks are not created between fully-powered desktop computers and servers, as is the case with the legacy networks. Nodes connected in ad hoc networks in most cases are tiny sensor nodes carried on the body or located within some larger mechanical device. Powering these devices is time-consuming and too expensive—in most of the cases it is much cheaper to simply replace them. Therefore, the requirement to extend the lifetime of such nodes becomes essential. Network protocols for ad hoc networks need to take this into consideration. Reliable end-to-end data delivery must not be based on a policy of extended retransmission of data, since this is considered to be a waste of limited power resources. Intelligent situation-aware solutions are needed at all network layers.

One of the most important requirements for ad hoc networks is scalability. There is a clear need for scalable networks, where adding new nodes should be as easy as possible. This is not an easy task, and a lot of effort is being put in developing the solutions for the process of node identification, service discovery, and connectivity. This is closely related to another important issue—quality of service (QoS). The traditional view of QoS in communication networks is concerned with end-to-end delay, packet loss, delay variation, and throughput. Other performance-related features, such as network reliability, availability, communication security, and robustness are often neglected in the QoS research. The Quality of Service provided by wireless ad hoc networks depends significantly on the level of interference in the environment, where the interference comes from other wireless and microwave devices, such as mobile phones, neon lights, or microwave ovens. The problems with overcoming interference and achieving satisfactory network availability present a major challenge in the design of wireless ad hoc networks.

The rest of this chapter is organised as follows. First, the activities in standardisation and development are presented, outlining the current technological solutions in low power wireless ad hoc networking. This is followed by a brief analysis of the general design principles of these networks, with emphasis on medium access control, routing, and reliable data transfer. Finally, the current research and development work in fine-tuning the basic design principles to further minimise the consumed energy is given.

STANDARDISATION AND DEVELOPMENT ACTIVITIES

The recent years have seen increased activity in the standardisation of mobile ad hoc network solutions. The most exciting standardisation activity has happened under the framework of the IEEE802.15 Working Group. The current 802.15 standards cover a range of networking solutions for ubiquitous computing. All of the standards in the IEEE802.15 family define the design principles for the physical and the link layer. The first standard, IEEE802.15.1, derives most of its text from the Bluetooth specification, defined by the Bluetooth Special Interest Group during the late 1990s. Bluetooth is characterised by time-division medium access control through polling, and the use of frequency hopping to avoid interference since the bandwidth is shared with the IEEE802.11 networks. We will discuss Bluetooth's link layer is more detail in the next section.

The IEEE802.15.2 standard deals with interoperability issues with other wireless networks, namely wireless LANs. This standard deals mostly with mitigating the negative effects of the fact that both IEEE802.11b and IEEE802.15.1 devices operate in the same 2.4GHz range. The standard defines the coexistence mechanisms in two main classes: collaborative and noncollaborative. In collaborative environments, a link is required between the 802.11 and 802.15 device. In noncollaborative the two (or more) devices are only using the same frequency spectrum at the same time.

The IEEE802.15.3 standard enables low-cost, low-complexity, low-power, high-speed communication between portable electronic devices. The data rates of up to 55Mbps are envisaged in the standard with ranges of around 70m. The IEEE802.15.3 standard defines a MAC protocol and a frequency hopping physical layer that operates in the unlicensed 2.4GHz band. The standardisation process started in 1999 and the standard was finally approved in 2003. The recent years have seen the emergence of IEEE802.15.3a standard which defines the physical layer and the medium access control for the emerging ultra wideband communication (UWB) systems (Reed, 2005). The two remaining solutions for the physical layer of UWB are based on orthogonal frequency division multiplexing (OFDM) and direct sequence (DS). More details about the 802.15.3 medium access control solution will be given in the MAC section of this chapter.

Finally, the IEEE802.15.4 standard addresses the low rate application space, with emphasis on ultralow power consumption and low cost and complexity. The applications using this standard include numerous wireless sensor networks. This standard defines the two bottom layers with the solutions for higher layers currently being extensively developed under the umbrella of the ZigBee Alliance. The term ZigBee originates from the communication method used by bees, which use zig-zag movement to communicate important issues such as location, distance, and direction of movement to other bees.

ZigBee solutions are essentially low-power ad hoc networks including features such as reliability and self-healing, scalability, security, low-cost, and vendor independence. ZigBee alliance coordinates the development of higher-layer solutions that are based on the MAC and physical layer of the IEEE802.15.4 standard. The IEEE802.15.4 standard allows for two types of devices: fully functional devices (FFD) and reduced-function devices (RFD). 802.15.4 defines a low-cost private communication networks that provides standardised data rates of 250Kbps, 40Kbps, and 20Kbps over 16 channels in the 2450MHz band (ISM band, used worldwide), 10 channels in the 915MHz band (used in Americas), and 1 channel in the 868MHz band (used in Europe).

The ZigBee Alliance has also been active in developing the two upper layers of the protocol stack—the network layer and the application layer. The responsibilities of the ZigBee network layer include mechanisms used to join and leave a network, to apply security to frames and to route frames to their intended destinations. In addition, the discovery and maintenance of routes between devices devolve to the network layer. Also the discovery of one-hop neighbors and the storing of pertinent neighbor information are performed by the network layer. The application layer responsibilities include maintaining tables for binding (the ability to match two devices together based on their services and their needs), forwarding messages between bound devices, defining the role of the device within the network (e.g., ZigBee coordinator or end device), discovering devices on the network and determining which application services they provide, initiating and/or responding to binding requests, and establishing a secure relationship between network devices.

In terms of power consumption and transmission range, IEEE802.15.4 defines very low power communication, with the output power at a nominal 0.5mW (-3dBm). Single hop ranges with this power are in the region of 10-100m. The data rate is from 250Kbps at 2.4GHz to 20Kbps at 868MHz. There is a clear need for high data rates to minimise the power consumption, because data transfer is much quicker in high data rates.

When it comes to available commercial products, wireless sensor networks appear to be the main application design space. Following a major hype in the early years on the 21st Century, the development of sensor networks is currently suffering from a reality check. In November 2006, the ZigBee Alliance finally announced the first four commercial products that satisfy the ZigBee testing requirements. In addition to this, most market research analysts point out that a number of potential users of the low power networking solutions are yet to be convinced. A large obstacle for the developers is also the fact that wireless systems they develop need to replace fast, reliable, and good-quality wired systems, for example, process control, or home monitoring and networking. The users will not be satisfied with any near-optimal solutions and will only be satisfied with products that have been meticulously tested.

On the other hand, the expectations are high. Numerous research projects, for example NEST (2000) or projects at CENS, are under way to develop solutions for wireless ad hoc systems, primarily in the wireless sensor network domain. Romer and Mattern (2004) present an excellent overview of a number of recent exciting research projects. Good list of links to important research activities is provided on the UK-Ubinet Web page.

Several research projects have produced successful design of nodes that can be used in wireless sensor networks. Several research projects at the University of California at Berkeley have produce a "Mica Mote" family of sensor nodes (Hill & Culler, 2002; Hill, Szewczyk, Woo, Hollar, Culler, & Pister, 2000), which are currently commercially available through the company Crossbow. The Scatterweb platform provides a comprehensive family of embedded nodes, starting from relatively standard sensor nodes to embedded Web servers. Infineon Technologies developed EYES nodes in the context of the EU project EYES. Good overview of current developments in wireless sensor networks can be found in Hill, Horton, Kling, and Krishnamurthy (2004).

WIRELESS AD HOC NETWORKS DESIGN

This section of the chapter will analyse the design requirements for the three crucial features of mobile ad hoc networks, namely the medium access control, routing, and reliable data transfer. The section will concentrate on the specific requirements mobile ad hoc networks have compared to traditional fixed or cellular mobile networks. By analysing the current state of research for each of the functionalities, this section will analyse how mobile ad hoc networks can be designed to increase the connectivity and therefore efficiency of the devices connected as part of a ubiquitous computing system.

Medium Access Control

Medium access control (MAC) is responsible for coordinating access to the shared medium and minimizing conflicts by defining rules that allow devices to communicate with each other in efficient manner. Designing an efficient and robust MAC protocol in ad hoc networks is a complex issue because of unique features including half-duplex operation, burst channel errors, lack of centralized coordinator, and scarce power resources. In addition, the nature of ad hoc networks, with a number of nodes contending for the use of the wireless medium, inevitably introduces probability for packet collisions. The medium access method needs to be designed to tackle this problem. On the basis of the rules assigning the medium access to nodes, the two main families of MAC methods are random access methods and fixed assignment methods. The following sections will analyse MAC in ad hoc networks in more detail.

Random Access MAC

The random access MAC methods are based on a concept that bursts of packets are transmitted towards the destination as they arrive at a node. The inherent feature of random access is the event of *collisions*, where neighbouring nodes transmit packets at the same time. At the event of collision, random access MAC methods define the retransmission policies to minimise the probability of further collisions.

We can further differentiate random access methods on the basis of whether the control includes the process of medium sensing or not. In random access with noncarrier sensing schemes, such as ALOHA (Abramson, 1977), a node may access the channel as soon as it has packet ready to be transmitted. The node will then wait for a certain period of time to receive an acknowledgement message.

Carrier sensing with multiple access (CSMA) is a typical example of random access with carrier sensing. In IEEE802.11 standard for wireless LANs, for example, CSMA is accompanied by a procedure for collision avoidance (CA) to form an efficient MAC solution. In CSMA/CA, when a node receives a packet to be transmitted, it first listens to the channel to ensure no other node is transmitting. In order to detect the status of the medium, the station performs carrier sensing at both the physical layer, referred to as physical carrier sensing, and at the MAC layer, referred to as virtual carrier sensing. A virtual carrier-sensing mechanism is used to minimise the impact of the so-called *hidden terminal* problem in larger networks. To see the cause of the hidden node phenomenon, let us consider Figure 1 where the transmission range of each node is determined by a circle around the node. Here node C is transmitting a data packet towards node D. Meanwhile, following the physical carrier sensing, node E detects the channel as idle (since C is hidden from E). Consequently, E also starts transmitting data to node D, causing collisions and bandwidth wastage as both data transmissions are destroyed.

To alleviate and tackle the hidden terminal problem in CSMA, researchers have come up with many protocols that involve some form of reservation resolution using special exchange messages. The reservation can be done through two mechanisms: handshaking and out-of-band approach. Dual Busy Tone Multiple Access (Haas & Deng, 2002) is one of the examples of reservation resolution protocols using out-of-band signalling.

Figure 1. Hidden and exposed terminal problem

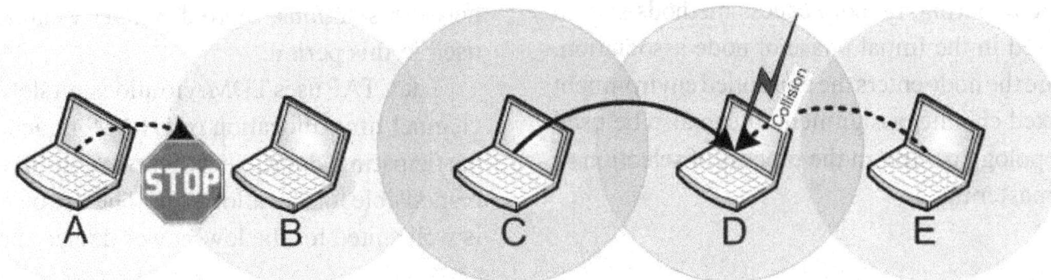

In the handshaking-based reservations, a node ready to transmit a packet first sends a control packet towards the destination. The destination, upon the reception of this control packet responds with another short control packet. All nodes that hear either the sender's or the receiver's control packet defer from accessing the channel for the duration of current transmission. However, while virtual carrier sensing eliminates the effect of hidden terminal, it introduces a new problem known as *exposed terminal.* In the same example depicted in Figure 1, after node C reserves the channel for transmitting packet to node D, node B is put in the silent mode by receiving the control message from node C. Hence, node A is unable to send any packet towards node B even this transmission does not interfere with node C to node D ongoing transmission. This clearly results to channel usage under-utilization and substantial throughput degradation. Examples of well-known and more adopted reservation resolution protocols using handshaking are IEEE 802.11, multiple access with collision avoidance (MACA) (Karn 1990), MACA for Wireless LAN (Bharghavan et al., 1994), MACA by Invitation (Talluci, Gerla, & Fratta, 1997), and Floor Acquisition Multiple Access (Garcia-Luna-Aveces & Fullmer, 1999)

From the above discussion, it is obvious that the operation of CSMA/CA algorithm is very complex. It requires continuous actions from all participants and the complexity introduced by adding new control messages is not suitable for the envisaged low-power participants in ad hoc networks. Further, random access methods such as CSMA/CA are more suitable for large data transfers. In a typical ad hoc network for ubiquitous computing, random access methods should be used in the initial phase of node association, before the node enters the controlled environment of fixed channel assignment. It can also be used in topology control in the process of selection of the master node.

Fixed Assignment MAC

The alternative solution to using random access methods is to use the fixed channel assignment methods. In wireless communications, under the term *channel* we can consider time, frequency, or code. Most of the emerging standards for wireless networks (802.16 and 802.15 families), define time division multiple access (TDMA) as the underlying principle of medium access. In general, in TDMA systems, participating stations are allocated precise time slots in which they can transmit data. The process of allocation of the time slots can be either centralised or distributed.

For example, the 802.15.1 standard, effectively defining the Bluetooth specification, defines the *polling* TDMA MAC algorithm where one node (a master) polls other nodes (slaves) in a round-robin fashion (see Figure 2). The master always transmits on even-numbered slots and the slave replies on odd-numbered slots, where a slot time is 625 μs. Master only transmits data when there is something to send. A slave may only transmit if it has been transmitted to. Such a scheme is only efficient in the low load environments or when the incoming traffic is symmetric in all slaves.

IEEE802.15.3 standard for MAC is a good example of a hybrid approach to medium access. In this solution, the channel time is divided into superframes, with each superframe composed of three main components (see Figure 3): the beacon, the optional contention access period (CAP), and the channel time allocation period (CTAP). In the standard definition, the use of CSMA/CA is envisaged in the CAP. Because carrier sensing may be difficult in certain UWB network solutions, Slotted ALOHA can also be used in this period.

The CTAP uses TDMA to allocate a slot (called channel time allocation or CTA) for each of the participating devices. A coordinator device is responsible for slot allocation. The use of TDMA is well suited for the low-power devices because

Figure 2. Polling MAC in Bluetooth

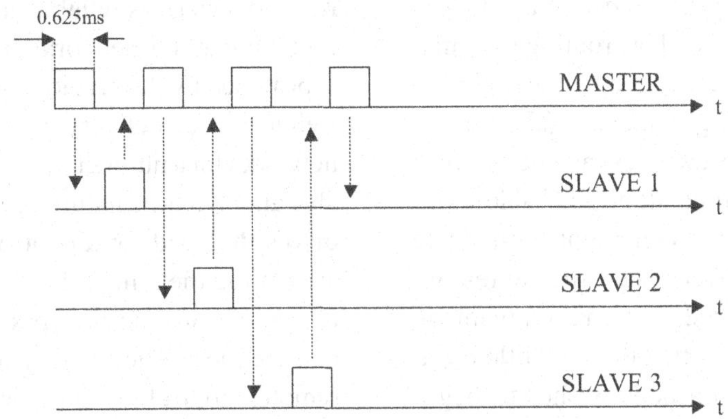

Figure 3. 802.15.3 superframe

Beacon	Contention Access Period	Channel Time Allocation Period						
			MCTA	CTA_1	CTA_1	…	CTA_{n-1}	CTA_n

they can remain in low-power mode in the slots used by other devices. The CTAs can be either dynamic or pseudo static. Dynamic CTAs can move within successive superframes, and they may be used for asynchronous streams. A pseudo-static CTA has a constant duration and position and a coordinator cannot reassign that slot in four successive superframes. In addition to the standard CTAs, Management CTAs (MCTAs) are used by the coordinator to transmit commands.

Routing and Reliable Data Transfer

Routing can be defined as a process of forwarding data from a remote sender to a remote receiver. Wireless ad hoc networks are specific from the routing point of view because each node in the network participates in the routing process. Contrary to the traditional networks where routers are specialised machines running highly sophisticated routing and switching procedures, the devices connected in the ad hoc mode operate as both senders/receivers of data and as routers, routing the data from a remote sender to a remote receiver. This operation duality presents one of the most important design problems in the ad hoc network domain. An excellent survey of routing techniques in wireless sensor networks is given in Al-Karaki and Kamal (2004).

The lack of infrastructure, the limited resources, and the inherent mobility in MANETs require a development of an intelligent routing protocol that can efficiently use the limited resources to adapt itself to the changing network conditions (network size, traffic density, and network partitioning). Wireless networks do not have fixed network topologies. Each node in a wireless network can potentially change the network topology by adjusting its transmission range or by selecting specific nodes to forward its messages. Nodes are able to control their set of neighbours in this way. This is called *topology control*. Topology control can be a powerful tool for lowering the power consumption in the network. This will be discussed in more detail in the next section.

The routing protocols used in ad hoc networks can be divided into *proactive*, *reactive*, and *hybrid* routing protocols based on how routing information is acquired and maintained by the nodes.

In proactive routing protocols (also called table-driven), nodes in a wireless ad hoc network continuously evaluate routes to all reachable nodes and attempt to maintain consistent, up-to-date routing information even when the routes are not currently being used. The main advantage of proactive protocols is that there is little or no latency involved when a node wishes to begin communicating with an arbitrary node that it has not yet been in communication with. Examples of pro-active protocols include the Destination Sequenced Distance Vector (Perkins & Bhagwat, 1994) and Optimized Link State Routing (Clausen & Jacquet, 2003).

In reactive routing protocols (also known as on-demand), routing paths are searched only when needed. Reactive protocols require less control traffic to maintain routes that are not in use in comparison to proactive protocols which in turn makes them more scalable than proactive protocols. More importantly, reactive protocols consume less energy in comparison to proactive routing protocols (Cano & Manzoni, 2000), enabling them to be an appropriate choice in low power ubiquitous computing networks. Examples on protocols using this approach are Dynamic Source Routing (Johnson, Maltz, & Hu, 2004) and Ad hoc On-Demand Distance Vector routing (Perkins, Belding-Royer, & Das, 2003).

Hybrid routing protocols are proposed to combine the merits of both proactive and reactive routing protocols and overcome their shortcomings by maintaining groups of nodes in which routing between members within a zone (cluster) is via proactive methods and routing between different groups of nodes is via reactive methods. zone routing protocol (Haas, Pearlman, & Samar, 2002) and cluster based routing protocol (Jiang, Li, & Tay, 1999) are examples of hybrid protocols proposed for ad hoc networks.

Another important issue in wireless ad hoc network design is reliable data transfer. In traditional computer networks, reliable data transfer is provided by the services of the transport layer. Reliable data delivery is important in ad hoc networks for a number of reasons. The unpredictable and dynamic nature of the wireless medium drives the need for a control system capable of estimating the reliability of the data transfer. By its nature, ad hoc networks are self-organized and the most efficient way of reconfiguring and remotely controlling the node activity would be by transmitting installation packages of application software onto networks nodes and reconfiguring them. For this to be done, the data transfer must be fully reliable.

The main issue in the reliable data transfer is how to guarantee that all fragments of a large packet will arrive at the destination point. We can recognize two fundamental solutions—end-to-end and hop-by-hop. In the *end-to-end* solution, the receiver would trigger the eventual retransmission of the lost packets. This is in a way similar to the operation of TCP in fixed networks. The operation of end-to-end transport control in wireless ad hoc networks is difficult, however, mostly because of the very harsh environment in which these networks operate. A large packet error rate due to the medium propagates through multiple hops making the process of reordering very difficult. In the *hop-by-hop* solution, the intermediate nodes will retransmit data segments until the data segment is safely forwarded to the following node. The intermediate hops will use a form of automatic repeat request (ARQ)—link-layer error recovery—to ensure the safe delivery of segments. Optimally, a balance of these two approaches would be the most beneficial. The local recovery of lost segments should be performed hop-by-hop, but the information about the process of local recovery (e.g., additional delay) will have to be relayed to the originating node where the window flow control mechanisms needs to follow the progress of the segments that have been sent in the network.

LOW POWER OPERATION OF WIRELESS AD HOC NETWORKS

Similar to other wireless systems, ad hoc networks have to be designed under a tight constraint of power consumption. For example, experimental results presented in (Kravets, 1998) show that power consumption related to networking activities is approximately 10% of the overall power consumption of a laptop computer, which can even rise up to 50% in handheld devices (Stemm & Katz, 1997). In addition to this, ad hoc networks usually consist of a large number of small-size nodes. It is clearly not cost-efficient to equip these nodes with rechargeable batteries. This is why the networks have to be designed to maximize the life span of individual nodes. In this section, we will analyze the principles of the so-called *power save* network design, specially designed to prolong the life of small-size nodes connected in ad hoc networks.

Nodes in ad hoc networks can be in one of four main states: transmitting, receiving, idle, and sleeping. When it comes to the power consumption, transmitting can be considered expensive, receiving typically costs just a little less, and idle state can be cheaper, but it can also be as expensive as receiving, as shown in experimental results presented in Feeney and Nilsson (2001). Sleeping state costs almost nothing, but results in a node not being able to participate in the network. It becomes obvious that to increase the battery lifetime of ubiquitous devices, it is necessary to maximize the time the interface spends in the sleep state by switching off the interface in idle time periods. On the other hand, the nodes must cooperate to provide routing services. The power management system needs to have minimal effect on the overall network performance in terms of data throughput and delay. Achieving this balance is very complicated and has been the subject of numerous research activities.

This chapter analyses the power management from the networking point of view. The next sections will introduce and analyse existing solutions for link-layer and network-layer power save protocols. An equally important development of low power sensors and in general low power computing devices is omitted. Good analysis of these issues is given by Min et al. (2001), Sinha and Chandrakasan (2001) and Karl and Willig (2005). The following two sections analyse the link-layer and the network-layer approach to power management.

Link-Layer Power Management

The power save mechanisms at the link layer are mostly concentrated around the medium access control (MAC). As we have seen in one of the previous chapters, MAC is a complex problem in ad hoc networks, because of the need for complex synchronisation, the hidden terminal problem, and the presence of half-duplex communication. The four main energy problems when it comes to the medium access are (Ye, Heidemann, & Estrin, 2004): collisions, overhearing, protocol overhead, and idle listening. Overhearing refers to packets received by the nodes that are not the destinations. Overhearing is desirable when collecting neighbourhood information, but it is generally considered as waste of energy. The overhead in MAC protocols can come from per-packet overhead (MAC headers and trailers), collisions, or from exchange of extra control packets.

Idle listening is especially important. The elimination of idle listening is based on a concept that nodes must spend as much time as possible in the sleeping state, waking up only to receive or send the data. Synchronisation of this activity presents a major problem. Distributing the information about the sleeping patterns of connected nodes is a major challenge. For example, Lin, Rabaey, and Wolisz (2004) present a good analysis of this problem. Schurgers, Tsiatsis, Ganeriwal, and Srivastava (2002) present the STEM method, where separate data and wakeup channels are used to minimise the idle listening periods using either periodic beacon signals or continuous busy signalling. Separate channel concept is also used by Singh and Raghavendra (1998) to develop PAMAS, a well-known solution that uses a control channel to send busy tones to prevent collisions. The S-MAC concept (Ye, Heidemann, & Estrin, 2002) uses a single channel and attempts to coordinate the schedules of neighbouring nodes such that their listening periods start at the same time. This solution enables the nodes to agree on wakeup patterns thus forming virtual clusters. The mediation device protocol (Callaway, 2003) uses a centralised energy unconstrained device to buffer request-to-send messages in order to forward them to the receivers once they wake up. Tseng, Hsu, and Hsieh (2002) present several solutions for better synchronisation of the sleeping and awake phases, based on sending more beacon packets and careful arrangement of sleeping and awake periods. The communication between the nodes and exchange of the information about the sleeping cycles and awake periods is essential for avoiding idle listening. Shi and Stromberg (2007) give a good analysis of this problem.

Multihop networks are, in general, very complex to model and optimal channel access scheduling is impossible to calculate (Arikan, 1984). For practical use, suboptimal solutions are needed. Sagduyu and Ephremides (2003) provided a heuristic to determine distinct receiver groups and determine temporal allocations based on cumulative battery energies left at transmitter groups to extend the node lifetimes is given. The Group TDMA concept (Nguyen, Weiselthier, & Ephremides, 2003) is based on identifying groups of transmitters and scheduling the available time into distinct large time slots, each to be used by a group of transmitters. To use this concept to create energy-efficient access scheduling, the node lifetimes and energy consumption rates can be used as measure for time allocation. A simple and straightforward approach to reduce collisions is to use a probabilistic scheme. The concept here is to partition the time into large time intervals and allow each source to randomly send packets in the allocated interval. Multihop Over-the-Air Programming (Stathopulos, Kapur, Heidemann, & Estrin, 2003) successfully uses such a scheme.

Bluetooth is another network where TDMA is in use at link layer. There are several proposals to minimise power consumption by modifying the MAC mechanism in Bluetooth. All solutions attempt to avoid empty slots in Bluetooth scheduling—that is, to avoid the cases when the master is polling a slave that has no data to send. The schemes differ on the basis of whether the polling is done in cycles—whether each slave is guaranteed at least one polling packet in a cycle, or the cycle does not exist. Most of the existing solutions have in common the need to prioritise among the slaves, and to use the queue length and traffic load to calculate the slave priority. Average waiting time (average packet delay) is the main metric used for the evaluation of these schemes. For example, Capone, Gerla, and Kapoor (2001) use the queue lengths at both the master and the slaves to identify the next slave. Das et al. (2001) analyse three different scheduling schemes based on a definition of a maximum time limit in which the master has to serve a slave. The polling interval for each slave is dynamic: it is longer for slaves with empty queues and shorter for slaves with high traffic load. Lapeyrie and Turletti (2003) analyse efficiency and fairness of polling schemes. They calculate the slave priority as a linear combination of the probability the queues are nonempty and the number of slots since the slave has last been polled.

Network-Layer Power Management

Network-layer activities in power management include power-efficient topology control and power-efficient routing. Topology control can be defined as a process of changing and optimising the network topology to satisfy some optimisation criterion. Topology control is an inherent feature of wireless networks. Each node in wireless networks can potentially change the network topology, either by moving, or by adjusting its transmission range, or by deciding which other nodes to use to forward messages. The neighbourhood relationship in wireless networks is therefore very dynamic. Power-efficient topology control is the process of controlling the network topology to maximise the network lifetime and enable power-efficient routing, while keeping the network connectivity intact.

The general principle of the power save topology control is that a set of nodes is awake all the time and this set of nodes is able to handle all the incoming traffic. Other nodes spend most of the time in the low-power mode and switch to the full-power mode only occasionally. The key problem is the process of identifying the subset of full-power nodes. This set is usually called the *dominating set,* and the nodes that are its members are called *coordinators*, or *clusterheads*, as typically they serve as gateways for *clusters* of low-power nodes.

Ad hoc networks in general consist of nodes with identical features, and the dominating set is not formed of any special nodes but nodes themselves elect the set. Most selection algorithms use a two-phase approach, as the one presented in Wu, Dai, Gao, and Stojmenovic (2002). The node membership in the dominating set is typically dynamic—the nodes join and leave the set during the network life. Finding a minimal set is known to be computationally hard, and most of the solutions attempt to find an algorithm that identifies approximate dominating set. The general concept is to keep adding and removing nodes from the set on the basis of some criteria (energy level, relative location), taking into consideration neighbouring nodes that are members of the set. For example, in Span (Chen, Jamieson, Balakrishnan, & Morris, 2002), a node makes itself eligible to be a coordinator (member of dominating set) if it discovers that its two neighbours cannot communicate directly or via other coordinators. Chen et al. (2002) show using simulation that Span can provide almost 50% power saving in dense networks compared to standard 802.11 network.

Optimization of the network topology is a complex problem. Chiasserini, Chlamtac, Monti, and Nucci (2002) present a scheme where an even share of the energy drain for all clusterheads is arranged to maximize the network lifetime. Energy is evenly drained from the clusterheads by optimally balancing the cluster traffic loads and regulating the clusterhead transmission ranges. In this way, the number of controlled nodes per cluster can be adjusted. Simulation results presented by Chiasserini et al. (2002) show excellent results in dynamic scenarios, with the improvement of 74% for the network lifetime.

Location information obtained externally (e.g., using GSP) can also be used for topology control. Example of this is the GAF protocol, presented in Xu, Heidemann, and Estrin (2001). In GAF, the network is divided in separate regions and at least one of the nodes within the region needs to be awake to enable the full network connectivity. In the particular solution of GAF, the nodes switch randomly between sleep, discovery, and active states. The problem with using location is that the path loss and therefore the size of network regions is not fixed and does not depend only on distance. GAF algorithm aims to identify routing equivalent nodes by associating each node with a square within the virtual grid using physical position.

Power-efficient routing in wireless ad hoc networks is one of the most widely analysed topics. The concept of power-efficient routing is that routes are selected with power consumption as one of the routing metrics. Traditionally, shortest path routing is used in networks. In a power scarce wireless ad hoc environment, new solutions are needed to optimise the overall power consumption. These solutions can shift the traditional routing decisions, so that very often the end-to-end path consisting of many intermediate hops will be chosen over the shortest path because the longer path consumes less power.

Feeney (2004) gives an excellent overview of power-efficient routing. She points out that there are three metrics commonly used in power-efficient routing: minimum-energy routing, max-min routing, and minimum-cost routing.

Minimum-energy routing minimizes the total energy consumed as packet is forwarded on a route. This can be achieved by taking the energy consumed as a routing metric. In comparison, the minimum-cost routing minimizes the total cost of using a specific end-to-end path. This may include additional parameters—for example, as proposed by Stojmenovic and Lin (2001), a hybrid routing metric can be used—a combination of node's lifetime and distance-based power metric. In addition, routing the packets through lightly loaded nodes is considered energy conserving since there is less likelihood for contention and therefore the number of link-layer retransmissions will be smaller.

Using relay regions (Rodoplu & Meng, 1999) also belongs to this family of solutions. The relay region for a particular source node and particular relay node is defined as a set of receivers for which transmitting via the relay node can minimise the total energy consumption. Once the source identifies the relay regions, a standard distributed routing algorithm can be used to identify the routes. A key problem with this type of schemes is the identification of transmission power of nodes, which is very difficult to do, mostly due to a very dynamic environment.

The problem with minimum energy routing is that while minimising the consumed power for a single packet, it does not take into consideration the power state of nodes, and thus does not optimise the network lifetime. Max-min routing selects the route that "maximizes the minimum residual energy of any node on the route" (Feeney, 2004). This will definitely increase the per-packet routing cost, but will improve the overall network lifetime. Finally, the *maximum lifetime routing* attempts to maximise the time before the first node in the network is left with no energy. Recently Madan and Lall (2006) presented two separate distributed algorithms for maximum lifetime routing.

CONCLUSION

This chapter introduced an exciting world of wireless ad hoc networks. In the future world of ubiquitous computing, networking small low-power devices will be essential. To increase the network efficiency and simplify the deployment, the devices need to be connected in the distributed, ad hoc mode—without the use of a centralised controller. Finally, to address the power consumption and reliability constraints, the network needs to be designed in a way substantially different from the standard five-layer network design used for the global TCP/IP Internet. This chapter introduced main design principles and main standardisation activities and especially pointed out the developments in the design of low power wireless ad hoc networks.

REFERENCES

Abramson, N. (1977). The throughput of packet broadcasting channels. *IEEE Trans. Commun., 25,* 117-128.

Al-Karaki, J.N., & Kamal, A.E. (2004). Routing techniques in wireless sensor networks: A survey. *IEEE Wireless Communications, 11*(6).

Arikan, E. (1984). Some complexity results about packet radio networks. *IEEE Trans. Info. Theory, IT-30, 681-85.*

Bharghavan, V. et al. (1994). MACAW: A media access protocol for wireless LANs. *Computer Communications Review, 24*(4).

Callaway, E.H. (2003). *Wireless sensor networks – architectures and protocols.* Boca Raton: Auerbach.

Cano, J.C., & Manzoni, P. (2000). Performance comparison of energy consumption for mobile ad hoc network routing protocols. In *Proceedings of the 8th International Symposium on Model-*

ing, Analysis and Simulation of Computer and Telecom System (pp. 57-64).

Capone, A., Gerla, M., & Kapoor, R. (2001). Efficient polling schemes for Bluetooth picocells. In *Proceedings of IEEE ICC 2001*, Helsinki, Finland.

Center for Embedded Networked Sensing, UCLA. Retrieved January 21, 2008, from http://research.cens.ucla.edu/research/

Chen, B., Jamieson, K., Balakrishnan, H., & Morris, R. (2002, September). Span: An energy-efficient coordination algorithm for topology maintenance in ad hoc wireless networks. *ACM Wireless Networks Journal, 8*(5), 481-494.

Clausen, T., & Jacquet, P. (2003). *Optimized link state routing protocol (OLSR)*. IETF Request for Comments 3626.

Chiasserini, C.-F., Chlamtac, I., Monti, P., & Nucci, A. (2002). *Energy efficient design of wireless ad hoc networks* (LNCS 2354).

Das, A. et al. (2001). Enhancing perfmance of asynchronous data traffic over the Bluetooth wireless ad hoc network. In *Proceedings of the IEEE INFOCOM.*

Edwards, W.K., Newman, M.W., Sedivy, J.Z., & Smith, T.F. (2005). Bringing network effects to pervasive spaces. *IEEE Pervasive Computing, 4*(3), 15-17.

European Union research project EYES. Retrieved January 21, 2008, from http://www.eyes.eu.org

Feeney, L.M. (2004). Energy-efficient communication in ad hoc wireless networks. In Basagni, Conti, Giordano, Stojmenovic (Eds.), *Mobile ad hoc networking.* IEEE.

Feeney, L.M., & Nilsson, M. (2001, April 24-26). Investigating the energy consumption of a wireless network interface in an ad hoc networking environment. In *20th Annual Joint Conference of the IEEE Computer and Communications Societies* (pp. 1548-1557).

Fifer, W., & Bruno, F. (1987). The low-cost packet ration. *Proceedings of the IEEE, 75*(1), 33-42.

Freebersyser, J.A., & Leiner, B. (2001). A DoD perspective on mobile ad hoc networks. *Ad Hoc Networking.* Addison Wesley.

Garcia-Luna-Aceves, J.J., & Fullmer, C.L. (1999). Floor acquisition multiple access (FAMA) in single-channel wireless networks. *Mobile Networks and Applications, 4*(3), 157-174.

Haas, Z.J, & Deng, J. (2002). Dual busy tone multiple access (DBTMA) - a multiple access control scheme for ad hoc networks. *IEEE Transactions on Communications, 50*(6), 975-985.

Haas, Z.J., Pearlman, M.R., & Samar, P. (2002). *Internet-draft - the zone routing protocol (ZRP) for ad hoc networks.*

Hill, J., & Culler, D. (2002). MICA: A wireless platform for deeply embedded network. *IEEE Micro, 22*(6), 12-24.

Hill, J., Horton, M., Kling, R., & Krishnamurthy, L. (2004). The platform enabling wireless sensor networks. *Communications of the ACM, 47*(6), 41-46.

Hill, J., Szewczyk, R., Woo, A., Hollar, S., Culler, D.E., & Pister, K.S.J. (2000). System architecture directions for networked sensors. *Architectural Support for Programming Languages and Operating Systems,* 93-104.

IEEE Standards for Wireless LAN Medium Access Control (MAC) and Physical Layer (PHY), Part 11:Technical Specifications. (1999).

Jiang, M., Li, J., & Tay, Y.-C. (1999). *Cluster based routing protocol functional specification.* Internet Draft, draft-ietf-manet-cbrpspec *.txt, work in progress.

Johnson, D.B., Maltz, D.A., & Hu, Y.-C. (2004). *Internet draft - the dynamic source routing protocol for mobile ad hoc networks (DSR).*

Karl, H., & Willig, A. (2005). *Protocols and architectures for wireless sensor networks.* Wiley.

Karn, P. (1990). MACA: A new channel access method for packet radio. In *Proceeding of 9th ARRL/CRRL Amateur Radio Computer Networking Conference.*

Kravets, R., & Krishnan, P. (1998). Power management techniques for mobile communication. In *Proceeding of 4th Annual ACM/IEEE International Conference on Mobile Computing and Networking* (pp. 157-168).

Lapeyrie, J.-B., & Turletti, T. (2003). FPQ: A fair and efficient polling algorithm with QoS support for Bluetooth piconet. In *Proceedings of the IEEE INFOCOM,* San Francisco, CA.

Lin, E.-Y.A., Rabaey, J.M., & Wolisz, A. (2004). Power-efficient rendez-vous schemes for dense wireless sensor networks. In *Proceedings of IEEE ICC 2004,* Paris.

Liu, C., & Kaiser, J. (2003). A survey of mobile ad hoc network routing protocols (Tech. Rep.).

Madan, R., & Lall, S. (2006). Distributed algorithms for maximum lifetime routing in wireless sensor networks. *IEEE Transactions on Wireless Communications, 5*(8).

Malkin, G.S., & Stenstrup, M.E. (1995). Distance-vector routing. In *Routing in Communications Networks,* 83-98. Prentice Hall.

Min, R., Bhadrwaj, M., Cho, S.-H., Shih, Sinha, A., Wang, A. et al. (2001). Low-power wireless sensor networks. In *Proceedings of the 14th International Conference on VLSI Design,* Bangalore, India.

NEST Project Web page. (2006). Retrieved January 21, 2008, from http://webs.cs.berkeley.edu/nest-index.html.

Nguyen, G.D., Weiselthier, J.E., & Ephremides, A. (2003). Multiple-access for multiple destinations in ad-hoc networks. In *Proceedings WiOpt 03.*

Perkins, C., Belding-Royer, E., & Das, S. (2003). Ad hoc on-demand distance vector (AODV) routing. *IETF Request for Comments, 3561.*

Perkins, C.E., & Bhagwat, P. (1994). Highly dynamic destination-sequenced distance-vector routing (DSDV) for mobile computers. *Computer Communications Review, 24*(4), 234.

Reed, J.H. (Ed.). (2005). *An introduction to ultra wideband communication systems.* Prentice Hall.

Rodoplu, V., & Meng, T.H.-Y. (1999). Minimum energy mobile wireless networks. *IEEE Journal on Selected Areas in Communications, 17*(8), 1333-1344.

Romer, K., & Mattern, F. (2004). The design space of wireless sensor networks. *IEEE Wireless Communications Magazine, 11*(6).

Sagduyu, Y.E., & Ephremides, A. (2003). Energy-efficient collision resolution in wireless ad hoc networks. In *Proceedings of IEEE Infocom.*

ScatterWeb. Retrieved January 21, 2008, from http://www.scatterweb.com

Schurgers, C., Tsiatsis, V., Ganeriwal, S., & Srivastava, M. (2002). Optimising sensor networks in the energy-latency-density design space. *IEEE Transactions on Mobile Computing, 1*(1), 7-80.

Shi, X., & Stromberg, G. (2007). SyncWUF: An ultra low power MAC protocol for wireless sensor networks. *IEEE Transactions on Mobile Computing, 6*(1).

Singh, S., & Raghavendra, C.S. (1998). PAMAS – power aware multi-access protocol with signalling for ad hoc networks. *ACM Computer Communication Review.*

Sinha, A., & Chandrakasan, A. (2001). Dynamic power management in wireless sensor networks. *IEEE Design and Test of Computers, 18*(2), 62-74.

Stathopulos, T., Kapur, R., Heidemann, J., & Estrin, D. (2003). A remote code update mechanism for wireless sensor networks (Tech. Rep. cens tr-30*). Centre for Embedded Networked Computing.*

Stemm, M., & Katz, R.H. (1997). Measuring and reducing energy consumption of network interfaces in hand-held devices. *IEICE Transactions on Communications, E80-B*(8), 1125-1131.

Stojmenovic, I., & Lin, X. (2001). Power aware localized routing in wireless networks. *IEEE Trans. On Parallel and Distributed Systems, 12*(10).

Talucci, F., Gerla, M., & Fratta, L. (1997). MACA-BI (MACA by Invitation) a receiver oriented access protocol for wireless multihop networks. In *Proceedings of International Symposium on Personal, Indoor and Mobile Radio Communications,* Helsinki, Finland (pp. 435-439).

Tseng, Y.-C., Hsu, C.-S., & Hsieh, T.-Y. (2002). Power-saving protocols for IEEE 802.11-based multi-hop ad hoc networks. In *Proceedings IEEE INFOCOM.*

UK Ubinet. Retrieved January 21, 2008, from http://www-dse.doc.ic.ac.uk/Projects/UbiNet/links.htm

Wu, J., Dai, F., Gao, M., & Stojmenovic, I. (2002). On calculating power-aware connected dominating sets for efficient routing in ad hoc wireless networks. *IEEE/KICS Journal of Communications and Networks, 4*(1), 59-70.

Xu, Y., Heidemann, J., & Estrin, D. (2001). Geography-informed energy conservation for ad hoc routing. In 7*th* *Annual International Conference on Mobile Computing and Networking* (pp. 70-84).

Ye, W., Heidemann, J., & Estrin, D. (2002). An energy efficient MAC protocol for wireless sensor networks. In *Proceedings of INFOCOM 2002,* New York.

Ye, W., Heidemann, J., & Estrin, D. (2004). Medium access control with coordinated adaptive sleeping for wireless sensor networks. *IEEE/ACM Transactions on Networking.*

KEY TERMS

Ad Hoc Networks: Networks of nodes that communicate without any centralized communication infrastructure. These are highly distributed systems characterized by self-organization and quick network formation.

Low Power Networking: A set of networking techniques and protocols aimed at minimizing the power consumption during the communication.

Network Design: A set of activities aimed at efficient choice and optimization of network hardware, protocols, and mechanisms to achieve the real-time goals of a communication network.

Network Resource Management: A set of activities aimed at efficient use of network resources: bandwidth, power, management capacity in a way that maximizes the benefit for the network users.

Sensor Networks: Distributed networks consisting of small networked nodes which are simultaneously used to monitor some physical event and collect data about it.

Ubiquitous Computing: The field of study in computer science dealing with the use of small specialized computing devices that fit naturally in their environment.

Wireless Networks: Communication networks in which networked nodes use wireless links to transmit data.

Chapter XI
TeleTables and Window Seat: Bilocative Furniture Interfaces

Yeonjoo Oh
Carnegie Mellon University, USA

Ken Camarata
KDF Architecture, USA

Michael Philetus Weller
Carnegie Mellon University, USA

Mark D. Gross
Carnegie Mellon University, USA

Ellen Yi-Luen Do
Georgia Institute of Technology, USA

ABSTRACT

People can use computationally-enhanced furniture to interact with distant friends and places without cumbersome menus or widgets. We describe computing embedded in a pair of tables and a chair that enables people to experience remote events in two ways: The TeleTables are ambient tabletop displays that connect two places by projecting shadows cast on one surface to the other. The Window Seat rocking chair through its motion controls a remote camera tied to a live video feed. Both explore using the physical space of a room and its furniture to create "bilocative" interfaces.

INTRODUCTION

Over a decade ago, Weiser predicted a shift in the dominant human computer interaction paradigm from mouse and keyboard based graphical user interface (GUI) to ubiquitous tangible computational artifacts embedded in our environment (Weiser, 1991). Traditional GUIs require a high level of attention, while ubiquitous computing promises to provide the power of computation in everyday settings without the overhead of having to focus on operating a computer. Furniture presents a familiar and promising platform for such investigation. During the course of several years, we have explored a variety of furniture interface projects. Our goal for these projects has been to develop interaction techniques appropriate to traditional pieces of furniture that enable people to leverage additional computational resources.

"Bilocative" interfaces leverage the intimate connection between furniture and place to create an intuitive physical interface to facilitate the navigation and transmission of information between remote places. A bilocative furniture interface is a piece of furniture that is computationally enhanced so that it can usefully be understood to be in two places at once. Instead of providing a screen-based interface that must be navigated to find information about different remote places, each bilocative furniture piece in a room represents a connection to a particular distant place, and that information stream can be engaged just by approaching the piece of furniture and using it in the traditional manner. To explore this idea, we built two computationally enhanced furniture pieces, the TeleTables and Window Seat. These projects represent quite different approaches to connecting people with a distant place. The TeleTables attempt to generate an ambient interpersonal awareness between households by relaying information about cast shadows between the two tables. The Window Seat provides a much more direct connection, but through a familiar interaction. It projects a live video feed from a distant camera that is controlled by rocking the chair. Both projects allow a distant place to be engaged without a traditional interface such as a GUI or keypad.

The TeleTables project explores the potential of ambient interpersonal communication devices. TeleTables are composed of a pair of tables that enable people in two distant locations to see shadows cast on the opposite table. The surface of each TeleTable contains an array of photo sensors and display pixels and when someone sits down at one table, for example to have breakfast, areas of the table that are shaded by the breakfast activities light up in one color on both tables. If someone else sits down at the other table to have breakfast at the same time, the shaded areas of the table light up in a different color on both tables, so that both people having breakfast see that there are similar breakfast activities taking place in the other location. The interaction is different than a phone call or a chat, as it does not require the explicit intention to communicate with the other person; casting shadows on our kitchen tables is a side effect of various common activities. This mode of communication allows people to develop an ambient awareness of events at another location with a low fidelity data stream that intrudes only minimally, and symmetrically, on the privacy of both participants.

Through our Window Seat project, we have investigated how a rocking chair can be tied to a view into a particular distant place. Rather than requiring the navigation of a Web interface to find a particular Web cam and adjust where it is looking, we lower the barrier to entry for using Web cam technology: it is accessed just by sitting in the rocking chair tied to a particular place and rocking to adjust the view. This interface brings information navigation out of the computer screen and into the physical space of a room and its furniture. We posit that the conceptual mapping of a chair to a view of a particular place will be accessible to people at any level of technological literacy.

The remainder of this chapter first describes related work and then each project with a use scenario, system overview, and demonstration. We also discuss future research directions and reflect on the implications for furniture interface design.

RELATED WORK

Many researchers have sought to leverage the familiarity of the interface afforded by furniture to create ubiquitous computational interfaces. We classify these computationally enhanced furniture projects into three groups by the functionality they afford: (1) providing a physical handle to control a virtual object, (2) retrieving useful information, and (3) supporting communication and awareness between distant places.

Tangible media projects have sought to provide direct control of virtual objects through physical handles. Much of the research involving furniture has focused on computationally enhanced tables, and there is even a conference devoted to "tabletop interaction" (Tabletop, 2006). Bricks (Fitzmaurice, Ishii, & Buxton, 1995), a graspable user interface, "metaDESK" (Ullmer & Ishii, 1997), and "DigitalDesk" (Newman & Wellner, 1992) all use the desk as an input device. Several projects have also sought to create computationally-enhanced furniture that can retrieve and present useful information. Samsung researchers (Park, Won, Lee, & Kim, 2003) built a computationally enhanced table, sofa, picture frame, and bed that attempt to provide useful information or services. For example, the picture frame provides local news, weather information, and stock market information and the bed gently wakes its occupant with a customized combination of smell, sound, light, and temperature. The Magic Wardrobe (Wan, 2000) is a computationally-enhanced wardrobe that identifies the clothes it contains using RFID tags and recommends new items for purchase from online stores. These projects are similar to ours in that they leverage the familiar interfaces presented by furniture. However, more relevant are computationally-enhanced furniture projects that attempt to support communication between places. Beckhaus, Blom, and Haringer (2005) built a stool to control a view of a virtual environment. The physical movement of the chair maps to movement in the virtual environment: (1) tilting the chair in any direction translates the current viewpoint; (2) rotating the seat rotates the virtual scene around the user's position. While the interaction for controlling the camera view is similar to our Window Seat, their stool does not attempt to bring information navigation out into physical space as does Window Seat, but merely serves as the joystick for a computer graphics workstation. The 6th Sense (Tollmar & Persson, 2002) is a lamp that encourages users to communicate with remote family members. With a family tree metaphor, each small light at the end of a branch represents a remote family member. A family member can turn on a small light to signal their presence to another member. The 6th Sense allows the users to feel "togetherness" with their loved ones without intruding on their lives. Similarly, our TeleTables project enables people to sense the presence of remote friends or family members. The 6th Sense interface introduces a novel interaction involving switches; our TeleTables leverage the traditional functions of a table, adding awareness feedback by illuminating patterns on the tabletop.

FURNITURE MEDIATING AMBIENT COMMUNICATION (TELETABLES)

While communication technologies such as cellular phones, e-mail, and instant messaging have made direct spoken and written communication channels easily accessible, they all require focused attention and serve best to transmit explicit messages. Our TeleTables are a bilocative tabletop interface that exists in two places at once in that they simultaneously display shadows cast from two different locations. They explore the potential of using projected shadows from a remote place as a means of creating a nonverbal unfocused communication channel between distant places. A pair of kitchen tables equipped with light sensors and LED displays are tied together through the Internet so that a shadow cast on one table is displayed on both in colored light, with different colors used to distinguish local and remote shadows.

For example, Angela is a college freshman living in Pittsburgh. She sits down to eat breakfast and the surface of the table is washed with red light reflecting the shadow of her cereal bowl, coffee cup, and the movement of her arms over the frosted Plexiglas surface. Three states away, at her parent's house, the red lights on the surface of her parents' table echo those on Angela's. Her father notices the lights and is reassured that Angela is not skipping breakfast and is on time for her morning class. As Angela gets up from the table she notices a series of amber circles appear on the surface as her father sets out plates and cups for his and her mother's breakfast. The shadow of her father's activity reminds her that she needs to call her parents tonight and ask them to deposit money in her account to cover the lab fee for her robotics course next semester. The shadows displayed by the TeleTables give Angela and her parents the sensation ofbeing close to each other, without overly intruding on their privacy or interrupting their busy lives.

Design Schematic and Diagram

TeleTables are two tables where each functions as both an input and an output device. The surface of each table contains eight modules; each module is divided into a 2 by 4 grid; each grid cell contains a red LED, an amber LED, and a photocell. Therefore, the surface of each table is divided into an 8 by 8 grid with 128 LEDs and 64 photocells (Figure 1). A microcontroller uses row-column scanning to illuminate the LEDs and to read values from the photocells. In the current version of TeleTables, a pair of radio frequency transceivers establishes a wireless connection between the tables allowing the microcontrollers to directly exchange data. (In the next version, data will be transmitted over the Internet). Figure 1 also shows the information flow in the TeleTables. When a user casts shadows over one table, the microcontroller reads the photocell values, lights the corresponding local LED lights, and also sends data to the other microcontroller to light the corresponding LEDs on the other table.

Each table has four major components: the array modules (photocells, red LEDs, and amber LEDs), microcontroller, a 22" by 22" table, and

Figure 1. Information flow in the TeleTables

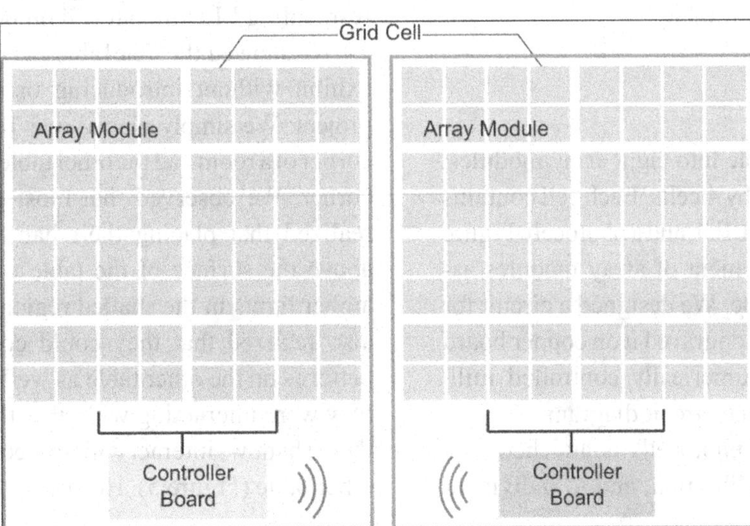

Figure 2. Table components: (1) array modules (photocells, red and amber LEDs); (2) microcontroller; (3) 22" x 22" table; (4) 1/8" Plexiglas

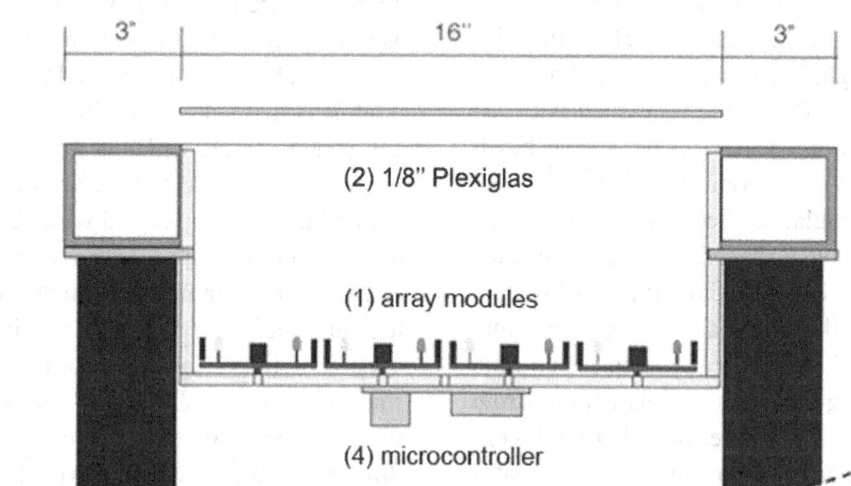

1/8" Plexiglas. We made a 3" deep compartment below the surface of an Ikea table to hold the printed circuit boards that constitute the eight array modules. A 1/8" translucent acrylic plastic forms the tabletop. We mounted a Basic Stamp 2 microcontroller with 16 digital I/O ports to the bottom surface of the table. Figure 2 illustrates the components of our table.

Electronics

We divided each table into eight array modules, each a subarray of 2 by 4 cells. Each cell contains a red LED, an amber LED, and a photocell. Figure 3 shows the arrangement of array modules assembled into the table. We designed a circuit for an array module and engraved it on copper board using a computer-numerically controlled mill. Figure 4 illustrates the circuit diagram.

Each column of photocells is attached to a potentiometer for calibration, and to individual pins on the microcontroller to make a voltage divider circuit. As the shift register powers each row, the microcontroller reads threshold values of photocells in that row as 8 bits of a byte. If the voltage on the pin is below the microcontroller's 1.5V internal threshold then the cell is considered "shaded" and the microcontroller lights the corresponding LED in that cell on both tables.

We showed the TeleTables as part of a public exhibit without introducing or explaining the project. We simply placed one TeleTable in one corner of a room and the other table in the opposite corner. We observed that most people quickly realized that placing their hands or an object above the surface of the table triggered red or amber lights in the shaded region. Many people also realized that they could control the light patterns on the other table as well as on the table they were interacting with directly, and through these shadows interact with someone sitting at the other table (Figure 5). However, the interactions

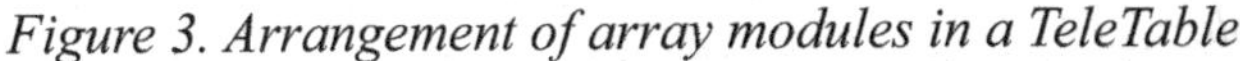

Figure 3. Arrangement of array modules in a TeleTable

Figure 4. Circuit diagram (a) array module schematic; (b) CAD drawing for copper board

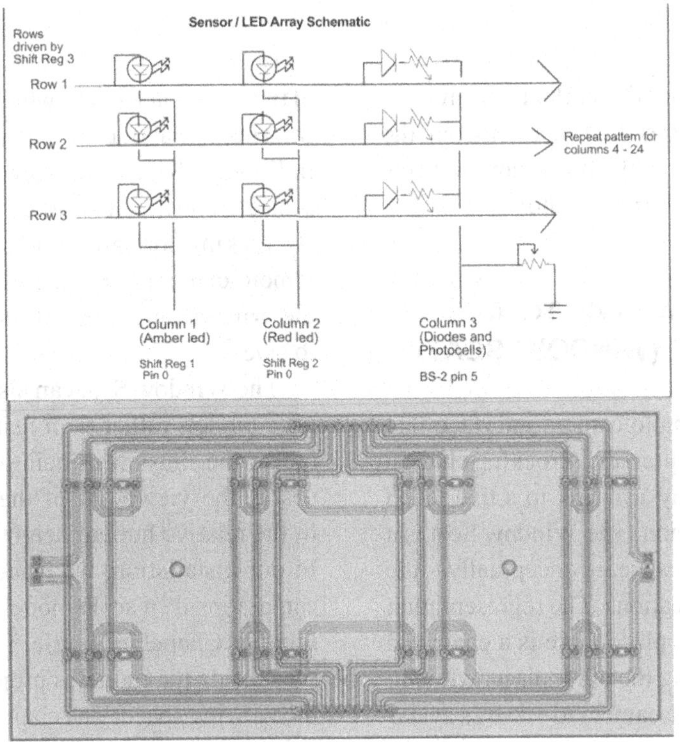

Figure 5. Two friends interact using the TeleTables

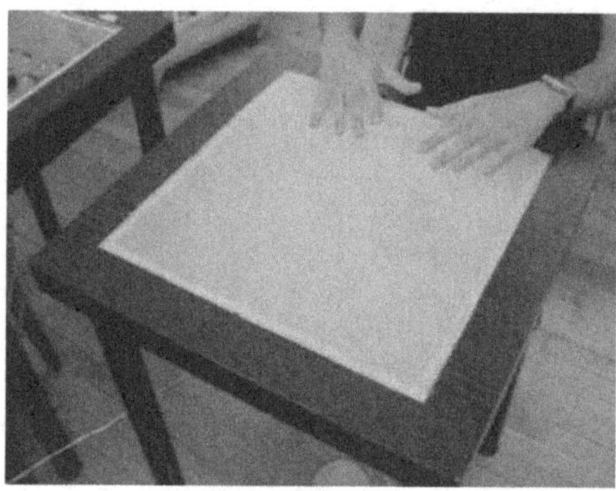

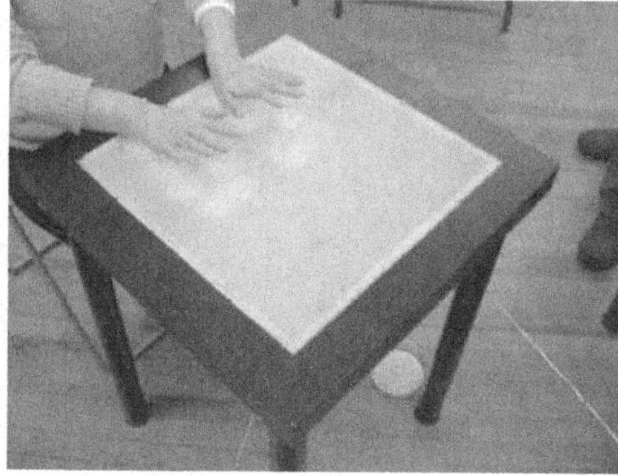

Figure 6. Real and projected images of Steven Holl's Chapel of St. Ignatius. The second and fifth pictures are projected images from the scale model. The others are photos taken on site.

we observed were more direct than we envision they would be when installed in a home, as the tables were not used as tables but as novel objects to be investigated by curious visitors.

FURNITURE AS A LINK TO A REMOTE PLACE (WINDOW SEAT)

Window Seat is a remote camera interface that requires no computer literacy. A rocking chair in a room serves as a physical link to a live video feed of a remote location. The Window Seat is a bilocative interface because—conceptually—the chair exists in both locations. The representation is asymmetric: in one place there is a chair and a video screen showing the other place, while in the other there is only a camera to serve as avatar of the viewer and chair, which provides very little information about the other side. While sitting in Window Seat, a live view of a remote space is projected on a video screen in front of the chair. By rocking forward and back in the chair, the remote camera view pans up and down. When the armrests are pressed, the camera pans side to side.

The Window Seat can also be used to experience models rather than real places. In order to create the illusion of being immersed in a real space, the viewpoint of the camera must map to the relative human height in the scale model. In our installation, we placed an actuated Web camera inside a scale model of Steven Holl's St. Ignatius Chapel in Seattle. The scene the camera sees inside the model is projected on the wall in the viewing space. The chair controls the camera tilt and pan to look in different directions within the model. As shown in Figure 6, images from inside the model are similar to what visitors might experience in the real chapel.

Design Schematic and Diagrams

The Window Seat has five major components. A physical chair serves as an input device; a Handyboard (Martin, 2001) microcontroller serves to orchestrate interaction; a camera captures remote images; and a projector displays them on a wall to provide a simulated immersive environment (Figure 7).

Figure 7 shows the flow of information in the Window Seat. As users rock the chair and press the armrests, the sensors transmit this information to the microcontroller. The microcontroller in turn drives two servomotors that control the camera angle. The remote view from the camera is then projected on the wall in front of the Window Seat rocking chair by a video projector housed inside the seat back (Figure 8).

The chair controls two axes of camera movement (up/down and left/right). When the user rocks the chair up and down, the camera tilts up and down. Control of panning is achieved by pressing on sensors attached to the armrests.

We used two kinds of sensors: an infrared sensor and two homemade pressure sensors. The infrared sensor is located beneath the seat (Figure 9) sensing the distance between the floor and the chair.

We made pressure sensors with conductive foam (easily obtained from standard electronics packing material) sandwiched between two washers (Figure 10). They act as variable resistors; when the foam is compressed the resistance is lower. When the user pushes the left pressure sensor, the camera pans left. As the user pushes harder, the microcontroller reads the lower resistance value and advances the servomotors further. If the user pushes both pressure sensors at the same time, the camera returns to a default position.

We considered several options to control camera panning. One option was to mount the chair on a swivel mount. However, if the chair swiveled, a wraparound screen would be needed. Another option was to mount pressure sensors on the seat cushion so that when the user shifts her center of gravity to the right, the camera pans to the right. However, preliminary user testing revealed this

Figure 7. Information flow in the window seat

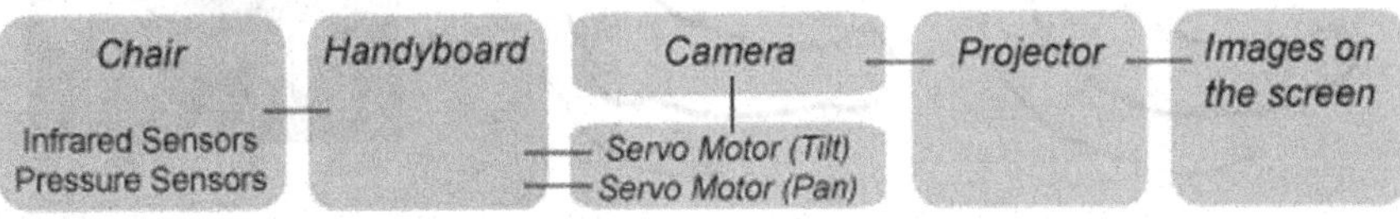

Figure 8. Window Seat components: (1) physical chair; (2) handyboard microcontroller; (3) remote camera; (4) projector; (5) wall as display device

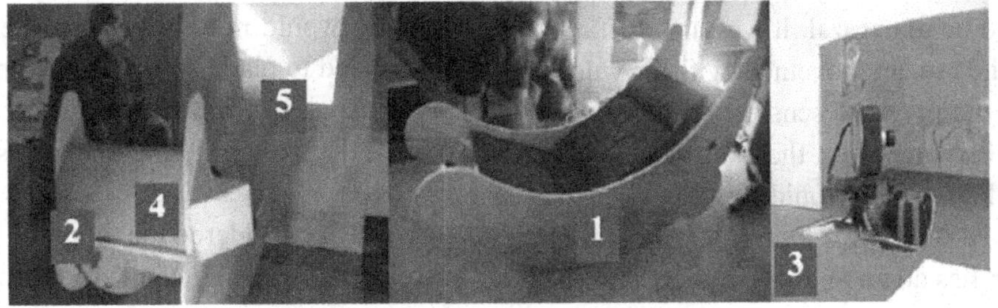

Figure 9. Camera movement and sensor placement

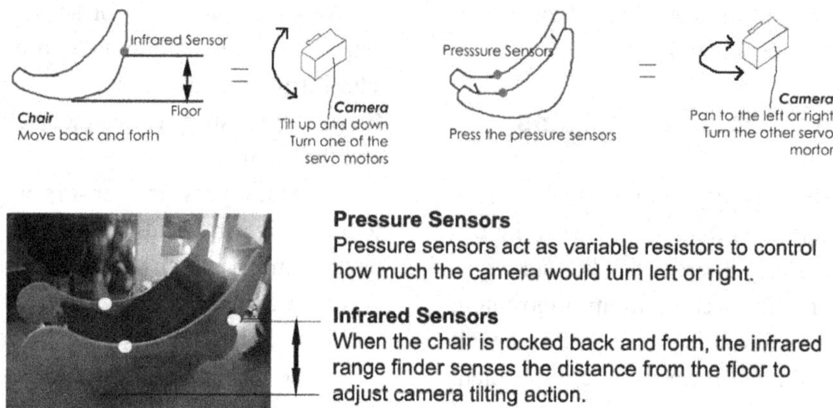

Figure 10. Homemade pressure switch with washers and conductive foam

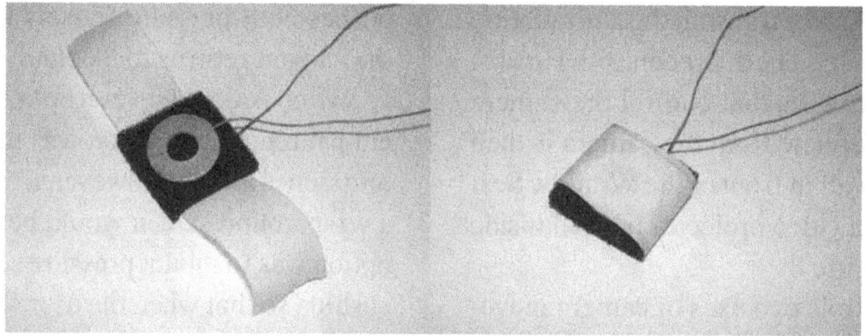

Figure 11. Stops for chair balance

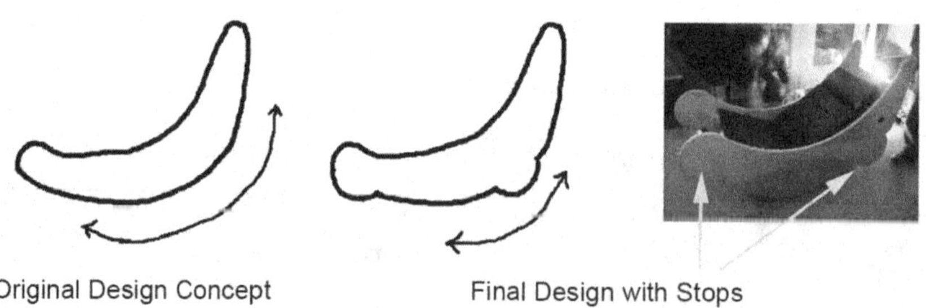

interaction to be unnatural. It was also difficult to calibrate the camera movement with the values reported by the pressure sensors. Another idea was to install switches on the chair base, close to the user's legs, which would activate when the user sits up. However, we found that if the user leans back or lies down on the rocking chair, the switches would not always activate. Therefore, we decided to place the panning control sensors on the armrests. This makes it easy for the user to press them regardless of the user's position on the chair.

We also considered the ergonomic aspects of sitting comfort using chair design standards for

Figure 12. Moving image on the screen

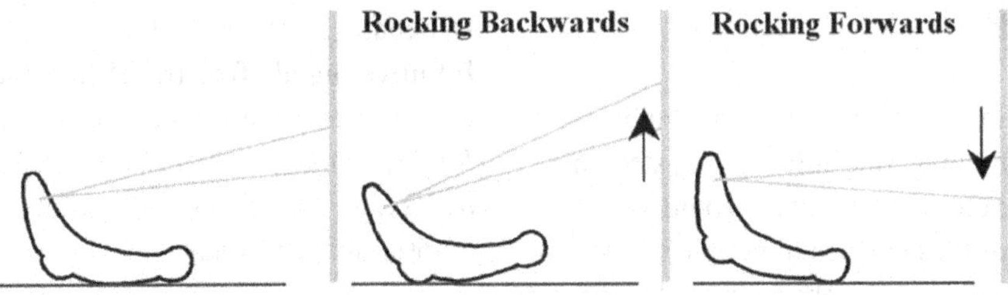

Figure 13. (a) Screen design alternatives, (b) chair balance, (c) projector, and mirror placement

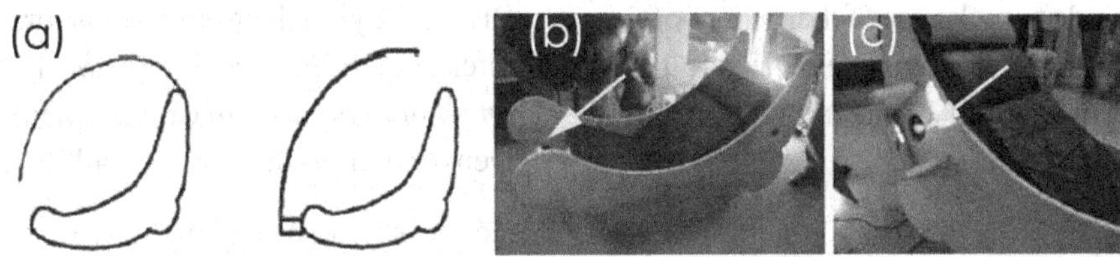

length and width of the seat and back (Cranz, 1998). The basic shape of the chair is a crescent curve (Hennessey & Papanek, 1974) made of plywood. We designed the chair to balance easily with stops, which we placed in the middle and the end of the chair curve (Figure 11). Without these stops, the crescent shaped chair could fall backwards or forwards.

In our Window Seat design, we developed a mapping scheme for motion translation and configured the camera movement to correspond to the user's viewing height. The projected visual images move up and down as the user rocks back and forth because the video projector is mounted on the chair (Figure 12).

Our original design considered connecting a screen to the rocking chair from either the top or the bottom of the chair (Figure 13). These alternatives have the merit that the projected images move simultaneously with users because the screen attached to the chair moves with chair. That, in turn, would allow the user to control the camera pan by swiveling the chair. However, attaching the screen on the chair top makes the chair harder to rock, and mounting the screen on the bottom of the chair makes it hard to sit comfortably. Despite the merits of these design alternatives, we decided on the armrest control for a static screen that can make use of any vertical wall. In order to project the images onto the front wall, we mounted the projector inside the back of the chair. We mounted a weight on the bottom of chair as a counterbalance (Figure 13).

Placement of Projector and Mirror Housing

We used a video projector to display interior space images onto the wall to create an immersive illusion for our users. We considered several alternatives for the projector position. We first tried to put the projector on the top of the chair, but learned that this placement of the projector is sensitive to the user's height and body shape. Instead we decided to put the projector inside the back of the chair (near its fulcrum) and used a mirror to reflect the image (Figure 13) out to the screen in front.

DISCUSSION AND FUTURE WORK

Future Work

To further evaluate bilocative furniture interfaces' utility for navigating information streams connecting remote locations, we would like to install several of these pieces in people's homes and observe their use. By observing bilocative interfaces in use in homes, we hope to be able to evaluate whether having a straightforward physical interface to information streams would encourage people to make use of them more often and provide a more satisfying experience than screen-based navigation of an interaction with remote information streams.

Discussion

We have explored the idea of using pieces of furniture as spatial links to information streams tied to remote locations. We call these bilocative furniture interfaces as they can be understood as being in two places at once, which provides a useful and intuitive conceptual map for the information stream provided. We believe that it is important to maintain the original interaction model afforded by a piece of furniture (to sit, to place objects) while extending its functionality to provide additional value such as remote presence awareness and immersive viewing.

ACKNOWLEDGMENT

We thank our TeleTables and Window Seat team members: Bridget Lewis, and Kursat Ozenc, who worked on the TeleTables, and Doo Young Kwon, Babak Ziraknejad, and Jennifer Lewis, who worked on the Window Seat. This work was supported by the U.S. National Science Foundation grant under Grant ITR-0326054.

REFERENCES

Beckhaus, S., Blom, K. J., & Haringer, M. (2005). Intuitive, hands-free travel interface for virtual environments. In *Proceedings of IEEE Virtual Reality Conference, Workshop on New Directions in 3D User Interfaces 2005,* Bonn, Germany (pp. 57-60). Shaker Verlag.

Cranz, G. (1998). *The chair: Rethinking culture, body, and design.* New York: Norton.

Fitzmaurice, G. W., Ishii, H., & Buxton, W. (1995). Bricks: Laying the foundations for graspable user interfaces. In *Proceedings of the ACM Conference on Human Factors in Computing Systems (CHI),* Denver, Colorado (pp. 442-449). ACM Press.

Hennessey, J., & Papanek, V. J. (1974). *Nomadic furniture: How to build and where to buy lightweight furniture that folds, collapses, stacks, knocks-down, inflates or can be thrown away and re-cycled.* New York: Pantheon Books.

Martin, F. G. (2001). *Robotic explorations: A hands-on introduction to engineering.* Prentice Hall.

Newman, W., & Wellner, P. (1992). A desk supporting computer-based interaction with paper documents. In *Proceedings of the ACM Conference on Human Factors in Computing Systems (CHI),* Monterey, California (pp. 587-592). ACM Press.

Park, S. H., Won, S. H., Lee, J. B., & Kim, S. W. (2003). Smart home - digitally engineered domestic life. *Personal and Ubiquitous Computing, 7*(3-4), 189-196.

Tabletop. (2006). *Proceedings of the First IEEE International Workshop on Horizontal Interactive Human-Computer Systems,* Adelaide, Australia. IEEE Press.

Tollmar, K., & Persson, J. (2002). Understanding remote presence. In *Proceedings of the Second*

ACM Nordic Conference on Human-Computer Interaction (NORDCHI), Aarhus, Denmark (pp. 41-50). ACM Press.

Ullmer, B., & Ishii, H. (1997). The metaDESK: Models and prototypes for tangible user interfaces. In *Proceedings of ACM Symposium on User Interface Software and Technology (UIST)* (pp. 223-232). ACM Press.

Wan, D. (2000). Magic wardrobe: Situated shopping from your own bedroom. *Personal and Ubiquitous Computing, 4*(4), 234-237.

Weiser, M. (1991). The computer for the 21st century. *Scientific American, 265*(3), 66-75.

Chapter XII
Using Multimedia and Virtual Reality for Web-Based Collaborative Learning on Multiple Platforms

Gavin McArdle
University College Dublin, Ireland

Teresa Monahan
University College Dublin, Ireland

Michela Bertolotto
University College Dublin, Ireland

ABSTRACT

Since the advent of the Internet, educators have realised its potential as a medium for teaching. The term e-learning has been introduced to describe this Internet-based education. Although e-learning applications are popular, much research is now underway to improve the features they provide. For example, the addition of synchronous communication methods and multimedia is being studied. With the introduction of wireless networks, mobile devices are also being investigated as a medium to present learning content. Currently, the use of 3-dimensional (3D) graphics is being explored for creating virtual learning environments online. Virtual reality (VR) is already being used in multiple disciplines for teaching various tasks. This chapter focuses on describing some VR systems, and also discusses the current state of e-learning on mobile devices. We also present the VR learning environment that we have developed, incorporating many of the techniques mentioned above for both desktop and mobile devices.

INSIDE CHAPTER

E-learning has become an established medium for delivering online courses. Its popularity is mainly due to the convenience and flexibility it provides for users, allowing them to learn without time or location restrictions. Many different e-learning systems are currently available, the majority of which are text-based and allow users to contact the course tutor via electronic mail or discussion forums. These courses essentially offer access to a common pool of resources that allow users to gain knowledge and often qualifications. Researchers are now exploring new ways of making the online learning experience more engaging and motivating for students. Multimedia and communication technologies are being added, and together with 3D graphics, are fast emerging as a means of creating an immersive online learning experience. With the advent of mobile technologies, m-learning is showing promise as an accompaniment to online courses, offering the prospect of a modern and pervasive learning environment.

This chapter discusses the benefits 3D environments offer the e-learning community. We outline how this type of system emerged and describe some currently available systems using these new technologies. In particular, we describe in detail our own virtual reality environment for online learning and the features it provides. We discuss the extension of this system to a mobile platform so that users have anytime, anywhere access to course materials. Finally, we put forward some thoughts on future technologies and discuss their possible contribution to the development of a truly ubiquitous and pervasive learning environment.

INTRODUCTION

Distance learning has gone through a number of iterations since its introduction in the 1800s. The notion of distance learning grew mainly out of necessity, and helped to overcome geographical, economical, and cultural barriers that prevented people from partaking in traditional classroom-based education. Over the years a number of distance learning applications have emerged to address these issues. The evolution of such systems can be clearly linked to the technological developments of the time. This chapter focuses on giving a brief overview of the changes in distance learning from its inception to today, before concentrating on the distance learning technologies currently in use. We provide details of how the latest technologies and demand from students have led to the development of 3-dimensional (3D) e-learning systems. We also look to the future, suggesting what the next generation of technology can bring to distance learning. We pay particular attention to the need for ubiquitous and pervasive means of e-learning, and in doing so describe our own system, which uses state of the art technologies to deliver learning material to students both on a desktop computer and while they are on the move.

In the background section, we describe how distance learning has evolved from a simple postal service offered by universities to a sophisticated tool that utilises the convenience of the Internet. As the discussion progresses toward the introduction of 3D graphical environments to distance learning applications, the origins of 3D graphics and their uses are also presented. Multi-user environments for distance education is a major area of research at present, and so the latter part of the section provides a synopsis of the history of multi-user computer applications. We also present a brief discussion on the current uses of mobile technologies, which are now emerging as promising tools for e-learning.

In the main section of this chapter, we describe how recent technological advancements and requirements of students and tutors have led to a new breed of computer-based learning systems utilising the latest 3D graphics and communication tools. We detail a number of such systems outlining their strengths and weaknesses, in particular

Figure 1. Chapter overview

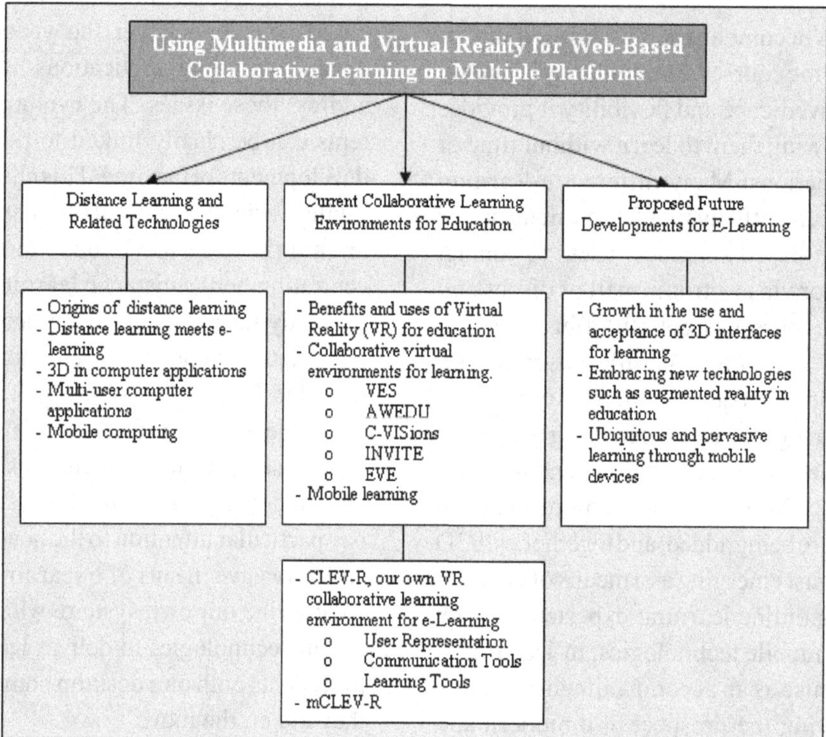

the system we are developing, which attempts to address some of these weaknesses. We describe how it uses the latest technologies to deliver a collaborative multi-user 3D learning system to students at fixed computer terminals and mobile devices. Finally we hypothesise how the current use of augmented reality (AR) technologies can be adapted to form a truly ubiquitous and pervasive learning environment. A summation and discussion of the chapter is provided in the concluding section.

BACKGROUND

This section gives the reader an overview of how distance learning has evolved from its early days as correspondence courses to the modern Internet based learning solution. It also charts the progression of computer-based 3D and multi-user tools, hinting at how they can be combined to form a new type of distance learning system. This new learning paradigm is made all the more powerful when combined with the latest mobile technologies, and a short overview of this emerging technology is provided below. Figure 2 provides an overview of the literature reviewed in this chapter, while Figures 3 and 4 highlight the main points of discussion in each subsection.

A Brief History of Distance Learning

Distance learning is a form of education that has emerged out of necessity. It is not always possible for a student and instructor to be present at the same location at the same time. Distance learning

Figure 2. Background

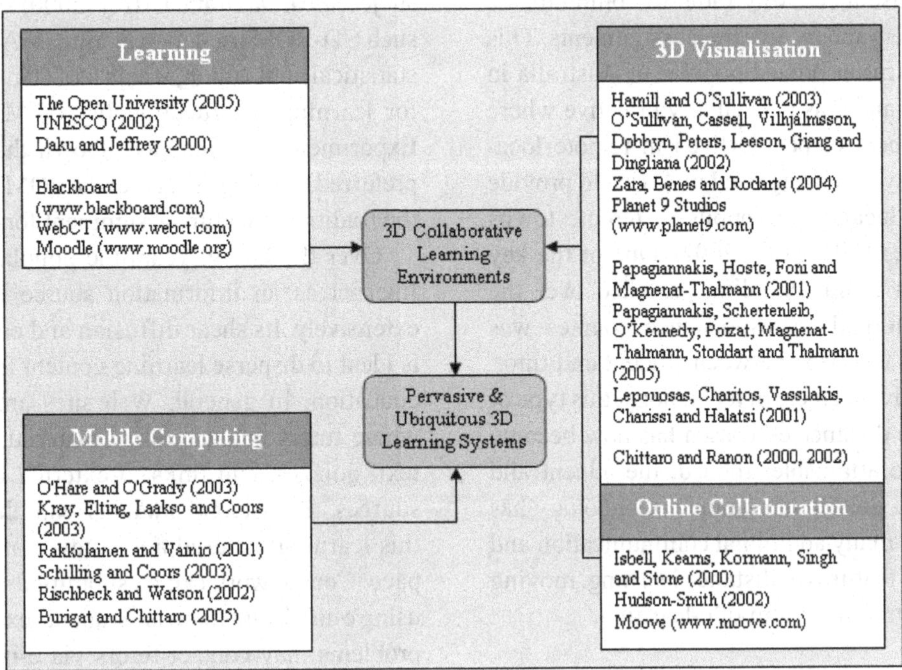

Figure 3. Progression of distance learning

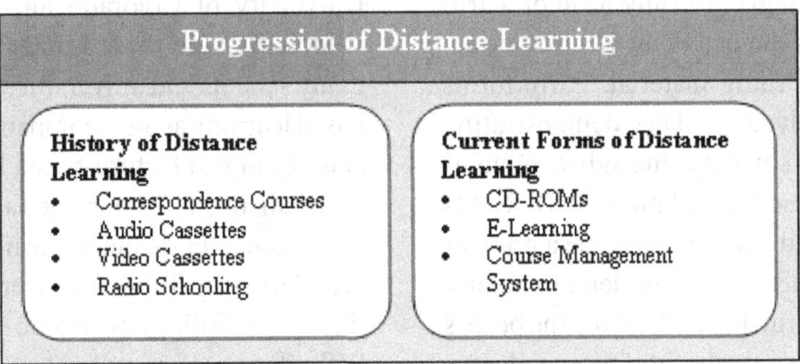

is not a new concept, and has been in use since the 1800s. Today, it can take a wide variety of forms, including correspondence courses, video and radio broadcasts, and e-learning. One of the earliest forms of distance learning was a correspondence course. Traditionally, these courses were a form of home study. Students receive printed or written course material via the postal service, complete assignments, and return them to their tutor for appraisal. These courses were later augmented with different types of media. For example, the Open University (2005) offered lectures on audio and video cassettes in the 1980s.

One major drawback of this form of distance education was the lack of interaction between student and teacher. Radio schooling provided a solution to this issue. Again, radio schooling is a form of home study, mainly used for primary and secondary education; pupils in remote locations can use a two-way radio to communicate with teachers and receive their assignments. This type of learning proved popular in Australia in the 1980s, and was particularly effective where large numbers of people lived in remote locations. Today it is being used in Africa to provide primary education for pupils in remote towns and villages (UNESCO, 2002). One of the key advantages radio schooling provided over the more traditional correspondence courses was the instant feedback between student and tutor. With the advancement of technology, this type of one-to-one distance education has now become much more attainable. Indeed, the advent and widespread growth of computer technology has introduced many additional communication and interactive features to distance learning, moving it forward into the realm of e-learning.

Distance Learning Meets E-Learning

E-learning is a term given to any form of learning which involves the use of an electronic medium to display learning material. Early forms of e-learning involved teachers demonstrating certain lessons to students through computer-based animations and simulations. CD-ROMs were then developed and soon became a popular accompaniment to textbooks. Students could use these CD-ROMs to further understand the book's content, and also as a study aid. Distance learning courses can also utilise this technology to distribute course material. The use of CD-ROMs means that the students' learning experience can be much more interactive and that learning content can be represented in different formats, including sound and video clips. For example, when studying historical events, news footage from the era can be displayed via the CD-ROM, helping to bring the learning material to life. CD- ROMs often provide interactive games (e.g., counting games) for younger students, helping them to improve their numerical skills. Automated quizzes provide instant feedback of a student's knowledge of a subject area. Daku and Jeffrey (2000) describe one such CD-ROM used for teaching, MATHLAB, a statistical application; it acts as a standalone tool for learning the functionality of MATHLAB. Experimental results have shown that students preferred learning using the CD-ROM rather than the traditional lecture/assignment format.

Over the last 10 years the popularity of the Internet as an information source has grown extensively. Its shear diffusion and convenience is ideal to disperse learning content for distance education. In general, Web sites are designed where tutors upload course material, including text, quizzes, and links to external knowledge sources. Registered students can then access this learning material and study it at their own pace. Course work can be submitted to the tutor using e-mail, and likewise students experiencing problems may contact tutors via e-mail. There are numerous examples of this type of distance learning system in use today. For example, the University of Colorado and the University of Illinois provide these kinds of courses. Indeed, many schools and universities now also use Web-based learning as an accompaniment to traditional classroom and lecture-based lessons.

Realising the importance and benefits of using the Internet for distance learning, much research is underway to improve the services and facilities that such learning portals can offer. Initially these Web sites were a mere bank of knowledge, simply providing the course material in HTML (Hyper Text Mark-up Language) format for students to access, read, and learn. Today, they are far more sophisticated. A number of successful companies have emerged which offer online course management tools for tutors to intuitively present course notes, lecture slides, and additional material online. All management, such as access rights and course registration, are provided by these applications. Blackboard (*www.blackboard.com*) is one such course management system, designed to facilitate teachers with the management of their online courses. It has been adopted as the e-learning platform by more than 2200 institutions, including Harvard University, the University of Maine, and the University College Dublin (Wikipedia, 2005). Web Course Tools (WebCT, *www.webct.com*) is another company involved in the provision of e-learning systems. Founded in 1995, it is currently the world's leading provider of e-learning systems, with institutes in over 70 countries relying on them for e-learning software. Like Blackboard, WebCT is an authoring environment for teachers to create online training courses. While these systems tend to be extremely costly, free systems with open source code have also been developed. Moodle (*www.moodle.org*) is one such learning system, which is in widespread use at institutions such as Dublin City University, University of Glasgow, and Alaska Pacific University, and looks like becoming the industry standard. Development of Moodle has been ongoing since 1999, and already it has a large user base. It offers a range of software modules that enable tutors to create online courses. One area that Moodle tries to address is the need for pedagogical support; this aspect is largely neglected in commercially available applications. In particular it promotes the notion of constructionist learning, where a student learns from his or her own experiences, resulting in a student-centred learning environment.

The current state of e-learning, and in particular distance learning, has been outlined above. Following the success of computers as a learning tool, much research is underway to enhance a user's learning environment. In particular, one area that is being researched is the use of 3D graphics in these systems. It is the examination of the use of 3D graphics and multimedia, combined with collaborative tools and mobile technologies within e-learning, that forms the focus of this chapter. The remainder of this section provides a brief description of the use of 3D graphics on computers, from their early days in computer games to its current role in visualisation. We also examine the emergence of 3D graphics on mobile devices such as personal digital assistants (PDAs). This section gives an insight into the previous use of collaboration tools and multi-user interaction on computers before the next section gives a detailed review of learning systems utilising these technologies.

3D, Collaborative, and Mobile Technologies

3D Computer Applications

For some time, 3D graphics have been an established means of entertainment, in particular within computer games. In 1993, ID Software released Doom, a first person shooter computer game. Like its predecessor Wolfenstein, 3D released in 1992, Doom was built using pseudo-3D, where images placed on a 2D plane give the impression of a 3D environment. The immersive game environment included advanced features such as stereo sound and multilevel environments with increased interaction for players. The popularity of these games and the 3D paradigm led to a succession of immersive 3D computer games using this formula, and ultimately led to the worldwide acceptance of this form of immersive environment. As technology improved, the complexity of the graphics used in such computers games increased. Today in games such as Half-Life, developed by Value Software, users take on roles of characters in stories with life-like scenes. Add-ons enable multi-user support for players to interact with each other in the game, although they may be geographically distant.

Another domain where 3D has been used for a long time is modelling; in particular engineering and architectural models can be effectively and efficiently modelled on a computer using 3D graphics. AutoCAD, developed by AutoDesk, is a computer aided drafting software application first developed in 1982 for use by mechanical engineers. It allows both 2D and 3D representation of objects to be rendered and has fast become

Figure 4. 3D, collaborative, and mobile technologies

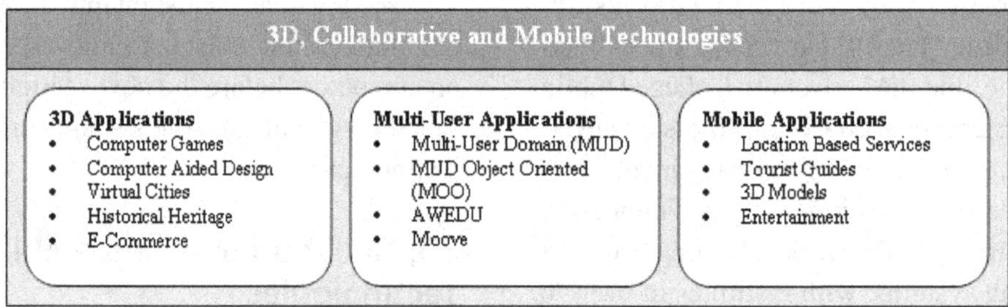

the industry standard. This form of modelling objects enables designers and customers to see how objects will look before they are built. Today property developers often produce 3D Virtual Reality (VR) models of houses in order to entice prospective buyers. This can be taken one step further as developers produce models of how new builds will affect the aesthetics of an area. Another area of interest in the research arena is that of modelling cities. Hamill and O'Sullivan (2003) describe their efforts in producing a large-scale simulation of Dublin City. The goal of their research is to allow users to navigate freely around the streets of Dublin. The city can be used as a test-bed for related work, such as simulating crowds in virtual environments (O'Sullivan, Cassell, Vilhjálmsson, Dobbyn, Peters, Leeson, et al, 2002). Zara, Benes, and Rodarte (2004) have produced a model of the old Mexican city of Campeche. This Internet-based application acts as a tourist aid and promotes the area as a tourist attraction. The area of urban modelling has much commercial interest. Planet 9 Studios (*www.planet9.com*), based in San Francisco and set up in the early 1990s, produces accurate and intricate 3D urban models for use in such diverse activities as homeland defence, military training, and tourism. It is tourism that has long been a driving force behind much of the development of the VR cities and has also led to a number of similar applications aimed at visitors and tourists. MIRALabs in Geneva have been investigating the area of virtual heritage. Much of this research focuses on enabling realistic models of historical sites to be created efficiently and in a means suitable for use on basic machines (Papagiannakis, Hoste, Foni, & Magnenat-Thalmann, 2001). Today, the work of MIRALab in the field of historical reconstructions involves the use of mixed realities; that is, augmenting real-world sites with VR 3D models of people and artefacts that would have once been there (Papagiannakis, Schertenleib, O'Kennedy, Poizat, Magnenat-Thalmann, Stoddart, et al, 2005). The benefits of using VR to host exhibitions in museums are outlined by Lepoursas, Charitos, Vassilakis, Charissi, and Halatsi (2001), where details on designing, such an exhibition, are also provided.

Several of the projects mentioned above use special features to allow users to interact with the environment. Often the environment acts as a 3D-Graphical User Interface (GUI) to access underlying information. E-commerce or purchasing products and services using Web sites on the Internet have long been popular. The number of people buying through this medium has increased dramatically over the last five years. According to Johnson, Delhagen, and Yuen (2003), online retail in the United States alone will have reached $229.9 billion by 2008, and so this is a natural area for researchers to investigate. While research has contributed to many improvements in this form of shopping, one area that is still emerging is the use of a 3D interface to browse for goods. Chittaro and Ranon (2002) have designed a virtual environment mimicking a traditional supermarket, where virtual products are placed on virtual shelves. Users navigate the store, selecting items they wish to purchase. They argue that this is a more natural way for consumers to shop online because it is more familiar to shoppers compared to lists of available items. These 3D department stores can be tailored and personalised to an individual user (Chittaro & Ranon, 2000). This can involve personalising the look and feel of the environment and user profiling to position relevant items in prominent positions. The extension of this 3D store paradigm to a multi-user platform is also discussed and proposed, where a number of shoppers are present in the one store. This, however, has drawbacks and provides difficultly in adapting the store for individuals. The next section provides a synopsis of the origins of multi-user computer applications and provides some details of their current uses.

Multi-User Applications

One of the earliest forms of multi-user interactivity using computers took the form of multi-user domains, known as MUDs. MUDs first appeared in 1978, and being primarily used for computer gaming purposes, quickly became popular. In a MUD, a text-based description of an environment is provided, with each user taking on the role of a character in that environment. Interaction with the system and with other users is achieved by typing commands in a natural language. Usually a fantasy game featuring goblins and other creatures, the purpose was to navigate through the virtual environment, killing as many demons as possible. While initially developed for entertainment, people saw the possibility of using this technology for other purposes, notably as a form of distance learning and as a means of virtual conferences. This move away from the use of MUDs for gaming led to the developments of a MOO (MUD Object Orientated) at the University of Waterloo in 1990. Again, MOO systems are text-based virtual environments, which were initially an academic form of a MUD. Isbell, Kearns, Kormann, Singh, and Stone (2000) discuss LambdaMoo, one of the longest running MOOs, created by Pavel Curtis in 1990. Today, it offers a social setting for connected users to engage in social interaction with similar functionality to that found in a chat room or online communities.

Improvements in technologies, along with increases in Internet connection speeds, have enabled a move away from the traditional text-based environments to more graphical-based communities. These communities, such as Active Worlds (Hudson-Smith, 2002), offer the same interaction as chat rooms. However, the rooms are designed as physical spaces complete with scenery and furniture. Each user is shown on-screen in the form of an avatar, a graphical representation visible to other users. A further extension of this type of environment is seen in the 3D online world of Moove (*www.moove.com*). Here, users maintain their own rooms in the 3D environment, which they can decorate to their own tastes and use to host chat sessions. Voice and video chat can also be used in many of the modern online 3D communities. In recent times, this type of 3D environment has been used for education, and this will be discussed later in this chapter.

Mobile Applications

In recent years, the use of mobile devices such as PDAs and cell phones has become prevalent, and this has led to a lot of research into providing applications on these devices. The widespread introduction of wireless networks has increased the use of these devices dramatically, and has helped fuel research in this area. People can now browse the Internet, send electronic mails (e-mails) and access their personal files while on the move. Many different applications have been developed for this mobile platform, the most popular of which utilise a global positioning system (GPS). These applications use a system of satellites and receiving devices to compute positions on the Earth, and therefore enable people to gain information relative to their position in the world. They are thus used mainly in providing location-based information to users, and in particular many tourist applications have been developed to help people find their way around foreign cities. For example, O'Hare and O'Grady (2003) have developed a context-aware tourist guide, which tracks a user's position and displays multimedia presentations for different attractions as the user approaches them. Their system uses images, videos, sound, and text to give the tourist information about the attraction. Kray, Elting, Laakso, and Coors (2003) developed an application to provide boat tourists with route instructions and information on services nearby.

A recent development in mobile technologies is the use of 3D graphics on these devices. Many large-scale 3D models have been successfully developed for use on laptop computers, but the challenge now is to extend these to smaller platforms, such as PDAs and even mobile phones. Rakkolainen and Vainio (2001) developed a Web-based 3D city model of Tampere and connected it to a database of relational information so that users can query the system about services available in the city. They customised it for mobile users by integrating a GPS receiver and have developed a fully working version for laptops. However, their 3D model is much too large to run on smaller devices such as PDAs, so they use only images and Web pages for these devices. Schilling and Coors (2003) have developed a system that provides a 3D map to help present route instructions to mobile users. In their model, landmarks and buildings of importance are visualised in detail through the use of textures, while less important buildings are rendered in grey. A user trial was carried out on a laptop running a mobile phone emulator. Results proved positive, with most users stating they would prefer to use the 3D maps than 2D paper maps and guidebooks. However, users did suggest that the 3D model should be more detailed and more realistic.

The major problem for extending these models to smaller mobile devices is their size in relation to processing power available, together with the users' desires for more detail and realism. Many researchers are exploring ways to achieve this using various culling techniques, parallelism, and information filtering (Burigat & Chittaro, 2005; Rischbeck & Watson, 2002). Smaller 3D models can, however, be displayed on smaller devices and are used in a variety of games on handheld devices and mobile phones, providing entertainment for their user. ParallelGraphics, a world leader in the provision of Web3D graphics solutions, describe uses of 3D for mobile devices, such as sales and marketing, real estate, and field maintenance.

The technologies presented in this section have been widely accepted by developers and computer users. As the next section shows, they have recently received attention from the educational research community. They show promise as a means of presenting learning material to students in an engaging and motivating way. A number of such systems using these technologies are presented in the following section before we discuss our own learning system, CLEV-R, which provides solutions to some of the issues that existing learning systems fail to address. In particular, the need for a range of communication and collaborative tools for both learning and socialising is dealt with. Also presented is a pervasive ubiquitous learning environment we developed for use on mobile devices as an accompaniment to the desktop system.

3D AND COLLABORATIVE VIRTUAL ENVIRONMENTS FOR E-LEARNING AND M-LEARNING

This section details the use of 3D as a learning aid. Firstly, we consider its use as a visualisation tool, and then discuss how multi-user technologies are being combined with 3D graphics to create effective online learning environments. We also discuss some current research into the provision of learning tools on mobile devices. Figure 5 provides an overview of the topics presented below.

3D Learning Tools

In addition to the uses of virtual reality (VR) and 3D graphics discussed in the previous section, these techniques have also been extended in various ways for use in education. The ability of these tools to model real-world objects and visualise complex data makes them an ideal learning tool. Users can explore these objects, interact with them, and discover their various features. Furthermore, the visualisation of complex data can greatly aid a person's comprehension of it. Thus, these models

Figure 5. 3D and collaborative virtual environments for e-learning and m-learning

3D and Collaborative Virtual Environments for E-Learning and M-Learning

3D Learning Tools	Collaborative 3D Learning Environments
Virtual Laboratories: *Casher, Leach, Page & Rzepa (1998)* Introduction to laboratory equipment, displays complex chemical structures *Dalgarno (2002)* Introduce undergraduate students to laboratory procedures.	**VES** *Bouras, Philopoulos & Tsiatsos (2001)* Interactive thematic rooms for teaching school children. **AWEDU** *Dickey (2003)* Web-based system where tutors can build an environment based on their requirements.
Medical Demonstrations: *Ryan, O'Sullivan, Bell & Mooney (2004)* Teaching medical students through organ modelling. *Raghupathiy, Grisoniz, Faurey, Marchalz, Cainy & Chaillouz (2004)* Preparing medical students to perform surgery.	**C-VISions** *Chee & Hooi (2002)* Interactive environment for teaching science and allowing students to conduct experiments **INVITE** *Bouras, Triantafiliou & Tsiatsos (2001)* Supports collaborative on the job training for staff who may be geographically distant
Embodied Agents: *Nijholt (2000)* Demonstrate solving a problem for example, the Towers of Hanoi problem. *Rickel & Johnson (1997)* Demonstrate the use of a specific piece of equipment	**EVE** *Bouras & Tsiatsos (2006)* Explores the used of shared training spaces for school children

Mobile Learning Environments

European m-Learning Projects: *MOBIlearn* Research pedagogy in mobile learning environments *M-learning* Deliver learning content to young adults and particularly those who do not enjoy traditional education	**Games:** *Ketamo (2002)* Teaches geometry to chidren in kindergarten who are experiencing difficulty with it *Göth, Hass & Schwabe (2004)* location-based game to help new students become familiar with the university *Luchini, Quintana & Soloway (2003)* Pocket PiCoMap – interactive tool that helps students to build concept maps
3D Models: *Lipman (2002)* Visualisation of structural steelwork models on construction sites *Zimmerman, Barnes & Leventhal (2003)* Teaching mobile users the art of origami	

provide users with an intuitive way to learn about natural objects by presenting them in a visually appealing way. As such, many 3D resources for education have been developed, both for online and individual applications.

Scientific and engineering visualisations use VR to represent complex chemical structures and to present experimental data in a more visual manner in order to gain a better understanding of the results. Casher, Leach, Page, and Rzepa (1998) describe the use of VR for chemical modelling, and outline the advantages that animation can bring to these models. They also describe how a virtual laboratory can introduce students to various laboratory instruments. In addition, Dalgarno (2002) has developed a virtual chemistry laboratory that allows undergraduate students to become familiar with the layout of the labs, and also to learn about procedures to follow while in the laboratory. VR has more recently been introduced in the field of medical training. Its use varies from modelling different organs and allowing students to interact with them freely to developing training application for specific procedures. Examples include Raghupathiy, Grisoniz, Faurey, Marchalz, Caniy, and Chaillouz (2004), who developed a training application for the removal of colon cancer, and Ryan, O'Sullivan, Bell, and Mooney (2004), who explore the use of VR for teaching electrocardiography. The major advantage of using VR in medicine is that students can repeatedly explore the structures of interest and can interactively view and manipulate them. Real training cases can be hard to come by, and so this extra practice and experience can be invaluable. Also, patients are not put at risk by having inexperienced students carry out procedures on them.

3D models can also be particularly useful in teaching younger students. Many games have been developed using 3D images that the user must interact with in order to learn a certain lesson. Interactive models increase a user's interest and make learning more fun. 3D animations can be used to teach students different procedures and mechanisms for carrying out specific tasks. Some researchers have combined the benefits of 3D and software agent technologies to provide intelligent models to teach certain tasks. For example, Jacob is an intelligent agent in a VR environment that guides the user through the steps involved in solving the towers of Hanoi problem, as described by Nijholt (2000). By following the directions of Jacob, the users learn how to solve the problem themselves. Likewise, STEVE, described by Rickel and Johnson (1997, 1999), is an intelligent agent that has been developed for use in naval training to show individuals or groups of students how to operate and maintain complex equipment. STEVE can demonstrate certain tasks and then observe while users carry out these tasks, correcting them when mistakes are made.

Collaborative 3D Learning Environments

VR also allows for the development of complete virtual environments that users can "enter" and navigate through as if it was a real environment. The most immersive of these environments require the user to wear a head mounted display and tracking gloves, while other VR environments are displayed on desktop computers, where users interact through the mouse and keyboard. As shown in the previous section, virtual environments like these have evolved from computer games, but are fast emerging in other areas such as e-commerce, chat-rooms, and indeed education. E-learning in particular is an ideal target for the development of an immersive VR environment. Here an entire VR environment is designed where all the learning takes place. This kind of system represents a shift in e-learning from the conventional text-based online learning environment to a more immersive and intuitive one. Since VR is a computer simulation of a natural environment, interaction with a 3D environment is much more intuitive than browsing through 2D Web pages looking for information. These environments tend to be multi-user, exploiting the notion of collaborative learning where students learn together. The benefits of collaborative learning have been researched extensively and are outlined in Laister and Kober (2002) and Redfern and Naughton (2002). The main advantage of this type of learning is that users no longer feel alone or isolated. This feeling of isolation can be particularly prevalent in online learning, where students do not attend actual classes or lectures. Thus, multi-user learning environments have proven very popular for online learning. The VES, AWEDU, C-VISions, EVE, and INVITE systems all concentrate on developing collaborative learning environments using VR to further immerse students in their learning. The following paragraphs outline the main features of these systems before we discuss our own research and what it has to offer.

In 1998, Bouras, Fotakis, Kapoulas, Koubek, Mayer, and Rehatscheck (1999) began research on virtual European schools (VES), the goal of which was to introduce computers to secondary school students and encourage teachers to use computers in the classroom. VES uses 3D to provide a desktop immersive environment. A different room in the 3D environment is used for each school subject, and these themed rooms provide information about the specific subject in the form of slide shows and animations, as well as links to external sources of information. The VES project was carried out in conjunction with book publishers, and these publishing houses provided much of the content that is displayed in the environment. VES is an example of a multi-user distributed virtual environment (mDVE). In an mDVE, more than one person can access the environment at the same time, and users are aware of one another. In the VES environment users can "talk" to each other using text chat facilities. The evaluation of VES took the form of questionnaires, which students and teachers completed. The results, which are presented in (Bouras, Philopoulos, & Tsiatsos, 2001) show that navigation in the 3D environment was difficult, the user interface was old fashioned, and there was not enough content to keep students amused and entertained. These points were taken on board and the system was improved. When launched, VES was used in 4 countries and had the cooperation of more that 20 publishers.

The Active Worlds Universe, a very popular and powerful Web-based VR experience, is a community of thousands of users that chat and build 3D VR environments in a vast virtual space. As discussed earlier, it provides thousands of unique worlds for shopping, chatting, and playing games. In 1999, an educational community known as the Active Worlds Educational Universe (AWEDU) was developed (Dickey, 2003). This is a unique educational community that makes the Active Worlds technology available to educational institutions. Through this community, educators can build their own educational environment using a library of customisable objects, and can then place relevant learning material in their environment. Through these environments, users are able to explore new concepts and learning theories and can communicate using text-chat. Users are represented in the environment by avatars which help them feel better immersed in the educational environment. Students from all over the world can be connected through this system, and it therefore aids cultural sharing and social learning. The AWEDU environment is extremely versatile and may be used for a number of types of learning. Dickey (2003) presents the use of the environment as a form of distance education within the university. Riedl, Barrett, Rowe, Smith and Vinson, (2000) provide a description of a class held within the Active Worlds environment. The course was designed for training teachers on the integration of technology into the classroom. Nine students took part in the class; their actions and group discussions were recorded during their online sessions and, along with results from questionnaires, are presented in the paper. While the majority of students were pleased with the freedom the virtual environment offered, not all adapted to this new form of learning. The evaluation discovered that one of the major benefits of this type of learning was that students were aware of the presence of others in the shared environment and this interaction with others kept students interested and motivated.

C-VISions was launched in 2000, and is a collaborative virtual learning environment that concentrates on supporting science learning. The system presents learning stimuli that help school children understand fundamental concepts from chemistry, biology and physics. C-VISions encourages active learners; students can run science experiments in the virtual world and view the outcomes as they change simulation parameters. Chee and Hooi (2002) describe their physics environment and in particular the Billiard World, a simulation to help students learn about mass, velocity, acceleration, conservation of momentum, friction, and the coefficient of restitution. This world contains a billiard table with two balls and a cue stick. Users can interact with a number of "live" objects that are provided within the world. For example, the cue stick can be aimed at a ball and then used to strike it. Students can replay the most recent simulation and can view the plotting of graphs of that event synchronously. This helps the students see the relation between their action and how it is plotted on a graph. It therefore helps them to understand the graph representations. Users can navigate around the world and change their viewpoints using buttons provided. The system is multi-user, and so events happening in one user's environment are propagated to all other connected users. Users may share video resources, and shared electronic whiteboards are also provided. The system provides a Social World where students can mingle and student-student communication is supported through text and audio chat. Chee (2001) describes a preliminary evaluation of the first prototype of this system. The study revealed that all students found the system "an enjoyable way to learn" and each felt they gained a better sense of understanding about the subject matter. Some problems using the collaboration tools were highlighted. For example, students found it difficult to work together on group tasks. This was put down to inexperience using the tools. While this study was small, involving only three students, the results proved encouraging that this type of 3D environment has something to offer students.

In April 2000, a consortium of companies and institutions began research into the design and development of a multi-user 3D collaborative environment for training. The goal of the environment was to support group learning, in particular on-the-job training, without the need for all those involved to be in the same location at the same time. Moving away from the traditional videoconferences, this system known as INVITE, the Intelligent Distributed Virtual Training Environment, had a fundamental objective of making people feel that they are working as a group rather than alone in front of a computer. The technologies required for such a system are described by Bouras, Triantafillou, and Tsiatsos (2001), along with implementation issues of the multi-user architecture. The project focuses on the importance of a social presence and the general sense of belonging within a learning environment, presenting the notion of photo-realistic avatars as a way to achieve this. The system design allows synchronous viewing of e-learning content within the 3D environment through a presentation table. Users can see pictures, presentations, 3D objects and prerecorded videos simultaneously, and collaboration is provided through application sharing. An initial prototype of the system was developed, and a first evaluation showed that INVITE could be a powerful tool for collaborative learning with test-users enjoying learning in the virtual environment. The INVITE project terminated prematurely, and so the main contribution it made to the area of virtual learning environments was a detailed system specification and outline of features that should be included in such a system.

The research group from the University of Patras in Greece who were involved in the development on the INVITE Project continued their work, leading to the development of EVE (Educational Virtual Environments). Like INVITE, EVE is a Web-based, multi-user environment that explores the use of shared virtual spaces for training. Their system addresses two main challenges. The first was a technological challenge to develop a learning environment that resembles the real world and that provides additional functionality to enhance the users' experience. Secondly, the pedagogical challenge of making an educational model that contributes in the most efficient way to the distribution of knowledge. EVE is organized into two types of place for each user, their personal desk space and the training area. The personal desk refers to a 2D place where all the asynchronous features of the system relating to that user can be accessed. Thus a user can access course and user information, upload and download files, view and reply to personal messages, and manage their profile. The training area is the virtual classroom where learning takes place, and consists of a presentation table, a whiteboard, and avatar representations for all connected students and a tutor. Features such as application sharing, brainstorming, and text and audio communication are also supported. The tutor has control over the course, learning material, and students. They decide what course content is displayed on the presentation board and when students may ask questions, and can also assign students to breakout session rooms during an e-learning class and monitor their text chat sessions. An evaluation of the system, provided by Bouras and Tsiatsos (2006), shows that test-users found the system interesting and promising for e-learning. The test users were chosen from a number of Greek schools and a teacher from each selected school also evaluated the system. The users' social presence and the intuitive virtual environment were highlighted as advantages of the system. Collaboration tools such as audio and text communication, application sharing, and visualisation on the presentation table also proved popular. Overall the feedback was positive, with both students and teachers seeing the appeal and usefulness of the 3D paradigm. Feedback was also taken from students about possible improvements that could be made to the system. The introduction of facial expressions, along with tool tips for assisting during navigation, are discussed. The future work of the EVE project therefore involves the implementation of these changes along with the addition of new rooms to the environment to support smaller groups for project work.

Mobile Learning Environments

The use of mobile devices for learning, termed m-learning, has been another area of interest for researchers of late. Their portable nature makes them convenient for many people to use while on the move. Therefore, the extension of e-learning to these devices seems a natural progression. While laptop computers are widely popular and capable of delivering large amounts of information efficiently, smaller mobile devices, such as PDAs, also show promise for learning. Oliver and Wright (2003) outline the main advantages of PDAs as their light weight and portability, their ease of use, and their low cost. Also, most are wireless enabled. Csete, Wong, and Vogel (2004) accredit the functionality provided on these devices as a reason for their growing popularity. Most mobile devices now include an address book, calendar, to-do list, and memo pad. Wireless enabled devices provide e-mail and Web browsing, and most support flash, audio, and movie files. Indeed, their functionality is continually increasing as companies are now developing versions of their software for these devices. Disadvantages of these devices, such as small screen size and limited processor power and memory, mean that applications for them must be lightweight and content needs to be adapted for this new platform. These drawbacks are, however, outweighed by their inexpensive and convenient nature, which makes them the ideal target for a learning application. The major advantage this mobile platform brings to e-learning is that students have "anytime-anywhere" access to course material.

Much research is now being carried out into providing services on these mobile devices for learning. The MOBIlearn project is a worldwide European-led research and development project exploring learning through a mobile environment (*www.mobilearn.org*). This project concentrates on creating pedagogy for learning in these environments, and looks at the adaptation of existing e-learning content for mobile devices. Their main objective is to enable content delivery for adult learning and professional development through collaborative spaces, context awareness, and adaptive human interfaces. M-learning is another European research and development programme that aims to deliver learning content to young adults who are no longer taking part in education or training (*www.m-learning.org*). In particular, they target those who are unemployed or homeless and those who do not enjoy traditional education. To engage the user in learning, themes of interest to young adults are used and are presented in the form of interactive quizzes and games. Modules include activities designed to develop aspects of literacy and numeracy. They have developed a number of learning tools ranging from interactive quizzes for teaching languages and driver theory test to giving the learners access to online Web page building and community tools.

Many researchers see games and interactive challenges as the way forward into mobile learning. Ketamo (2002) has designed a game for handheld devices that teaches geometry to 6-year-old kindergarten kids. The system proved effective and in particular helped low-skilled students understand geometry better. Göth, Hass, and Schwabe (2004) have developed a location-based game to help new university students become familiar with the university and its surroundings. Students are grouped into teams and have to carry out a number of tasks at certain locations on the campus. Pocket PiCoMap, as described in Luchini, Quintana, and Soloway (2003), is another interactive tool for mobile learning which helps students build concept maps (i.e., graphical representations of complex ideas and the relationships between them). Students draw a link between two concepts on their map and can then add a descriptive label to this linking edge. An English sentence describing the visual representation is dynamically created and displayed, thus helping the students understand how the relationship between the concepts is interpreted.

Some applications using 3D graphics on mobile devices are now also being developed offering a wide range of services to their users. For example, Lipman (2002) explored the use of 3D models on mobile devices for the visualisation of structural steelwork models on construction sites. Zimmerman, Barnes, and Leventhal (2003) designed an effective system for teaching mobile users the art of origami. A 3D model is provided showing the different steps involved in creating a particular shape. The user follows a set of instructions and uses the 3D model as a visual aid to gain a better understanding of the action they are to perform. This rendering of 3D graphics on mobile devices is an area of interest to us, and together with the potential of these devices to provide tools for collaboration, we feel a mobile learning system with these technologies could be very effective.

Above, we have outlined ways in which 3D graphics have been used for learning. Initially, 3D was used as a means of training within specific fields. For example, it proved popular for teaching medical students to perform surgery. More recently, 3D graphics have been amalgamated with multi-user technologies to form complete learning environments. A number of projects using this technology have been identified and discussed above. Within these environments, students take on the role of a character and navigate through a virtual on-screen location to access course notes and interact with each other. Each of the systems described have their own merits and limitations. Building on the strengths of the systems above and proposing a solution to their limitations, we have developed a system that recognises the importance of social learning as part of an individual's education. This aspect was not fully addressed by other systems. Many of the traditional text-based e-learning systems discussed previously are aimed at third level students, providing diploma and degree qualifications. To date, no collaborative VR learning environment has been developed to solely cater to this particular market. Our research investigates the benefits that a 3D learning environment can bring to this domain. As the prevalence of mobile devices increases, their use as a learning tool is now being researched. Above, we have presented some currently available m-learning systems, and we too are exploring this area. In the next section we discuss our research, as we develop both a desktop 3D collaborative learning environment and a mobile application to supplement this. In particular, our system examines the use of 3D graphics in conjunction with various collaborative tools to act as a medium for learning.

COLLABORATIVE LEARNING ENVIRONMENT WITH VIRTUAL REALITY (CLEV-R)

The system which we are developing is entitled collaborative learning environment with virtual reality (CLEV-R) and addresses problems with current e-learning systems. The main objectives of the research underlying the development of CLEV-R include:

- Exploring the use of a 3D multi-user environment for e-learning, both to supplement traditional learning and for use in distance education.
- Supporting both social interaction and collaboration among system users.
- Developing the system so that it is cost-effective and requires minimal software on the client side.
- Exploring the extension of 3D interfaces for learning to mobile devices.
- Evaluating the resulting systems in terms of usability and effectiveness as a learning solution.

The following scenario indicates some issues faced by people wishing to take part in online courses. It highlights how a system like CLEV-R can address many of the concerns which people experience when using distance learning tools online.

Sample Scenario

Mary has been working for several years as an administrator in a legal firm. She wishes to further her career by obtaining a professional qualification. As she is working full time, she is unable to attend a university. Her employer suggests that she takes an online course. She has reservations about doing this because she knows of others who have found it difficult to complete courses online. They found them to be challenging; the lack of contact with others was isolating and it was difficult to maintain motivation for the duration of the course. Her friend Rachel recommends CLEV-R, an e-learning system that she found very convenient. She completed a business course using this system and said it was an enjoyable way to learn. Rachel attended university once a month; however, the rest of the course took place in a 3D virtual environment online. CLEV-R is also available on mobile devices and so she often used her PDA to access course content and communication tools while on the move. She particularly liked the collaborative aspects of CLEV-R and used them for both learning and socialising with others. Mary is convinced that this is an ideal solution for her learning needs.

The problem that Mary faced is a typical one, encountered by many people wishing to take up online courses. The social isolation, ennui, and lack of support within e-learning applications are all issues which we are addressing through the development of an online collaborative learning environment that uses 3D graphics and VR to engage and motivate the user. Our VR environment for e-learning concentrates on providing collaborative tools so students can work, learn, and socialise together (Monahan, McArdle, Bertolotto, & Mangina, 2005). Mimicking a real university, it consists of a central common area surrounded by lecture rooms, meeting rooms, and social rooms. Learning materials are presented within the environment through various multimedia techniques and communication controls, such as text and audio chat, allow students and tutors to converse easily (Monahan, McArdle, & Bertolotto, 2005). The following paragraphs outline some of the most important features of the system and explain their use in an e-learning application.

User Representation

One of the main disadvantages people see with existing e-learning applications is the lack of social presence and the feeling of isolation that can be experienced while partaking in an online course. Thus, one of the primary objectives of our environment is to remove this sense of loneliness and create a greater sense of community within each online course. The basis for our online collaborative learning environment is to facilitate multi-user support, allowing many users to be present and navigate around the same environment simultaneously. It is also vitally important that users of the environment are aware of all other connected users at any one point in time. Users are represented within the system by avatars. Upon registering for a course, each student and tutor is required to select a character to represent him or her in the VR environment. This 3D character is the user's on-screen persona for the duration of a course. In order to create an effective learning community, it is imperative that these avatars are distinctive for each individual user. In this way, avatar representations allow users of the system to recognize others, and hence feel a social presence in the learning environment. Applying different clothing or hairstyles to each character can create unique avatars.

Communication Tools

In order to support collaboration, communication technologies are imperative. In fact, it is the lack of support for real-time communication that we feel is a major drawback in current e-learning systems. In any learning scenario, it is imperative that students have a lot of communication with course tutors and also with their fellow students. Much research has been carried out to determine the importance of communication in learning, and it been has shown that students often learn from each other in informal chats as well as from lecture content (Redfern et al., 2002; Laister et al., 2002). Communicating with others who are partaking in the same course makes students feel more involved in the learning environment and removes any sense of isolation that may occur in single-user learning environments. As such, a major aspect of CLEV-R is the provision of multiple communication methods. The communication controls for CLEV-R are provided in a graphical user interface (GUI), as shown in Figure 6. Text and audio chat communication is supported. Students can send both public and private messages via text-chat and can broadcast audio streams into specific areas of the VR environment. Also users may broadcast Web-cams into the 3D environment and so have real-time face-to-face conversations with other connected users. The avatars in our system are enabled with gesture animations, which are a further form of communication. For example, avatars can raise their hand if they wish to ask a question and can

Figure 6. The communication controls of CLEV-R

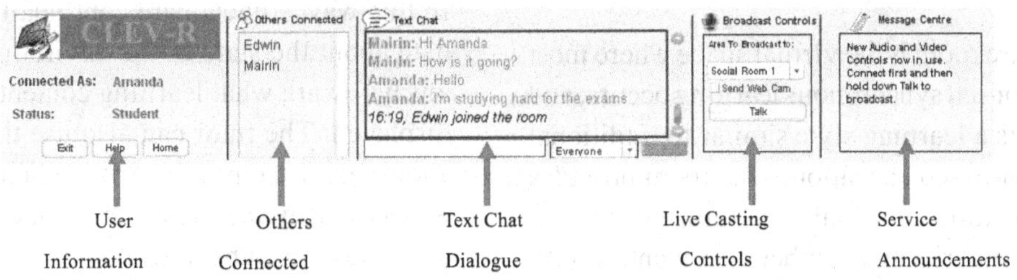

User Information
Others Connected
Text Chat Dialogue
Live Casting Controls
Service Announcements

Figure 7. Virtual university structure within CLEV-R

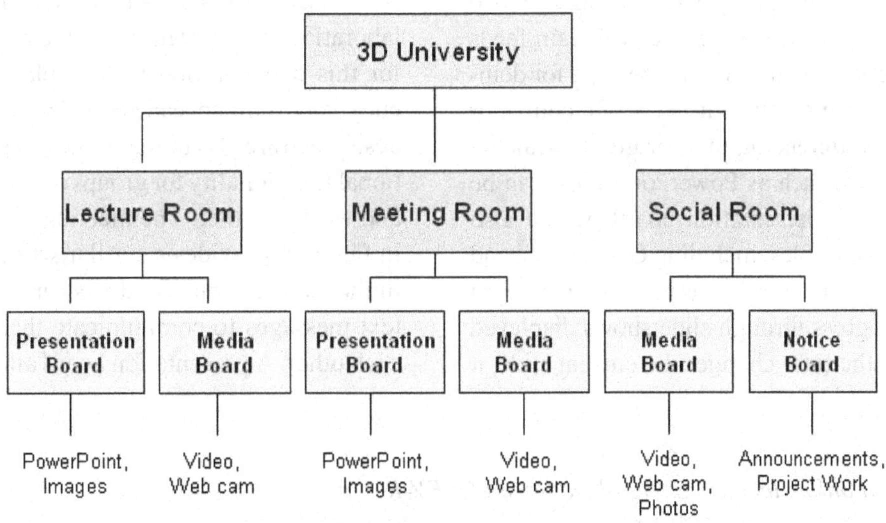

also nod or shake their head to show their level of understanding of a certain topic. Of course users can also communicate asynchronously with others via e-mail.

Interactive Tools

Another common problem with Web-based learning environments is that the learning content is primarily presented through various forms of text, including word files, PDF documents, HTML, and so forth. While these may be effective for presenting the learning material, they do not portray course content in a motivating or engaging way for the students. Thus, within the development of CLEV-R, we provide different multimedia methods for presenting course content within the learning environment. The system supports features such as PowerPoint slides, movies, audio, animations, and images. Rather than downloading these media files to the students' own PC, they can be experienced from within the virtual environment in real-time with other students. Many different features are available within the various virtual rooms of CLEV-R to support these file types. These are outlined in Figure 7, and the remainder of this section describes the different areas in our virtual university and the support for learning that each provides.

Lecture Room

The lecture room is the virtual space where most of the tutor-led synchronous learning occurs, and it supports a learning style similar to traditional classroom-based education. This room provides several features to enable a tutor to present learning material to a number of students simultaneously. An example of an online lecture can be seen in Figure 8. A media board is provided, where the lecturer can upload both audio and video files. Where appropriate, the lecturer also has the option of streaming live Web-cam feeds into the lecture room. This can be used for demonstrating more practical aspects of a course or as a video conferencing tool for guest speakers. Lecture slides, such as PowerPoint files, can be displayed on a presentation board, which also supports images files, including GIFs, JPGs, and PNGs. The tutor controls this presentation board and can progress through slide shows displayed here. Once the tutor changes the current slide, it is changed in the worlds of all connected students. In this way, students are continually kept up-to date about the state of the environment and are always aware what learning content is currently displayed. The tutor can also use the streaming audio facility to provide live audio commentary to accompany the presentation and address any questions raised by students.

Meeting Rooms

As one of the main focuses of CLEV-R is collaboration, it is very important to provide an area for this collaboration to take place. While the entire environment can be used for collaboration, designated areas of the environment provide additional functionality for groups of students to meet and work together. The meeting room as shown in Figure 9 provides a similar set of tools found in the lecture room. Students can use audio and text messages to communicate their ideas with each other. A presentation board allows students

Figure 8. An online lecture taking place within CLEV-R

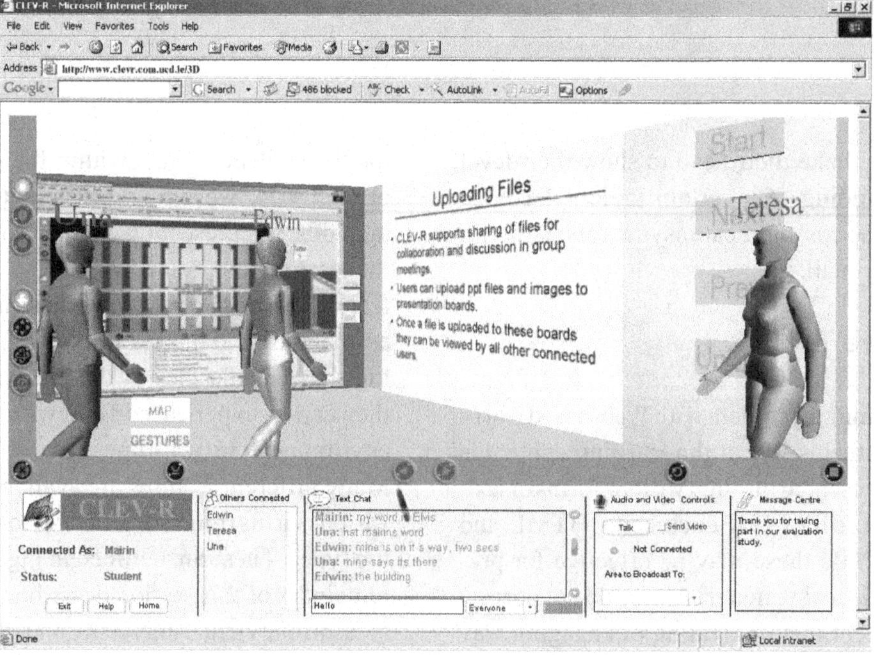

to upload their own material to the room for discussion. Each student can bring slideshows, animations, and media clips for discussion and viewing by the entire group. Live video can also be streamed into this room via a student's Web-cam to aid with the discussion.

Social Rooms

Social interaction is a key component of CLEV-R, and therefore nominated areas of the 3D university have been specifically created for users to mingle and partake in informal conversation with each other. While students can use these areas to discuss the course they are attending, they can also use them for social purposes. In a similar way to the meeting rooms, small numbers of students can gather together to share their experiences and stories as well as photos, pictures, and movies. Social rooms exist where a media board is available for students to upload images, videos, and Web-cam broadcasts. A centrally located lobby also serves as an informal setting, where students can chat and build rapports with others. Here users can talk informally about the course material. Students can display their project work on special notice boards provided; others can then peruse these posters at their own pace and in their own time. Students can also place advertisements for upcoming events and other general notices in this common area.

Library

As CLEV-R is primarily a learning environment, it provides easy access to learning material through a library. The library contains a bookcase and a number of desks. Lecture notes, which have been uploaded to the lecture room by the tutor, are automatically represented in the form of a book in the bookcase. When a student clicks on one of the books, the lecture notes associated with that book are displayed on a desk in the library. The student can then peruse the notes in situ within

Figure 9. Media board displaying a video within CLEV-R

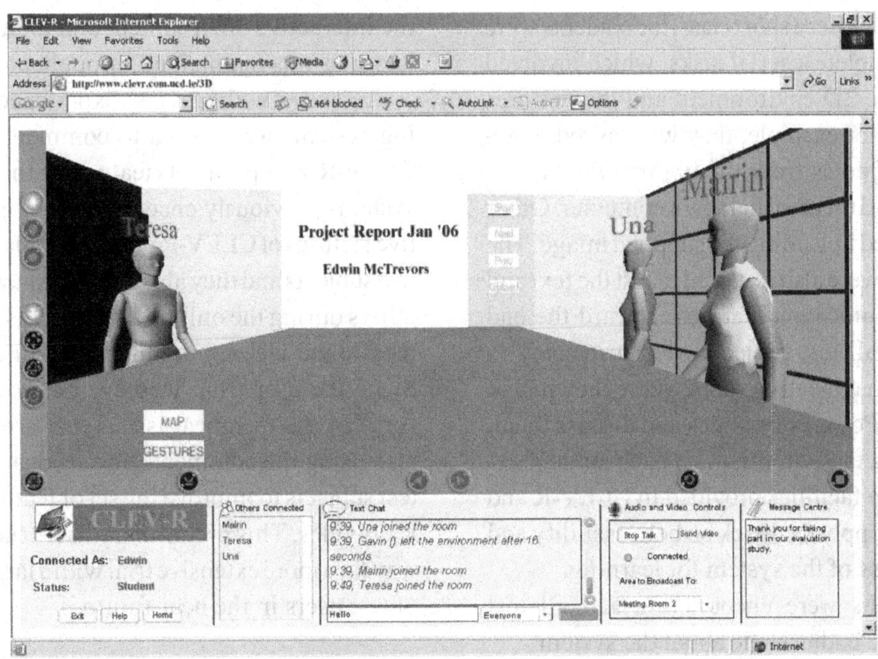

the 3D environment or download them to their own computer. The bookcase in the library also contains a number of links to external information sources such as online dictionaries and encyclopaedias.

Evaluation and Discussion

A usability study has been conducted to obtain user feedback on the CLEV-R system and also to ensure the standard of the functionality was adequate for users' needs. The test subjects took on the role of students within the 3D environment. They consisted of 7 postgraduate students, one secondary school teacher, and one college lecturer. The user trial was set up to ensure each user was exposed to all the features of CLEV-R. The test subjects registered for the system and choose an avatar to represent them in the 3D environment. Prior to the trial, each test subject received an image and a PowerPoint file via e-mail. They were also supplied with instructions for completing the user trial and an evaluation sheet. At an appointed time, those taking part in the trail attended a synchronous lecture in which a tutor presented slides and gave instructions on how to use CLEV-R. After a short class, the students were asked to complete a set of tasks, which involved exploring the 3D environment and the features it provides. For example, they were asked to access a set of notes from the library, view them, and download them to their own computer. Other tasks included uploading the supplied image. The participants were also required to test the text and audio communication features. Toward the end of the trial, all test subjects were instructed to attend a virtual meeting room where they had to upload their PowerPoint slides and discuss them. By assigning tasks in this way, each student experienced the facilities provided in CLEV-R and was able to supply feedback on both usability and the usefulness of the system for learning.

The results were encouraging and all test subjects were enthusiastic about the system.

As intuitive navigation within the 3D environment is a key aspect of the system, we were particularly interested in user-feedback on this matter. The feedback relating to navigation was mixed. While those who had prior experience of using 3D environments found manoeuvring easy, it took novice users some time to become familiar with the controls. Entering rooms proved particularly difficult and so we are improving the situation by removing doors and making the doorways wider. Test subjects found the communication controls easy to use, although some experienced an echo while using the audio controls. This can occur if speakers are too close in proximity to the microphone and so clearer instructions on this could resolve this issue. The lecture room was seen as an effective medium for teaching, and the participants particularly liked the real-time communication features. All users successfully uploaded files to the CLEV-R environment and collaborated on a task. Another key area of interest to us during this evaluation was the users' sense of immersion and presence within the 3D learning environment. Most of the test users felt part of a group and no one felt isolated during the evaluation. All of the subjects were engaged in the interactive environment and their interest in learning was maintained throughout the trial.

Test users with previous experience of e-learning systems were asked to comment further on CLEV-R, comparing its features to the e-learning systems previously encountered. The collaborative features of CLEV-R proved popular with these test subjects and they also liked their awareness of others during the online session. This is a feature they found lacking in other e-learning systems. Since the user trial, we have begun to address some of the technical issues that arose. We are also using the comments and feedback from the test subjects to improve the set of features CLEV-R provides. This preliminary user-trial paves the way for a more extensive trial with a larger number of test users in the near future.

mCLEV-R

We are developing a mobile version of CLEV-R that will provide "anytime-anywhere" access to learning resources. This mobile version is called mCLEV-R and provides the opportunity for people on the move to work through course material and to communicate with course tutors and other users in real time when they cannot be stationed at a fixed location. Our research in this field has focused on the following aspects:

- Exploring the use of a 3D interface for m-learning.
- Examining the technical capabilities of small mobile devices with regard to 3D graphics. In particular, we are exploring the use of the Virtual Reality Modelling Language (VRML) on personal digital assistants (PDAs).
- Facilitating the use of PDAs as a collaboration tool for e-learning.
- Evaluating this ubiquitous and pervasive system for learning.

Mobile devices have certain limitations when it comes to developing any application for them. Small screen sizes with low resolution make it difficult to ensure an application looks well and displays all necessary information. Limited memory for running applications, and also for storage, means applications need to be light weight. Also, lack of software support is another concern. Their inexpensive and convenient nature, however, makes them the ideal target for a learning application, and once mCLEV-R has been developed, we feel it will be of great benefit to any mobile student.

Due to the device limitations mentioned above, the system needs to be greatly modified for this new platform. Firstly, the 3D environment provided in mCLEV-R is much simpler than that of the full-scale system. Only features absolutely necessary are downloaded to mobile devices, and even then may need to be simplified for more efficient rendering. For example, textures can be replaced with simple colours and complex shapes can be simplified or removed altogether depending on their importance in the environment. It is also necessary to reduce the functionality for the mobile system. Thus, we must prioritise the

Figure 10. The mCLEV-R interface on PDA

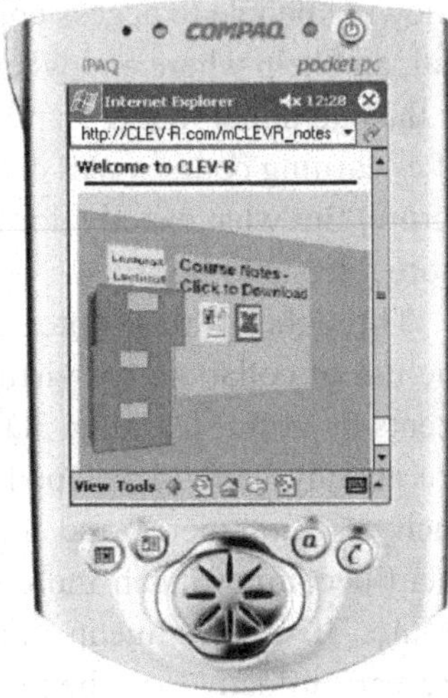

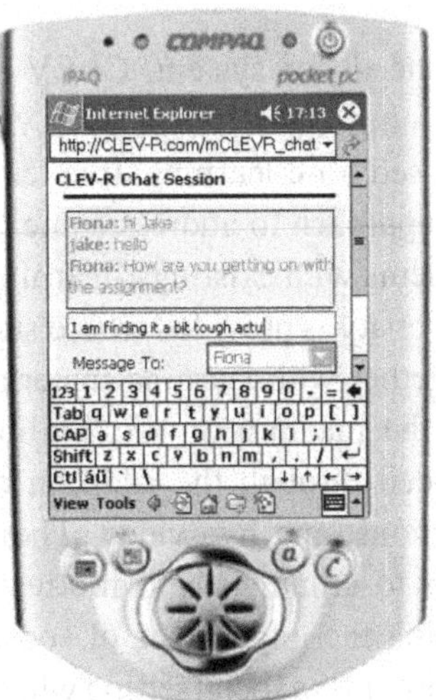

features of the system, carefully selecting those best suited to a mobile platform. The two most important features of our system are firstly to present learning content to users, and secondly to support social interaction among connected users. Thus mCLEV-R supports both these features.

Access to course content is supported through synchronisation with a desktop PC and by download from the 3D interface on the mobile device (see Figure 10). Due to small screen size and low resolution of the PDAs, course notes cannot be displayed clearly within the 3D environment. Therefore, we use external applications such as Pocket Word, Pocket Slideshow, and Pocket Adobe Acrobat Reader to open course files on these devices. Technological limitations of these devices, including lack of software support, mean it is unfortunately not possible to ensure full consistency with the desktop version of CLEV-R. Thus students on mobile devices are not aware when a tutor changes a lecture slide and are not updated about other users' locations in the environment. They can, however, be notified about important changes in the environment through the communication techniques provided. Both text chat, as seen in Figure 7, and audio chat are available in the mobile system. Thus, mCLEV-R users are continually aware of other connected users and can converse via these communication modes in real time, making them feel part of the learning community.

We have introduced our system, CLEV-R, a collaborative learning environment with virtual reality that is used for e-learning. It takes a novel and modern approach to address some of the issues and problems with existing e-learning systems. A 3D university is provided where students can learn together with learning material delivered through the medium of VR. Online lectures are enhanced through the addition of multimedia, animations, and live video. These enhancements help to stimulate and motivate students. Recognising the importance of social learning, CLEV-R provides a social setting where students can interact with one another. Collaboration on group and project work is also possible using designated areas and special tools within the environment. CLEV-R promises to improve the usability of online learning and enhance the students' learning experience. The extension of the system to mobile devices is highly innovative and presents interesting research challenges. A subset of the functionality is provided on PDAs, and we feel mCLEV-R will be an invaluable accompaniment to the full-scale system, giving students the opportunities an ubiquitous learning environment provides. Once development is complete, we look forward to the results of an extensive evaluation determining their true value for online learning.

FUTURE TRENDS FOR COLLABORATIVE LEARNING ENVIRONMENTS WITH VIRTUAL REALITY

The e-learning domain is set to increase, as the focus in society shifts to life-long learning. People of all ages are now partaking in education courses, older generations are returning to the classroom to learn new skill sets, and younger generations are staying in education longer. E-learning is an ideal solution for the needs of life-long learning, allowing people to access course content, material, and help where and when they want. There is thus no doubt that research into the provision of e-learning courses will continue well into the future. But what exactly does the future have in store for e-learning?

Throughout this chapter, we have examined the use of collaborative virtual reality environments for online learning. 3D interfaces like this are already being developed in other domains, such as e-commerce and tourism, and we see them becoming much more widespread in the future. 3D environments for online education are very effective, as they are stimulating and motivating and so engage the student in their learning. They are made all the more amenable and inviting when combined with the multi-user and collaborative features discussed above. As more of these systems emerge, the advantages (such as better retention rates for online courses and more interaction, discussion, and cooperation between students) will be seen by educators. We feel this will ultimately lead to a general acceptance of VR and 3D as a medium for learning. Of course, it would be naïve for us to think that this concludes research into e-learning. E-learning and distance learning are continually evolving, adapting to new technologies and new requirements. We have no doubt that this will continue in the future and so, based on current state of the art technologies, we now surmise what the next milestones in e-learning will be.

There is great potential within these 3D learning environments to further enhance a user's learning experience. Firstly, the environment could be personalised to each user's individual preferences, thus making the environment even more welcoming to them. Personalisation and adaptive user interfaces are areas of high interest at the moment (Liu, Wong, & Hui, 2003; Ye & Herbert, 2004) and they could also be applied to these 3D learning environments. These techniques examine user profiles and preferences, and subsequently adjust system features for each user accordingly. Therefore, a user could alter the physical appearance of the virtual world and state how they wish course notes to be displayed, what format they want them to be in for download, whether they want them to appear online to other users, and so forth. Software agents could also be added to the system to remove some mundane tasks for the user and oversee the management of the environment (McArdle, Monahan, Bertolotto, & Mangina, 2005). They could be used to make recommendations to the users about course material and other similar users, and indeed to help tutors keep track of students' progress and results.

While the use of VR on desktop computers continues to grow in popularity, research is now being carried out on the possible uses of augmented reality (AR). This branch of computer science is concerned with augmenting a real world environment or scene with computer-generated objects. This is often achieved through the use of head mounted displays (HMDs); the user wears a special pair of glasses and as they look at objects in the real world, computer generated 3D objects and data are superimposed into their view via the glasses. While AR research has been taking place for some time, it is only now that hardware is able to deliver results which are satisfactory to the user. One of the driving forces behind this technology is the area of medical visualisation. An example of a system using a HMD to project a 3D model of a patient's liver is described by Bornik, Beichel, Reitinger, Sorantin, Werkgartner, Leberl, et al. (2003). This tool renders the patient's liver from an x-ray computed tomography (CT) scan and enables surgeons to measure the dimensions of the liver to locate a tumour prior to surgery. The surgeon can then manipulate this model to obtain different viewing angles and see features in more detail. One drawback of using head mounted displays is that they tend to be cumbersome to wear and do not feel very natural. Again, it is in the medical visualisation arena in which strides are being made to alleviate this issue. Schnaider, Schwald, Seibert, and Weller (2003) have developed MEDARPA, a tool to assist with minimal invasive surgery. It consists of the practitioner looking through a screen, which is placed over the patient. Based on information from previous scans, an internal view of the patient is displayed on the screen; sensors track the position of the screen and the doctor's tools and update the image accordingly. The doctor can then use the on screen image as a guide for the keyhole surgery.

These two examples from within the medical domain show where this technology is heading. As mentioned earlier, distance learning and learning in general, has always evolved with technology and there is no reason why it will not embrace this new AR technology. One can easily see how this technology could be adapted for education. The very fact that 3D models themselves can be projected into the real world provide a means for students to see for themselves things that may have been dealt with in a theoretical way within the traditional classroom. For example, complex chemical structures, human organs, computer components, and sophisticated machinery can be projected into the real world for students to interact with and manipulate, therefore increasing their understanding of a topic. We see the future of collaborative learning environments as discussed above adapting to augmented reality. A student, or indeed a teacher who is not able to attend the physical classroom setting, may have their representation projected into the classroom. They can then see the lecture taking place, and others are aware of their presence and can interact with them in a natural way. An alternative to this idea is for a holographic representation of the teacher to be projected to the location where the remote student is, in a similar style to that seen in the Star Wars movie series. Unfortunately, acceptance and widespread availability of this form of technology is a long way off.

Before the advent of AR technologies that offer truly ubiquitous and pervasive learning environments, the use of mobile computers as a supplement to e-learning will increase. As people lead busier and more hectic lives, the need to access learning content while on the move will become paramount, and m-learning will emerge as a solution to this. We envisage great improvements in mobile technologies that will allow people to access vast amounts of learning content from PDAs and mobile phones in the future. Improvements and growth in wireless networks will allow more sophisticated communication and collaborative techniques, and will also make it possible for mobile users to download large detailed virtual environments and fully partake in synchronous and interactive learning scenarios like the one CLEV-R permits. Systems like ours, with its collaborative tools supporting interaction between students, will be particularly beneficial and will play an important role in moulding the future of m-learning.

CONCLUSION

This chapter gives a brief insight into the history of distance learning, outlining how it is continually evolving and adapting to new technologies, and arguing that e-learning will embrace the current range of VR technologies now available. We particularly focus on the need for collaboration within e-learning systems. This chapter shows how 3D graphics, with its roots as a modelling tool for engineers, has been used in the past for computer games, and outlines how it is being used today in activities such as urban planning, tourism, and e-commerce. Online collaboration tools initially grew out of text-based fantasy computer games, and this chapter charts how they evolved, becoming conference tools and later acting as social aids. The use of 3D, combined with collaboration techniques, is a more recent phenomenon and several examples of such systems being developed have been discussed. These systems offer a new form of e-learning, addressing many of the issues, such as isolation and lack of motivation, which students often experience while using text-based e-learning environments. The benefits and weaknesses of these new VR e-learning systems are presented.

This chapter describes our efforts in developing a VR e-learning system called CLEV-R. Like some of the other systems, CLEV-R has the remit of providing a motivating and stimulating multi-user 3D environment; however, our research recognises the importance of social learning within groups of students, and so offers specific features to facilitate this. CLEV-R is an intuitive, multimedia rich Web-based environment, which can be used both as a complete distance learning solution and as an accompaniment to traditional classroom-based teaching. Unlike the other systems presented in this chapter, CLEV-R uniquely offers support for providing learning material and collaboration tools on mobile devices, such as PDAs. This addition provides anytime, anywhere access to course material and allows students to interact while they are away from their desktop computer. The use of mobile devices is a new avenue in the e-learning paradigm, which has recently been termed m-learning. As the need for pervasive learning environments comes to the forefront of the research community, the use of m-learning is sure to increase. We have also discussed some interesting future trends within 3D visualisations, particularly demonstrating how the need for improvements in medical visualisation is fuelling research in Augmented Reality. We conclude this chapter by proposing how AR can be adapted for use as a tool within e-learning to provide a truly pervasive and ubiquitous learning environment.

REFERENCES

Bornik, A., Beichel, R., Reitinger, B., Sorantin, E., Werkgartner, G., Leberl, F., et al. (2003). Augmented reality based liver surgery planning. *Computer Graphics Forum, 22*(4), 795-796.

Bouras, C., Fotakis, D., Kapoulas, V., Koubek, A., Mayer, H., & Rehatscheck, H. (1999, June 7-11). In *Proceedings of the Virtual European School-VES, IEEE Multimedia Systems'99, Special Session on European Projects,* Florence, Italy (pp. 1055-1057).

Bouras, C., Philopoulos, A., & Tsiatsos, T. (2001, July). E-learning through distributed virtual environments. *Journal of Network and Computer Applications, 24*(3), 175-199.

Bouras, C., Triantafillou, V., & Tsiastsos, T. (2001, June 25-30). Aspects of collaborative environments using distributed virtual environments. In *Proceedings of the ED-MEDIA 2001 World Conference on Educational Multimedia, Hypermedia & Telecommunications* (pp. 173-178). Tampre, Finland.

Bouras, C., & Tsiatsos, T. (2006, June). Educational virtual environments: Design rationale and architecture. *Multimedia tools and applications, 29*(2), 153-173.

Burigat, S., & Chittaro, L. (2005, April). *Location-aware visualization of VRML models in GPS-based mobile guides. In Proceedings of the Web3D 2005: The 10th International Conference on 3D Web Technology* (pp. 57-64). New York.

Casher, O., Leach, C., Page, C., & Rzepa, H. (1998). Virtual reality modelling language (VRML) in Chemistry. *Chemistry in Britain* (pp 34-26).

Chee, Y.S. (2001). Networked virtual environments for collaborative learning. In *Proceedings of the Ninth International Conference on Computers in Education (ICCE/SchoolNet)* (pp. 3-11), Seoul, South Korea.

Chee, Y.S., & Hooi, C.M. (2002). C-VISions: Socialized learning through collaborative, virtual, interactive simulations. In *Proceedings of the Conference on Computer Support for Collaborative Learning (CSCL)* (pp. 687-696), Boulder, Colorado.

Chittaro, L., & Ranon, R. (2000). Virtual reality stores for 1-to-1 commerce. In *Proceedings of the CHI2000 Workshop on Designing Interactive Systems for 1-to-1 E-Commerce,* The Hague, The Netherlands.

Chittaro, L., & Ranon, R. (2002, May). New directions for the design of virtual reality interfaces to e-commerce sites. In *Proceedings of the AVI 2002: 5th International Conference on Advanced Visual Interfaces* (pp. 308-315). New York: ACM Press.

Csete, J., Wong, Y.H., & Vogel, D. (2004). Mobile devices in and out of the classroom. In *Proceedings of the 16th World Conference on Educational Multimedia and Hypermedia & World Conference on Educational Telecommunications,* Lugano, Switzerland (pp. 4729-4736).

Daku, B.L.F., & Jeffrey, K. (2000, October 18-21). *An interactive computer-based tutorial for MATLAB.* In *Proceedings of the 30th ASEE/IEEE Frontiers in Education Conference* (pp. F2D:2-F2D:7). Kansas City, Missouri.

Dalgarno, B. (2002). The potential of 3D virtual learning environments: A constructivist analysis. *Electronic Journal of Instructional Science and Technology, 5*(2).

Dickey, M.D. (2003). 3D Virtual worlds: An emerging technology for traditional and distance learning. In *Proceedings of the Ohio Learning Network; The Convergence of Learning and Technology – Windows on the Future.*

Göth, C., Häss, U.P., & Schwabe, G. (2004). Requirements for mobile learning games shown on a mobile game prototype. *Mobile Learning Anytime Everywhere*, 95-100. Learning and Skills development agency (LSDA).

Hamill, J., & O'Sullivan, C. (2003, February). Virtual Dublin – A framework for real-time urban simulation. *Journal of the Winter School of Computer Graphics, 11*, 221-225.

Hudson-Smith, A. (2002, January). 30 days in active worlds – Community, design and terrorism in a virtual world. In *The social life of avatars.* Schroeder, Springer-Verlag.

Isbell, C.L., Jr., Kearns, M., Kormann D., Singh, S., & Stone, P. (2001, July 30-August 3). Cobot in LambdaMOO: A social statistics agent. In *Proceedings of the Seventeenth National Conference on Artificial Intelligence AAAI 2000* (pp. 36-41). Austin, Texas.

Johnson, C.A., Delhagen, K., & Yuen, E.H. (2003, July 25). *Highlight: US e-commerce hits $230 billion in 2008.* (Business View Brief). Retrieved October 11, 2006, from Forester Research Incorporated at http://www.forrester.com

Ketamo, H. (2002). mLearning for kindergarten's mathematics teaching. In *Proceedings of IEEE International Workshop on Wireless and Mobile Technologies in Education* (pp. 167-170). Vaxjo, Sweden.

Kray, C., Elting, C., Laakso, K., & Coors, V. (2003). Presenting route instructions on mobile devices. In *Proceedings of the 8th International Conference on Intelligent User Interfaces* (pp. 117-124). Miami, Florida.

Laister, J., & Kober, S. (2002). Social aspects of collaborative learning in virtual learning environments. In *Proceedings of the Networked Learning Conference,* Sheffield, UK.

Lepouosas, G., Charitos, D., Vassilakis, C., Charissi, A., & Halatsi, L. (2001, May 16-18). Building a VR museum in a mueseum. In *Proceedings of Virtual Reality International Conference,* Laval Virtual, France.

Lipman, R.R. (2002, September 23-25). Mobile 3D visualization for construction. In *Proceedings of the 19th International Symposium on Automation and Robotics in Construction* (pp. 53-58). Gaithersburg, Maryland.

Liu, J.,Wong, C.K., & Hui, K.K. (2003). An adaptive user interface based on personalized learning intelligent systems. *IEEE Intelligent Systems, 18*(2), 52-57.

Luchini, K., Quintana, C., & Soloway, E. (2003, April 5-10). Pocket PiCoMap: A case study in designing and assessing a handheld concept mapping tool for learners. In *Proceedings of the ACM Computer-Human Interaction 2003, Human Factors in Computing Systems Conference* (pp. 321-328). Ft. Lauderdale, Florida.

McArdle, G., Monahan, T., Bertolotto, M., & Mangina, E. (2005). Analysis and design of conceptual agent models for a virtual reality e-learning environment. *International Journal on Advanced Technology for Learning, 2*(3), 167-177.

Monahan, T., McArdle, G., & Bertolotto, M. (2005, August 29-September 2). Using 3D graphics for learning and collaborating online. In *Proceedings of Eurographics 2005: Education Papers* (pp. 33-40). Dublin, Ireland.

Monahan, T., McArdle, G., Bertolotto, M., & Mangina, E. (2005, June 27- July 2). 3D user interfaces and multimedia in e-learning. In *Proceedings of the World Conference on Educational Multimedia, Hypermedia & Telecommunications (ED-MEDIA 2005),* Montreal, Canada.

Nijholt, A. (2000). Agent-supported cooperative learning environments. In *Proceedings of the International Workshop on Advanced Learning Technologies* (pp. 17-18). Palmerston North, New Zealand.

O'Hare, G.M.P., & O'Grady, M.J. (2003). Gulliver's genie: A multi-agent system for ubiquitous and intelligent content delivery. *Computer Communications, 26*(11), 1177-1187.

Oliver, B., & Wright, F. (2003). E-learning to m-learning: What are the implications and possibilities for using mobile computing in and beyond the traditional classroom? In *Proceedings of the 4th International Conference on Information Communication Technologies in Education,* Samos, Greece.

Open University. (2005). *Media relations, fact sheet series, history of the open university.* Retrieved October 11, 2006, from http://www3.open.ac.uk/media/factsheets

O'Sullivan, C., Cassell, J., Vilhjálmsson, H., Dobbyn, S., Peters, C., Leeson W., et al. (2002). Crowd and group simulation with levels of detail for geometry, motion and behaviour. In *Proceedings of the Third Irish Workshop on Computer Graphics* (pp. 15-20).

Papagiannakis, G., Hoste, G.L., Foni, A., & Magnenat-Thalmann, N. (2001, October 25-27). Real-time photo realistic simulation of complex heritage edifices. In *Proceedings of the 7th International Conference on Virtual Systems and Multimedia VSMM01* (pp. 218-227). Berkeley, California.

Papagiannakis, G., Schertenleib, S., O'Kennedy, B., Poizat, M., Magnenat-Thalmann, N., Stoddart, A., et al. (2005, February). Mixing virtual and real scenes in the site of ancient Pompeii. Computer Animation and Virtual Worlds, 16(1), 11-24.

Raghupathiy, L., Grisoniz, L., Faurey, F., Marchalz, D., Caniy, M., & Chaillouz, C., (2004). An intestinal surgery simulator: Real-time collision processing and visualization. *IEEE Transactions on Visualization and Computer Graphics, 10*(6), 708-718.

Rakkolainen, I., & Vainio, T. (2001). A 3D city info for mobile users. *Computers & Graphics (Special Issue on Multimedia Appliances), 25*(4), 619-625.

Redfern, S., & Naughton, N. (2002). Collaborative virtual environments to support communication and community in Internet-based distance education. In *Proceedings of the Informing Science and IT Education, Joint International Conference* (pp. 1317-1327). Cork, Ireland.

Rickel, J., & Johnson, W.L. (1997). Integrating pedagogical capabilities in a virtual environment agent. In *Proceedings of the First International Conference on Autonomous Agents* (pp. 30-38). California.

Rickel, J., & Johnson, W.L. (1999). Virtual humans for team training in virtual reality. In *Proceedings of the Ninth International Conference on AI in Education* (pp. 578-585).

Riedl, R., Barrett, T., Rowe, J., Vinson, W., & Walker, S. (2001). Sequence independent structure in distance learning. In *Proceedings of Society for Information Technology and Teacher Education INternational Conference* (pp. 1191-1193)

Rischbeck, T., & Watson, P. (2002, March 24-28). A scalable, multi-user VRML server. In *Proceedings of the IEEE Virtual Reality Conference* (pp. 199-207). Orlando, Florida.

Ryan, J., O'Sullivan, C., Bell, C., & Mooney, R. (2004). A virtual reality electrocardiography teaching tool. In *Proceeding of the Second International Conference in Biomedical Engineering* (pp. 250-253), Innsbruck, Austria.

Schilling, A., & Coors, V. (2003, Septmeber). 3D maps on mobile devices. In *Proceedings from the Design Kartenbasierter Mobiler Dienste Workshop,* Stuttgart, Germany.

Schnaider, M., Schwald, B., Seibert, H., & Weller, T. (2003). MEDARPA - An augmented reality system for supporting minimally invasive interventions. In *Proceedings of Medicine Meets Virtual Reality 2003* (pp. 312-314). Amsterdam, The Netherlands.

UNESCO (2002). *Open and distance learning, trends policy and strategy consideration. United Nations Educational Scientific and Cultural Organisation (UNESCO)* Report 2002. Retrieved October 11, 2006, from http://unesdoc.unesco.org/images/0012/001284/128463e.pdf

Wikipedia Blackboard Incorporated. *In The Wikipedia Encyclopedia.* Retrieved October 11, 2006, from http://en.wikipedia.org/wiki/Blackboard_Inc

Ye, J.H., & Herbert, J. (2004, June 28-29). Framework for user interface adaptation. In *Proceedings from the 8th ERCIM Workshop on User Interfaces for All* (vol. 3196, pp. 167-174). Vienna, Austria: Springer Verlag.

Zara, J., Benes, B., & Rodarte, R.R. (2004, September 20-24). Virtual campeche: A Web based virtual three-dimensional tour. In *Proceeding of the 5th Mexican International Conference in Computer Science*, (pp. 133-140). Colima, Mexico.

Zimmerman, G., Barnes, J., & Leventhal, L.M. (2003). A comparison of the usability and effectiveness of Web-based delivery of instructions for inherently-3D construction tasks on handheld and desktop computers. In *Proceedings of Web3D 2003* (pp. 49-54). Saint Malo, France.

APPENDIX I: INTERNET SESSION

C-VISions: Collaborative Virtual Interactive Simulations

The C-VISions research group develop interactive simulations to help students learn (*http://yamsanchee.myplace.nie.edu.sg/NUSprojects/cvisions/cvisions.htm*). The Web site above provides details of their work along with relevant publications. Use this information to prepare a presentation, outlining the background to the research along with a synopsis of the systems they have developed.

APPENDIX II: CASE STUDY

A university has been offering a virtual reality learning environment as an accompaniment to classes and as a distance learning solution for three years now. Students' acceptance of the technology has been high; however, faculty have been slow to adopt this new method of teaching.

Comp 4015 is a software engineering module offered by the university. The course involves the tutor giving a number of lectures detailing best practice methods for Java Programming; this generally takes the form of a PowerPoint presentation showing examples of poor coding. The tutor then asks individual pupils how they would fix the problem. This creates interaction and discussion within the class. Another aspect of the Comp 4015 module involves students working together on a group project, where each team must design a program to address a fictional company's needs. At the end of the course they must present their work to the class. The tutor is very reluctant to offer this course via the virtual reality environment. He feels the dialog in which the students engage in during the actual lectures will be lost. He is particularly worried that the group project will no longer be possible and it may have to become a project for individual students instead. Thirty percent of a student's final grade for this module comes from the final presentation, which students give, and the tutor is concerned that the student's presentations will no longer be possible if the module is offered via the virtual environment.

Taking the CLEV-R system described above, encourage the tutor to offer the Comp 4015 module in the virtual environment by offering advice on the following points and questions raised by the tutor:

1. The tutor has been teaching this module for many years and has all the lecture slides and material ready. He does not want to change the material in order to tailor it for the virtual environment.
2. How can the interaction, which his classes are well known for, be maintained when the module is offered in the virtual reality environment?
3. Can people who may never meet really partake in a group project and give a presentation at the end? What tools support this?
4. Students will just be anonymous, with no personality and no way for them to be distinguished or to get to know each other. Is there any way to address this?
5. Suggest how mCLEV-R, the mobile accompaniment to CLEV-R could be introduced and used on this course.

APPENDIX III: USEFUL LINKS

Human Computer Interaction Laboratory
http://hcilab.uniud.it/

MIRALab
http://www.miralab.unige.ch/

Research Unit 6
http://ru6.cti.gr/ru6/

M-Learning World
http://www.mlearningworld.com/

MOBIlearn
http://www.mobilearn.org/

TECFA
http://tecfa.unige.ch/

Augmented Reality
http://www.uni-weimar.de/~bimber/research.php

APPENDIX IV: FURTHER READING

Adelstein F., Gupta S., Richard G., III, & Schwiebert, L. (2004). *Fundamentals of mobile and pervasive computing.* McGraw-Hill Professional.

Bimber, O., & Raskar, R. (2005). *Spatial augmented reality: Merging real and virtual worlds.* A.K. Peters, Ltd.

Bowman, D.A., Kruijff, E., LaViola, J.J., & Poupyrev, I. (2004). *3D User interfaces: Theory and practice.* Addison-Wesley Professional.

Burdea, G.C., & Coiffer, P. (2003). *Virtual reality technology* (2nd ed.). Wiley-IEEE Press.

Comeaux, P. (2002). *Communication and collaboration in the online classroom: Examples and applications.* Anker Pub Co.

Mahgoub, I., & Ilyas, M. (2004). *Mobile computing handbook.* CRC Press.

McLennan, H. (1999). *Virtual reality: Case studies in design for collaboration and learning.* Information Today Inc.

Palloff, R.M., & Pratt, K. (2004). *Collaborating online: Learning together in community.* Jossey-Bass guides to online teaching and learning. Jossey-Bass.

Sherman, W.R., & Craig, A. (2002). *Understanding virtual reality: Interface, application and design.* The Morgan Kaufmann series in computer graphics. Morgan Kaufmann.

APPENDIX V: POSSIBLE PAPER TITLES/ ESSAYS

- Issues with traditional text-based e-learning systems
- Combining collaborative tools and virtual reality
- Embracing new technologies to deliver learning material over the Internet
- Mobile technologies to offer ubiquitous learning environments
- Augmented Reality: The future for education?

This work was previously published in Ubiquitous and Pervasive Knowledge and Learning Management: Semantics, Social Networking and New Media to Their Full Potential, edited byM. Lytras and A. Naeve, pp. 118-157, copyright 2007 by IGI Publishing, formerly known as Idea Group Publishing (an imprint of IGI Global).

Chapter XIII
Leveraging Pervasive and Ubiquitous Service Computing

Zhijun Zhang
University of Phoenix, USA

ABSTRACT

The advancement of technologies to connect people and objects anywhere has provided many opportunities for enterprises. This chapter will review the different wireless networking technologies and mobile devices that have been developed, and discuss how they can help organizations better bridge the gap between their employees or customers and the information they need. The chapter will also discuss the promising application areas and human-computer interaction modes in the pervasive computing world, and propose a service-oriented architecture to better support such applications and interactions.

INTRODUCTION

With the advancement of computing and communications technologies, people do not have to sit in front of Internet-ready computers to enjoy the benefit of information access and processing. Pervasive computing, or ubiquitous computing, refers to the use of wireless and/or mobile devices to provide users access to information or applications while the users are on the go. These mobile devices can be carried by the users, or embedded in the environment. In either case, these devices are connected, most likely through a wireless network, to the Internet or a local area network (LAN).

Mobile technologies come in a large variety and are ever changing. In order to gain the business value of pervasive computing, and at the same time keep the supporting cost under control, it is important to develop an architecture solution. A service-oriented architecture (SOA) would allow an enterprise to easily provision functions to be accessible by certain types of pervasive channels. A service-oriented architecture would also make it possible to quickly integrate data generated by pervasive devices and make them available in the form of an information service.

In this chapter, we will first look at the communication networks and mobile devices that create the various information-access and information-generation touch points in a pervasive computing environment. Then we will discuss the applications and interaction models for pervasive computing. Finally, we will describe a service-oriented architecture that an enterprise can adopt in order to effectively and efficiently support pervasive computing.

MOBILE COMMUNICATION NETWORKS

Mobile communication technologies range from personal area networks (PANs; a range of about 10 meters) and local area networks (a range of about 100 meters) to wide area networks (WANs; a few kilometers). From a network-topology perspective, most networks are based on a client-server model. A few are based on the peer-to-peer model.

Wireless PANs

A wireless personal area network allows the different devices that a person uses around a cubicle, room, or house to be connected wirelessly. Such devices may include the computer, personal digital assistants (PDA's), cell phone, printer, and so forth.

Bluetooth is a global de facto standard for wireless connectivity (Bluetooth SIG, 2005). The technology is named after the 10th-century Danish King Harald, who united Denmark and Norway and traveled extensively.

HomeRF is an early technology for wireless home networking, first marketed in 2000.

The Institute of Electrical Engineers (IEEE) 802.15 wireless-PAN effort (IEEE, 2005a) focuses on the development of common standards for personal area networks or short-distance wireless networks. One technology out of this effort is ZigBee, which is based on the IEEE 802.15.4 standard.

ZigBee is a low-cost, low-power-consumption, wireless communication-standard proposal (ZigBee Alliance, 2005). Formerly known as FireFly, ZigBee is being developed as the streamlined version of HomeRF. A streamlined version would allow most of the functionality with less integration and compatibility issues.

ZigBee's topology allows as many as 250 nodes per network, making the standard ideal for industrial applications. Radio-frequency-based ZigBee is positioned to eventually replace infrared links. To achieve low power consumption, ZigBee designates one of its devices to take on the coordinator role. The coordinator is charged with waking up other devices on the network that are in a sleep mode, moments before packets are sent to them. ZigBee also allows coordinators to talk to one another wirelessly. This will allow for opportunities for wireless sensors to continuously communicate with other sensors and to a centralized system.

For enterprise computing, the wireless PANs are within the corporate firewall. They do not create new requirements for the enterprise architecture to extend access to applications. However, they do require security measures to make sure the device that is receiving information is a rec-

Table 1. Summary of the wireless PANs

Technology	Radio Frequency	Maximum Distance	Data Capacity
Bluetooth	2.4 GHz	10 meters	721 Kbps
HomeRF	2.4 GHz	50 meters	0.4-10 Mbps, depending on distance
ZigBee	2.4 GHz	75 meters	220 Kbps

ognized device. It also creates an opportunity for the computing infrastructure to potentially know where a particular device, and most likely the associated user, is located. How these are handled will be discussed later in the description of the proposed service-oriented architecture.

Wireless LANs

The set of technical specifications for wireless local area networks (WLANs), labeled 802.11 by IEEE, has led to systems that have exploded in popularity, usability, and affordability. Now wireless LAN can be found in many organizations and public places.

With a wireless LAN, a user's device is connected to the network through wireless access points (APs). APs are inexpensive—many are available for less than $100—and will usually work perfectly with little or no manual configuration.

Wireless LANs use a standard, called IEEE 802.11, that provides a framework for manufactures to develop new wireless devices. The first two standards released for wireless LANs were 802.11b and 802.11a. The 802.11b standard was used in most wireless devices in the early adoption of wireless LAN. A new standard, called 802.11g, combines data-transfer rates equal to 802.11a with the range of an 802.11b network (Geier, 2002). It uses access points that are backward compatible with 802.11b devices.

Wireless technology has become so popular that many new devices, especially laptop computers, have built-in wireless LAN capabilities. Windows XP, Mac OS, and Linux operating systems automatically configure wireless settings, and software such as NetStumbler and Boingo provides automatic connections to whatever WLANs they encounter. What is more, community-based groups have furthered neighborhood area networks (NANs) to share wireless Internet access from one building to the next.

Besides 802.11a/b/g technologies that have shipped products, new technologies are emerging, including 802.11h, 802.11i, and 802.1x. The most important developments for wireless security will be contained in the 802.11i and 802.1x specifications. The 802.11i specification addresses encryption (securing the communication channel), whereas 802.1x will address authentication (verifying individual users, devices, and their access levels).

IEEE 802.1x is another authentication protocol, not an encryption protocol. 802.1x by itself does not fix the existing problems with WLAN security that relate to encryption. Therefore, attackers can still easily read network traffic on 802.1x networks. The 802.11i standard will address communication-channel encryption.

In order to increase the throughput of wireless LANs, a technology called Mimo (multiple input-multiple output) has been developed. Mimo allows for transmission rates of more than 100 Mbps,

Table 2. Summary of wireless LAN technologies

Technology	Radio Frequency	Maximum Distance	Data Capacity
802.11a	5 GHz	20 meters	54 Mbps
802.11b	2.4 GHz	100 meters	11 Mbps
802.11g	2.4 GHz	100 meters	54 Mbps
802.11i	A security standard for encryption on wireless LANs		
802.11n	Varies	Varies	> 100 Mbps
802.1x	A standard security protocol for user authentication on wireless LANs		

which is much greater than existing wireless LANs. Presently, wireless LANs use a single antenna operating at only one of a limited number of frequencies (channel) that are shared by all users. Mimo technology allows the use of two or more antennas operating on that channel. Normally, this would cause interference degradation of the signal because the radio waves would take different paths—called multipath distortion. However, Mimo uses each of these different paths to convey more information. The Mimo technology corrects for the multipath effects. IEEE is standardizing the technology as IEEE 802.11n.

For an enterprise, wireless LAN technologies allow pervasive information access throughout the campus. Employees with authorized mobile devices such as wireless laptops and PDAs will be able to get online wherever they are on the campus.

Table 2 summarizes the wireless LAN technologies.

Wireless MANs

A wireless metropolitan area network (MAN; also referred to as broadband wireless access, or WiMAX) can wirelessly connect business to business within the boundary of a city. It is becoming a cost-effective way to meet escalating business demands for rapid Internet connection and integrated data, voice, and video services.

Wireless MANs can extend existing fixed networks and provide more capacity than cable networks or digital subscriber lines (DSLs). One of the most compelling aspects of the wireless MAN technology is that networks can be created quickly by deploying a small number of fixed-base stations on buildings or poles to create high-capacity wireless access systems.

In the wireless MAN area, IEEE has developed the 802.16 standard (IEEE, 2005b), which was published in April 2002, and has the following features.

- It addresses the "first mile-last mile" connection in wireless metropolitan area networks. It focuses on the efficient use of bandwidth between 10 and 66 GHz.
- It enables interoperability among devices so carriers can use products from multiple vendors. This warrants the availability of lower cost equipment.
- It defines mechanisms that provide for differentiated quality of service (QoS) to support the different needs of different applications. The standard accommodates voice, video, and other data transmissions by using appropriate features.
- It supports adaptive modulation, which effectively balances different data rates and link quality. The modulation method may be adjusted almost instantaneously for optimal data transfer. Adaptive modulation allows efficient use of bandwidth and fits a broader customer base.

The WiMAX technical working group has developed a set of system profiles, standards for protocol-implementation conformance, and test suites (http://www.wimaxforum.org).

One particular technology for WiMAX is non line of sight (NLOS) networking (Shrick, 2002). NLOS networks provide high-speed wireless Internet access to residential and office facilities. NLOS uses self-configuring end points that connect to a PC (personal computer). The end point has small attached antennas and can be mounted anywhere without the need to be oriented like satellite antennas. Two major vendors are Navini Networks and Nokia.

With the wireless MAN technology, enterprises can quickly set up a network to provide wireless access to people in a certain area. It is very useful in situations such as an off-site working session or meeting.

Wireless NANs

Wireless neighborhood area networks are community-owned networks that provide wireless broadband Internet access to users in public areas (Schwartz, 2001). To set up a wireless NAN, community group members lend out access to the Internet by linking wireless LAN connections to high-speed digital subscriber lines or cable modems. These wireless LAN connections create network access points that transmit data for up to a 1-kilometer radius. Anyone possessing a laptop or PDA device equipped with a wireless network card can connect to the Internet via one of these community-established access points.

Wireless NANs have been established in more than 25 cities across the United States. Community-based networks differ from mobile ISPs (Internet service providers) such as MobileStar and Wayport that offer subscribers wireless access to the Internet from hotels, airports, and coffee shops. Wireless NANs extend access to consumers in indoor as well as outdoor areas, and the access is typically offered at no charge. For instance, NYC Wireless (http://www.nyc-wireless.net) provides Internet access to outdoor public areas in New York City. In addition, this organization is negotiating with Amtrak to bring wireless Internet access to Penn Station.

Enterprises could leverage the existing wireless NANs and equip employees with the right devices and security mechanisms in order to use these wireless networks to securely connect to the corporate network.

Wireless WANs

Wireless wide area networks are commonly known as cellular networks. They refer to the wireless networks used by cell phones.

People characterize the evolution of wireless WAN technology by generation. First generation (1G) started in the late 1970s and was characterized by analog systems. The second generation of wireless technology (2G) started in the 1990s. It is characterized by digital systems with multiple standards and is what most people use today. 2.5G and 3G are expected to be widely available 1 to 3 years from now. 4G is being developed in research labs and is expected to launch as early as 2006.

Wireless WAN originally only offered voice channels. Starting from 2G, people have used modems to transmit data information over the voice network. More recent generations offer both voice and data channels on the same cellular network.

One of the major differentiating factors among the wireless generations is the data transmission speed in which the wireless device can communicate with the Internet. The table below is a comparison of the data transmission rates of the 2G, 2.5G, 3G, and 4G technologies (3Gtoday, 2005). Both 2G and 2.5G include different technologies

Table 3. Data transmission speed of wireless wide area networks

Technology	Maximum	Initial	Typical
2G: GSM	9.6 Kbps	—	—
2G: CDMA	14.4 Kbps	—	—
2.5G: GPRS	115 Kbps	< 28 Kbps	28-56 Kbps
2.5G: CDMA 1x	144 Kbps	32 Kbps	32-64 Kbps
2.5G: EDGE	384 Kbps	64 Kbps	64-128 Kbps
3G	2 Mbps	< 128 Kbps	128-384 Kbps
4G	20 Mbps	TBD	TBD

with different data transmission rates. Global Systems for Mobile Communications (GSM) and Code Division Multiple Access (CDMA) are 2G technologies. General Packet Radio Service (GPRS), CDMA 1x, and Enhanced Data for GSM Environment (EDGE) are 2.5G technologies.

In the United States, cellular carriers Verizon and Sprint use CDMA technology. Cingular uses GSM, GPRS, and EDGE technologies. Both Verizon and Sprint have rolled out their CDMA 1x services, which is 2.5G. Cingular has rolled out GRPS service and is starting to roll out EDGE service in selected markets.

Wireless WANs are available wherever cell phones can be used. For now, they are the most pervasive wireless networks. By subscribing to a service plan, an enterprise user's laptop computer or other mobile device can connect to the Internet through the service provider's cellular towers.

Ultrawideband (UWB)

Traditional radio-frequency technologies send and receive information on particular frequencies, usually licensed from the government. Ultrawideband technology sends signals across the entire radio spectrum in a series of rapid bursts.

Ultrawideband wireless technology can transmit data at over 50 Mbps. A handheld device using this technology consumes 0.05 milliwatts of power as compared to hundreds of milliwatts for today's cell phones. Ultrawideband signals appear to be background noise for receivers of other radio signals. Therefore it does not interfere with other radio signals. Ultrawideband is ideal for delivering very high-speed wireless-network data exchange rates (up to 800 Mbps) across relatively short distances (less than 10 meters) with a low-power source.

Another feature of ultrawideband signals is that they can penetrate walls. Therefore, this technology would allow a wireless device to communicate with a receiver in a different room. This feature can also be used to detect buried bodies, people in a building, or metal objects in concrete.

Mesh Radio and Mess Networks

Mesh radio is a wireless network technology that operates in the 28-GHz range of the radio spectrum and provides high-speed, high-bandwidth connectivity to the Internet (Fox, 2001). A mesh radio network consists of antennas connected in a web-like pattern to a fiber-optic backbone. A single antenna attached to the roof of a building could provide Internet access to all of the subscribers residing in the building. Each node on the network has a small, low-power, directional antenna that is capable of routing traffic for other nodes within a 2.8-kilometer radius. In contrast to other wireless networks, mesh radio avoids many of the line-of-sight issues between the base station and each node on the network. Consequently, the configuration of mesh radio reduces the chance of encountering physical obstructions that could impede access to the network.

Mesh radio networks are being developed in two different ways. CALY Networks has developed a system that utilizes the Internet protocol (IP) as its communication mechanism, while Radiant Networks has created a system that communicates using the asynchronous transfer mode (ATM). Providers of mesh radio services include British Telecommunications, TradeWinds Communications (http://www.tnsconnects.com), and Nsight Teleservices (http://www.nsighttel.com).

Features of mesh radio include the following:

- Provides upload and download data rates of up to 25 Mbps
- Supports up to 600 subscribers per square kilometer without degradation of service
- Provides cost-effective access to broadband services in rural communities or urban areas

- Increases network capacity and resilience as the customer base grows

Different from the mesh radio technology, mesh networks enable wireless devices to work as a peer-to-peer network, using the handsets themselves instead of the radio towers to transmit data (Blackwell, 2002). Each handset would be capable of transmitting data at rates from 6 Mbps to 18 Mbps. This technology can be used for a group of users or devices communicating with each other in a peer-to-peer mode without needing an established wireless network. The technology was developed by Mesh Networks Inc., which has been acquired by Motorola.

Sensor Networks

Motes (also called sensor networks or Smart Dusts; Culler & Hong, 2004) are small sensing and communication devices. They can be used as wireless sensors replacing smoke detectors, thermostats, lighting-level controls, personal-entry switches, and so forth. Motes are built using currently available technology and are inexpensive enough to be deployed in mass quantities. Depending on the sensors and the capacity of the power supply, a mote can be as big as 8 cubic centimeters (the size of a matchbox) or as small as one cubic millimeter.

Motes are the result of a joint effort between Defense Advanced Research Projects Agency (DARPA) and the University of California, Berkeley, research labs. Most initial applications are positioned to helping the military for tasks such as surveillance of war zones, the monitoring of transportation, and the detection of missiles and/or biological weapons. Commercial mote sensors are available from Crossbow Technology.

A mote is typically made up of the following:

- A scanner that can scan and measure information on temperature, light intensity, vibrations, velocity, or pressure changes
- A microcontroller that determines tasks performed by the mote and controls power across the mote to conserve energy
- A power supply that can be small solar cells or large off-the-shelf batteries
- TinyOS, an open-source software platform for the motes. TinyOS enables motes to self-organize themselves into wireless network sensors.
- TinyDB, a small database that stores the information on a mote. With the help of TinyOS, the mote can process the data and send filtered information to a receiver.

These motes enable enterprises to constantly collect important information and send the information to the appropriate server for processing so that the appropriate response can be initiated when necessary. The motes become the generator of pervasive information that reflects the status of business processes or environmental conditions.

Pervasive Devices

Pervasive devices come in different forms and shapes. Compared to a networked computer, some pervasive devices, such as landline or cell phones, are more widely available. Other devices are simply more portable and thus can be easily carried around. Yet other devices are embedded in the environment and are able to deliver specialized information. In terms of their functions, some are for accessing the Internet, some are just for entering information while the user is on the go, and others are for storing large amounts of information and can be easily carried around.

Traditional Telephones, Pagers, and Cell Phones

Traditional landline telephone has been the most pervasive communication device around

Figure 1. Voice gateway connects the phone network with the data network

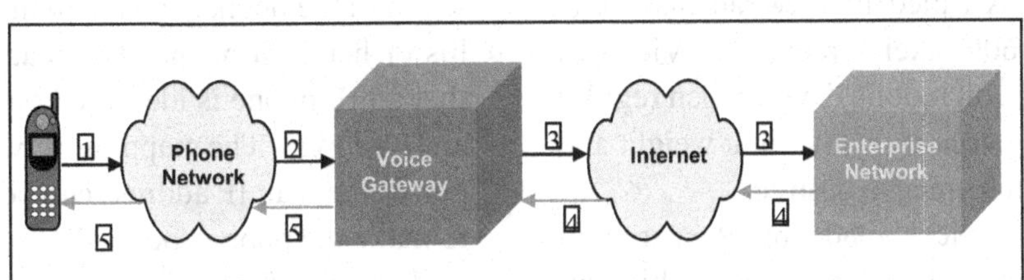

the world. Voice markup languages such as VoiceXML (voice extensible markup language; Rubio, 2004), together with supporting technologies such as the voice browser and voice gateway, has made the traditional telephone yet another device for connecting the user to the Internet. With speech recognition, users can choose to use touch tone or simply say what they need. Figure 1 shows how a telephone can be used to connect to the Internet.

1. The user dials the number from any phone (landline or mobile).
2. The call is routed to the corresponding voice gateway, which maps the phone number to a particular application hosted at the enterprise network.
3. The voice gateway knows the URL (uniform resource locator) of the application. It uses an HTTP (hypertext transfer protocol) request to fetch the first dialog of the application.
4. The enterprise Web server and application server return the dialog to the gateway in the form of a VoiceXML document.
5. The gateway interprets the VoiceXML document, plays the greeting, and asks the user for input. Now the user can use touch tone or speech to provide input. Based on the user input and the application logic as described in the VoiceXML file, the voice gateway decides what dialog to fetch next from the enterprise network.

Pagers allow users to receive alerts with a limited amount of text. With two-way pagers, users can also reply with a text message.

With cell phones (not smart phones), besides the same communication capabilities of a landline telephone, most users can use short-message service (SMS) to send and receive text messages. This is good for near-real-time conversational communications.

Smart Phones, Wireless PDAs, and Blackberry Devices

Smart phones are cells phones that have both voice and data capabilities. Such a cell phone comes with a mini Web browser and thus can be used to access Internet content. However, since the smart phones typically have rather small screens, they can only access pages specifically designed for small screens and coded in a special markup language such as Wireless Markup Language (WML). Some smart phones are equipped with a computing platform such as the Java Virtual Machine that can run applications written in J2ME (Java 2 Micro Edition).

Wireless PDAs typically have larger screens than cell phones and can directly access HTML (hypertext markup language) pages. Some wireless PDAs can also be used to make phone calls, and are referred to as PDA phones. Since many people prefer to carry only one of such mobile device around, there is a competition between PDA phones and smart phones, a war in which the smart phones seem to be winning.

ViewSonic (http://www.viewsonic.com) made a super-sized PDA, called the ViewPad, that offers a regular 800x600-pixel screen. The ViewPad can be a very useful mobile device when regular screen size is a necessity while light weight and zero-boot-up time are also desired.

Blackberry devices made by Research in Motion (http://www.rim.com) has been a big success for enterprise users as they provide a very convenient way for reading and typing e-mails while being away from the office.

Laptop or Tablet PCs with Wireless Access

When size and weight are not inhibitive, mobile users may choose to carry a laptop or tablet PC while on the go. These mobile PCs use wireless cards to connect to either a wireless LAN or wireless WAN. Many such laptops now have built-in wireless LAN cards, and have slots for users to insert a wireless WAN card such as the AirCard made by Sierra Wireless (http://www.sierrawireless.com). An enterprise also needs to be prepared to provide support to mobile users in order to help them connect to the Internet through Wi-Fi hot spots (Hamblen, 2005).

Wireless LAN is often available at a corporation campus, or at public hot spots such as many airports and Starbucks Cafés. Wireless WAN is available wherever cellular service is available for the specific provider that the wireless card is registered with.

IP Phones

IP phones are telephones that use a TCP/IP (transmission-control protocol/Internet protocol) network for transmitting voice information. Since IP phones are attached to the data network, makers of such devices often make the screens larger so that the phones can also be used to access data. What makes IP phones pervasive devices is that a user who is away from his or her own desk can come to any IP phone on the same corporate network, log in to the phone, and make the phone work as his or her own phone. The reason is for this is that an IP phone is identified on the network by an IP address. The mapping between a telephone number and an IP address can be easily changed to make the phone "belong" to a different user.

In terms of the information-access capability, Cisco (http://www.cisco.com) makes IP phones that can access information encoded in a special XML format. Example applications on the phone include retrieving stock quotes, flight departure and arrival information, news, and so forth.

Pingtel (http://www.pingtel.com) developed a phone that runs a Java Virtual Machine. This makes the phone almost as powerful as a computer.

Mitel (http://www.mitel.com) made an IP phone that allows a user to dock a PDA. With this capability, users can go to any such IP phone, dock their PDA into the phone, and immediately have their address books on the PDA available to the telephone. Users can also have their personal preferences transferred from the PDA to the phone and start to use the phone the way they prefer. In addition, users can benefit from new applications on the PDA, such as portable voice mail and dialing by the address book.

The Mitel IP phone seamlessly blends the wired and wireless world for the user so that they are no longer dealing with two separate communication tools. It also provides users with location transparency within the network.

Orbs (Ambient Devices)

Orbs are simple devices that convey information at a glance in a manner that is easy to observe and comprehend (Feder, 2003). Orbs only present a visual indication of the data, not detailed information or actual numbers. Orbs come in different forms. One common orb is a simple globe that changes color and intensity. Other forms include the following:

- Wall panels that adjust color or blink
- Pens, watch bezels, and fobs that change color
- Water tubes that vary the bubble rate
- Pinwheels that change speed

Orbs operate via wireless pager networks under the command of a server. This server gathers pertinent information from sources, including the Web, condenses it to a simple value, and periodically sends the information to the orbs.

Orbs are currently available from several retailers. The wireless service costs about $5 per month per device. Ambient Devices (http://www.ambientdevices.com) sells orbs and provides the communications service.

The information displayed by orbs is configurable. There are currently available data feeds for stock-market movement and weather forecasts.

Input Technologies: Dictation, Anoto Pen, and Projection Keyboard

Two natural ways for mobile users to input information are speech and handwriting.

Speech input can be at two levels: question-and-answer vs. dictation. Question-and-answer speech input is useful for entering structured information where the answers can be predefined using a grammar. Dictation technology allows users to speak freely and tries to recognize what the user has said. Diction technology typically requires a training phase to tune the speech recognizer to each particular speaker in order to achieve high recognition accuracy. Leading dictation products are Dragon NaturallySpeaking from ScanSoft (http://www.scansoft.com) and ViaVoice from IBM (http://www.ibm.com).

The Swedish company Anoto (http://www.anoto.com) invented a technology for pen-based input (McCarthy, 2000). It consists of a digital pen that feels like a regular ballpoint pen, a special paper with patterns of dots printed on it, and a wireless technology such as Bluetooth that sends handwritten information stored in the pen to a computer. As the user writes, the pen not only records what has been written, but also the order in which the user writes it. Anoto has partnered with companies such as Logitech (http://www.logitech.com) and Nokia (http://www.nokia.com) to bring this technology to end users.

For users who want to use a keyboard without carrying one, Canesta (http://www.canesta.com) developed the projection keyboard, in which the image of a keyboard is projected on a surface. By typing on the projection keyboard, information is entered into the associated PDA device.

Application Scenarios

From an enterprise's perspective, the following applications areas are where pervasive computing brings business value.

- Allow employees to stay in touch with phone calls, voice mail, e-mail, and so forth while being away from the office.
- Give employees access to information or transactions via mobile devices while on the road.
- Provide employees with access to the corporate network from anywhere on the Internet (i.e., remote access).
- Send location-based information to employees and customers.
- Monitor device status, perimeter security, and so forth using a wireless sensor network.

COMMUNICATION: UNIFIED COMMUNICATION AND INSTANT COMMUNICATION

With cell phones and pagers, it is not very hard to keep mobile users in touch. But some pervasive communication technologies have reached a higher level. Let us look at two such technologies:

unified communication and instant communication.

Unified communications refers to technologies that allow users access to all their phone calls, voice mails, e-mails, faxes, and instant messages as long as they have access to either a phone or a computer. With a computer, a software phone allows the user to make or receive phone calls. Voice-mail messages can be forwarded to the e-mail box as audio files and played on the computer. Fax can be delivered to the e-mail box as images. With a phone, a user can listen to e-mail messages that the system would read using the text-to-speech technology. A user can request a fax to be forwarded to a nearby fax machine.

Unified communications services are offered by most traditional telecommunications technology providers such as Cisco, Avaya, and Nortel.

Instant communication refers to the ability of reaching someone instantly via a wearable communication device. Vocera (http://www.vocera.com) offers a system that uses 802.11b wireless local area networks to allow mobile users to instantly communicate with one another. Each user only needs to have a small wearable device to stay connected. To reach someone, the user would only need to speak a name, a job role, a group, or a location to the system, and the system will take care of the rest. By combining a small wearable device and the speech-recognition capability, Vocera offers a highly usable solution for mobile communication within an organization.

The functions and features of Vocera include the following:

- Instant communication via a small wearable device and speech commands
- Hands-free communication. Except for pressing the button to start and stop a conversation, a user's hands are free during the communication.
- Flexibility in how to specify the recipients. A user can use a name, role, group, or location to tell the system whom to contact.
- The option of having a conversation or leaving a message, for both one-to-one and group communications
- Call controls such as call transfer, blocking, or screening
- Outside calling through the private branch exchange (PBX). The Vocera server can be connected to the PBX to allow users of Vocera to contact people outside the organization.

The Vocera technology has been well received in organizations such as hospitals where users' hands are often busy when they need to communicate with others.

Mobile Access to Information and Applications

Organizations can benefit significantly by allowing mobile access to information and applications. Here are a few examples.

Sales-Force Automation

Salespeople are often on the road. It is important for them to have access to critical business information anywhere at anytime. Pervasive access to information increases their productivity by using their downtime during travel to review information about clients and prospects, about the new products and services they are going to sell, or to recap what has just happened during a sales event when everything is still fresh in their memory. Being able to use smart phones or wireless PDAs to conduct these activities is much more convenient for salespeople as opposed to having to carry a laptop PC.

Dashboard or Project-Portfolio Management

For busy executives, it is very valuable for them to be able to keep up to date on the dashboard while they are away from the office and to take actions when necessary. It is also very helpful for them to be able to look at the portfolio of projects they are watching, update information they have just received during a meeting or conversation, and take notes or actions about a specific project.

Facility Management and Other On-Site Service Applications

Mobile access to information can significantly boost the productivity of on-site service people such as facility- or PC-support staff. With mobile access, they can retrieve ticket information on the spot, update the ticket as soon as they are done with the work, and get the next work order without having to come back to the office. Mobile access also reduces the amount of bookkeeping, which requires a lot of manual intervention, and thus reduces the chance of human errors.

Remote Access to Corporate Network

Allowing employees access to the corporate network from anywhere on the Internet could certainly bring convenience to employees and boost productivity. There are two primary fashions of allowing remote access.

One approach is through a technology called virtual private network, or VPN. This typically requires the user to carry a laptop offered by the employer. Once the user is connected to the Internet, a secure connection (called a VPN tunnel) is established between the laptop and the corporate network after both user and device are authenticated. Then the user will have access to all the information and applications just as if the user were in the office.

The other approach does not require the user to carry a corporate laptop. It simply requires that the user has access to a Web browser. In this case, for security reasons, two-factor authentication is often employed, in which the user not only needs to provide a user ID and password, but also something else, such as the security code generated by a hard token. With this approach, an enterprise can choose which applications to make available for remote access. Terminal service technology offered by Citrix (http://www.citrix.com) can be used to offer browser-based remote access to applications, both Web based and desktop based.

Location-Based Services

A special type of pervasive application is location-based service. With wireless LANs, when a mobile user is in the vicinity of an access point, location-specific information can be delivered to the user's mobile device. With wireless WANs, a user's location can be determined by the cellular tower(s) that the user's handset is communicating with, or by the GPS (Global Positioning System) receiver the user is using. Location-based services include pushing information about local businesses, sending promotions to the user's device based on the user's profile and preferences, and showing meeting agendas and meeting material if the user is on the meeting attendee list for the room at the time.

If location needs to be accurately determined, an ultrasonic location system called the bat system can be used. This 3-D location system uses low power and wireless technology that is relatively inexpensive. An ultrasonic location system is based on the principle of *trilateration*: position finding by the measurement of distances. A short pulse of ultrasound is emitted from a transmitter or bat that is attached to a person or object to be located. On the ceiling are receivers mounted at known points. These receivers can measure the pulse and length of travel.

An ultrasonic location system is composed of three main components.

- **Bats:** Small ultrasonic transmitters worn by an individual or on an object to be located
- **Receivers:** Ultrasonic signal detectors mounted in the ceiling
- **Central controller:** Coordinator of the bats and receivers

To locate a bat, the central controller will send the bat's ID via a 433-MHz bidirectional radio signal. The bat will detect its ID through the embedded receiver and transmit an ultrasonic signal containing a 48-bit code to the receiver in the ceiling. The central controller will measure the elapsed time that it took for the pulse to reach the receiver. The system developed at the AT&T Cambridge facility can provide an accuracy of 3 centimeters.

Overall, location-based services are still in research mode. Once the technology becomes mature and "killer apps" are identified, there could be an explosive adoption.

User-Interaction Models

In the context of pervasive computing, it is usually inconvenient, if not impossible, for the user to enter text using a regular keyboard. Sometimes, it is also inconvenient for the user to read text. Therefore, other input and output mechanisms have to be employed.

Nontraditional input mechanisms include speech recognition, gesture, touch screen, eye gazing, software keyboard, and projection keyboard. Among these, a combination of speech-recognition and pen-based touch-screen input is most natural for most situations. This is also what PDAs and tablet PCs typically offer.

Nontraditional output mechanisms include converting text to speech and using sound, blinking, and vibration to convey information (as in ambient computing described earlier in this chapter).

Multimodal interaction allows a user to choose among different modes of input and output. For mobile users, speech is typically the most convenient way for input, while visual means may still be the most powerful way of seeing the output (especially when the output includes pictures or diagrams).

Kirusa (http://www.kirusa.com) has developed technologies to support multiple levels of multimodal interaction. SMS multimodality allows users to ask a question in voice and have the answers delivered to their mobile devices in the form of an SMS message. Sequential multimodality allows users to use the interaction mode deemed most appropriate for each step of the process. Simultaneous multimodality lets users combine different input and output modes at the same time. For example, for driving directions, a user can say "I need directions from here to there," while pointing to the start and end points.

Both IBM and Microsoft have developed technologies that will support multimodal interaction. IBM's solution is based on the XHTML+VoiceXML (or simply X+V) specification. Microsoft's solution is based on the speech application language tags (SALT) specification, which defines speech input and output tags that can be inserted into traditional Web pages using XHTML.

Besides deciding on what interaction mode to support, much effort is needed to apply user-centered design in order to deliver a good use experience for mobile users (Holtzblatt, 2005).

A Service-Oriented Architecture to Support Pervasive Computing

For an enterprise to leverage pervasive computing, instead of deploying various point solutions, the better way is to build an architecture that is well positioned to support pervasive devices and usage.

Figure 2. A service-oriented architecture that supports pervasive computing

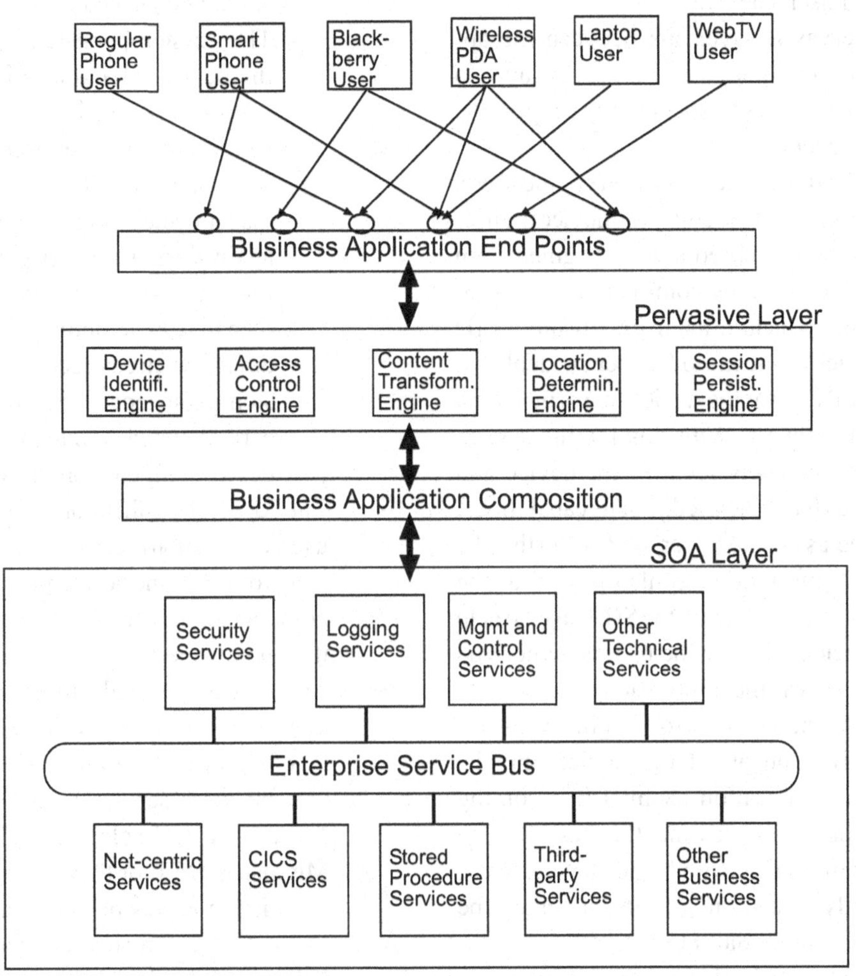

In order to provide mobile users with maximum access to enterprise information and applications with customized interaction methods and work flow, and at the same time minimize the extra cost in supporting pervasive access, a service-oriented architecture should be established.

The following picture shows a service-oriented architecture that supports pervasive computing. Let us look at this architecture from the top to the bottom.

- Users access applications from different devices. Some devices, such as the regular telephone, have only the voice channel. Some, such as the Blackberry devices, only have the visual display. Others may have both voice and visual channels. The size of the visual display ranges from 1 inch for cell phones, several inches for the PDA and Blackberry, and 15 or more inches for laptops.
- The user devices may be on different network connections, ranging from wireless LAN and wireless WAN to telephone networks.
- Users access applications through the applications' end points. This could be a URL,

a phone number, or a start screen stored on the end user's device.

- The pervasive layer sits between the application end points and the SOA layer to provide services to specifically support the mobile users.
  - The device identification engine uses a unique ID to identify the device the user is using. This requires the augmentation of some of the communication protocols to include a universally unique ID (such as the radio frequency identifier, or RFID) of the device that is initiating the request. With this ID, the system can uniquely identify the device and thus have knowledge of its capabilities, the associated user, and so forth. The ID information is also passed to the security service in the SOA layer to help decide whether the user is authorized to access the application.
  - The access-control engine uses information about the device and the communication channel it is coming from to determine the best way to communicate with the device: voice only, visual only, SMS, or some type of multimodal interaction.
  - Based on the desired interaction mode with the user, the content-transformation engine either calls the appropriate version of the application or dynamically transforms the information into the appropriate markup language: HTML, WML, VoiceXML, X+V, and so forth, using the eXtensible Stylesheet Language transformation (XSLT) technology.
  - The location-determination service uses mechanisms built into the networks to determine the geographic location of the user, and then decides whether the information should be tailored based on the location and whether additional location-based information should be pushed to the user.
  - The session-persistence engine uses the device ID and user-identity information to keep the user in the same session while the user is roaming from one network to another, or from disconnected mode to connected mode again during a short period of time. For smart-client applications, where data may be temporarily stored on the device when connection is lost, the session-persistence layer would also take care of synchronizing the data on the device with data on the server.
- The business-application composition layer uses information received from the pervasive layer to determine how to integrate the business services together to best fit the need of this mobile user.
- The SOA layer provides the business services and technical services that are integrated together through the enterprise service bus. The business services can be built using Net-centric technologies such as Java or Microsoft .NET, or they can be built based on existing legacy business functions such as customer information control system (CICS) transaction and stored procedures. They can also be based on business functions built using third-party tools or existing in-house business modules developed in C or C++, COBOL, and so forth.

After the establishment of such an architecture (which can be gradually built across multiple projects), when building an application that supports pervasive access, business services are either reused or built. When an existing business service is reused, the project team needs to go through the service's specification to verify that the service will work well with the pervasive layer to support all the pervasive channels that the application is going to support. If not, the first thing the project team should try to modify is the pervasive layer. If the issue really lays in the fact that the business service is not a "pure" service, that is, the service is tied to access methods, then the service needs to be either modified or wrapped in order to support the new requirements. When such a modification occurs, the service needs to be made backward compatible, and existing applications that use the service need to be regression tested. Eventually, the service definition needs to be modified to reflect the changes.

With this architecture, when a new pervasive access channel appears, or there is a change in an existing channel, then the only thing that needs to be modified is the pervasive channel. All business services can remain the same.

FUTURE DIRECTIONS

Moving forward, there needs to be much research and development work on building a system infrastructure that can use different sources of information to judge where the user is, and what devices and interaction modes are available to the user during a pervasive session. This will enable smarter location-based information push to better serve the user.

A related research topic is how to smoothly transition an interaction to a new device and interaction mode as the user changes locations and devices. Some initial work on this subject, referred to as seamless mobility, is being conducted at IBM and other organizations.

Another area that deserves much attention is the proactive delivery of information that users will need based on their profiles and information such as activities on their calendars or to-do lists. This relates to previous research efforts on intelligent personal assistants with integration into the pervasive computing environment.

REFERENCES

3Gtoday. (2005). Retrieved November 5, 2005, from http://www.3gtoday.com

Blackwell, G. (2002, January 25). Mesh networks: Disruptive technology? *Wi-Fi Planet.* Retrieved October 25, 2005, from http://www.wi-fiplanet.com/columns/article.php/961951

Bluetooth SIG. (2005). *The official Bluetooth wireless info site.* Retrieved November 3, 2005, from http://www.bluetooth.com

Culler, D. E., & Hong, W. (Eds.). (2004). Wireless sensor networks. *Communications of the ACM, 47*(6), 30-57.

Feder, B. (2003, June 10). Glass that glows and gives stock information. *New York Times*, P.C1.

Fox, B. (2001, November 21). "Mesh radio" can deliver super-fast Internet for all. *New Scientist.* Retrieved November 15, 2005, from http://www.newscientist.com/news/news.jsp?id=ns99991593

Geier, J. (2002, April 15). Making the choice: 802.11a or 802.11g. *Wi-Fi Planet.* Retrieved October 16, 2005, from http://www.wi-fiplanet.com/tutorials/article.php/1009431

Hamblen, M. (2005). Wi-Fi fails to connect with mobile users. ComputerWorld, *39*(37), 1, 69.

Henderson, T. (2003, February 3). Vocera communication system: Boldly talking over the wireless LAN. *NetworkWorld.* Retrieved November 12, 2005, from http://www.networkworld.com/reviews/2003/0203rev.html

Holtzblatt, K. (Ed.). (2005). Designing for the mobile device: Experiences, challenges, and methods. *Communications of the ACM, 48*(7), 32-66.

IEEE. (2005a). *IEEE 802.15 Working Groups for WPAN.* Retrieved November 7, 2005, from http://www.ieee802.org/15/

IEEE. (2005b). *The IEEE 802.16 Working Group on Broadband Wireless Access Standards.* Retrieved November 22, 2005, from http://www.wirelessman.org

McCarthy, K. (2000, April 7). Anoto pen will change the world. *The Register.* Retrieved September 14, 2005, from http://www.theregister.co.uk/2000/04/07/anoto_pen_will_change/

Rubio, D. (2004, October 20). VoiceXML promised voice-to-Web convergence. *NewsForge.* Retrieved November 23, 2005, from http://www.newsforge.com/article.pl?sid=04/10/15/1738253

Schrick, B. (2002). Wireless broadband in a box. *IEEE Spectrum.* Retrieved November 19, 2005, from http://www.spectrum.ieee.org/WEBONLY/publicfeature/jun02/wire.html

Schwartz, E. (2001, September 26). Free wireless networking movement gathers speed. *InfoWorld.* Retrieved December 5, 2005, from http://www.infoworld.com/articles/hn/xml/01/09/26/010926hnfreewireless.xml

ZigBee Alliance. (2005). Retrieved November 11, 2005, from http://www.zigbee.org/en/index.asp

This work was previously published in Enterprise Service Computing: From Concept to Deployment, edited by R. Qiu, pp. 261-284, copyright 2007 by IGI Publishing, formerly known as Idea Group Publishing (an imprint of IGI Global).

Section IV
New Usability Engineering Approaches

Chapter XIV
A Software Engineering Perspective on Ubiquitous Computing Systems

Emerson Loureiro
Federal University of Campina Grande, Brazil

Loreno Oliveira
Federal University of Campina Grande, Brazil

Frederico Bublitz
Federal University of Campina Grande, Brazil

Angelo Perkusich
Federal University of Campina Grande, Brazil

Hyggo Almeida
Federal University of Campina Grande, Brazil

ABSTRACT

We are now facing a migration from the traditional computing, based on personal computers, to an era of pervasiveness, on which computing devices will be spread all around us, seamlessly integrated into our lives. It is this new stage of computing that researchers have named of ubiquitous computing, also known as pervasive computing. There is no doubt that this vision is certainly a promising computing paradigm for the 21st Century. However, its completely new characteristics have an impact on the way that software is developed. We should emphasize that, for example, to achieve the seamless integration characteristic of ubiquitous computing environments, applications must implement mechanisms for discovering the needs of users in order to present them with relevant information at the right place and at the right time. This, and other intrinsic features of ubiquitous computing systems, makes necessary the use of different software engineering techniques. Within this scope, we claim that service-oriented computing, component-based development, plug-in-based architectures, event-based systems, and dynamic software evolution are the main techniques that can be used in the development of ubiquitous systems. The purpose of this chapter is then to review the challenges involved in ubiquitous systems development as well as present a software engineering perspective for tackling such challenges. In addition, we will also present the way these techniques have been used by outlining some of the current ubiquitous computing solutions.

INTRODUCTION

Much has been said recently about the advances in computing-related technology. It is not hard to notice, for example, the shrink in the size of electronic components like memories, hard disks, and microprocessors. A direct consequence of this fact is the emergence of mobile devices like handhelds, cellular phones, and tablet PCs. Another interesting point within this scope is the increase of the computational power of such devices, which has enabled them to execute more complex applications. Electronic games, both 2D and 3D, and multimedia players are just some examples of these applications.

Looking at these advances from the viewpoint of computer networks, one cannot avoid mentioning the evolution that has taken place on the networking interfaces, which has culminated on the wireless solutions we have nowadays. Bluetooth, Wi-Fi (Wireless Fidelity), and Zigbee are maybe the examples that best represent such solutions. In addition, some of these interfaces are embedded with energy consumption techniques. As a mobile device works by using limited batteries, this feature has been providential as a way of extending their lifetime.

Considering all these advances, the popularity these mobile devices have gained is not surprising. Just take a quick look around and you will notice that many people carry a cellular phone nowadays. In addition, the use of other mobile devices like smart phones and handhelds has considerably grown in some industry sectors. They can be found, for example, in solutions for supply chain management[1] and support for hospitals,[2] amongst others.

What can be perceived from all these facts is that there is, indeed, a migration from the traditional computing, based on personal computers, to an era of pervasiveness, on which computing devices will be spread all around us, seamlessly integrated into our lives. It is this new stage of computing that researchers have named of *ubiquitous computing*, also known as *pervasive computing*. Its ideas have been first exposed in 1991 by Mark Weiser (Weiser, 1991), a researcher of the Xerox Palo Researcher Center at that time. The primary vision of Weiser (1991) is a world where computing is embedded in every day objects, like televisions and cars, which will work in the background for performing tasks on our behalf.

Within this scope, the advances in hardware and networking technologies we have delineated previously are now leveraging the realization of the first environments contemplating the features of ubiquitous computing. It is not a surprise, thus, to see the emergence of many solutions in this field nowadays, like *Wings* (Loureiro, Bublitz, Barbosa, Perkusich, Almeida, & Ferreira, 2006), *Plug-in ORB* (d'Acierno, Pietro, Coronato, & Gugliara, 2005), *RUNES* (Costa, Coulson, Mascolo, Picco, & Zachariadis, 2005), and *PDP* (Campo, Rubio, López, & Almenárez, 2006).

There is no doubt that the vision conceived by Weiser (1991) is certainly a promising computing paradigm for the 21st Century. However, its completely new characteristics have an impact on the way that software is developed. Developing software targeted at such a paradigm involves, thus, the need for dealing with such characteristics, though the use of different software engineering techniques.

Based on this trend, the purpose of this chapter is to review the software engineering issues involved in the development of ubiquitous computing systems. To this end, we start by reviewing the features of ubiquitous computing in the Features of Ubiquitous Computing section. After that, we examine the challenges and requirements related to ubiquitous systems, respectively, in the Challenges of Ubiquitous Computing Systems and Requirements for Ubiquitous Computing Systems sections. Next, in the Software Engineering for Ubiquitous Computing section, we present the main software engineering techniques for tackling such challenges. We also review how these techniques have been applied in real pervasive computing solutions in the Ubiquitous Computing Systems Engineering in Practice section. Some of the future trends with the scope of software engineering for ubiquitous systems will also be presented in the Future Trends section. Finally, in the Conclusions Section, we conclude this chapter, presenting our vision about the status of software engineering for ubiquitous computing and our overall expectation about this chapter.

FEATURES OF UBIQUITOUS COMPUTING

As the reader could have noted in the beginning of this chapter, ubiquitous computing is completely different from the current computing paradigm. Today we use computers mainly for playing electronic games and working. No matter what the task is, the fact is that today computers require our full attention at what we are performing. Ubiquitous computing requires us to change completely the way we view and use computers (Saha & Mukherjee, 2003). In such a paradigm, a computer is just another appliance somehow integrated into human environments, which communicate wirelessly with others and perform tasks on behalf of people.

One of the issues that can be extracted from these initial concepts is that, as Weiser (1991) already declared, ubiquitous computing is not just about the anytime and anywhere presence of computing appliances like sensors and mobile devices. According to Weiser (1991), ubiquitous computing goes further, by specifying a seamless integration of such appliances into our lives. This integration should be so transparent that people should barely perceive that computing is pervaded in their environments. As a consequence, the usage of ubiquitous computing appliances should be done in a very natural way, just like electricity. We do not need to know how electricity is generated and delivered to our homes or how the electric power grid is configured; we simply plug an electronic device into a socket and use it. Ubiquitous computing should be exactly this way.

Another issue to be noted, which turns to be a very important one, is that ubiquitous computing is centered on the user. In other words, applications within this scope must be executed based on their needs/interests, using information from the environment, and past experiences, amongst others. An application should not notify you that the shoes you were looking for have just become available in the shopping mall if you are in a movie, and mainly if it "knows" that you did not like the last time it disturbed you in a similar situation. Conversely, when it detects that you have already left the movie, it should "know" that now is a good moment to warn you about the availability of the shoes you wanted.

Finally, two main characteristics of some ubiquitous computing devices are that they are small and battery-based. Such characteristics enable the users of such devices to move around different environments in an unpredictable way. A user carrying a cellular phone, for example, will take it to most of the places he/she goes, or maybe to all of them. It should also be considered the mobility of applications between devices (Benavar & Bernstein, 2003), as computing appliances will be available everywhere. The purpose of such an approach to mobility is to enable ubiquitous applications to follow their users no matter where they go. Within this scope, approaches like mobile agents have been claimed as a suitable approach to the ubiquitous computing vision (Cardoso & Kon, 2002). Your personal agent, for example, could migrate from your cellular phone to your desktop, as soon as you get to work, and back to the former when it detects that you are going home.

CHALLENGES FOR DEVELOPING UBIQUITOUS COMPUTING SYSTEMS

As we have seen in the last section, pervasive computing brings a new set of features for computing systems. Building software that contemplates such features may be, however, a challenging task, and, thus, many studies today are trying to identify the main problem in such a task (Henricksen, Indulska & Rakotonirainy, 2001; Niemalä & Latvakoski, 2004; Raatikainen, Christensen, & Nakajima, 2002).

If we take seamless integration, for instance, one of the first things that may come to our minds is that ubiquitous computing applications should not annoy us with irrelevant information, services, or requests. We should not be asked, for example, to select the components and services that should be used for deploying a new application into our device. This is clearly not a seamless integration. Another point to be highlighted is that such an integration of computing appliances into our lives requires ubiquitous applications to have access to information like the people in the vicinity, environmental conditions (e.g., lighting and temperature levels), current needs and interests of the users, and services and devices available in the environment, among others. It is based on this kind of information that ubiquitous computing applications would be able to provide us with relevant services, as we move from one environment to another.

On the other hand, when thinking about the user-centered execution, it is easy to note that, many times, pervasive computing systems will need to provide functionalities that they were not initially designed to deal with. This is because it is not possible to provide such systems with all the needed functionalities. There is no way to predict, at development time, all the functionalities that users will require. A tourist, for example, could be interested on a nearby all you can eat restaurant at some moment and a few minutes later on the weather forecast for the next day. It is probable that the application executing on the tourist's personal device had not been conceived to provide one of these functionalities, though it will still have to find a way of doing so. If ubiquitous computing applications are supposed to act on our behalf, they will have to cope with situations like this one. In other words, they will need to (1) keep track of the current needs of the user, (2) synthesize tasks for fulfilling such needs, (3) find appropriate components and services for accomplishing the synthesized tasks, (4) put these components and services together into a single application, and (5) deploy the application in the user's device.

Another feature of ubiquitous computing systems, mobility, both physical and logical, also brings some challenges. These kinds of mobility make such systems be faced with all sorts of environments, populated by a wide range of devices. Personal digital assistants (PDAs), cellular phones, smart phones, and Internet tablets are some examples. Due to physical mobility, applications will sometimes find themselves placed in environments inhabited by devices having different networking interfaces (e.g., Wi-Fi, Bluetooth, and Zigbee). Therefore, if ubiquitous computing appliances are supposed to interact with each other and become truly invisible, there should be some level of interoperability among such interfaces. The logical mobility, on the other hand, will make applications to be hosted by devices with different screen size and resolution, memory, processing, and storage capacities, and input methods (i.e., keyword, voice speech), among other different features. Another problem brought by mobility is that as users migrate from one environment to another, services that were available in the former may not be accessible in the latter. The Internet access service you were using while walking in the shopping mall will probably not be accessible when you leave it. In this situation, your device would have to find another service for enabling you to access the Internet when outside the shopping mall, preferably without interrupting your current task.

REQUIREMENTS FOR UBIQUITOUS COMPUTING SYSTEMS

From the challenges we have drawn in the last section, three requirements for ubiquitous computing systems can be stressed: *adaptation*, *dynamic extensibility*, and *context awareness*. We will describe each of these requirements in the following sections.

Adaptation

We have showed how ubiquitous computing systems are supposed to track user's needs and interests and tune themselves accordingly. Getting back to the tourist example we presented, remember that the user required two completely different functionalities in two different moments. Such an example, however, was too simplistic. In real world situations, the tourist would certainly require a wider range of functionalities. Car renting, hotel booking, entertainment guide, city maps, buses and metros timetables, and Internet access, are just some of such functionalities.

In face of all these abrupt changes in the requirements imposed by mobile users, ubiquitous computing systems must be able to *adapt* themselves according to such changes. Adaptation, in this case, means the addition and removal of components as well as changes in the links between them (Schilit, Adams, & Want, 1994). In our previous example, when the tourist requested the weather forecast, the ubiquitous system running in the tourist's personal device could, for example, inquiry a remote server for a component providing this functionality and, if there is such a component, deploy it in the user's device. Another option is to search in the environment where the user is situated or in the Internet for a service which implements the tourist's needs. If such a service is found, the ubiquitous system would then create and deploy in the device a component linked to this remote service.

We now reach an interesting point in our discussion. As we mentioned in the last section, when users move between environments, not only new services will become available to them but also old ones (i.e., those already known by the user) might become unavailable. In the latter case resides the problem we want to highlight. The natural choice, when a system detects that a service has become unavailable, is to search for a substitute for it, as in the example of the Internet access service presented in the last section. Unfortunately, this is not always possible. In some cases, there is no service similar to the unavailable one. Enabling users to perform the current task continuously will then require integrating disparate services into a single composite one. In both cases, from a structural perspective, there is nothing to be changed in the ubiquitous computing system. The only required change is that the component linked to the old service will have to be relinked to the recently composed one.

Adaptability is also a fundamental requirement for solving device heterogeneity problems. Sometimes, the different physical features ubiquitous computing systems will face, when migrating from one device to another, will force them to adapt themselves. If your personal agent is currently hosted on your cellular phone and using Bluetooth for communicating with other devices, when migrating to your personal computer it will probably have to change its communication layer for an Ethernet-based one. In this case, the adaptability was necessary; otherwise your personal agent would not be able to communicate with the outer world. There are situations, however, on which adaptability is not necessary, yet desirable. When your personal agent migrates from the cellular phone to the personal computer, its user interface could be adapted to fit the larger dimensions of the latter's screen. In this case, the personal agent adapted itself for better using the resources of the device it was hosted, not because it really needed that, as in the first example.

Dynamic Update

When foreseeing the ubiquity concept of Mark Weiser (1991), one could wonder how ubiquitous computing systems will be able to adapt, sometimes by changing the set of its internal components, and yet not disturb the user. Some of us could ask what is the relation between this kind of adaptation and the user disturbance. I will start illustrating this relation with a simple example. Although the way that software is engineered has been improved through the years, we still see applications which are not able to be updated without a restart. Now imagine this situation in a ubiquitous computing system. Considering the dynamic changes in its requirements, imposed by the user, if this kind of system could not be updated without annoying us, then we should change the name of ubiquitous computing to "disturbing computing." After all, which user would like to be frequently asked to restart the ubiquitous system running on a personal device just because it has been recently updated? It is not hard to realize that the seamless integration concept has been violated.

For tackling this kind of scenario, ubiquitous computing systems should be able to be updated dynamically, that is, at runtime. Based on the idea of adaptation we used previously, this implies that a ubiquitous computing system is supposed to have components inserted/removed and the links between them re-established without stopping it. Therefore, in the tourist example, a component providing the weather forecast could be downloaded, inserted in the application, and linked with the other components in a completely transparent way to the user. In addition, this component could also be transparently removed when no longer needed.

Context Awareness

As we have discussed, ubiquitous computing systems need some information for acting on our behalf. The application of the shoes example needed to be informed about your current location so that it could decide a good moment for notifying about the availability of the shoes you are looking for. Information like this one, as well as any other used by applications for improving their interaction with users has been named context (Dey, 2001). In the same way, the ability of sensing and reasoning over this information has been named *context awareness*. Context is an important element for ubiquitous computing, as it enables applications to act in a personalized way, which in turns helps on increasing the users' satisfaction (Tiengo, Costa, Tenório, & Loureiro, 2006).

Although human beings are very good at using the context to guide their actions, embedding this feature in a pervasive computing system is not that simple. First, because three tasks must be performed in order to be aware of the context (Loureiro, Ferreira, Almeida, & Perkusich, 2006): *context acquisition*, *context modeling*, and *context reasoning*. The former involves the acquisition of the information available in the context, and can be performed, for example, through sensors (i.e., lighting and temperature sensors). Context modeling is about representing the context in a way that applications can "understand" it. Finally, context reasoning is the task on which the information acquired from the context is used to guide the actions of an application.

We should remind the reader that, besides being able to retrieve the information available in the context, ubiquitous systems must also be able to detect changes in the context. Such changes can be either between contexts (e.g., when you leave the movie context to the shopping mall context) or within the same context (e.g., changes in the entities of the context) (Coutaz, Crowley, Dobson, & Garlan, 2005). They would have to know, for example, when a new device or service has become available in the environment, when the location of the user has changed, and many other changes. This is a fundamental feature for ubiquitous applications, as a way of enabling them to define a set of actions to be triggered when some specific changes are detected (Schilit, Adams, & Want, 1994). In the example about the shoes, the application should be aware that your location has changed, from inside to outside the movie, for automatically notifying you about the availability of the shoes you wanted.

SOFTWARE ENGINEERING FOR UBIQUITOUS COMPUTING

Now that the main requirements of ubiquitous computing systems are well understood, we can start describing how some of current of software engineering techniques can aid when dealing with such requirements. More precisely, we will cover the following techniques: *component-based development*, *plug-in-based architectures*, *service-oriented computing*, *event-based systems*, and *dynamic software evolution*.

Component-Based Development

Component-based development (CBD) enables the development of applications through the assembly of software modules, named *components*. A component can be viewed as units of software, which are developed and deployed independently, interacting with each other to build a functional system (Szypersky, 1999). One major advantage of CBD is that the dependencies among components are defined at the functionality level (i.e., the components' interfaces), not tightening them at specific implementation details. As a consequence, components can be reused in different applications. This feature is very helpful for software evolution because it enables components to be updated with less impact on the rest of an application.

In the context of pervasive computing, component-based development provides an elegant way of allowing ubiquitous systems to update its internal components. We mentioned that the logical mobility causes such systems to be faced with heterogeneous devices. Therefore, it would be reasonable to update the system in order to make better use of the resources available in each host the system migrates. From an engineering perspective, this could be solved by structuring the application in a component-based fashion. Your personal agent could have, for example, a component named *networking component*, among others. Such a component would be responsible for enabling the agent to communicate with the outer world. Therefore, when the personal agent migrates from the cellular phone to the desktop, it could automatically download an ethernet-based networking component, change it by the Bluetooth-based one, which is currently in use, and finally continue executing. Since the dependencies of the networking component with the other is in terms of their interfaces, no impact would be caused in the application.

A similar idea could be applied when a device migrates from one environment to another. In this case, the communication protocols used in the former may be different from the ones used in the latter. In addition, the networking interfaces used by the devices of the new environment may also be different from those used by the ones of the old environment. A ubiquitous application could turn around these problems by defining two software components: one for the protocols used in a specific environment, called *protocol component*, and another for the networking interfaces, called *network interface component*. Now, imagine that the protocol component uses the network interface component for sending data to the other hosts, and also that their initial implementations are based, respectively, on UPnP and Bluetooth. If the device joins an environment where the interactions are based on Wi-Fi, for example, all the ubiquitous system needs to do is to download a Wi-Fi-based networking component and then substitute the Bluetooth-based one. Similarly, if the protocol used in the environment is not UPnP, (e.g., Zeroconf (Guttman, 2001)), the ubiquitous system needs just to download the correct protocol component and replace the UPnP-based one.

Plug-In-Based Architectures

Plug-in-based architectures are based on the concepts of *core* and *extension point*. The core is where the basic application functionalities are implemented. Extension points, on the other hand, are well-defined places in the application core where extensions (i.e., plug-ins) can be plugged. As plug-ins are intended to increase the set of functionalities provided by an application (Birsan, 2005), they can be safely removed when no longer necessary. The Mozilla Firefox[3] Web browser and the Eclipse IDE[4] are some examples of plug-in-based applications.

Applying the concepts of plug-in-based architectures in ubiquitous computing has proven to be a reasonable solution for enabling applications to be extended on demand. It would be possible to deliver applications with only a minimal set of functionalities, enabling them to download and install plug-ins for fulfilling the users' needs whenever needed. In the tourist example, the application executing on the tourist's cellular phone could query a plug-in database trying to find a weather forecast plug-in. Once such a plug-in is found, it could thus be downloaded and installed in the users' device.

Another important usage of plug-ins in ubiquitous computing systems is to enable extensions over a particular functionality of the application. A multimedia player, for instance, could define an extension point for video plug-ins, enabling it to play different video formats. In ubiquitous environments, where multimedia content can be delivered in a wide range of formats, such a feature permits ubiquitous applications to play all kinds of video formats, needing only to download and install the correct plug-ins. This approach has also been used for coping with the diversity of networking protocols. As we will show , some ubiquitous computing middlewares define extensions for the addition of networking plug-ins, thus enabling them to communicate with other hosts using heterogeneous networking protocols (Loureiro, Oliveira, Almeida, Ferreira, & Perkusich, 2005).

The last aspect to be observed when applying plug-in-based architectures in ubiquitous computing applications is the fact that, as we mentioned, plug-ins can be removed without halting the host application. In the ubiquitous computing world this can be very useful, considering the storage constraints presented by some mobile devices. Therefore, users could remove nonused plug-ins in order to make room for other plug-ins.

Event-Based Systems

In an event-based system, communication is performed by generating and receiving events. This process starts when some component within the system fires an event, representing some changes internal or external to the system. The event will then be delivered to a set of other components, who have previously registered their interest in such an event. This process of event notification can be implemented in two different ways (Fiege, Mühl, & Gärtner, 2002): either through the *event-based* cooperation model or through the *callback* cooperation model. In the former, a centralized event-service is responsible for receiving these events when they are fired and delivering them to the interested components. It is thus through this event service that components register their interest in a particular event. Conversely, in the callback model, the delivery of each event is performed by the component which provides it. Therefore, in order to receive a particular event, the interested components must register themselves with the component providing it. The so-called *Observer* design pattern (Gamma, Helm, Johnson, & Vlissides, 1995) is an abstraction of the callback event cooperation model.

It is not hard to note how the event approach is useful when monitoring changes in the context. Particularly, the event service cooperation model, due to its decoupled characteristic, can be successfully applied for the monitoring of changes in the environment. A centralized event service deployed in the environment could be responsible for notifying events fired by the devices available in it. Getting back to the shoes example, the application running in your cellular phone could register your interest on a specific kind of shoe in the event service. Then, when a new shipment of shoes is delivered to the shoe store located in the mall, the ubiquitous application of the store could fire an event to the centralized event service. In such an event, it could be included information about the types of shoes that have been delivered as well as their prices. If the information contained in the fired event matches the shoes specified by the user, the event service would thus notify the ubiquitous application of your device, which would then choose the best moment for notifying you.

Another usage of events, in the scope of ubiquitous computing, is applying the callback model for notifying about changes in the context related to the local device. A networking component executing on a personal device could fire events when the network bandwidth reaches a low level. Other applications in this device could then register to this event directly with the networking component, in order to perform some network congestion algorithm when the bandwidth is low.

Service-Oriented Computing

Service-oriented computing is a paradigm for building distributed applications through the integration of remote resources known as *services* (Huhns & Singh, 2005). To this end, four operations are defined (Papazoglou & Georgakopoulos, 2003): *publication*, *discovery*, *selection*, and *binding*. Publication makes a service available to the ones interested in it. Therefore, once services are published, the discovery operation is used to search for them, by using criteria like keywords representing the desired functionalities. As more then one service can be returned by the discovery operation, it is necessary to select a single one, which is performed through the selection operation. When a service is finally selected, it is possible to establish a connection with it, using the binding operation, in order to make use of its functionalities. Through these four operations, a distributed application can then bind to required services in a dynamic way, providing it with a high a degree of flexibility.

This facility of binding to remote services at runtime is straightforward for ubiquitous computing applications. As mentioned, mobility may cause the unavailability of some services. If these services are currently in use, then we would have trouble. If you are using the shopping mall's Internet access service for listening to an online radio through your cellular phone, you might not be able to continue listening to it when leaving the mall, because the service will probably be unavailable. Using the service oriented computing paradigm, the ubiquitous computing player in your cellular phone could instantly search and bind to a substitute Internet access service. Maybe, the most interesting point in this aspect is the fact that all this process could be performed in a very transparent way. In other words, you would not be aware that the service you were using became unavailable and a substitute one was found and relinked to the ubiquitous player.

The way that services are discovered is another feature that fits very well to the ubiquitous computing scenario. As we mentioned, in the service-oriented paradigm, services are discovered through a set of requirements. These requirements will then be matched against the services' description, for determining how close it is to the users' needs. These requirements can be, for example, the users' required functionalities, represented as a set of keywords. In the Internet access service example, the ubiquitous player could use keywords such as "Internet" and "access" when searching for the substitute service. Such a service could have a description like "Service for enabling Internet access," allowing the discovery operation to detect that this service is relevant enough for you. Therefore, this way of discovering services provides a very effective way for providing anytime and anywhere access to needed services on demand.

Dynamic Software Evolution

The term dynamic software evolution, as well as variants like unanticipated software evolution (Ebraert, Vandewoude, Cazzola, D'Hondt, & Berbers, 2005) and dynamic software updating (Hicks & Nettles, 2005), have been used to refer to the process of adapting software systems without stopping and restarting them.

In a world where devices should provide us with needed functionalities when demanded and still be as transparent as possible to us, dynamic software evolution becomes an essential tool for achieving such a goal. Dynamic software evolution could be useful, for example, in the tourist scenario we have been presenting throughout this chapter. Remember that, for enabling the tourist to check the weather forecast, the application in his personal device had to download and deploy pieces of software (e.g., components or services) which, together, perform the desired task. Therefore, performing all these steps in a transparent way is straightforward to Weiser's (1991) vision of invisibility. With dynamic software evolution, these pieces of software could be deployed in the tourist's device on the fly, not bothering users with requests to restart any of the ubiquitous application of his device.

UBIQUITOUS COMPUTING SYSTEMS ENGINEERING IN PRACTICE

Now that we have seen the challenges and requirements of ubiquitous computing systems as well as the software engineering techniques that can be used for coping with them, it is time to present some of the current ubiquitous middleware solutions that make use of them.

JCAF

The Java context awareness framework (JCAF) (Bardan, 2005), is a ubiquitous computing middleware based on events and services. This middleware defines the idea of *context services*, which are supposed to handle the context information of a specific environment (e.g., a room, a bedroom). To this end, all context services are connected in a peer-to-peer fashion, in order to exchange context information among each other. The context model of each context service is based on three elements: *context*, *entity*, and *context item*, where context represents the environment being modeled, entity represents real world objects in a specific context (e.g., chairs, beds, light bulbs), and context items represent the context information that can be assigned to and acquired from each entity. Based on these elements, JCAF presents an event-based mechanism for enabling the retrieval of context information about the environment. More precisely, applications can register their interest in the changes of a particular context. For example, an application could be interested when the entity "John" enters in the context "Bedroom." The context services in charge of this context thus cooperate in order to deliver such events to the interested applications.

Wings

Wings (Loureiro et al., 2006) is a ubiquitous computing middleware based on the provision of services and discovery of hosts across heterogeneous protocols as well as the reuse of context information in different applications. To this end, the middleware has been based on the concepts of service-oriented computing, plug-in based architectures, and dynamic software evolution. Service-oriented computing has been used to enable users to publish, discover, and use remote services on demand and on the fly, using his interests and preferences as the guide for this process. The plug-in-based approach has been used to encapsulate the basic functionalities of Wings in plug-ins. Therefore, the middleware presents three kinds of plug-ins, *Service Provision Plug-ins* (SPPs), *Host Discovery Plug-ins* (HDPs), and *Context Awareness Plug-ins* (CAPs), respectively for service provision, host discovery, and context awareness. The general idea is that each SPP and HDP is associated with a specific protocol, enabling the middleware to provision services and discover services across different kinds of networks, possibly at the same time. An example of such an idea is presented in Figure 1, where we illustrate the service discovery process in Wings. In Figure 1, four SPPs are installed in the middleware, and thus, once an application requests a service discovery operation, the middleware passes this request for all these four SPPs. On the other hand, the use of CAPs permits to encapsulate the acquisition of context information in software plug-ins, freeing the application from this burden. In this way, different applications could easily use context information from different CAPs. Finally, in order to insert, remove, and update these plug-ins at runtime, Wings has been based on a dynamic component model, named of Compor (Almeida, Perkusich, Ferreira, Loureiro, & Costa, 2006), enabling it to evolve in a dynamic and transparent way.

RUNES

RUNES, which stands for *reconfigurable, ubiquitous, networked embedded systems*, is a ubiquitous computing middleware which focuses on reconfiguration (Costa et al., 2005). The basic idea behind this middleware is to define different component frameworks, each one with a specific purpose. Therefore, each of these component

Figure 1. Service discovery in the Wings middleware

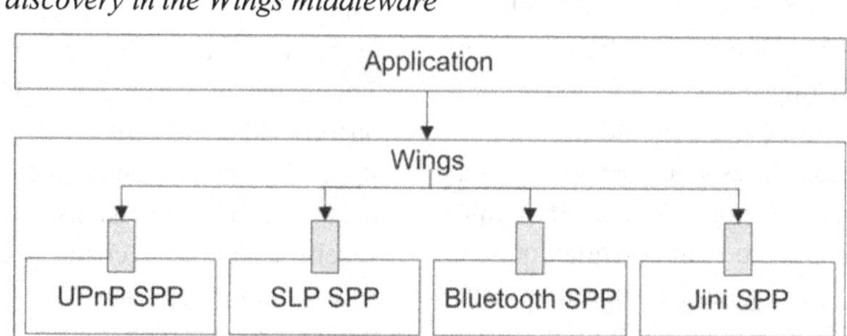

frameworks specifies the kinds of extensions that can be plugged into it. Examples of component frameworks defined by this middleware are the Network Services, Location Services, and Advertising and Discovery Service, which provide, respectively, networking communication, information about the location where the middleware is running, and the advertisement/discovery of components and services. Each component framework uses concepts from dynamic software evolution, through the RUNES component model, to enable the insertion and removal of extensions without stopping and restarting the middleware. Therefore, by plugging and unplugging extensions into the middleware's component frameworks, it is possible to change its functionalities in a completely transparent way, for both users and applications. For example, it is possible to use a networking communication extension for infrastructure-based networks at one moment, and change it for an ad hoc-based one later on. As in the Wings middleware, the use of services enables RUNES to discover services at runtime, with the goal of fulfilling the users' current needs.

Draco

The Draco middleware (Preuveneers, Rigole, Vandewoude, & Berbers, 2005) has been developed with the goal of providing a support for component-based ubiquitous applications. More precisely, it acts as a component container, instantiating application components and managing the interactions among them. Applications can thus be split into a set of interacting and replaceable components, managed internally by the middleware. Therefore, Draco can easily substitute one application component by another, for better using the resources of the device where such application is running. This is illustrated in Figure 2, which presents a personal agent application composed of two kinds of components, a streaming component, for video streaming over a network, and a user interface (UI) component, for displaying

Figure 2. Different configurations of a personal agent and its components in the Draco middleware

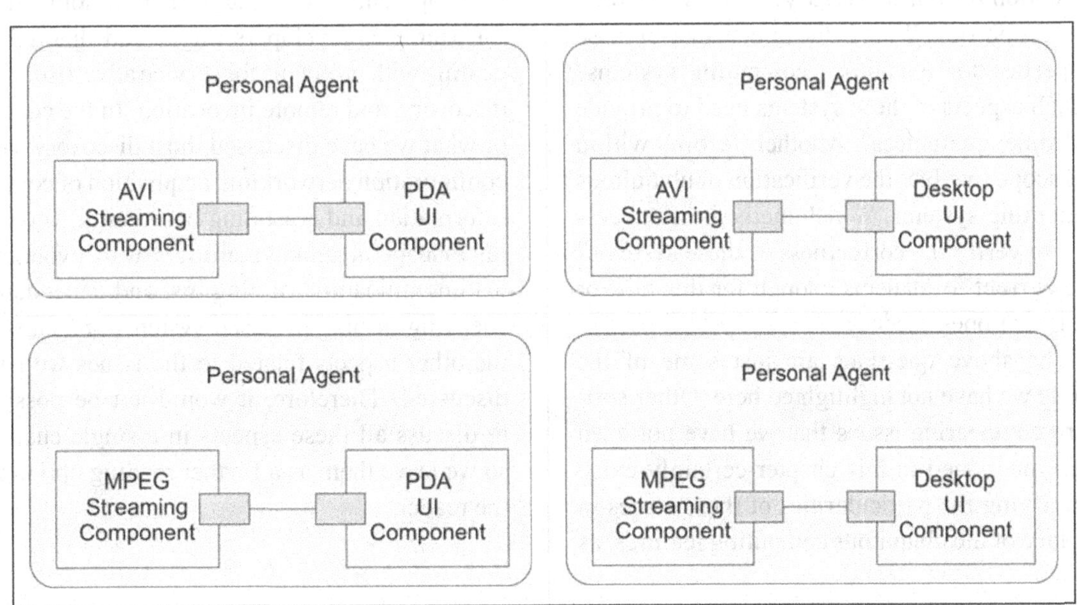

the video content received by the streaming component. Note that both components communicate with each other through well-defined interfaces (the gray squares in each component). Therefore, these components can be changed with a lesser impact on the remaining ones. This enables to set different configurations for the personal agent application, enabling it to be reconfigured when needed and according to the hardware available in the host it is executing.

FUTURE TRENDS

The engineering of ubiquitous computing systems is a broad field of research. Besides the issues we discussed in here, many other ones are involved in this field. An example is the management of ubiquitous computing systems as a whole. For instance, how faults and system malfunctioning could be automatically and transparently detected. Does the scale of ubiquitous computing systems affect the detection of these faults and malfunctioning? If yes, how to deal with it? Could such systems recover from faults and malfunctioning by themselves? In which cases does human intervention become necessary? What about real-time properties? What is the importance of these properties for ubiquitous computing systems? Which aspects of these systems need to provide real-time guarantees? Another feature within this scope involves the verification of ubiquitous computing systems. Which methods are necessary to verify the correctness of these systems? Are current formalisms enough for this task or are newer ones needed?

The above questions are just some of the points we have not highlighted here. Other software engineering issues that we have not even been mentioned in this chapter certainly exist. Identifying the particularities of these issues in the face of the ubiquitous computing features, as well as new software engineering issues exclusive of ubiquitous computing systems, is thus an important task towards the development of more dependable ubiquitous software systems.

CONCLUSION

In this chapter, we presented a software engineering perspective for ubiquitous computing systems. To this end, we reviewed the challenges, requirements, and techniques involved both in the design and implementation of these systems. Our aim, however, is not to cover nor define all aspects of software engineering for ubiquitous computing systems. Instead, we have tried to present what we believe to be the tip of the iceberg, and based on this, open the way for further research on the field of software engineering for ubiquitous computing systems.

As we have seen, there are many issues involved in the task of engineering these systems. Although we have presented these issues in a very high-level way, it is worth mentioning that many other aspects, not necessarily involved with software engineering, are involved in each of them. In service-oriented computing, for example, developers might find themselves dealing with protocols for service advertisement, discovery, and remote invocation. In the context of what we have discussed, host discovery, zero configuration networking, acquisition of context information and reasoning based on it, versioning management in dynamic software evolution, loading/unloading of plug-ins, and dependency checking in plug-in-based systems are some of the other aspects related to the issues we have discussed. Therefore, it would not be possible to discuss all these aspects in a single chapter, so we leave them as a further reading option for the reader.

REFERENCES

Almeida, H., Perkusich, A., Ferreira, G., Loureiro, E., & Costa, E. (2006, July). A component model to support dynamic unanticipated software evolution. In *Proceedings of the 18th International Conference on Software Engineering and Software Engineering.* San Francisco, CA.

Banavar, G., & Bernstein, A. (2002, December). Software infrastructure and design challenges for ubiquitous computing, *Communications of the ACM, 45*(12), 92-96.

Bardram, J. E. (2005, May). The Java context awareness framework (JCAF) - a service infrastructure and programming framework for context-aware applications. In H. Gellersen, R. Want, & A. Schmidt (Eds.), *Proceedings of the 3rd International Conference on Pervasive Computing* (pp. 98-115). Munich, Germany: Spinger-Verlag.

Birsan, D. (2005, March). On plug-ins and extensible architectures. *ACM Queue, 3*(2), 40-46.

Campo, C., Rubio, C. G., López, A. M., & Almenárez, F. (in press). PDP: A lightweight discovery protocol for local-scope interactions in wireless ad hoc networks. *Computer Networks.*

Cardoso, R. S., & Kon, F. (2002, November). Mobile agents: A key for effective pervasive computing. In *2002 OOPSLA Workshop on Pervasive Computing.* Seattle, WA.

Clarke, M., Blair, G. S., Coulson, G., & Parlavantzas, N. (2001, November). An efficient component model for the construction of adaptive middlewares. In *Proceedings of the IFIP/ACM International Conference on Distributed Systems Platforms* (pp. 160-178). Heidelberg, Germany: Springer-Verlag.

Costa, P., Coulson, G., Mascolo, C., Picco, G. P., & Zachariadis, S. (2005, September). The RUNES middleware: A reconfigurable component-based approach to networked embedded systems. In *Proceedings of the 16th IEEE International Symposium on Personal Indoor and Mobile Radio Communications.* Berlin, Germany: IEEE Communications Society.

Coutaz, J., Crowley, J. L., Dobson, S., & Garlan, D. (2005, March). Context is key. *Communications of the ACM, 48*(3), 49-53.

d'Acierno, A., Pietro, G. D., Coronato, A., & Gugliara, G. (2005, June). Plugin-orb for applications in a pervasive computing environment. In *Proceedings of the 2005 International Conference on Pervasive Systems and Computing* (pp. 140-146). Las Vegas, NE: CSREA Press.

Dey, A. K. (2001, February). Understanding and using context. *Personal and Ubiquitous Computing, 5*(1), 4-7.

Ebraert, P., Vandewoude, Y., Cazzola, W., D'Hondt, T., & Berbers, Y. (2005, July). Pitfalls in unanticipated dynamic software evolution. In *Proceedings of the workshop on reflection, AOP and meta-data for software evolution.* Glasgow, Scotland.

Fiege, L., Mühl, G., & Gärtner, F. C. (2002, December). Modular event-based systems. *The Knowledge Engineering Review, 17*(4), 359-388

Gamma, E., Helm, R., Johnson, R., & Vlissides, J. (1995, January). *Design patterns: Elements of reusable object-oriented software.* Addison-Wesley Professional.

Grace, P., Blair, G. S., & Samuel, S. (2005, January). A reflective framework for discovery and interaction in heterogeneous mobile environments. *Mobile Computing and Communications Review, 9*(1), 2-14.

Guttman, E. (2001, May). Autoconfiguration for IP networking: Enabling local communication. *IEEE Internet Computing, 5*(3), 81-6.

Henricksen, K., Indulska, J., & Rakotonirainy, A. (2001, September). Infrastructure for pervasive computing: Challenges. In *Proceedings of Informatik 01: Workshop on Pervasive Computing* (pp. 214-222).

Hicks, M., & Nettles, S. (2005, November). Dynamic software updating. *ACM Transactions on Programming Languages and Systems, 27*(6), 1049-1096.

Huhns, M. N., & Singh, M. P. (2005, January). Service-oriented computing: Key concepts and principles. *IEEE Internet Computing, 9*(1), 75-81.

Loureiro, E., Bublitz, F., Barbosa, N., Perkusich, A., Almeida, H., & Ferreira, G. (2006, June). A flexible middleware for service provision over heterogeneous pervasive networks. In *4th International Workshop on Mobile and Distributed Computing.* Niagara Falls, NY: IEEE Computer Society.

Loureiro, E., Ferreira, G., Almeida, H., & Perkusich, A. (2006). Pervasive computing: What is it anyway? In M. Lytras & A. Naeve (Eds.), *Ubiquitous and pervasive knowledge and learning management: Semantics, social networking and new media to their full potential.* Hershey, PA: Idea Group.

Loureiro, E., Oliveira, L., Almeida, H., Ferreira, G., & Perkusich, A. (2005, November). Improving flexibility on host discovery for pervasive computing middlewares. In *3rd International Workshop on Middleware for Pervasive and Ad hoc Computing.* Grenoble, France.

Niemalä, E., & Latvakoski, J. (2004, October). Survey of requirements and solutions for ubiquitous software. In *Proceedings of the 3rd International Conference of Mobile and Ubiquitous Multimedia* (pp. 71-78). College Park, MD: ACM Press.

Papazoglou, M. P. (2003, December). Service-oriented computing: Concepts, characteristics and directions. In *Proceedings of Fourth International Conference on Web Information Systems Engineering* (pp. 3-12). Rome, Italy: IEEE Computer Society.

Papazoglou, M. P., & Georgakopoulos, D. (2003, April). Service oriented computing. *Communications of the ACM, 46*(10), 24-28.

Preuveneers, D., Rigole, P., Vandewoude, Y., & Berbers, Y. (2005, November). Middleware support for component-based ubiquitous and mobile computing applications. In *Demo Session of the 7th International Middleware Conference.* Grenoble, France.

Raatikainen, K., Christensen, H. B., & Nakajima, T. (2002, October). Application requirements for middleware for mobile and pervasive systems. *Mobile Computing and Communications Review, 6*(4), 16-24.

Saha, D., & Mukherjee, A. (2003, March). Pervasive computing: A paradigm for the 21st Century. *Computer, 36*(3), 25-31.

Shilit, B. N., Adams, N., & Want, R. (1994, December). Context-aware computing applications. In *Proceedings of the IEEE Workshop on Mobile Computing Systems and Applications* (pp. 85-90). Santa Cruz, CA: IEEE Computer Society.

Szypersky, C. (1999, December). *Component software - beyond object-oriented programming.* Addison Wesley Longman.

Tiengo, W., Costa, E., Tenório, L. E., & Loureiro, E. (2006, January). An architecture for personalization and recommendation system for virtual learning community libraries. In *Proceedings of The Fifth IASTED International Conference on Web-based Education.* Puerto Vallarta, Mexico: Acta Press.

Weiser, M. (1991, September). The computer for the 21st century. *Scientific American, 265*(3), 94-104.

KEY TERMS

Computing Devices: Every day objects embedded with computing and communication capabilities.

Context: Any information that can be used to characterize the situation of an entity.

Context-Awareness: To be aware of the context in order to give relevant services to the user.

Mobile Devices: Any low-sized portable device used to interact with other mobile devices and resources from smart spaces. Examples of mobile devices are cellular phones, smart phones, PDAs, notebooks, and tablet PCs.

Pervasive Computing: The vision conceived by Mark Weiser which consists of a world where computing will be embedded in everyday objects.

Sensor Networks: Network of many spatially distributed devices using sensors to monitor conditions at different locations, such as temperature, sound, vibration, pressure, motion, or pollutants.

Service: A software entity that can be integrated to a remote distributed application.

Service Oriented Computing: The newest paradigm for distributed computing where applications should be built by dynamically integrating services.

ENDNOTES

1 Source: SAP Global (http://www.sap.com)

2 Source: Mimosa Medical Information Systems (http://www.mimosa.com)

3 http://www.mozilla.com/firefox

4 http://www.eclipse.org

Chapter XV
When Ubiquitous Computing Meets Experience Design:
Identifying Challenges for Design and Evaluation

Ingrid Mulder
Telematica Instituut and Rotterdam University, The Netherlands

Lucia Terrenghi
Vodafone Group R&D, Germany

ABSTRACT

In this chapter we provide an overview of the main implications of emerging ubiquitous computing scenarios with respect to the design and evaluation of the user experience. In doing that, we point out how these implications motivate the evolution of the human-computer interaction discipline towards a more interdisciplinary field of research requiring a holistic approach as well as new adequate research methods. We identify challenges for design and evaluation and consider different classes of methods to cope with these challenges. These challenges are illustrated with examples in which ubiquitous technology is used both for its design and for the study of the users' everyday life. In our discussion we support the idea that ubiquitous technology provides new means for the study of human experiences as well as human deliberate engagement with technology; the latter as an alternative to automation and invisible technology.

INTRODUCTION

The vision of ubiquitous computing foresees novel scenarios of highly interactive environments in which communication takes place between single users and devices, between devices and devices, and between users and users. The novel possibilities enabled by embedded technology have motivated most of the research on context sensitive systems, automation, and invisible technology. Next to that type of scenario, novel and ubiquitous possibilities for capturing, authoring, editing, and transferring multimedia content provide new means for people's interaction, performance, communication, and storytelling. This in turn allows for the design of new stimuli from which people can create their own meaningful experiences. These new design possibilities raise potentials as well as challenges, and ask for new methods and forms of interaction between users and environments, and between different groups of users.

Furthermore, an overview of the main implications of emerging ubiquitous computing scenarios with respect to the design and evaluation of the user experience will be provided. In doing that, we point out how these implications motivate the evolution of the Human-Computer Interaction (HCI) discipline towards a more interdisciplinary field of research, which requires a more holistic approach as well as new adequate research methods. In our discussion we support the idea that ubiquitous computing technologies provide new means for the study of human experiences as well as human deliberate engagement with technology, in contrast to automation and invisible technology.

This chapter addresses the point "where ubiquitous computing meets experience design." In other words, the question "how can the design of products and services benefit from the potential of ubiquitous computing?" is central. We identify challenges for design and evaluation and consider different types of methods to cope with them. Then, these challenges are illustrated by examples in which ubiquitous technology is used both for the design of innovative products and services as well as for the study of the users' everyday life experiences.

FEATURES OF UBIQUITOUS COMPUTING

In this section, the features of ubiquitous computing that are most relevant to experience design are described.

A key implication of ubiquitous computing on the design of the user experience is the extension of human-human and human-computer interactions across a broader range of time and location. The individual, situated interaction setting, characteristic for the personal computer (PC) is augmented by a more distributed and casual interaction with computing, or with information in a broader sense. As a consequence, the level of complexity of the humans' activities dealing with technology increases.

Users' interactions with technology become much more continuous and overlapping in time. While it is still possible to distinguish single goal-driven tasks when analyzing users' interactions on a desktop PC, this becomes harder with ubiquitous computing. We can talk on the phone while moving in the street, listen to music while writing an SMS, or purchase a bus ticket with our mobile phone while riding on the train. Our activities become more and more concurrent and our accessibility to social interaction broadened. This implies the chance of more frequent interruptions and the difficulty to clearly identify a beginning and an end of our activities (Abowd, Mynatt, & Rodden, 2002; Fogarty et al., 2004).

Ubiquitous networks have a large impact on how we organize our daily life, how we work, make friends, and look for entertainment. In short, they are changing our behaviors and social patterns. The increasing use of mobile telephones affects our expectations for availability and accessibility. When setting an appointment with someone somewhere, for example, we tolerate and actually expect more flexibility in punctuality, due to the fact that it is possible to inform each other in case of delay. With the reduction of cost and effort in communicating with others through these devices, the likelihood of communication increases. Despite the possibility of communication with "anyone, anytime, anyplace" that these ubiquitous networks allow for, people do not always want to be accessible.

Another attribute of ubiquitous computing is its invisibility. In ubiquitous technology the miniaturization of computing, such as, RFID, "smart dust" technologies, and wireless data connections (i.e., Bluetooth) makes interactions potentially seamless and invisible; whereas the desktop work station has its own recognizable physical appearance and a fixed location, even though the activities that can be operated on a PC are very diverse. Due to ubiquitous computing, implicit interactions can take place, consequently the level of user control over ubiquitous technology is not always straightforward; issues such as transparency, control, and feedback should be considered in designing the user interface.

Finally, ubiquitous computing brings human interaction with digital technology out of the office and into our everyday lives. In this sense, digital and physical layers of interaction might blur in hybrid contexts of interaction requiring the design and analysis of experience on both levels. This means that we need to understand the critical factors that make and affect an experience in order to design and evaluate them in the novel settings of computing.

UBIQUITOUS COMPUTING AND EXPERIENCE DESIGN: WHEN BOTH WORLDS MEET

The specific aspects brought along by the development of ubiquitous computing have generated some changes in the disciplines that are involved in the research, design, and development of new systems.

The above mentioned features of ubiquitous computing raised the need for a broader design perspective and extension of the traditional HCI community in terms of competences and individuals involved, including the design of experiences for the use of interactive products asks for interdisciplinary teams as well as for the user involvement in the design process. This trend has contributed to the adoption of a more holistic point of view in the analysis and design of human-computer and human-human interaction, which takes time and space dimensions into account. In the following paragraphs, we review some of the present thoughts on this topic.

New Design Dimensions

The focus of HCI on usability has broadened because of the sensorial, cognitive, and emotional aspects of ubiquitous interaction, which become more evident in such dynamic and distributed contexts of experience. Jordan (2000) to this respect conceptualizes pleasure with products beyond usability. He defines pleasure with products as the emotional, hedonic, and practical benefits associated with products. Norman (2004) describes studies that suggest there are three levels of processing information, the visceral level, dealing with instinct, the behavioral level, dealing with behavior and use, and the reflective level, dealing with contemplation.

These different levels demand different kinds of design. In traditional usability studies time and space dimensions have been "crystallized" to unpack activities into single tasks that can be analyzed and formalized. HCI has mostly dealt with usability, looking at the cognitive level of information processing. Experience design embraces a broader perspective and focuses on the quality of the whole relationship between a user and a product during the whole period of engagement: from the first approach and impression (visceral level), through its usage, cultural relevance, and durability (behavioral level), and to the reflection and memory of the complete relationship (reflective level). Indeed when technology enters our daily environments and activities, the way we experience it is strongly related to our physical, social, and cognitive context. This implies that ergonomic as well as social and psychological dimensions need to be addressed in the design and evaluation of the experience. Experience design includes deriving plausible user intentions and requires a new class of contextualized systems, also referred to as pragmatic systems (van Kranenburg, Bargh, Iacob, & Peddemors, 2006; van Kranenburg, Snoeck, & Mulder, 2006).

New Design Goals

Another new and extended definition of user experience has been proposed by Dillon (2000). He writes that the user experience is the sum of behaviors, its result as emotion, including aesthetics, perceived usability, cognitive effort, perception of information shapes, acceptance level, and self-efficacy. In such a scenario, traditional usability goals (i.e., effectiveness, efficiency, safety, utility, learnability, and memorability, as defined by Preece, Rogers, & Sharp, 2002) fall short in covering the complexity of experience and new goals such as fun, entertainment, motivation, engagement, and reward need to be considered. A main issue remains open though: how to define such goals and to set priorities? These are obviously different for different experiences and different individuals. Morville (2004) proposes a user experience honeycomb in which he defines general qualities of experience: useful, usable, desirable, findable, accessible, credible, and valuable. Such honeycomb, even though conceived for Web-based experiences, aims to serve as design tool to define priorities. Priorities vary in dependence of context, content, and users.

Another related term in use is "value sensitive design." Friedman (2004) conceptualizes "value sensitive design" as an approach that methodologically integrates and iterates three types of investigations: conceptual, physical, and technical. One of the distinguishing features of such an approach is that it maintains certain values, such as those relative to human welfare, that are universally held, despite their different roles in different cultures. For Friedman (2004), the more concretely one conceptualizes a value, the more its cultural dependency becomes stronger; on the other hand, the more abstractly one conceptualizes it, the more universally it will be recognized. In a similar vein Shedroff (1995) suggests the identification of persistent human values and emotions as guidance for the design of experiences: for example, spirituality, playing, love, creativity, enjoyment, sport, art, and creativity are values, which have not changed over thousands of years. In keeping with Friedman (2004) and Shedroff (1995), however, we argue that what has changed and where design probably has an influence and responsibility, are *behaviors*. The experience of interacting with SMS is a good example. In terms of efficiency, the usability of the interactions when texting with mobile devices is low, but the perceived value of the SMS experience is high. This is because of the underlying motivation, which deals with the value of social communication and social connectedness. In this respect, the understanding of people's values and needs is crucial in the definition of experience goals.

New Designers' Roles

The shift of perspective in HCI from a utilitarian focus towards a moral one has been coupled with the emergence of a design approach that strives for openness rather than for efficiency. It is the intention that users actively are completing the experience for themselves and may even turn the design into unintended or unpredicted directions. Ambiguity and interpretation are embraced by design as fertile terrain for creativity and interactivity (Gaver, Beaver, & Benford, 2003; Sengers & Gaver, 2005). This has fostered the idea of looking at performing arts such as scriptwriting, storytelling, and performance as sources for design guidance. Storytelling is a fruitful method to recall memories and experiences. These disciplines are particularly concerned with the communication of varied stories and messages through the creation of interesting and wonderful experiences (Laurel, 1991; Shedroff, 2004). At this rate, designers can be compared to skilled theatre play-writers or directors who write the plot and design everything that is necessary for the play to take place, knowing that they cannot control what the actors will really say or do on stage.

Users' creativity (or *actors'* creativity, in the metaphor) on stage is generally motivated by individual values and cultures; this in turn raises ethics questions in terms of design responsibilities and design roles. Are designers responsible for dictating values and shaping cultures? To which extent can they have an influence on these? Are there any generally acceptable values that we, as designers, can rely on in the definition of design goals?

Laurel (2001) states:

The stories, movies, videogames, and Web sites don't have to be about values to have a profound influence on values. Values are everywhere, embedded in every aspect of our culture and lurking in the very natures of our media and technologies. Culture workers know the question isn't whether they are there, but who is taking responsibilities for them, how they are being shaped, and how they are shaping us for the future (p. 62).

FROM INTERACTION DESIGN TO USER EXPERIENCE DESIGN

The changes in HCI described above have generated a vivid discussion about the differences and analogies between interaction and experience design. Even though a clear distinction is still missing in the community, and the borders between the two fields remain subtle, we attempt to clarify this by providing a definition of interaction and experience and by reviewing some related work.

Winograd (1996) refers to interaction design as design of spaces for human communication and interaction between humans (or their agents), mediated by products. Interaction design deals with the design of any artifact, be it an object, system, or environment, whose primary aim is to support either an interaction of a person with the artifact, or an interaction among people that is mediated by the artifact (Erickson, 2006). Interaction therefore involves users and products and is about the relationship between them.

Experience design is focused on the interaction between people and products and the resulting experience (Forlizzi & Ford, 2000). It includes all aspects emerging from the interaction with a product across time and space: emotionally, intellectually, and sensually. Experience design focuses on the quality of the user experience during the whole period of interaction with a product. In this sense, interaction is the means and method by which humans experience the world. According to Kankainen (2003), a user's experience is a result of a motivated action in a certain context. This definition illustrates that the intention and expectations of a person using a product or service influence the experience, and that using and evaluating a product in turn influences future experiences.

In comparison to interaction, experience differs in the following aspects:

- Experience is continuous; it can be made of sequence of several concrete interactions;
- Experience is subjective; the same product can be experienced in different ways from different users, on sensorial, cognitive, and especially emotional levels;
- Experience is about values; that is, the value proposition.

Though the differences between interaction and experience, the link between the two remains tight. Some work has been done in describe this relationship in a systematic way. Shedroff (2000) defines the dimensions of interactivity as feedback, control, productivity, creativity/cocreativity, communication, and adaptivity. According to Shedroff (2000), such dimensions have to be thought of and displayed as continuous: all experiences (and products) inhabit such a continuum of interactivity. It is important to tune the level of interactivity in a way which is appropriate for the goals of experience we design for. Forlizzi and Ford (2000) worked on a framework of interaction and experience as it relates to design. In this framework they define three types of user-product interactions, namely fluent, cognitive, and expressive, which unfold in a particular situation, generating three types of experience, namely experience, an experience, and co-experience. The relationship between interaction and experience types is not one-to-one, though, and it actually remains unclear to some extent how designers are supposed to use such a framework in practice.

DESIGN AND EVALUATION CHALLENGES

The difficulties in defining the goals of experience—and designing for it—are obviously affecting the evaluation phase as well. Indeed, the goals of experience are determining what kind of parameters to observe and assess in the evaluation phase as well as and the priorities of requirements. Referring to some particular aspects of ubiquitous computing and to some features of the experience previously introduced, we reflect on the main emerging issues that experience design and evaluation need to cope with (Terrenghi, Kronen, & Valle, 2005):

- The holistic aspect of experience requires for an even more extended set of dimensions to be assessed, which are often dependent on subjective values. This asks for a combination of quantitative and qualitative data to be collected and interpreted.
- The context of use of ubiquitous computing is highly mutable since users are mostly mobile in time and place and their goals are variable; thus, it is hard to track their cognitive and operative workflows, together with their emotional states.
- Ubiquitous technology mostly deals with communication systems and social interfaces: this means that the same system should accomplish different goals for different users.
- Ubiquitous computing scenarios are often based on middle-long term horizons, for which technology is not yet available: users might not know the technological possibilities, and therefore it is hard to envision needs for unfamiliar scenarios.
- Prototyping for ubiquitous computing often needs to rely on new technologies and protocols that are not yet mature and grounded, so that many assumptions about performance and reliability are needed.
- Interfaces can migrate across different communication means, using different modalities, thus requiring a multiplatform interface design and evaluation tools.
- The continuity feature of experience makes it difficult to disassemble and decompose it for analysis: previous interaction with other kinds of systems, for instance, can deeply affect the expectations of interaction and resulting experience with other ones;
- New aspects, such as outdoor setting, multitasking and intermittent activities, multiuser interaction, new business models, and communication patterns affect the whole usage experience and need to be assessed in different times and places.

Achieving a product that satisfies the users' needs normally requires an iterative approach to software development with continuous feedback from users throughout the process. Additionally, the social and economic role of communication is leading to more and more discussion about the best way to include the user in the design process. In the next section we reflect on the research methods currently available as well as on their suitability to cope with the issues presented above.

EVALUATING EXPERIENCE USING UBIQUITOUS COMPUTING

The increasing complexity of organizations and systems of communication, and the fast pace of technological change and adaptation poses a challenge for studying the resulting experience of new products and services in relation to design. Interestingly, ubiquitous computing offers several possibilities to study such experiences in novel ways.

Several tools to study experiences and human behavior exist to study different aspects of experiences, such as emotions or fun. However, methodologies that study experience in a coherent and comprehensive way are admittedly still in their infancy, although many ingredients are available. Ethnographic studies, user profiles, contextual inquiries, participatory design sessions, focus groups, paper prototypes, in depth interviews, cultural probes, and technology probes are some of the tools that design research has been using to the purpose of understanding users. While most of these tools engage the users' collaboration in an explicit way, ubiquitous technology also provides tools to get such information in an implicit and less obtrusive manner. For instance, by embedding a sensor network in an environment, it is possible to draw users' patterns of interaction with appliances, usage patterns, and movements from one location to the other. Such usages of ubiquitous technology have been particularly motivated by the wish either to monitor elderly or disabled people's behavior, or to optimize resource consumption. Another way in which ubiquitous technology supports the evaluation analysis is the adoption of biosensors, measuring phenomena such as skin temperature or heart beat frequency: in this way it is possible to infer stress and excitements level, for instance while the user is playing with an interactive game. Furthermore, the location and log tracking of mobile users allow inferences on the usage of mobile services across time and space.

Methods and techniques that can be used to study different aspects of experiences can be distinguished between "explicit" and "implicit," referring to users' engagement in the analysis, and present pros and cons that need to be considered, depending on the experience to be evaluated.

Explicit Methods

This class of methods can benefit from users' conscious and deliberate participation: this can be very helpful when the researcher wants to establish a high level of empathy with the user. However there are drawbacks of these explicit methods:

- The high cost in terms of researcher's time
- The difficulty to formalize and quantify results
- The risk of biased results;
- The risk of flow interruption, if the analysis takes place during the interaction
- The asynchronous reflection on an experience, which either has not taken place yet, or is a past event

This last point is due to the continuity of experience, and refers to the fact that when people describe their experiences *a posteriori* (or *a priori*), they have obviously a different cognitive, emotional, and sensorial state than while they experience it *there and then*. Techniques of psychoanalysis promise to provide a useful and grounded methodology to this respect (Israel, 2003). Talking loud or cognitive walkthrough techniques, which try to assess the experience in the meanwhile of interaction, may interrupt the flow of such interaction, alienating users from immersion in their activities; besides they may provide results that are valid only for a specific and limited set in time and space, but cannot cover the overall experience.

Implicit Methods

This class of methods can cope with the last issue presented in the previous section by invisibly tracking interactions, without interrupting them. Additionally, these methods provide quantitative results, which are easier to analyze than qualitative ones. The limits of these methodologies are:

- The mapping between sensed values and inferred emotional or cognitive states can be incorrect, as there is not always a universal and well established relationship between them (e.g., a higher skin temperature can be due to a positive or negative emotional stress, and can highly vary from person to person);
- They deal with privacy sensitive content, and often users feel uncomfortable and can behave unnaturally if they know that they are being observed.

Given the benefits and limitations of both classes, it is our suggestion that a heterogeneous and well-thought application of such methodologies provides the best potential for success in the hard task of designing for and evaluating the complexity of user experiences. In the following section we report on two examples in which ubiquitous technology is used both as a design and evaluation tool.

A DESIGN RESEARCH STUDY: EXPERIENCE DESIGN FOR POLICE OFFICERS

The study reported here concentrates on the experience of police officers that interact using ubiquitous computing and context sensitive systems (see, for more details, Steen, de Koning, & Mulder, 2005; Steen, van Eijk, Gunther, Hooreman, & Koning, 2005). For instance, an experience offered by police officers might be a safety bundle for retailers. In case retailers collaborate in solving criminality problems, the police force could award their initiative and offer these retailers a special telephone number for direct help (retailer is identified, and their trust relation confirms that such a call involves a serious robbery) or appropriate forms that ease reporting a crime, or prosecuting the shoplifter.

In order to adequately design for police officers we needed to understand their activities. In this phase we adopted explicit methods with an empathic and participatory design approach. Thus we interacted directly with police officers so as to share and collaboratively reflect on their experience. Special attention was paid to the several groups and distinctive contexts in which police officers work; their roles and tasks, and processes of communication and cooperation.

Rapid Ethnography: Developing Storylines

To advance our understanding of the daily work of police officers was observed in order to identify problems police officers might encounter regarding communication and cooperation in different contexts. Seven researchers shadowed police officers for a day, either during a day shift or during a night shift. The researcher accompanied the police officer during the entire working day, in the office as well as on the street and in the car. Each researcher made a report of his observations. A few days after the observations all researchers came together to report and share their findings. Some aspects and problems of the daily work of the police officers were mentioned repetitively during the workshop. We observed that police officers' work is driven by incidents and requires much improvisation. Police officers communicate with different people and often need information that is not easily available, and have to call a colleague at the office for this information, or have to go to the office to look it up. For communication between police officers, they use radio telephones (porto-phones) or cell phones, and for communication with others they use cell phones. Additionally, they spend considerable time at their desk in order to process and file information. On many occasions, police officers need to cooperate with other officers, school directors, and with people from the municipality. Police officers on the beat often work for years in one area and have their contacts there. They gain a lot of knowledge about this, whereas police officers within emergency response go to emergencies in different areas around the clock, and gain another type of knowledge focused on emergencies. Experts from the police speculate that the performance of these two police tasks can improve if these different police officers could more easily access each other's knowledge, and if they would be more aware of each other.

The "WijkWijzer" (in English: Neighbourhood Pointer) application, developed in the FRUX project, is a novel application, which we tested in the police domain. The WijkWijzer points you to people who are relevant for you—given your context, whom you may contact, or who may most likely contact you. The WijkWijzer taps into the police's real-time database of reports (e.g., emergency calls by citizens), combines current reports, a history of reports, the current availability of police officers, and composes a list of people who are potentially relevant for each other in working on that report. The WijkWijzer presents these people, and hints to contact them, on a PDA. During the summer of 2006, the WijkWijzer has been applied in small-scale test with five police-officers using the prototype (Steen, van Eijk et al., 2005).

However, several issues still remain open: which contextual information should be displayed in the list or on the screen at a certain moment? Put differently, which contact is most relevant for a police officer in a certain situation? To answer those questions measurement tools for capturing and analyzing the usage of FRUX services were adopted to study the relationship between service usage and the user's experience. To describe context variables, other measurements such as experience sampling are being developed within the FRUX project.

Also, in the FRUX project, mobile devices are used as the primary data capturing devices, supported by sensors and beacons in other infrastructures, where this is possible and appropriate. SocioXensor is an experience measurement tool that responds to the goal of doing in-situ research using the peculiarities of context-sensitive systems and the capabilities of mobile and wearable devices (Mulder, ter Hofte, & Kort, 2005). Put differently, ubiquitous computing is used as a means to get closer to the user and therefore to the user experience. SocioXensor is a toolkit that makes use of the hardware (sensors) and software functionalities built into mobile devices (e.g., PDAs and smartphones). The goal is to collect information about how users experience a setting or applications. Examples of this include not only aspects of functionality and usability, but also emotional ones. SocioXensor collects objective information of human behaviour within a specific context, such as where and how communication takes place. More specifically, SocioXensor typically collects data at times and locations, which would be impractical or very costly with ethnography and lab studies, while maximizing the chance that subjects exhibit their natural behaviour in their natural context. Information about the use of applications, such as the registration of keystrokes and the duration of use, is also collected. Finally, SocioXensor also record subjective data, reflecting the mood of the user, for example, stressed, happy, sad. SocioXensor can be more obtrusive than logging, but it is typically less obtrusive than direct observation methods such as ethnography (which allow for very rich data capturing) or lab experiments or more details.

UBICOMP IN THE KITCHEN

In this example, we report on the Living Cookbook project (Terrenghi, Hilliges, & Butz, 2007) in order to reflect on some of the design and evaluation issues that the introduction of ubicomp in everyday life activities brings along.

The Living Cookbook is an appliance for the exchange of multimedia cooking experiences in the kitchen. It consists of a client application running on a tablet PC mounted on a kitchen cabinet. It is implemented in Macromedia Flash and connected to a server implemented in Java, which in turn controls a camera for recording video, and a video projector for playing back the video. Via the client interface, a user can insert new recipes, choose already inserted recipes, and control video recording and playback. The video is projected onto a wall above the counter in order to provide a good view and still keep the counter clear of devices. The content of the cookbook is stored in an XML File on the server side. Video material is referenced externally from the server's file system. Another XML file stored on the server side defines all ingredients including appropriate ranges and units.

When designing such an appliance our aim was to cultivate communication and collaboration in the kitchen by making people's cooking experiences recordable and shareable in an interactive digital cookbook. The goal is to preserve cultural and social roots on the one hand, and stimulate cultural and generational fertilization on the other. Instead of simply exchanging written instructions, we capture the whole cooking process with annotated audio and video and make it available for others so that they can asynchronously reproduce the dish. When users give instructions for a recipe, they author a multimedia cookbook. We therefore rely on people's interest in communication and story telling, as they are turned into actors of a participatory theater, who interact with their audience via technology.

The technical setup and the user tests of the appliance took place in the small kitchen of our lab. As we will point out later this implies a certain complexity in terms of evaluation, as the testers were not as familiar with such a kitchen as they are with their own domestic one. The design of the interface underwent an iterative process. In an early stage of development four members of the design and development team tested the application with real cooking sessions. Two of them recorded recipes, and the other two played them back. Considering that everyone is familiar with cooking, it made sense to directly involve ourselves (i.e., researchers), in the test, so as to have a first hand experience. Everyone, indeed, has his personal way to deal with household activities, which justifies the direct involvement of team members. These sessions were concluded by four meals in which the team dined and watched the videos of the cooking sessions, discussed the application, improvements to be done on the interface, changes in the setting of the camera and projector, and the experience delivered by the application.

In a second phase, four people from outside of the team, two men and two women with an age range of 22 to 45 were invited to test the application. In this phase a cognitive walkthrough method was adopted, so as to evaluate the user interface. Testers were given tasks and asked to report and talk aloud when they did not understand what to do or encountered any difficulty. These tests also ended up in meals and discussions, jointly with the team members. In this setting, the discussion addressed both the user interface (e.g., whether it was clear how to interact), and the whole experience (e.g., how they felt about recording or playing a video of a personal cooking session). During the meal with the team, testers were invited to present their impressions of the application, to discuss whether they would use it in their homes, and how it could be improved.

In this context, ubiquitous technology supports our design in such a way that is rather different from automation and optimization of efficiency. Instead, we exploit the potential of ubiquitously capturing and displaying experiences, in a multimodal fashion, so as to enhance users' deliberate intention of authoring and communicating. The emotional quality of content created by family members or intimate friends is expected to be very different in comparison to the cooking sessions broadcast on TV shows for a large audience. This aspect promises to affect motivation and engagement. People can customize each recipe with personal tips and tricks, make explicit reference to their well known target users, and thereby create a very personal experience.

Furthermore we exploit ubiquitous technology for our analysis of the experience. Reviewing the videos that were stored together with the authors of such videos (i.e., our invited cooks), we have the possibility to reflect on both technical issues (e.g., placement of cameras, set up of the hardware) as well as experience ones (e.g., some testers were very keen on having a copy of the video to demonstrate their cooking skills to their buddies).

For more details about the results of our evaluation, we refer to Terrenghi et al. (2007). What is more important for the current discussion is that the experiences with ubiquitous computing outside the office raise questions in terms of focus and methods of evaluation.

The introduction of computing technology into everyday life implies hybrid contexts of interaction in which physical and digital features of our design affect each other and the resulting experience. During the design and evaluation of our appliance it became clear how the design of new experiences enhanced by available technology needs to cope with both the traditional constraints of the physical environment and mundane activities (e.g., accessing the kitchen cabinet, sink, dirty hands, heating sources), and at the same time with the novel issues brought along by new appliances and new technology (e.g., visual feedback of the activity, additional interactions, expectation of performance, and communication).

From a user's point of view, the two aspects blur and their combination affects the whole experience. For design research and evaluation, this raises the challenge of distinguishing the critical factors, that is, whether these reside in the physical environment, for example, on the screen placement in relationship to other artefacts and to the users, whether on the interface, whether on the cognitive effort required from the computer supported activity, and so forth. The users' possibility to move around in the space and to directly manipulate objects and information items needs to be supported by interfaces that are properly scaled to users' metrics, locations in the space, reciprocal distance among users and motor capabilities. Issues such as the user's height, her visual angle, the ability to reach displayed objects, the proportion between objects and hands sizes, and environmental factors such as sound, smoke, and heat, assume an important role. Interior designers, product designers, and ergonomists have been working on the kitchen in terms of space and artefacts for some time; the design of affordances for digital information embedded in a real physical environment implies the consideration of new aspects which differ from the desktop PC environment.

Furthermore, the design of experiences that build on social relationships and imply social contexts needs to find novel approaches to prototype, test and assess such experiences. In this sense the collaboration between design research and the behavioural sciences promises to provide novel methods for experience simulation and assessment.

So far, most of the research in domestic technology has focused on making the environment aware of the context: this requires definition and description of parameters, assessment of their relevance, interpretation of sensed data, and design of relative system reactions. It remains an open issue, though, how to make users aware and knowledgeable of the hybrid context in which they interact. Furthermore, how to make designers knowledgeable about the complexity of the hybrid contexts of interaction for which they design is not straightforward.

CONCLUSION AND DISCUSSION

In this chapter, we described how the introduction of ubiquitous technology into everyday life has raised novel design and evaluation challenges that justify a shift in the perspective of HCI research towards more holistic interdisciplinary approaches. We reflected on the meaning of experience and how it is conceived in different research fields, and we considered the implications and potential effect of ubiquitous computing on human experiences. In particular, we focused on the new possibilities that ubiquitous computing offers in terms of the design of contextualized learning experiences, design of social experiences, and evaluation methodologies.

Given the complexity of experience, we argue that the definition of design goals needs to take different dimensions into account, which include usability as well as human values. This requires new evaluation approaches and methods.

By reflecting on pros and cons of different methods, we support the idea that a combination of quantitative and qualitative data, using explicit and implicit methods of analysis, is necessary. The combination of quantitative data tracked by the system (e.g., location, proximity, communication) with qualitative data provided by the users (e.g., availability, feeling, experience sampling) contributes to the acquisition of a deeper and more holistic insight of people's context.

Recently, the role of psycho-physiological data has been discussed during the "Probing Experience" symposium (Westerink, de Ruyter, Overbeek, Ouwerkerk, & Pasveer, 2008). These psycho-physiological data are expected to become key factors in differentiating benefits of products for a diversity of user experiences. In this sense, evaluating the user's experience plays a central role, not only during the design and evaluation processes, but also during the interaction itself. A video recorder that recommends TV programs that fit the user's current mood, a module that alerts a factory operator when he is getting drowsy are possible applications. Systems that detect and render psycho-physiological data are then required to assess and interpret user experiences (almost) in real-time. How to achieve this? What are potential applications of psycho-physiological measurements? Are real-time assessments based on monitoring of user behavior possible at all? (see, for more details, Westerink et al., 2008).

A lot of issues remain open in the research agenda, which ask for interdisciplinary collaboration towards the understanding of human experiences. Some examples are:

- When designing for context adaptive systems we make inferences on users' needs, based on contextual data implicitly sensed by the system, on which criteria should we draw a meaning out of these data? And how should the system adapt to that?
- Given that quantitative data are more exact; to what extent are they suitable for the understanding of the emotional aspects of experiences?
- Given the subjectivity of experience, what are the parameters to be assessed for different users?

In order to answer these questions, we believe that the collaboration of design research with social and psychological sciences will become a key point in the next user experience research agenda.

ACKNOWLEDGMENT

Our insights and experiences for writing this chapter are mainly based on participating in two projects, namely Flexible User Interfaces for Distributed Ubiquitous Machinery (FLUIDUM) and Freeband User Experience (FRUX). The FLUIDUM project (www.fluidum.org) has been funded by the Deutsche Forschungsgemeinschaft (DFG) and is hosted in the Media Informatics

Department at the LMU University Munich. The project deals with scenarios of ubiquitous computing for everyday life environments. The project Freeband User Experience (FRUX) is part of the research program Freeband Communication (www.freeband.nl), which aims at the generation of public knowledge in advanced telecommunication technology and applications in The Netherlands. FRUX is a joint effort of Ericsson, ISC (Dutch Police ICT service organization), Telematica Instituut, TNO ICT, Delft University of Technology, Free University Medical Centre, Waag Society, and Web Integration. In addition, several international discussions inspired us in writing this work. For this, we thank our project members, and the participants of the workshop on "User Experience Design for Pervasive Computing" associated with the Pervasive 2005 Conference co-organized by Lucia Terrenghi. Last but not least, special thanks go to Susan Whyche and Herma van Kranenburg for their helpful comments to the chapter.

REFERENCES

Abowd, G.D., Mynatt, E., & Rodden, T. (2002). The human experience. *Pervasive Computing, IEEE, 1*(1), 48-57.

Dillon, A. (2000). *Understanding and evaluating the user experience with information spaces.* Indiana University, HCI Lab.

Erickson, T. (2006). Five lenses: Towards a toolkit for interaction design. In S. Bagnara, G. Crampton-Smith & G. Salvendy (Eds.), *Theories and practice in interaction design.* Lawrence Erlbaum.

Fogarty, J., Hudson, S., Atkeson, C., Avrahami, D., Forlizzi, J., Kiesler, S. et al. (2004). Predicting human interruptability with sensors. *ACM Transactions on Computer-Human Interaction, 12*(1), 119-146.

Forlizzi, J., & Ford, S. (2000). The building blocks of experience: An early framework for interaction designers. In *Proceedings of DIS'00* (pp. 419-423). Brooklyn, NY: ACM Press.

Friedman, B. (2004). Value sensitive design. In *Encyclopedia of human-computer interaction* (pp. 769-774). Great Barrington, MA: Berkshire Publishing Group.

Gaver, W., Beaver, J., & Benford, S. (2003). Ambiguity as a resource for design. In *Proceedings of the ACM CHI 2003 Human Factors in Computing Systems Conference* (pp. 233-240). Ft. Lauderdale, FL.

Israel, T. (2003). *Some place like home: Using design psychology to create ideal places.* Academy Press.

Jordan, P. (2000). *Designing pleasurable products: An introduction to the new human factors.* London: Taylor & Francis.

Kankainen, A. (2003). UCPCD: User-centered product concept design. In *Proceedings of the conference on Designing for user experiences* (pp. 1-13). San Francisco, CA: ACM Press.

Laurel, B. (1993). *Computers as theatre.* Boston, MA: Addison-Wesley Longman Publishing Co., Inc.

Laurel, B. (2001). *Utopian entrepreneur.* Cambridge, MA: MIT Press.

Morville, P. (2004, June). *User experience design.* Retrieved January 24, 2008, from http://semanticstudios.com/publications/semantics/000029.php

Mulder, I., ter Hofte, G.H., & Kort, J. (2005, August 30 – September 2). SocioXensor: Measuring user behaviour and user eXperience in conteXt with mobile devices. In L.P.J.J. Noldus, F. Grieco, L.W.S. Loijens & P.H. Zimmerman (Eds.), *Proceedings of Measuring Behavior 2005, the 5th International Conference on Methods and Techniques in Behavioral Research* (pp. 355-358). Wageningen, The Netherlands.

Norman, D.A. (2004). *Emotional design: Why we love (or hate) everyday things*. New York: Basic Books.

Preece, J., Rogers, Y., & Sharp, H. (2002). *Interaction design: Beyond buman-computer interaction*. New York: John Wiley and Sons Ltd.

Sengers, P., & Gaver, W. (2005). Designing for interpretation. In *Proceedings of Human-Computer Interaction International (HCII) Conference,* Las Vegas, NV.

Shedroff, N. (1995). *100 years*. Paper presented at the VISCOMM 1995conference, San Francisco, CA. Retrieved January 24, 2008, from http://www.nathan.com/thoughts/100/index.html

Shedroff, N. (2000). Information interaction design: A unified field theory of design. In R. Jacobson (Ed.), *Information design*. Cambridge, MA: MIT Press.

Shedroff, N. (2004). Research methods for designing effective experiences. InB. Laurel (Ed.), *Design research: Methods and perspectives*. Cambridge, MA: MIT Press.

Steen, M., de Koning, N., & Mulder, I. (2005). *Empathic design and participatory research for the development of we-centric services for a police organisation*. Enschede, The Netherlands: Freeband.

Steen, M., van Eijk, R., Gunther, H., Hooreman, S., & Koning, N. (2005, October 13). We-centric services for police officers and informal carers. In *Proceedings HCI Close to you*. The Hague, The Netherlands.

Terrenghi, L., Hilliges, O., & Butz, A. (2007). Kitchen stories: Sharing recipes with the living cookbook [Special issue]. *Personal and Ubiquitous Computing, 11*(5), 409-414. London: Springer.

Terrenghi, L., Kronen, M., & Valle, C. (2005). Usability requirement for mobile service scenarios. In *Proceedings of HCI International Conference*, Las Vegas, NV.

van Kranenburg, H., Bargh, M.S., Iacob, S., & Peddermors, A. (2006). A context management framework for supporting context aware distributed applications. *IEEE Communications Magazine, 44*(8), 67-74.

van Kranenburg, H., Snoeck, N., & Mulder, I. (2006, April 26-28). Context aware support targeting plausible and usable results - from reactive, via pro-active to pragmatic systems. In *Proceedings of the 16th Wireless World Research Forum Meeting the needs of Emerging Markets (WWRF16),* Shanghai, China.

Westerink, J. H. D. M., Ouwerkerk, M., Overbeek, Th. J. M., Pasveer, W. F., & de Ruyter, B. (Eds.) press). *Probing experience: From assessment of user emotions and behaviour to development of products.*. Philips Research Book Series, Vol. 8. Dordrecht, The Netherlands: Springer.

Winograd, T. (1996). *Bringing design to software*. Addison-Wesley.

KEY TERMS

Experience Design is a highly multi-disciplinary field within human-computer interaction which embraces quality of the whole relationship between a user and a product during the whole period of engagement to design an artifact.

Human–Computer Interaction (HCI) is the study of interaction between people and computers.

Interaction Design is the discipline of defining the behavior of products and systems that a user can interact with.

Methodology is the systematic study of methods that are, can be, or have been applied within a discipline (Merriam–Webster).

Ubiquitous Computing (or ubicomp) is a field within human-computer interaction in which information processing has been thoroughly integrated into everyday objects and activities.

User Experience is a term used to describe the overall experience and satisfaction a user has when using a product or system.

Chapter XVI
Building Applications to Establish Location Awareness:
New Approaches to Design, Implementation, and Evaluation of Mobile and Ubiquitous Interfaces

D. Scott McCrickard
Virginia Polytechnic Institute and State University (Virginia Tech), USA

Miten Sampat
Feeva Technoology, Inc., USA

Jason Chong Lee
Virginia Polytechnic Institute and State University (Virginia Tech), USA

ABSTRACT

An emerging challenge in the design of interfaces for mobile devices is the appropriate use of information about the location of the user. This chapter considers tradeoffs in privacy, computing power, memory capacity, and wireless signal availability that accompany the obtaining and use of location information and other contextual information in the design of interfaces. The increasing ability to integrate location knowledge in our mobile, ubiquitous applications and their accompanying tradeoffs requires that we consider their impact on the development of user interfaces, leading to an agile usability approach to design borne from agile software development and usability engineering. The chapter concludes with three development efforts that make use of location knowledge in mobile interfaces.

INTRODUCTION

A key challenge in the emerging field of ubiquitous computing is in understanding the unique user problems that new mobile, wearable, and embedded technology can address. This chapter focuses on problems related to location determination—different ways to determine location at low cost with off-the-shelf devices and emerging computing environments, and novel methods for integrating location knowledge in the design of applications. For example, many Web sites use location knowledge from IP addresses to automatically provide the user with relevant weather and traffic information for the current location. There is significant opportunity in the use of location awareness for human-computer interaction (HCI) researchers to explore information-interaction paradigms for the uncertainty and unpredictability that is inherent to many location detection systems—particularly indoor systems that use Wifi signals which can be blocked by roofs, walls, shelves, and even people!

The prior knowledge of location to make such decisions in the presentation of information affords it to be categorized as *context awareness*, the use information that can be used to identify the situation of an entity to appropriately tailor the presentation of and interaction with information to the current situation (Dey, 2001). While context awareness can include a wide variety of information—including knowledge of who is in your surrounding area, events that are happening, and other people in your vicinity—this chapter focuses on the identification and use of location information, perhaps the most cheaply and readily available type of context information. This chapter considers the tradeoffs in privacy, computing power, memory capacity, and wireless (Wifi) signal availability in building interfaces that help users in their everyday tasks. We discuss our own SeeVT system, which uses Wifi signals in location determination (Sampat, Kumar, Prakash, & McCrickard, 2005). The SeeVT system provides the backbone for supplying location information to mobile devices on a university campus. Numerous interfaces built on SeeVT provide timely and appropriate location information to visitors in key areas of the campus.

The increasing ability to integrate location knowledge in our mobile, ubiquitous applications requires that we consider its impact on the development of user interfaces. This chapter describes the merging of agile software development methods from software engineering with the scenario-based design (SBD) methodology from usability engineering to create a rapid iteration design approach that is heavy in client feedback and significant in its level of reusability. Also presented are three interfaces developed using our Agile Usability methodology, focusing on the benefits found in using the Agile Usability approach and the tradeoffs made in establishing location awareness.

BACKGROUND

From the early days, navigation has been central to progress. Explorers who set sail to explore the oceans relied on measurements with respect to the positions of celestial bodies. Mathematical and astronomical techniques were used to locate oneself with respect to relatively stationery objects. The use of radio signals proved to be fairly robust and more accurate, leading to the development of one of the first modern methods of navigation during World War II, called long range navigation (LORAN). LORAN laid the foundation of what we know as the Global Positioning System or GPS (Pace et al., 1995). Primarily commissioned by the United States Department of Defense for military purposes, GPS relies on 24 satellites that revolve around the Earth to provide precision location information in three dimensions. By relying on signals simultaneously received by four satellites, GPS provides much higher precision than previous techniques. GPS navigation is used in a wide range of applications from in-car navigation, to geographic information system (GIS)-mapping, to GPS-guided bombs.

GPS has become the standard for outdoor location-awareness as it provides feedback in a familiar measurement metric. Information systems like in-car navigators have adopted GPS as the standard for obtaining location, since it requires little or no additional infrastructure deployments and operates worldwide. However, GPS has great difficulty in predicting location in dense urban areas, and indoors, as the signals can be lost when they travel through buildings and other such structures. With an accuracy of about 100 meters (Pace et al., 1995), using GPS for indoor location determination does not carry much value. Along with poor lateral accuracy, GPS cannot make altitude distinctions of three to four meters—the average height of a story in a building—thus making it hard to determine, for example, whether a device is on the first floor or on the second floor. Despite continued progress through technological enhancements, GPS has not yet evolved sufficiently to accommodate the consumer information-technology space. This chapter primarily focuses on technologies making inroads for indoor location determination.

While GPS has clear advantages in outdoor location determination, there have been other efforts focused around the use of sensors and sensing equipment to determine location within buildings and in urban areas. Active Badges was one of the earliest efforts at indoor location determination (Want, Hopper, Falcao, & Gibbons, 1992). Active Badges rely on users carrying badges which actively emit infrared signals that are then picked up by a network of embedded sensors in and around the building. Despite concerns about badge size and sensor deployment costs, this and other early efforts inspired designers to think about the possibilities of information systems that could utilize location-information to infer the context of the user, or simply the context of use. One notable related project is MIT's Cricket location system, which involved easy-to-install motes that acted as beepers instead of as a sensor network (Priyantha, Chakraborty, & Balakrishnan, 2000). The user device would identify location based on the signals received from the motes rather than requiring a broadcast from a personal device. Cricket was meant to be easy to deploy, pervasive, and privacy observant. However, solutions like Cricket require deployment of a dense sensor network—reasonable for some situations, but lacking the ubiquity necessary to be an inexpensive, widely available, easy-to-implement solution.

To provide a more ubiquitous solution, it is necessary to consider the use of existing signals—many of which were created for other purposes but can be used to determine location and context. For example, mobile phone towers, IEEE 802.11 wireless access points (Wifi), and fixed Bluetooth devices (as well as the previously mentioned GPS) all broadcast signals that have identification information associated with them. By using that information, combined with the same sort of triangulation algorithms used with GPS, the location of a device can be estimated. The accuracy of the estimation is relative to the number and strength of the signals that are detected, and since one would expect that more "interesting" places would have more signals, accuracy would be greatest at these places—hence providing best accuracy at the most important places. Place Lab is perhaps the most widespread solution that embraces the use of pre-existing signals to obtain location information (LaMarca et al., 2005). Using the broadcasted signals discussed previously, Place Lab allows the designer to establish location information indoors or outdoors, with the initiative of allowing the user community to contribute to the overall effort by collecting radio environment signatures from around the world to build a central repository of signal vectors. Any client device using Place Lab can download and share the signal vectors for its relevant geography—requiring little or no infrastructure deployment. Place Lab provides a location awareness accuracy of approximately 20 meters.

Our work focuses specifically on the use of Wifi access networks, seeking to categorize the benefits according to the level of access and the amount of information available in the physical space. We propose three categories of indoor location determination techniques: *sniffing* of signals in the environment, *Web-services access* to obtain information specific to the area, and *smart algorithms* that take advantage of other information available on mobile devices. In the remainder of this chapter, we describe these techniques in more detail, and we discuss how these techniques have been implemented and used in our framework, called SeeVT using our Agile Usability development process.

CATEGORIZING INDOOR LOCATION DETERMINATION TECHNIQUES

When analyzing location awareness, it is clear that the goal is not just to obtain the location itself, but information associated with the location—eventually leading to full context awareness to include people and events in the space, as described in Dey (2001). For example, indoor location awareness attributes such as the name of the building, the floor, surrounding environments, and other specific information attributed with the space are of particular interest to designers. Designers of systems intended to support location awareness benefit not only from location accuracy, but also from the metadata (tailored to the current level of location accuracy) that affords several types of cross-interpretations and interpolations of location and other context as well.

Access to this information can be stored with the program, given sufficient computing power and memory. This approach is reasonable for small areas that change infrequently—a library or a nature walk could be examples. Information about the area can be made accessible within the application with low memory requirements and rapid information lookup. However, changes to the information require updates to the data, a potentially intolerable cost for areas where location-related changes occur frequently. For example, a reconfigurable office building where the purpose and even the structure of cubicles change frequently would not be well served by a standalone application. Instead, some sort of Web-based repository of information would best meet its needs. Taking this model another step, a mobile system could request and gather information from a wide range of sources, integrating it for the user into a complete picture of the location. As an example, a university campus or networked city would benefit from a smart algorithm that integrated indoor and outdoor signals of various types to communicate a maximally complete picture of the user's location.

Of course, each added layer of access comes with additional costs as well. Simple algorithms may sense known signals from the environment (for example, GPS and wireless signals) to determine location without broadcasting presence. However, other solutions described previously might require requesting or broadcasting of information, revealing the location to a server, information source, or rogue presence—potentially resulting in serious violations of privacy and security. The remainder of this section describes the costs and benefits for three types of indoor location determination approaches: sniffing, Web services, and smart algorithms.

Sniffing

As the name suggests, sniffing algorithms sense multiple points of a broadcast environment, using the points to interpret the location of a device. The radio environment is generally comprised of one or more standard protocols that could be used to interpret location—modern environments include radio signals including Wifi, Bluetooth, microwaves, and a host of other mediums—creating interesting possibilities for location interpolation. Sniffing is also desirable because all location interpolation and calculations are performed on the client device, eliminating the need for a third-party service to perform the analysis and produce results. As mentioned previously, there are some benefits and disadvantages to this approach.

Performing the location determination on the client device eliminates the need for potentially slow information exchange over a network. This approach gives designers the flexibility they need in order to perform quick and responsive changes to the interfaces as well as decision matrices within their applications. For example, a mobile device with a slow processor and limited memory will need a highly efficient implementation to achieve a speedy analysis. A limiting factor for this approach is the caching of previously known radio vectors. Since most analysis algorithms require a large pool of previously recorded radio-signal vectors to interpolate location, it translates into large volumes of data being precached on the client device. A partial solution for this exists already, precaching only for regions that the user is most likely to encounter or visit. Though this is not a complete solution to the resource crunch, it is a reasonable approach for certain situations with periodic updates or fetches when radio-vectors are upgraded or the system encounters an unknown location.

Herecast is an example of a system using the sniffing model (Paciga & Lutfiyya, 2005). It maintains a central database of known radio vectors, which are then published to client devices on a periodic basis. The clients are programmed to cache only a few known locations that the user has encountered, and relies largely on user participation to enter accurate location information when they enter new areas that the system has not encountered before. The accuracy for these systems is generally acceptable, but there is always the worry of not having a cache of an area that the application is about to encounter. The lack of linking to a service also means that other contextual information associated with the location is hard to integrate with this approach due to device caching constraints and metadata volatility.

Web-Services Model

Keeping with the fundamental idea of mobile devices facing a resource crunch, this approach has client devices and applications use a central service for location determination. This means that the client device simply measures or "sees" the radio environment and reports it to the central service. The service then performs the necessary computation to interpolate the user location (potentially including other timely information) and communicates it back to the client. This also allows the client to store a minimal amount of data locally and to perform only the simplest of operations—important for mobile devices that often trade off their small size for minimal resources.

The approach is elegant in many ways, but faces several challenges in its simplistic approach such as the problem of network latency leading to lengthy times to perform the transactions. However, as the speed and pervasiveness of mobile networks is on the rise, as is the capability of silicon integration technologies for mobile platforms, designing large-scale centralized systems based on the Web-services model will be a reasonable approach for many situations. Mobile online applications such as Friend Finders and child tracking services for parents are classic examples of tools that require central services to allow beneficial functionality to the end user.

Our own SeeVT system uses the Web services model by allowing its clients to perform Simple Object Access Protocol (SOAP) Web service calls to a standard Web interface, and submit a radio vector for analysis. It then performs the necessary location determination using a probabilistic algorithm and returns the location to the client. SeeVT provides the interface designer access to functionality on the service end as well. It allows the designers to control sessions and monitor the progress of clients by using a logging feature, and provides handles to integrate other widgets as well. For example, if an application wants to perform a search based on the user's current location, SeeVT allows the designer to add functionality to its modules to perform further server-side computations.

Smart Algorithms

Looking ahead, algorithms that span large and diverse geographic areas will require the integration of many signals, information requests, and additional inputs. Place Lab attempts to address this issue for all radio signals (LaMarca et al., 2005). Currently it can compute location using mobile phone tower signals, Wifi, fixed Bluetooth devices, and GPS. However, we expect that other information will be used for location determination in the near future. For example, the ARDEX project at Virginia Tech seeks to use cameras—quickly becoming commonplace on mobile devices—to create a real-time fiducially-based system for location determination based on augmented reality algorithms (Jacobs, Velez, & Gabbard, 2006). The goal of the system is to integrate it with SeeVT such that anyone at defined hot spots can take a picture of their surrounding area and obtain information about their location. In an interesting twist on this approach, the GumSpots positioning system allows users to take a picture of the gum spots on the ground in urban areas and performs image recognition on them to return user location (Kaufman & Sears, 2006). Other information recording devices could be used in similar ways to help determine or enhance the understanding of our current location.

BUILDING INTERFACES FOR LOCATION-KNOWLEDGEABLE DEVICES

This section begins with a discussion on possible application scenarios that can leverage location knowledge in mobile devices. This section first describes *Agile Usability*, an extension of agile software development methodologies to include key aspects of usability engineering—resulting in an interface building technique that is well suited to ubiquitous and location-knowledgeable computing devices, both from the standpoint of interaction as well as development processes. Next, three case studies illustrate real world applications that have been built using these processes. Each case study describes key aspects of the application, illustrating one of the indoor location determination techniques and highlighting key lessons learned from the use of Agile Usability.

Agile Software Development, Usability Engineering, and Agile Usability

Ubiquitous and pervasive systems are often introduced to augment and support everyday tasks in novel ways using newly developed technology or by using existing technology in different ways. Since end-user needs are often ill-defined for ubiquitous systems, development needs to quickly incorporate stakeholder feedback so the systems can be iteratively improved to address new and changing requirements. This section discusses the use of an agile development methodology to build ubiquitous systems. Based on our own work (Lee et al., 2004; Lee, Chewar, & McCrickard, 2005; Lee & McCrickard, 2007) and on prior investigation of agile development methods (Beck, 1999; Constantine, 2001; Koch, 2004), we present a usability engineering approach for the construction of interfaces for mobile and ubiquitous devices.

Agile software development methodologies have been developed to address continuous requirements and system changes that can occur during the development process. They focus on quick delivery of working software, incremental releases, team communication, collaboration, nd the ability to respond to change (Beck et al., 2001). One stated benefit of agile methods is a flattening of the cost of change curve throughout the development process. This makes agile methods ideally suited to handle the iterative and incremental development process needed to effectively

Figure 1. The agile usability process. The central design record bridges interface design with implementation issues. This enables incremental improvement incorporating feedback from project stakeholders and usability evaluations.

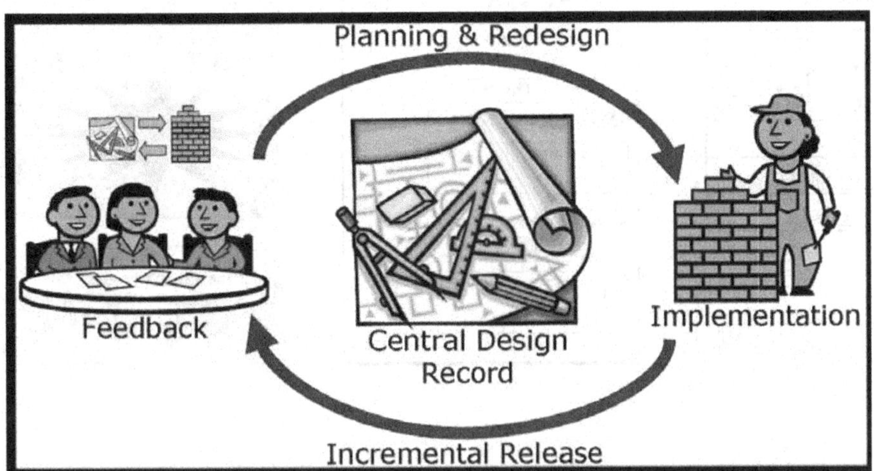

engineer ubiquitous systems. One shortcoming of many agile methods is a lack of consideration for the needs of end users (Constantine, 2001). Current agile development methodologies have on-site clients to help guide the development process and ensure that all required functionality is included. However, many ubiquitous and pervasive systems require continuous usability evaluations involving end-users to ensure that such systems adequately address their needs and explore how they are incorporated in people's daily tasks and affect their behavior. Researchers, including Miller (2005), Constantine (2001), and Beyer, Holtzblatt, and Baker (2004) have developed ways to integrate system and software engineering with usability engineering. We present our approach to agile usability engineering, henceforth referred to as Agile Usability, with the added benefit of usability knowledge capture and reuse.

Our approach combines the software development practices of extreme programming (XP) with the interaction design practices of scenario-based design (SBD) (Beck, 1999; Rosson & Carroll, 2002). The key features of this process are an incremental development process supported by continual light-weight usability evaluations, close contact with project stakeholders, an agile interface architecture model, known as a central design record (CDR), that bridges interface design and system implementation issues, and proactive knowledge capture and reuse of interface design knowledge (Figure 1).

Running a large-scale requirements analysis process for developing ubiquitous systems is not as beneficial as when designing other types of systems as it can be very difficult to envision how a ubiquitous system will be used in a specific situation or how the introduction of that system will affect how people behave or use it. In this type of development process, portions of the system are developed and evaluated by end users on a continual basis. This helps developers in uncovering new requirements and dealing with changing user needs as development proceeds. This type of development process requires some amount of discipline and rigor in terms of the types of development practices to follow. Specific details of these XP programming practices are detailed in Beck's book on the subject (Beck, 1999). Our use of these practices are elaborated in a techni-

Figure 2. Screenshots from three applications built on SeeVT. From the left, the alumni tour guide, VTAssist, and SeeVT-ART

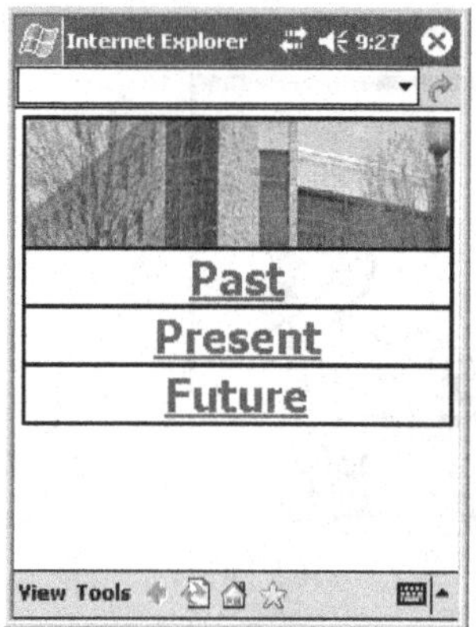

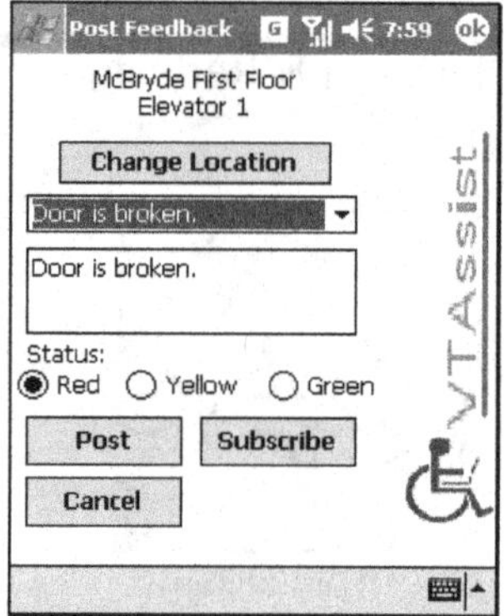

cal report (Lee, Wahid, McCrickard, Chewar & Congleton, 2007).

An incremental development process necessitates close collaboration with customers and end users to provide guidance on what features are needed and whether the system is usable. Ideally, representatives from these groups will be onsite with the developers working in the same team. Our customers were not strictly on site, although they were in the same general location as the developers. Regularly scheduled meetings and continual contact through e-mail and IM were essential to maintaining project velocity.

The key design representation is the central design record (CDR), which draws on and makes connections between design artifacts from XP and SBD. Stories that describe individual system features are developed and maintained by the customer with the help of the developers. They are prioritized by the customer and developed incrementally in that order. These include all features needed to develop the system including underlying infrastructure such as databases, networking software, or hardware drivers. Scenarios, which are narratives describing the system in use, are used to communicate interface design features and behaviors between project stakeholders. Claims, which describe the positive and negative psychological effects of interface features in a design, are developed from the scenarios to highlight critical interaction design features. Story identification and development may lead to changes to the scenarios and claims. The reverse may also be true. This coupling between interface design and system implementation is critical for ubiquitous systems as developers must deal with both interactional and technological issues when deploying a system to the population.

In addition to acting as a communication point between stakeholders and highlighting connections between interface design and implementation, the CDR is important as a record of design decisions. As developers iterate on their designs, they often need to revisit previous design decisions. The explicit tradeoffs highlighted in the claims can be used by developers and clients to determine how best to resolve design issues that come up. Perhaps most important, Agile Usability drives developers to explore key development techniques in the development of location-based interfaces—the techniques used advance the field and can be reused in other situations.

Agile Usability has been applied in numerous situations, three of which are highlighted in this chapter as case studies. Each case study describes how the user tasks were identified, how stakeholder feedback was included, how our agile methodology was employed, and how appropriate location detection technologies were integrated. The discussion portion of this section will compare and contrast the lessons learned in the different case studies—highlighting specific usability engineering lessons and advancements that can be used by others.

Case Study 1: Alumni Tour Guide

The alumni tour guide application was built for visitors to the Virginia Tech (VT) campus. The system notifies users about points-of-interest in the vicinity as and when they move about the VT campus (Nair et al., 2006). This image-intensive system provides easy-to-understand views of the prior and current layout of buildings in the current area. By focusing on an almost exclusively image-based presentation, users spend little time reading text and more time reflecting on their surroundings and reminiscing about past times in the area. See Figure 2 for a screenshot of the guide.

The earliest prototypes of the tour guide proposed a complex set of operations, but task analyses and client discussions performed in the Agile Usability stages indicated that many alumni—particularly those less familiar with handheld and mobile technology—would be unlikely to want to seek out solutions using the technology. Instead, later prototypes and the final product focused on the presentation and contrast of historical and modern images of the current user location. For example, alumni can use the tour guide to note how an area that once housed some administrative offices in old homes has been rebuilt as a multistory technology center for the campus. This pictorial comparison, available at any time with only a few clicks, was well received by our client as an important step in connecting the campus of the past with the exciting innovations of the present and future.

As the target users are alumni returning to campus, most are without access to the wireless network, and the logistics are significant in providing access to the thousands of people who return for reunions, sporting events, and graduations. As such, the Alumni Tour Guide uses the sniffing location detection method to identify current location. This method fits well with the nature of the tasks of interest to alumni: they care most about the general space usage and the historical perspectives of a location that change little over time.

Case Study 2: VTAssist

Building interfaces is often difficult when the target audience has needs and skills different than those of the developer: for example, users with mobility impairments. It often takes many iterations to focus on the most appropriate solutions—a perfect candidate for Agile Usability. A pair of developers used our methodology to build VTAssist, a location-aware application to enable users with mobility impairments, specifically users in wheelchairs, to navigate a campus environment (Bhatia, Dahn, Lee, Sampat, & McCrickard, 2006). VTAssist helps people in wheelchairs navigate in an environment more conducive to those who are not restricted in movement. Unlike typical handhelds and Tablet PC applications (the two platforms for which VTAssist was created), the VTAssist system must attract the user's attention at times of need or danger, guide them to alternate paths, and provide them with a means to obtain personal assistance when necessary. Perhaps most importantly, VTAssist allows users to quickly and easily supply feedback on issues and difficulties at their current location—both helping future visitors and building a sense of community among those who traverse the campus. See Figure 2 for a screenshot of the VTAssist.

In developing VTAssist using Agile Usability, we found that needs and requirements changed over time requiring that the methodology account for those changes. For example, the original design was intended to help wheelchair users find location accessible resources and locations, but later the need was identified to keep that information constantly updated, resulting in the addition of the collaborative feedback feature. It was this feature that was deemed most important to the system—the feature that would keep the information in VTAssist current, and would enable users to take an active role in maintaining the information, helping others, and helping themselves.

Due to the importance of the feedback feature in maintaining up-to-date information for those in wheelchairs, VTAssist uses the Web services model. Certainly it would be possible to obtain some benefit from the sniffing model, but the client reaction indicated the importance of user feedback in maintaining an accurate database of problems and in providing feedback channels to frustrated users looking for an outlet for their comments. In addition, the server-side computations of location and location information (including comments from users and from facility administrators) results in faster, more up-to-date reports about the facilities.

Case Study 3: Conference Center Guide

The conference center guide, known as SeeVT-ART, addresses the desires of visitors and alumni to our area in coming to, and generally in returning to, our university campus—specifically the campus alumni and conference center (Kelly, Hood, Lee, Sampat, & McCrickard, 2006). SeeVT-ART provides multimodal information through images, text, and audio descriptions of the artwork featured in the center. Users can obtain alerts about interesting regional and university-specific features within the center and they can be guided to related art by the same artist or on the same topic. The alerts were designed to be minimally intrusive, allowing users to obtain more information if they desired it or to maintain their traversal through the center if preferred. See Figure 2 for a screenshot of SeeVT-ART.

Agile Usability was particularly effective in this situation because of the large amount of input from the client, who generated a lot of ideas that, given unlimited time and resources, would have contributed to the interface. Agile Usability forced the developers to prioritize—addressing the most important changes first while creating placeholders illustrating where additional functionality would be added. Prioritization of changes through Agile Usability also highlighted the technological limitations of the underlying SeeVT system, specifically those related to the low accuracy of location detection, and how that influenced the system design. For example, when a user enters certain areas densely populated with artistically interesting objects, SeeVT-ART requires the user to select from a list of the art pieces, as it is impossible to determine with accurate precision where the user is standing or (with any precision) what direction the user is facing. These limitations suggested the need for smart algorithms that use information about the area and that integrate additional location determination methods.

Smart algorithms that store location data over time and use it to improve location detection can be useful in determining data such as the speed at which a user is walking and the direction a user is facing. SeeVT-ART can use this data to identify the piece of art at which a user most likely is looking. Our ongoing work is looking at integrating not only the widely accessible broadcast signals from GPS, cellular technology, and fixed Bluetooth, but also RFID, vision algorithms, and augmented reality (AR) solutions. Our early investigation into a camera-based AR solution combines information about the current location with image processing by a camera mounted on the handheld to identify the artwork and augment the user's understanding of it with information about the artist, provenance, and so forth. These types of solutions promise a richer and more complete understanding of the importance of a location than any one method could accomplish alone.

CONCLUSION AND FUTURE DIRECTIONS

The three location-knowledgeable SeeVT applications described in this document offer a glimpse into the possibilities for location-knowledgeable mobile devices. The increasing presence of wireless networks, improvements in the power and utility of GPS, and development of other technologies that can be used to determine location portends the ubiquity of location-knowledgeable applications in the not-too-distant future. Delivery of location-appropriate information in a timely and useful manner with minimal unwanted interruption will be the goal of such systems. Our ongoing development efforts seek to meet this goal.

In support of our development efforts, we explore new usability engineering approaches particularly appropriate for location-knowledgeable applications. The use of stories and the knowledge capturing structures of Agile Usability combined with its rapid multiple iterations enable convergence on solutions to the most important issues faced by emerging application areas. We repeatedly found that designers are able to identify issues of importance to the target users, while keeping in perspective the design as a whole. Our ongoing work seeks ways to capture and share the knowledge produced from designing these applications not only within a given design but across designs, leading to the systematic scientific advancement of the field.

In the future, these developing Agile Usability techniques will be supported by specific tools and toolkits for leveraging the location-awareness needs of on-the-go users. An early contribution that can be drawn from this work is the novel methods for supporting location awareness in users—browseable historical images of the current location, rapid feedback methods for reporting problems, new map presentation techniques—all methods that should be captured in a toolkit and reused in other location awareness situations.

REFERENCES

Bahl, P., & Padmanabhan, V. N. (2000). RADAR: An in-building RF-based user location and tracking system. In *Proceedings of IEEE INFOCOM*, Tel Aviv, Israel, (Vol. 2, pp. 775-784).

Beck, K. (1999, October). Embracing change with extreme programming. *IEEE Computer, 32*(10), 70-77.

Beck, K., Beedle, M., van Bennekum, A., Cockburn, A., Cunningham, W., Fowler, M. et al. (2001). *The Agile Manifesto.* Retrieved January 25, 2008, from http://agilemanifesto.org

Beyer, H. R., Holtzblatt, K., & Baker, L. (2004). An agile customer-centered method: Rapid contextual design. In *Proceedings of Extreme Programming and Agile Methods 2004 (XP/Agile Universe)*, Calgary, Canada (pp. 50-59).

Bhatia, S., Dahn, C., Lee, J. C., Sampat, M., & McCrickard, D. S. (2006). VTAssist-a location-based feedback notification system for the disabled. In *Proceedings of the ACM Southeast Conference (ACMSE '06)*, Melbourne, FL (pp. 512-517).

Constantine, L. L. (2001). Process agility and software usability: Toward lightweight usage-centered design. *Information Age, 8*(2). In L. Constantine (Ed.), *Beyond chaos: The expert edge in managing software development.* Boston: Addison-Wesley.

Dey, A. K. (2001). Understanding and using context. *Personal and Ubiquitous Computing, 5*(1), 4-7.

Jacobs, J., Velez, M, & Gabbard, J. (2006). ARDEX: An integrated framework for handheld augmented reality. In *Proceedings of the First Annual Virginia Tech Center for Human-Computer Interaction Research Experience for Undergrads Symposium*, Blacksburg, VA (p. 6).

Kaufman, J., & Sears, J. (2006). GSPS: GumSpots positioning system. In *IPT 2006 Spring Show.*

Retrieved January 25, 2008, from http://itp.nyu.edu/show/detail.php?project_id=539

Kelly, S., Hood, B., Lee, J. C., Sampat, M., & McCrickard, D. S. (2006). *Enabling opportunistic navigation through location-aware notification systems.* Pending paper submission.

Koch, A. S. (2004). *Agile software development: Evaluating the methods for your organization.* Artech House Publishers.

LaMarca, A., Chawathe, Y., Consolvo, S., Hightower, J., Smith, I., Scott, J., et al. (2005). Place lab: Device positioning using radio beacons in the wild. In *Proceedings of the 3rd International Conference on Pervasive Computing (Pervasive 2005),* Munich, Germany (pp. 134-151).

Lee, J. C., Chewar, C. M., & McCrickard, D. S. (2005). Image is everything: Advancing HCI knowledge and interface design using the system image. In *Proceedings of the ACM Southeast Conference (ACMSE '05),* Kennesaw, GA (pp. 2-376-2-381).

Lee, J. C., Lin, S., Chewar, C. M., McCrickard, D. S., Fabian, A., & Jackson, A. (2004). From chaos to cooperation: Teaching analytic evaluation with LINK-UP. In *Proceedings of the World Conference on E-Learning in Corporate, Government, Healthcare, and Higher Education (E-Learn '04),* Washington, D.C. (pp. 2755-2762).

Lee, J. C., & McCrickard, D. S. (2007). Towards extreme(ly) usable software: Exploring tensions between usability and agile software development. In *Proceedings of the 2007 Conference on Agile Software Development (Agile '07)*, Washington DC, (pp. 59-70).

Lee, J. C., Wahid, S., McCrickard, D. S., Chewar, C. M., & Congleton, B. (2007). Understanding Usability: Investigating an Integrated Design Environment and Management System. *International Journal of Information Technology and Smart Education (ITSE), 2*(3), 161-175.

Miller, L. (2005). Case study of customer input for a successful product. In *Proceedings of the Agile 2005 Conference,* Denver, CO (pp. 225-234).

Nair, S., Kumar, A., Sampat, M., Lee, J. C., & McCrickard, D. S. (2006). Alumni campus tour: Capturing the fourth dimension in location based notification systems. In *Proceedings of the ACM Southeast Conference (ACMSE '06),* Melbourne, FL (pp. 500-505).

Pace, S., Frost, G. P., Lachow, I., Frelinger, D., Fossum, D., Wassem, D. et al. (1995). *The global positioning system: Assessing national policies* (Ref. No. MR-614-OSTP). Rand Corporation.

Paciga, M., & Lutfiyya, H. (2005). Herecast: An open infrastructure for location-based services using WiFi. In *Proceedings of Wireless and Mobile Computing, Networking, and Communications (WiMoB 2005),* Montreal, Canada (pp. 21-28).

Priyantha, N. B., Chakraborty, A., & Balakrishnan, H. (2000). The cricket location-support system. In *Proceedings of the Sixth Annual International Conference on Mobile Computing and Networking (MOBICOM 2000),* Boston, MA (32-43).

Rosson, M .B., & Carroll, J. M. (2002). *Usability engineering: Scenario-based development of human-computer interaction.* New York: Morgan Kaufman.

Sampat, M., Kumar, A., Prakash, A., & McCrickard, D. S. (2005). Increasing understanding of a new environment using location-based notification systems. In *Proceedings of 11th InternationalConference on Human-Computer Interaction (HCII '05).* Las Vegas, NV.

Sciacchitano, B., Cerwinski, C., Brown, I., Sampat, M., Lee, J. C., & McCrickard, D. S. (2006). Intelligent library navigation using location-aware systems. In *Proceedings of the ACM Southeast Conference (ACMSE '06),* Melbourne, FL (pp. 371-376).

Tom, H. (1994). The geographic information systems (GIS) standards infrastructure. *StandardView, 2*(3), 33-142.

Want, R., Hopper, A., Falcao, V., & Gibbons, J. (1992). The active badge location system. *ACM Transactions on Information Systems, 40*(1), 91-102.

Youssef, M., & Agrawala, A. K. (2004). Handling samples correlation in the Horus system. In *Proceedings of IEEE INFOCOM.* Hong Kong, China.

KEY TERMS

Agile Usability: Design methodologies that incorporate practices from agile software development methods and usability engineering methods to enable the efficient development of usable software.

Extreme Programming: An agile software development methodology centered on the values of simplicity, communication, feedback, courage, and respect.

Location Awareness: Functionality in mobile devices that allows them to calculate their current geographic location.

Mobile Devices: Handheld, portable computing devices such as smart phones and personal digital assistants.

Scenario-Based Design: Usability engineering methodology that uses descriptions of how people accomplish tasks—scenarios—as the primary design representation to drive the development and analysis of systems.

SeeVT: Location aware system that uses Wifi signals to calculate the position of wireless-enabled mobile devices.

Ubiquitous Computing: Technology embedded in the environment that becomes implicit and tightly integrated into peoples' day to day tasks.

Wifi: Wireless local area networking technology and standards developed to improve the interoperatility of wireless communication devices.

Chapter XVII
Interactive Tables:
Requirements, Design Recommendations, and Implementation

Michael Haller
Upper Austria University of Applied Sciences–Digital Media, Austria

Mark Billinghurst
Human Interface Technology Laboratory New Zealand–University of Canterbury, New Zealand

ABSTRACT

Interactive tables are becoming increasingly popular. In this chapter, we describe a collaborative tabletop environment that is designed for brainstorming meetings. After describing the user requirements, we demonstrate different possible solutions for both the display and the tracking implementation, and summarize related work. Finally, we conclude with a more detailed description of the Shared Design Space. Using a digital pen, participants can annotate not only virtual paper, but also real printouts. By integrating both forms of physical and digital paper, we combine virtual and real drawings, three-dimensional models, and digital data in a single information space. We discuss the unique way that we have integrated these devices and how they can be used efficiently during a design process.

INTRODUCTION AND MOTIVATION

An interactive table combines the benefits of a traditional table with all the functionalities of a digital computer, including the combination of both real and virtual paper. Although interactive tabletop environments are becoming increasingly popular, there are few applications which fully show their potential. One area where they could be expected to be very useful is in supporting creative collaboration. In the creative process, people often use real paper and sketching tables to capture their ideas, so digital tabletop setups could provide an ideal interface for supporting computer-based collaboration. Blinn (1990) postulates that the creative process occurs in two-phases: first

Figure 1. Separation of person space and task space

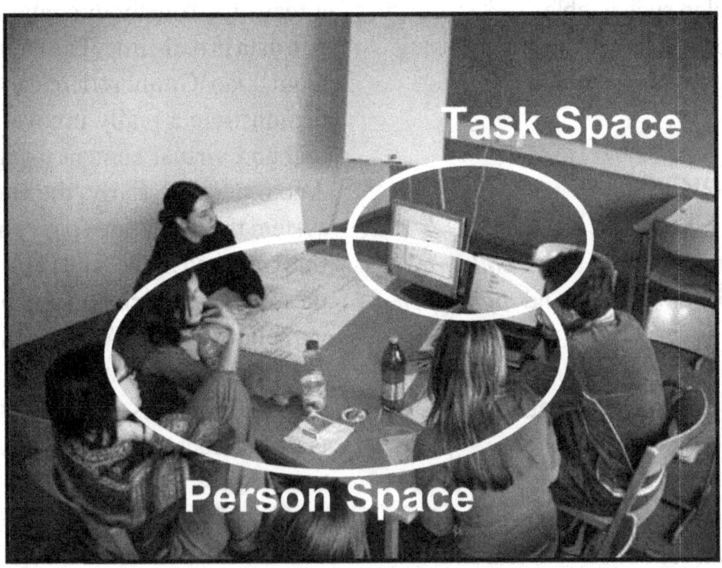

moving from chaos to order and second from ideation to implementation. Most computer-based design tools are primarily focused on the second phase and there is limited support for digital tools where people can play with ideas in a free form manner. In this chapter we describe an interactive digital table which supports the first phase, moving from chaos to order.

Introducing a computer into a face-to-face meeting changes the group dynamic. In general, users focus more on their own device and pay less attention to the coparticipants. Buxton (1992) uses the terminologies *person space* and *task space* to describe the spaces used for communication and for working on a task (Figure 1). Computers in face to face collaboration often cause an artificial separation between the person space and task space.

In this chapter, we describe how to use a digital tabletop system for enhancing face-to-face collaboration. Interactive tables combine the physical and social affordance of a traditional table with the advantages of digital technology (Morris, 2006). Enhanced with virtual elements, a tabletop setup becomes an ideal input and output device around which people can share a wide range of verbal and nonverbal cues to collaborative effectively. The digital data, projected onto the table, can be stored, moved, re-arranged, and manipulated in an intuitive way.

In contrast to vertical displays, such as interactive SmartBoards,[1] horizontal displays have several advantages: in a meeting with a vertical display, the participants usually have a single leader who stands in front of the display and controls most of the session. The horizontal display, however, facilitates a discussion where all participants interact in the same way without any leadership (Morris, 2006).

It is very challenging to develop an interactive table which can be used under different conditions and there are a lot of requirements and constraints that have to be considered. These requirements and the proposed solutions are often diverging. Summarizing, the key questions of this chapter are:

- What are the (most important) requirements for designing an interactive table?

- Which technology possibilities do we have to use to develop such a table?
- How can people interact intuitively using an interactive table?

RELATED WORK

Our work draws on work in two areas: *collaborative interactive tabletop systems* and *digital pen technology.*

Collaborative Interactive Tabletop Systems

Wellner's (1992) DigitalDesk was one of the first interactive tables that combined both real and virtual paper into a single workspace environment. In this case he used computer vision technology to track user input. Current digital tabletops vary widely in their size and shapes (Dietz et al., 2001; Ishii et al., 2002; Streitz, Prante, Rocker, van Alphen, Magerkurth, & Stenzel 2003). Since many tabletops have a physically shared space, it becomes difficult for people to reach digital items that are across the table. Scott, Carpendale, and Inkpen (2004) investigated tabletop territoriality in digital tabletop workspaces and found that users automatically create their own territories and their private storage places. Based on this phenomenon, Parker, Mandryk, and Inkpen (2006) demonstrated different interaction techniques for tabletop displays which support the interaction with distant objects. A closer description of current interactive tables is given in the chapter "Tracking."

Digital Pen

An alternative to using computer vision or other technology for hand tracking is capturing input through digital pens. Many researchers are working with digital pens from Anoto.[1] Although the Anoto technology has been available for more than 5 years, in the last year it became possible to use a real-time Bluetooth connection to retrieve the pen data in real-time. The PapierCraft application from Liao Guimbretiere, and Hinckley (2005) demonstrate a really innovative combination of real and virtual content using printouts and the Anoto pen. Similarly, the ButterflyNet shows a system that integrates paper notes with information captured in the field (Yeh et al., 2006). While these systems focus on a paper-based interface, we believe that the Anoto technology can be used in a different context, namely interactive tabletop setups. Using this technology allows us to create large horizontal displays with easy-to-use interaction devices.

Our work is influenced by this previous work in interactive tables and digital pens, but is different from it in a number of important ways. The most important difference is the fact that we use the digital pen as a stylus and track large augmented surfaces. The setup itself is scalable, easy-to-manufacture, and accurate—even on really large surfaces.

DESIGN REQUIREMENTS

We carried out an explorative field study at the Voestalpine, an Austrian steel company, and identified the following design requirements that are necessary for developing a successful interactive table:

- Scalability of both the display and the interactive (tracking) surface
- Multipoint interaction to support simultaneous touches
- Robust tracking and easy-to-use calibration
- Integration of physical objects should not interfere with the tracking system
- Ability to identify which of the participants is interacting with the surface
- Inexpensive to manufacture

Based on our experiences with interactive tabletop environments, we have developed a set of design requirements that can inform future work in this area. The following list is an extension of the requirements presented by Scott, Grant, and Mandryk (2003).

Integration and Combination with Traditional Tables

Working around a table is still the most convenient and comfortable way of face-to-face communication. Instead of creating a completely novel interface, the interactive (digital) table should be *integrated* in the environment instead of *replacing* the current hardware device. All the benefits that a conventional table has should remain.

Shape, Size, and Height of the Interactive Table

The shape, size, and height are important parameters for designing a good table. Different shapes can influence the users' attitudes to sit either closer or further away from each other (Ramsborg, 2002). Rectangular tables, for example, invite participants to form teams that are sitting at opposite ends of the table; see section (a) of Figure 2. An advantage of this shape is the motivation of discussion, which mostly happens across the table.

In contrast, U-shaped tables, see section (b) of Figure 2, are mostly designed for larger groups (more than 7 people), formal discussions

Figure 2. Different shapes and sizes influence the behavior of the participants. (a) Rectangular table, (b) U-shape table, (c) Circular table, and (d) Oval table are the most important shapes. The dark-gray bodies represent the leaders' position

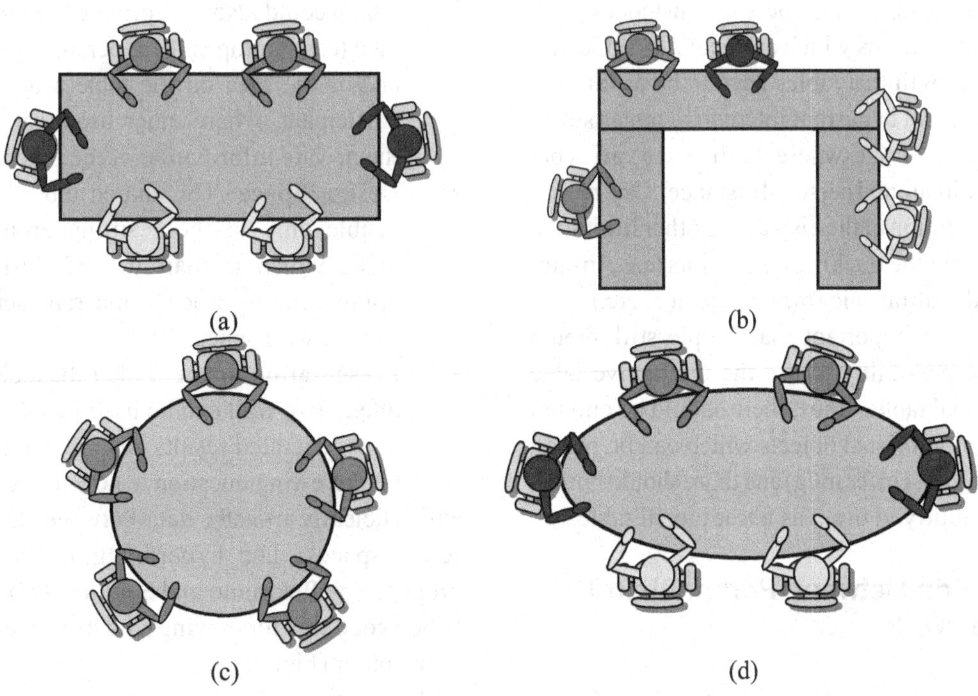

Table 1. Interpersonal distances in the social interactions which should be considered during the design process of an interactive table

Distance	Approximate distance	Interaction
Intimate distance	< 0.5 meters	Restricted to private encounters
Personal distance	0.5 – 1.25 meters	Between friends
Social distance	1.25 – 3.5 meters	Impersonal business dealing
Public distance	> 3.5 meters	Addressing a crowd

and presentations. Circular tables, see section (c) of Figure 2, de-emphasize the importance of the leader. Finally, oval tables, see section (d) of Figure 2, combine the benefits and advantages of a rectangular table and a circular table. They promote discussion and give greater possibilities for eye contact to each participant. In addition, a leader can still sit in a position of control.

Depending on the type of meeting the distance between participants can differ. In an informal meeting, people sit closer than in a business meeting with different partners. The size requirements for the table are determined by the preferred mode of use, that is, whether users sit or stand. This fact also influences the height of a table. Hall (1966) found four different interpersonal distances in the social interactions which are listed in Table 1.

It is a myth that tables have to be as large as possible. A lot of current interactive tables suffer from the small size (where the distance varies between intimate and personal distance). One reason is the limitation of the display. Another limitation comes from the tracking constraints (e.g., limitation of the ultrasonic tracking device, etc.).

It is also important that people still should have the possibility to use the interactive table as a normal table—thus, there should be enough space for additional objects which can be put on the table (e.g., coffee mug) and there should be also the possibility to use it as a traditional table.

Transition Between Personal and Group Work

The table is an ideal interface for sharing data as everybody can easily access to objects placed on the table. Around the table, it is essential that participants have access to their personal workspaces; in addition they still need easy access to the group data and shared workspace. Figure 3 depicts this arrangement on a traditional table.

Territories and the users' physical reach are also important features that have to be designed with care. Scott et al. (2004) investigate the phenomena of different territories in a tabletop setup. Using their approach, we can three identify different working areas (spaces/territories) that have to be projected in a collaborative tabletop setup. See section (d) of Figure 3:

- **Private Space:** The users' private territory, which could also be a private hardware device (e.g., laptop screen, personal printout) and/or the area on the table around each participant, where other users cannot see the private information of the others.
- **Design Space:** The shared table surface, visible only to those sitting around the table, which is mainly used during the brainstorming process and represents the chaotic workspace.
- **Presentation Space:** Either the table or an interactive wall can be used for presenting final generated results during a meeting.

The interesting question is how to intuitively and efficiently transfer data between these different spaces. The hyperdragging metaphor, proposed by Rekimoto and Saitho (1999), seems to be a good way for moving data from one device to the other (Figure 4).

Users can click on a note on their laptop computer desktop and drag it to the augmented

Figure 3. A face-to-face communication setup (a) with different data views, (b) different storage attitudes, (c) and "interacting"-territories. We identified three different spaces, the private workspace, the design space, and the presentation space (d)

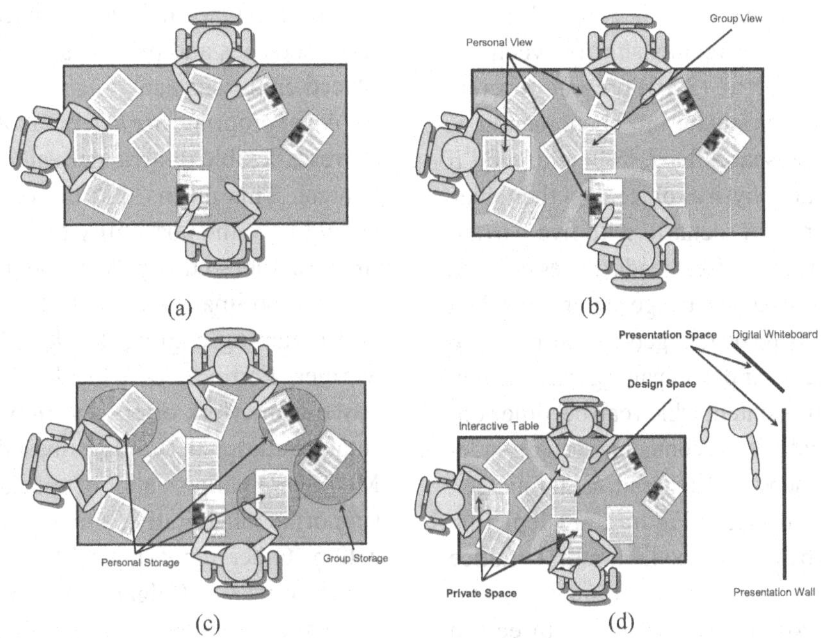

Figure 4. The hyper-dragging metaphor; the user can drag the data from the personal device to the augmented surface

tabletop surface. Once the mouse reaches the edge of the physical display, the note appears on the table connected by a virtual line to the centre of the desktop. Dragging with the mouse continues to move the note across the tabletop. The hyper-dragging metaphor can have a problem with users losing their mouse cursor among several cursors on the table. To address this problem, we propose a visual extension cursor, a radar-mouse-cursor that shows inside the private space the position of the actual cursor on the table. This appears as a line on the private screen space that connects with the projected virtual mouse line on the display space. A closer description can be found in Haller, Billinghurst, Leithinger, Leitner, and Seifried (2005).

Appropriate Arrangements of Users

Usually, people are sitting or standing around the table, having different "distance zones" which are dependent on the relationship between the participants. Scott et al. (2003) present different constraints and investigate the phenomenon of territories. These spaces have to be enlarged if people put a lot of physical objects on the table.

Figure 5 depicts a scenario with five participants, where one of the users leads the session and presents the results using a huge paper sheet. Not surprisingly, only the leader gets the best view to the data. All the other participants get a different perspective to the content which can become confusing—especially if the content is seen up-side-down (Morris, Paepcke, Winograd, & Stamberger, 2006). The four images of Figure 5 are depicting the views seen by the four collaborators—notice that especially for people who are sitting too far away from the content (as participants three and four), the distorted view can become too much and important messages can get lost.

However, the table has to be large enough so that participants can arrange comfortably. They should not have to sit too close together, have an adequate distance and enough space for additional large sketches and printouts that should still be placed on the surface.

An appropriate arrangement of users also requires a flexible re-arrangement of the projected content. This means that the rendering engine should have the possibility to rotate the content in any angle, so that each of the participants can have an optimal view to it. The DiamondSpin is a rendering engine, developed by the Shen, Vernier, Forlines, & Ringel (2004). The Java based framework offers a variety of features to rotate traditional Windows-based applications. Moreover, it allows a lot of special features that support a collaborative and a multimouse interaction. Other rendering tabletop engines (e.g., the University of Calgary Tabletop Framework[3]) are mainly developed on top of OpenGL and/or DirectX, where the Windows content is mainly grabbed and visualized as a texture. The col-

Figure 5. Different views; not every participant can get an optimal view to the content

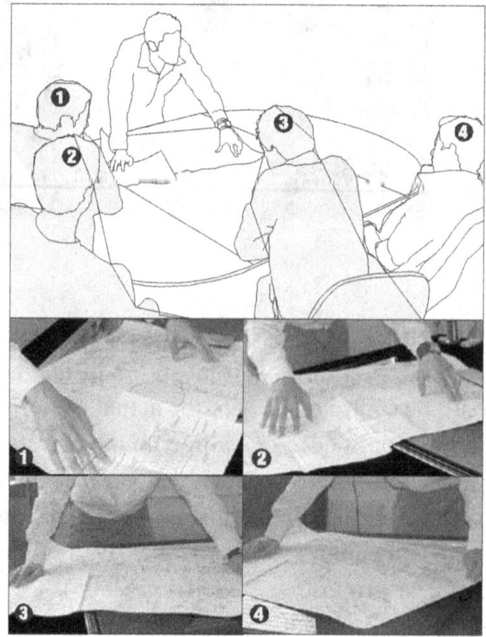

laboration and multimouse functionality, which is not supported by the operating system, usually have to be emulated (Tse, 2004).

Support for Interpersonal Interaction

At no point should the technology interrupt the natural flow of a conversation (Inkpen, 1997). Instead, the interface should support people during the discussion. Not surprisingly, using laptops and other input devices can reduce the conversational awareness and interfere with the exchange of communication cues. Although many researchers try to integrate mobile devices in a tabletop environment (Rekimoto & Saitoh, 1999), we noticed that the usage of the digital pen, with the possibility to make annotations directly onto real paper, improved the discussion a lot.

Fluid Transitions Between Activities

People should not have to actively switch between different tasks. We also noticed this phenomenon between different devices, which were used simultaneously in one of our testing scenarios. In most cases, people felt confused in using more than one device at a time. Once multiple control elements are placed on the table, it becomes especially difficult to understand which device is to be used for which task. Therefore, the benefits of each tool have to be considered carefully and participants should always know how to use the different tools.

Transition Between Collaboration and External Work

Although the main research focuses is on how to find adequate interaction metaphors on the tabletop setup, it is important that data, created in the interface, can be accessible in other environments without additional special software.

Support of Physical Objects

People want to place objects and items on the table surface during the collaboration. Due to the tracking restrictions a lot of interactive tabletop systems do not allow physical objects to be placed on the table surface. In our setup, people interact with real objects, such as printouts. In addition, participants should also be able to include task-specific devices (e.g., personal laptops, tablet PCs) and physical objects (e.g., paper, notebooks). However, people often tend to put physical objects on the table. Using pressure-sensitive surfaces, physical objects result in unwanted touches.

Shared Access to both Physical and Digital Objects

There is no doubt that a table is an ideal interface for sharing data. Therefore, the data access has to be easy-to-use and fast, and there should be a seamless integration of both the real and virtual content.

Support of Simultaneous User Interaction

At no point should the system create an atmosphere where only part of the group can get control of the discussion. In our first experiments, we noticed that each participant has to have the same control elements. If the system supports special control devices (e.g., a wireless control device), it should be clear which of the participants can use it and how they can use it. Therefore, all participants should be able to interact simultaneously.

TECHNICAL IMPLEMENTATION

There are two technical aspects that have to be considered during the design and implementation phase of an interactive table:

- The display, which should be large, bright, and high-resolution
- The tracking system, which should enable users to interact with the table in a natural and intuitive way

Display

There are several ways to display digital content on the table. The most popular system is a projector setup, mounted on the ceiling. Today's standard projectors' resolution is 1024x768 pixels, which obviously limits the size of the table. The image size can be increased by mounting the projector a bit higher, but this does not automatically increase the display resolution. Multiple-projector systems are a logical consequence to increase the resolution. Some graphics cards (e.g., Quadvision' Xentera GT8 PCI) can drive up to eight displays. Two or more graphics cards can be connected to a single PC. A cost-effective solution is to upgrade the system by connecting the video output with a Matrox DualHead2Go box. The output signal simply gets split and can result in a dual monitor upgrade with few performance penalties. It is still a challenging task to calibrate the individual projectors. A detailed background and a good overview of using multiple projectors simultaneously are given in Bimber and Raskar (2005). Although plasma displays would be an attractive alternative, they are usually very cost-prohibitive and limited in size (Streitz et al., 2003). Another problem is the sensible surface which is at high risk of getting scratched.

Tracking

The DigitalDesk was one of the first tabletop displays that combined augmented interaction with physical documents using computer vision technology (Wellner, 1992). In contrast, the DiamondTouch system from the Mitsubishi Electric Research Lab (MERL) is based on measuring the capacitance of users. Up to four users can sit on special chairs around the DiamondTouch table interface (Dietz & Leigh, 2003). Signals, which are transmitted through antennas, embedded in the table, are then capacitively coupled through the users and chairs to the receivers, mounted on the chair. A similar setup is presented by Rekimoto (2002) with the SmartSkin project, where he uses a mesh-shaped sensor grid to determine the hand position. Both systems are highly robust and accurate. Unfortunately, both systems are expensive to manufacture.

The InteracTable, a single-user system, allows an interaction using a stylus. In contrast to the related research, this system is based on a plasma display (Streitz et al., 2003). The DViT[4] (Digital Vision Touch) technology uses smart cameras mounted in each of the four corners of the table to track the user input (Morrison, 2005). Thus, the lens of each camera has a 90-degree field of view. The current version allows two simultaneous touches. Unfortunately, people cannot place any physical objects (e.g., a coffee mug) on the surface without achieving un-wanted touches. While DViT is mainly used for the SmartBoards, NextWindow,[5] a company from New Zealand has developed a similar system. This setup is mainly designed for touch-enabling existing LCD and/or plasma displays. The MIMIO[6] and eBeam[7] ultrasonic tracking devices, where participants use special styli, are a good and cheap alternative tracking surface. However, they are limited in the range and a lot of objects on the table can interfere the tracking.

The LumiSight table captures the objects on the table using cameras (Kakehi, Iida, Naemura, Shirai, Matsushita, & Ohguro, 2005). Using a transparent surface, both the cameras and the projectors are mounted inside the table. The advantage is that no additional hardware has to be placed on the ceiling. One of the first larger tabletop setups was been presented by Ishii et al. (2002). In their installation, they implemented a setup for engineers discussing urban planning. The system supports multilayering of 2d sketches, drawings, and maps in combination with 3d physical (tangible) objects and is primarily designed for group sizes up to 10 people. The setup consists of two projectors hanging from the ceiling. Two cameras (also mounted above the setup) capture all the users' activities.

SHARED DESIGN SPACE

Shared Design Space (Haller et al., 2006) is a collaborative tabletop environment that is mainly designed for brainstorming based on the design requirements mentioned in the previous sections. The main goal of the Shared Design Space project was to develop a large interaction surface which should be inexpensive to manufacture, scalable, and robust (Figure 6).

Hardware Setup

The current hardware setup consists of four projectors (with a high-resolution of 2048 x 1536 pixels) mounted above the interactive table (Figure 7a).

The tracking is realized by using a large Anoto pattern[8] and digital pens; see section (b) of Figure 7. Anoto-based pens are ballpoint-pens with an embedded infrared (IR) camera that tracks the pen movements simultaneously. The pen has to be used on a specially printed paper with a pattern of tiny dots. Each paper sheet is unique. The pattern is protected by a transparent Plexiglas cover; see section (c) of Figure 7. Once the user touches the table with the pen, the camera tracks the underlying Anoto paper. Instead of using a normal pen tip, we used a stylus tip that does not leave a mark on the Plexiglas. Both the surrounding light and the light of the projectors do not interfere with the pen tracking, because the camera tracks the pattern with its IR camera. We also noticed that the Plexiglas cover does not diffract the Anoto pattern. From the pen, we receive the ID of the pen, the ID of each paper sheet, and the position of the pen tip on the page. In our setup, we used two A0 (118,0cm x 84,1cm) sized paper sheets. The data can be collected in real-time and sent to the PC via Bluetooth. Currently, Anoto pens with Bluetooth are available from Nokia (SU-1B), Logitech (io-2), and Maxell (PenIT). All of these pens are pressure sensitive which allows for additional functionalities (i.e., better control in a sketching/drawing application).

Figure 6. The shared design space application: Users are interacting with digital pens on a large tabletop surface

Figure 7. The shared design space setup consists of an interactive table and an interactive wall (a). 36 tiny dots are arranged on a square area of 1.5 x 1.5 mm² (b). The Anoto pattern, placed under the Plexiglas, allows accurate tracking of digital data and the projected content does not interfere with the tracking of the digital pen (c)

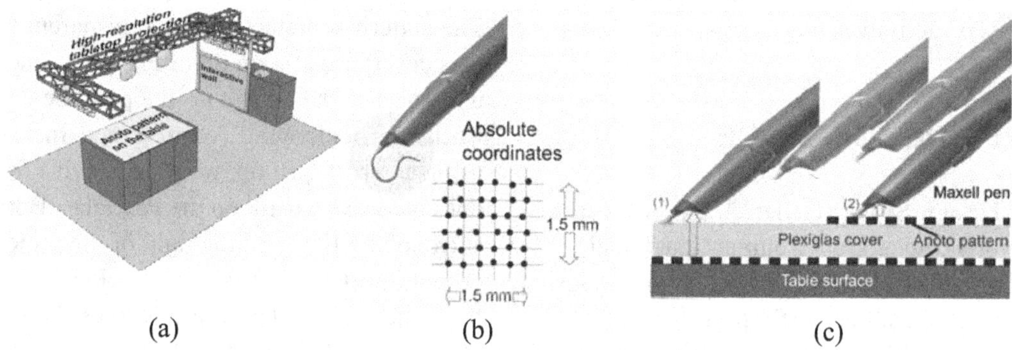

Our setup can identify simultaneous touches by using multiple styli. Whenever the pen touches the table's surface, the system identifies the ID of the pen and the action of the users they want to perform. Theoretically, there is no limit to how many people interact simultaneously. We have tested our setup with twelve participants interacting simultaneously. Surprisingly, people never mentioned problems with occlusion and shadows after testing the setup. We recognized that the users' focus is always on the tip of the pen while working with the interactive table and the shadows never occur on the relevant area. Nevertheless, we have also started exploring a rear-projection setup using a special semi-transparent projection foil in combination with the Anoto pattern. Although the Anoto tracking performs well on transparent foil, we have not been successful yet in printing the high-resolution pattern on the special rear-projection foil.

In our setup, we use the Anoto technology in different ways (Figure 8). In the first scenario, we combine real printouts with digital augmented content (similar to Mackay, Velay, Carter, Ma, & Pagani, 1993). In a second setup, we only work with digital paper and digital ink. Participants can interact with tangible (graspable) interfaces (e.g., with a real color box). In each of the color tiles of the box, we used again the Anoto tracking technology. Thus, the pen does not track directly the color, but the underlying pattern. For all these different patterns, we implemented a calibration tool, which allows a fast and robust calibration and registration of the pattern. After choosing a color, participants can draw with the digital ink or combine it with virtual content (e.g., images, videos, or 3d geometries). We used the Pick-and-Drop metaphor, proposed by Rekimoto (1997), instead of using the Drag-and-Drop paradigm. Thus, users can pick-up digital data from the table and drop-it on the private workspace by using the digital pen. Figure 9 depicts a modified state transition diagram based on the idea of Rekimoto (1997).

Once the user taps a digital object on the interactive table, our system automatically binds it (virtually) to the pen. Users can either drag it or lift the pen and move the pen to their own workspace. Once the users tap again to the private workspace, they can either drag the content again or put it to the desired position.

Figure 8. The current version of shared design space allows the interaction with real paper and real ink in combination with augmented content (a) or the interaction with digital paper and digital ink (b). Participants can annotate the real paper. The digital pen recognizes the corresponding color by the Anoto pattern, printed under the color label (c).

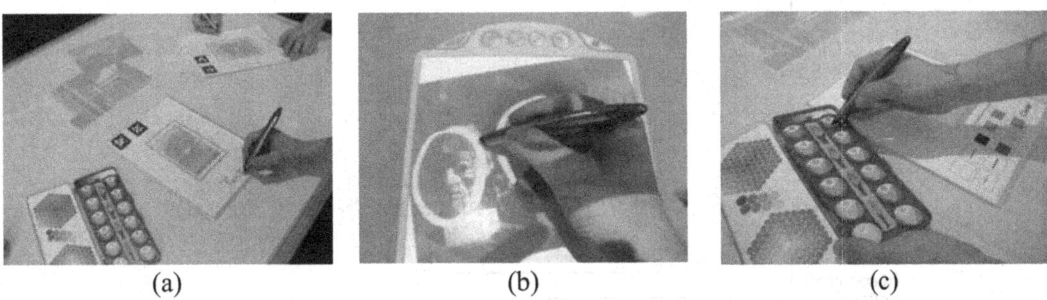

(a) (b) (c)

Figure 9. The state transition diagram of the pick and drop paradigm

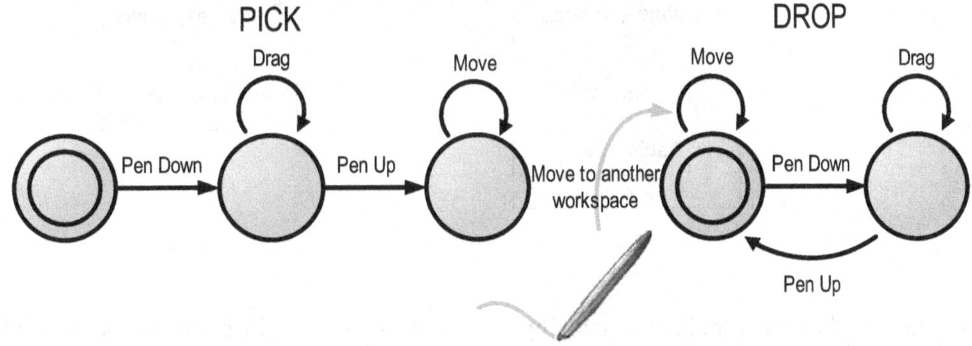

Implementation

Figure 10 depicts the implementation concept of the Shared Design Space. As mentioned, a virtually infinite number of digital pens can be linked together without any system-inherent limitations.

The digital pen server is implemented in C# using the digital pen SDKs from Maxell and the Tablet-PC API for gesture recognition. Whenever the users touch the table surface, the digital pen sends its data via Bluetooth to the digital pen sever. Thereafter, the resulted data are sent to the tabletop application, which maps the data to the local table coordinate system and which interprets the different pen inputs. Alternatively, we also connected an ultrasonic MIMIO tracking device to the gesture recognition component for testing the flexibility of our system. Again, the strokes are then directly interpreted and sent to the tabletop application. The digital pen server always sends the raw data (in the case of the Anoto paper, it sends the coordinates relative to the upper left corner of the paper). The tabletop application itself stores the digital content in a "scenegraph" and transforms the raw positions of the digital pen to the image space. Whenever, the user touches a digital content, it will be transformed accordingly depending where the user is interacting. Actually, we support simple transformations (translations by

Figure 10. Shared design space implementation

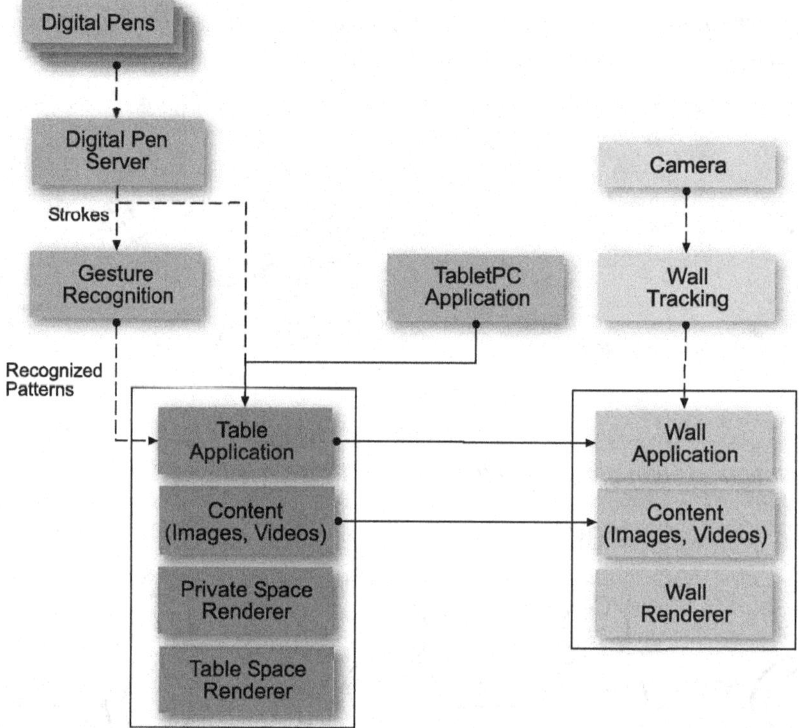

pointing to the middle of a digital content and by moving the digital pen, rotations and scaling by clicking to the anchors (handles), which are placed on the lower left of each widget). Thus, for each graphical object, we simply store its matrix which will be modified, whenever the user manipulates it with the digital pen.

There are several ways that participants can interact with the table. They can use the private space projected in front of their place or use a personal device (e.g., tablet PC), which is wirelessly connected to the table application. The personal workspace is rendered on the same machine as the rest of the design space. We simply implemented a huge rendering window, which is then split into the four different video outputs.

Participants can create new content on their own device and move it by hyper-dragging to the design table. The client application is also implemented in C++ in combination with OpenGL. The communication is realized by TCP/IP and the "dragged" objects are moved to the server's shared folder. The rendering engine of the tabletop application is realized using C++ and OpenGL. Similar approaches are implemented on top of the Mac OS X using Quartz and on Linux using the XRender Extension render engine. But it is still an open question if the system will support a multi-user input.

We used the ClanLib[9] library for rendering the applications' graphical user interface. The advantage of the ClanLib library is that the system is based on top of OpenGL and can therefore be combined easily with the basic rendering system of the 3d graphics library. In addition, we used the component model of the ClanLib library for the inter-component communication and the network extension for the communication between the clients and the server (e.g., communication with the gesture recognition engine).

The real paper, as depicted in section (a) of Figure 8, is tracked by using ARTag markers, placed on top of each piece of paper (Fiala, 2005). We use small markers (2cm x 2cm) in combination with a standard WATEC WAT-502B camera with manual focus, mounted on top of the table. There is some noise in the ARTag tracker output which means the virtual, augmented content is not 100% projected on the exact position and orientation of the paper. This was one of the main reasons, why we changed our primary focus to the digital paper in combination with digital ink.

The interactive wall, which consists of a rear-projection screen, provides a simple gesture tracking environment and allows for a multitouch interface for manipulating digital content, which can be moved from the interactive table to the wall and vice versa. The tracking on the interactive wall is mainly based on the JazzUp[10] library and on the OpenCV computer vision library.

USER STUDY

We conducted a user study to explore how well the Shared Design Space can solve some of the design challenges described before.

Apparatus

The participants performed the experiment while standing around the large table (183cm x 122cm), with a high-resolution (2048 x 1536 pixels) tabletop display. Three private workspaces were fixed in placed on the longer edges of the table. Two people were standing closer together—the third person was on the opposite edge of the table. A digital video camera, mounted on top of the table, was used to record the participant's interactions and movements.

Task

We designed a task that required a lot of collaboration, participants were provided with 60 images which included hidden shapes that the participants had to find (section (a) of Figure 11). There were three copies of each image on the table. Solving the task could be done by selecting a separate image for each participant or by using references. In this case, all users had the same view of the image and all annotations were seen by all participants simultaneously.

At the beginning of each session, the digital images were randomly placed in the middle of the table (Figure 11b). Some of them were overlapping and they needed to be examined in order to reveal the hidden shapes. The goal was to work together as a group to identify as many of the shapes as possible. There was a time limit set to 5 minutes and the participants were encouraged to make the most of the time and to discuss with their team members while finding the solutions. In order to test, whether the Shared Design Space setup has an impact on the overall workflow and the user performance, we repeated the test by using paper printouts of the hidden images and using real ink for annotations; section c of Figure 11. In contrast to the Shared Space Design setup, there were no fixed workspaces, and it was not possible to scale the images or create references. Task assignment, table, and content were the same under both conditions.

Participants

Results of the primary user study were gathered from 48 participants who used the Shared Design Space setup. The participants were recruited during a local festival. Of these, there were 28 males and 18 females between the ages of 11 and 54 years. The mean age of the participants was 28.8 (SD = 9.29) years. Two participants did not report age and gender. We formed 16 groups consisting of three members. The comparison group that

Figure 11. Participants had to find all hidden shapes (a) of the images. In the first scenario, participants were using the interactive table (b). In the second scenario, we repeated the test using real images (c)

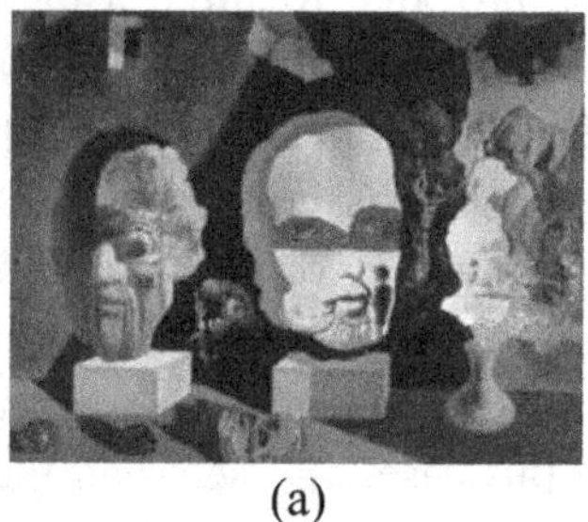

(a)

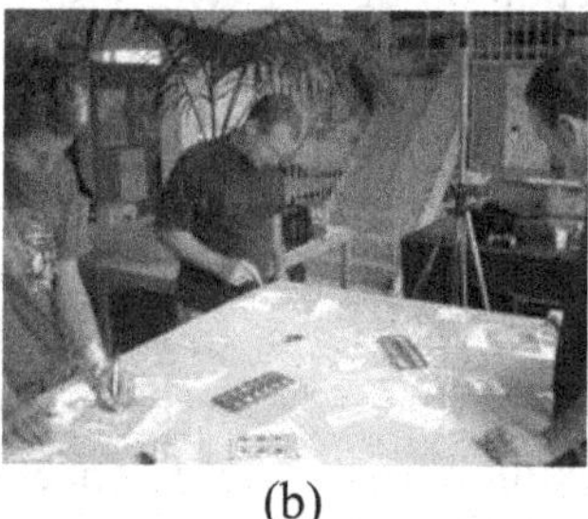

(b)

(c)

worked under the paper condition consisted of 12 participants recruited from the local university. Of these were nine males and three females between ages of 23 and 39 years ($\bar{x}$ = 27.6, SD = 4.48). We formed 4 groups of three members each. In both cases most of the participants reported that they had good computer skills, using a computer more than 15 hours a week.

Procedure

Before starting with the usability study, the participants were able to get familiar with the system. We demonstrated to them how to interact with the setup for about 5 minutes and allowed them to practice with the system themselves. Not all participants did the warm-up phase.

After each session, a survey was presented to the participants with a number of statements and they were asked how much they agreed or disagreed with the statement. The participants were also asked for general comments and feedback about the experience. In addition we tracked the movements of the participants in both setups, by using a camera mounted above the table.

RESULTS

Although the task had a fixed time limit of 5 minutes, participants had the possibility to "play" with the system before completing the task. Around 40% of the participants spent between 6 and 10 minutes around the table (including the warm-up phase and the test). Eighteen point three percent took between 11 and 20 minutes, only 26.7% played with the table for just 5 minutes. Fifteen percent of the users spent more than 20 minutes around the interactive table. The questionnaires were made up of 20 items, using a 5-point Likert-scale (1 = totally disagree, 5 = totally agree). The data were analyzed by using SPSS and the main effects were tested with a pair-wise t-test to determine if there was a statistical significance between the two conditions.

The questionnaires were grouped into the categories of learnability, interaction, interaction devices, collaboration and awareness, and space.

Learnability

Two items of the questionnaires addressed the learnability and ease-of-use of the system:

- **Q1:** It was always clear to me how to use the system.
- **Q2:** It was very easy to learn how to use the system.

Several participants were concerned that it was not immediately clear how to use the interactive table setup ($\bar{x}$ = 3.75, SD = 1.02). However, after a short introduction, people also mentioned that the application itself was easy-to-learn ($\bar{x}$ = 4.67, SD = 0.63) and they were more comfortable with the different interaction metaphors (e.g., the pick-and-drop). Thus, the way to use the pen was obvious and intuitive for the participants.

Interaction

At the beginning of each session, a lot of people found it difficult to move data from the table using the pick-and-drop metaphor without support. However, they immediately understood it once we demonstrated it in the warm-up phase. Three questions addressed the interaction with data:

- **Q3:** It was easy to select/grab an image from the table.
- **Q4:** It was easy to move an image on the table.
- **Q5:** It was easy to rotate an image on the table.

Overall, participants did not find it very difficult to select data sets, as indicated by the Likert-scale responses to the statement "I found it easy to select/grab an image from the table" ($\bar{x}$ = 4.44, SD = 0.65). People also did not have a lot of problems moving data ($\bar{x}$ = 4.56, SD = 0.68), nor did they find it very difficult to rotate data ($\bar{x}$ = 4.45, SD = 0.90). Surprisingly, the pick-and-drop metaphor was not as intuitive as expected. The first approach of most participants was to move data into their private workspace using drag-and-drop. As images can be moved by dragging with the pen, they tried the same technique to place them in their private workspace. Explaining the difference between moving data inside a workspace and changing the workspace location from public to private or vice versa clarified the two ways of handling digital content.

While tipping once with the pen to the digital images, a lot of persons were confused where the content has gone and images got selected by fault. Dropping them and selecting a new image confused users. They tried to select a new image while they had the one still selected. This resulted in dropping the old image at the next click instead of picking up the new one. But not all of participants had this problem. Especially those who spent more time in the warm-up phase reported encountering fewer problems.

Interaction Devices

In the category *interaction devices*, we mainly focused on the tangible interfaces and the pen interaction asking the following four questions:

- Q6: The palettes were very intuitive.
- **Q7:** The pen tracking was really accurate and robust.
- **Q8:** The pen vibrated really often.
- **Q9:** I would rather prefer interacting with the fingers instead of using the pen.

Not all users found the palettes very intuitive ($\bar{x}$ =3.94, SD=1.00). Many participants remarked that the icons on the palettes were not always clear. The color boxes however, as tangible interfaces were evaluated positively. Another problem was that real objects were hard to be detected on the table once they were illuminated by the projector's image (Figure 13). So, for instance, it is not only hard to detect the right color, but also to find the color box itself, once many images are projected onto the table.

Most of the participants had the feeling that the pen tracking was really accurate and robust ($\bar{x}$ = 4.13, SD = 0.89). This was also confirmed while asking if the participants noticed the vibration of the pen which occurred whenever the pen camera could not track the tiny dots of the paper ($\bar{x}$ = 2.58, SD = 1.25). The pen mostly itself vibrated when people held the pen too flat, which caused bad tracking results.

When asked "Would you rather prefer interacting with your fingers instead of using the pen," the average of all responses was 2.2 (SD = 1.37). The relatively high standard deviation indicates that in this question not all participants had the same opinion: interviewing participants, a lot of users thought that the pen should be mainly used for writing and for typing (e.g., onto a virtual keyboard). In contrast, some activities are more intuitive using the fingers (e.g., rotating content).

Space

Four questions focused on the space and workspace:

- **Q10:** I could easily see all images and all details of the images on the table.
- **Q11:** I mostly focused on my private workspace.
- **Q12:** I mostly focused on the common workspace.
- **Q13:** The size of the interactive table was too small.

Table 2 summarizes the average results on space and workspaces using the paper and interactive table condition.

During the tests, we recognized that most of the participants mainly focused on their private workspace working on the interactive table. The public workspace was only used by one group. They discussed the selected image placed in the public workspace and used different scale levels and rotations to solve the task.

We tracked the movements of the participants in both setups and measured the "level of interactivity," by using a camera mounted on top of the setups. Figure 12 depicts the results of the movement analysis over the five minutes. The black areas represent the movements and the interactions of the participants. The red areas show the movements standing around the table. The green area is depicting the interaction area on the table. Under the paper condition, the participants were grouping to one position; see section (a) of Figure 12.

The participants arranged the paper images in front of them and chose a common location to access them. Interaction across the table only happened at the beginning the focus then shifted to the near area directly in front of them. In contrast, in the interactive table setup, the main interaction happened in front of each participant; see section (b) of Figure 12). Participants stayed at the position of their workspaces and we can distinguish three separate areas.

After the experiment was completed, the participants were also briefly interviewed about their experience. The participants were more active during the discussion using the interactive table; see section (b) of Figure 12. In general, people neither changed their position on the interactive table, nor did they walk around it. Users commented that the private workspace should be larger and not have a fixed position. One of the participants

Table 2. Average results on space and workspaces

Condition	Paper	Interactive Table
Q10	3.63 (SD = 1.21)	3.47 (SD = 1.17)
Q11	3.50 (SD = 1.38)	3.98 (SD = 0.99)
Q12	2.91 (SD = 1.16)	2.68 (SD = 1.00)
Q13	3.58 (SD = 0.67)	2.96 (SD = 0.45)

Figure 12. Participants' movements and interactions in paper scenario (a) and using the interactive table setup (b). While the red areas mark the location of the participants, the green areas visualize the main interaction areas

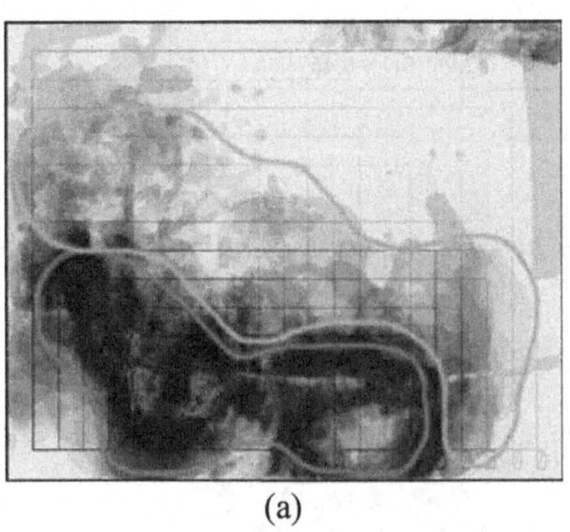

(a)

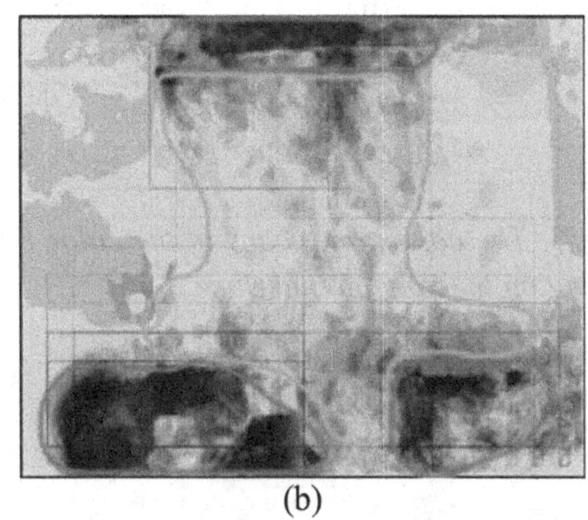

(b)

noticed that the printed pictures were too small, which forced him to actually pick-up the pictures so that he could recognize the hidden shapes. This, however, brought the focus away from the shared workspace. Although we used the same table size under both conditions, we found a significant difference in the assessment of the size of the table, $t(58) = 9.227$, $p < 0.05$. While those working in the Shared Design Space agreed that the table was rather a bit too small ($\bar{x} = 2.69$, SD = 0.46), those using the paper setup confirmed that the table was too large ($\bar{x} = 3.58$, SD = 0.67).

Finally, it was not immediately clear to everyone that the whole table was interactive. Some people just thought that they could interact with their private workspace.

Awareness and Collaboration

We asked two questions about the awareness and collaboration both in the interactive table as well as the paper condition:

- **Q14:** How often were you aware of what your partner was doing?
- **Q15:** Coordinating with your partner was easy.

Table 3 shows the average results for each of these questions. The t-test found no significant difference for question Q14 and a significant difference for question Q15, $t(58) = 5.606$, $p < 0.05$.

Participants felt that they were more aware of what their partners were doing under the paper condition. It was interesting to see that under the paper condition the participants got really close to each other to solve the problem; see section (a) of Figure 12). Initially, most of the participants were standing around the table and had a larger distance to each other. Once they had to solve the problem, they immediately moved away from their initial position and got closer to each other to focus on the same image. In most cases, one person became the leader of the session and the other two mostly agreed or disagreed with their comments. In contrast to the paper condition, more people got actively involved under the interactive table condition. Nevertheless, due to the longer distances and the fixed private workspaces, people were less aware of what their partner was doing.

An average of four correct images was found by the participants using the interactive table setup. In contrast, the users found mostly different solutions under the paper condition (an average of only one common solution was found by all par-

Table 3. Average results on collaboration and awareness

Condition	Paper	Interactive Table
Q14	3.00 (SD = 1.13)	2.92 (SD = 0.85)
Q15	3.58 (SD = 0.67)	2.96 (SD = 0.46)

Figure 13. The colors and icons of the color box can become hardly to read once digital content is projecting on the tangible interface

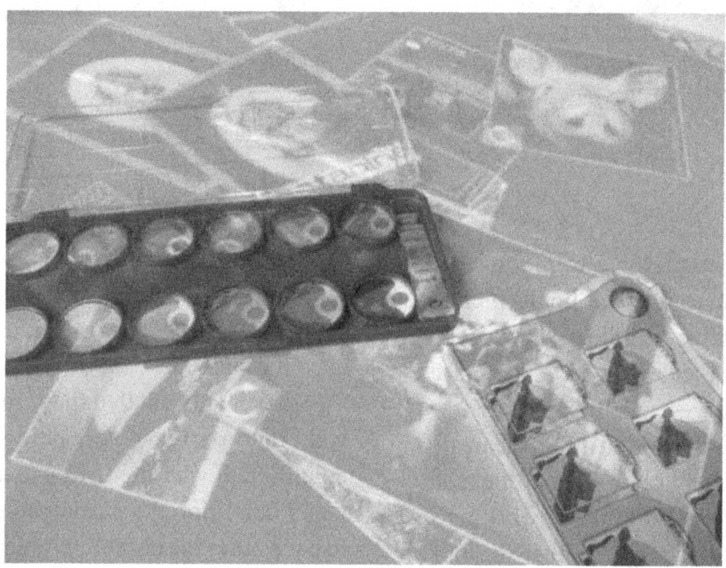

ticipants). Although most of them thought to have a single solution, we noticed that the annotations of the printouts were mostly different. Thus, the participants thought they were talking about the same thing, but in reality they were not.

CONCLUSION AND FUTURE WORK

Although there are already several projects focusing on ubiquitous environments, it is still challenging to design a digital table which is seamlessly embedded in an existing environment. In this chapter, we mainly focused on design requirements we achieved from discussions with our customers. After the requirements, we presented the most important related projects highlighting both their display and tracking technologies. Finally, we described the Shared Design Space, a scalable tabletop setup, which allows for development of a very large interactive table at low cost. The interaction is realized using digital pens with embedded cameras which track a special pattern (with tiny dots) mounted on the table surface. The installation provides a cooperative and social experience by allowing multiple face-to-face participants to interact easily around a shared workspace, while also having access to their own private information space and a public presentation space combining both virtual and real sketches. The project is different from typical screen-based collaboration because it uses advanced interface technologies to merge the personal and task space.

Using the Anoto paper pattern creates a flexible, easy-to-use, and cheap interface. Very large displays can easily be built, while keeping the price low. Using no special surface allows users to sit freely around the table and to put additional physical objects onto the table surface without interfering the tracking. Moreover, the system can identify who is interacting with the interface without any additional hardware requirements, for example, capacitive measurement on the chairs (Dietz & Leigh, 2001). One drawback with the digital pens is the lack of free fingers for simple user gesture inputs (e.g., the movement of digital paper can be done easily and faster using the hand instead of using digital pens).

Although a lot of people were not disturbed by self-occlusions and shadows which occur using a tabletop projection setup, we recognized that real objects were hard to detect on the table once they were illuminated by the projector's image (Figure 13).

One possible solution for this problem would be to mask the real objects and not project digital content on these areas.

The most critical questions are the rendering engine and the framework. Using an OpenGL/DirectX based approach always raises the question about the possible combination with desktop-based applications (e.g., the integration of Powerpoint slides, Excel sheets, or PDF documents). For each of these formats, we would have to write a separate viewer (renderer). Similarly, the lack of multi-user support is a serious problem which can not be solved easily.

Another problem is an adequate user interface for the large surface. The Windows-based applications are mainly optimized for desktop setups. Therefore, applications cannot just be projected on the table without modifications. How can we create new content on the table efficiently? Which user interfaces should we use to achieve an optimal performance? How can we move the data around the table efficiently?

In the future, we would like to employ our setup in a collaborative remote setup and conduct more in-depth user studies. Moreover, we will develop further applications to explore other aspects of collaborative applications.

ACKNOWLEDGMENT

The authors gratefully acknowledge the entire research lab of the Upper Austria University of Applied Sciences. In particular, we would like to thank Peter Brandl, Daniel Leithinger, Jakob Leitner, Thomas Seifried, and Jürgen Zauner. This work is funded by the FFG FHPlus Program (No. 811407) and by Voestalpine Informationstechnologie GmbH. We would like to acknowledge Anoto and Maxell for their technical support. Finally, we would also thank all participants for joining the user study.

REFERENCES

Bimber, O., & Raskar, R. (2005). *Spatial augmented reality: Merging real and virtual worlds*. A K Peters LTD.

Blinn, J. (1990, November/December). The ultimate design tool. *IEEE Computer Graphics and Applications, 10*(6), 90-92.

Buxton, W. (1992). Telepresence: Integrating shared task and person spaces. In *Proceedings of Graphics Interface '92* (pp. 123-129).

Dietz, P.H., & Leigh, D.L. (2001, November). DiamondTouch: A multi-user touch technology.

In *ACM Symposium on User Interface Software and Technology (UIST)* (pp. 219-226). ISBN: 1-58113-438-X.

Fiala, M. (2005, June 20-26). ARTag, a fiducial marker system using digital techniques. In *Proceedings of the 2005 IEEE Computer Society Conference on Computer Vision and Pattern Recognition (CVPR '05)* (Vol. 2) (pp. 590-596). Washington, DC: IEEE Computer Society

Hall, E. (1966). *Distances in man: The hidden dimension.* Garden City, NY: Double Day.

Haller, M., Billinghurst, M., Leithinger, D., Leitner, J., & Seifried, T. (2005, December 5-8). Coeno, enhancing face-to-face collaboration. In 15th International Conference on Artificial Rea*lity and Telexistence (ICAT).* Christchurch, New Zealand.

Haller, M., Leithinger, D., Leitner, J., Seifried, T., Brandl, P., Zauner, J. et al. (2006, August). The shared design space. In *ACM SIGGRAPH 2006, Emerging Technologies*, Boston, MA.

Inkpen, K. (1997). *Adapting the human computer interface to support collaborative learning environments for children.* Ph.D. Dissertation, Department of Computer Science, University of British Columbia.

Ishii, H., Underkoffler, J., Chak, D., Piper, B., Ben-Joseph, E., Yeung, L. et al. (2002). Augmented urban planning workbench: Overlaying drawings, physical models and digital simulation. In *IEEE and ACM International Symposium on Mixed and Augmented Reality ACM Press,* Darmstadt, Germany.

Kakehi, Y., Iida, M., Naemura, T., Shirai, Y., Matsushita, M., & Ohguro, T. (2005). Lumisight table: Interactive view-dependent tabletop display surrounded by multiple users. *IEEE Computer Graphics and Applications, 25*(1), 48-53.

Liao, C., Guimbretière, F., & Hinckley, K. (2005, October 23-26). PapierCraft: A command system for interactive paper. In *Proceedings of the 18th Annual ACM Symposium on User interface Software and Technology*, Seattle, WA (pp. 241-244). New York, NY: ACM Press.

Mackay, W.E., Velay, G., Carter, K., Ma, C., & Pagani, D. (1993, July). Augmenting reality: Adding computational dimensions to paper. *Communications of the ACM, 36*(7), 96-97.

Morris, M.R. (2006, April). *Supporting effective interaction with tabletop groupware.* Ph.D. Dissertation, Stanford University Technical Report.

Morris, M.R., Paepcke, A., Winograd, T., & Stamberger, J. (2006). TeamTag: Exploring centralized versus replicated controls for co-located tabletop groupware. In *Proceedings of CHI.*

Morrison, G. (2005, July/August). A camera-based input device for large interactive displays. *IEEE Computer Graphics and Applications, 25*(4), 52-57.

Parker, J. K., Mandryk, R. L., & Inkpen, K. M. (2006, September). Integrating point and touch for interaction with digital tabletop displays. *IEEE Computer Graphics and Applications, 26*(5), 28-35.

Ramsborg, G. (2002). *Dynamics of seating arrangements: Identification of points of power around a conference table.* Retrieved January 27, 2008, from http://www.ramsborg.com/etopic/Nov_2002/index.html

Rekimoto, J. (1997, October 14-17). Pick-and-drop: A direct manipulation technique for multiple computer environments. In *Proceedings of the 10th Annual ACM Symposium on User Interface Software and Technology*, Banff, Canada (pp. 31-39).

Rekimoto, J. (2002). SmartSkin: An infrastructure for freehand manipulation on interactive surfaces. In *CHI 2002.*

Rekimoto, J., & Saitoh, M. (1999). Augmented surfaces: A spatially continuous work space for hybrid computing environments. In *CHI '99, Proceedings of the SIGCHI conference on Human Factors in Computing Systems.*

Scott, S.D., Carpendale, M.S.T., & Inkpen, K.M. (2004). Territoriality in collaborative tabletop workspace. In *Proceedings of CSCW 2004 (pp.* 294-303).

Scott, S.D., Grant, K.D., & Mandryk, R.L. (2003, September). System guidelines for co-located, collaborative work on a tabletop display. In *Proceedings of ECSCW'03, European Conference Computer-Supported Cooperative Work 2003.*

Shen, C., Vernier, F.D., Forlines, C., & Ringel, M. (2004, April 24-29). DiamondSpin: An extensible toolkit for around-the-table interaction. In *Proceedings of the SIGCHI Conference on Human Factors in Computing Systems*, Vienna, Austria (pp. 167-174). New York, NY: ACM Press.

Streitz, N., Prante, P., Röcker, C., van Alphen, D., Magerkurth, C., & Stenzel, R. (2003). Plewe ambient displays and mobile devices for the creation of social architectural spaces: Supporting informal communication and social awareness in organizations. In *Public and situated displays: Social and interactional aspects of shared display technologies* (pp. 387-409). Kluwer Publishers.

Tse, E. (2004, November). *The single display groupware toolkit.* M.Sc. Thesis, Department of Computer Science, University of Calgary, Calgary, Alberta, Canada.

Wellner, P. (1992, November 11-13). The DigitalDesk calculator: Tactile manipulation on a desktop display. In *Proceedings of UIST'92, the ACM Symposium on User Interface Software and Technology,* Hilton Head, SC. New York: ACM.

Yeh, R., Liao, C., Klemmer, S., Guimbretière, F., Lee, B., Kakaradov, B. et al. (2006). ButterflyNet: A mobile capture and access system for field biology research. In *Proceedings of the SIGCHI Conference on Human Factors in Computing Systems CHI '06* (pp. 571-580). New York, NY: ACM Press.

ENDNOTES

1 http://www.smarttech.com/
2 www.anoto.com
3 http://grouplab.cpsc.ucalgary.ca/cookbook/index.php?n=Toolkits.TableTopFramework
4 http://www.smarttech.com/DViT/
5 http://www.nextwindow.com/
6 http://www.mimio.com
7 http://www.e-beam.com
8 http://www.anoto.com
9 http://www.clanlib.org
10 http://SourceForge.net/projects/JazzUp/

Chapter XVIII
A Case Study of Icon-Scenario Based Animated Menu's Concept Development

Lim Chee Koon
Motorola Electronics Pte. Ltd, Singapore

Henry B. L. Duh
National University of Singapore, Singapore

ABSTRACT

This chapter will first describe the development workflow of graphical user interface (GUI) design and the implementation that is adopted across a 2G platform. It describes the development workflow of graphical user interface (GUI) design and the implementation that is adopted across a 2G platform. The authors then describe the implementation process of developing Icon-Scenario Based Animated Menu GUI. The same design process developed is implemented in the other models when the authors develop another set of GUIs for different customers using the same workflow. The chapter concludes by describing the concept development process of the phone's menu enhanced by the use of a captivating Icon-Scenario Based Animated Menu, followed by demonstrating how it takes usability into consideration, bringing delight to users.

INTRODUCTION

It was over the recent years that the 2G platform has become a mandatory technology in a mobile phone design house. Presently, most of the phones in the market adopted the icon based menu which is becoming mundane. Redesigning the Graphic Design of the icons and user interface was one of our solutions to redefine the user experience in menu navigation.

There was a need to differentiate the phone from what is seen in the market; we have implemented the element of fun into the menu by animating scenarios in the menu. When the user navigates the menu, the user can experience the different animated scenarios. With the aid of the engineering capability, we were able to compress high density animation and apply the compressed format of the animation into the menu. This enables us to create the new style of menu.

With the new method of menu presentation, we have developed and followed through a design methodology that enables us to create and generate different concepts. This chapter describes the methodology from the conceptualization stage to the implementation of the Icon-Scenario Based Animated Menu. We then conduct a usability test to evaluate the new menu developed for E1200 and discuss the results.

THE DESIGN WORKFLOW

The flow chart (see Figure 1) describes the process in its initial stage and the development stage. When the initial Industrial Design Rendering of mobile phone was approved, information regarding the project was given to the GUI design team. Among the information, a design brief which described the target audience and technical specification was given. The GUI designers then began the conceptualization stage where the themes for the phone were explored. GUI storyboarding on different themes and scenarios was presented in the first draft to our customer. The concept theme was iterated until approved. The concepts were illustrated using Adobe Illustrator. With the selected theme, the GUI designers will proceed to the stage of prototyping. The equipment and software used for our GUI prototype involved HP iPAQ Pocket PC h4100 series, HP workstation xw4100, Adobe Creative Suite Premium, Macromedia Studio MX 2004. The scenario was animated and then downloaded into the Pocket PC. The GUI on the phone was simulated and implemented into the pocket PC to achieve high fidelity prototyping effect. The system was prototyped from idle stage to submenu stage. The main objective was to allow the customers and engineers to experience the look and feel of the Icon-Scenario Based Animated GUI through interactive navigation. Iteration began from the prototyping stage onward, taking into account the customer's feedback.

The software engineer on the team created the simulation on workstation using C++. At this

Figure 1. Flow chart for GUI design process

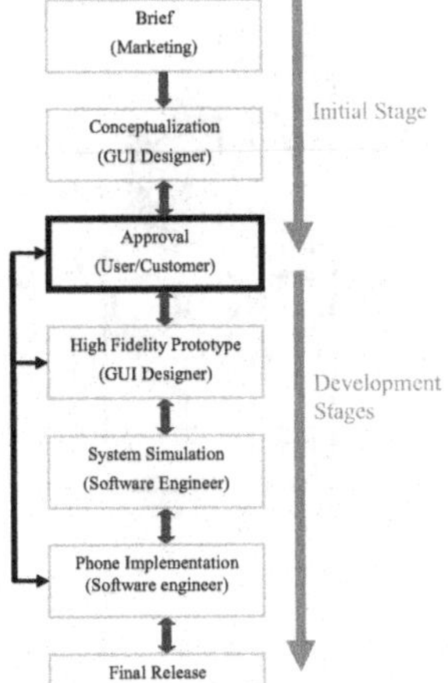

stage, we were able to get a better distribution of memory space allocation for the animation frames that were to be implemented into the menu. The frames usually ranged from five to eight depending on the memory space in the phone. The frames would be compressed and converted from the BMP format to ASCII format; information within this file would then be embedded into the source code. This conversion process was handled by our software engineers. The coded simulation will be the actual system that could be downloaded into the actual phone when ready. From this moment, we used the actual phone with the downloaded system to evaluate the acceptance of the GUI.

Case Study: E1200

E1200, one of the mobile phones developed by Newgen Telecom, is a bar type phone. The E1200 has a compact dimension of 78.5mm x 47mm x 17.6mm. It utilizes a 65,000 TFT color LCD 1.3" TFT Screen with a resolution of 160x128. One of our motivations to innovate the animated style menu was due to the small screen size and miniature form factor of the phone design.

We also needed to include text information as well as icon cue to assist the user on the status of navigation. The UI structure was adopted from the previous platform, which consists of left, right soft keys, send, end keys, numeric keys, and navigation jog key (see Figure 2).

E1200 Task Flow

The female avatar was selected in E1200 and there were details refined in the development stage. A description of the work flow is usually illustrated to state the application of the animated frames. We start from idle stage to the submenu stage (see Figure 3). This stage will show the original status when the phone is switched on. When the user pressed the left soft key, the display will show the sequence of animation. After the animation, it will display the menu at the phonebook feature by default. Upon activating the "OK" key, the screen will display the submenu options.

Figure 2. Operation keys for E1200

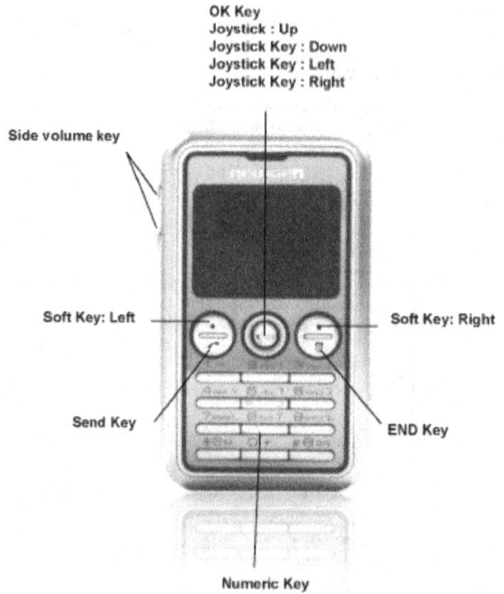

Figure 3. Task flow

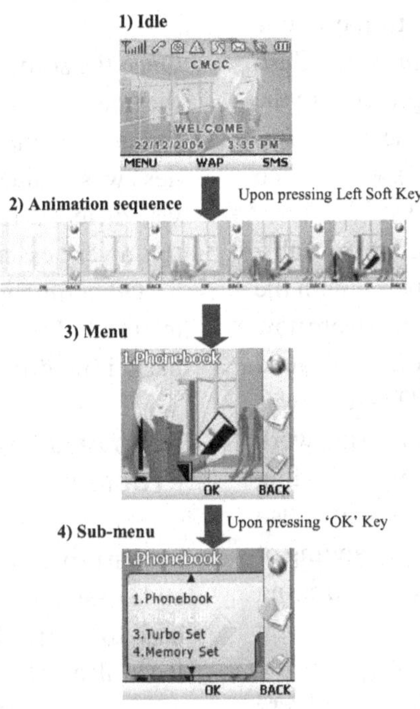

Figure 4. GUI Specification for scenario based menu

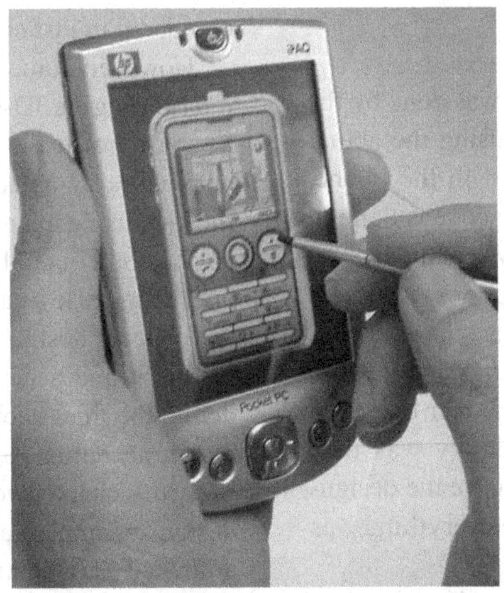

Prototype

We understood that there is some slight difference when we view the animation on workstation monitor screens and on the actual phone. The pixel size and resolution differs, but at this stage, we did not have the luxury to download the graphics in the actual phone for viewing, as the phone was still under prototyping and development. To simulate the closest experience in relation to the phone and the application, we made an animated flash file with the visual of the phone together with the application and downloaded it into the Pocket PC. Using Flash Assist 1.3 (see Figure 4), we are then able to play it full screen in the PDA.

With the flash output as SWF file, we were able to demonstrate and communicate better with the customer as well as our engineers. They were now able to interact and get a feel for how we wanted the graphic user interface to work. This stage was practiced to avoid unnecessary engineering work by the software engineers, for example the coding to accommodate the animated frames. We also wanted the team to have a clear understanding of the interaction concept, at the same time ironing out the constraints of the platform. Prototyping was typically done from the idle stage till the submenu stage. The details of the functions were usually omitted as most of them were standard across the 2G platform used.

Simulation

A simulation of the Phone GUI was done by the Software team. This involved using the actual software code that will be used in the phone, therefore superior in a way. The code is done in the C language using the ARM compiler. The software used to simulate the phone environment was done in Visual Studio 6. Once the code was modified and images converted and inserted into the code, it was compiled. This was then uploaded into the simulator. The interactivity was then tested from the simulator. This gave the designers the ability to visually ensure everything was working according to design.

This helped to speed up the development time when the actual phone was still under development/testing. Furthermore uploading of the software into the phone took about 15 minutes. Only after the simulation worked fine was the software uploaded to the phone.

Implementation

Once the software was uploaded into the phone, the final evaluation was carried out. At this point, the speed of the animation and menu responsiveness was evaluated as the speed of the processor was different from that of a PDA or PC making this a very essential step.

Other functions of the phone also went through testing at this point in time. Again, iteration took place if modification was needed.

Pros and Cons of the Design Process

Scenario based menu allowed us to customize the style to suit the phone. This style can be changed based on the platform and size of the mobile phone. It can also be localized to suit the market trends or even customer requirements. If we were to sell this phone to a particular customer, the whole phone GUI style could be customized easily to appeal to user. This would create much more impact when compared to just changing the icon.

However, some users may find difficulty in interpreting the 3D-style scenarios. They may not be able to relate the scene to the function. For example, the original scene used for settings involved the lady using a laptop and icon of laptop which our customer could not relate to and which was later changed to a garage and icon of gears during the concept design stage for E1200. Stereotype feedback and acceptance by the user/customer define the final decision of adoption within our recommendations and proposals.

In this chapter we have reported the process of design and implementation of the scenario based animated GUI menu of E1200. We developed this method to give the team a better understanding of the processes involved in the design and implementation of the particular GUI mentioned.

By having a system of early prototyping using flash and the software simulator, we allowed for designer, customer/user, and engineer to easily communicate with each other. This allowed us to immediately get creative and technical feedback in an early stage while the actual physical product was still under development and not available.

For this process, we need skilled GUI designers with an animation skill set, which in turn contributed to churning out the prototype in shorter time. We adopted this method in other projects and have contributed well in terms of presentation and communication.

There are technical issues like speed of the processor which could affect the animation effect. As we knew, phones of different platforms may differ in the processor speed. An area to investigate further is to look into details such as when the mobile phone varieties diverse. We also hoped to improve the versatility of prototypes so that the speed of process can be best simulated.

DESIGN METHODOLOGY

In the design process, we prepared the graphic user interface design of the Icon Based Menu, Scenario Based Animated Menu, and Icon-Scenario Based Animated Menu. The development of concepts for Icon-Scenario Based Animated menu, followed by usability test evaluation of these different types of menus, are shown.

Icon Based Menu

The icon based menu (see Figure 5) is commonly used in many phones. The icons created are in 3D and a grey box is used as an indication for the icon selected. The layout is similar to that of the menu adopted in Newgen S410. The icon animates when the feature is selected.

Figure 5. Icon based menu

Figure 6. Scenario based animated menu

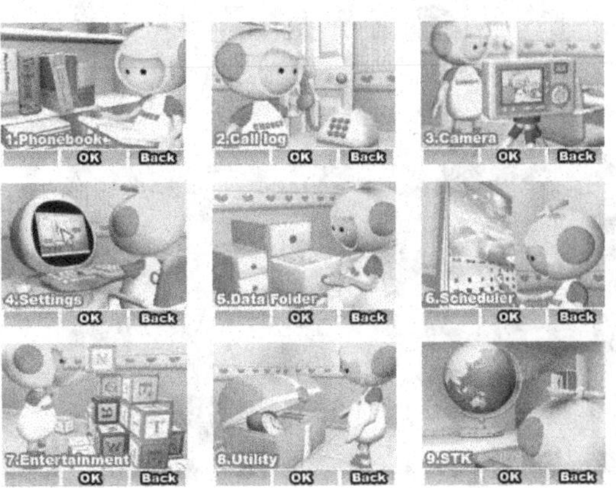

Scenario Based Animated Menu

The scenario based animated menu (see Figure 6) is one of the earlier menu designs which we have previously adopted in Newgen C620. It is based on a cute humanoid character in the settings of an interior of a room churned out in 3D style. Instead of using desktop icons, the menu illustrates a series of scenario which consist of a character performing an action in relation to the particular feature. This concept consists of nine animated scenarios. In each animation, text was included to provide information display (Jenny P., Yvonne R., Helen S., David B., Simon H., & Tom C., 1994). for the user navigating through the menu. This text can be changed based on language settings.

The concern about the present Scenario Based Animated Menu is that the graphical user interface design is not customized for E1200. The graphics user interface design is based on the user group study for teenagers who are receptive to 3D animated graphics. There is also a lack of affordance to guide the user in navigation.

Icon-Scenario Based Animated Menu

With the concern regarding the two types of menu mentioned earlier, we were motivated to develop a new concept to display the menu on the mobile phone. Nonetheless, it was important for us to implement design concept with usability that is able to bring delights to the specific users. With that in consideration, we needed to develop a concept based on the design criteria and specifications in the process of concept development.

DESIGN CRITERIA

In order to take usability into consideration and find out the acceptability of the concepts, we have set the following criteria for consideration in the process of design:

1. **Navigation:** The ease of selection of features in conjunction with the joy key
2. **Recognition:** The ease of recognizing the features represented by icons and/or scenarios
3. **Feedback:** The clarity of visual and audio feedback
4. **Consistency:** The level of consistency in the layout of menu during navigation
5. **Efficiency:** The level of efficiency in achieving the task
6. **Aesthetic:** The level of good visual appearance to user

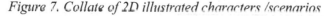

Figure 7. Collate of 2D illustrated characters /scenarios

7. **Fun:** The level of fun element in the event of navigation

These criteria were also used in the usability study. The users were asked to compare and comment on the Icon Based Menu, Scenario Based Animated Menu, and Icon-Scenario Based Animated Menu design based on these criteria.

DESIGN SPECIFICATIONS

In this case study, we were required to design a new set of GUI menus for E1200. E1200 is a bar type phone that has a compact dimension of 78.5mm x 47mm x 17.6mm. It utilizes a 65,000 TFT color LCD 1.3" TFT Screen with a resolution of 160x128. One of our motivations to improve the animated style menu is due to the following:

- Small screen size and miniature form factor of the phone design
- The implementation of fun and a pleasing aesthetic into the menu

The intention of target market for E1200 was for women between 21 to 25 years of age. We were required to design a new menu based on these specifications. This menu also needs to appeal to targeted users and fun to use at the same time. The criteria mentioned earlier were also part of the considerations for the GUI menu design. The UI structure was adopted from the previous platform, which consists of left, right soft keys, send, end keys, numeric keys, and navigation jog key.

CONCEPT DEVELOPMENT

Theme Inspiration

There are various sources of themes we considered during the conceptualization of the theme for the menu. Icon-Scenario Based Animated Menu is based on the new female avatar concept that we created. The source for the female avatar was an inspiration from collates of images from female magazines that were in trend. We then created our own lady avatar from the inspirations using 2D illustrated style (see Figure 7).

Animated Scenarios

The Icon-Scenario Based Animated Menu consists of nine main menu items of which the user has to cycles through to find the one user needs. We created new scenes for each of the nine main menu items. Each scene's environment was designed to relate to the feature. For instance, the "entertainment" feature is illustrated with the avatar holding poker cards in a casino environment.

We decided to place and pose the avatar in different scenes according to the menu item function. Users would experience nine sets of animating scenarios of different animations (see Figure 8). The animation will start from the faded view of the environment, followed by the gradual appearance of the avatar. Each animation was limited to five frames to avoid lag in processing.

Color Selection

Different colors were used in each scenario to give each page its own feel. This was done to give the user a cue that they have already moved on to a different feature (see figure 8). There may not be any significance in the color used but we make the point to use different tones and shades for each scenario set up. We have applied a different wear for the avatar, each wear represents a different theme and further enhanced by the environment. In the environment of each scenario, we added shadow of objects and figures which make more sense in the scenario set up. They are described as follow:

1. In the "**Phonebook**" feature, the avatar is in office wear standing outside an office en-

vironment holding a diary. We had selected blue to give the feel of clarity and seriousness. There were two figures in dark blue tones standing outside the office door.

2. In the "**Call log**" feature, the avatar is in violet dress holding a phone by her ear in a city landscape environment. We have selected peach to give the feeling of sun setting. There were passerby figures in their dark peach tones.
3. In the "**Camera**" feature, the avatar is in an evening gown posing in front of a camera in an outdoor setup. We have selected violet to relate photography session in a mystic night. There was a photographer in the dark violet tone.
4. In the "**Setting**" feature, the avatar is in her singlet standing behind the car garage. The environment is illustrated in tones of green to simulate dim room set up. There was a male figure holding boxes in his dark green tones.
5. In the "**Data folder**" feature, the avatar again is in another set of office wear standing next to a file cabinet holding a file in the air. The background is in different tone of blue to relate the office environment. There is a lady holding a document, in dark blue tones.
6. In the "**Schedule**" feature, the avatar is in an office wear, talking on the phone holding a schedule sheet at the same time. The color of the background is in lighter tone of cyan to relate to the office environment. There is a man sitting at the desk thinking, in the dark cyan tone.
7. In the "**Entertainment**" feature, the avatar is in a gown, standing in a casino pub environment holding poker cards. The color of the background is in tones of red to relate the

Figure 8. Icon-scenario based animated menu

classy set up in a pub environment. There is a waiter in the dark red tone.

8. In the "**Utilities**" feature, the avatar is in the washroom with her make up box, again she is in a different dress. Tones of light green were used to relate a room set up. There is a lady figure in front of a mirror; she is in the dark green tone.
9. In the "**STK**" feature, the avatar is in an office environment with a globe on a table. The color used is in tones of brown. There is a figure sitting at the desk writing, in the dark brown tone.

Icons

One of the requirements developed in this concept was that there has to be a way for the user to know what are the next page and the previous page item. This was achieved through the use of icons. In each of these pages, three icons are shown. The center icon represents the page the user is currently in, the size is also bigger, and the remaining two icons represent the next and previous pages. The icons style was designed to represent the function yet being compatible to the whole theme. We used the following icons for its feature:

1. **Phonebook feature:** Phonebook as icon
2. **Call log:** Mobile phone as icon
3. **Camera:** Camera as icon
4. **Setting:** Gears as icons
5. **Data Folder:** File cabinet as icon
6. **Schedule:** Desk Calendar as icon
7. **Entertainment:** Poker card as icon
8. **Utilitie:** Make-up box as icon
9. **STK:** Globe as icon

Text

The text display (Jenny P., Yvonne R., Helen S., David B., Simon H., & Tom C., 1994) design is similar to that seen in the icon based menu and scenario based animated menu. In each animation, text was included to provide information display for the user in the navigation through the menu. This text can be changed based on language settings.

Figure 9. GUI Specification for scenario based menu

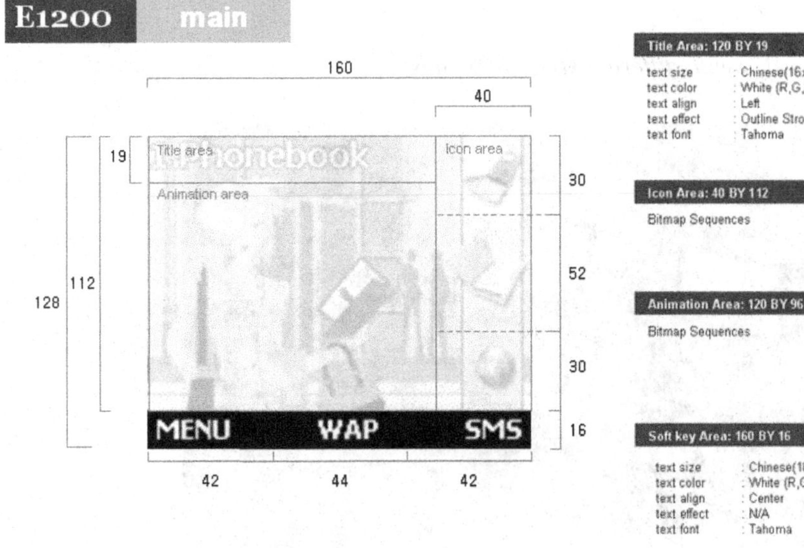

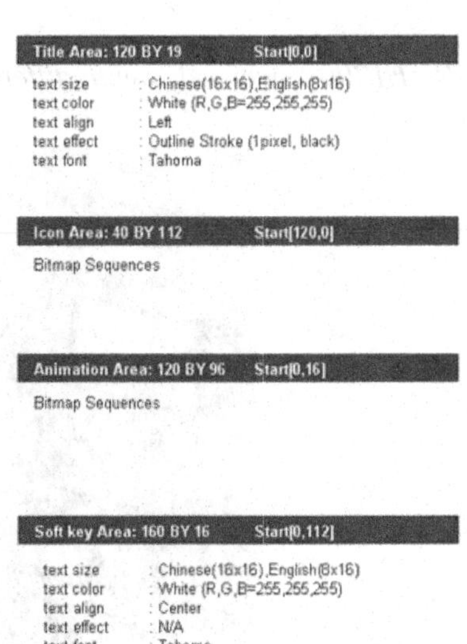

GUI Specification

The dimension and position of the component layout is stated in the specification. This GUI specification guide is a reference to our team (see Figure 9) during the implementation. The guide also defines the icon area, animation area, title area, soft key area, text size, and so forth, which will be consistently used across the menu.

USABILITY EVALUATION

Method

In an effort to investigate the usability between the three menu concepts, we conducted a heuristic evaluation (Nielsen, 1993) to gather information in which requirements were redefined to improve the acceptability of the menu. Users were each given three phones of the same model. A different style of menu was downloaded on each phone, namely Icon based menu, Scenario based animated menu, and Icon-Scenario based animated menu (see Figure 10).

Participants

Participants for the study were working class females aged between 21 to 25 years old. Participants for the study were randomly selected from the streets. They were 10 in number. The participants were office bound working class executives. The participants were experienced mobile phone users.

Procedure

The test was conducted outdoor while we met participants. We sought permission from participants before conducting the test. The participants were briefed on the expectation. During the test, each participant was required to navigate from the menu stage. They were then required to make a comparison between the three types of menu style. Users were also asked to select their preference type of menu in each criterion and state the reason why they prefer each. Their overall preferences were logged down for reference (see Figure 11). We also gathered their feedbacks for analysis (Nielsen, 1993) which is discussed later.

Figure 10. E1200 downloaded with different styles of menus

Figure 11. Result of user preference over the different types of menus

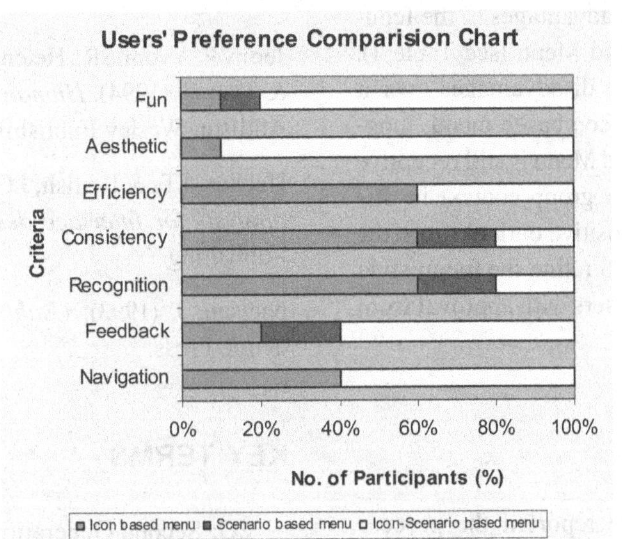

Table 1. Advantages and disadvantages of icon-scenario based animated menu

Advantages	Disadvantages
1. Able to scroll through menu to view animated scenarios	1. No overview of menu icons
2. Navigating in menu was made refreshing and more fun	2. Orientation in navigation
3. Icons displayed allow preview	3. Icons displayed insufficient due to space constraint
4. Captivating graphics are customizable	4. Less effective in navigating task

Results and Discussion

In this test, we found out that most users prefer to navigate the Icon based menu. They were able to get an overview of the features available in the phone. Nonetheless, the Icon-Scenario Based Animated Menu was selected as well due to some preview of icons. Users also provided feedback regarding difficulties in recognizing the feature represented by the scenario, but with the help of the text display, this gap was bridged. In the event of navigation, users commented that the efficiency level of the Scenario Based Animated Menu was the lowest due to the lack of preview of the feature coming next. With regards fun and aesthetic, most users preferred the refreshing style of Icon-Scenario Based Animated Menu. Some users commented that the animated scenario in Icon-Scenario Based Animated Menu with the graphic of the lady avatar makes the phone lady like.

Different colored scenarios in Icon-Scenario Based Animated Menu could actually bring in the element of refreshment and delight when navigating. Users felt that the phone was customized for them. Some users found difficulty in interpreting the 3D scenarios in Scenario Based Animated Menu and hence Icon-Scenario Based Animated Menu was preferred.

From the user study, we were able to deduce some advantages and disadvantages of the Icon-Scenario Based Animated Menu (see Table 1). Although there are some disadvantages over it in comparison with the icon based menu, Icon-Scenario Based Animated Menu is still receptive with its style in this user group context in this case study. With some positive outlook from the analysis, we proceeded to refine the menu style with feedback from the users with approval from our client.

CONCLUSION

In this chapter we have reported the process of design development of the scenario based animated GUI menu of E1200. By conducting a heuristic evaluation on the different types of menu set on the same type of phone, we were able to experience and compare the effect of these different types of menu. The criteria set are particularly useful for evaluating the menu type. The feedback gathered also assists in the refinement of the graphics before implementation. We also learned the importance of customizing a theme in this kind of menu; it helps to create a sense of identification with the users.

Iteration (Hackos & Redish, 1998) three of the process can take place if there is luxury of time in the running the project to further improve interface. Nonetheless, we are still testing out on other styles of graphics that can be appealing to other user group. Our future plan is to develop an animated scenario based menu that can be customized to bring more delight to the users.

ACKNOWLEDGMENT

We would like to thank Howard Chun, Design Director of Newgen Telecom in Korea, and his team members for their contribution to this chapter.

REFERENCES

Jenny P., Yvonne R., Helen S., David B., Simon H., & Tom C. (1994). *Human computer interaction.* Addison-Wesley Publishing Company.

Hackos, J.T., & Redish, J.C. (1998). *User and task analysis for interface design.* Wiley Computer Publishing.

Nielsen, J. (1993). *Usability engineering,* Academic Press.

KEY TERMS

2G: Second Generation.

American Standard Code for Information Interchange (ASCII): A code for representing English characters as numbers.

ARM Compiler: Tool used by software engineers to script code.

BMP: An image file format used to store bitmap digital images.

GUI: Graphic User Interface.

Icon Based Menu: Menu with represented icon for each feature.

Icon-Scenario Based Animated Menu: Menu with represents animated sequence and Icon for each feature.

PDA: Personal Digital Assistance

Scenario Based Animated Menu: Menu with represented animated sequence for each feature.

SWF: Vector graphics file format produced by the Adobe Flash software.

Chapter XIX
Formalizing Patterns with the User Requirements Notation

Gunter Mussbacher
University of Ottowa, Canada

Daniel Amyot
University of Ottowa, Canada

Michael Weiss
Carleton University, Canada

ABSTRACT

Patterns need to be described and formalized in ways that enable the reader to determine whether the particular solution presented is useful and applicable to his or her problem in a given context. However, many pattern descriptions tend to focus on the solution to a problem, and not so much on how the various (and often conflicting) forces involved are balanced. This chapter describes the user requirements notation (URN), and demonstrates how it can be used to formalize patterns in a way that enables rigorous trade-off analysis while maintaining the genericity of the solution description. URN combines a graphical goal language, which can be used to capture forces and reason about trade-offs, and a graphical scenario language, which can be used to describe behavioral solutions in an abstract manner. Although each language can be used in isolation in pattern descriptions (and have been in the literature), the focus of this chapter is on their combined use. It includes examples of formalizing Design patterns with URN together with a process for trade-off analysis.

INTRODUCTION

Patterns document common solutions to recurring problems in a specific context. They enable an efficient transfer of experience and skills. However, many pattern descriptions tend to focus on the solution to a problem, and not so much on how the various (and often conflicting) forces involved are balanced. Therefore, patterns need to be described and formalized in ways that enable the reader to determine whether the particular solution presented is useful and applicable to his or her problem in a given context.

A large body of patterns has been documented to date, and the different efforts are not well-connected. The Pattern Almanac (Rising, 2000) alone, a major effort summarizing and linking the patterns published at patterns conferences and in books prior to the year 2000, lists over 1,200 patterns contained in over 800 different publications. Most of those are publications with a single pattern. The number of patterns has only increased since, but estimates are harder to obtain lacking a similar effort to the Pattern Almanac.

Much work on pattern formalization focuses on the solution domain. For instance, Taibi and Ngo (2001) describe why patterns should be formalized and suggest combining formal specifications of structural and behavioral aspects of Design patterns in one specification. However, the problem domain and relevant trade-offs are seldom handled formally.

In this chapter, we propose a formalization of patterns using the user requirements notation (URN) in a way that supports a rigorous trade-off analysis. In the following sections we first present the background for patterns and the formalization of patterns. Then, we review related work on reasoning about the trade-offs between patterns. We then introduce the user requirements notation, and our explicit model of the forces addressed by a pattern, which provides the basis for the trade-off analysis. The description of the approach is followed by a case study from the literature to which we have applied our approach. Finally, we present future trends and present our concluding remarks.

FORMALIZING PATTERNS

Patterns are three-part rules that describe a recurring problem that occurs in a specific context and its solution (Alexander, 1979). They capture important practices and existing methods uncodified by conventional forms of communicating design experience. The structure they capture is usually not immediately apparent. Perhaps the most significant contribution of patterns is that they make the trade-offs between forces explicit.

Each pattern describes the situation when the pattern can be applied in its context. The context can be thought of as a precondition for the pattern. This precondition is further refined in the problem description with its elaboration of the forces that push and pull the system to which the pattern is applied in different directions. Here, the problem is a precise statement of the design issue to be solved. Forces are design trade-offs affected by the pattern. They can be documented in various forms. One popular approach is to document the trade-offs as sentences like "on one hand …, but on the other hand …".

The solution describes a way of resolving the forces. Some forces may not be resolved by a single pattern. In this case, a pattern includes references to other patterns, which help resolve forces that were unresolved by the current pattern. Together, patterns connected in this way are often referred to as a pattern language. Links between patterns can be of different types, including uses, refines, and conflicts. Patterns that need another pattern link to that pattern with *uses*. Patterns specializing the context or problem of another pattern *refine* that pattern. Patterns that offer alternative solutions *conflict*.

Current pattern representations are textual. They include the gang-of-four (GoF) form, the Coplien form, and the Alexandrian form. The GoF form (Gamma, Helm, Johnson, & Vlissides, 1994) includes sections for intent, motivation, structure, participants, and collaborations. The emphasis of this format is on the structure of the solution. However, the discussion of the forces is spread out over multiple sections, which makes it challenging for a developer to get an overview of when to apply a particular pattern and the consequences of using it.

Motivated by this drawback of the GoF form, the Coplien form (Coplien, 1996) defines a more rigid pattern structure. It includes explicit sections for forces and consequences, in which the forces and the implications of using the patterns are presented in bullet form. This provides quick access to the reasons for applying a pattern. Variations of this format have been proposed that present the forces and consequences as tables.

Recently, many pattern authors have returned to the Alexandrian pattern form (Alexander, 1979). It resolves the trade-off between the needs to have structure on the one hand, and the desire to create more easily readable pieces of literature, on the other. In practical use for documenting software designs, the Alexandrian form has been adapted to include the concept of explicit lists of forces and consequences from the Coplien form.

Nonetheless, with these formats there are still open issues, such as how to recognize under what conditions a given pattern should be selected, how to compare between different patterns that address the same problem, and how to integrate the consequences of applying a pattern or a combination of patterns into a model of the resulting system. It is with these issues in mind that we propose a formalization of patterns using the user requirements notation (URN) in a way that supports a rigorous trade-off analysis during the application of Design patterns while maintaining the generality of the solution description.

RELATED WORK

Previously, Araujo and Weiss (2002) have proposed an explicit representation of the forces involved in a pattern and their interrelationships. This representation suggests interpreting forces as functional and, mainly, as non-functional requirements, and uses the non-functional requirements (NFR) framework (Chung, Nixon, Yu, & Mylopoulos, 2000) to analyze forces and the trade-offs made by a pattern.

In related earlier work, Ong, Weiss, and Araujo (2003) derived the forces affected by a pattern through a close reading of the textual pattern description. The extended pattern representation enabled them to discover contributions made by the patterns to overall system concerns that were only implicit in their textual descriptions. Their main finding was that the contributions of each pattern to overall system concerns became much more apparent when compared to reading the pattern descriptions alone.

Our approach is similar, at the level of individual patterns, to the work by Gross and Yu (2001), as well as Chung, Supakkul, and Yu (2002). Both present ways of reasoning about patterns using NFRs. However, there are important differences. We are also concerned with the connections between patterns at the pattern language level, as well as with establishing models of the forces and their trade-offs that exist in a particular domain. As a result, we feel that our results are farther-reaching, and will lead to a more objective approach.

Also in related work, use case map scenarios have been used by Andrade and Logrippo (2000) to describe patterns of behavior in wireless systems and by Billard (2004) to capture agent interaction patterns. In addition, such scenarios have been the object of patterns themselves. For instance, Mussbacher and Amyot (2001) proposed use case map modeling patterns for describing and composing features. Our approach also captures pattern solutions with abstract scenarios, but we do so in a context where scenarios are explicitly linked to forces.

USER REQUIREMENTS NOTATION

Several years ago, the standardization sector of the International Telecommunications Union initiated work toward the creation of a *user requirements notation* (URN) in the Z.150 series of Recommendations (ITU-T, 2003). The purpose of URN is to support, prior to detailed design, the modeling and analysis of user requirements in the form of goals and scenarios, in a formal way. URN is generally suitable for describing most types of reactive and distributed systems and services. It is also a convenient notation for business process modeling and evolution (Weiss & Amyot, 2005). An overview of URN with a tutorial example from the wireless communication domain is presented in Amyot (2003). The appendix at the end of this chapter also includes a summary of the main notation elements.

URN has concepts for the specification of behavior, structure, and goals, which are all relevant for the formalization of pattern forces and solutions, and for trade-off analysis. URN is, in fact, composed of two complementary notations, which build on previous work. The first is GRL, the *goal-oriented requirement language* (URN Focus Group, 2003a). GRL borrows its main concepts from the NFR (Non-functional requirements) framework published in Chung et al. (2000), and complements them with agent modeling concepts from the *i** framework (Yu, 1997). GRL captures business or system goals, alternative means of achieving goals, and the rationale for goals and alternatives. The notation is applicable to functional requirements, but it is especially good for capturing and reasoning about the interaction of non-functional requirements.

The second part of URN is the *use case map* (UCM) notation, described in URN Focus Group (2003b). The UCM notation was developed by Buhr and Casselman (1995) to depict emerging behavioral scenarios during the high-level design of distributed object-oriented reactive systems. It was later considered appropriate as a notation for describing operational requirements and services, at a higher level of abstraction. A UCM model depicts scenarios as causal flows of responsibilities that can be superimposed on underlying structures of components. UCM responsibilities are scenario activities representing something to be performed (operation, action, task, function, etc.). Responsibilities can potentially be allocated to components, which are generic enough to represent software entities (e.g., objects, processes, databases, or servers) as well as nonsoftware entities (e.g., actors or hardware resources). With UCMs, different structures suggested by architectural alternatives that were identified in a GRL model can be expressed and evaluated by moving responsibilities from one component (the UCM equivalent of a GRL actor) to another, or by restructuring (for example, decomposing) components.

FORMALIZING FORCES FOR TRADE-OFF ANALYSIS

Our pattern representation uses GRL to add an explicit model of the forces addressed by a pattern, and the rationale behind them. It also allows us to model relationships between patterns. Figure 1 shows the elements of the notation, and their interpretation in the context of representing patterns. The diagram on the left shows how an individual pattern, its contributions to forces, and the desired functionality of the system can be modeled as a goal hierarchy.

Non-functional requirements are represented as softgoals (clouds). The notation suggests that these cannot be achieved in an absolute manner. We use them to represent forces. Functional requirements are represented as (hard) goals (rounded rectangles). They allow us to reason about the functional requirements to which a pattern contributes.

Patterns are modeled as tasks (hexagons), which are ways of achieving a goal or softgoal. The nodes of this goal graph can be connected by different types of links. Direct contributions of a pattern on goals are shown as straight lines. Side effects (indirect contributions called correlations) are shown as dotted lines. Contributions can be labeled with a + (the default value if none is present) or - to indicate that they are positive

Figure 1. Elements of the notation used to model forces and their resolution

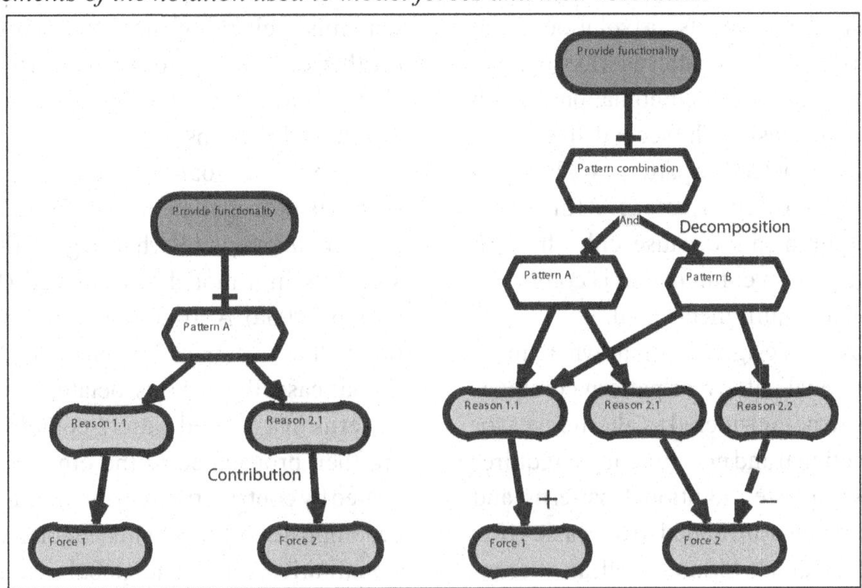

Figure 2. Considering alternative pattern combinations

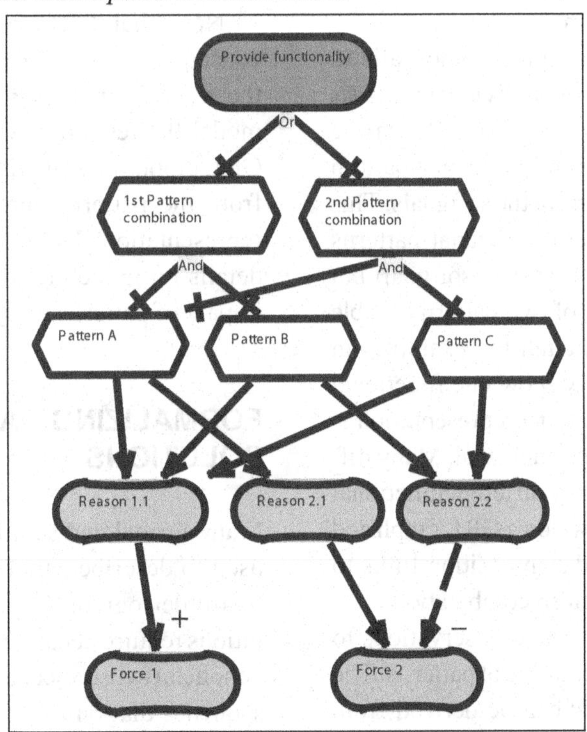

or negative. Note that GRL also offers a richer set of labels, which allows us to represent different levels of strength of a contribution or correlation (see Figure 12e). Uses, refines, and conflict relationships between patterns are modeled as AND or OR decomposition links between tasks (barred lines).

In order to achieve the desired functional and non-functional requirements, a solution often requires the use of several patterns. Hence, there is a need to model pattern combinations which are also depicted as tasks. The second diagram in Figure 1 indicates that only a pattern combination (which involves the original pattern A) fulfills the functional requirements because only the task describing the pattern combination is connected to the functional requirements goal.

There also exist design situations where more than one individual pattern or pattern combination may have to be considered as alternatives for achieving functional and non-functional requirements. In such a case, additional patterns and pattern combinations are added to the basic GRL graph. Figure 2 extends Figure 1 with an alternative pattern combination. The functional goal is now connected to the two pattern combinations with an OR decomposition.

Note that our pattern representation allows contributions to be made by individual patterns as well as pattern combinations. The latter can be modeled with a contribution link from a pattern combination task to any one of the softgoals. This is useful in the case where individual patterns alone cannot balance a force (i.e., softgoal) but only the combined usage of two patterns is able to do so. Finally, even though the examples in Figure 1 and Figure 2 only show one functional requirements goal, our pattern representation is not at all limited to just one such goal. Many different goals describing many different functional requirements may be shown on a GRL graph and may be connected with decomposition links to individual patterns or pattern combinations.

There are several important observations to be made about our representation of patterns. The bottom half of the figures can be derived from other GRL graphs that focus on one individual pattern at a time and show the pattern's contribution to forces. GRL graphs for an individual pattern only need to be created once and establish reusable models of forces applicable to many domains. Several of these focused GRL graphs are then combined into our pattern representation shown above in order to highlight the differences of selected patterns.

Like most goal-oriented languages, GRL supports propagation algorithms to evaluate, for a given *strategy*, to what degree the goals and softgoals in a model are satisfied (URN Focus Group, 2003a). A strategy assigns initial satisfaction values to some of the elements in the model (in our case, the tasks associated with individual patterns in a desired pattern combination) which are then propagated to the other elements connected by contribution, correlation, and AND/OR decomposition links. This enables one to make a qualitative, rapid, and global assessment of the impact of a particular choice and hence to find the most appropriate trade-off in a given context.

Note that GRL graphs do not model the consequences of applying patterns in terms of the architectural design of a system. UCMs will model the resulting system, and links between GRL graphs and UCMs will provide traceability from the pattern representation to the system representation. The next section provides more details on modeling the solution space and the impact of patterns on system design.

FORMALIZING PATTERN SOLUTIONS

Many formal and semiformal languages can be used to describe pattern solutions, for instance, first-order logic or UML class diagrams. When solutions require behavioral descriptions, it is often beneficial to use a scenario notation such as UML sequence diagrams or message sequence charts. However, when the solution does not require the definition of message exchanges between components, then the use case map scenario notation becomes an interesting option. UCM models can

Figure 3. Use case map for the Observer pattern

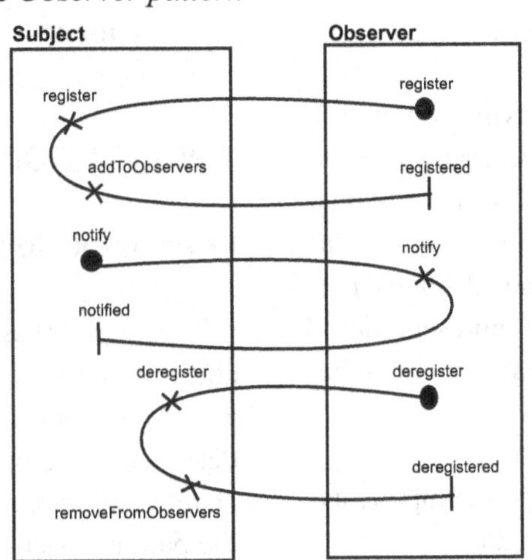

show both structure and behavior of a solution at an abstract level (e.g., see Figure 3 for a UCM of the observer pattern).

In the UCM notation (summarized in Figure 13), scenarios are initiated at start points, represented as filled circles, which correspond to preconditions or triggering events. Scenarios terminate at end points, shown as bars, which correspond to postconditions or resulting events. Paths show the causal relationships between start and end points, and (guarded) alternative and concurrent paths can be expressed. Generic components are shown as rectangles, and they are responsible for the various activities (called responsibilities and indicated by X's on a path) allocated to them. Diamonds are used to represent stubs, which are containers for submaps called plug-ins. Components can also be assigned roles, which further contributes to the reusability and adaptability of the solution in similar contexts. For instance, the two component roles in Figure 3 can be assumed by concrete components when the map is used in a stub.

Similar to GRL graphs for individual patterns, UCMs for individual patterns have to be created only once and can be plugged into any system description with the help of stubs. UCMs for individual patterns can also package different scenario fragments meant to be used by different stubs. For example, in a stub handling the registration phase of the Observer pattern, the "register" start point of the top scenario fragment in Figure 3 is bound to the input segment of a stub and the "registered" end point to the output segment of that stub.

The paths and their elements can easily be allocated to different underlying structures of components, which could represent different architectural alternatives. Different path structures could also share similar component structures. A GRL model could provide the details of the trade-offs involved in choosing one solution over another, in context.

OVERVIEW OF PROPOSED PROCESS

The pattern forces and solutions formalized as suggested in the previous sections can be integrated with regular pattern descriptions, independently of the template used. Although such patterns can be useful on their own, this section introduces a process that will take full advantage of the new formalized aspects of these patterns. Essentially, some aspects of the system to be designed should also be described with GRL and UCM, hence enabling global impact and trade-off analysis in context.

A precondition to our process is that individual patterns should include forces formalized with GRL (see first diagram in Figure 1) and solutions formalized with UCM (as in Figure 3). Note that the presence of GRL/UCM models does not preclude the existence of other representations and formalizations. The process can then be summarized as follows:

1. Extract a preliminary list of components from the system requirements.
2. Construct a GRL actor diagram for the system:
   a. Identify actors together with their interdependencies and the objects of these dependencies (e.g., goals, softgoals, and resources). Include the system itself as a GRL actor. Refer to Figure 12 for corresponding notation elements.
   b. Expand the system's internal goal model, determine its main functional subgoals, and connect the relevant elements to the actor's external dependencies.
3. For each subgoal, select candidate patterns. Most of the time, a number of patterns can be selected from experience. Additionally, candidate patterns may be found by matching the goals and softgoals identified in the GRL graphs of the candidate patterns to the goals and softgoals found in step 2.b.
4. For each subgoal, connect alternative candidate patterns or combinations of patterns in an AND/OR graph, as illustrated in Figure 2.
5. Determine the most suitable pattern or combination of patterns by using trade-off analysis based on GRL strategies.
6. Assess architectural ramifications based on a UCM model of the system that contains stubs where the selected pattern plug-ins are used.

APPLICATION TO A CASE STUDY

Feedback Control Framework

Our example is based on a case study from Yacoub and Ammar (2004). In this case study, a reusable framework for feedback control systems is designed by composing Design patterns. In this chapter, we focus on the pattern selection stage of the pattern-oriented design approach advocated by Yacoub and Ammar (2004). We illustrate how URN can be used to support the matching of requirements to patterns.

A schematic representation of a feedback control system is provided in Figure 4. It consists of a feedforward controller, the controlled system or plant, and a feedback controller. The user applies a desired output value (configuration data) to the control system, which is then compared to the actual output observed in the system. The difference between the desired output and the actual output (error) is applied as input to the feedforward controller. In simple systems, an identity function is often used as the feedback controller.

A cruise-control system is a typical example of a feedback control system. It is used to maintain the velocity of a vehicle at a constant speed. Deviations from the desired speed are fed back to the controller as an error, and a corrective action (slowing down, speeding up) is applied to align the actual speed with the desired speed once again. Our goal is to design a generic framework for the development of such feedback control systems.

In Yacoub and Ammar (2004), five high-level components are already identified:

- A feedforward component that applies a control algorithm to the plant;

Figure 4. Schematic representation of a feedback control system

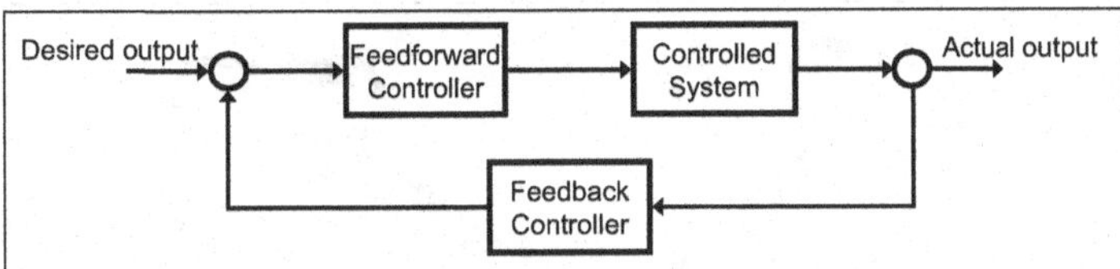

Figure 5. Feedback control system dependencies

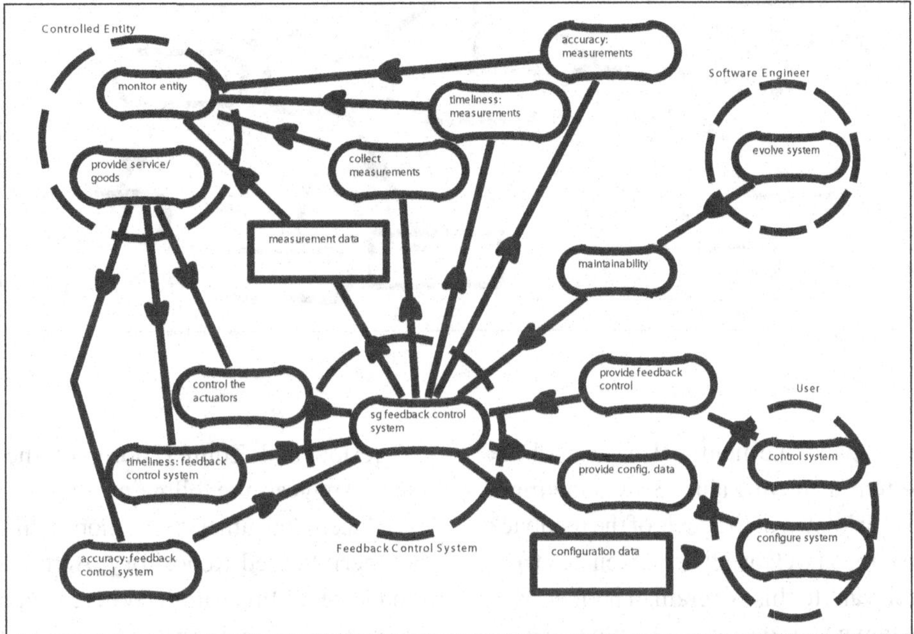

- A measurement component that collects measurements coming from the plant;
- A feedback component that observes measurements and aggregates them into feedback data representing the actual output measured at the plant;
- An error calculation component that compares the desired output and feedback data and computes the error provided as input to the feedforward component; and
- A plant or the external component controlled by the feedback control system.

The second step of our approach is to map the requirements into an actor diagram that shows the system to be designed as an actor, the external actors using or affected by the system, and the dependencies between the external actors and the system. In the case study, we identify three external actors: the user who applies the desired output to the plant, the plant (controlled entity), as well as the software engineer who develops and maintains the system. Figure 5 shows the resulting actor diagram for the feedback control system. For example, the user depends on the feedback control system to provide feedback control (shown as a goal dependency), and, in turn, the feedback control system depends on the user to provide configuration data (a goal and a resource dependency).

Figure 6. Internal goal breakdown of the feedback control system

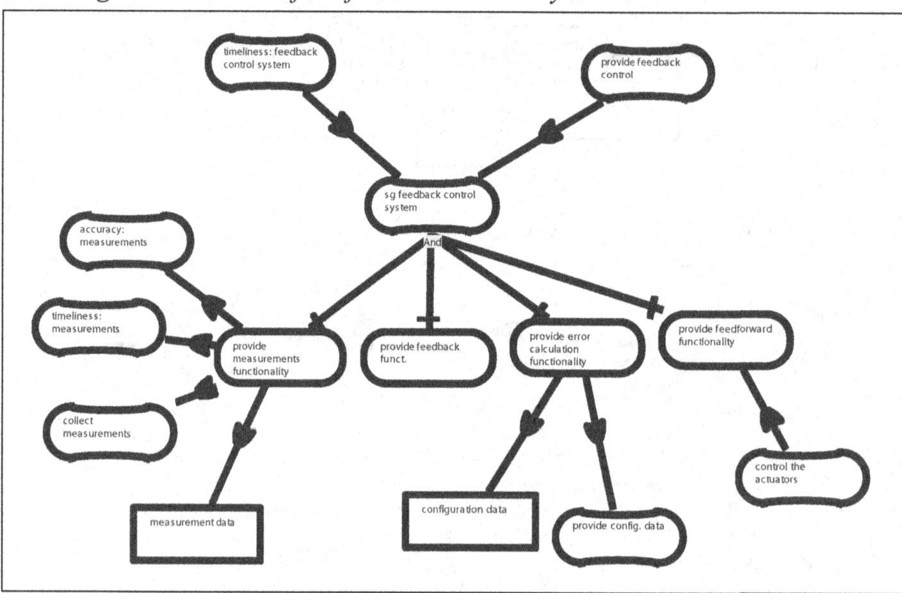

Figure 6 expands the main goal of the feedback control system actor in Figure 5 by showing a high-level breakdown of the goals of the feedback control system, as well as all dependencies from Figure 5 relevant to this diagram. The feedback control system goal is decomposed into subgoals which can be derived from four of the five high-level components identified earlier.

The next step introduces several pattern combinations as design alternatives for each of the four subgoals. It makes use of the pattern representation discussed earlier.

Candidate Patterns for the Case Study

The authors of the original case study (Yacoub & Ammar, 2004) identify three patterns that should be considered during the design of the feedback control framework: Strategy (Gamma et al., 1994), Observer (Gamma et al., 1994), and Blackboard (Shaw & Garlan, 1996). Further exploration, under consultation of the pattern catalogs of Buschmann, Meunier, Rohnert, Sommerlad, Stal (1996) and Avgeriou and Zdun (2005), of the candidate space suggests the following additional patterns: Producer-Consumer (a variation of Publisher-Subscriber), Shared Repository, Active Repository, and Explicit Invocation. Whereas in the original case study, all patterns were used in the design, with the revised list of candidate patterns, there are trade-offs to be made between the patterns. Pattern selection will take into account functional and non-functional requirements and their priorities. Figure 7 shows the alternatives considered for the design of the feedback component of the system, as well as all relevant dependencies from Figure 5. Four combinations make use of different subsets of five individual patterns. The observer pattern, for instance, has a positive contribution toward the decoupling of processing stages but, on the other hand, it negatively impacts the reduction of the complexity.

Trade-Off Analysis

Two of the four alternatives depicted in Figure 7 are evaluated. The first alternative involves the

Figure 7. Alternatives for the feedback goal

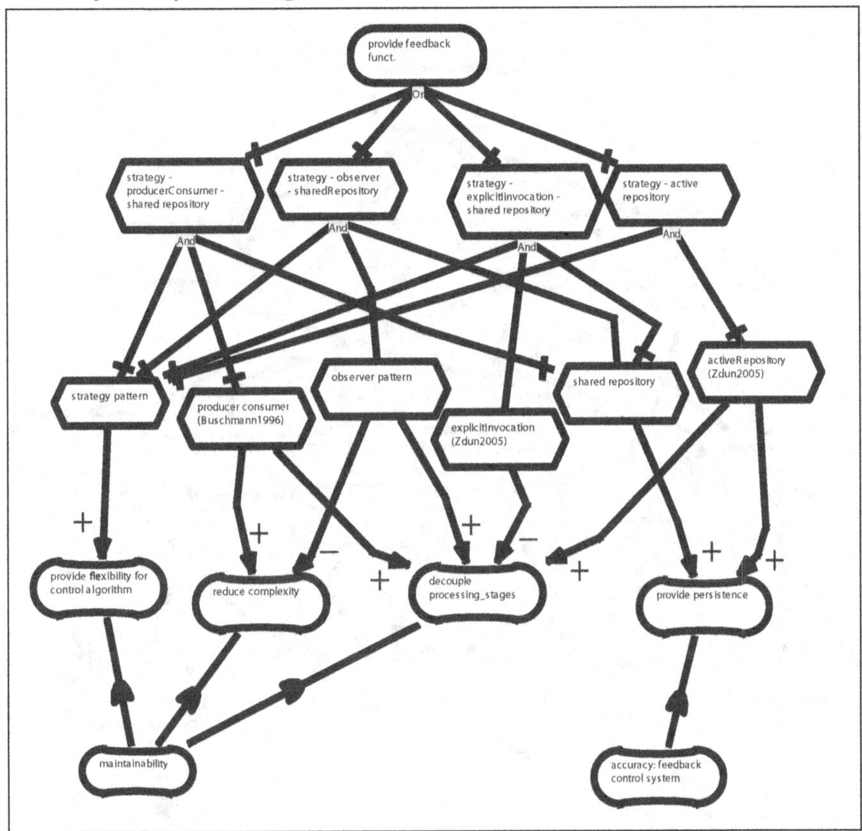

use of the strategy pattern combined with the observer pattern and a shared repository. The trade-off analysis is done for all subgoals in Figure 6, but only the GRL graph for the feedback subgoal is shown here.

The starting points of the evaluation are the candidate patterns (strategy, observer, and shared repository in this case) which have been assigned an initial satisfaction level. To do so, we have used the jUCMNav tool, an Eclipse-based editor for URN models that supports GRL model evaluation based on GRL strategies and propagation algorithms (Roy, Kealey, & Amyot, 2006). jUCMNav is a generic editor for the URN notation, with no specific support for patterns, and all the diagrams in this chapter were produced with this tool.

We assigned an initial satisfaction value of 100 to the three patterns (Figure 8). The star (*) next to the task symbol indicates that this value was entered by the user. A collection of such initial assignments represents in fact a GRL strategy definition, and these assignments are usually done to a subset of the leaves in the GRL graph (the bottom contributors, that contribute to or refine higher-level goals). In jUCMNav, a positive number between 1 and 100 next to a node indicates the degree of satisfaction achieved for the node. A negative number between -1 and -100 next to a node indicates the degree of dissatisfaction suffered for the node. Zero indicates that there is no evaluation available for the node (the node is undecided). Corresponding GRL satisfaction level

Figure 8. Evaluating one alternative for the feedback goal

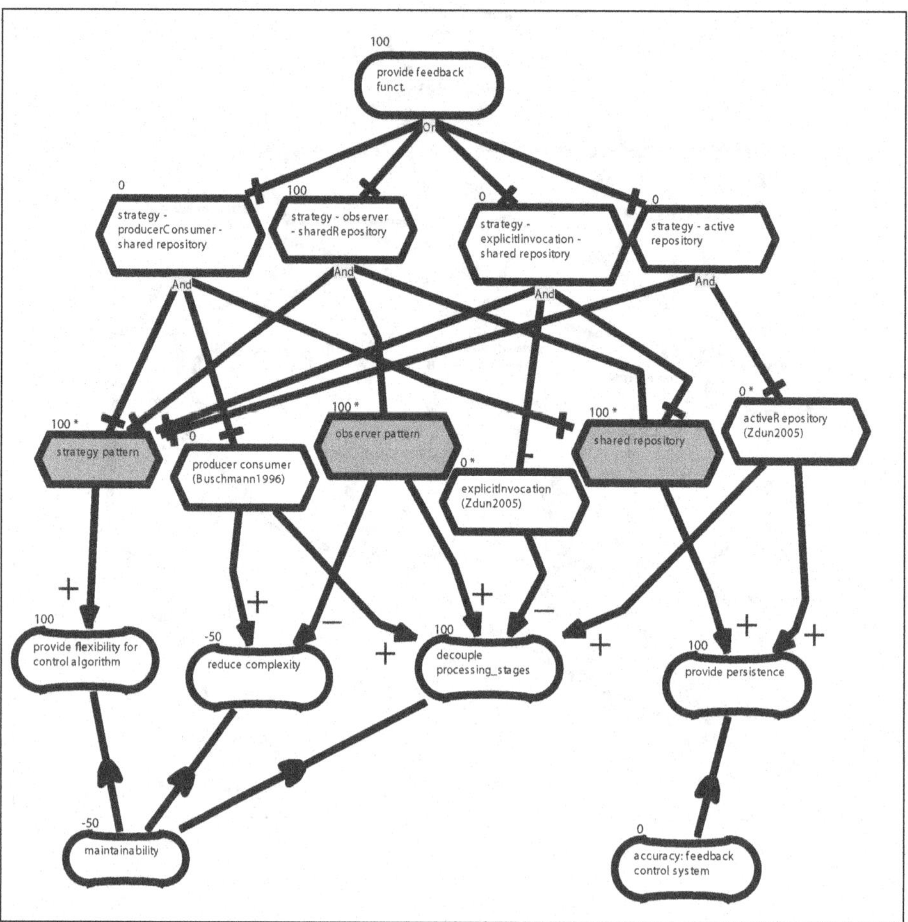

icons (Figure 12b) and colors are also used in the diagrams for improved visual feedback.

Based on the decomposition, contribution, and dependency links, the initial evaluation is now propagated to other nodes in the GRL graph. In a nutshell, the propagation procedure from Roy et al. (2006) first considers the decomposition links, as a standard AND/OR graph. For an AND decomposition, the result corresponds to the minimal evaluation of the source nodes, and for an OR decomposition, the result corresponds to the maximal evaluation of the source nodes. The propagation algorithm then evaluates the contribution links. Each contribution type is given a numerical value between -1 (for break) and 1 (for make). The satisfaction level of the source element is normalized to a value between 0 (denied) and 100 (satisfied) which is multiplied by the contribution level. The results of each of the contributions are summed up and normalized to provide the total contribution as a value between -100 and 100. Finally, the dependency links are evaluated. The minimal value among the dependees is compared with the current evaluation of the source node. The resulting evaluation corresponds to the minimum value of those two evaluations, the rationale being that an intentional element cannot have a higher value than those it depends

Figure 9. Use case map for first alternative

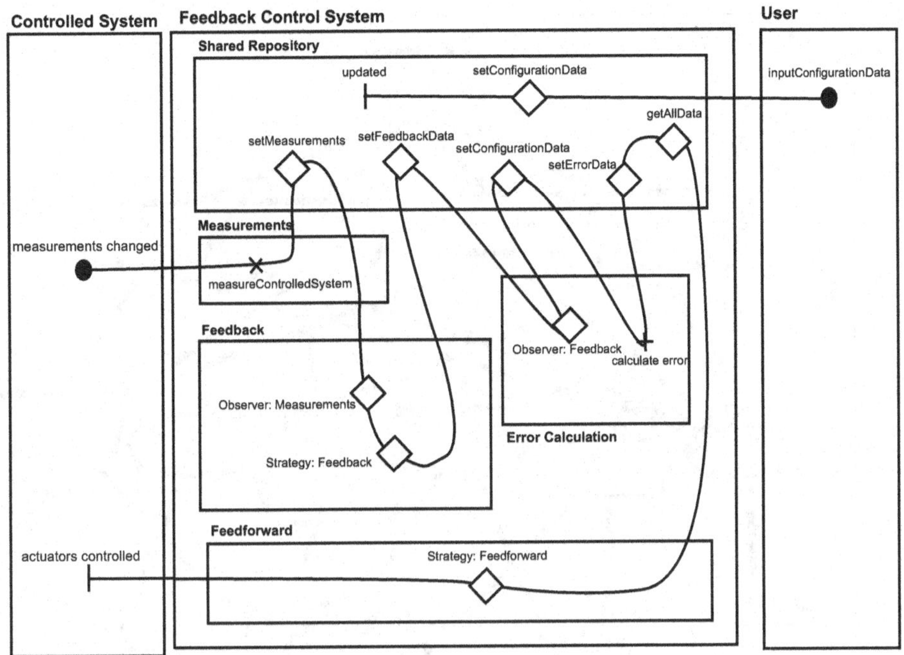

on. This is the default propagation algorithm supported in jUCMNav, but the tool is flexible enough to support other approaches.

Using this algorithm, the particular alternative evaluated in Figure 8 satisfies the feedback goal and most softgoals except complexity reduction, upon which maintainability depends.

In addition to the GRL graph explaining the impact of the proposed alternative on the forces, a corresponding UCM describes the architectural ramifications. The UCM model in Figure 9 shows the complete system summarizing all design decisions from all four subgoals. It also contains the five components previously discovered for this case study, as well as the actors involved in the use of the feedback control system (namely, the user and the controlled system itself). Links between the GRL graphs and the UCM model ensure traceability. For instance, the strategy pattern task is mapped onto the stub "Strategy: Feedback," the observer pattern task is mapped onto the stub "Observer: Measurements" and "Observer: Feedback," and the shared repository pattern task is mapped to the stub "setFeedbackData" (and many others). The stubs on the UCM can be expanded into submaps which give further details on the application of the pattern in this context. For instance, the middle scenario fragment in Figure 3 is connected to "Observer: Feedback" and the "Error Calculation" component assumes the role of "Observer" while the "Feedback" component assumes the role of "Subject."

The second alternative still uses the strategy pattern but replaces the observer and shared repository with an active repository (Figure 10). Again, the GRL graph is linked to the UCM (Figure 11). The strategy pattern task is mapped onto the stub "Strategy: Feedback" and the active repository pattern maps to the four "setNotify" stubs. In this alternative, the trade-off is different; there is no impact on complexity and maintainability, at the cost of a lower satisfaction level of the decoupling of processing stages. From a maintainability and accuracy point of view, this

Figure 10. Evaluating a second alternative for the feedback goal

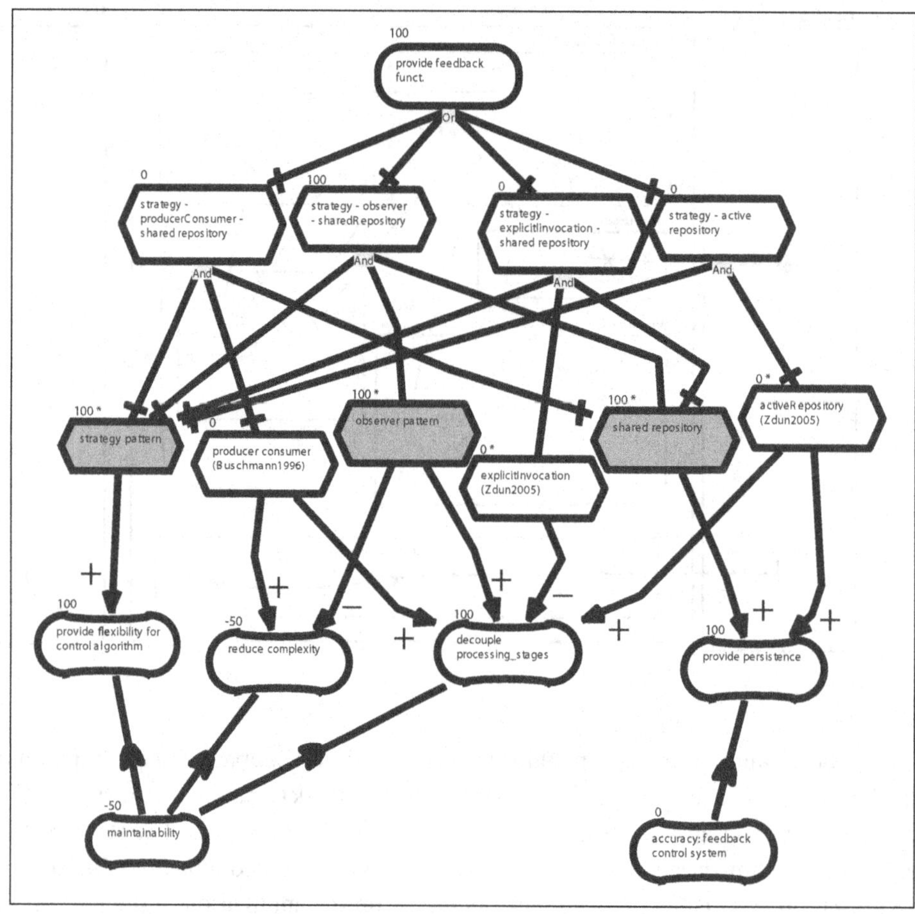

solution is better than the first one, although there is still room for improvement.

DISCUSSION AND FUTURE TRENDS

This example demonstrates how GRL graphs capture pattern forces and can be used to assess the qualitative impact of various solutions to a functional goal, in context. The benefits of the proposed process become even more interesting as the system gets more complex and trade-offs are more difficult to assess due to numerous inter-related contributions and side-effects.

The proposed process for URN-based trade-off analysis is not limited to individual subgoals. It can easily be extended to pattern combinations addressing all subgoals at once, hence providing for global impact analysis and guidance, at the system level. This may go beyond the needs of designers and system architects who may only be interested in solving a focused design problem, but this level of evaluation is nevertheless possible.

The UCM models resulting from a particular selection of patterns can be used for guiding developers into making low-level decisions, and can be used as a basis for the generation of test goals (Amyot, Weiss, & Logrippo, 2005). They can also help in quantifying some of the performance

Figure 11. Use case map for second alternative

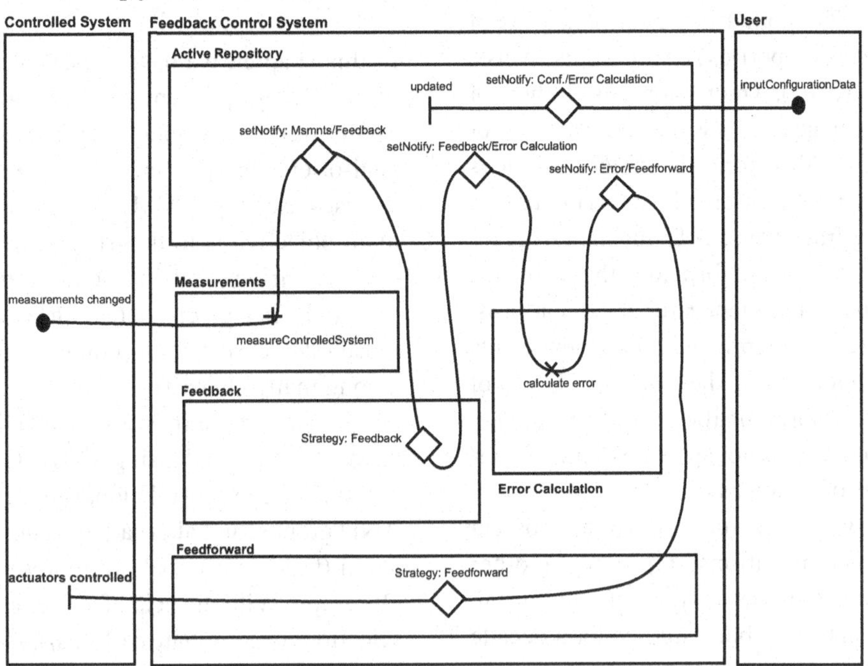

aspects by providing means to specify more precisely the contribution levels in GRL models and the satisfaction levels in strategy initializations. For instance, Petriu and Woodside (2002) propose a tool-supported transformation from annotated UCM models to performance models that can be formally analyzed and simulated. Analysis results could be fed back to the system-level GRL model to fine-tune some of the weights and reach better conclusions.

Although many graphical approaches often tend not to scale very well for the description and analysis of large systems, this issue is handled to some extent by the high level of abstraction at which URN is used and by several mechanisms such as decomposition (stubs/plug-ins in UCMs, decomposition links in GRL). In addition, URN and jUCMNav distinguish diagrams from models, that is, an element defined in a model can be reused or referenced in many diagrams, which then act like partial views. Complex systems can hence easily be composed of many such diagrams or views, both in UCM and in GRL.

Obviously, in addition to having patterns formalized with URN, the more advanced benefits require additional investments that not all modelers may be willing to make: a system-level GRL model for assessing the global impact of selected patterns, a system-level UCM model (where the pattern solutions will be plugged-in) to perform UCM-level analysis and test generation, and additional performance-level annotations to the UCM model to perform quantitative performance analysis.

There is also a general trend toward formalizing aspects of patterns, whether they are related to the relationships between patterns, or to properties of individual patterns. Often, these efforts have been confined to certain domains, which are more amenable to formalization, such as the area of security patterns. One example is the formalization of security properties that are satisfied by application of a pattern (Wassermann & Cheng, 2003), another is the formalization of security pattern properties in Mouratidis, Weiss, and Giorgini (2005), which allows the authors of a pattern language to assess the completeness of the language. In this work, the pattern solutions are modeled in agent-oriented models in the Tropos modeling framework. A formal language for Tropos models is used to formalize the problems, solutions, and consequences of these patterns. These properties are expressed in logic statements over the components of the solutions. Some of this logic-based formalization could be added to GRL, although it does not appear essential in our current trade-off analysis context.

Aspects, which are concerns that crosscut dominant decompositions, represent another trend identifiable in the software community in general. Aspects have been studied for a decade and are used to compensate several weaknesses of object-oriented programming languages (e.g., scattering and tangling of functionalities and other concerns). Existing Design patterns have been recast for new aspect-oriented languages, for example, see Hannemann and Kiczales (2002), whereas new patterns specific to such languages have started to appear. More recently, aspect-oriented concepts have been included in modeling languages, closer to design and requirements. For instance, Jacobson and Ng (2004) present an approach where aspects are derived from UML use cases, whereas Yu, Leite, and Mylopoulos (2004) present an approach where aspects are inferred from goal models. The impact of the availability of such enhanced modeling languages requires further exploration. For instance, Mussbacher, Amyot, and Weiss (2006) believe aspect-oriented concepts can easily be added to URN. This could help close the gap between aspect-oriented modeling and programming languages and, at the same time, open the door to new types of patterns that are more abstract or closer to requirements than the current generation of Design patterns.

CONCLUSION

In this chapter, we have presented an approach where Design patterns are formalized with the user requirements notation, which combines the goal-oriented requirements language (GRL) and the use case map (UCM) scenario notation. Our main objective is to describe patterns in a way that the various and conflicting forces involved can guide, in a given context, the selection of the most suitable patterns or combinations of patterns among many alternatives.

Forces and contributions for individual patterns are captured using GRL. Combinations and side effects (correlations) are described with AND graphs, and alternative combinations for a given (functional) goal are represented with an OR graph. With the help of strategies (i.e., initial selections of candidate patterns) and propagation rules, designers can assess the impact of their selection on the forces and find a suitable solution in their context. This context can itself be modeled with GRL, first at the actor/dependency level, and then at the level of intentional elements (goals, softgoals, tasks, etc.) for the system. This enables global and rigorous assessments to be made, even when many functional subgoals are considered.

Pattern solutions are formalized at an abstract level with UCM. Such models package many scenario segments that can be plugged into stubs belonging to a description of the system's main operational scenarios (also a UCM model). The availability of such a scenario model enables further analysis and transformations, including simulation, performance evaluation, and test goal generation.

To take full advantage of URN-based formalization of Design patterns, a process was briefly introduced and illustrated with a case study where many combinations of patterns could be used to achieve the same functionality while leading to different trade-offs involving non-functional aspects, such as maintainability and accuracy.

A prototype tool, which was used to create and evaluate the URN models presented here, already exists to support such process, and is still evolving to support new types of analyses and transformations, including patterns-oriented ones.

We believe this formalization approach will provide means to get rapid and global trade-off analysis results in context and make better use of current and future Design patterns.

REFERENCES

Alexander, C. (1979). *A pattern language*. Oxford University Press.

Amyot, D. (2003). Introduction to the user requirements notation: Learning by example. *Computer Networks, 42*(3), 285-301.

Amyot, D., Weiss, M., & Logrippo, L. (2005). UCM-based generation of test purposes. *Computer Networks, 49*(5), 643-660.

Andrade, R., & Logrippo, L. (2000, July). Reusability at the early development stages of the mobile wireless communication systems. In *Proceedings of the 4th World Multiconference on Systemics, Cybernetics and Informatics (SCI 2000),* Orlando, FL (Vol. VII, Part I, pp. 11-16).

Araujo, I., & Weiss, M. (2002). Linking non-functional requirements and patterns. In *Proceedings of the 9th Conference on Pattern Languages of Programs (PLoP).* Retrieved November, 16, 2006, from http://jerry.cs.uiuc.edu/~plop/plop2002/final/PatNFR.pdf

Avgeriou, P., & Zdun, U. (2005, July). Architectural patterns revisited: A pattern language. In *Proceedings of the 10th European Conference on Pattern Languages of Programs (EuroPlop),* Irsee, Germany.

Billard, E.A. (2004, August). Patterns of agent interaction scenarios as use case maps. *IEEE Transactions on Systems, Man, and Cybernetics. Part B, Cybernetics, 34*(4), 1933-1939.

Buhr, R.J.A., & Casselman, R.S. (1995). *Use case maps for object-oriented systems.* Prentice Hall.

Buschmann, F., Meunier, R., Rohnert, H., Sommerlad, P., Stal, M. (1996). *Pattern-oriented software architecture.* Wiley.

Chung, L., Nixon, B., Yu, E., & Mylopoulos, J. (2000). *Non-functional requirements in software engineering.* Kluwer Academic Publishers.

Chung, L., Supakkul, S., & Yu, A. (2002, July 8-11). Good software architecting: Goals, objects, and patterns. In *Proceedings of the Information, Computing & Communication Technology Symposium (ICCT- 2002), UKC'02,* Seoul, Korea.

Coplien, J. (1996). *Software patterns.* SIGS. Retrieved November 16, 2006, from http://users.rcn.com/jcoplien/Patterns/WhitePaper/SoftwarePatterns.pdf

Gamma, E., Helm, R., Johnson, R., & Vlissides, J. (1994). *Design patterns: Elements of reusable object-oriented software.* Addison-Wesley.

Gross, D., & Yu, E. (2001). From non-functional requirements to design through patterns. *Requirements Engineering, 6*(1), 18-36.

Hannemann, J., & Kiczales, G. (2002, November). *Design pattern implementation in Java and AspectJ. In Proceedings of the 17th OOPSLA* (pp. 161-173).

ITU-T (2003). *Recommendation Z.150 (02/03), user requirements notation (URN) – Language requirements and framework.* Geneva, Switzerland.

Jacobson, I., & Ng, P.-W. (2004). *Aspect-oriented software development with use cases.* Addison-Wesley.

Mouratidis, H., Weiss, M., & Giorgini, P. (2005). Security patterns meet agent oriented software engineering: A complementary solution for developing secure information systems. *Conceptual modeling (ER)* (LNCS 2716, pp. 225-240). Springer-Verlag.

Mussbacher, G., & Amyot, D. (2001, October 3-5). A collection of patterns for use case maps. In *Proceedings of the 1st Latin American Conference on Pattern Languages of Programming (SugarLoafPLoP 2001)*, Rio de Janeiro, Brazil.

Mussbacher, G., Amyot, D., & Weiss, M. (2006, September 11). Visualizing aspect-oriented requirements scenarios with use case maps. In *Proceedings of the International Workshop on Requirements Engineering Visualization (REV 2006)*, Minneapolis/St. Paul, Minnesota.

Ong, H., Weiss, M., & Araujo, I. (2003, March). Rewriting a pattern language to make it more expressive. *Hot topic on the expressiveness of pattern languages, ChiliPLoP*. Carefree, USA.

Petriu, D., & Woodside, M. (2002). Software performance models from system scenarios in use case maps. *Computer performance evaluation / TOOLS 2002* (LNCS 2324, pp. 141-158). Springer-Verlag.

Rising, L. (2000). *Pattern almanac 2000*. Addison-Wesley.

Roy, J.-F., Kealey, J., & Amyot, D. (2006, May). Towards integrated tool support for the user requirements notation. In *Proceedings of the Fifth Workshop on System Analysis and Modelling (SAM'06)*, Kaiserslautern, Germany.

Shaw, M., & Garlan, D. (1996). *Software architecture: Perspectives on an emerging discipline*. Prentice Hall.

Taibi, T., & Ngo, D.C.L. (2001). Why and how should patterns be formalized. *Journal of Object-Oriented Programming (JOOP), 14*(4), 8-9.

URN Focus Group (2003a, September). *Draft Rec. Z.151 – Goal-oriented requirement language (GRL)*. Geneva, Switzerland.

URN Focus Group (2003b, September). *Draft Rec. Z.152 – Use case map notation (UCM)*. Geneva, Switzerland.

Wassermann, R., & Cheng, B. (2003). *Security patterns* (Tech. Rep. No. MSU-CSE-03-23). Michigan State University.

Weiss, M., & Amyot, D. (2005, July-September). Business process modeling with URN. *International Journal of E-Business Research, 1*(3), 63-90.

Yacoub, S., & Ammar, H. (2004). *Pattern-oriented analysis and design: Composing patterns to design software systems*. Addison-Wesley.

Yu, E. (1997, January 6-8). Towards modelling and reasoning support for early-phase requirements engineering. In *Proceedings of the 3rd IEEE International Symposium on Requirements Engineering (RE'97)* (pp. 226-235). Washington, DC.

Yu, Y., Leite, J.C.S.P., & Mylopoulos, J. (2004, September). From goals to aspects: Discovering aspects from requirements goal models. In *Proceedings of the 12th IEEE International. Conference on Requirements Engineering (RE 2004)* (pp. 38-47). Kyoto, Japan.

APPENDIX

Figure 12. Summary of the GRL notation

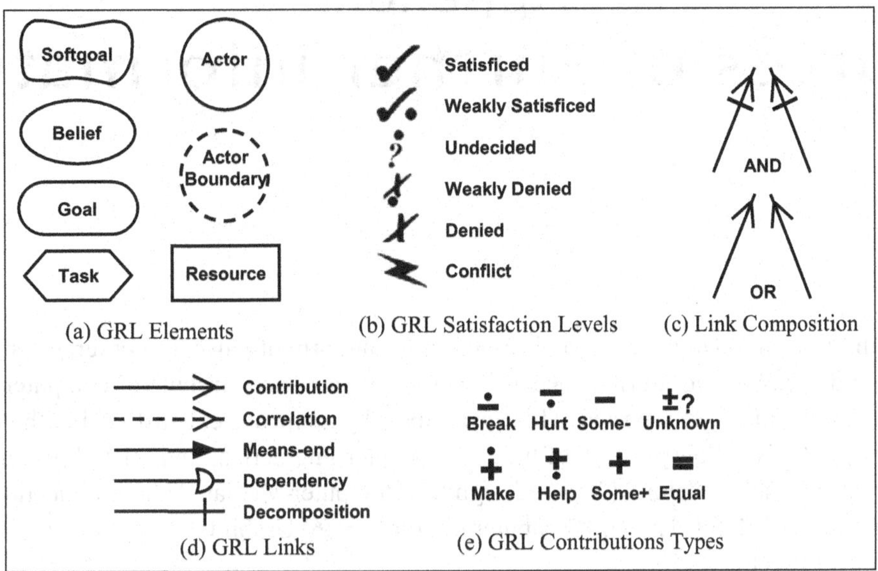

Figure 13. Summary of the UCM notation

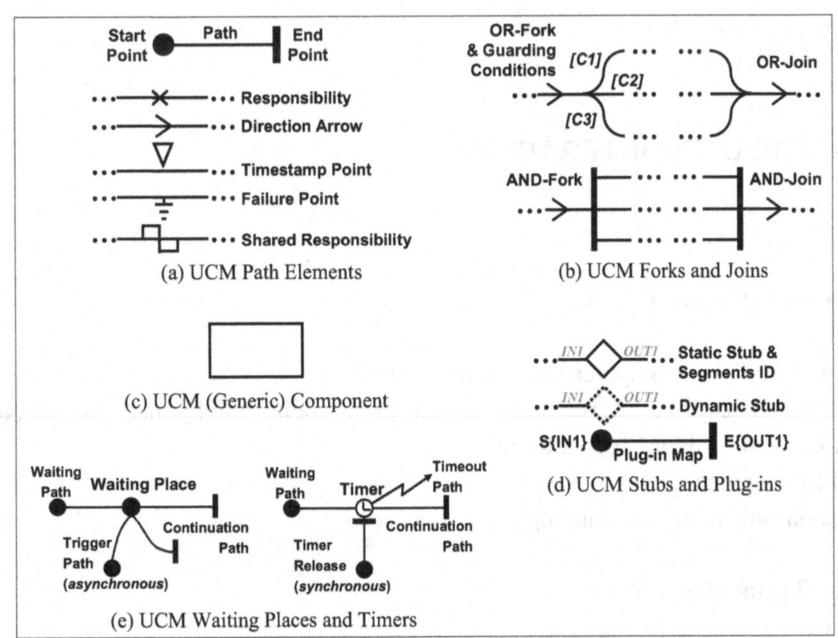

This work was previously published in Design Pattern Formalization Techniques, edited by T. Taibi, pp. 302-323, copyright 2007 by IGI Publishing, formerly known as Idea Group Publishing (an imprint of IGI Global).

Appendix
Sources of Further Information

This Appendix is a compilation of selected resources in the form of journals, conference/proceedings, portals/online databases, and journal special issues where advances in human-computer interaction research and development are reported. This appendix is by no means exhaustive, but the listing aims to surface the multidisciplinary nature of human-computer interaction, and related disciplines in the following areas: (1) user modeling; (2) user design; (3) Computer-Mediated Communication; (4) Ubiquitous Computing; (5) Mobile Human-Computer Interaction; (6) Usability Evaluation; (7) Ergonomics; and (8) Cognitive Psychology.

We hope the appendix will serve as a starting point to locate important sources for the human-computer interaction researcher.

1. HUMAN-COMPUTER INTERACTION

Journals

- ACM Computing Surveys
- ACM Queue
- ACM Transactions on Computer-Human Interaction
- Applied Intelligence: The International Journal of Artificial Intelligence, Neural Networks, and Complex Problem-Solving Technologies
- Artificial Intelligence
- Behavior and Information Technology
- Chaos
- Cognition, Technology & Work
- Computer
- Computer Integrated Manufacturing Systems
- Computer Methods and Programs in Biomedicine
- Computer Speech and Language

- Computer Supported Cooperative Work
- Computers & Graphics
- Computers in Education Journal
- Computers in Human Behavior
- Cybernetics and Systems
- Data Mining and Knowledge Discovery
- Digital Creativity
- Education & Computing
- Expert Systems
- High Technology Letters (English Language Edition)
- Human Factors
- Human-Computer Interaction
- IBM Systems Journal
- IEEE Annals of the History of Computing
- IEEE Transactions on Education
- IEEE Transactions on Neural Networks
- IEEE Transactions on Pattern Analysis and Machine Intelligence
- Information Processing Letters
- Information Technology & People
- Interacting with Computers
- Interactions
- International Journal of Human-Computer Interaction
- International Journal of Human-Computer Studies
- International Journal of Man-Machine Studies
- International Journal of Medical Informatics
- International Journal of Modeling & Simulation
- ISPRS Journal of Photogrammetry and Remote Sensing
- Journal of Aircraft
- Journal of Biomedical Informatics
- Journal of Computer Information Systems
- Journal of Information Science and Engineering
- Journal of Information Technology
- Journal of Management Information Systems
- Journal of Process Control
- Journal of the American Society for Information Science
- Journal of VLSI Signal Processing Systems for Signal, Image, and Video Technology
- Minds and Machines
- Neural Networks
- OCLC Systems & Services
- Speech Communication
- Structural Engineering and Mechanics
- Universal Access in the Information Society
- WSEAS Transactions on Computers

Others

- Encyclopedia of Human-Computer Interaction
- Handbook of Human-Computer Interaction
- SIGCHI Bulletin
- SIGCSE Bulletin

Conferences/Proceedings/Workshops

- ACIS International Conference on Software Engineering Research and Applications
- ACM CHI 2007 Conference on Human Factors in Computing Systems
- ACM International Conference on Multimedia
- Conference of the Human-Computer Interaction Group of the British Computer Society
- East-West International Conference on Human-Computer Interaction
- European Conference on Software Maintenance and Reengineering
- HCI Conference on People and Computers
- IEEE International Conference on Robotics and Automation
- IEEE International Conference on Systems, Man and Cybernetics
- IEEE Technical Exhibition Based Conference on Robotics and Automation, Proceedings
- IFIP INTERACT: Human-Computer Interaction
- International Conference on Human-Computer Interaction

2. USER MODELING

Journals

- AI & Society
- Automation in Construction
- Behavior and Information Technology
- British Journal of Educational Technology
- Computer Graphics Forum
- Computers & Education
- Computers in Industry
- Computing and Informatics
- Control and Cybernetics
- Data & Knowledge Engineering
- Electronic Government
- Expert Systems with Applications
- Human-Computer Interaction
- IBM Systems Journal
- IEE Proceedings-Computers and Digital Techniques
- IEEE Transactions on Knowledge and Data Engineering
- IEEE Transactions on Systems, Man & Cybernetics, Part A (Systems & Humans)
- IEICE Transactions on Communications

- Information Processing & Management
- Information Retrieval
- Information Systems Journal
- Interacting with Computers
- International Journal of Expert Systems Research and Applications
- International Journal of Human Computer Interaction
- International Journal of Human-Computer Studies
- International Journal of Information Management
- International Journal of Man-Machine Studies
- International Journal of Modeling and Simulation
- International Journal of Uncertainty, Fuzziness and Knowledge-Based Systems
- Journal of Artificial Intelligence in Education
- Journal of Digital Information Management
- Journal of Documentation
- Journal of End User Computing
- Journal of Intelligent Systems
- Journal of the American Society for Information Science and Technology
- Knowledge Organization
- Materials Science and Technology
- Multimedia Systems
- Personal and Ubiquitous Computing
- Software Testing, Verification and Reliability
- Universal Access in the Information Society
- User Modeling and User-Adapted Interaction
- WSEAS Transactions on Systems

Conferences/Proceedings/Workshops

- ACM CHI Conference on Human Factors in Computing Systems
- ACM Conference on Assistive Technologies
- ACM Conference on Electronic Commerce
- ACM Symposium on User Interface Software and Technology
- ACM/IEEE-CS Joint Conference on Digital Libraries
- Annual International ACM SIGIR Conference on Research and Development in Information Retrieval
- Annual Symposium on Human Interaction with Complex Systems
- Computational Linguistics and its Applications International Workshop Proceedings
- ERCIM Workshop on "User Interfaces for All"
- European Conference on Artificial Intelligence
- Human Factors and Ergonomics Society Annual Meeting
- IEE Colloquium on Computers in the Service of Mankind: Helping The Disabled
- IEE Seminar Scenarios through the System Life Cycle
- IEEE International Conference on Fuzzy Systems

- IEEE International Conference on Fuzzy Systems
- IFIP INTERACT: Human-Computer Interaction
- International Conference on Conceptual Structures
- International Conference on Formal and Applied Practical Reasoning
- International Conference on Human-Computer Interaction
- International Conference on Intelligence in Services and Networks
- International Conference on Intelligent Environments
- International Conference on Intelligent User Interfaces
- International Conference on Multi Media Engineering Education
- International Conference on Networking
- International Conference on User Modeling
- International Workshop on Advances in Databases and Information Systems
- International Workshop on Computational Linguistics and its Applications
- International Conference on Information Technology: Coding and Computing
- UK Mechatronics Forum International Conference
- UK/International Conference on Electronic Library and Visual Information Research

Others

- Artificial Intelligence Review
- Knowledge Engineering Review
- New Review of Hypermedia and Multimedia

Journal Special Issue

- User Modeling and User-Adapted Interaction [Special Issue on Statistical and Probabilistic Methods for User Modeling], March 2007, 17, 93-117

3. USER DESIGN

Journals

- ACM Transactions on Computer-Human Interaction
- ACM Transactions on Information Systems
- Behavior and Information Technology
- Communications of the ACM
- Computer Design's Electronic Systems Technology & Design
- Computing Systems in Engineering
- Design Studies
- Education and Information Technologies
- Educational Technology, Research and Development
- Human Factors
- Information Systems Journal
- Information Systems Management

- Information Technology and Libraries
- Interacting with Computers
- Interactions
- International Journal of Human-Computer Interaction
- International Journal of Human-Computer Studies
- International Journal of Man-Machine Studies
- Internet Research: Electronic Networking Applications and Policy
- Journal of Education for Library and Information Science
- Journal of Engineering and Applied Science
- Journal of Librarianship and Information Science
- Journal of Systems and Software
- Journal of Visual Languages and Computing
- OCLC Systems & Services
- Universal Access in the Information Society

Others

- SIGCHI Bulletin

Conferences/Proceedings/Workshops

- ACM CHI Conference on Human Factors in Computing Systems
- ACM Conference on Assistive Technologies
- ACM International Conference on Design of Communication
- Conference of the Human-Computer Interaction Group of the British Computer Society
- DIS: Designing Interactive Systems: Processes, Practices, Methods, & Techniques
- Hawaii International Conference on System Sciences
- Human Factors and Ergonomics Society Annual Meeting
- IEE Colloquium on "Human Centred Automation"
- IEE Colloquium on Making User-Centred Design Work in Software Development
- IEE Colloquium on Man-Machine Interfaces for Instrumentation
- IEEE International Conference on Systems, Man, and Cybernetics
- IFIP INTERACT: Human-Computer Interaction
- International Conference on Applied Ergonomics (ICAE)
- International Conference on Commerce and Web Technologies
- International Conference on Human-Computer Interaction
- Proceedings IEEE Virtual Reality

4. COMPUTER MEDIATED COMMUNICATION

Journals

- AI & Society
- Behavior and Information Technology

- Computer and Composition
- Computers & Education
- Computers in Human Behavior
- Educational Technology
- European Journal of Information Systems
- Human-Computer Interaction
- Information Processing & Management
- Interacting with Computers
- International Journal of Human-Computer Studies
- International Journal of Man-Machine Studies
- Internet Research
- Journal of Computer Assisted Learning
- Journal of Computer-Mediated Communication
- Journal of Educational Computing Research
- Journal of Information Technology
- Journal of Management Information Systems
- Journal of Organizational Computing
- Journal of Organizational Computing and Electronic Commerce
- Management Science

Others

- SIGCSE Bulletin

Conferences/Proceedings/Workshops

- ACM CHI Conference on Human Factors in Computing Systems
- ACM CSCW Conference on Computer-Supported Cooperative Work
- ACM International Conference on Systems Documentation
- Americas Conference on Information Systems
- Conference of the Human-Computer Interaction Group of the British Computer Society
- Conference on Computers and the Quality of Life
- Conference on Human Factors in Computing System
- Conference on Human-Computer Interaction with Mobile Devices and Services
- Conference on Integrating Technology into Computer Science Education
- Conference on Office Automation Systems
- Conference on Office Information Systems
- DIS: Designing Interactive Systems: Processes, Practices, Methods, & Techniques
- East-West International Conference on Human Computer-Interaction
- European Conference on Computer-Supported Cooperative Work
- GROUP: International Conference on Supporting Group Work
- Hawaii International Conference on System Sciences
- IEEE International Conference on Advanced Learning Technologies
- IFIP INTERACT: Human-Computer Interaction

- INTERCHI Conference on Human Factors in Computing Systems
- International Conference on Automatic Face and Gesture Recognition
- International Conference on Intelligent User Interfaces
- International Cyberspace Conference on Ergonomics
- Nordic Conference on Human-Computer Interaction
- Workshop on Embodied Conversational Characters

Other Related Conferences

- ACM International Conference on Digital Libraries

5. UBIQUITOUS COMPUTING

Journals

- ACM Transactions on Computer-Human Interaction
- ACM Transactions on Information Systems
- Communications of the ACM
- Computer Journal
- Computer Supported Cooperative Work
- Educational Media International
- IEEE Pervasive Computing
- IEEE Transactions on Information Technology in Biomedicine
- IEEE Transactions on Parallel and Distributed Systems
- IEEE Transactions on Systems, Man and Cybernetics, Part C (Applications and Reviews)
- IEICE Transactions on Communications
- IEICE Transactions on Information and Systems
- Information Systems Management
- Interacting with Computers
- International Journal of Ad Hoc and Ubiquitous Computing
- International Journal of Human-Computer Interaction
- International Journal of Human-Computer Studies
- International Journal of Medical Informatics
- Journal of Computer Assisted Learning
- Journal of Educational Computing Research
- Journal of Organizational Computing and Electronic Commerce
- Journal of The Communications Network
- Personal and Ubiquitous Computing
- Pervasive and Mobile Computing
- Software - Practice and Experience
- Universal Access in the Information Society
- Wireless Communications and Mobile Computing
- WSEAS Transactions on Computers

Others

- EDUCAUSE Review
- SIGCHI Bulletin

Conferences/Proceedings/Workshops

- ACM CHI Conference on Human Factors in Computing Systems
- ACM Conference on Assistive Technologies
- ACM Conference on Universal Usability
- ACM CSCW Conference on Computer-Supported Cooperative Work
- ACM IDC: Interaction Design and Children
- ACM Symposium on User Interface Software and Technology
- CHI Workshops
- Conference on Human-Computer Interaction with Mobile Devices and Services
- DIS: Designing Interactive Systems: Processes, Practices, Methods, & Techniques
- Embedded and Ubiquitous Computing Workshops
- ERCIM Workshop on "User Interfaces for All"
- IEEE International Conference and Security Informatics
- IEEE International Conference on Pervasive Computing and Communications Workshop
- IEEE International Conference on Sensor Networks, Ubiquitous and Trustworthy Computing,
- IEEE International Workshop on Wireless and Mobile Technologies in Education
- IFIP INTERACT: Human-Computer Interaction
- IFIP International Conference on Network and Parallel Computing
- International ACM SIGIR Conference on Research and Development in Information Retrieval
- International Conference on Computational Science (ICCS)
- International Conference on Computational Science and its Applications (ICCSA)
- International Conference on Embedded Software and Systems
- International Conference on Intelligent User Interfaces
- International Conference on Software Engineering Research, Management and Applications
- International Conference on Ubiquitous Intelligence and Computing (UIC)
- International Conferences on Service-Oriented Computing (ICSOC)
- International Symposium on Applications and the Internet
- International Workshop on Information Security Applications
- Nordic Conference on Human-Computer Interaction
- World Congress on Intelligent Control and Automation

Other Related Conferences

- **ACM Conference on Hypertext.**
- **ACM Conference on Hypertext and Hypermedia**
- ACM/IEEE-CS Joint Conference on Digital Libraries
- Symposium on the Interface

6. MOBILE HCI

Journals

- ACM Transactions on Computer-Human Interaction
- Behaviour and Information Technology
- Business Process Management Journal
- Computer Supported Cooperative Work
- IEEE Intelligent Systems
- IEEE Software
- IEEE Transactions on Mobile Computing
- IEEE Transactions on Systems, Man and Cybernetics, Part C (Applications and Reviews)
- Interacting with Computers
- International Journal of Human-Computer Studies
- Journal of Human-Computer Interaction
- Journal of Internet Technology
- Journal of Organizational Computing and Electronic Commerce
- Journal of Software
- Manager-British Journal of Administrative Management
- Personal and Ubiquitous Computing
- Psychology Journal, Presence and Embodiment in Mobile Phone Communication, http://www.psychnology.org/
- Universal Access in the Information Society
- WSEAS Transactions on Information Science and Applications

Others

- ACM SIGCHI Bulletin
- New Review of Hypermedia and Multimedia

Conferences/Proceedings/Workshops

- ACM CHI Conference on Human Factors in Computing Systems
- ACM CSCW Conference on Computer-Supported Cooperative Work
- ACM Symposium on User Interface Software and Technology
- ERCIM Workshop on "User Interfaces for All"
- Human-Computer Interaction with Mobile Devices and Services
- IEEE International Conference on e-Commerce and Technology
- IEEE International Conference on Enterprise Computing, e-Commerce and e-Services
- IEEE International Conference on Wireless and Mobile Computing, Networking and Communications
- IEEE International Workshop on Mobile Commerce and Wireless Services
- IFIP INTERACT: Human-Computer Interaction
- International Conference on Human-Computer Interaction

- International Conference on Information & Communication Technologies: from Theory to Applications
- International Conference on Intelligent User Interfaces
- International Conference on Mobile Technology, Applications and Systems
- International Workshop on Programming Multi-Agent Systems
- International Workshop on Security, Privacy and Trust in Pervasive and Ubiquitous Computing
- Nordic Conference on Human-Computer Interaction
- Pacific Rim International Workshop on Multi-Agents
- The International Conference on "Computer as a Tool"
- Workshop on Human Computer Interaction with Mobile Devices

Other Related Conferences

- ACM International Conference on Digital Libraries

7. USABILITY EVALUATION

Journals

- Behavior and Information Technology
- Computer
- Computers and Education
- IEEE Security and Privacy
- IEEE Transactions on Industrial Electronics
- Interacting with Computers
- Interactions
- International Journal of Advanced Manufacturing Technology
- International Journal of Human-Computer Studies
- International Journal of Industrial Ergonomics
- International Journal of Man-Machine Studies
- International Journal of Software Engineering and Knowledge Engineering
- Journal of Systems and Software
- Performance Evaluation
- Universal Access in the Information Society
- Wireless Communications and Mobile Computing

Conferences/Proceedings/Workshops

- ACM Conference on Assistive Technologies
- ACM CSCW Conference on Computer-Supported Cooperative Work
- Conference on Human Factors in Computing Systems
- HCI Conference on People and Computers

- HFS INTERFACE
- Human Factors and Ergonomics Society Annual Meeting
- IEEE Pacific Rim Conference on Communications, Computers and Signal Processing
- International ACM SIGIR Conference on Research and Development in Information Retrieval
- International Conference on Intelligent User Interfaces
- International Conference on Internet and Multimedia Systems and Applications

Other Related Conferences

- ACM/IEEE-CS Joint Conference on Digital Libraries
- JCDL: ACM/IEEE-CS Joint Conference on Digital Libraries

8. ERGONOMICS

Journals

- Applied Ergonomics
- Behavior and Information Technology
- Business Equipment Digest
- Cognition, Technology & Work
- Computers & Industrial Engineering
- Computers in Libraries
- Control Engineering
- Digital Creativity
- Electronic Library
- Engineering Designer
- Ergonomics
- Ergonomics in Design
- Facilities
- Health & Safety at Work
- Human Factors and Ergonomics in Manufacturing
- IEEE Transactions on Neural Systems and Rehabilitation Engineering
- IEEE Transactions on Visualization and Computer Graphics
- Industrial Engineering
- Informatica
- Information Visualization
- International Journal of Computer Integrated Manufacturing
- International Journal of Human-Computer Interaction
- International Journal of Human-Computer Studies
- International Journal of Industrial Ergonomics
- International Journal of Operations & Production Management
- International Journal of Vehicle Design

- Journal of Computing and Information Science in Engineering
- Journal of Engineering Design
- Journal of Ergonomics
- Journal of Occupational and Environmental Hygiene
- Journal of Zhejiang University
- JSME International Journal, Series C (Mechanical Systems, Machine Elements and Manufacturing)
- Machine Design International
- Managing Office Technology
- Material Handling Management
- Modern Materials Handling
- Occupational Ergonomics
- Office & Information Management International
- Online
- Physiological Measurement
- Professional Safety
- Remittance and Document Processing Today
- Risk Management
- Technology and Health Care
- Theoretical Issues in Ergonomics Science
- Work Process Improvement Today
- Work, a Journal of Prevention, Assessment & Rehabilitation

Conferences/Proceedings/Workshops

- ACM Conference on Human-Robot Interaction
- Annual Meeting of the Human Factors and Ergonomics Association, Ergonomics for the New Millennium
- Applied Ergonomics Conference
- Conference on Human-Robot Interaction
- Human Factors and Ergonomics Society Annual Meeting
- IEEE Power India Conference
- Innovative Applications of Artificial Intelligence Conference
- Innovative Applications of Artificial Intelligence Conference
- International Conference on AI, Simulation, and Planning in High Autonomy Systems
- International Conference on Applied Simulation and Modeling
- International Conference on Management Science and Engineering
- International Cyberspace Conference on Ergonomics
- International Multiconference on Engineers and Computer Scientists
- International Power Engineering Conference
- Joint Asia-Pacific Computer Human Interaction/ ASEAN Ergonomics
- Symposium on Eye Tracking Research and Applications
- Triennial Congress of the International Ergonomics Association
- Winter Simulation Conference

Others

- Bulletin of the Transilvania University of Brasov

9. COGNITIVE PSYCHOLOGY

Journals

- ACM Transactions on Computer-Human Interaction
- ACM Transactions on Office Information Systems
- AI & Society
- Australian Journal of Scientific Research
- Behavior Research Methods, Instruments, & Computers
- Behavioral and Brain Sciences
- Behavior and Information Technology
- British Journal of Psychology
- Cognitive Brain Research
- Cognitive Science
- Communications of the ACM
- Design Studies
- Educational Technology, Research and Development
- Electronics & Communication Engineering Journal
- European Journal of Neurosciences
- European Psychologist
- Human Communication Research
- Human-Computer Interaction
- Information and Decision Technologies
- Information Sciences
- Intelligence
- Interacting with Computers
- International Journal of Advanced Robotic Systems
- International Journal of Cognitive Technology
- International Journal of Engineering Education
- International Journal of Human-Computer Studies
- International Journal of Man-Machine Studies
- Journal of Applied Developmental Psychology
- Journal of Applied Psychology
- Journal of Behavioral Therapy & Experimental
- Journal of Computer-Based Instruction
- Journal of Consumer Research
- Journal of Educational Computing Research
- Journal of Educational Psychology

- Journal of End-User Computing
- Journal of Experimental Psychology: Learning, Memory & Cognition
- Journal of Human Evolution
- Journal of Learning Sciences
- Journal of Management Information Systems
- Journal of Memory and Language
- Journal of Neurolinguistics
- Journal of Occupational and Organizational Psychology
- Journal of Organizational Computing
- Journal of Verbal Learning and Verbal Behavior
- Learning and Instruction
- Medical Engineering & Physics
- Metaphor and Symbolic Activity
- Nature Neuroscience
- NeuroImage
- New Review of Hypermedia and Multimedia
- Perception & Psychophysics
- Psychnology Journal, Review of How Space Affords Socio-Cognitive Processes during Collaboration, http://www.psychnology.org/
- Quarterly Journal of Experimental Psychology
- The Journal for the Integrated Study of Artificial Intelligence, Cognitive Science and Applied Epistemology
- The Journal of Social Psychology
- Training Research Journal

Others

- Annual Review of Psychology
- Encyclopedia of cognitive science
- Handbook of Applied Cognition
- Handbook of human-computer interaction
- International encyclopedia of social and behavioral sciences
- Neuropsychology Review
- Psychological Bulletin
- Psychological Review
- Review of Information Science
- The MIT encyclopedia of the cognitive sciences

Conferences/Proceedings/Workshops

- ACM CHI Conference on Human Factors in Computing Systems
- Conference on Cognitive Ergonomic-Cognition and Cooperation
- East-West International Conference on Human-Computer Interaction
- European Conference on Cognitive Ergonomics

- European Conference on Cognitive Modeling
- HCI Conference on People and Computers
- Human Factors and Ergonomics Society Annual Meeting
- International Conference on Cognitive Modeling
- International Conference on Computer Support fro Collaborative Learning
- International Conference on Computer-Based Learning in Science
- International Conference on Human-Computer Interaction
- OZCHI, the CHISIG Annual Conference on Human-Computer Interaction

Compilation of References

3Gtoday. (2005). Retrieved November 5, 2005, from http://www.3gtoday.com

Aaron, A., & Weng, J. (2001). *Performance comparison of ad-hoc routing protocols for networks with node energy constraints.* Retrieved January 19, 2008, from http://ivms.stanford.edu/~amaaron/ee360/EE360_FINAL_PAPER.pdf

Aarts, E. (2004, January-March). Ambient intelligence: A multimedia perspective. *IEEE Multimedia, 11*(1), 12-19.

Abowd, G. (1999). *Software engineering issues for ubiquitous computing.* ACM Press.

Abowd, G..D., & Mynatt, E.D. (2000). Charting past, present, and future research in ubiquitous computing. *ACM Transactions on Computer-Human Interaction, 7*(1), 29-58.

Abowd, G.D., Mynatt, E., & Rodden, T. (2002). The human experience. *Pervasive Computing, IEEE, 1*(1), 48-57.

Abramson, N. (1977). The throughput of packet broadcasting channels. *IEEE Trans. Commun., 25,* 117-128.

Acampora, G., & Loia, V. (2005, May 22-25). Using fuzzy technology in ambient intelligence environment. In *Proceedings of the IEEE International Conference on Fuzzy Systems*, Reno, NV.

Acampora, G., & Loia, V. (2005). Fuzzy control interoperability and scalability for adaptive domotic framework. *IEEE Transactions on Industrial Informatics, 1*(2), 97-111.

Agarwal, R., & Karahanna, E. (2000). Time flies when you're having fun: Cognitive absorption and beliefs about information technology. *MIS Quarterly, 24*(4), 665-694.

Agrawal, R., & Srikant, R. (1994). Fast algorithms for mining association rules. In *Proceedings of the 20th International Conference on Very Large Databases,* pp. 487-499. Santiago, Chile.

Alben, L. (1996). Quality of experience: Defining the criteria for effective interaction design. *Interactions, 3(*3), 11.

Albrecht, M., Frank, M., Martini, P., Schetelig, M., Vilavaara, A., & Wenzel, A. (1999). IP services over Bluetooth: leading the way to a new mobility. In *Proceedings of 24th Annual Conference on Local Computer Networks (LCN'99),* pp. 2-11.

Aldestein, F., Gupta, S.K.S., Richard, G.G., & Schwiebert, L. (2005). *Fundamentals of mobile and pervasive computing.* McGraw-Hill.

Alexander, C. (1979). *A pattern language.* Oxford University Press.

Al-Karaki, J.N., & Kamal, A.E. (2004). Routing techniques in wireless sensor networks: A survey. *IEEE Wireless Communications, 11*(6).

Almeida, H., Perkusich, A., Ferreira, G., Loureiro, E., & Costa, E. (2006, July). A component model to support dynamic unanticipated software evolution. In *Proceedings of the 18th International Conference on Software Engineering and Software Engineering.* San Francisco, CA.

Amann, P., Bright, D., Quirchmayr, G., & Thomas, B. (2003). Supporting knowledge management in context aware and pervasive environments using event-based co-ordination. *In Proceedings of the 14th International Workshop on Database and Expert Systems Applications*, Prague, Czech Republic.

Amyot, D. (2003). Introduction to the user requirements notation: Learning by example. *Computer Networks, 42*(3), 285-301.

Amyot, D., Weiss, M., & Logrippo, L. (2005). UCM-based generation of test purposes. *Computer Networks, 49*(5), 643-660.

Analysys. (2001). *Mobile location services and technologies.* Retrieved January 21, 2008, from http://www.gii.co.jp/english/an6596_mobile_location.html

Anderson, R. (1994). Representation and requirements: The value of ethnography in system design. Human-Computer Interaction, 9(2), 151-182.

Andrade, R., & Logrippo, L. (2000, July). Reusability at the early development stages of the mobile wireless communication systems. In *Proceedings of the 4th World Multiconference on Systemics, Cybernetics and Informatics (SCI 2000),* Vol. VII, Part I, pp. 11-16. Orlando, FL.

Apostolopoulos, T.K., & Kefala, A. (2003). A configurable middleware architecture for deploying e-learning services over diverse communication networks. In V. Uskov (Ed.), *Proceedings of the 2003 IASTED International Conference on Computers and Advanced Technology in Education*, pp. 235-240. Rhodes, Greece: Acta Press.

Araujo, I., & Weiss, M. (2002). Linking non-functional requirements and patterns. In *Proceedings of the 9th Conference on Pattern Languages of Programs (PLoP).* Retrieved November, 16, 2006, from http://jerry.cs.uiuc.edu/~plop/plop2002/final/PatNFR.pdf

Arikan, E. (1984). Some complexity results about packet radio networks. *IEEE Trans. Info. Theory, IT-30, 681-85.*

Astrom, K. J. (1987). Adaptive feedback control. *Proceedings of the IEEE, 75*(2), 185-217.

Avgeriou, P., & Zdun, U. (2005, July). Architectural patterns revisited: A pattern language. In *Proceedings of the 10th European Conference on Pattern Languages of Programs (EuroPlop),* Irsee, Germany.

Bachman, F., Bass, L., Buhman, C., Dorda, S.C., Long, F., Robert, J., Seacord, R., & Wallnau, K. (2000). *Technical concepts of component-based software engineering* (vol. 2). Pittsburgh, PA. EUA: Carnegie Mellon Software Engineering Institute. Retrieved October 10, 2006, from http://www.sei.cmu.edu/pub/documents/00.reports/pdf/00tr008.pdf

Bahl, P., & Padmanabhan, V. N. (2000). RADAR: An in-building RF-based user location and tracking system. In *Proceedings of IEEE INFOCOM,* Tel Aviv, Israel, (Vol. 2, pp. 775-784).

Ballou, D., Wang, R., Pazer, H., & Tayi, G. (1998). Modeling information manufacturing systems to determine information product quality. *Management Science, 44*(4), 462-484.

Banavar, G., & Bernstein, A. (2002, December). Software infrastructure and design challenges for ubiquitous computing, *Communications of the ACM, 45*(12), 92-96.

Bardram, J. (2005, July 23). *The trouble with login: On usability and computer security in ubiquitous computing.* Springer-Verlag London Limited.

Bardram, J. E. (2005, May). The Java context awareness framework (JCAF) - a service infrastructure and programming framework for context-aware applications. In H. Gellersen, R. Want, & A. Schmidt (Eds.), *Proceedings of the 3rd International Conference on Pervasive Computing* (pp. 98-115). Munich, Germany: Spinger-Verlag.

Bardram, J.E., & Christensen, H.B. (2001). Middleware for pervasive healthcare: A white paper. In G. Banavar (Ed.), *Advanced topic workshop: Middleware for mobile computing*, Heidelberg, Germany.

Barros, G., Zuffo, M. K., & Benini, J. (2006). *Home entertainment UI continuum:Cellphone, HTPC and iTV.* Paper presented at Investigating New User Experience Challenges in iTV: Mobility & Sociability Workshop, CHI'06. Retrieved January 16, 2008, from http://soc.kuleuven.be/com/mediac/chi2006workshop/files/home_entertainment_ui_continuum.pdf

Basangi, S., Conti, M., Giordano, S., & Stojmenovic, I. (2004). *Mobile ad-hoc networking.* Wiley Inter-Science.

Bayne, K.M. (2002). *Marketing without wires: Targeting promotions and advertising to mobile device users.* New York: John Wiley & Sons Ltd.

Beck, K. (1999, October). Embracing change with extreme programming. *IEEE Computer, 32*(10), 70-77.

Beck, K., Beedle, M., van Bennekum, A., Cockburn, A., Cunningham, W., Fowler, M. et al. (2001). *The Agile Manifesto.* Retrieved January 25, 2008, from http://agilemanifesto.org

Becker, C., Handte, M., Schiele, G., & Rothermel, K. (2004). PCOM: A component system for pervasive computing. In *Proceedings of the 2nd IEEE International Conference on Pervasive Computing and Communications* (pp. 67-76). Orlando, FL: IEEE Computer Society.

Becker, C., Schiele, G., Gubbels, H., & Rothermel, K. (2003). BASE-A micro-broker-based middleware for pervasive computing. In *Proceedings of the First IEEE International Conference on Pervasive Computing and Communications*, pp. 443-451. Fort Worth, USA: IEEE Computer Society.

Beckhaus, S., Blom, K. J., & Haringer, M. (2005). Intuitive, hands-free travel interface for virtual environments. In *Proceedings of IEEE Virtual Reality Conference, Workshop on New Directions in 3D User Interfaces 2005,* Bonn, Germany (pp. 57-60). Shaker Verlag.

Bell, G., & Dourish, P. (2007, January). Yesterday's tomorrows: Notes on ubiquitous computing's dominant vision. *Personal Ubiquitous Computing, 11*(2), 133-143.

Benford, S., Flintham, M., Drozd, A., Anastasi, R., Rowland, D., Tandavanitj, N., et al. (2004, July). Uncle Roy all around you: Implicating the city in a location-based performance. In *Proceedings of ACM Advanced Computer Entertainment*, Singapore. ACM Press.

Berzowska, J., & Yarin, P. (2005). Memory rich garments: Body-based displays. In *Proceedings of the ACM SIGGRAPH 05 Electronic Art and Animation Catalog*, pp. 168-171. Los Angeles, CA.

Beyer, H. R., Holtzblatt, K., & Baker, L. (2004). An agile customer-centered method: Rapid contextual design. In *Proceedings of Extreme Programming and Agile Methods 2004 (XP/Agile Universe),* pp. 50-59. Calgary, Canada.

Bharghavan, V. et al. (1994). MACAW: A media access protocol for wireless LANs. *Computer Communications Review, 24*(4).

Bhatia, S., Dahn, C., Lee, J. C., Sampat, M., & McCrickard, D. S. (2006). VTAssist-a location-based feedback notification system for the disabled. In *Proceedings of the ACM Southeast Conference (ACMSE '06),* pp. 512-517. Melbourne, FL.

Billard, E.A. (2004, August). Patterns of agent interaction scenarios as use case maps. *IEEE Transactions on Systems, Man, and Cybernetics. Part B, Cybernetics, 34*(4), 1933-1939.

Bimber, O., & Raskar, R. (2005). *Spatial augmented reality: Merging real and virtual worlds.* A K Peters LTD.

Birsan, D. (2005, March). On plug-ins and extensible architectures. *ACM Queue, 3*(2), 40-46.

Blackwell, G. (2002, January 25). Mesh networks: Disruptive technology? *Wi-Fi Planet.* Retrieved October 25, 2005, from http://www.wi-fiplanet.com/columns/article.php/961951

Blinn, J. (1990, November/December). The ultimate design tool. *IEEE Computer Graphics and Applications, 10*(6), 90-92.

Bluetooth SIG. (2005). *The official Bluetooth wireless info site.* Retrieved November 3, 2005, from http://www.bluetooth.com

Bornik, A., Beichel, R., Reitinger, B., Sorantin, E., Werkgartner, G., Leberl, F., et al. (2003). Augmented reality based liver surgery planning. *Computer Graphics Forum, 22*(4), 795-796.

Bose, I. (2006). Fourth generation wireless systems: A review of technical and business challenges for the next frontier. *Communications of AIS, 17*(31), 693-713.

Bouch A., & Sasse, M. A. (2001, August 20-24). A user-centered approach to Internet quality of service: Why value is everything. In *Proceedings of IT-COM'2001,* Denver, Colorado.

Bouras, C., & Tsiatsos, T. (2006, June). Educational virtual environments: Design rationale and architecture. *Multimedia tools and applications, 29*(2), 153-173.

Bouras, C., Fotakis, D., Kapoulas, V., Koubek, A., Mayer, H., & Rehatscheck, H. (1999, June 7-11). In *Proceedings of the Virtual European School-VES, IEEE Multimedia Systems'99, Special Session on European Projects,* pp. 1055-1057. Florence, Italy.

Bouras, C., Philopoulos, A., & Tsiatsos, T. (2001, July). E-learning through distributed virtual environments. *Journal of Network and Computer Applications, 24*(3), 175-199.

Bouras, C., Triantafillou, V., & Tsiastsos, T. (2001, June 25-30). Aspects of collaborative environments using distributed virtual environments. In *Proceedings of the ED-MEDIA 2001 World Conference on Educational Multimedia, Hypermedia & Telecommunications* (pp. 173-178). Tampre, Finland.

Boyera, S., & Lewis, R. (2005, May 2). *Device independence activity.* Retrieved October 10, 2006, from http://www.w3.org/2001/di

Bray, J., & Sturman, C.F. (2000). *Bluetooth: Connect without cables.* Prentice Hall.

Buhr, R.J.A., & Casselman, R.S. (1995). *Use case maps for object-oriented systems.* Prentice Hall.

Burigat, S., & Chittaro, L. (2005, April). *Location-aware visualization of VRML models in GPS-based mobile guides. In Proceedings of the Web3D 2005: The 10th International Conference on 3D Web Technology* (pp. 57-64). New York.

Burrell, J., & Gay, G.K. (2002). E-graffiti. Evaluating realworld use of a context-aware system. Interacting with Computers, 14.

Buschmann, F., Meunier, R., Rohnert, H., Sommerlad, P., Stal, M. (1996). *Pattern-oriented software architecture.* Wiley.

Businessweek. (2005, November 21). Special advertising section: 3G the mobile opportunity [Asian ed.]. *BusinessWeek,* 92-96.

Button, G. (2000). The ethnographic tradition and design. Design Studies, 21, 319-332.

Buxton, W. (1992). Telepresence: Integrating shared task and person spaces. In *Proceedings of Graphics Interface '92* (pp. 123-129).

Callaway, E.H. (2003). *Wireless sensor networks – architectures and protocols.* Boca Raton: Auerbach.

Campo, C., Rubio, C. G., López, A. M., & Almenárez, F. (in press). PDP: A lightweight discovery protocol for local-scope interactions in wireless ad hoc networks. *Computer Networks.*

Cano, J.C., & Manzoni, P. (2000). Performance comparison of energy consumption for mobile ad hoc network routing protocols. In *Proceedings of the 8th International Symposium on Modeling, Analysis and Simulation of Computer and Telecom System* (pp. 57-64).

Capone, A., Gerla, M., & Kapoor, R. (2001). Efficient polling schemes for Bluetooth picocells. In *Proceedings of IEEE ICC 2001,* Helsinki, Finland.

Cappiello, C., Francalanci, C., & Pernici, B. (2003). Time-related factors of data quality in multichannel information systems. *Journal of Management Information Systems, 20*(3), 71-91.

Cardoso, R. S., & Kon, F. (2002, November). Mobile agents: A key for effective pervasive computing. In *2002 OOPSLA Workshop on Pervasive Computing.* Seattle, WA.

Caroll, J. M., & Rosson, M. B. (1992). Getting around the task-artifact cycle: How to make claims and design by scenario. *ACM Transactions on Information Systems, 10*(2), 181-212.

Carroll, J. M. (2000). *Making use: Scenario-based design of human-computer interactions.* Cambridge, MA: Massachusetts Institute of Technology Press.

Casher, O., Leach, C., Page, C., & Rzepa, H. (1998). Virtual reality modelling language (VRML) in Chemistry. *Chemistry in Britain* (pp 34-26).

Center for Embedded Networked Sensing, UCLA. Retrieved January 21, 2008, from http://research.cens.ucla.edu/research/

Cereijo, R.A., & Johnson, S. (2006). Unfolding the user experience in new scenarios of pervasive interactive TV. In Proceedings of CHI 2006, Interact. Inform. Inspire.

Cereijo, R.A., & Sala, R. (2004, March-April). Main HCI issues for the design of interfaces for ubiquitous interactive multimedia broadcast. Interactions Magazine, 51-53. ACM.

Chee, Y.S. (2001). Networked virtual environments for collaborative learning. In *Proceedings of the Ninth International Conference on Computers in Education (ICCE/SchoolNet)* (pp. 3-11), Seoul, South Korea.

Chee, Y.S., & Hooi, C.M. (2002). C-VISions: Socialized learning through collaborative, virtual, interactive simulations. In *Proceedings of the Conference on Computer Support for Collaborative Learning (CSCL)* (pp. 687-696), Boulder, Colorado.

Chen, B., Jamieson, K., Balakrishnan, H., & Morris, R. (2002, September). Span: An energy-efficient coordination algorithm for topology maintenance in ad hoc wireless networks. *ACM Wireless Networks Journal, 8*(5), 481-494.

Chen, G., & Kotz, D. (2000). *A survey of context-aware mobile computing research* (Tech. Rep. No. TR2000-381). Hanover: Dartmouth College.

Chen, G., & Kotz, D. (2002). *Solar: A pervasive computing infrastructure for context-aware mobile applications* (Tech. Rep. No. TR2002-421). Hanover: Dartmouth College.

Chen, H., Finin, T., & Joshi, A. (2003). An ontology for context-aware pervasive computing environments. *Knowledge Engineering Review, 18*(3), 197-207.

Cheverst, K., Dix, A., Fitton, D., & Rouncefield, M. (2003). Out to lunch: Exploring the sharing of personal context through office door displays. In S. Viller & P. Wyeth (Eds.), Proceedings of the 2003 Australasian Computer-Human Conference, OzCHI 2003, CHISIG, Canberra, Australia (pp. 74-83).

Chiasserini, C.-F., Chlamtac, I., Monti, P., & Nucci, A. (2002). *Energy efficient design of wireless ad hoc networks* (LNCS 2354).

Chittaro, L., & Ranon, R. (2000). Virtual reality stores for 1-to-1 commerce. In *Proceedings of the CHI2000 Workshop on Designing Interactive Systems for 1-to-1 E-Commerce,* The Hague, The Netherlands.

Chittaro, L., & Ranon, R. (2002, May). New directions for the design of virtual reality interfaces to e-commerce sites. In *Proceedings of the AVI 2002: 5th International Conference on Advanced Visual Interfaces* (pp. 308-315). New York: ACM Press.

Chlamtac, I., Conti, M., & Liu, J.J.N. (2003). Mobile ad hoc networking: Imperatives and challenges. *Ad hoc Networks, 1*(1), 13-64.

Choo, C.W. (1997). IT2000: Singapore's vision of an intelligent island. In P. Droege (Ed.), *Intelligent environments.* North-Holland, Amsterdam.

Chung, D. (2005). Something for nothing: Understanding purchasing behaviors in social virtual environments. *CyberPsychology & Behavior, 8*(6), 538-554.

Chung, L., Nixon, B., Yu, E., & Mylopoulos, J. (2000). *Non-functional requirements in software engineering.* Kluwer Academic Publishers.

Chung, L., Supakkul, S., & Yu, A. (2002, July 8-11). Good software architecting: Goals, objects, and patterns. In *Proceedings of the Information, Computing & Communication Technology Symposium (ICCT- 2002), UKC'02,* Seoul, Korea.

Churchill E. (Ed.). (2000). *Embodied conversational agents*. Cambridge, MA: The MIT Press.

Clarke, M., Blair, G. S., Coulson, G., & Parlavantzas, N. (2001, November). An efficient component model for the construction of adaptive middlewares. In *Proceedings of the IFIP/ACM International Conference on Distributed Systems Platforms* (pp. 160-178). Heidelberg, Germany: Springer-Verlag.

Clausen, T., & Jacquet, P. (2003). *Optimized link state routing protocol (OLSR)*. IETF Request for Comments 3626.

Cohen, J., Aggarwal, S., & Goland, Y.Y. (2000, September 6). *General event notification architecture base: Client to arbiter*. Retrieved October 10, 2006, from http://www.upnp.org/download/draft-cohen-gena-client-01.txt

Constantine, L. L. (2001). Process agility and software usability: Toward lightweight usage-centered design. *Information Age, 8*(2). In L. Constantine (Ed.), *Beyond chaos: The expert edge in managing software development*. Boston: Addison-Wesley.

Cope, B., Kalantzis, M., & New London Group. (2000). Multiliteracies: Literacy learning and the design of social futures. South Yarra, Vic: Macmillan.

Coplien, J. (1996). *Software patterns*. SIGS. Retrieved November 16, 2006, from http://users.rcn.com/jcoplien/Patterns/WhitePaper/SoftwarePatterns.pdf

Cordeiro, C., Abhyankar, S., Toshiwal, R., & Agrawal, D. (2003). A novel architecture and coexistence method to provide global access to/from Bluetooth WPANs by IEEE 802.11 WLANs. In *Proceedings of IEEE Performance, Computing and Communications Conference (IPCCC 2003)* (pp. 23-30).

Costa, P., Coulson, G., Mascolo, C., Picco, G. P., & Zachariadis, S. (2005). The RUNES middleware: A reconfigurable component-based approach to network embedded systems. In *Proceedings of the 16th Annual IEEE International Symposium on Personal Indoor and Mobile Radio Communications* (pp. 11-14). Berlin, Germany.

Costa, P., Coulson, G., Mascolo, C., Picco, G. P., & Zachariadis, S. (2005, September). The RUNES middleware: A reconfigurable component-based approach to networked embedded systems. In *Proceedings of the 16th IEEE International Symposium on Personal Indoor and Mobile Radio Communications*. Berlin, Germany: IEEE Communications Society.

Coulson, G., Grace, P., Blair, G., Duce, D., Cooper, C., & Sagar, M. (2005). *A middleware approach for pervasive grid environments*. Paper presented at the Workshop on Ubiquitous Computing and E-research, Edinburgh, Scotland.

Coutaz, J., Crowley, J. L., Dobson, S., & Garlan, D. (2005, March). Context is key. *Communications of the ACM, 48*(3), 49-53.

Cranz, G. (1998). *The chair: Rethinking culture, body, and design*. New York: Norton.

Crnkovic, I. (2001). Component-based software engineering: New challenges in software development software. *Software Focus, 4*, 127-133.

Csete, J., Wong, Y.H., & Vogel, D. (2004). Mobile devices in and out of the classroom. In *Proceedings of the 16th World Conference on Educational Multimedia and Hypermedia & World Conference on Educational Telecommunications*, Lugano, Switzerland (pp. 4729-4736).

Culler, D. E., & Hong, W. (Eds.). (2004). Wireless sensor networks. *Communications of the ACM, 47*(6), 30-57.

d'Acierno, A., Pietro, G. D., Coronato, A., & Gugliara, G. (2005, June). Plugin-orb for applications in a pervasive computing environment. In *Proceedings of the 2005 International Conference on Pervasive Systems and Computing* (pp. 140-146). Las Vegas, NE: CSREA Press.

dAcierno, A., Pietro, G.D., Coronato, A., & Gugliara, G. (2005). Plugin-orb for applications in a pervasive computing environment. In *Proceedings of the 2005 International Conference on Pervasive Systems and Computing*. Las Vegas, Nevada: CSREA Press.

Daku, B.L.F., & Jeffrey, K. (2000, October 18-21). *An interactive computer-based tutorial for MATLAB.* In *Proceedings of the 30th ASEE/IEEE Frontiers in Education Conference* (pp. F2D:2-F2D:7). Kansas City, Missouri.

Dalgarno, B. (2002). The potential of 3D virtual learning environments: A constructivist analysis. *Electronic Journal of Instructional Science and Technology, 5*(2).

Das, A. et al. (2001). Enhancing perfmance of asynchronous data traffic over the Bluetooth wireless ad hoc network. In *Proceedings of the IEEE INFOCOM.*

Dey, A. K. (2001). Understanding and using context. *Personal and Ubiquitous Computing, 5*(1), 4-7.

Dey, A.K., & Abowd, G.D. (1999). Towards a better understanding of context and context-awareness (GVU Tech. Rep. GIT-GVU-99-22). College of Computing, Georgia Institute of Technology. Retrieved January 18, 2008, from ftp://ftp.cc.gatech.edu/pub/gvu/tr/1999/99-22.pdf

Dey, A.K., Abowd, G.D., & Salber, D. (2001). Toolkit for supporting the rapid prototyping of context-aware applications. *Human-Computer Interaction, 16*, 97-166.

Dickey, M.D. (2003). 3D Virtual worlds: An emerging technology for traditional and distance learning. In *Proceedings of the Ohio Learning Network; The Convergence of Learning and Technology – Windows on the Future.*

Dieberger, A., & Lönnqvist, P. (2000). Visualizing interaction history on a collaborative Web server. In *Proceedings of Hypertext'2000* (pp. 220-221).

Dieberger, A., Dourish, P., Höök, K., Resnick, P., & Wexelblat, A. (2000). Social navigation: Techniques for building more usable systems. *Interactions, 7*(6), 36-45.

Dietz, P.H., & Leigh, D.L. (2001, November). DiamondTouch: A multi-user touch technology. In *ACM Symposium on User Interface Software and Technology (UIST)* (pp. 219-226). ISBN: 1-58113-438-X.

Dillon, A. (2000). *Understanding and evaluating the user experience with information spaces.* Indiana University, HCI Lab.

Ditze, M., Kamper, G., Jahnich, I., & Bernhardi-Grisson, R. (2004, June 24-26). Service-based access to distributed embedded devices through the open service gateway. In *Proceedings of the 2nd IEEE International Conference on Industrial Informatics*, Berlin, Germany (pp. 493-498).

DuCharme, B. (1999). *XML: The annotated specification.* Upper Saddle River, NJ: Prentice Hall.

Ebraert, P., Vandewoude, Y., Cazzola, W., D'Hondt, T., & Berbers, Y. (2005, July). Pitfalls in unanticipated dynamic software evolution. In *Proceedings of the workshop on reflection, AOP and meta-data for software evolution.* Glasgow, Scotland.

Edwards, W. K., & Mynatt, E. D. (1997). Timewarp: Techniques for autonomous collaboration. In *Proceedings of Conference on Human Factors in Computing Systems (CHI'97)* (pp. 218-225), New York: ACM Press.

Edwards, W.K., Newman, M.W., Sedivy, J.Z., & Smith, T.F. (2005). Bringing network effects to pervasive spaces. *IEEE Pervasive Computing, 4*(3), 15-17.

Erickson, T. (2006). Five lenses: Towards a toolkit for interaction design. In S. Bagnara, G. Crampton-Smith & G. Salvendy (Eds.), *Theories and practice in interaction design.* Lawrence Erlbaum.

Esler, M., Hightower, J., Anderson, T., & Borriello, G. (1999). Next century challenges: Data-centric networking for invisible computing (The Portolano Project at the University of Washington). In *Proceedings of the 5th International Conference on Mobile Computing and Networking* (pp. 24-35). Seattle, Washington: ACM Press.

European Union research project EYES. Retrieved January 21, 2008, from http://www.eyes.eu.org

Feder, B. (2003, June 10). Glass that glows and gives stock information. *New York Times*, P.C1.

Feeney, L.M. (2004). Energy-efficient communication in ad hoc wireless networks. In Basagni, Conti, Giordano, Stojmenovic (Eds.), *Mobile ad hoc networking.* IEEE.

Feeney, L.M., & Nilsson, M. (2001, April 24-26). Investigating the energy consumption of a wireless network interface in an ad hoc networking environment. In *20th Annual Joint Conference of the IEEE Computer and Communications Societies* (pp. 1548-1557).

Fiala, M. (2005, June 20-26). ARTag, a fiducial marker system using digital techniques. In *Proceedings of the 2005 IEEE Computer Society Conference on Computer Vision and Pattern Recognition (CVPR '05)* (Vol. 2) (pp. 590-596). Washington, DC: IEEE Computer Society

Fiege, L., Mühl, G., & Gärtner, F.C. (2002). Modular event-based systems. *The Knowledge Engineering Review, 17*(4), 359-388.

Fifer, W., & Bruno, F. (1987). The low-cost packet ration. *Proceedings of the IEEE, 75*(1), 33-42.

Fischer, C.S. (1992). America calling: A social history of the telephone. Berkeley, CA: University of California Press.

Fischer, G., & Nakakoji, K. (1991). Making design objects relevant to the task at hand. In *Proceedings of the Ninth National Conference on Artificial Intelligence (AAAI-91)* (pp. 67-73). Cambridge, MA: AAAI Press/The MIT Press.

Fitzmaurice, G. W., Ishii, H., & Buxton, W. (1995). Bricks: Laying the foundations for graspable user interfaces. In *Proceedings of the ACM Conference on Human Factors in Computing Systems (CHI),* Denver, Colorado (pp. 442-449). ACM Press.

Fjermestad, J., Pattern, K., & Bartolacci, M.R. (2006). Moving towards mobile third generation telecommunications standards: The good and bad of the anytime/anywhere solutions. *Communications of AIS, 17,* 71-89.

Fleck, M., Frid, M., Kindberg, T., O'Brien-Strain, E., Rajani, R., & Spasojevic, M. (2002). Rememberer: A tool for capturing museum visits. In *Proceedings of Ubicomp 2002* (pp. 48-55).

Fodor, G. A. (1998). *Ontologically controlled autonomous systems: Principles, operations, and architecture.* Kluwer Academic.

Fogarty, J., Hudson, S., Atkeson, C., Avrahami, D., Forlizzi, J., Kiesler, S. et al. (2004). Predicting human interruptability with sensors. *ACM Transactions on Computer-Human Interaction, 12*(1), 119-146.

Forlizzi, J., & Ford, S. (2000). The building blocks of experience: An early framework for interaction designers. In *Proceedings of DIS'00* (pp. 419-423). Brooklyn, NY: ACM Press.

Foster, I., Kesselman, C., Nick, J., & Tuecke, S. (2002). Grid services for distributed system integration. *Computer, 35*(6), 37-46.

Fox, B. (2001, November 21). "Mesh radio" can deliver super-fast Internet for all. *New Scientist.* Retrieved November 15, 2005, from http://www.newscientist.com/news/news.jsp?id=ns99991593

Freebersyser, J.A., & Leiner, B. (2001). A DoD perspective on mobile ad hoc networks. *Ad Hoc Networking.* Addison Wesley.

Friedman, B. (2004). Value sensitive design. In *Encyclopedia of human-computer interaction* (pp. 769-774). Great Barrington, MA: Berkshire Publishing Group.

Gadamer, H.G. (1982). *Reason in the age of science* (Trans.). Cambridge: MIT Press.

Gamma, E., Helm, R., Johnson, R., & Vlissides, J. (1994). *Design patterns: Elements of reusable object-oriented software.* Addison-Wesley.

Gamma, E., Helm, R., Johnson, R., & Vlissides, J. (1995). *Design patterns: Elements of reusable object-oriented software.* Addison-Wesley Professional.

Garcia-Luna-Aceves, J.J., & Fullmer, C.L. (1999). Floor acquisition multiple access (FAMA) in single-channel wireless networks. *Mobile Networks and Applications, 4*(3), 157-174.

Garlan, D., Siewiorek, D., Smailagic, A., & Steenkiste, P. (2002). Project Aura: Toward distraction-free pervasive computing. *IEEE Pervasive Computing, 1*(2), 22-31.

Gast, M.S. (2002). *802.11 wireless networks–the definitive guide.* CA: O'Reilly.

Gaver, W., Beaver, J., & Benford, S. (2003). Ambiguity as a resource for design. In *Proceedings of the ACM CHI*

2003 Human Factors in Computing Systems Conference (pp. 233-240). Ft. Lauderdale, FL.

Gaver, W.W., Dunne, A., & Pacenti, E. (1999). Cultural probes. Interactions Magazine, vi(1), 21-29.

Geier, J. (2002, April 15). Making the choice: 802.11a or 802.11g. *Wi-Fi Planet.* Retrieved October 16, 2005, from http://www.wi-fiplanet.com/tutorials/article.php/1009431

Gemmell, J., Lueder, R., & Bell, G. (2003). The MyLifeBits lifetime store. In *Proceedings of ACM SIGMM 2003 Workshop on Experiential Telepresence.*

Gong, L. (2001). JXTA: A networking programming environment. *IEEE Internet Computing, 5*(3), 88-95.

Göth, C., Häss, U.P., & Schwabe, G. (2004). Requirements for mobile learning games shown on a mobile game prototype. *Mobile Learning Anytime Everywhere*, 95-100. Learning and Skills development agency (LSDA).

Grace, P., Blair, G. S., & Samuel, S. (2005, January). A reflective framework for discovery and interaction in heterogeneous mobile environments. *Mobile Computing and Communications Review, 9*(1), 2-14.

Gross, D., & Yu, E. (2001). From non-functional requirements to design through patterns. *Requirements Engineering, 6*(1), 18-36.

Gu, T., Pung, H.K., & Zhang, D.Q. (2004). A Bayesian approach for dealing with uncertain contexts. In G. Kotsis (Ed.), *Proceedings of the 2nd International Conference on Pervasive Computing,* Vienna, Austria. Austrian Computer Society.

Gu, T., Pung, H.K., & Zhang, D.Q. (2004). Toward an OSGi-based infrastructure for context-aware applications. *IEEE Pervasive Computing, 3*(4), 66-74.

Guttman, E. (2001, May). Autoconfiguration for IP networking: Enabling local communication. *IEEE Internet Computing, 5*(3), 81-6.

Gwizdka. J. (2000). *What's in the context?* (Position Paper for Workshop on the What, Who, Where, When, Why, and How of Context-Awareness). The Hague: The Netherlands.

Haas, Z.J, & Deng, J. (2002). Dual busy tone multiple access (DBTMA) - a multiple access control scheme for ad hoc networks. *IEEE Transactions on Communications, 50*(6), 975-985.

Haas, Z.J., Pearlman, M.R., & Samar, P. (2002). *Internet-draft - the zone routing protocol (ZRP) for ad hoc networks.*

Hackos, J.T., & Redish, J.C. (1998). *User and task analysis for interface design.* Wiley Computer Publishing.

Hagen, P., Robertson, T., Kan, M., & Sadler, K. (2005). Emerging research methods for understanding mobile technology use. In Proceedings of the 19th Conference of the Computer-Human Interaction Special Interest Group (CHISIG) of Australia on Computer-human Interaction, ACM International Conference Proceeding Series (Vol. 122). Camberra, Australia.

Hall, E. (1966). *Distances in man: The hidden dimension.* Garden City, NY: Double Day.

Haller, M., Billinghurst, M., Leithinger, D., Leitner, J., & Seifried, T. (2005, December 5-8). Coeno, enhancing face-to-face collaboration. In 15th International Conference on Artificial Rea*lity and Telexistence (ICAT).* Christchurch, New Zealand.

Haller, M., Leithinger, D., Leitner, J., Seifried, T., Brandl, P., Zauner, J. et al. (2006, August). **The shared design space. In** *ACM SIGGRAPH 2006, Emerging Technologies,* Boston, MA.

Hamblen, M. (2005). Wi-Fi fails to connect with mobile users. ComputerWorld, *39*(37), 1, 69.

Hamill, J., & O'Sullivan, C. (2003, February). Virtual Dublin – A framework for real-time urban simulation. *Journal of the Winter School of Computer Graphics, 11*, 221-225.

Hannemann, J., & Kiczales, G. (2002, November). *Design pattern implementation in Java and AspectJ. In Proceedings of the 17th OOPSLA* (pp. 161-173).

Harper, R. (2003). People versus information: The evolution of mobile technology. In L. Chittaro (Ed.), Human computer interaction with mobile devices (pp. 1-15). Berlin, Germany: Springer, Berlin.

Heidegger, M. (1955, 1977). The question concerning technology (Trans.). In *The question concerning technology and other essays* (pp. 3-35). New York: Harper & Row Publishers.

Held, A., Buchholz, S., & Schill, A. (2002). Modeling of context information for pervasive computing applications. In *Proceedings of the 6th World Multiconference on Systemics Cybernetics and Informatics*, Orlando, Florida.

Held, G. (2003). *Securing wireless LANs.* Sussex: John Wiley & Sons.

Henderson, T. (2003, February 3). Vocera communication system: Boldly talking over the wireless LAN. *NetworkWorld.* Retrieved November 12, 2005, from http://www.networkworld.com/reviews/2003/0203rev.html

Hennessey, J., & Papanek, V. J. (1974). *Nomadic furniture: How to build and where to buy lightweight furniture that folds, collapses, stacks, knocks-down, inflates or can be thrown away and re-cycled.* New York: Pantheon Books.

Henricksen, K., Indulska, J., & Rakotonirainy, A. (2001, September). Infrastructure for pervasive computing: Challenges. In *Proceedings of Informatik 01: Workshop on Pervasive Computing* (pp. 214-222).

Henricksen, K., Indulska, J., & Rakotonirainy, A. (2002). Modeling context information in pervasive computing systems. In F. Mattern & M. Naghshineh (Eds.), In *Proceedings of the First International Conference on Pervasive Computing* (pp. 167-180). Zurich, Switzerland: Springer-Verlag.

Henricksen, K., Livingstone, S., & Indulska, J. (2004). Towards a hybrid approach to context modeling, reasoning, and interoperation. In *Proceedings of the First International Workshop on Advanced Context Modeling, Reasoning, and Management,* Nottingham, UK (pp. 54-61). ACM Press.

Hicks, M., & Nettles, S. (2005, November). Dynamic software updating. *ACM Transactions on Programming Languages and Systems, 27*(6), 1049-1096.

Hill, J., & Culler, D. (2002). MICA: A wireless platform for deeply embedded network. *IEEE Micro, 22*(6), 12-24.

Hill, J., Horton, M., Kling, R., & Krishnamurthy, L. (2004). The platform enabling wireless sensor networks. *Communications of the ACM, 47*(6), 41-46.

Hill, J., Szewczyk, R., Woo, A., Hollar, S., Culler, D.E., & Pister, K.S.J. (2000). System architecture directions for networked sensors. *Architectural Support for Programming Languages and Operating Systems,* 93-104.

Hill, W. C., Hollan, J. D., Wroblewski, D., & McCandless, T. (1992). Edit wear and read wear. In *Proceedings of ACM Conference on Human Factors in Computing Systems (CHI'92)* (pp. 3-9). New York: ACM Press.

Hill, W., & Hollan, J. (1993). History-enriched digital objects. In *Proceedings of Computers, Freedom: And Privacy (CFP'93).* Retrieved January 18, 2008, from http://archive.cpsr.net/conferences/cfp93/hill-hollan.html

Holtzblatt, K. (Ed.). (2005). Designing for the mobile device: Experiences, challenges, and methods. *Communications of the ACM, 48*(7), 32-66.

Hristova, N., & O'Hare, G.M.P. (2004). Ad-me: Wireless advertising adapted to the user location, device and emotions. In *Proceedings of the 37th Annual Hawaii International Conference on System Science.*

Hudson-Smith, A. (2002, January). 30 days in active worlds – Community, design and terrorism in a virtual world. In *The social life of avatars.* Schroeder, Springer-Verlag.

Hughes, C.E., Stapleton, C.B., Hughes, D.E., & Smith, E.M. (2005). Mixed reality in education, entertainment, and training. *IEEE Computer Graphics and Applications, 25*(6), 24-30.

Huhns, M. N., & Singh, M. P. (2005, January). Service-oriented computing: Key concepts and principles. *IEEE Internet Computing, 9*(1), 75-81.

Hulkko, S., Mattelmäki, T., Virtanen, K., & Keinonen, T. (2004). Mobile probes. In Proceedings of the Third

Nordic Conference on Human-Computer Interaction (pp. 43-51). ACM Press.

IDA Infocomm Survey. (2006). Annual survey of Infocomm usage in households and individuals 2006. Retrieved January 16, 2008, from http://www.ida.gov.sg/doc/Publications/Publications_Level2/2006_hh_exec%20summary.pdf

IDA. (2005). *Enhancing service, enriching experience, differentiating Singapore.* iN2015 (p. 14). Retrieved January 16, 2008, from http://www.in2015.sg/download_file.jsp?file=pdf/11_Tourism_Hospitality_and_Retail.pdf

IDA. (2005). *Innovation. Integration. Internationalisation.* iN2015 (p. 92). Retrieved January 16, 2008, from http://www.in2015.sg/download_file.jsp?file=pdf/01_iN2015_Main_Report.pdf

IDA. (2006). iN2015. Retrieved January 16, 2008, from http://www.in2015.sg/about.html

IEEE Standards for Wireless LAN Medium Access Control (MAC) and Physical Layer (PHY), Part 11:Technical Specifications. (1999).

IEEE. (2005). *IEEE 802.15 Working Groups for WPAN.* Retrieved November 7, 2005, from http://www.ieee802.org/15/

IEEE. (2005). *The IEEE 802.16 Working Group on Broadband Wireless Access Standards.* Retrieved November 22, 2005, from http://www.wirelessman.org

Inkpen, K. (1997). *Adapting the human computer interface to support collaborative learning environments for children.* Ph.D. Dissertation, Department of Computer Science, University of British Columbia.

INSTINCT Project home page. Retrieved January 16, 2008, from http://www.ist-instinct.org/

Isbell, C.L., Jr., Kearns, M., Kormann D., Singh, S., & Stone, P. (2001, July 30-August 3). Cobot in LambdaMOO: A social statistics agent. In *Proceedings of the Seventeenth National Conference on Artificial Intelligence AAAI 2000* (pp. 36-41). Austin, Texas.

Ishii, H., Underkoffler, J., Chak, D., Piper, B., Ben-Joseph, E., Yeung, L. et al. (2002). Augmented urban planning workbench: Overlaying drawings, physical models and digital simulation. In *IEEE and ACM International Symposium on Mixed and Augmented Reality ACM Press,* Darmstadt, Germany.

Israel, T. (2003). *Some place like home: Using design psychology to create ideal places.* Academy Press.

Issac, B., Hamid, K., & Tan, C.E. (2006). Analysis of demand driven ad-hoc routing protocols on performance and mobility. In *Proceedings of the International Wireless and Telecommunication Symposium 2006 (IWTS 2006),* Malaysia (136-141).

Issac, B., Hamid, K., & Tan, C.E. (2006). Analysis of single and mixed 802.11 networks and mobility architecture. In *Proceedings of the International Conference on Computing and Informatics (ICOCI 2006),* Malaysia.

ITU-T (2003). *Recommendation Z.150 (02/03), user requirements notation (URN) – Language requirements and framework.* Geneva, Switzerland.

Jacobs, J., Velez, M, & Gabbard, J. (2006). ARDEX: An integrated framework for handheld augmented reality. In *Proceedings of the First Annual Virginia Tech Center for Human-Computer Interaction Research Experience for Undergrads Symposium,* Blacksburg, VA (p. 6).

Jacobson, I., & Ng, P.-W. (2004). *Aspect-oriented software development with use cases.* Addison-Wesley.

Jambon, F. (2006, Aoruk 22-27). Reality testing of mobile devices: How to ensure analysis validity? In *Proceedings of CHI 2006,* Montreal, Canada.

Jenny P., Yvonne R., Helen S., David B., Simon H., & Tom C. (1994). *Human computer interaction.* Addison-Wesley Publishing Company.

Jiang, M., Li, J., & Tay, Y.-C. (1999). *Cluster based routing protocol functional specification.* Internet Draft, draft-ietf-manet-cbrpspec *.txt, work in progress.

Johnson, C.A., Delhagen, K., & Yuen, E.H. (2003, July 25). H*ighlight: US e-commerce hits $230 billion in 2008.*

(Business View Brief). Retrieved October 11, 2006, from Forester Research Incorporated at http://www.forrester.com

Johnson, D.B., Maltz, D.A., & Hu, Y.-C. (2004). *Internet draft - the dynamic source routing protocol for mobile ad hoc networks (DSR).*

Jones, M., & Marsden, G. (2006). *Mobile interaction design.* John Wiley & Sons Ltd.

Jordan, P. (2000). *Designing pleasurable products: An introduction to the new human factors.* London: Taylor & Francis.

Kaikkonen, A., Kallio, T., Kekäläinen, A., Kankainen, A., & Cankar, M. (2005, November). Usability testing of mobile applications: A comparison between laboratory and field testing. *Journal of Usability Studies, 1*(1), 4-16.

Kakehi, Y., Iida, M., Naemura, T., Shirai, Y., Matsushita, M., & Ohguro, T. (2005). Lumisight table: Interactive view-dependent tabletop display surrounded by multiple users. *IEEE Computer Graphics and Applications, 25*(1), 48-53.

Kankainen, A. (2003). UCPCD: User-centered product concept design. In *Proceedings of the conference on Designing for user experiences* (pp. 1-13). San Francisco, CA: ACM Press.

Karl, H., & Willig, A. (2005). *Protocols and architectures for wireless sensor networks.* Wiley.

Karn, P. (1990). MACA: A new channel access method for packet radio. In *Proceeding of 9th ARRL/CRRL Amateur Radio Computer Networking Conference.*

Kaufman, J., & Sears, J. (2006). GSPS: GumSpots positioning system. In *IPT 2006 Spring Show.* Retrieved January 25, 2008, from http://itp.nyu.edu/show/detail.php?project_id=539

Keefe, D., & Zucker, A. (2003). Ubiquitous computing projects: A brief history. In *Ubiquitous Computing Evaluation Consortium.* Arlington, VA: SRI.

Kelly, S., Hood, B., Lee, J. C., Sampat, M., & McCrickard, D. S. (2006). *Enabling opportunistic navigation through location-aware notification systems.* Pending paper submission.

Kelsey, J., Schneier, B., & Wagner, D. (1999). Key schedule weaknesses in SAFER+. In *Proceedings of the 2nd Advanced Encryption Standard Candidate Conference* (pp. 155-167).

Ketamo, H. (2002). mLearning for kindergarten's mathematics teaching. In *Proceedings of IEEE International Workshop on Wireless and Mobile Technologies in Education* (pp. 167-170). Vaxjo, Sweden.

Kjeldskov, J., & Graham, C. (2003). A review of mobile HCI research methods. In *Proceedings of 5th International Mobile HCI Conference*, Udine, Italy. Springer-Verlag.

Koch, A. S. (2004). *Agile software development: Evaluating the methods for your organization.* Artech House Publishers.

Kohonen, T. (1995) *Self-organizing maps.* Berlin, Germany: Springer.

Kravets, R., & Krishnan, P. (1998). Power management techniques for mobile communication. In *Proceeding of 4th Annual ACM/IEEE International Conference on Mobile Computing and Networking* (pp. 157-168).

Kray, C., Elting, C., Laakso, K., & Coors, V. (2003). Presenting route instructions on mobile devices. In *Proceedings of the 8th International Conference on Intelligent User Interfaces,* pp. 117-124 . Miami, Florida.

Kress, G.R., & Van Leeuwen, T. (2001). Multimodal discourse: The modes and media of contemporary communication. London: Hodder Headline.

Kurkovsky, S., & Harihar, K. (2006). Using ubiquitous computing in interactive mobile marketing. *Personal and Ubiquitous Computing, 10*(4), 227-240.

Laister, J., & Kober, S. (2002). Social aspects of collaborative learning in virtual learning environments. In *Proceedings of the Networked Learning Conference,* Sheffield, UK.

LaMarca, A., Chawathe, Y., Consolvo, S., Hightower, J., Smith, I., Scott, J., et al. (2005). Place lab: Device positioning using radio beacons in the wild. In *Proceedings of the 3rd International Conference on Pervasive Computing (Pervasive 2005),* Munich, Germany (pp. 134-151).

Lamming, M., & Flynn, M. (1994). Forget-me-not: Intimate computing in support of human memory. In *Proceedings of the FRIEND21 Symposium on Next Generation Human Interfaces* (pp. 125-128).

Lapeyrie, J.-B., & Turletti, T. (2003). FPQ: A fair and efficient polling algorithm with QoS support for Bluetooth piconet. In *Proceedings of the IEEE INFOCOM,* San Francisco, CA.

Laurel, B. (1993). *Computers as theatre.* Boston, MA: Addison-Wesley Longman Publishing Co., Inc.

Laurel, B. (2001). *Utopian entrepreneur.* Cambridge, MA: MIT Press.

Lee, A.J., & Wang, Y-T. (2003). Efficient data mining for calling path patterns in GSM network. *Information Systems, 28,* 929-948.

Lee, B., & Lee, R.S. (1995). How and why people watch TV: Implications for the future of interactive television. Journal of Advertising Research, 35(6).

Lee, C., Nordstedt, D., & Helal, S. (2003). Enabling smart spaces with OSGi. *IEEE Pervasive Computing, 2*(3), 89-94.

Lee, J. C., & McCrickard, D. S. (2007). Towards extreme(ly) usable software: Exploring tensions between usability and agile software development. In *Proceedings of the 2007 Conference on Agile Software Development (Agile '07),* Washington DC, (pp. 59-70).

Lee, J. C., Chewar, C. M., & McCrickard, D. S. (2005). Image is everything: Advancing HCI knowledge and interface design using the system image. In *Proceedings of the ACM Southeast Conference (ACMSE '05),* Kennesaw, GA (pp. 2-376-2-381).

Lee, J. C., Lin, S., Chewar, C. M., McCrickard, D. S., Fabian, A., & Jackson, A. (2004). From chaos to cooperation: Teaching analytic evaluation with LINK-UP. In *Proceedings of the World Conference on E-Learning in Corporate, Government, Healthcare, and Higher Education (E-Learn '04),* Washington, D.C. (pp. 2755-2762).

Lee, J. C., Wahid, S., McCrickard, D. S., Chewar, C. M., & Congleton, B. (2007). Understanding Usability: Investigating an Integrated Design Environment and Management System. *International Journal of Information Technology and Smart Education (ITSE), 2*(3), 161-175.

Lee, Y., Kozar, K.A., & Larsen, K.R.T. (2003). The technology acceptance model: Past, present, and future. *Communications of the Association for Information Systems, 12,* 752-780.

Leed, E.J. (1991). The mind of the traveller. New York: Basic Books.

Leow, M.C.L. (2005). *Exploring effectiveness of augmented reality for learning geometry in primary schools: A case study.* Unpublished masters thesis, Nanyang Technological University, Singapore.

Lepouosas, G., Charitos, D., Vassilakis, C., Charissi, A., & Halatsi, L. (2001, May 16-18). Building a VR museum in a mueseum. In *Proceedings of Virtual Reality International Conference,* Laval Virtual, France.

Liao, C. J., Yang, F. C., Hsu, K. (2005). A service-oriented approach for the pervasive learning grid. *Journal of Info. Science and Engineering, 21*(5), 959-971.

Liao, C., Guimbretière, F., & Hinckley, K. (2005, October 23-26). PapierCraft: A command system for interactive paper. In *Proceedings of the 18th Annual ACM Symposium on User interface Software and Technology,* Seattle, WA (pp. 241-244). New York, NY: ACM Press.

Lim, Y., Kim, J., Min, S., & Ma, J. (2001). Performance evaluation of the Bluetooth based public Internet access point. In *Proceedings of the 15th International Conference on Information Networking (ICOIN 2001)* (pp. 643-648).

Lin, E.-Y.A., Rabaey, J.M., & Wolisz, A. (2004). Power-efficient rendez-vous schemes for dense wireless sensor networks. In *Proceedings of IEEE ICC 2004,* Paris.

Lipman, R.R. (2002, September 23-25). Mobile 3D visualization for construction. In *Proceedings of the 19th International Symposium on Automation and Robotics in Construction* (pp. 53-58). Gaithersburg, Maryland.

Liu, C., & Kaiser, J. (2003). A survey of mobile ad hoc network routing protocols (Tech. Rep.).

Liu, J.,Wong, C.K., & Hui, K.K. (2003). An adaptive user interface based on personalized learning intelligent systems. *IEEE Intelligent Systems, 18*(2), 52-57.

Loureiro, E., Bublitz, F., Barbosa, N., Perkusich, A., Almeida, H., & Ferreira, G. (2006). A flexible middleware for service provision over heterogeneous networks. In *Proceedings of the 4th International Workshop on Mobile Distributed Computing*, Niagara Falls, New York. IEEE Computer Society. (Accepted for publication)

Loureiro, E., Ferreira, G., Almeida, H., & Perkusich, A. (2006). Pervasive computing: What is it anyway? In M. Lytras & A. Naeve (Eds.), *Ubiquitous and pervasive knowledge and learning management: Semantics, social networking and new media to their full potential.* Hershey, PA: Idea Group.

Loureiro, E., Oliveira, L., Almeida, H., Ferreira, G., & Perkusich, A. (2005, November). Improving flexibility on host discovery for pervasive computing middlewares. In *3rd International Workshop on Middleware for Pervasive and Ad hoc Computing.* Grenoble, France.

Luchini, K., Quintana, C., & Soloway, E. (2003, April 5-10). Pocket PiCoMap: A case study in designing and assessing a handheld concept mapping tool for learners. In *Proceedings of the ACM Computer-Human Interaction 2003, Human Factors in Computing Systems Conference* (pp. 321-328). Ft. Lauderdale, Florida.

Lull, J. (1980). The social uses of television. Human Communication Research, 6(3).

Lytras, M., Pouloudi, A., & Poulymenakou, A. (2002). Knowledge management convergence: Expanding learning frontiers. *Journal of Knowledge Management, 6*(1), 40-51.

Lyytinen, K., Varshney, U., Ackerman, M.S., Davis, G., Avital, M., Robey, D. et al. (2004). Surfing the next wave: Design and implememtation challenges of ubiquitous computing environments. *Communications of AIS, 13*, 697-716.

Ma, T., Kim, Y.D., Ma, Q., Tang, M., & Zhou, W. (2005). Context-aware implementation based on CBR for smart home. In *Proceedings of IEEE International Conference on Wireless and Mobile Computing, Networking and Communications,* Montreal, Canada (pp. 112-115). IEEE Computer Society.

Mackay, W.E., Velay, G., Carter, K., Ma, C., & Pagani, D. (1993, July). Augmenting reality: Adding computational dimensions to paper. *Communications of the ACM, 36*(7), 96-97.

Madan, R., & Lall, S. (2006). Distributed algorithms for maximum lifetime routing in wireless sensor networks. *IEEE Transactions on Wireless Communications, 5*(8).

Maitland, C.F., Van der Kar, E.A.M., Wehn de Montalvo, U., & Bouwman, H. (2005). Mobile information and entertainment services: Business models and service networks. *International Journal of Management and Decision Making, 6*(1), 47-63.

Malkin, G.S., & Stenstrup, M.E. (1995). Distance-vector routing. In *Routing in Communications Networks*, 83-98. Prentice Hall.

Mamdani, E. H. (1974). Applications of fuzzy algorithms for simple dynamic plants. *Proceedings of IEEE, 121*, 1585-1588.

Mankoff, J., Dey, A. K., Hsieh, G., Kientz, J., Lederer, S., & Ames, M. (2003). Heuristic evaluation of ambient displays. In *Proceedings of ACM Conference on Human Factors in Computing Systems 2003, CHI Letters, 5* (pp. 169-176). New York: ACM Press.

Marriott A., & Stallo, J. (2002, July 16).VHML: Uncertainties and problems, a discussion. In *Proceedings of the AAMAS-02 Workshop on Embodied Conversational Agents*, Bologna, Italy.

Marshall, B., Zhang, Y., Chen, H., Lally, A., Shen, R., Fox, E., & Cassel, L. (2003). Convergence of knowledge management and e-learning: The GetSmart experience.

In *Proceedings of the Joint Conference on Digital Libraries,* Houston, Texas (pp. 135-146). IEEE Computer Society.

Martin, F. G. (2001). *Robotic explorations: A hands-on introduction to engineering.* Prentice Hall.

Marwick, A.D. (2001). Knowledge management technology. *IBM Systems Journal, 40*(4), 814-831.

Mascolo, C., Capra, L., & Emmerich, W. (2002). Mobile computing middleware. *Advanced Lectures on Networking* (pp. 20-58). Springer-Verlag.

Masuoka, R., Labrou, Y., Parsia, B., Sirin, E. (2003). Ontology-enabled pervasive computing applications. *IEEE Intelligent Systems, 18*(5), 68-72.

Matthews, T., Dey, A. K., Mankoff, J., Carter, S., & Rattenbury, T. (2004). A toolkit for managing user attention in peripheral display. In *Proceedings of the Symposium on User Interface Software and Technology (UIST2004)* (pp. 247-256).

Mayer, J., Melzer, I., & Schweiggert, F. (2002). Lightweight plug-in-based application development. In M. Aksit, M. Mezini, & R. Unland (Eds.), *Revised Papers from the International Conference on Objects, Components, Architectures, Services, and Applications for a Networked World,* Erfurt, Germany (pp. 87-102). Springer-Verlag.

McArdle, G., Monahan, T., Bertolotto, M., & Mangina, E. (2005). Analysis and design of conceptual agent models for a virtual reality e-learning environment. *International Journal on Advanced Technology for Learning, 2*(3), 167-177.

McCarthy, J., Sasse, M. A., & Miras, D. (2004, April 20-24). Sharp or smooth? Comparing the effects of quantization vs. frame rate for streamed video. In *Proceedings of CHI 2004,* Vienna, Austria.

McCarthy, K. (2000, April 7). Anoto pen will change the world. *The Register.* Retrieved September 14, 2005, from http://www.theregister.co.uk/2000/04/07/anoto_pen_will_change/

McCarthy, M. (2005). *Adidas puts computer on new footing.* Retrieved January 16, 2008, from http://www.usatoday.com/money/industries/2005-03-02-smart-usat_x.htm

McGuigan, J. (2005, April). Towards a sociology of the mobile phone. *Human Technology.* Retrieved January 16, 2008, from http://www.humantechnology.jyu.fi/archives/april05.html

Mikropoulos, T.A., Chalkidis, A., Katsikis, A., & Emvalotis, A. (1998). Students' attitudes towards educational virtual environments. *Education and Information Technologies, 3,* 137-148.

Miller, L. (2005). Case study of customer input for a successful product. In *Proceedings of the Agile 2005 Conference,* Denver, CO (pp. 225-234).

Min, R., Bhadrwaj, M., Cho, S.-H., Shih, Sinha, A., Wang, A. et al. (2001). Low-power wireless sensor networks. In *Proceedings of the 14th International Conference on VLSI Design,* Bangalore, India.

Min, S.-H., & Han, I. (2005). Detection of the customer time-variant pattern for improving recommender systems. *Expert Systems with Applications, 28*(2), 189-199.

Mobile Taiwan Initative. (2004). Retrieved January 16, 2008, from http://www.roc-taiwan.org/uk/TaiwanUpdate/nsl022005h.htm

Monahan, T., McArdle, G., & Bertolotto, M. (2005, August 29-September 2). Using 3D graphics for learning and collaborating online. In *Proceedings of Eurographics 2005: Education Papers* (pp. 33-40). Dublin, Ireland.

Monahan, T., McArdle, G., Bertolotto, M., & Mangina, E. (2005, June 27- July 2). 3D user interfaces and multimedia in e-learning. In *Proceedings of the World Conference on Educational Multimedia, Hypermedia & Telecommunications (ED-MEDIA 2005),* Montreal, Canada.

Morley, D. (1986). Family television. Cultural power and domestic leisure. London, UK: Comedia.

Morris, M.R. (2006, April). *Supporting effective interaction with tabletop groupware.* Ph.D. Dissertation, Stanford University Technical Report.

Morris, M.R., Paepcke, A., Winograd, T., & Stamberger, J. (2006). TeamTag: Exploring centralized versus replicated controls for co-located tabletop groupware. In *Proceedings of CHI.*

Morrison, G. (2005, July/August). A camera-based input device for large interactive displays. *IEEE Computer Graphics and Applications, 25*(4), 52-57.

Morville, P. (2004, June). *User experience design.* Retrieved January 24, 2008, from http://semanticstudios.com/publications/semantics/000029.php

Mostéfaoui, G.K., Rocha, J.P., & Brézillon, P. (2004). Context-aware computing: A guide for the pervasive computing community. In F. Mattern & M. Naghshineh (Eds.), *Proceedings of the 2004 IEEE/ACS International Conference on Pervasive Services,* Beirut, Lebanon (pp. 39-48). IEEE Computer Society.

Mouratidis, H., Weiss, M., & Giorgini, P. (2005). Security patterns meet agent oriented software engineering: A complementary solution for developing secure information systems. *Conceptual modeling (ER)* (LNCS 2716, pp. 225-240). Springer-Verlag.

Mulder, I., ter Hofte, G.H., & Kort, J. (2005, August 30 – September 2). SocioXensor: Measuring user behaviour and user eXperience in conteXt with mobile devices. In L.P.J.J. Noldus, F. Grieco, L.W.S. Loijens & P.H. Zimmerman (Eds.), *Proceedings of Measuring Behavior 2005, the 5th International Conference on Methods and Techniques in Behavioral Research* (pp. 355-358). Wageningen, The Netherlands.

Mussbacher, G., & Amyot, D. (2001, October 3-5). A collection of patterns for use case maps. In *Proceedings of the 1st Latin American Conference on Pattern Languages of Programming (SugarLoafPLoP 2001),* Rio de Janeiro, Brazil.

Mussbacher, G., Amyot, D., & Weiss, M. (2006, September 11). Visualizing aspect-oriented requirements scenarios with use case maps. In *Proceedings of the International Workshop on Requirements Engineering Visualization (REV 2006),* Minneapolis/St. Paul, Minnesota.

Myers, E. (2003). *HomeRF overview and market positioning.* Retrieved January 19, 2008, from http://www.palowireless.com/homerf/

Mynatt, E.D., Back, M., Want, R., Baer, M., & Ellis, J.B. (1998). Designing audio aura. In Proceedings of CHI '98, Los Angeles, California (pp. 566-573). ACM.

Nair, S., Kumar, A., Sampat, M., Lee, J. C., & McCrickard, D. S. (2006). Alumni campus tour: Capturing the fourth dimension in location based notification systems. In *Proceedings of the ACM Southeast Conference (ACMSE '06),* Melbourne, FL (pp. 500-505).

Nakakoji, K., & Fischer, G. (1995). Intertwining knowledge delivery, construction, and elicitation: A process model for human-computer collaboration in design. *Knowledge-Based Systems Journal: Special Issue on Human-Computer Collaboration, 8*(2-3), 94-104. Oxford, UK: Butterworth-Heinemann Ltd.

National Computer Board. (1992). *A vision of an intelligent island: IT2000 report.* Singapore: National Computer Board.

Navarro-Prieto, R., & Conaty, G. (2003). User requirements for SDR terminals. In M. Dillinger, K. Madani & N. Alonistioti (Eds.), *Software defined radio: Architectures, systems and functions* (pp. 27- 45). John Wiley & Sons.

NEST Project Web page. (2006). Retrieved January 21, 2008, from http://webs.cs.berkeley.edu/nest-index.html.

Newman, W., & Wellner, P. (1992). A desk supporting computer-based interaction with paper documents. In *Proceedings of the ACM Conference on Human Factors in Computing Systems (CHI),* Monterey, California (pp. 587-592). ACM Press.

Nguyen, G.D., Weiselthier, J.E., & Ephremides, A. (2003). Multiple-access for multiple destinations in ad-hoc networks. In *Proceedings WiOpt 03.*

Nielsen, J. (1993). *Usability engineering,* Academic Press.

Niemalä, E., & Latvakoski, J. (2004, October). Survey of requirements and solutions for ubiquitous software. In *Proceedings of the 3rd International Conference of Mobile and Ubiquitous Multimedia* (pp. 71-78). College Park, MD: ACM Press.

Nijholt, A. (2000). Agent-supported cooperative learning environments. In *Proceedings of the International Workshop on Advanced Learning Technologies* (pp. 17-18). Palmerston North, New Zealand.

Nishigaki, K., Yasumoto, K., Shibata, N., Ito, M., & Higashino, T. (2005). Framework and rule-based language for facilitating context-aware computing using information appliances. In *Proceedings of the First International Workshop on Services and Infrastructure for the Ubiquitous and Mobile Internet* (pp. 345-351). Columbus, Ohio: IEEE Computer Society.

Noguchi, H., Mori, T., & Sato, T. (2003, October). Network middleware for utilization of sensors in room. In *Proceedings of IEEE/RSJ International Conference on Intelligent Robots and Systems,* Las Vegas, NV (Vol. 2, pp. 1832-1838).

Nokia press release. (2006, March 8). *Mobile TV set to be very popula*r. Retrieved January 16, 2008, from http://press.nokia.com/PR/200603/1038209_5.html

Norman, D. (1998). *The psychology of everyday things.* Basic Books.

Norman, D.A. (2004). *Emotional design: Why we love (or hate) everyday things.* New York: Basic Books.

O'Hare, G.M.P., & O'Grady, M.J. (2003). Gulliver's genie: A multi-agent system for ubiquitous and intelligent content delivery. *Computer Communications, 26*(11), 1177-1187.

O'Sullivan, C., Cassell, J., Vilhjálmsson, H., Dobbyn, S., Peters, C., Leeson W., et al. (2002). Crowd and group simulation with levels of detail for geometry, motion and behaviour. In *Proceedings of the Third Irish Workshop on Computer Graphics* (pp. 15-20).

Okoli, C., Ives, B., Jessup, L.M., & Valacich, J.S. (2002). The mobile conference information system: Unwiring academic conferences with wireless mobile computing. *Communications of AIS, 9,* 180-206.

Oliver, B., & Wright, F. (2003). E-learning to m-learning: What are the implications and possibilities for using mobile computing in and beyond the traditional classroom? In *Proceedings of the 4th International Conference on Information Communication Technologies in Education,* Samos, Greece.

Ong, H., Weiss, M., & Araujo, I. (2003, March). Rewriting a pattern language to make it more expressive. *Hot topic on the expressiveness of pattern languages, ChiliPLoP.* Carefree, USA.

Open University. (2005). *Media relations, fact sheet series, history of the open university.* Retrieved October 11, 2006, from http://www3.open.ac.uk/media/factsheets

Pace, S., Frost, G. P., Lachow, I., Frelinger, D., Fossum, D., Wassem, D. et al. (1995). *The global positioning system: Assessing national policies* (Ref. No. MR-614-OSTP). Rand Corporation.

Paciga, M., & Lutfiyya, H. (2005). Herecast: An open infrastructure for location-based services using WiFi. In *Proceedings of Wireless and Mobile Computing, Networking, and Communications (WiMoB 2005),* Montreal, Canada (pp. 21-28).

Page, C. (2005). Mobile research strategies for a global market. *Communications of ACM, 48*(7), 42-48.

Palen, L., Salzman, M., & Youngs, E. (2000). Going wireless: Behavior of practices of new mobile phone users. In Proceedings of CSCW 2000 (pp. 201-210).

Pan, Z., Cheok, A.D., Yang, H., Zhu, J., & Shi, J. (2006). Virtual reality and mixed reality for virtual learning environments. *Computers & Graphics, 30,* 20-28.

Papagiannakis, G., Hoste, G.L., Foni, A., & Magnenat-Thalmann, N. (2001, October 25-27). Real-time photo realistic simulation of complex heritage edifices. In *Proceedings of the 7th International Conference on Virtual Systems and Multimedia VSMM01* (pp. 218-227). Berkeley, California.

Papagiannakis, G., Schertenleib, S., O'Kennedy, B., Poizat, M., Magnenat-Thalmann, N., Stoddart, A., et al. (2005, February). Mixing virtual and real scenes in the site of ancient Pompeii. Computer Animation and Virtual Worlds, 16(1), 11-24.

Papazoglou, M. P. (2003, December). Service-oriented computing: Concepts, characteristics and directions. In *Proceedings of Fourth International Conference on Web Information Systems Engineering* (pp. 3-12). Rome, Italy: IEEE Computer Society.

Papazoglou, M. P., & Georgakopoulos, D. (2003, April). Service oriented computing. *Communications of the ACM, 46*(10), 24-28.

Park, S. H., Won, S. H., Lee, J. B., & Kim, S. W. (2003). Smart home - digitally engineered domestic life. *Personal and Ubiquitous Computing, 7*(3-4), 189-196.

Parker, J. K., Mandryk, R. L., & Inkpen, K. M. (2006, September). Integrating point and touch for interaction with digital tabletop displays. *IEEE Computer Graphics and Applications, 26*(5), 28-35.

Pascoe, J., Ryan, N.S., & Morse, D.R. (1999). Issues in developing context-aware computing. In Proceedings of the International Symposium on Handheld and Ubiquitous Computing (pp. 208-221). Karlsruhe, Germany: Springer-Verlag.

Perkins, C., Belding-Royer, E., & Das, S. (2003). Ad hoc on-demand distance vector (AODV) routing. *IETF Request for Comments, 3561.*

Perkins, C.E. (1997). Mobile IP. *IEEE Communications, 35*(5), 84-99.

Perkins, C.E., & Bhagwat, P. (1994). Highly dynamic destination-sequenced distance-vector routing (DSDV) for mobile computers. *Computer Communications Review, 24*(4), 234.

Perry, M., O'Hara, K., Sellen, A., Harper, R., & Brown, B.A.T. (2001). Dealing with mobility: Understanding access anytime, anywhere. ACM Transactions on Computer-Human Interaction, 4(8), 1-25. ToCHI.

Petrelli, D., Not, E., Strapparava, C., Stock, O., & Zancaro, M. (2000). Modeling context is like taking pictures. In *Proceedings of the Workshop on Context Awareness.* The Hague: The Netherlands

Petriu, D., & Woodside, M. (2002). Software performance models from system scenarios in use case maps. *Computer performance evaluation / TOOLS 2002* (LNCS 2324, pp. 141-158). Springer-Verlag.

Pooley, C.G., Turnbull, J., & Adams, M. (2005). A mobile century? Changes in everyday mobility in Britain in the Twentieth Century. Aldershot, Hampshire: Ashgate.

Preece, J., & Maloney-Krichmar, D. (2003). Online communities: Focusing on sociability and usability. In J.A. Jacko & A. Sears (Eds.), Handbook of human-computer interaction. London: Lawrence Erlbaum Associates Inc.

Preece, J., Rogers, Y., & Sharp, H. (2002). *Interaction design: Beyond buman-computer interaction.* New York: John Wiley and Sons Ltd.

Prendinger, H., Descamps, S., & Ishizuka, M. (2004). MPML: A markup language for controlling the behavior of life-like characters. *Journal of Visual Languages and Computing, 15*, 183-203.

Preuveneers, D., Rigole, P., Vandewoude, Y., & Berbers, Y. (2005, November). Middleware support for component-based ubiquitous and mobile computing applications. In *Demo Session of the 7th International Middleware Conference.* Grenoble, France.

Priyantha, N. B., Chakraborty, A., & Balakrishnan, H. (2000). The cricket location-support system. In *Proceedings of the Sixth Annual International Conference on Mobile Computing and Networking (MOBICOM 2000),* Boston, MA (32-43).

Raatikainen, A.K., Christensen, H.B., & Nakajima, T. (2002). Application requirements for middleware for mobile and pervasive systems. *Mobile Computing Communication Review, 6*(4), 16-24.

Raatikainen, K., Christensen, H. B., & Nakajima, T. (2002, October). Application requirements for middleware for mobile and pervasive systems. *Mobile Computing and Communications Review, 6*(4), 16-24.

Raghupathiy, L., Grisoniz, L., Faurey, F., Marchalz, D., Caniy, M., & Chaillouz, C., (2004). An intestinal surgery simulator: Real-time collision processing and visualization. *IEEE Transactions on Visualization and Computer Graphics, 10*(6), 708-718.

Rakkolainen, I., & Vainio, T. (2001). A 3D city info for mobile users. *Computers & Graphics (Special Issue on Multimedia Appliances), 25*(4), 619-625.

Ramsborg, G. (2002). *Dynamics of seating arrangements: Identification of points of power around a conference table.* Retrieved January 27, 2008, from http://www.ramsborg.com/etopic/Nov_2002/index.html

Ranganathan, A., Muhtadi, J.A., & Campbell, R.H. (2004). Reasoning about uncertain contexts in pervasive computing environments. *IEEE Pervasive Computing, 3*(2), 62-70.

Rao, B., & Minakakis, L. (2003). Evolution of mobile location-based services. *Communications of the ACM, 46*(12), 61-65.

Redfern, S., & Naughton, N. (2002). Collaborative virtual environments to support communication and community in Internet-based distance education. In *Proceedings of the Informing Science and IT Education, Joint International Conference* (pp. 1317-1327). Cork, Ireland.

Reed, J.H. (Ed.). (2005). *An introduction to ultra wideband communication systems.* Prentice Hall.

Reid, N.P., & Seide, R. (2002). *Wi-Fi (802.11) network handbook.* McGraw-Hill.

Rekimoto, J. (1997, October 14-17). Pick-and-drop: A direct manipulation technique for multiple computer environments. In *Proceedings of the 10th Annual ACM Symposium on User Interface Software and Technology,* Banff, Canada (pp. 31-39).

Rekimoto, J. (1999). Time-machine computing: A time-centric approach for the information environment. In *Proceedings of the ACM Symposium on User Interface Software and Technology (UIST'99)* (pp. 45-54).

Rekimoto, J. (2002). SmartSkin: An infrastructure for freehand manipulation on interactive surfaces. In *CHI 2002.*

Rekimoto, J., & Saitoh, M. (1999). Augmented surfaces: A spatially continuous work space for hybrid computing environments. In *CHI '99, Proceedings of the SIGCHI conference on Human Factors in Computing Systems.*

Rickel, J., & Johnson, W.L. (1997). Integrating pedagogical capabilities in a virtual environment agent. In *Proceedings of the First International Conference on Autonomous Agents* (pp. 30-38). California.

Rickel, J., & Johnson, W.L. (1999). Virtual humans for team training in virtual reality. In *Proceedings of the Ninth International Conference on AI in Education* (pp. 578-585).

Riedl, R., Barrett, T., Rowe, J., Vinson, W., & Walker, S. (2001). Sequence independent structure in distance learning. In *Proceedings of Society for Information Technology and Teacher Education INternational Conference* (pp. 1191-1193)

Rischbeck, T., & Watson, P. (2002, March 24-28). A scalable, multi-user VRML server. In *Proceedings of the IEEE Virtual Reality Conference* (pp. 199-207). Orlando, Florida.

Rising, L. (2000). *Pattern almanac 2000.* Addison-Wesley.

Robinson, J., & Wakeman, I. (2003). The scooby event based pervasive computinginfrastructure. In *Proceedings of the Postgraduate Networking Conference,* Liverpool, UK.

Rodoplu, V., & Meng, T.H.-Y. (1999). Minimum energy mobile wireless networks. *IEEE Journal on Selected Areas in Communications, 17*(8), 1333-1344.

Rogers, Y., Price, S., Randell, C., Fraser, D. S., & Weal, M. (2005). Ubi-learning integrates indoor and outdoor experiences. *Communications of the ACM, 48*(1), 55-59.

Romer, K., & Mattern, F. (2004). The design space of wireless sensor networks. *IEEE Wireless Communications Magazine, 11*(6).

Rosson, M.B., & Carroll, J. M. (2002). *Usability engineering: Scenario-based development of human-computer interaction.* New York: Morgan Kaufman.

Rosson, M. B., & Carroll, J. M. (2002). Usability engineering in practice. In *Usability Engineering-Scenario-Based Development of Human-Computer Interaction* (pp. 349-360). San Francisco: Morgan Kaufmann Publishers.

Rouhana, N., & Horlait, E. (2002). BWIG: Bluetooth Web Internet Gateway. In *Proceedings of IEEE Symposium on Computer and Communications (ISCC 2002)* (pp. 679-684).

Roy, J.-F., Kealey, J., & Amyot, D. (2006, May). Towards integrated tool support for the user requirements notation. In *Proceedings of the Fifth Workshop on System Analysis and Modelling (SAM'06)*, Kaiserslautern, Germany.

Royer, E.M., & Toh, C-K. (1999). A review of current routing protocols for ad hoc mobile wireless networks. *IEEE Personal Communications*, 46-55.

Rubio, D. (2004, October 20). VoiceXML promised voice-to-Web convergence. *NewsForge.* Retrieved November 23, 2005, from http://www.newsforge.com/article.pl?sid=04/10/15/1738253

Ryan, J., O'Sullivan, C., Bell, C., & Mooney, R. (2004). A virtual reality electrocardiography teaching tool. In *Proceeding of the Second International Conference in Biomedical Engineering* (pp. 250-253), Innsbruck, Austria.

Ryan, N. (1999, August 6). *ConteXtML:* Exchanging contextual information between a mobile client and the FieldNote server. Retrieved October 10, 2006, from http://www.cs.kent.ac.uk/projects/mobicomp/fnc/ConteXtML.html

Sagduyu, Y.E., & Ephremides, A. (2003). Energy-efficient collision resolution in wireless ad hoc networks. In *Proceedings of IEEE Infocom.*

Saha, D., & Mukherjee, A. (2003). Pervasive computing: A paradigm for the 21st century. *Computer, 36*(3), 25-31.

Sampat, M., Kumar, A., Prakash, A., & McCrickard, D. S. (2005). Increasing understanding of a new environment using location-based notification systems. In *Proceedings of 11th InternationalConference on Human-Computer Interaction (HCII '05).* Las Vegas, NV.

Satyanarayanan, M. (1996). Fundamental challenges in mobile computing. In *Proceedings of the 15th Annual ACM Symposium on Principles of Distributed Computing* (pp. 1-7). Philadelphia: ACM Press.

Satyanarayanan, M. (2001). Pervasive computing: Vision and challenges. *IEEE Personal Communication, 8*(4), 10-17.

Satyanarayanan, M. (2002). The evolution of coda. *ACM Transactions on Computer Systems, 20*(2), 2-25.

ScatterWeb. Retrieved January 21, 2008, from http://www.scatterweb.com

Schilit, B., & Theimer, M. (1994). Disseminating active map information to mobile hosts. *IEEE Network, 8*(5), 22-32.

Schilling, A., & Coors, V. (2003, Septmeber). 3D maps on mobile devices. In *Proceedings from the Design Kartenbasierter Mobiler Dienste Workshop,* Stuttgart, Germany.

Schnaider, M., Schwald, B., Seibert, H., & Weller, T. (2003). MEDARPA - An augmented reality system for supporting minimally invasive interventions. In *Proceedings of Medicine Meets Virtual Reality 2003* (pp. 312-314). Amsterdam, The Netherlands.

Schrick, B. (2002). Wireless broadband in a box. *IEEE Spectrum.* Retrieved November 19, 2005, from http://www.spectrum.ieee.org/WEBONLY/publicfeature/jun02/wire.html

Schurgers, C., Tsiatsis, V., Ganeriwal, S., & Srivastava, M. (2002). Optimising sensor networks in the energy-latency-density design space. *IEEE Transactions on Mobile Computing, 1*(1), 7-80.

Schwartz, E. (2001, September 26). Free wireless networking movement gathers speed. *InfoWorld.* Retrieved

December 5, 2005, from http://www.infoworld.com/articles/hn/xml/01/09/26/010926hnfreewireless.xml

Sciacchitano, B., Cerwinski, C., Brown, I., Sampat, M., Lee, J. C., & McCrickard, D. S. (2006). Intelligent library navigation using location-aware systems. In *Proceedings of the ACM Southeast Conference (ACMSE '06),* Melbourne, FL (pp. 371-376).

Scott, S.D., Carpendale, M.S.T., & Inkpen, K.M. (2004). Territoriality in collaborative tabletop workspace. In *Proceedings of CSCW 2004 (pp.* 294-303).

Scott, S.D., Grant, K.D., & Mandryk, R.L. (2003, September). System guidelines for co-located, collaborative work on a tabletop display. In *Proceedings of ECSCW'03, European Conference Computer-Supported Cooperative Work 2003.*

Sengers, P., & Gaver, W. (2005). Designing for interpretation. In *Proceedings of Human-Computer Interaction International (HCII) Conference,* Las Vegas, NV.

Shardanand, U., & Maes, P. (1995). Social information filtering: Algorithms for automating word of mouth. In *Proceedings of the ACM Conference on Human Factors in Computing Systems (CHI'95)* (pp. 210-217). New York: ACM Press.

Shaw, M., & Garlan, D. (1996). *Software architecture: Perspectives on an emerging discipline.* Prentice Hall.

Shedroff, N. (1995). *100 years.* Paper presented at the VISCOMM 1995conference, San Francisco, CA. Retrieved January 24, 2008, from http://www.nathan.com/thoughts/100/index.html

Shedroff, N. (2000). Information interaction design: A unified field theory of design. In R. Jacobson (Ed.), *Information design.* Cambridge, MA: MIT Press.

Shedroff, N. (2004). Research methods for designing effective experiences. InB. Laurel (Ed.), *Design research: Methods and perspectives.* Cambridge, MA: MIT Press.

Shen, C., Vernier, F.D., Forlines, C., & Ringel, M. (2004, April 24-29). DiamondSpin: An extensible toolkit for around-the-table interaction. In *Proceedings of the SIGCHI Conference on Human Factors in Computing Systems,* Vienna, Austria (pp. 167-174). New York, NY: ACM Press.

Shi, X., & Stromberg, G. (2007). SyncWUF: An ultra low power MAC protocol for wireless sensor networks. *IEEE Transactions on Mobile Computing, 6*(1).

Shilit, B. N., Adams, N., & Want, R. (1994, December). Context-aware computing applications. In *Proceedings of the IEEE Workshop on Mobile Computing Systems and Applications* (pp. 85-90). Santa Cruz, CA: IEEE Computer Society.

Shin, Y.S. (2003). Virtual experiment environments design for science education. In *Proc. Int'l Conference on Cyberworlds 2003, IEEE Computer Society* (pp. 388-395).

Shirai, Y., Nakakoji, K., Yamamoto, Y., & Giaccardi, E. (2005). A framework for presentation and use of everyday interaction histories. In *Proceedings of 1st Korea-Japan Joint Workshop on Ubiquitous Computing and Networking Systems (ubiCNS2005)* (pp. 257-261).

Shirai, Y., Owada, T., Kamei, K., & Kuwabara, K. (2003). Optical stain: Amplifying vestiges of a real environment by light projection. In *Proceedings of the 10th International Conference on Human-Computer Interaction (HCI International 2003), 2* (pp. 283-287).

Sicre, J. L., Duffy, A., Navarro-Prieto, R. et al. (2004, November 3-4). Three user scenarios on the joint usage of mobile telco and TV services for customers on the move. In *WWRF12 meeting – WG1.* Toronto, Canada.

Singh, S., & Raghavendra, C.S. (1998). PAMAS – power aware multi-access protocol with signalling for ad hoc networks. *ACM Computer Communication Review.*

Sinha, A., & Chandrakasan, A. (2001). Dynamic power management in wireless sensor networks. *IEEE Design and Test of Computers, 18*(2), 62-74.

Skog, T. (2004). Activity wallpaper: Ambient visualization of activity information. In *Proceedings of the 2004 Conference on Designing Interactive Systems (DIS2004)* (pp. 325-328).

Södergård, C. (2003). *Mobile television - technology and user experiences. Report on the Mobile-TV project.* Espoo: VTT Information Technology.

Spiekermann, S. (2004). General aspects of location-based services. In J. Schiller & A. Voisard (Eds.), *Location-based service* (pp. 9-26). California: Morgan Kaufmann.

Spigel, L. (1992). Make room for TV: Television and the family ideal in postwar America. Chicago: University of Chicago Press.

Stanford, V., Garofolo, J., Galibert, O., Michel, M., & Laprun, C. (2003). The NIST smart space and meeting room projects: Signals, acquisition, annotation and metrics. In *Proceedings of the 2003 IEEE Conference on Acoustics, Speech, and Signal Processing*, Hong Kong, China. IEEE Computer Society.

Stasko, J. T., Miller, T., Pousman, Z., Plaue, C., & Ullah, O. (2004). Personalized peripheral information awareness through information art. In *Proceedings of Ubicomp 2004* (pp. 18-25).

Stathopulos, T., Kapur, R., Heidemann, J., & Estrin, D. (2003). A remote code update mechanism for wireless sensor networks (Tech. Rep. cens tr-30*). Centre for Embedded Networked Computing.*

Steen, M., de Koning, N., & Mulder, I. (2005). *Empathic design and participatory research for the development of we-centric services for a police organisation.* Enschede, The Netherlands: Freeband.

Steen, M., van Eijk, R., Gunther, H., Hooreman, S., & Koning, N. (2005, October 13). We-centric services for police officers and informal carers. In *Proceedings HCI Close to you.* The Hague, The Netherlands.

Stemm, M., & Katz, R.H. (1997). Measuring and reducing energy consumption of network interfaces in hand-held devices. *IEICE Transactions on Communications, E80-B*(8), 1125-1131.

Stojmenovic, I., & Lin, X. (2001). Power aware localized routing in wireless networks. *IEEE Trans. On Parallel and Distributed Systems, 12*(10).

Strategies Group. (2000). *European wireless location services.* Retrieved January 21, 2008, from http://www.findarticles.com/p/articles/mi_m0BFP/is_2000_April_10/ ai_61430512

Streitz, N., Prante, P., Röcker, C., van Alphen, D., Magerkurth, C., & Stenzel, R. (2003). Plewe ambient displays and mobile devices for the creation of social architectural spaces: Supporting informal communication and social awareness in organizations. In *Public and situated displays: Social and interactional aspects of shared display technologies* (pp. 387-409). Kluwer Publishers.

Streitz, N., Prante, T., Rocker, C., Alphen, D.V., Magerkurth, C., Stenzel, R., et al. (2003). Ambient displays and mobile devices for the creation of social architectural spaces. In K. O'Hara et al. (Eds.), *Public and situated displays: Social and interactional aspects of shared display technologies* (pp. 387-409). Dordrecht, The Netherland: Kluwer Academic Publisher.

Strong, D.M., Lee, Y.W., & Wang, R.Y. (1997). Data quality in context. *Communications of the ACM, 40*(5), 103-110.

Suchman, L. A. (1987). *Plans and situated actions: The problem of human-machine communications.* Cambridge, UK: Cambridge University Press.

Sun, J.Z., & Savoula, J. (2002). Mobility and mobility management: A conceptual framework. In *Proceedings of the 10th IEEE International Conference on Networks* (pp. 205-210). Singapore: IEEE Computer Society.

Szypersky, C. (1999, December). *Component software - beyond object-oriented programming.* Addison Wesley Longman.

Tabletop. (2006). *Proceedings of the First IEEE International Workshop on Horizontal Interactive Human-Computer Systems,* Adelaide, Australia. IEEE Press.

Taibi, T., & Ngo, D.C.L. (2001). Why and how should patterns be formalized. *Journal of Object-Oriented Programming (JOOP), 14*(4), 8-9.

Takagi, T., & Sugeno, M. (1985) Fuzzy identification of systems and its applications to modeling and control.

IEEE Transactions on Systems, Man and Cybernetics, 15(1), 116-132.

Talucci, F., Gerla, M., & Fratta, L. (1997). MACA-BI (MACA by Invitation) a receiver oriented access protocol for wireless multihop networks. In *Proceedings of International Symposium on Personal, Indoor and Mobile Radio Communications,* Helsinki, Finland (pp. 435-439).

Terrenghi, L., Hilliges, O., & Butz, A. (2007). Kitchen stories: Sharing recipes with the living cookbook [Special issue]. *Personal and Ubiquitous Computing, 11*(5), 409-414. London: Springer.

Terrenghi, L., Kronen, M., & Valle, C. (2005). Usability requirement for mobile service scenarios. In *Proceedings of HCI International Conference*, Las Vegas, NV.

Terveen, L., Hill, W., Amento, B., McDonald, D., & Creter, J. (1997). PHOAKS: A system for sharing recommendations. *Communications of the ACM, 40*(3), 59-62.

Theng, Y.L., Lim, M.L., Liu, W., & Cheok, A. (2007, July 22-27). Mixed reality systems for learning: A pilot study understanding user perceptions and acceptance. Full Paper. Accepted to HCI International 2007 (HCII2007), Beijing, China.

Three.com.hk. (2006). *Location-based mobile workforce management (WorkPlace).* Retrieved January 21, 2008, from http://dualband.three.com.hk/website/template?pageid=d81240&lang=chi

Tiengo, W., Costa, E., Tenório, L. E., & Loureiro, E. (2006, January). An architecture for personalization and recommendation system for virtual learning community libraries. In *Proceedings of The Fifth IASTED International Conference on Web-based Education.* Puerto Vallarta, Mexico: Acta Press.

Tollmar, K., & Persson, J. (2002). Understanding remote presence. In *Proceedings of the Second ACM Nordic Conference on Human-Computer Interaction (NORDCHI),* Aarhus, Denmark (pp. 41-50). ACM Press.

Tom, H. (1994). The geographic information systems (GIS) standards infrastructure. *StandardView, 2*(3), 33-142.

Tse, E. (2004, November). *The single display groupware toolkit.* M.Sc. Thesis, Department of Computer Science, University of Calgary, Calgary, Alberta, Canada.

Tseng, Y.-C., Hsu, C.-S., & Hsieh, T.-Y. (2002). Power-saving protocols for IEEE 802.11-based multi-hop ad hoc networks. In *Proceedings IEEE INFOCOM.*

Turner, N., Cairns, P., & Jones, M. (2006). *Dispersing the interactivity: Mobiles and electronic programme guides.* Paper presented at the Investigating New User Experience Challenges in iTV: Mobility & Sociability Workshop CHI'06. Retrieved January 16, 2008, from http://soc.kuleuven.be/com/mediac/chi2006workshop/files/dispersing_the_interactivity.pdf

UK Ubinet. Retrieved January 21, 2008, from http://www-dse.doc.ic.ac.uk/Projects/UbiNet/links.htm

Ullmer, B., & Ishii, H. (1997). The metaDESK: Models and prototypes for tangible user interfaces. In *Proceedings of ACM Symposium on User Interface Software and Technology (UIST)* (pp. 223-232). ACM Press.

UNESCO (2002). *Open and distance learning, trends policy and strategy consideration. United Nations Educational Scientific and Cultural Organisation (UNESCO)* Report 2002. Retrieved October 11, 2006, from http://unesdoc.unesco.org/images/0012/001284/128463e.pdf

URN Focus Group (2003, September). *Draft Rec. Z.151 – Goal-oriented requirement language (GRL).* Geneva, Switzerland.

URN Focus Group (2003, September). *Draft Rec. Z.152 – Use case map notation (UCM).* Geneva, Switzerland.

van Kranenburg, H., Bargh, M.S., Iacob, S., & Peddemors, A. (2006). A context management framework for supporting context aware distributed applications. *IEEE Communications Magazine, 44*(8), 67-74.

van Kranenburg, H., Snoeck, N., & Mulder, I. (2006, April 26-28). Context aware support targeting plausible and usable results - from reactive, via pro-active to pragmatic systems. In *Proceedings of the 16th Wireless World Research Forum Meeting the needs of Emerging Markets (WWRF16),* Shanghai, China.

Vemuri, S., Schmandt, C., Bender, W., Tellex, S., & Lassey, B. (2004). An audio-based personal memory aid. In *Proceedings of Ubicomp2004* (pp. 400-417).

Venkatesh, V., & Davis, F.D. (2000). A theoretical extension of the technology acceptance model: Four longitudinal field studies. *Management Science, 46*(2), 186-204.

Venkatesh, V., & Morris, M.G. (2000). Why don't men ever stop to ask for directions? Gender, social influence, and their role in technology acceptance and usage behavior. *MIS Quarterly, 24*(1), 115-139.

Vogel, D., & Balakrishnan, R. (2004). Interactive public ambient displays: Transitioning from implicit to explicit, public to personal, interaction with multiple users. In *Proceedings of ACM Symposium on User Interface Software and Technology (UIST2004)* (pp. 137-146).

Waldo, J. (1999). The Jini architecture for network-centric computing. *Communications of the ACM, 42*(7), 76-82.

Wan, D. (2000). Magic wardrobe: Situated shopping from your own bedroom. *Personal and Ubiquitous Computing, 4*(4), 234-237.

Want, R., & Pering, T. (2005). System challenges for ubiquitous & pervasive comput-ing. In *ICSE'05, ACM* 1-58113-963-2/05/00.

Want, R., Hopper, A., Falcao, V., & Gibbons, J. (1992). The active badge location system. *ACM Transactions on Information Systems, 40*(1), 91-102.

Wassermann, R., & Cheng, B. (2003). *Security patterns* (Tech. Rep. No. MSU-CSE-03-23). Michigan State University.

Watson, A., & Sasse, M.A. (1996). Evaluating audio and video quality in low-cost multimedia conferencing systems. Interacting with Computers, 8(3), 255-275.

Weiser, M. (1991). The computer for the 21st century. *Scientific American, 265*(3), 94-104.

Weiser, M. (1993). Ubiquitous computing. *Computer, 26*(10), 71-72.

Weiser, M. (1993). Some computer science issues in ubiquitous computing. *Communications of the ACM, 36*(7), 75-84.

Weiser, M., & Brown, J. S. (1996). Designing calm technology. *PowerGrid Journal, 1*(1).

Weiss, M., & Amyot, D. (2005, July-September). Business process modeling with URN. *International Journal of E-Business Research, 1*(3), 63-90.

Weiss, S. (2002). Handheld usability. New York: Wiley.

Wellner, P. (1992, November 11-13). The DigitalDesk calculator: Tactile manipulation on a desktop display. In *Proceedings of UIST'92, the ACM Symposium on User Interface Software and Technology,* Hilton Head, SC. New York: ACM.

Westerink, J. H. D. M., Ouwerkerk, M., Overbeek, Th. J. M., Pasveer, W. F., & de Ruyter, B. (Eds.) press). *Probing experience: From assessment of user emotions and behaviour to development of products..* Philips Research Book Series, Vol. 8. Dordrecht, The Netherlands: Springer.

Wexelblat, A., & Maes, P. (1999). Footprint: History-rich tools for information foraging. In *Proceedings of Conference on Human Factors in Computing Systems (CHI'99)* (pp. 270-277). New York: ACM Press.

Wikipedia Blackboard Incorporated. *In The Wikipedia Encyclopedia.* Retrieved October 11, 2006, from http://en.wikipedia.org/wiki/Blackboard_Inc

Wildman, D. (1995, July). Getting the most from paired user testing. *Interactions.*

Winograd, T. (1996). *Bringing design to software.* Addison-Wesley.

Winograd, T., & Flores, F. (1986). *Understanding computers and cognition: A new foundation for design.* Norwood, NJ: Ablex Publishing Corp.

Wireless@SG project. (2006). Retrieved January 16, 2008, from http://www.ida.gov.sg/Infrastructure/20070202144018.aspx

Wisneski, C., Ishii, H., & Dahley, A. (1998). Ambient displays: Turning architectural space into an interface between people and digital information. In *Proceedings of International Workshop on Cooperative Buildings (CoBuild'98)* (pp. 22-32).

Wu, J., Dai, F., Gao, M., & Stojmenovic, I. (2002). On calculating power-aware connected dominating sets for efficient routing in ad hoc wireless networks. *IEEE/KICS Journal of Communications and Networks, 4*(1), 59-70.

Xu, Y., Heidemann, J., & Estrin, D. (2001). Geography-informed energy conservation for ad hoc routing. In *7th Annual International Conference on Mobile Computing and Networking* (pp. 70-84).

Yacoub, S., & Ammar, H. (2004). *Pattern-oriented analysis and design: Composing patterns to design software systems.* Addison-Wesley.

Yamada, S. (2003). *Overview of privacy management.* Ubiquitous Computing Environments, National Institute of Informatic.

Yamamoto, Y., & Nakakoji, K. (2005). Interaction design of tools for fostering creativity in the early stages of information design. *International Journal of Human-Computer Studies (IJHCS), 63*(4-5), 513-535.

Yarin, P., & Ishii, H. (1999). TouchCounters: Designing interactive electronic labels for physical containers. In *Proceedings of Conference on Human Factors in Computing Systems (CHI'99)* (pp. 362-369). New York: ACM Press.

Ye, J.H., & Herbert, J. (2004, June 28-29). Framework for user interface adaptation. In *Proceedings from the 8th ERCIM Workshop on User Interfaces for All* (Vol. 3196), pp. 167-174. Vienna, Austria: Springer Verlag.

Ye, W., Heidemann, J., & Estrin, D. (2002). An energy efficient MAC protocol for wireless sensor networks. In *Proceedings of INFOCOM 2002,* New York.

Ye, W., Heidemann, J., & Estrin, D. (2004). Medium access control with coordinated adaptive sleeping for wireless sensor networks. *IEEE/ACM Transactions on Networking.*

Yeh, R., Liao, C., Klemmer, S., Guimbretière, F., Lee, B., Kakaradov, B. et al. (2006). ButterflyNet: A mobile capture and access system for field biology research. In *Proceedings of the SIGCHI Conference on Human Factors in Computing Systems CHI '06* (pp. 571-580). New York, NY: ACM Press.

Youssef, M., & Agrawala, A. K. (2004). Handling samples correlation in the Horus system. In *Proceedings of IEEE INFOCOM.* Hong Kong, China.

Yu, E. (1997, January 6-8). Towards modelling and reasoning support for early-phase requirements engineering. In *Proceedings of the 3rd IEEE International Symposium on Requirements Engineering (RE'97)* (pp. 226-235). Washington, DC.

Yu, Y., Leite, J.C.S.P., & Mylopoulos, J. (2004, September). From goals to aspects: Discovering aspects from requirements goal models. In *Proceedings of the 12th IEEE International. Conference on Requirements Engineering (RE 2004)* (pp. 38-47). Kyoto, Japan.

Zadeh, L. A. (1965). Fuzzy sets. *Information and Control, 8*, 338-353.

Zara, J., Benes, B., & Rodarte, R.R. (2004, September 20-24). Virtual campeche: A Web based virtual three-dimensional tour. In *Proceeding of the 5th Mexican International Conference in Computer Science*, (pp. 133-140). Colima, Mexico.

Zeithaml, V.A. (1988, July). Consumer perceptions of price, quality, and value: A conceptual model and synthesis of research. *Journal of Marketing, 52*, 2-22.

Zhang, D. (2003). Delivery of personalized and adaptive content to mobile devices: a framework and enabling technology. *Communications of AIS, 12*, 83-202.

ZigBee Alliance. (2005). Retrieved November 11, 2005, from http://www.zigbee.org/en/index.asp

Zimmerman, G., Barnes, J., & Leventhal, L.M. (2003). A comparison of the usability and effectiveness of Web-based delivery of instructions for inherently-3D construction tasks on handheld and desktop computers. In *Proceedings of Web3D 2003* (pp. 49-54). Saint Malo, France.

About the Contributors

Henry B.L. Duh is, currently, an assistant professor in the Department of Electrical and Computer Engineering/ Interactive and Digital Media Insititute at National University of Singapore. He received degree in psychology, industrial design and industrial engineering respectively. After graduating from Human Interface Technology Laboratory (HIT Lab) at University of Washington, he went to NASA-Johnson Space Center as a postdoctoral fellow involving in virtual reality training project. Dr. Duh's research interests include human-computer interaction, virtual interface design, interface usability testing and mobile interactions. His current research focuses on user experiences in interaction design, behavioral responses in virtual environments and game effects. He has published numerous papers in HCI relevant journals and conferences, and has served as a full paper reviewer for ACM CHI, UIST, CSCW and DIS in the past five years.

Yin-Leng Theng is currently an associate professor at the Wee Kim Wee School of Communication and Information, Nanyang Technological University (NTU, Singapore). She teaches in the Information Studies and Information Systems Master Programme: human-computer interaction, usability engineering, information architecture, and digital libraries. She was awarded two research grants from EPSRC (UK) during her 4 years of teaching at Middlesex University. Recently, she was also awarded an NTU grant to work on usability techniques on the Web and mobile environments, and two A*Star grants to work on e-learning systems and mobile media.

* * *

Hyggo Almeida has been an electrical engineer PhD candidate at the electrical engineering department (DEE), Federal University of Campina Grande (UFCG), since 2004. He earned his Master's in Computer Science with focus in software engineering for multiagent systems from the Federal University of Campina Grande, in 2004. He is currently an assistant professor in the computer and systems department at the Federal University of Campina Grande. He is leading activities related to component-based development and pervasive computing. He has more than 70 papers published in conferences and journals.

Nídia Berbegal is a Computer Engineer at Universitat Pompeu Fabra (2004). She has been a researcher at the User Center Design Lab at Barcelona Media Innovation Center (Barcelona, Spain) and at the Interactive Technologies Group of the Universitat Pompeu Fabra (Barcelona). She has participated in several European funded projects such as ICING, INSTINCT, UNFOLD, and eTITLE. She has also worked at Fundació Televall (Ribes de Freser, Spain), the first teleworking centre in Catalonia. Nídia started a PhD program at the Universitat Politècnica de Catalunya investigating human interfaces for welfare-robotic systems.

Mark Billinghurst is a researcher developing innovative computer interfaces that explore how virtual and real worlds can be merged. Director of the HIT Lab (New Zealand) at the University of Canterbury, he has produced over 80 technical publications and presented demonstrations and courses at a wide variety of conferences. He has a PhD from the University of Washington and conducts research in augmented and virtual reality, wearable computing, and conversational interfaces. He has previously worked at ATR Research Labs, British Telecom, and the MIT Media Laboratory. One of his research projects, the MagicBook, was winner of the 2001 Discover award for Best Entertainment Application.

Indranil Bose is associate professor of information systems at school of business, the University of Hong Kong. His degrees include B.Tech from the Indian Institute of Technology, MS from University of Iowa, and an MS and PhD from Purdue University. He has research interests in telecommunications, data mining, electronic commerce, and supply chain management. His teaching interests are in telecommunications, database management, data mining, and decision science. His publications have appeared in Communications of AIS, Communications of the ACM, Computers and Operations Research, Decision Support Systems, and Electronic Commerce, Ergonomics, European Journal of Operational Research, Information and Management, and Operations Research Letters.

Frederico Bublitz received a BS in Computer Science from the Federal University of Alagoas, Brazil, in 2005. He is an MSc student at the Federal University of Campina Grande, Brazil. His MSc work is focused on context-awareness in pervasive environments. He is involved in an affiliated Nokia project for the development of embedded systems applications for mobile devices, the Percomp project, in the Embedded Systems and Pervasive Computing Laboratory.

Ken Camarata has taught and conducted research at the University of Washington and Carnegie Mellon University. His work focused on the blending of computation and the built environment through the development of tangible interfaces, interactive furniture, and computational spaces. He received a bachelor's of arts in architectural studies and a master's of architecture at the University of Washington. He is now at KDF Architecture where he works with an experienced team of architects and interior designers to create healing environments.

Lim Chee Koon has been working in the design industry for more than 5 years and is presently the Industrial Design Lead in Motorola, Enterprise Mobility Singapore. He graduated from Temasek Polytechnic Singapore with a Diploma in Product Design in 1997, Umeå University Institute of Design Sweden with a Master in Interaction Design in 2001, and Nanyang Technological University (Singapore) with a Master in Human Factor Engineering in 2006. He has won a few design awards and scholarships such as Birka Energi & Thorn Lighting Design Competition in Sweden and Trade Development Board (TDB) Design Scholarship in Singapore. He is also a certified instructor for Autodesk Alias Studio Tools and he enjoys coaching and giving lectures in design schools occasionally. Currently, he serves as the Vice-President of the Usability Professional Association (UPA), Singapore Chapter 2007. His mission is to increase design and usability awareness and integrate them seamlessly to improve design efficiency.

Adrian David Cheok is the Director of the Mixed Reality Lab, National University of Singapore. He is associate professor in the department of electrical and computer engineering. He leads a team of over 20 researchers and students. He has been a keynote and invited speaker at numerous international and local conferences and events. He has won several awards and is the editor/associate editor of several academic journals. He has been working on research covering mixed reality, human-computer interaction, wearable computers and smart spaces, fuzzy systems, embedded systems, power electronics, and multimodal recognition, and has successfully obtained funding for externally funded projects in the area of wearable computers and mixed reality from many agencies/organisations. Research outputs include high quality academic journal papers, research prototypes demonstrations to the President and Deputy Prime Minister of Singapore, broadcasts on television worldwide (such as CNN/CNBC/Discovery/National Geographic), and international invited new media exhibits such as in Ars Electronica and Wired Nextfest.

Jimmy Chong is currently an IT manager supporting the business needs and operational efficiencies of DHL Express Asia Pacific Regional Office, which is the business HQ in AP. He has been in DHL for more than 7 years and has been instrumental in the implementation of latest technology to the business. His last appointment was the IT Manager of DHL Singapore HUB, which is the operations gateway for South East Asia. He is a recent graduate of the MSc (Information Systems) programme from the Wee Kim Wee School of Communication and Information, Nanyang Technological University. He received his Bachelor's Degree in Computer Science from NUS in 1997.

Dr. Tan Chong Eng is a lecturer in the Faculty of Computer Science and Information Technology, University Malaysia Sarawak (UNIMAS), Malaysia. He has a PhD from Cambridge University. He is also the head of the computer systems and communication technologies department and the head for Information Infrastructure Core Research Group in UNIMAS. His research interests are in Wireless Networks, Broadband Communications, and Mobile IP. He has published a number of international conference papers and other research publications, along with supervising postgraduate research students. He has been a member of IEEE since 1998. His e-mail address is cetan@fit.unimas.my

Jason Chong Lee is a PhD student in the Department of Computer Science at Virginia Tech, and a member of Virginia Tech's Center for Human-Computer Interaction. His interests are in usability engineering, agile software development, notification systems, and mobile and ubiquitous computing. He received his BS in Computer Science from the University of Virginia in 2003.

Mark D. Gross is Professor at Carnegie Mellon University in the School of Architecture's Computational Design program. He has worked on constraint-based models to support design, as well as (pen based) diagram and sketch recognition as interfaces to knowledge based systems. In recent work he has investigated the design space of computationally enhanced construction kits and craft activities made possible by advances in microelectronics and rapid prototyping and manufacturing. He holds a BS in architectural design and a PhD in design theory and methods from Massachusetts Institute of Technology.

Michael Haller is a researcher developing innovative computer interfaces that explore how virtual and real worlds can be merged to enhance and improve computer systems. Currently, he is working at the department of digital media of the Upper Austria University of Applied Sciences and is responsible for computer graphics, multimedia programming, and augmented reality. He has produced technical publications and his work has been demonstrated at a wide variety of conferences. Furthermore, he is active in several research areas, including augmented and virtual reality, and human computer interfaces. In 2004, he received the Erwin Schroedinger fellowship award presented by the Austrian Science Fund for his stay at the HITLabNZ, University of Canterbury (New Zealand) and the CGIT, University of Southern California (USA).

Ehsan Hamadani received his BSc degree in Control Engineering in 2003 at Isfahan University of Technology, Iran. He then joined the Mobile Networks Research Group at City University, London, where he is currently doing his PhD in the area of ad hoc networks. His main research interest is the cross layer analysis of TCP performance over 802.11 multihop ad hoc networks with special emphasis on instability and unfairness issue. He has also worked on mathematical modeling and testbed implementations of 802.11 ad hoc networks.

Biju Issac is a lecturer in the School of IT and Multimedia in Swinburne University of Technology (Sarawak Campus). He is also the head of Network Security Research Group in the iSECURES (Information Security Research) Lab at Swinburne University Sarawak. His research interests are in wireless and network security, spam detection, wireless mobility, and IPv6 networks. He has published various IEEE conference papers and other research publications. His e-mail address is bissac@swinburne.edu.my

Sze Ling Koh works in information systems with the IT department at the Center for IT Services, Nanyang Technological University (NTU, Singapore). Currently, she is involved in the technology groups of the User Interface Web Services and Multimedia, which aims to equip the development team with advanced knowledge to design user-centered interface which assist users to complete their business processes with accuracy and efficiency. She is a recent graduate of the MSc (Information Systems) programme from the Wee Kim Wee School of Communication and Information, NTU. She received her BASc (Computer Engineering) from NTU in 1996.

Charissa Lim Mei-Ling is a recent graduate of the MSc (Information Studies) programme from Nanyang Technological University. She received her BBus (majoring in IT) with First Class Honours from Nanyang Technological University in 2005. She is currently a Systems Planner in Singapore Airlines.

Emerson Loureiro received an MSc in Informatics from the Federal University of Campina Grande, at Campina Grande, Brazil, in 2006, and a BS in Computer Science from the Federal University of Alagoas, at Maceió, Brazil, in 2004. His current research activities are focused on pervasive computing, mainly on the aspects of middleware, software engineering, adaptation, context awareness, and service provision.

D. Scott McCrickard is an Associate Professor in the Department of Computer Science at Virginia Tech, and a member of Virginia Tech's Center for Human-Computer Interaction. His interests lie in the areas of human-computer interaction, notification systems, design knowledge capture and reuse, and mobile and ubiquitous computing. McCrickard received his BS degree from the University of North Carolina in 1992 and an MS and PhD from Georgia Institute of Technology in 1995 and 2000.

Ingrid Mulder holds a Master's degree in Policy and Organization Sciences (University of Tilburg) and a PhD in Behavior Sciences (Twente University). Since 1998, Ingrid works as a scientific researcher at Telematica Instituut, Enschede, The Netherlands. She specializes in methodological innovation in the domain of psychometrics, such as methods and techniques for eliciting experiences and user needs, as well as methods for the design of human-centered technology. She authored more than 75 articles for international conferences and journals, and is an experienced international reviewer (e.g., Computer in Human Behavior).

Kumiyo Nakakoji is Full Professor at RCAST, University of Tokyo, Japan, and Senior Research Fellow at SRA Key Technology Laboratory, Inc., Japan. She received a BA in computer science from Osaka University, Japan, and a PhD in computer science from University of Colorado, Boulder. She has served as chair, editor, and committee member for a number of research communities, journals, and conferences, and was recently awarded Distinguished Engineering Alumni Award from College of Engineering, University of Colorado, Boulder. She is currently chairing IPSJ SIGHCI. Her research interests include human-computer interaction design, software engineering, and collective creativity, specifically Knowledge Interaction Design, which is a framework for the design and development of computational tools for creative knowledge work.

Raquel Navarro-Prieto is currently the director of the User Centred Design lab at the Barcelona Media Innovation Centre (Spain). She has lead the Human Factors' work in numerous projects, including European funded projects like ICING (studying innovative service to that meet the needs of specific communities and citizens) and INSTINCT (studying the convergence between digital broadcasting and mobile networks). Previously, she coordinated the research at the Interaction Lab (Open University of Catalonia). She also worked at Motorola Research Lab (UK) and has industrial experience at Apple Inc. (USA), and HP (Spain). Raquel obtained her PhD in Cognitive Psychology in 1998 at the University of Granada. She has written numerous papers and participated in several program committees. Her research interests include applying the user centred approach to the development of applications, specifically mobile multimedia applications.

Yeonjoo Oh is a PhD student in the Computation Design Lab (CoDeLab) at Carnegie Mellon University. Her research interests include developing computational design environments—sketch interfaces and intelligent design tools—based on an understanding of design processes and design activities. She received a BS in architecture, a BA in art history, and an MS in architecture history and criticism at Ewha Womans University. She received an MS in design computing at University of Washington.

Loreno Oliveira is currently an MSc candidate at the Federal University of Campina Grande, Brazil. His ongoing thesis consists of designing an infrastructure of hand-off management aimed at multimedia applications. Research interests include pervasive computing, distributed computing, multimedia, streaming applications, and hands-off management.

Angelo Perkusich received a PhD and an MSc in electrical engineering from the Federal University of Paraíba, at Campina Grande, Brazil, in 1994 and 1987, respectively. In 1982 he received a BS in electrical engineering from the Engineering Faculty of Barretos. From 1988 to 1990, he was an assistant professor of the electronic and systems department at the Federal University of Pernambuco. From 1992 to 1993, he was a visiting researcher at the University of Pittsburgh, United States. From 1991 to 1994, he was an assistant professor of the electrical engineering department at the Federal University of Paraíba. Since 1994 he has been an adjunct professor in the same department. He is a project leader/consultant at the affiliated Nokia project for the development of embedded systems applications for mobile devices. His research interest include software engineering for embedded systems, dynamic software composition, formal methods, and pervasive computing.

Dr Veselin Rakocevic is currently a Senior Lecturer at City University, London, UK, where he leads the Mobile Networks Research Group. His main research interests include wireless ad hoc networks, quality of service in mobile networks, and network reliability. He published over 25 papers in journals and conferences and is a member of the TPC for a number of conferences, including IEEE Globecom, MASS, and WCNC. He holds a PhD in Telecommunications from University of London, UK, and a Dipl-Ing Degree in electronic engineering from University of Belgrade, Serbia.

Dr. Anxo Cereijo Roibás is Senior Lecturer at the University of Brighton, visiting lecturer at Westminster University, at the Politecnico di Milano and the National Institute of Design (India). His expertise resides in the user experience in pervasive communication systems. He has been HCI manager at the Mobile Internet Services Provider, HiuGO SpA, and User Experience Consultant for Vodafone and, since 2000, he has been collaborating with the Nokia Research Center. He has coordinated an ethnographic research addressing the future use of mobile phones as multimedia tools in collaboration with the Vodafone Group Foundation and the British Royal Academic of Engineering. He has been British Telecom Fellow at the BT IT Mobility Research Centre and Executive Committee member of the British HCI Group.

Miten Sampat is an MS student in the department of computer science at Virginia Tech, and a member of Virginia Tech's Center for human-computer interaction at Virginia Tech. As an undergraduate, he was a founding member of the CHCI's location-based services research through the SeeVT initiative. Miten continues to lead this effort in prototyping interfaces for the geospatial Web and exploring different mobile-spatial interaction methods. He received his BS in computer science from Virginia Tech in 2005.

Lily Seah is currently a senior assistant director at the Centre for IT Services, Nanyang Technological University. She is a recent graduate of the MSc (Information Systems) programme from the Wee Kim Wee School of Communication and Information, Nanyang Technological University. She received her degree from the British Computer Society (UK). In 2001, she became the leader of the GUI Team which standardised the interface for applications developed for the Web platform for the university. Currently she is a member of the User Interface Web Services (UIWS) and Multimedia technology groups which involves setting the usability guidelines and standards for the development team.

Stanley See is currently a vice-president (consultancy) in Spiral Communications offering IT consultancy for diverse industries from schools to technology companies. He is a recent graduate of the MSc (Information Systems) programme from the Wee Kim Wee School of Communication and Information, Nanyang Technological University. He received his B.Comm. (majoring in Information Systems) from Curtin University of Technology in 1996 and started his career at PricewaterhouseCoopers working on infrastructure and later on systems development. In 1999, he cofounded Postkid.com that delivered one of the first e-learning portal solutions to 170 Singapore schools and also introduced wireless solutions in an education environment.

Yoshinari Shirai is a researcher at the NTT Communication Science Laboratories at NTT Corporation and is a PhD candidate in the Graduate School of Engineering at the University of Tokyo. He received a BA in environmental information and an M.M.G. (Master of Media and Governance) from Keio University in 1998 and 2000, respectively. His research interests include ubiquitous computing and interaction design. He is a member of the Information Processing Society of Japan (IPSJ) and the Human Interface Society.

Lucia Terrenghi is a designer and a researcher working in the field of Human-Computer Interaction at Vodafone R&D in Munich, Germany. Prior to that, she worked as research assistant at the Ludwig-Maximilians-Universität München, in Germany, where she has recently attained with honor her PhD in Computer Sciences. Her research has developed in the context of the FLUIDUM project (www.fluidum.org), which explores techniques for interacting with ubiquitous computing technologies, in settings of everyday life. In the past, she also did an internship at Microsoft Research Cambridge. Before that, she worked as user interface designer at the Fraunhofer Institute for Applied Information Technology, in Sankt Augustin, Germany, and as brand designer for the Organizing Committee of the XX Olympic Winter Games, Torino 2006. Lucia also holds a Master of Science in Industrial Design from the Politecnico di Milano, in Italy. Her interests address the relationship between humans and technologies and the ways in which technological artifacts can enhance social engagement, self-expression, and creativity.

Liu Wei is a Research Fellow at the Mixed Reality Lab, Singapore. She received her Master of Computer Engineering in 2002 from National University of Singapore. She has previously worked at the Xian Jiaotong Univerisity, China (department of electrical engineering) as a lecturer. Her research interests include mixed and virtual reality, human-computer interface, computer graphics, and edutainment. She joined the Mixed Reality Lab in January 2002, and since then has been involved in many projects such as Digital Sand Table, Human Pacman, Kyoto Garden, and Magic Land, and her recent works are the Solar System and the Plant Story.

Michael Philetus Weller is a PhD Candidate in the CoDe Lab at Carnegie Mellon University. He is experimenting with ways computation can be embedded in buildings and furniture to reimagine our relationship with the built environment. He holds a BA in philosophy, a BA in architecture, and a Master's of architecture from the University of Washington. He believes in Open Source, and believes everyone should read Daniel Dennett.

Chen Xi is doctoral candidate in Information Systems at School of Business, the University of Hong Kong. His degrees include a BS from Fudan University and an MS from National University of Singapore. He has research interests in data mining, electronic commerce, and mobile service.

Yasuhiro Yamamoto is an associate professor at Research Center for Advanced Science and Technology (RCAST), University of Tokyo, where he codirects Knowledge Interaction Design (KID) laboratory. He received a BS in information engineering from Kyoto University, an MS and a PhD in information science from Nara Institute of Science and Technology (NAIST), Japan. He worked as a post-doctoral researcher at the Japan Society for the Promotion of Science (JSPS), Japan Science and Technology Corporation (JST), and RCAST. His research interests include human-computer interaction, interaction design, and design process design. He is a member of ACM and the IEEE Computer Society.

Ellen Yi-Luen Do is associate professor in the College of Architecture's Design Computing PhD program and the College of Computing's Human Centered Computing Program at Georgia Institute of Technology. Her research interests include sketch understanding, intuitive design interfaces, creativity and cognition, intelligent systems and toys, ubiquitous computing, ambient intelligence, and smart living technologies. She received a Bachelor's degree of architecture (Honors) from National Cheng-Kung University in Taiwan, with a minor in urban planning, a Master's of design studies from the Harvard Graduate School of Design, and a PhD in design computing from Georgia Tech, with a minor in cognitive science.

Index

Symbols

2.5G 208
2G platform 288
3-dimensional (3D) 172
3G 208
4G 208
802.11 networks 114

A

access-control engine 218
access points (APs) 206
Active Worlds Educational Universe (AWEDU) 183
activities, environments, interactions, objects, users (ABOU), 61
adaptive frequency hopping (AFH) 125
ad hoc networks 120
ad hoc on-demand routing (AODV) 120
advanced encryption standard (AES) 115, 116
advancement of technologies 204
agile software development 258
agile usability approach 253
ambient devices 212, 213
ambient intelligence (AmI) 99
ambient intelligence environment 106
animated scenarios 295
Anoto Pen 213
application areas 204
application scenarios 213
asynchronous transfer mode (ATM) 209
augmented reality (AR) 174, 195, 262
automatic repeat request (ARQ) 152

B

bats 216
Bellman-Ford algorithm 120
biometric features 99
Blackberry devices 211, 217
Blackboard 176
BlueStar architecture 124
Bluetooth 13, 213, 223, 240, 255
Bluetooth networks 114
Bluetooth Public Access (BLUEPAC) network 124
Bluetooth specification 146
Bluetooth Web Internet Gateway (BWIG) 123
Boingo 206
British Telecommunications 209
broadcast and mobile networks 37
business-application composition 218

C

calm technology 10
Canesta 213
carrier sensing with multiple access (CSMA) 149
central controller 216
central design record (CDR) 259, 260
channel time allocation period (CTAP) 150
Cisco 212
Citrix 215
clusterheads 155
code division multiple access (CDMA) 133
collaborative learning environment with virtual reality (CLEV-R) 187, 194
component-based development (CBD) 228
component-based software 19
computed tomography (CT) 195
computer supported collaborative care (CSCC) 59
computing context 17–18
connection point (CP) 126
contention access period (CAP) 150
context acquisition 18
context aware applications 18
context reasoning 18
context representation 18

context sensitive mobile services (CSMS) 130, 131
context sensitive services, benefits of 132
contracts 20
corporate network 215
cruise-control system 308

D

DARPA 210
dashboard or project-portfolio management 215
denial of service (DoS) 119
destination-sequenced distance vector (DSDV) 120
device identification engine 218
DigitalDesk 268
digital pen 268
digital subscriber lines (DSLs) 207
direct-sequence spread spectrum (DSSS) 115
direct sequence (DS) 147
discovery messages 17
document type definition (DTD) 102
domain-specific ontologies 25
draco middleware 233
dynamic host configuration protocol (DHCP) 15
dynamic software evolution, definition of 231
dynamic source routing (DSR) 120

E

Eclipse-based editor 311
Eclipse IDE 229
embedded agents 108
energy restrictions 14
event-based systems 229
event service 22
EVE project 185
Experience Clip 58
extensible markup language (XML) 102
extreme programming (XP) 259

F

facility management and Other On-site service applications 215
FireFly 205
first generation (1G) 208
first mile-last mile 207
fourth generation of mobile telecommunication network (4G) 141
frequency-hopping spread spectrum (FHSS) 115
frequency hopping (FH) 123
fully functional devices (FFD) 147
fuzzy control 99
fuzzy logic control (FLC) 101
fuzzy markup language (FML) 99
fuzzy object model (FOM) 102

G

gang of four (GoF) 302
general event notification architecture (GENA) 23
general packet radio service (GPRS) 15, 133
geographic information system (GIS) 254
global positioning system (GPS) 133, 137, 179
global system for mobile (GSM) 132
goal-oriented requirement language (GRL) 304, 316
graphical user interface (GUI) 160, 188, 288

H

H2ML 99
head-mounted display (HMD) 88, 195
hierarchical fuzzy control 106
Home Radio Frequency Working Group (HomeRF WG) 126
HomeRF networks 114, 204
HTML (hypertext markup language) 211
HTTP (hypertext transfer protocol) 211
human-computer interaction (HCI) 38, 238, 204, 254
human to markup language (H2ML) 106
hybrid protocols, for ad hoc networks 152
Hyper Text Mark-up Language (HTML) 176

I

IBM 216
icon-scenario based animated menu 288, 294
icon based menu 293
Icon Recognition test 48
IEEE802.15.4 148
independent basic service set (IBSS) 119
information-access 205
information-generation 205
information quality (IQ) 135
information technology (IT) 27
innovative convergence services 37
instant communication 213
instant messaging system (IM) 67
INSTINCT project 37
interaction mode 218
interactive table 266
interactive tables, collaborative systems 268
interactive TV 56
internet protocol (IP) 209
intrusion detection software (IDS) 119
Isochronous data device (I-node) 126
ISPs (Internet service providers) 208

J

J2ME (Java 2 Micro Edition) 211
Java context awareness framework (JCAF) 231
Java Virtual Machine 211

K

Kirusa (http://www.kirusa.com) 216

L

LAN technologies 206
learning objects (LOs) 27
Living Cookbook 247
local area network (LAN) 115, 204
location, alphabetical, time, category hierarchy (LATCH) 61
location based services (LBS) 136, 138, 215
location knowledge 253
Logitech 213
long range navigation (LORAN) 254
Low-Fi prototypes 67

M

Mac OS 206
management CTAs (MCTAs) 151
mCLEV-R 193
medium access control (MAC) 115, 119, 126, 147, 148, 153
megabits per second (mbps) 133
mesh radio 209
mess networks 209
metropolitan area network (MAN) 207
microcontroller 210
Microsoft 216
Mitel 212
mixed reality (MXR) 87
mobile access to information and applications 214
mobile ad hoc networks (MANETs) 119
mobile devices 204, 253
moodle 177
moove 179
morphological recognition subsystems 106
motes 210
Mozilla Firefox3 Web browser 229
MUD object orientated (MOO) 179
multi-agents system 104
Multi-Modal Presentation Markup Language 107
multi-user distributed virtual environment (mDVE) 183
multilayer controller 106
multimodal interaction 216
multiple-input multiple-output (MIMO) 127
multiple access with collision avoidance (MACA) 150

N

neighborhood area networks (NANs) 206
NetStumbler 206
non-functional requirements (NFR) 303
non line of sight (NLOS) 207
notification-based 16
Nsight Teleservices 209
NYC Wireless 208

O

OA layer 218
oiceXML 216
Orbs (ambient devices) 212
orthogonal frequency division multiplexing (OFDM) 116, 147

P

pattern
  almanac 302
peer-to-peer network 210
perceived quality of experience (PQoE) 55
person, objects, situations, time, and activity (POS-TA) framework 61
personal area networks (PANs) 205
personal computer (PC) 207, 239
personal digital assistants (PDAs) 123, 205, 213, 217, 225
pervasive communication 15
pervasive computing 216, 217, 222
pervasive computing world 204
pervasive devices 210
physical context 18
physical layer (PHY) specifications 115
Pingtel 212
plant mixed reality system (PMRS) 87
plug-in-based architectures 229
point-to-point protocol (PPP) 125
projection keyboard 213
pull model 136
push model 135

Q

quality of experience (QoE) 54, 55
quality of service (QoS) 55, 146
quality of transmission (QoT), 55

query-based 16
question-and-answer speech input 213

R

Radiant Networks 209
Radio-frequency-based ZigBee 205
radio frequency identification (RFID) 133
radio telephones (porto-phones) 246
rapid ethnography 245
receivers 216
reconfigurable, ubiquitous, networked embedded systems (RUNES) 232
reconfigurable context-sensitive middleware (RCSM) 25
reduced-function devices (RFD) 147
remote access 215
remote procedure call (RPC) 24
Research in Motion 212
route replay (RREP) 120
route request (RREQ) 120

S

sales-force automation 214
scenario-based design (SBD) 254, 259
scenario based animated menu 294
second generation of wireless technology (2G) 208
sensor networks 210
service-oriented architecture (SOA) 204, 216, 217
service-oriented computing 230
service-oriented context-aware middleware (SO-CAM) 25
session-persistence engine 218
Shared Design Space, setup 279
shared wireless access protocol (SWAP) 126
short-message service (SMS) 211
smart algorithms 256, 258
smart phones 211
SMS multimodality 216
sniffing algorithms 256
SocioXensor 246
speech application language tags (SALT) 216
STEM method 153

T

table, as an interface 270
tablet PCs 212
Takagi-Sugeno-Kang (TSK) 102
TCP/IP (transmission-control protocol/Internet protocol) 212
technology acceptance model (TAM) 87, 88, 89
TeleTables 161, 162
temporal key integrity protocol (TKIP) 115
temporally-ordered routing algorithm (TORA) 121
text-to-speech technology. 214
third generation (3G) wireless systems 141
time context 18
time division multiple access (TDMA) 150
TinyDB, 210
TinyOS 210
TradeWinds Communications (http://www.tnsconnects.com) 209
trilateration 215

U

Ubicomp Conference Series 2
ubicomp paradigm 4
ubiquitous applications 253
ubiquitous computing 1, 222, 224, 238, 239, 240
ubiquitous computing systems, challenges of developing 225, 226
ubiquitous technology 239
ultra wideband communication (UWB) 147, 209
unified communication 213
URL (uniform resource locator) 211
use case map (UCM)
user-centered design (UCD) 37, 38
user context 17, 18
User Interface Continuum 40
user requirements notation (URN) 301, 302, 303
uses and gratifications (U&G) 57

V

ViewPad 212
ViewSonic 212
Virginia Tech (VT) 261
virtual European schools (VES) 183
Virtual Human Markup Language (VHML) 107
virtual private network (VPN) 119, 215
virtual reality (VR) 172, 178, 181
Vocera 214
voice gateway 211
VoiceXML 211

W

Web-services access 255
Wi-Fi 13, 225
WiMAX 207
Window Seat 161, 166
Windows XP 206
Wings middleware 232

wired equivalent privacy (WEP) 115
wireless access 212
wireless ad hoc networks 151
wireless fidelity (WiFi) 127, 223
wireless LAN 208, 217
wireless local area networks (WLANs) 206
wireless mesh networks (WMN) 119
wireless metropolitan area network (MAN) 207
wireless NAN 208
wireless networking technologies 204
wireless PANs 205
wireless PDAs 211
wireless personal area network 205
wireless sensor networks (WSNs) 119
Wireless technology 206
wireless WAN 208, 217
Wizard of Oz testing 57
WML (wireless markup language) 211

Z

ZigBee 205, 223
ZigBee Alliance, testing requirements 148